Effective Technical Communication

SECOND EDITION

About the Author

M Ashraf Rizvi is currently Director, Jaipuria Institute of Management, Lucknow. An eminent academician with more than thirty years of teaching, training, consulting and research experience in India and abroad, Dr. Rizvi has taught in top institutes including Indian Institute of Management Indore, Indian Institute of Technology Dhanbad, and Sultan Qaboos University, Muscat, Oman. He is widely credited for positioning IIM Indore as a national leader in executive education. He has also served as Chairman of Executive PGP Programme of IIM Indore; Coordinator for Collaboration with University of Pittsburgh, USA; and headed Media Management Centre of IIM Indore from 2007–2012.

Professor Rizvi has delivered various lectures, presentations and keynote addresses at premier universities, institutes and business schools around the world including IIMs, NITs, Preston University, Sharjah, American University of Emirates, UAE, MARA University, Kuala Lumpur, and BITS Pilani Dubai Campus.

Dr. Rizvi has trained and coached thousands of professionals including CEOs, top MNC executives, civil servants, judges, army officers, police officers, scientists, doctors, engineers, journalists, writers, university teachers, academic administrators, etc. His consulting and executive education experiences include engagements with several national and multinational organizations. Dr. Rizvi has designed and conducted innovative management and leadership development programmes for public sector as well as private sector companies including LG India, ONGC, Alstom, GAIL, Thomas Cook, Honeywell, Birla, Eicher, Godrej, NTPC, Vodafone, Reliance, Bharat Petroleum, EIL, SBI Life, PNB, and several other organizations. He has served as a consultant to a number of companies and government departments and agencies including Ministry of Home, Government of India, Ministry of Health, Government of Madhya Pradesh, IPCA Pharmaceuticals, Kotak Life Insurance, ONGC, etc.

Dr. Rizvi is an author of eleven books, some of which include Communication for Retail Professionals (McGraw Hill Education, New Delhi, 2009), Effective Technical Communication: KIIT (McGraw Hill Education, New Delhi, 2009) Business Communication: Challenges and Prospects, (Paragon International Publishers, New Delhi, 2008); Resumes and Interviews: The Art of Winning, (McGraw Hill Education, New Delhi, 2007); Effective Technical Communication (McGraw Hill Education, New Delhi, 2005), Professional Communication (McGraw Hill Education, New Delhi, 2005). Professor Rizvi is also the author of over 60 journal articles, book chapters, reviews, working papers, cases, role plays, simulations, and notes. He is on the Editorial Boards and Review Panels of many scholarly journals including Profile: A Journal of Columbia University, Asian Case Research Journal, National University of Singapore, How: A Colombian Journal for English Teachers, Columbia, SEARCH Journal, Malaysia, Indore Management Journal, and IMT Case Journal, India.

EFFECTIVE TECHNICAL COMMUNICATION

SECOND EDITION

M ASHRAF RIZVI
Director
Jaipuria Institute of Management, Lucknow
Former Professor
Indian Institute of Management, Indore
Indian Institute of Technology, Dhanbad

McGraw Hill Education (India) Private Limited

Published by McGraw Hill Education (India) Private Limited,
Registered Office: Anjana Complex No: 5/90 A, Butt Road, St. Thomas Mount, Chennai – 600016, Tamil Nadu, India.

Effective Technical Communication

Fourteenth reprint 2023

Print Edition
ISBN -13: 978-93-5260-578-1
ISBN -10: 93-5260-578-0

E-book Edition
ISBN -13: 978-93-5260-610-8
ISBN -10: 93-5260-610-8

15 16 17 18 19 SDR 27 26 25 24 23

Managing Director: *Lalit Singh*
Head—Production: *Pankaj Manohar*
Manager—Production: *Reji Kumar*

Typeset at Text-O-Graphics, B-1/56, Arawali Apartment, Sector 34, Noida 201301 and printed and bound in India at SDR Printers, A-7, Sector B-3, Trans Delhi Signature City, Ghaziabad (U.P.)

Visit us at: www.mheducation.co.in
Toll free in India: 1800 103 5875
Write to us at: info.india@mheducation.com
CIN: U80302TN2010PTC111532

To my late father

M MUSLIM RIZVI,

who has always been a source of inspiration to me

Preface to the Second Edition

Introduction

Effective Technical Communication is designed to enhance the communication skills for students pursuing technical courses. This book aims to enable the reader to master all the four dimensions of communication—listening, speaking, reading and writing. Simple language, step-by-step approach and practice modules will help students in mastering the subject.

Target Audience

This textbook has been designed to cater to needs of students of various technical and management courses as well as for working professionals. The content offers a complete training programme, which can be used to build effective communication skills by engineering and management students in IITs, IIMs, NITs, RECs, deemed universities, state and private technical universities, and similar educational institutes in other Asian countries.

Objective of the Revision

The main objective of the revision was to align this extremely popular content with the latest advancements in the professional communication domain. The previous edition has been prescribed in most of the technical institutes and universities in India for undergraduate and postgraduate courses, and has been freely used by the instructors, academicians, researchers, and professionals in different fields. It is a comprehensive learning resource on technical communication and the revised edition has further strengthened the utility of this book.

New to this Edition

The text has been thoroughly revised to include:

- **New chapter!!** Chapter on *Communication Today* highlights new topics such as methods of communication, networks of communication, online communication, communication at the workplace, and corporate communication.
- **Enriched content!!** The content on oral communication skills and professional speaking has been improved and enriched by adding new inputs, including strategies of effective oral communication, problem sounds, conversation and telephone media, non-verbal communication elements such as kinesics, paralinguistics, proxemics, chronemics, oral practice, etc.

- **Coverage of emerging issues** and topics that are reshaping professional and technical communication, including digital content creation, passages to test the analytical skills and expression, blog and website, etc.
- With **focus on developing linguistic ability of students** of science and technology, some new topics have been included such as writing definitions of engineering terms.
- The content on reading skills and professional reading has been updated by adding topics such as reading and analysis, analytical reading skills, passages to test analytical skills and expression, reading comprehension, and summarizing.
- **Learning objectives** have been added and restructured in each chapter to make the content more streamlined and learner centric.

Online Learning Centre

Supplementary resources related to the text can be accessed from the web link:
https://connect.mheducation.com.

Organisation of the Book

The revised version consists of nine sections. The *fi rst section* deals with the fundamentals of communication. It contains four chapters. Chapter 1 discusses communication in the professional world today and focuses on basics and methods of communication, channels and networks of communication, online communication, barriers to communication, and communication at the workplace including challenges of workplace communication. Chapter 2 discusses the nature and dimensions of technical communication, including importance and forms of technical communication, aspects of technical competence, and technical communication skills. Chapter 3 deals with linguistic ability, style in technical communication, the ABC of technical communication, objectivity in speaking and writing, and use of formal language. Chapter 4 deals with structuring and organisation in technical communication and concentrates on several methods of organising information in speaking and writing.

The *second section* concentrates on listening comprehension and includes two chapters. Chapter 5 discusses the listening process, types of listening, listening with a purpose, and barriers to listening while Chapter 6 concentrates on improving listening comprehension and focuses on effective listening strategies, listening in conversational interaction, listening to structured talks, team listening, and listening and note taking.

Section three discusses speaking strategies and consists of three chapters. Chapter 7 deals with the speech process and focusses on conversation and oral skills, strategies for good conversation, improving fl uency and self-expression, and body language. Chapter 8 covers key topics in phonetics and spoken English such as basics in phonetics, phonetic transcription, pronunciation guidelines, and problems sounds and differences in pronunciation. Chapter 9 deals with oral communication and speaking techniques and focuses on effective oral communication strategies, speaking including techniques of effective word accent, voice quality, rhythm in connected speech, and developing the correct tone. The *fourth section* is an extensive treatment of three important forms of professional speaking, i.e., job interviews, group discussions, and oral presentations.

The *fi fth section* concentrates on reading and language comprehension. Chapter 13 discusses the reading process, reading with a purpose, reading different kinds of texts, active and passive reading, and reading speed. Chapter 14 concentrates on reading skills, vocabulary skills, eye reading and visual perception, prediction techniques, scanning skills, skimming skills, and intensive reading skills, such as distinguishing between facts and opinions, and drawing inferences and conclusions. Chapter 15 focuses on reading scientific and technical texts, reading methods, reading instructions and manuals, and reading and interpreting graphic information. The *sixth section* discusses important study skills such as note-writing, summarising, parapharsing, and referencing.

The *seventh section* deals with writing strategies whereas the *eighth section* is an exhaustive treatment of professional writing and covers routine business letters, sales letters, resumes and job applications, business memos, e-mails, reports, proposals, and technical articles. The *ninth section* includes three appendices that contain a comprehensive review of functional grammar, problem areas and grammatical analysis, and vocabulary development.

Features and Resources to Improve the Course Experience

With its clear focus on learning outcomes, *Effective Technical Communication,* is ideal for comprehensive technical and professional communication courses in any curriculum and any set-up.

The professor/instructor may also customize the use of the book keeping in view the linguistic level of their students and focus of their course. For courses with an emphasis on a particular skill-area of technical communication such as oral communication or professional speaking, the instructor may find comprehensive material in Chapters 5–12 useful while for courses with a focus on technical writing, Chapters 21–28 give comprehensive coverage of all aspects of technical writing. For a simple course on Technical English, Chapters 3, 4, 19, and 20 can add great value to the course. For instructors who are keen to improve the reading skills of their students, Chapters 13–17 offer balanced coverage of reading skills in all contexts.

M Ashraf Rizvi

Publisher's Note

McGraw Hill Education (India) invites suggestions and comments from you, all of which can be sent to *info.india@mheducation.com* (kindly mention the title and author name in the subject line). Piracy-related issues may also be reported.

Preface to the First Edition

The IT revolution and globalisation of business have brought technical communication to the forefront of academia and industry. With the whole world becoming a global market and businesses becoming diverse and result-oriented, professionals and technocrats are facing newer challenges in communication every day. Success in this competitive environment depends not just on acquiring knowledge and hard skills, but also on developing effective technical communication skills.

Effective Technical Communication is designed as a textbook on communication skills for students of technical and management courses as well as for working professionals. Consistent with its aim to help the reader master the entire gamut of skills required of a successful professional, this book provides a comprehensive coverage of all the four dimensions of communication skills, namely, listening, speaking, reading, and writing. I have tried to make the contents appropriate for a wide range of readers so that any student or professional, regardless of his or her field of specialisation, will find the desired ingredients in this book.

The book offers a complete training programme, which can be used as a self-study resource, as a core text for classes, as a 'refresher,' or as a supplement by engineering and management students in IITs, IIMs, NITs, RECs, deemed universities, state technical universities and colleges, private engineering and management colleges and institutes, and similar educational institutes in other Asian countries. I have tried to make the coverage comprehensive and the presentation simple, and have supplemented the texual matter with examples, illustrations and exhibits.

Structure

The book consists of eight parts and three appendices. The *first part* deals with the **fundamentals of technical communication**. It contains three chapters. Chapter 1 discusses the nature of technical communication and focuses on the stages and channels of communication, nature and importance of technical communication, and barriers to effective communication. Chapter 2 deals with organisation in technical communication and concentrates on several methods of organising information in speaking and writing. Chapter 3 deals with technical style, the ABC of technical communication, objectivity in speaking and writing, and use of formal language.

The *second part* concentrates on **listening and language development**. Chapter 4 discusses the listening process, types of listening, listening with a purpose, and barriers to listening. Chapter 5 concentrates on improving listening comprehension and focuses on effective listening strategies, listening in conversational interaction, listening to structured talks, team listening, and listening and note taking.

Part three discusses **speaking strategies**. It contains three chapters. Chapter 6 deals with the speech process and concentrates on conversation and oral skills, strategies for good conversation, improving fluency and self-expression, and body language. Chapter 7 covers key topics in phonetics and spoken English such as basics in phonetics, phonetic transcription, and pronunciation guidelines. Chapter 8 deals with speaking techniques and focuses on techniques of effective word accent, voice quality, rhythm in connected speech, and developing the correct tone. The fourth part is an extensive treatment of three important forms of professional speaking, that is, job interviews, group discussions, and oral presentations.

The *fifth part* concentrates on **reading and language comprehension**. Chapter 12 discusses the reading process, reading with a purpose, reading different kinds of texts, active and passive reading, and reading speed. Chapter 13 concentrates on reading skills, vocabulary skills, eye reading and visual perception, prediction techniques, scanning skills, skimming skills, and intensive reading skills, such as distinguishing between facts and opinions, and drawing inferences and conclusions. Chapter 14 focuses on reading scientific and technical texts, reading methods, reading instructions and manuals, and reading and interpreting graphic information.

The *sixth part* discusses important study skills such as note-writing, summarising, parapharsing, and referencing.

The *seventh part* deals with **writing strategies** where as the *eighth part* is an exhaustive treatment of **professional writing** and covers routine business letters, sales letters, resumes and job applications, business memos, e-mails, reports, proposals, and technical articles. The appendices contain a comprehensive review of functional grammar, problem areas and grammatical analysis, and vocabulary development.

Learning Aids Some of the learning aids, which I have included in this book, to make it completely learner-centric, are:

1. **Learning Objectives** These promote focused learning.
2. **Review Tips** These end-of-the-chapter tips provide a quick review and summary of the topic discussed.
3. **Progress Checks** These are short modules of question answer sessions given after every important topic, as a reinforcement aid before moving on to the next topic
4. **Recap Boxes** The important points within each chapter have been highlighted in a box in the corresponding sections.
5. **Figures and Tables** They provide easy comprehension.
6. **Functional Grammar Review** Given as an appendix (Appendix A) at the end of the book, this feature will help the students in refreshing essential grammar.
7. **Common Errors in English Communication** A short course designed to make the students aware of the very common mistakes that they make unknowingly and to help students master the art of communicating in correct English (Appendix B).
8. **Vocabulary Development** Another special feature of this book, this module will help students choose the apt word and add to their word power to help them communicate powerfully, and of course, effectively (Appendix C).

While my endeavor has been to give a good book to the students, I will welcome any critical suggestion on this book. Please write to me at ashrafrizvi@yahoo.co.uk or drop a letter at the publisher's address.

M Ashraf Rizvi

Foreword

Communication is as fundamental to our social living as eating is to our biological existence. Naturally, even without any special training everyone develops proficiency in it. Why then do we need books on communication? For the same reason we need books that advise us on eating. If we ignore the expert advice and let our instincts prevail, we may develop faulty eating habits and ruin our health. The rich and the poor are equally at risk although in vastly different ways. Something similar may happen with our communication. We may be able to articulate words but not communicate well. We may hear or read and recognize words, but not comprehend well. If we do not master communication skills, we may ruin our social and professional relationships.

There was a time, not long ago, when soft skills including communication were thought of as poor cousins of the hard skills. While investing considerable time and resources to acquire the hard skills, bright students ignored the soft skills. Once you mastered the hard skills, they thought, the lowly soft skills would follow without any special effort. Teachers and parents often endorsed this lop-sided view of social and technical skills.

In the globalized world, 'techies' are discovering the harsh reality that technical skills without soft ones would make them knowledge workers, not managers or leaders. Hard skills are perishable and machine-replaceable. Those who cannot communicate well will lose out; they get much less credit for their contributions than they deserve.

It is in this context that Dr. Ashraf Rizvi's *Effective Technical Communication* has to be viewed. For this edition, he has revised the text thoroughly incorporating the rapid changes in the field of technical and professional communication during the last ten years. With the revision ETC, which has been popular with students and teachers of technical communication alike as a comprehensive guide, has now become even more reader-friendly. Dr. Rizvi takes the reader through the whole spectrum of communication. He takes into account the needs of students and practicing professionals. He meshes sound theory with pragmatic advice. He treats discrete skills such as sentence construction with as much felicity and clarity as integrated communication skills such as writing technical articles and proposals.

As a large part of technical and professional communication the world over is through the medium of the English language, Dr. Rizvi also pays attention to it. He has three very useful appendices on functional grammar, common errors, and vocabulary building.

Effective Technical Communication is undoubtedly a student-friendly book. In order to help the learner cope with the wide range of concepts and skills that he covers, Dr. Rizvi has thoughtfully inserted learning aids such as Review Tips, Checklists, and Progress Checks.

I congratulate Dr. Rizvi on bringing out a thoroughly revised, updated edition of *Effective Technical Communication* and warmly recommend it to students and professionals of all shades everywhere.

M M Monippally
Former Professor, Communications
Indian Institute of Management, Ahmedabad

Acknowledgements

The revised edition of *Effective Technical Communication* echoes the professional experience of a large team of contributors, mentors, and advisors who immensely contributed to add value to the book in several ways. I express my thanks to many academicians, professionals, faculty colleagues, mentors, advisors, and my students from IIT, Dhanbad, IIM Indore, and Sultan Qaboos University, whose valuable advices, observations, helpful suggestions, and comments helped the book to become so successful.

First of all, I thank Sri Sharad Jaipuria, Chairman, Jaipuria Institute of Management, and Sri Shreevats Jaipuria, Vice-Chairman, Jaipuria Institute of Management for promoting a research culture in the institute by encouraging intellectual output from faculty by providing a conducive environment to pursue research interests, resulting in high quality publications in form of books, articles, and cases. All this has encouraged me to revise the existing edition to suit the changing needs of our audience. I also thank my colleagues at IIM Indore and Jaipuria Institute of Management Lucknow whose input enriched the revised content of the book.

I would also like to thank my former colleagues at IIT Dhanbad (Earlier ISM Dhanabd), who made the publication of the book possible. Firstly, I thank Sri P.K. Lahiri, I.A.S. (Retd.), Chairman, Indian School of Mines for inspiring the faculty of our university to achieve academic excellence and providing us a positive academic work environment, which made it possible for me to write a book. I also thank Professor S N Mukherjee, Director, Indian School of Mines for encouraging and supporting my academic efforts. My thanks are also due to Professor R K Singh, Head of the Department of Humanities and Social Sciences, Indian School of Mines for providing constructive suggestions to improve the quality of the work. I also thank my colleagues Col. S. M. Mehta, Dr. Partha De, Dr. Vishnu Priye, Dr. Atul Kumar Verma, Dr. V. Kumar, Professor S. B. Srivastava, Dr. V. M. S. R. Murthy, Professor T. Kumar, Professor Gurdeep Singh, and Dr. Ashish Sarkar, for providing sample material for examples and illustrations throughout the book. My thanks are also due to my colleagues at Sultan Qaboos University, including Professor David Kirk Vaughan, Dr. Ronald Peterson, Dr Felix Paul, Mr. Ian Robertson, Ms Asma Bhatti and Ms Naveen Saa for their enlightening views on several topics covered in the book. I am also grateful to Professor M. M. Monipally, Indian Institute of Management, Ahmedabad, Professor Maya Khemlani David of University of Malaya, Malaysia, Professor K M Tiwary of Taiz University, Yemen, Professor P N Pandit of Arab Open University, Kuwait; and Professor Sherwin Peng of Shantou University, China for valuable comments.

My sincere thanks to the team at McGraw-Hill Education whose professional commitments and devotion made value addition to the book.

Above all, I thank my wife Tamanna and my children Asfar and Anum for bearing with my busy schedule during the project.

While my endeavor has been to give a good book to the students, I will welcome any critical suggestion on this book. Please write to me at mashrafrizvi@gmail.com or drop a letter at the publisher's address.

M Ashraf Rizvi

Contents

SECTION 2: LISTENING COMPREHENSION

SECTION 3: SPEAKING STRATEGIES

SECTION

1

Fundamentals

CHAPTERS

1 CHAPTER

Communication Today

Communication is the transfer of information and understanding from one person to another person. It is a way of reaching others with facts, ideas, thoughts and values.

—Keith Davis

LEARNING OBJECTIVES

- Understanding the concept of communication
- Grasping stages of the communication process
- Understanding the methods of communication
- Identifying channels and networks of communication
- Understanding online communication
- Identifying the barriers that disrupt the communication process as well as appropriate steps to overcome these barriers
- Learning about communication at the workplace and its challenges

1.1 BASICS OF COMMUNICATION

Communication is a process of sharing information.

Look around and you will find people involved in several activities, which involve informal conversations, discussions, meetings, presentations, phone calls, teleconferencing, videoconferencing, gossiping, net surfing, chatting, and so on. In short, we need to communicate in order to interact. Communication is one of the essential conditions of social interaction. Without communication, social interaction may not be possible because human interaction is essentially communicative interaction. It pervades the entire range of social and professional relationships, and plays a key role in our life. It is the reciprocal stimulation and response between individuals, and makes social as well as professional interaction possible.

Now, let us try to understand what the term 'communication' means. The term has been defined at various levels. As it comes from the Latin word *communicare*, meaning 'to share, to impart, or to commune', its literal meaning is 'giving or sharing information'. It is this sharing of information that makes the process of communication so important to us.

> Communication is any behavior that results in an exchange of meaning.
>
> **American Management Association**

Communication is an exchange of meaning and understanding. Meaning is central to communication, and transmission of meaning is the central objective of communication. Communication begins with the sender sending out message cues, which are perceived by the receiver who assigns meaning to them and responds to them accordingly. Communication is not complete unless the message is decoded and understood by the receiver. Moreover, communication can be considered effective only when the receiver's response is congruent with the meaning the sender wants to convey.

> Communication is the process involving the transmission and reception of symbols eliciting meaning in the minds of the participants by making common their life experiences.
>
> **Baird Jr. E John**

Communication is symbolic because it involves not only words but also symbols and gestures that accompany the spoken words. Infact, our ability to symbolise makes communication possible.

> Effective communication is purposive symbolic interchange resulting in workable understanding and agreement between the sender and the receiver.
>
> **George T Vardaman**

Communication is an interactive process. The two communication agents involved in the communication process are the sender (S) and the receiver (R). Both the communication agents exert a reciprocal influence on each other through interstimulation and response.

To conclude, we can define communication as a multidimensional interactive process of sharing common sets of signs, symbols, and language from one person to another person so that a suitable response results.

Progress Check 1

1. **Study the following statements about the process of communication and tick True or False against each of them.**
   (a) Communication directs the flow of information to help people interact with each other.
   (b) Communication is always a one-way process of passing information and ideas to someone else.
   (c) You may use a specific set of words, gestures, and images to convey what you want to say.
   (d) Symbolic action is limited to verbal communication.
   (e) Communication involves only words.
   (f) Human interaction is not communicative interaction.
   (g) Meaning is crucial to communication.
   (h) Communication achieves shared understanding.
   (i) Communication is designed to achieve a goal.
   (j) In order to achieve desired objectives, the sender and the receiver must share common understanding.

1.2 PROCESS OF COMMUNICATION

Whether it is an informal social situation or a formal academic or professional situation, we need to share information, ideas, and knowledge with others. However, this process of sharing information is a symbolic interchange, which is both dynamic and interactive, and results in an exchange of meaning and understanding. Let us look more closely at the whole process of communication.

Firstly, communication is a dynamic interactive process that involves the effective transmission of facts, ideas, thoughts, feelings, and values. It is not passive and does not just happen; we actively and consciously engage in communication in order to develop the information and understanding required for effective group functioning. It is dynamic because it involves a variety of forces and activities interacting over a period of time. The word 'process' suggests that communication exists as a flow through a sequence or series of steps. The term 'process' also indicates a condition of flux and change. The relationships of people engaged in communication continuously grow and develop.

As noted earlier, communication is a dynamic interactive process. It consists of five steps, namely, ideation, encoding, transmission, decoding, and response. Study Fig. 1.1, to understand the different stages of communication.

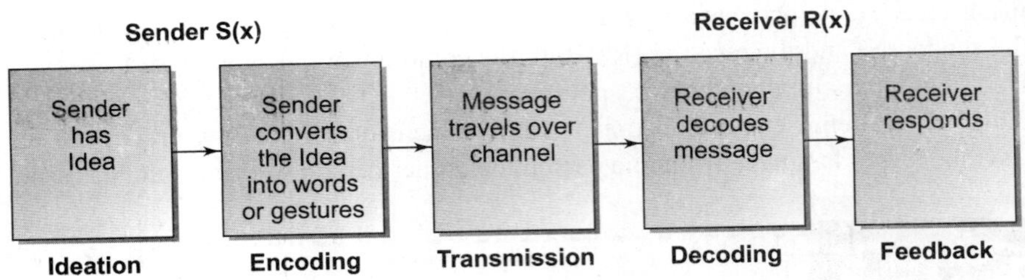

Fig. 1.1 The Communication Process

1.2.1 Ideation

The process of communication begins with ideation, which refers to the formation of the idea or selection of a message to be communicated. It consists of the 'What' of communication and is concerned with the content of the specific message to be presented. The scope of 'ideation' is generally determined by the sender's knowledge, experiences, and abilities, as well as the purpose of communication and the context of the communicative situation. However, the form of ideation depends on several other factors.

Messages generally have two kinds of content, logical and emotional. Logical messages consist of factual information, while emotional messages consist of feelings and emotions. In a formal communicative situation, 'ideation' may consist of finding and selecting a subject or general topic, looking for ideas and thoughts, and deciding the type, scope, and sources of information.

1.2.2 Encoding

Encoding is the next step in communication. It is the process of changing the information into some form of logical and coded message. The encoding process is based on the purpose of communication and the relation between the sender and the receiver. In a formal situation, encoding involves:

(a) Selecting a language
(b) Selecting a medium of communication
(c) Selecting an appropriate communication form

Selecting the right language is essential for effective encoding. Verbal messages need a common language code, which can be easily decoded by the receiver. If the receiver is not able to decode or understand the message, communication will fail. For example, a person who does not understand Tamil cannot decode a message encoded in Tamil. We generally use our first language (L 1) in informal situations while we prefer official language in formal business, academic, or professional situations.

As selecting the right medium of communication involves making the right choice out of many available options, it determines the effectiveness of encoding. This is vital as there are so many options available to a communicator for transmitting interpersonal messages that he or she may get confused. Making the right choice is the beginning of effective communication. There are three basic options for sending interpersonal messages, that is speaking, writing, and non-verbal signs and symbols. The spoken word involves vocalisation while non-verbal message cues are generally visual (auditory and tactile). Non-verbal cues play a significant role in oral communication. These cues include body movements, facial expressions, touching patterns, speech mannerisms.

The selection of the appropriate form (Table 1.1) largely depends on the sender-receiver relationship and the overall goal of the communicative situation. Oral communication may be face-to-face interpersonal communication, group communication, speaker-audience communication, or telephonic communication. The choice depends on the need and purpose of the communication. Writing involves the selection of the correct written form, that is, letter, memo, notice, report, proposal, and so forth.

TABLE 1.1 Communication Forms

Forms	*Examples*
Interpersonal face-to-face communication	Casual conversations, formal interactions, student-student negotiations, job interviews
Group communication	Meetings, conferences, group discussions, panel discussions
Speaker-audience communication	Speeches, debates, seminars, workshops, oral presentations
Telephonic communication	Personal interactions, business deals, telephone interviews
Written communication	Reports, proposals, memos, letters, emails

1.2.3 Transmission

Transmission refers to the flow of message over the chosen channel. Transmission confirms the medium selected during the process of encoding and keeps the communication channel free from interference or noise so that the message reaches the receiver without any disturbance. It is one of the most basic aspects of communication because it also involves choosing the proper time (when to communicate), proper place (where to communicate), and a proper way (how to communicate). For example, when you want to tell your teacher that you will not be able to attend his or her next class, you decide whether you should tell him/her before the class or after the class; in the class room itself or in his/her chamber. For communication to be effective, it is essential that the right time, the right place, and the right method is chosen.

1.2.4 Decoding

Decoding is the process of converting a message into thoughts by translating the received stimuli into an interpreted meaning in order to understand the message communicated. It is important to note that it is the message that is transferred, as meaning cannot be transferred from one person to another. The receiver has to assign meaning to a message in order to understand it.

The process of decoding involves interpretation and analysis of a message. Decoding in written communication refers to reading and understanding a written message. On the other hand, in oral communication, decoding includes listening and understanding. Effective decoding is very important for successful communication as any misinterpretation of a message leads to communication breakdown and creates confusion and misunderstanding.

1.2.5 Response

Response is the last stage in the communication process. It is the action or reaction of the receiver to the message. It helps the sender know that the message was received and understood. The feedback that goes to the sender makes it clear whether the receiver has accepted the information and filed it in his/her memory or rejected it. He or she may ask for more information or clarification. Response is, thus, the key to communication as the effectiveness of communication depends on how congruent a receiver's response is with the meaning intended by the sender.

Progress Check 2

1. **Which of the following statements about the steps of communication are not True?**
   (a) The process of communication begins when the sender converts the idea into words or gestures.
   (b) Ideation is shaped by assumptions based on the sender's experiences.
   (c) The scope of 'ideation' is not determined by the situation.
   (d) Transmission confirms the medium selected during the process of encoding.
   (e) Noise is anything that interrupts the transmission of a message.
   (f) Decoding relates to the sender of a message.
   (g) The sender is the person initiating the communication.
   (h) The sender often expects a response from the receiver.
   (i) The responses of the receiver create feedback.
   (j) It is the duty of the receiver to keep the communication channel free from interference.

1.3 METHODS OF COMMUNICATION

There are various methods used for communication. Communication between two people or groups of people can take place verbally or non-verbally in a formal or an informal setting. This can be done within an internal setting or with the world outside. Let us understand these methods in detail.

1.3.1 Verbal Communication, Written and Non-Verbal Communication

Verbal Communication

Verbal communication is communication done orally between people. If done properly, it helps both the parties involved understand each other better. The biggest advantage of verbal communication is that it provides immediate feedback to the sender of the message. It also gives a personal touch to the communication. Certain aspects like gestures, facial expressions, voice modulation, tone, making the other person at ease, etc., can all be done using verbal communication. In fact, the sender can even modify his/her message based on the feedback he/she gets during the conversation.

This method of communication is given less preference over written communication in business scenarios because any mistake made during a conversation, is difficult to correct.

Written Communication

Written communication is a widely used form of communication. The biggest advantage of written communication is that it leaves a permanent record. It, therefore, facilitates organised messages to be communicated. However, unlike oral communication, the sender does not get instant feedback for his/her message. Also, he/she cannot add a personal touch to the message.

This form of communication is preferred in business scenarios because it leaves a proof of the communication and ensures formality and correctness in formal correspondence.

Non-Verbal Communication

The third category of communication that is used widely but seldom recognised, is non-verbal communication. This refers to communication done through gestures, facial expressions, eye contact, touch, tone of voice, dress, space between the people communicating, and ambience, to name a few. Even while sitting quietly, two people can communicate using one of the aforementioned forms of communication.

Let us now study various forms of non-verbal communication in detail.

Kinesics

Kinesics refers to communication through the body language of the parties communicating. Let us understand the concept through some examples.

Sometimes people use signs for communicating their message. For example, when a boss gestures a thumbs up to his/her colleague, it could mean that he/she liked the idea or is giving him/her a go-ahead.

Sometimes during a conversation, a person may pound the table to express anger or disagreement over something. Though this is a negative form of expression, it is still not uncommon.

Think of the stare that your father may have given you when you may have said something inappropriate. This is another example of non-verbal communication through affective displays.

Many times, during face-to-face interaction, people may nod to show their agreement or even disagreement over what is being discussed. This nodding too delivers the message without the use of any words.

During interviews or situations where a person is uncomfortable, some people are seen shaking their legs, constantly. Such a body language clearly shows nervousness or a lack of confidence in the person shaking his/her legs. Therefore, even without the person realising that he/she is communicating something, the message is sent to others around him/her.

Paralinguistics

Paralinguistics refers to spoken communication through changes in the rate of speech, accent, volume, voice modulation, pitch, and fluency. It is not only what is being said is important but also how it is said plays a role in communication. For example, a simple sentence like “Come here!” can be said authoritatively or endearingly, depending on the tone of voice of the sender.

Proxemics

Ever wondered how some people stand very close to another person while talking. Some people may be okay with it, while others may take offence. This aspect of communication is called proxemics.

This aspect of communication goes as far as to study the impact of objects around the room where people are communicating. For example, if during a meeting, a fountain is kept in the room, people may get distracted.

Not only the objects in a room, the room itself can have an impact on a conversation. Imagine an interview taking place in an office cafeteria. How comfortable would the interviewee be? Compare this situation to giving an interview in a closed room only in the presence of the interviewer. The answer is a no-brainer.

Chronemics

Chronemics refers to communication using time as a factor. Let us understand this with the help of an example. A boss who comes to office on time every day, subtly communicates it to his/her employees that they too are expected to be on time every day.

To conclude, we can say that non-verbal messages are as important or sometimes even more important than their verbal or written counterparts. Therefore, while communicating, especially in professional settings, non-verbal gestures should also be taken care of.

1.3.2 Formal and Informal Communication

Formal communication refers to communication taking place through pre-planned channels in an organised setting. On the other hand, informal communication refers to casual conversations in personal setting or even in formal settings. For example, communication between team members during a meeting is formal communication. Later on, when these team members form sub-groups and discuss about the meeting casually, it is informal communication.

Formal communication may be more time consuming than informal communication, but it has the advantage of having a proof later on unlike its informal counterpart.

Even though one may be tempted to undermine the importance of informal channels of communication, they are equally important. Many a times, relationships are built over such casual conversations; some crucial ideas come up; sometimes a colleague may even extract some information from another only to be used later on. Therefore, one must always be careful while communicating when in a formal setting, irrespective of the method.

1.3.3 Internal and External Communication

Communication can also be categorised on the basis of location or the relationship with a person or an organisation. Any communication done within an organised set up like an organisation or a department or even a team, is internal communication. On the other hand, communication done with people outside an organised setup, i.e., an organisation, is external communication.

External communication is always formal because in these types of communications, a person deals with external parties that may quote the person later on. On the other hand, internal communication can be both, formal and informal.

1.4 CHANNELS OF COMMUNICATION

Communication is essential for the internal functioning of any organisation. By integrating the managerial functions and serving to influence the behaviour and attitudes of people through persuasion, it encourages them to perform in order to achieve organisational objectives. The interaction between the different individuals working in a company or organisation takes place through different channels. These channels could be both informal and formal.

Informal channels transmit official news through unofficial and informal communicative interactions known as the 'grapevine'. This informal communication network includes tea time gossip, casual gatherings, lunch time meetings and so on. These channels may not be very reliable as they may be company rumours or just gossip. Such channels are more active in organisations that are not transparent. As employees want to know what is going on in their organisation, they seek out unofficial sources of information. The grapevine is not always negative for an organisation and can, infact, be helpful as it helps in positive group building by acting as a safety valve for pent-up emotions. It may help in building up organisational solidarity and harmony.

> Informal channels transmit official news through unofficial and informal communicative interactions known as the 'grapevine'.

A formal communication channel, on the other hand, refers to the formal methods of communication that are followed in management. As illustrated in Fig. 1.2, four different channels of communication are used within an organization which are listed as follows:

- Downward communication
- Upward communication
- Horizontal communication
- Diagonal communication

Downward Channel	Upward Channel	Horizontal Channel	Diagonal Channel
Communication from the decision makers to workers.	Communication from employees to management	Communication among workers at the same level	Communication flows in all directions
Seniors → subordinate employees	Subordinate employees → seniors	Seniors → seniors employees → employees	No protocol

Fig. 1.2 Channels of Communication

1.4.1 Downward Communication

As the main function of downward communication is providing direction and control, it refers to communication from the higher level in managerial hierarchy to the lower ones. A communication from the general manager of a company to the branch managers is an example of downward communication. Other examples of downward communication include annual confidential reports, performance appraisals, notices, project feedback, announcements of company policies, official instructions, and so on. Forms of downward communication may include notes, notices, memos, telephone conversations, voice mails, emails, or face-to-face conversations.

> There are four formal channels of communication: downward channel, upward channel, horizontal channel, and diagonal channel.

Downward communication is essential for the functioning of any organisation as it involves the transfer of information, instruction, advice, request, feedback, and ideas to subordinate staff. It increases staff awareness and facilitates implementation of new policies, guidelines, decisions, and evaluation and appraisal of the performance of employees. However, too much downward communication can lead to reaction from subordinates and can hamper better employee-employer relationship.

1.4.2 Upward Communication

As the main purpose of upward communication is to provide feedback on several areas of organisational functioning, it refers to communication from subordinates to superiors. A business report from the branch manager of a company to the managing director of the company is an example of upward communication. Other examples of upward channel include business proposals, suggestion box, exit interviews, grievance committees, and so forth.

Since upward communication involves the transfer of information, request, and feedback from the subordinates to their seniors, it promotes better working relationships within an organisation by giving the subordinate staff opportunities to share their views and ideas with their supervisors. It facilitates employee involvement in the decision-making process. Nevertheless, in any organization there has to be a balance between downward and upward communication channels.

1.4.3 Horizontal Communication

The main objective of horizontal communication is to develop teamwork, and promote group coordination within an organisation. It takes place between professional peer groups or people working on the same level of hierarchy. Horizontal communication is less formal and structured than both downward communication and upward communication, and may be carried out through informal discussions, management gossip, telephone calls, teleconferencing, videoconferencing, memos, routine meetings, and so on.

1.4.4 Diagonal Communication

Diagonal communication is the product of modern changes in information technology and management and is a result of the growing realisation of fraternity and equality in the corporate sector. It is basically a response to the market needs that demand speed and efficiency. As the diagonal channel occurs between people who do not have to follow rigid norms of communication protocol, it flows in all directions.

Progress Check 3

1. **Which of the following statements about channels of communication are TRUE?**
   (a) The main function of upward communication is providing direction and control.
   (b) Communication from the chief executive officer of a company to the personnel manager of the company is an example of upward communication.
   (c) Formal communication channels are based on social relationships in which employees talk about work during informal social gatherings.
   (d) The main objectives of horizontal communication are developing teamwork and promoting group coordination within an organisation.
   (e) Informal communication channels transmit official news through unofficial means.
   (f) A formal communication channel is the process of communication that is followed in organizational management.
   (g) A business proposal from the branch manager of a company to the managing director of the company is an example of horizontal communication.
   (h) Horizontal communication takes place between professional peer groups or people working at the same level of hierarchy.

(i) The main purpose of upward communication is to provide feedback on several areas of organisational functioning.
(j) Diagonal channels flow in all directions.

1.5 NETWORKS OF COMMUNICATION

The concept of networks of communication is related to the channels of communication discussed in the previous section. Based on these channels, the networks of communication can be divided into two major types—centralised communication and decentralised communication.

1.5.1 Centralised Communication

As the name suggests, in such a network, communication is centralised with a leader. It is the leader who directs the flow of communication. An example of centralised communication is a chain network (Fig. 1.3)

Fig. 1.3 Chain Network

As must be clear, 'A' is the leader from whom the communication flows down the hierarchy. In such a network, communication channel can be both, upward and downward. This means, 'E' can give some information to 'C' through 'D'. However, it is only the leader, 'A', that decides what messages should be passed and how. In most organisations, it is usually the Chief Executive Officer or the Managing Director who decides this.

1.5.2 Decentralised Communication

Unlike the centralised communication, communication is not centralised with a leader in a decentralised network of communication. Here, everybody is a leader and can communicate freely with other members of the group. An example of decentralised communication is the circle network (Fig. 1.4).

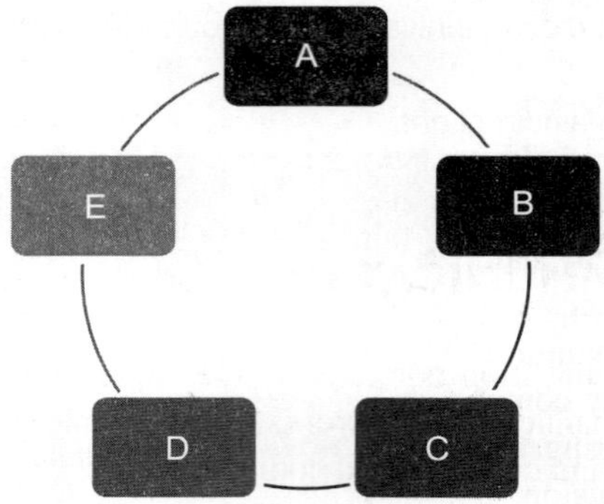

Fig. 1.4 Circle Network

In a circle network, nobody is the leader. 'A' can communicate with 'E' or any other member like they can communicate with him/her or any other member. Here, nobody is the leader who gets to decide the flow of communication.

1.6 ONLINE COMMUNICATION

Information Technology has changed the way people communicate and how businesses run. IT has opened a new world called the online or web or digital world. New dimensions have been added to the way organisations and people communicate.

Digital content comprises of websites, e-commerce sites, blogs, online feedback forms, interactive chats, discussion boards, and social media like Facebook, Twitter, LinkedIn, Instagram, and Pinterest, to name a few.

Basic rules for communication and content creation remain the same as those in offline communication. However, newer dimensions get added to each type of content. This is best understood with the help of some examples.

Any business communication through a platform like Twitter has to be short, crisp, and responsive. The user needs to be conversant with functions like hashtags, twitter handles, and re-tweets.

Website is the first face of an organisation that everybody sees. These days, it is not an option to not have one. A badly designed website or a website with poor content, can drive customers away. While creating content for a website, there are many aspects that need to be taken care of. The following are some pointers though the list is not exhaustive:

- Content should facilitate search engine optimisation
- Content should be crisp
- Information about the organisation should be up-to-date
- Content should be customised keeping the target audience in mind
- The website and its content should be compatible across platforms
- The content and the design should be mobile-friendly

There are different rules and guidelines for different media like blogs, or LinkedIn, or Facebook, or e-commerce sites. Each of them requires an in-depth discussion, which is beyond the scope of this book.

However, the above-mentioned guidelines must have given some idea about the process of digital content creation. To succeed in any sphere, a working knowledge of digital content is a must.

1.7 BARRIERS TO EFFECTIVE COMMUNICATION

As communication is a complex process, it is desirable to take care of communication interference and the barriers in communication that may hamper the smooth flow of effective communication. These barriers may emanate from either the sender/receiver or the circumstances of communication. However, we need to avoid them to become effective communicators. In real communicative situations, any interference or noise, as it is commonly referred to, may complicate the communication process and interfere with our message. Communication barriers arise during the communication process and may confuse the listener or reader, create misunderstanding and confusion, and may sometimes lead to communication breakdown.

A careful analysis of communication barriers reveal that they are generally created by:

- Improper encoding
- Bypassing
- Frame of reference
- Physical distractions
- Psychological and emotional interference
- Cultural differences

Let us discuss some of these barriers to communication in greater detail.

1.7.1 Improper Encoding

Improper encoding is a recurrent barrier in the process of communication. Since there is a lack of understanding on the part of the receiver, it leads to confusion and misunderstanding. Messages should be presented in a linguistic code familiar to one's audience. The sender must consider the cognitive knowledge the receiver has of the communicative code that is being used. If the audience is not able to follow the language/dialect, a communication breakdown will definitely occur. In addition, selection of an inappropriate medium or linguistic form also leads to communication breakdown due to misunderstanding or confusion.

1.7.2 Bypassing

The term 'bypassing' refers to misunderstanding resulting from missed meanings because of the use of abstract words and phrases on which both senders and receivers do not agree. Bypassing is probably the most common communication barrier that you have to deal with. Words mean different things to different people. Age, education, and cultural background are three of the more obvious variables that influence the language a person uses. In order to avoid bypassing, you should use familiar words with concrete meanings so that there is no scope for confusion. Moreover, it is also necessary to know the background of your audience.

> 'Bypassing' refers to misunderstanding resulting from missed meanings because of the use of abstract words and phrases on which both senders and receivers do not agree.

For instance, an Indian asked his Arab colleague why he was a bachelor at the age of forty. The Arab replied innocently, "because of dowry…". The Indian responded,

'You should not have been so greedy." The Arab was upset and confused because he could not understand why his Indian friend considered him greedy. There was a communication breakdown.

'Dowry' for an Indian is the money that the groom takes from the family of the bride while 'dowry' for an Arab is the amount of '*mehar*' that the groom has to pay to the father of the bride.

1.7.3 Frame of Reference

Your weakness in viewing others within your frame of reference may also lead to confusion and misunderstanding. The moment you interpret others' point of view from your angle, you allow your preconceived notions and prejudices to start working for you. Your frame of reference is individual to you as it is based on your experiences, exposure, education, personality, and several other elements peculiar to you. In order to avoid communication failure, you have to be sensitive to this fact and try to put yourself in the other person's position.

> The moment you interpret others' point of view from your angle, you allow your preconceived notions and prejudices to start working for you.

1.7.4 Physical Distractions

Physical distractions can easily disrupt communication. For example, you are trying to give an oral presentation in the classroom but the room temperature is very high and there is no air-conditioner or fan in the room. Your discomfort may cause communication failure because a person who is physically uncomfortable can be neither a good speaker nor a good listener. You should avoid any physical discomfort during communication.

1.7.5 Psychological and Emotional Interference

Any psychological or emotional turbulence or disturbance can prove to be a barrier to effective communication because it leads to lack of interest and concentration. Feelings of sadness, fear, anger, anxiety, or jubilation influence our reception and receptivity to others' ideas. Communication is a purposeful activity based on rationality and reason and one must assure that one is not emotionally charged (for example, very excited/angry/nervous) before one takes part in a communicative interaction. One may find it difficult to concentrate on the content of the message if one is emotionally charged. Over arousal of emotions may adversely affect both encoding and decoding. Whether you are a sender or a receiver, it is necessary that you try to focus on the content of the message.

> Over arousal of emotions may adversely affect both encoding and decoding.

1.7.6 Intercultural Differences

As noted earlier, it is the receiver who assigns meaning to message cues and meanings are assigned in terms of a receiver's frame of reference. This interpretation of meaning can create misunderstandings during intercultural communication because the sender and the receiver belong to different cultures and share different values. In fact, our values are our personal guides to thought and behaviour, and exert a strong influence on us. We should be sensitive to cultural differences and take into account the values of our listeners/readers while communicating with them.

Checklist for Communication Barriers

- Know your audience before you communicate with them. Try to know their needs, perceptions, and expectations from you.
- Try to experience the world from the receiver's perspective.
- Use an appropriate and effective personal style and avoid using a negative or angry tone.
- Use an appropriate form and style of communication.
- Encode your message well.
- Avoid physical and psychological barriers.
- Listen and read carefully.
- Be precise and to the point. Avoid information overload.
- Be open, frank, and positive.
- Appreciate and understand cultural differences.

Progress Check 4

1. Study the following communicative situations to identify communication barriers in them. If the situation involves a communication barrier, tick Yes but if it does not involve a barrier, tick No.

(a) One of your colleagues has misbehaved with you. You are very upset and you want to complain to the director of your company.
Yes/No

(b) Suppose you are working in a company and you have thought of a brilliant idea to solve the technical problems of your company but you are not sure whether your colleagues will agree with you or not. You are very nervous as you do not know the response of your colleagues. However, you want to share your ideas with all your colleagues.
Yes/No

(c) A friend wants to know why you are doing B.Tech in Computer Science and Engineering. You are not very clear about the reasons for joining the course but want to respond to his query.
Yes/No

(d) You have some problems with one of your assistants. He has insulted you. You are very angry and upset, and immediately want to express your feelings to your immediate boss.
Yes/No

(e) You have to attend a meeting where you have to present a proposal but you are very disturbed because your sister is very sick.
Yes/No

(f) You are not happy with the internet facilities in your department and want to propose major changes. You want to share your innovative ideas with the head of the department.
Yes/No

(g) You want to propose major changes in the computer facilities provided by your institution. You want to share your innovative ideas with all the students of your class.
Yes/No

(h) Your communication teacher is very angry with you because you did not submit an important assignment as per the deadline set by him. You want to explain the reasons for the delay. You go and meet him personally.
Yes/No

1.8 COMMUNICATION AT THE WORKPLACE

Ultimately, the whole purpose of reading this book is to be able to apply the learning in a working environment. Communication cannot be ignored even if one is in a technical job. Good or bad communication can make or break careers. In fact, organisations take communication very seriously not only for their employees, but also for their own good. Many organisations, therefore, have a specialised function or department for this is called corporate communication.

1.8.1 Corporate Communication

Most organisations have a specialised department that deals with the internal and external communication of an organisation. This department is called the Corporate Communications Department. It handles information dissemination to the outside world in a manner that is in congruence with the corporate policy. In some organisations, it is referred to as Public Relations or Public Affairs department. This department is ultimately responsible for maintaining a good image of the organisation. In times of crisis or any allegation against the organisation, it is the Corporate Communications Department that comes to the rescue.

1.8.2 Communication Challenges at the Workplace

No matter how prepared or adept one is at communication, there will always be challenges while communicating in a workplace. The reasons are galore. Given below are some common challenges faced by people in the workplace. The list is not and cannot be exhaustive, given the dynamic nature of communication and people interaction.

1. **Different backgrounds of employees:** Given the multicultural and global nature of organisations these days, employees come from varied backgrounds in terms of nationality, location, ethnicity, religion, economic status, etc. Therefore, communication styles need to be altered when dealing with different people.
2. **Different accents:** An offshoot of different backgrounds is different languages, accents and fluency. When dealing with people with different accents and fluency or language competence, one should make an effort to go slow or modify the communication style to ensure the message is being understood by the other party.
3. **Different organisation culture:** Some organisations have an open door policy where the seniors can be approached any time, while some have a policy of following the hierarchy before reaching the top. Therefore, any new employee needs to adapt himself/herself to the culture prevalent in the organisation and modify his/her communication style.
4. **Closed groups:** When an organisation has a lot of old employees, sometimes new hires are seen as a threat and are not accepted within the closed groups that may have been formed over a period of time. This hinders communication and can be very daunting for the new employee.

5. **Direct versus indirect feedback:** Some organisations appreciate direct feedback however negative it may be. On the other hand, some organisations may not take in the right spirit. Therefore, an employee needs to be aware of the culture and tweak his/her communication accordingly.
6. **Personality traits:** No matter how much homogeneity a group of employees have in an organisation, there will still be some communication challenges because each individual is different. Personality of one person can never be the same as that of the other. Therefore, one needs to tweak one's communication style keeping the receiver in mind.
7. **Differences in experience:** Many a times, technical jargon or terms or organisation-specific abbreviations may be alien to freshers or a person who may be new to an organisation. Therefore, while communicating, one should do an audience analysis in terms of their background and experience.

Exercise

1. **Please list below the names of persons with whom you have communicated in English during the last three days–even if only for a moment. Answering the following questions will provide you with the guidelines and basics of your communication:**
   (a) List of names
   (b) With how many people did you actually communicate?
   (c) What were the reasons for communicating with each person?
   (d) What did they communicate about?
   (e) What were the forms of communication that you used?
   (f) How important is it to be able to communicate?
   (g) What would it be like if we could not communicate with others?
2. **Write short notes on the following:**
   (a) Informal channels of communication
   (b) Downward communication
   (c) Communication barrier
   (d) Workplace communication
   (e) Online communication
3. **Answer the following questions as briefly as possible:**
   (a) What is communication?
   (b) What are the steps in communication?
   (c) Which communication channel is the most important? Give reasons to support your answer.
   (d) Which are the different methods of communication?
   (e) When communicating with people from different cultures/regions, what can you do to reduce misunderstandings?
   (f) Have you experienced any communication barrier in understanding this chapter? How can we eliminate communication barriers, so that we can work and understand better?

Key to Progress Check

Progress Check 1

1. (a) True (b) False (c) True (d) False (e) False
   (f) False (g) True (h) True (i) True (j) True

Progress Check 2

1. (a), (c), (g)

Progress Check 3

1. (d), (e), (f), (h), (i), (j)

Progress Check 4

1. (a) Yes (b) Yes (c) Yes (d) Yes (e) Yes
   (f) No (g) No (h) Yes

2 CHAPTER

Nature and Dimensions of Technical Communication

Communication is a key strategy, both human communication and technical communication.

—Helene Nelson

LEARNING OBJECTIVES

- Understanding the nature of technical communication
- Learning various forms of technical communication
- Understanding the need for technical communication
- Learning effective technical communication skills

2.1 ASPECTS OF TECHNICAL COMPETENCE

Technical communication is a central factor in the emerging knowledge society, where technocrats and professionals in different areas face new communication challenges. In order to be an effective technical communicator, one needs to understand the process of technical communication. We may define technical communication as a transmission of scientific and technical information from one individual or group to another. This exchange of professional information may include simple definitions of tools, complex descriptions of machines and processes, or sophisticated explanation and interpretation of scientific principles. Effective technical communication is a dynamic interchange that may involve a systematic understanding of scientific and technical subjects.

> Technical communication is a transmission of technical and professional information from one individual or group to another.

The three important requirements of effective technical communication are:

- Subject competence
- Linguistic competence
- Organisational competence

2.1.1 Subject Competence

Ideation in the technical communication process, which depends on the sender's subject competence, i.e., his or her professional knowledge, experiences, and abilities. Subject competence is the first requirement of technical communication. It is the possession of appropriate knowledge of a particular technical subject-matter as well as the possession of highly sophisticated technical or professional skills. An inadequate background in the subject or lack of information might lead to incomplete and ineffective communication.

> Subject competence is the first requirement of technical communication.

2.1.2 Linguistic Competence

Linguistic competence, on the other hand, is the possession of appropriate language skills and the ability to present scientific facts or information clearly and objectively. As technical communication involves technical presentation of data in reports, proposals, research papers, technical bulletins, manuals, and handbooks, linguistic competence includes several functional skills. Lack of these skills may lead to ineffective or incomplete communication. These skills include the ability to:

- Analyse facts or information for clear presentation
- Use appropriate rhetorical devices to present scientific data
- Use graphs, charts, and diagrams systematically

> Linguistic competence is the ability to present scientific facts or information clearly and objectively.

2.1.3 Organisational Competence

> Organisational competence is the ability to organise technical information in a logical and structured way.

Since technical communication is a systematic and structured presentation of information, it involves a process of logical and thematic organisation. Organisational competence is the ability to organise technical information in a logical and structured way. It includes several skills such as the ability to sequence thoughts in a sentence, organise a paragraph according to the needs of the reader and the topic, use appropriate logical ordering, and provide thematic coherence to expression.

2.2 FORMS OF TECHNICAL COMMUNICATION

The fast growth of technical knowledge coupled with the development of sophisticated information technology has changed the way we communicate in professional situations. We prefer fast, interactive, and result-oriented forms of communication such as voice-mail, email, video transmission, teleconferencing, videoconferencing, intranet transmission, and so on to the traditional and slow forms of communication such as letters, memos, newsletters, and so forth. Today, one may find a range of interactive technologies for communication. However, technical communication still depends on the two basic forms of communication: oral and written.

2.2.1 Oral and Written Communication

Each form of communication has its merits and demerits. While oral communication provides immediate feedback and promotes better understanding, written communication provides a permanent record and facilitates the creation of organised messages. Oral communication gives a personal touch to the communication process whereas written communication is impersonal as the two communicators cannot see each other. The choice of an appropriate form of communication may depend on the need and purpose of the communicative situation.

> Oral communication provides immediate feedback, written communication provides a permanent record.

2.2.2 External and Internal Communication

There are two widely recognised categories of technical communication: *external communication* and *internal communication*. External communication consists primarily of describing the areas of expertise technical people or professionals provide. This may include any communication that an organisation does with people belonging to other organisations. Internal communication includes memos describing problems or requesting additional resources, different kinds of reports and proposals, internal presentations, company meetings, policy statements, office instructions, and office descriptions to be used for public releases or company websites.

2.2.3 General and Technical Communication

Technical communication is the process of communicating a specific message to a specific audience with a specific purpose. The repetition of the word 'specific' indicates the special nature of technical communication. It is this need-based specific characteristic of technical communication that makes it different from general or literary communication.

There are several characteristic features of technical communication that makes it different from general communication. As shown in Table 2.1, technical communication differs from general communication in content, style and approach of presentation, attitude, organisation, and language.

TABLE 2.1 Differences Between General and Technical Communication

General Communication	*Technical Communication*
• General content	• Technical content
• General vocabulary	• Specialised vocabulary
• Usually no formal elements	• Formal elements
• Both, formal and informal in style	• Always formal in style
• Both, factual and non-factual	• Always factual
• Both, objective and subjective	• Objective
• Not always structured	• Logically organised and structured
• Usually no specific exposition techniques	• Complex and important exposition techniques
• Not always for a specific audience	• Specific audience
• May or may not involve graphics	• Usually, involves graphics

Progress Check 1

1. Which of the following statements about technical communication are not True?

(a) Technical communication is the transfer of technical information from one individual or group to another.

(b) Linguistic competence is the possession of appropriate language skills and the ability to present facts or information clearly and objectively.

(c) Ideation in technical communication does not depend on the sender's subject competence.

(d) Technical communication involves complex and important exposition techniques.

(e) Inadequate knowledge regarding the subject might lead to incomplete and ineffective communication.

(f) Technical communication does not involve understanding and analysis of graphical information.

(g) Technical communication is less formal and structured than general communication.

(h) Technical communication makes professional interaction possible and directs the flow of technical information and knowledge for the guidance of technocrats, engineers, and others in their professional activities.

(i) Technical communication skills are crucial to professional success today.

(j) The revolution in information technology is having a profound impact on technical communication tasks.

2.3 IMPORTANCE OF TECHNICAL COMMUNICATION

The functional importance of technical communication for an individual or an organisation cannot be overemphasised. Whether you are an executive working in a multinational company, an engineer working at the shop floor level, a scientist working in a premier scientific lab, or a technical student studying in a professional institution, you need effective technical communication skills in order to be successful.

Technical communication is the essence of organisational life and a prerequisite to effective management. The list of its multipurpose functions is very long. It not only makes professional interaction possible but also directs the flow of technical information and knowledge for the guidance of technocrats, engineers, and others in their professional activities. It stimulates scientists and researchers to act to achieve individual as well as social and organisational objectives and develops information and understanding essential for effective group functioning. Moreover, it leads to unification between the activities of individuals as a work team and helps to foster positive attitudes required for motivation, cooperation, and other important organisational processes. Finally, it ensures free exchange of information and ideas and promotes scientific temper and maintenance of professional relations.

> Success in the highly competitive environment of today will depend not just on your professional knowledge and skills but on the ability to analyse, organize, and present essential information effectively.

With the information revolution and socio-economic changes in the new millennium, the importance of effective technical communication skills has increased. The whole world has become a global market and the transfer of technology is playing a key role in economic growth and transformation. As the professional world becomes more diverse, competitive, and result-oriented, the importance of technical communication skills continues to increase. In fact, technical communication skills are crucial to professional success today because success in communicating in the technical environment will depend not just on an effective style but on the ability to analyse, organise, and present essential information effectively.

Revolution in information technology is having a profound impact on technical communication tasks, and new kinds of communications tasks or skills will be required in the changed technological environment. These skills include knowledge of high-tech communication capabilities, ability to present and explain complex technical information in a simple and familiar style, ability to understand and explain quantitative data, cultural awareness capability, and ability to analyse and prioritise information.

The changes that have taken place in the field of science and technology reflect several developments in the way technical communication skills are viewed. In fact, there has been a shift in perspective, so that communication skills take priority over technical and professional skills. There is no doubt that good writing and speaking skills are essential to have success in job. It is also true that some technical skills are as important as communication skills but knowledge of highly sophisticated technical or professional skills will be useless if one does not know how to communicate the information and insights that result from the use and application of these technical and professional skills.

> Knowledge of highly sophisticated technical or professional skills will be useless if one does not know how to communicate.

Progress Check 2

1. **Which of the following factors is not responsible for the increasing importance of technical communication?**
   (a) Highly competitive environment
   (b) Information revolution
   (c) Changed technological environment
   (d) Socio-economic changes in the new millennium
   (e) Changes in the field of politics
   (f) Growing diversity of the business world
   (g) Globalisation
   (h) Growing complexity of technical information

2.4 TECHNICAL COMMUNICATION SKILLS

As technical communication may be oral or written, it may involve all the skills of language: listening, speaking, reading, and writing. Let us discuss each skill in some detail. Please note that many of the aspects discussed here are applicable to general communication also.

2.4.1 Listening

Technical communication involves all the four skills of language: listening, speaking, reading, and writing.

Listening skills, as summarised in Table 2.2, are probably one of the most important language skills that you need in order to be successful in your academic and professional pursuits. As students, you have to listen to lectures, explanations during tutorials and practical sessions, seminars and workshops, technical presentations, academic discussions, academic interactions, viva voce tests, and so on. Once you join a profession, you may be required to listen to discussions in meetings and conferences, seminars, business presentations, news bulletins, pre-recorded talks, telephonic conversations, teleconferences and videoconferences, and so forth. In fact, it is hard to imagine any academic, professional, or business work that does not require efficient listening skills.

TABLE 2.2 Listening Skills*

General	*Academic Listening to/during*	*Professional*
• Casual conversation	• Lectures	• Professional interaction
• Formal conversation	• Tutorials and practicals	• Meetings
• Social interaction	• Seminars and workshops	• Conferences
• Public speeches	• Technical presentations	• Interviews
• Announcements	• Academic discussions	• Professional discussions
• Radio	• Academic interaction	• Professional presentations
• Television programmes	• Viva voce	• Teleconferencing
• News reports		• Videoconferencing

*The list is not exhaustive.

One cannot be an effective communicator unless one is an effective listener.

Moreover, one needs effective listening skills as it is a state of receptivity that permits understanding of what is heard and grants the listener full partnership in the communication process. One cannot be an effective communicator unless one is an effective listener. In any oral communicative situation, listening is of special significance because oral communication cannot be complete without listening. One's response in an oral communication situation largely depends on one's ability to understand and appreciate the speaker's perspective. A student requires quick, efficient, and imaginative listening techniques in order to achieve academic success because his/her academic performance partly depends on the quantity and quality of listening. By listening to classroom lectures, academic discussions in seminars and workshops, and academic speeches the student acquires the professional knowledge and expertise needed to excel in his/her profession.

The importance of listening also lies in its multipurpose functions. As a purposeful communicative activity, listening serves individual needs and aids in implementing oral communication goals. There are many ways by which decisions are made in an organisation—by discussion in meetings and conferences, by negotiation in business dealings, by voting in democratic processes, and so on. In each instance, listening plays an important role as it aids in analysing a problem, understanding the possible solutions, and making a decision. In brief, listening:

- Makes oral interaction possible
- Aids in decision making
- Stimulates others to act to achieve individual as well as professional objectives
- Develops information and understanding essential for decision-making in meetings and conferences
- Leads to unification between the activities of individuals as a work team, towards achievement of common business, professional, or organisational goals
- Promotes maintenance of professional relations.

2.4.2 Speaking

Speaking skills, as summarised in Table 2.3, are also very important for a person's professional survival and growth. One needs them to be successful in one's academic and professional pursuits. In fact, every academic, professional, or business work requires effective speaking skills. Whether you are a scientist engaged in technical research, a business executive involved in business activities, or a student working for a professional degree, you need effective speaking skills in order to take an active part in oral communicative processes.

Every academic, professional, or business work requires effective speaking skills.

TABLE 2.3 Speaking Skills*

General	*Academic Speaking in/during*	*Professional*
• Casual conversation	• Lectures	• Professional interaction
• Formal conversation	• Tutorials and practicals	• Oral reports
• Social interaction	• Seminars and workshops	• Oral presentations
• Public speeches	• Technical presentations	• Group discussions/Meetings
• Small talks on local topics	• Academic discussions	• Conferences
• Negotiating meanings in social situations	• Academic interaction	• Workshops
• Conversation tasks in a given social milieu	• Viva voce	• Interviews
	• Oral interaction	• Professional discussions
	• Oral reports	• Teleconferencing
		• Videoconferencing

*The list is not exhaustive.

A person requires effective oral communication skills in several formal communicative situations, i.e. meetings, conferences, group discussions, panel discussions, interviews, teleconferencing, videoconferencing, seminars, workshops, and symposiums. Some of the sub-skills of oral communication that one may need include the following:

Asking and Answering Questions

- Asking questions in meetings, talks, business presentations, lectures, seminars, conferences, training sessions, fieldwork, and laboratory work
- Asking questions related to non-verbal data, formulae, equations, measures, numbers, fractions, and cardinal and ordinal numbers
- Answering questions, providing clarification, and giving explanations in the above situations

Expressing Opinions and Comments

- Asking for opinions
- Expressing criticism, objections, and doubt
- Expressing general comments
- Agreeing and disagreeing
- Seeking suggestions
- Giving suggestions
- Stating points of view

Academic and Professional Oral Interaction

- Interacting during interviews and viva voce tests
- Interacting orally with experts or professionals

Academic/Professional Discussions

- Discussing academic matter with fellow students
- Inviting to discuss
- Initiating discussion
- Initiating topic shift
- Giving information
- Coordinating in discussions

Meetings/Conferences

- Coordinating in meetings
- Conducting meetings
- Participating in meetings
- Summarizing and concluding in meetings

Oral Presentations

- Making oral presentations
- Orally describing and interpreting non-verbal data, *e.g.*, graphs, tables, diagrams, charts, plans, maps, and so on

- Persuading
- Using visual aids effectively

Several factors have contributed to the increased importance of speaking skills today. The information revolution along with globalisation and other social and economic changes in the new millennium have increased the importance of speaking skills. Look around and you will find people involved in oral communication: conversations, meetings, discussions, presentations, telephone calls, voice mails, teleconferencing, videoconferencing, gossiping, and so on. Speaking pervades the entire range of social and professional relationships, and plays a key role in our life. Without oral communication, social as well as professional interactions may not be possible.

The growth and expansion of service oriented industry has also increased the significance of oral competence for professionals in different fields. As the economy becomes less dependent on manufacturing, and more service oriented, the need for students with good speaking skills has become more acute. Media reports frequently highlight employers' complaints that graduates' oral skills require considerable improvement. Students, thus, need to develop speaking skills if they are to be successful in their careers. Speaking skills are the single most important criterion in hiring professionals. Most of the professionals are hired through a selection process, which involves speaking skills in the form of group discussion/case discussion/personal interview/oral presentation or some other form of oral communication.

Moreover, increasing reliance on oral communication forms such as meetings, group discussions, conferences, seminars, workshops, and other forms of oral interaction in democratic decision-making today has given increased significance to the need for effective speaking skills. Oral communication not only makes professional interaction possible, it develops information and understanding essential for decision-making in meetings, conferences, and other similar oral communicative situations. Moreover, it leads to unification between the activities of individuals as a work team, towards achievement of common business, professional, or organisational goals; and promotes maintenance of business and professional relations.

As oral communication is a tool of professional and business interaction, one should be able to use it fluently, effectively, and confidently. A person should know how to speak using appropriate grammatical and lexical forms and how to sound using appropriate phonological and graphical forms. One should have the ability to be an understanding interlocutor, create coherent discourse, and take appropriate turns in conversations, as well as have the ability to negotiate meanings with others by creating reciprocity of perspectives on the topic of discussion.

> As oral communication is a tool of professional and business interaction, one should be able to use it fluently, effectively, and confidently.

2.4.3 Reading

Like listening and speaking, reading is crucial to effective communication. You need effective reading skills as you may be required to read several kinds of reading materials for different general, academic, and professional purposes (summarised in Table 2.4). Both professionals and students need excellent reading skills to be successful in their pursuits as it is hard to imagine any academic, professional, or business work that does not require efficient reading skills.

TABLE 2.4 Reading Skills*

General	*Academic Reading*	*Professional*
• Newspapers	• Text books	• Business reports
• Magazines	• Journals	• Proposals
• Journals	• Research papers	• Business letters
• Novels	• Scientific articles	• Memos
• Stories	• Classroom notes	• Email messages
• Articles	• Lecture notes	• Notes
• Personal letters	• Thesis	• Notices
• Emails	• Dissertations	• Circulars
• General books	• Abstracts	• Promotional bulletins
• Entertainment literature		• Catalogues
		• Instruction manuals
		• Corporate brochures

*The list is not exhaustive.

The changes in business and industrial fields, coupled with the development of advanced information technology have greatly changed the way we receive and interpret information. Reading is not merely reading of letters and memos; it includes receiving and interpreting sophisticated technical material, email messages, intranet information, information on websites, and so on. Reading has new dimensions in industrial and technical organisations.

It is important that you are able to read and analyse scientific texts, instruction manuals, and technical materials in different forms. Comprehension of technical materials requires basic understanding of the technical subject, familiarity with scientific/technical terms, words and phrases, familiarity with scientific formulae/equations/abbreviations and with the discourse features of technical writing. It also includes the ability to understand and interpret graphic information.

2.4.4 Writing

The significance of writing skills (summarised in Table 2.5) cannot be overemphasised because writing is so important for students of all kinds and professionals in all fields. As a student, a person needs effective writing skills because one has to write examination answers, project reports, lab reports, summaries, synopsis, abstracts, and subject notes. Professionals are required to write business letters, memos, email messages, reports, proposals, minutes, notes, professional summaries, and so on. Both professionals and students need excellent writing skills to survive and excel in their pursuits as there is hardly any academic or professional activity that does not require writing skills.

TABLE 2.5 Writing Skills*

General	*Academic Writing*	*Professional*
• Personal letters • Personal e-mail messages • Notes • Comments • General articles	• Examination answers • Project reports • Lab reports • Synopsis • Thesis • Dissertations • Abstracts • Research papers • Scientific articles • Classroom notes • Lecture notes	• Technical reports • Industrial reports • Project proposals • Business proposals • Business letters • E mails • Memos • Notices • Agenda • Minutes of meeting • Technical abstracts • Job applications • Resumes

*The list is not exhaustive.

Exercise

1. **Answer the following questions as briefly as possible:**
   (a) Listening, speaking, reading, and writing skills are essential to be an effective technical communicator. Explain with examples.
   (b) Subject competence alone can suffice for success in technical fields. Linguistic and organisational competences are not required for a person with good subject knowledge. Do you agree?
2. **Give two differences between each of the following:**
   (a) Oral and Written Communication
   (b) External and Internal Communication
   (c) General and Technical Communication

Key to Progress Check

Progress Check 1

1. (c), (f), (g)

Progress Check 2

1. (e)

CHAPTER 3

Linguistic Ability and Style in Technical Communication

Style is the dress of thoughts.

—Lord Chesterfield

LEARNING OBJECTIVES

- Understanding style in technical communication
- Learning to apply techniques of precision in writing and speech
- Achieving clarity in communication
- Communicating in formal, direct, and specific language
- Learning to apply techniques of conciseness in technical communication
- Identifying characteristics of objectivity in communication
- Learning to use impersonal passive
- Knowing the use of formal language

3.1 TECHNICAL STYLE

When you write a letter to your friend, you try to be personal and subjective. On the other hand, you are impersonal, objective, and direct when you write your project report. Similarly, when you talk to a friend, you use informal language and casual style. In contrast, you use formal language when you make an oral presentation. The reason is obvious. You may like to express your feelings, emotions, and sentiments through a letter or an informal casual conversation, but you are only concerned with facts when you are writing a technical report or making an oral presentation. This difference of attitude and approach determines the characteristic features of 'general style' and 'technical style'.

> Style in technical communication is the way one speaks or writes to convey technical information.

Since 'style' is a major consideration in technical communication, we need to look more closely at the concept of style in technical communication. What is style? Style refers to the way something is said rather than what is said. For our purposes, style is the distinctive mode or manner of expressing ideas in language. But what is this distinctive mode or manner of expression? This distinctive manner may refer to the process of choosing appropriate:

- Words and phrases (formal, informal, technical, and so on)
- Sentence structure (simple, complex, compound, mixed, and so on)
- Sentence type (affirmative, negative, questions, question tags, and so on)
- Rhetorical devices or discourse writing techniques (description, narration, explanation, comparison and contrast, and so on)
- Effective logical structure and organisation.

Style in communication depends on several factors. It largely depends on:

- The audience—for example, the same message when addressed to a superior is expressed more diplomatically and tactfully, but when addressed to subordinates it is more direct and forceful.
- The communicative context—for example, conveying routine information and making requests, communicating good or bad news, conveying goodwill or trying to persuade someone.
- The purpose—for example, the way one conveys good news is not the same as conveying bad news.

Style could be very formal, as in a technical report or a professional presentation, or very informal, as in a personal letter or casual conversation. The most effective style is the one that accurately encodes the thought content of the message into appropriate language. It is important to adopt and use an appropriate style in order to be effective.

> Style in communication depends on the audience, the communicative context, and the purpose of communication.

Thus, style in technical communication may refer to the way a person puts words together into sentences, arranges sentences into paragraphs, and organises paragraphs to frame a piece of writing or an appropriate oral discourse to convey technical information clearly and accurately. In short, it is the way one speaks or writes when one deals with a technical or scientific subject. Let us try to understand this with the help of an example. Read the following short passage about sounds and note its style and language:

"For a sound to be produced and heard, a source of vibratory energy, a material medium, and a receiver are required. Some of the energy from a vibrating source is transmitted as a longitudinal wave through the medium to the ear. Sound waves will not travel through a vacuum. The ear is sensitive to the small pressure variations caused by the sound wave and is able to convert these small pressure changes into electrical impulses. These are transmitted by auditory nerves to the brain, where they produce the sensation of sound.

Sound sources are present almost everywhere in our environment, and the control of sound is a major problem. Unwanted sounds are called noise. The control of noise is becoming an important consideration in our everyday lives. Excessive noise is known to produce drastic changes in our personalities; it is fatiguing; and it may cause deafness and even a reduction in our life span."

Now let us examine the salient features of this passage.

- The passage describes the topic with objectivity as the writer does not use personal pronouns, subjective comments, or emotional expressions. The writer uses formal words and makes the passage objective and impersonal by choosing passive constructions such as "to be produced and heard", "are required", "is transmitted", "caused by", "are called", "is known to", and so forth.
- The writer uses compact phrases containing scientific words/technical terms such as "vibratory energy", "vibrating source", "longitudinal wave", "pressure variations", "electrical impulses", and "auditory nerves", and so on.
- The language is simple, direct, factual, and precise. There is no use of decorative language, figures of speech, or roundabout expressions.
- The author uses the rhetorical technique of description with linear logical organisation to present the information.

Technical communication skills can be improved by learning to recognise the essential features of technical style. The most important elements that one needs to keep in mind are appropriateness, brevity, clarity, objectivity, and formal language.

> Technical communication skills can be improved by learning to recognise the essential features of technical style.

Progress Check 1

1. **Study the following statements about technical style and write True or False against each of them:**
   (a) When you write a project report, you try to be personal and subjective.
   (b) Style is a major consideration in technical communication.
   (c) Style is the distinctive mode or manner of expressing ideas in language.
   (d) Style in technical communication does not depend on the purpose of communication.
   (e) The most effective style is the one that accurately encodes the thought content of the message into appropriate language.
   (f) Technical style is the way one speaks or writes when one deals with a technical or scientific subject.

3.2 ABC OF TECHNICAL COMMUNICATION

Remember that the acronym ABC denotes the three basic elements of technical communication: Accuracy, Brevity, and Clarity.

3.2.1 Accuracy

The first characteristic feature of technical communication is accuracy, which includes accuracy of information as well as accuracy of expression. One must assure oneself of the accuracy of information before communicating. For example, if a person has to write a technical report or give an oral presentation, he/she should repeatedly check all the facts that need to be included in the report/presentation. Any factual error will put a question mark on the reliability of the report or presentation and thereby reduce its effectiveness. Moreover, facts have to be recorded carefully and appropriately.

Accuracy demands exactness and precision.

Accuracy of expression demands that there should be no errors of grammar, spelling, punctuation, or usage. One has to be careful about grammar and punctuation mistakes and should review and revise the draft thoroughly for these errors. If a person is making a professional oral presentation, or taking part in a conversation, meeting, or discussion, he/she should take care of pronunciation, accent, intonation, and non-verbal mannerisms. Accuracy is essential for a professional and technical communicator.

Accuracy of expression also demands 'precision' in the use of words, phrases, sentences, and paragraphs. One must be certain that one is expressing one's ideas precisely and exactly so that the reader/audience is able to understand without confusion or misunderstanding.

Characteristics of Precision

Precision is the quality of being exact, accurate, and definite. In technical communication, precision refers to the art of attaining exact correspondence between the matter to be communicated and its presentation. It is an essential feature of technical style. As words are the symbols of ideas and the ingredients of thought, an effective sentence cannot be made from imprecise, incorrect, or inappropriate words. Words shape thought and help us to organise ideas and facts into manageable larger units. To use words in their appropriate places one must select words that convey the precise meaning from among the synonyms at one's disposal. Thus, precision demands an exact knowledge of the meaning of words and involves the use of simple, familiar, and concrete words instead of vague, abstract, difficult, and unfamiliar words, clichés, and technical jargon.

Precision is the quality of being exact, accurate, and definite.

Techniques of Precision

The various techniques that can be used to make expression precise and exact include:

- Use of simple and familiar words
- Use of exact words and phrases
- Use of avoiding excessive use of jargon

Using Simple and Familiar Words

Some people fancy big words. They seem to believe that big and difficult words reflect one's depth of understanding and command of language. The truth is just the opposite. Simplicity is an art and it is not easy to be simple. Using easy, simple, and familiar words demand a better understanding and command of the language. The use of simple and familiar words makes it easier for the reader or listener to understand the message transmitted. On the other hand, difficult words and phrases are barriers to effective communication. A message may not be understood just because the words used to present the information are too difficult for the reader/listener.

Techniques of precision include using simple, familiar, and exact words.

Read the following passage about metals:

> *"Although all metals react with oxygen, their reactivity is different. Some metals, such as sodium and potassium, react with oxygen trenchantly. They ignite even if retained unenclosed in the air. Magnesium needs to be inflamed before it combines with oxygen. Once inflamed to an ignition temperature, magnesium ribbon blazes with fire, yielding intense heat and light."*

You will find this passage difficult to understand because it contains unfamiliar and difficult words like "trenchantly", "ignite", "retained", "unenclosed", "inflamed", "blazes", and "yielding".

Now, read the following improved version of the passage. The words underlined in the above passage have been replaced. Simple and familiar equivalents of the underlined words are used here.

> *"Although all metals react with oxygen, their reactivity is different. Some metals, such as sodium and potassium, react with oxygen vigorously. They catch fire even if kept open in the air. Magnesium needs to be heated before it combines with oxygen. Once heated to an ignition temperature, magnesium ribbon burns, producing intense heat and light."*

You will agree that this passage is better because it contains simple and familiar words, i.e., vigorously, catch fire, kept, open, heated, burns, producing.

Study the list of some of the most commonly used difficult words and their plain equivalents given in Table 3.1.

TABLE 3.1 Use of Simple and Familiar Words

Difficult	*Simple*	*Difficult*	*Simple*
Abandon	Give up	Accumulate	Collect
Abashed	Embarrassed	Accustomed	Used to
Ablaze	On fire	Amalgamate	Mix
Absolute	Complete	Amenable	Responsive
Absolutely	Completely	Assassin	Killer
Attainment	Achievement	Activate	Start
Ascertain	Find out	Bespeak	Suggest
Colloquial	Informal	Combustion	Burning
Commence	Begin	Commute	Travel
Confer	Grant	Configuration	Arrangement
Consequence	Result	Discard	Reject
Dissent	Disagree	Dissuade	Discourage
Emanate	Originate	Exuberant	Lively
Excommunicate	Officially exclude	Furore	Uproar
Facsimile	Exact copy	Futile	Useless

(Contd.)

Forefront	Leading position	Glimpse	Brief view
Impel	Force	Inevitable	Unavoidable
Inexorable	Unstoppable	Intercept	Seize
Juvenile	Youthful	Litigate	Go to law
Manifest	Clear	Numerous	Many
Overwrought	Nervous	Partisan	Biased
Ravishing	Beautiful	Skirmish	Minor battle
Snapshot	Casual photograph	Tantamount	Equivalent to
Tumultuous	Noisy	Unscramble	Interpret
Vociferous	Noisy	Whiff	Breath of air

3.2.2 Using Exact Words and Phrases

The technical communicator must have an exact knowledge of the meaning of words and phrases, and should avoid using confusing words. Study the list of some of the confusing words given in Table 3.2.

TABLE 3.2 Use of Exact Words and Phrases

Confusing Words	*Meaning*
Advise/inform	To give advice/tell
Affect/effect	Influence/result
All ready/already	Completely prepared/ beforehand
All together/altogether	United/thoroughly
Appraise/apprise	Evaluate/inform
Allusion/illusion	An indirect reference to something or someone/a mistaken assumption
Assume/presume	Take to be true/take for granted
Between/among	Involving two persons/involving more than two persons or groups
Complement/compliment	Something that completes/an expression of praise or recognition
Confident/confidant	Full of assurance and self-reliance/a person one trusts
Continuous/continual	Constantly/on a regular basis
Council/counsel	Policy making body/to offer someone advice
Discrete/discreet	Separate/tactful, judicious
Uninterested/disinterested	Not interested/impartial
Forward/foreword	To advance/introductory remarks
Imply/infer	Suggest/come to a conclusion
Practical/practicable	Functional/possible in practice
Principle/principal	Rule or law/most important
Sensual/sensuous	Of physical pleasure/affecting the senses
Stationary/stationery	Not moving/writing materials

Avoiding Difficult Words and Complex Jargon

Technical jargon is an integral part of technical communication but using too much jargon, which the audience may not understand, will be inappropriate. Before you use specialized vocabulary and terminology, you must try to consider whether your audience has:

- Sufficient education
- Considerable knowledge of your subject
- The ability to understand the technical details that you want to give

Checklist for Achieving Accuracy and Precision

- Check facts for accuracy of information
- Revise your draft for grammar, usage, spelling, and punctuation errors
- Take care of your pronunciation, accent, intonation, and non-verbal mannerisms during oral communication
- Use simple, familiar, and exact words
- Avoid difficult and unfamiliar words
- Use words carefully with proper discretion
- Avoid excessive jargon

3.2.3 Brevity

Brevity is the quality of being brief but comprehensive in expression. You must try to be as brief as possible and give maximum information in the minimum number of words possible. Nobody has the time to read or listen to long and dull discourses. Lengthy documents or speeches and presentations with unnecessary details bore readers or listeners. A document can be made brief and concise by avoiding wordiness and repetition.

> Brevity can be achieved by avoiding wordiness and repetition.

Avoiding Wordiness

Wordiness normally results from the desire to impress the reader with learning, language skills, or intellect by substituting words for thoughts. Read the following passage and note the use of a wordy style:

> *Blasting is a very important and significant process, which can be defined as a process where rock is broken into fragments for a remarkable purpose, that is, recovery of valuable ore. It cannot be denied that modern technology has led to the advent of modern earth moving and rock-breaking equipment, but the advent of such sophisticated equipment has not diminished the value of explosives, which still remain the cheapest method of rock-breaking. However, there is no doubt that rock breakage by explosives has a negative impact on the environment, resulting in certain negative environmental consequences. These negative environmental consequences include ground vibration, air-overpressure, noise, dust, and toxic fumes.* *(Number of words:111)*

You will notice that the writer uses wordy expressions and repeats several points in order to increase the effectiveness of communication but the result is an ineffective wordy passage.

Now read the following version of the same passage:

> *Blasting is a process where rock is broken into fragments for recovery of valuable ore. Despite the advent of modern earthmoving and rock breaking equipment, explosives still remain the cheapest method of rock breaking. However, rock breakage by explosives has environmental consequences which include ground vibration, air-overpressure, noise, dust, and toxic fumes.* *(Number of words: 54)*

You will agree that the second passage is concise as it conveys the same message in only 54 words.

Wordiness has no place in technical communication. You can avoid wordiness by excluding unnecessary or trivial details, substituting one precise word for several words or phrases, and avoiding fancy words.

Study the list of wordy phrases and their simple substitutes given in Table 3.3.

TABLE 3.3 Word Phrases with their Simpler Substitutes

Phrase	*Word Substitution*	*Phrase*	*Word Substitution*
At a low ebb	Exhausted	Bad blood	Enmity
To beat about the bush	Digress	Be taken aback	Surprised
Blow one's own trumpet	Self-praise	Grease the palm of	Bribe
Broadly speaking	Generally	Call in question	Doubt
From the bottom of one's heart	Earnestly	Fall through	Collapse
Snap one's fingers at	Defy	Tooth and nail	Completely
Goes without saying	Self-evident	Throw dust in the eyes of	Cheat
On the face of it	Apparently	Throw cold water on	Discourage
Throw mud at	Abuse	Up one's sleeve	Concealed
To the backbone	Thoroughly	All in all	Everything

Avoiding Repetition

Repetition is a recurrent problem in the writing and speech of people who fail to consider meaning. You may repeat an idea or a fact because you want to be forceful but you should always remember that brevity cannot be sacrificed for eloquence in technical writing or a professional speech.

Now, examine the following examples of wordy sentences and their concise equivalents given in Table 3.4.

TABLE 3.4 Sentences with their Concise Equivalents

Wordy Style	*Concise Style*
A computer performs several important functions, which include performing fast and accurate calculations. (Number of words: 13)	A computer performs fast and accurate calculations. (Number of words: 07)
It has been noticed that during recent years, several groups of people, which primarily includes scientists and policy makers, have paid substantial attention to airborne substances that threaten human health or environmental quality. (Number of words: 33)	During recent years, scientists and policy makers have paid substantial attention to airborne substances that threaten human health or environmental quality. (Number of words: 21)

(Contd.)

It is a known fact that there is a natural source of hydrocarbons and this source is none other than petroleum (crude oil), which is preserved by nature in some reservoirs of porous rocks in the earth. (Number of words: 37)	The natural source of hydrocarbons is petroleum (crude oil), which is preserved by nature in some reservoirs of porous rocks in the earth. (Number of words: 23)
An important aspect of the process of withdrawing petroleum from reservoirs is the fact that petroleum is withdrawn from such reservoirs through wells driven in them by puncturing the cap of protective impervious rocks that prevented it from seeping away. (Number of words: 40)	Petroleum is withdrawn from reservoirs through wells driven in the latter by puncturing the cap of protective impervious rocks that prevented the petroleum from seeping away. (Number of words: 26)
An important characteristic feature of chromium metal is the fact that it is very hard and, although it is quite reactive in the powdered form, it is quite resistant to corrosion in the massive form. (Number of words: 35)	Chromium metal is very hard and, although quite reactive in the powdered form, in the massive form is quite resistant to corrosion. (Number of words: 22)
Computer network is a unique system of networks, including a chain of computers connected to each other for the purpose of communicating information to one another. (Number of words: 26)	Computer networks include interconnected computers, which communicate information to one another. (Number of words: 11)

Checklist for Conciseness

- Avoid repetition
- Avoid using wordy phrases and expressions
- Do not include unnecessary details
- Revise your document thoroughly in order to make it concise
- Avoid exaggeration

3.2.4 Clarity

Clarity in communication is the quality of being unambiguous and easily understood. Clarity is achieved when the communicator has communicated his or her meaning to the reader or listener. In technical communication, clarity contributes to communicative effectiveness. You will not be able to achieve your communicative objective if you are not clear.

> Clarity in communication is the quality of being unambiguous and easily understood.

Since clarity is the art of making your meaning clear to your audience, it is essential for you to understand your audience before you try to communicate. Audience adaptation can only come from a proper audience analysis. Audience analysis involves defining your audience in terms of their background, subject competence, linguistic competence, and familiarity with the topic or content of your communication. A better understanding of your audience will give you clarity of thought as well as clarity of expression.

> Clarity can be achieved by using direct language, specific and concrete words, and clear expressions.

Clarity involves both clarity of expression as well as clarity of thought. The secret of clear expression is clear thinking. Sloppy, illogical, or incomplete thinking causes lack of clarity in technical communication.

The various techniques that you can use to make your expression clear include use of:

(a) Direct language
(b) Specific words and expressions

Using Direct Language

Clarity involves the use of direct language. There is no scope for roundabout constructions, indirect expressions, exaggeration, artificial eloquence, and ornamentation in technical communication. Unlike a literary writer who needs imagery to express his abstract feelings, a technical writer does not need any literary device to convey his ideas. The technical communicator is concerned with the description, narration, explanation, and analysis of facts, and does not need to compose a piece of rhetoric charged with emotion. Unlike a public speaker whose main aim of communication may be to appeal to the emotions of the audience, a person presenting a paper at a technical seminar will have to give a matter-of-fact account of the research carried out by him or her.

Using Specific and Concrete Words and Expressions

As an effective technical communicator, one should use concrete words because they tend to be specific, narrow, and particular. Readers and audiences respond more predictably to concrete language. By using concrete language, one can ensure clarity of expression. The use of concrete and specific words and phrases bring vividness and clarity. On the other hand, obscure, abstract, and vague words and phrases confuse the audience, as they do not convey the exact meaning, and the speaker may be called upon to repeat certain phrases or give detailed clarifications. The following expressions are common:

1. I beg your pardon.
2. Could you please repeat?
3. What do you mean?
4. Could you please explain?
5. What did you say?
6. Do you mean……?

For example, examine the sentence: I will contact you later. What does the speaker mean by the word 'contact'? Will he call, send an email, write a letter, or make a personal visit? What does the word 'later' mean? Does it mean next week, next month, or next year? A better version of this sentence would be: I will visit your office on Monday, or, I will send you an email next week.

Examine another example: This television set is of high quality. What does 'high quality' refer to? It is a very subjective expression as quality for different people may mean different standards of perfection. A better version can be: This television set meets or exceeds standard government specifications.

Let us take a third example: He will meet you soon. What does the word 'soon' mean here? Does it mean tomorrow, or the day after tomorrow, or the next month? The audience will definitely be confused. A better version will be: He will meet you by March 15.

You must understand the need for using specific language. While vague and abstract words create ambiguity and lead to incomplete communication or miscommunication, the use of specific and concrete words ensures limited interpretation, reducing the risk of confusion and misunderstanding.

Checklist for Achieving Clarity

- Do not use indirect expressions.
- Use specific words and phrases.
- Avoid exaggeration, artificial eloquence, and ornamentation.
- Use direct sentences.

Progress Check 2

1. **The following passages are full of wordy phrases, repetitions, trivial details, and vague words. Rewrite them, making them clear and concise.**
   (a) Every student of science is aware of the fact that when we subject a material to repeated varying loads over a very long period, it gradually loses its strength. This important feature is known as fatigue. We may notice that it occurs more rapidly if the material that we are subjecting to repeated, varying loads has a flaw. We cannot deny the fact that fatigue is a common cause of failure in machinery.
   (b) Local Area Network (LAN) can be easily understood if we try to understand it with reference to its definition. It is a very common term that refers to a group of desktop computers that are located relatively close to one another through a system called a cabling system in order to enable them to be able to share access to computing resources.
   (c) There are several metals, which are characterized by hardness. Manganese is one such metal. Infact, manganese is a very hard metal, which we do not use industrially in its pure form. We generally use it as an addition to various ferrous metals and alloys to render them more forgeable. Manganese does this perfectly by combining with the sulphur present as an impurity. You must be aware that manganese is commercially available. However, it is commercially available as manganese metal which we prepare by reduction with aluminum, or ferromanganese which we prepare in the electric furnace.
   (d) Lead refining is a very significant process. In this process, we can easily obtain precious metals such as gold, silver, and platinum in the zinc crust of the Parkes process. We place this crust in a retort and then the next thing that we do is to distill off the zinc. We may find that the residue is an alloy, which contains gold, silver, and platinum, in addition to lead. We cupell this alloy, i.e., we heat it in an oxidising atmosphere until the lead is oxidised, leaving an alloy of the precious metals.

3.3 OBJECTIVITY IN TECHNICAL COMMUNICATION

> Technical communication is a systematic discussion, analysis, and interpretation of facts rather than expression of sentiments and emotions.

An important characteristic of technical style is objectivity. As technical communication is a systematic discussion, analysis, and interpretation of facts rather than expression of sentiments and emotions, the speaker or writer is not concerned with subjective comments and personal feelings. The concentration is on an objective and impersonal presentation of facts.

3.3.1 Objectivity in Technical Writing

Characteristics of Objectivity

Let us compare the following two passages: A and B.

> ***Passage A***
> We know that chemical reactions involve the breaking of bonds and the making of new ones. We often need to supply energy to get the reaction going. The energy that we supply may be in the form of heat, light, or mechanical shaking for proper contact between the reactant molecules and electricity. When chemical reactions occur, we can see a great variety of rearrangements of atoms.

> ***Passage B***
> Chemical reactions involve the breaking of bonds and the making of new ones. Energy is supplied to get the reaction going. The energy that is supplied may be in the form of heat, light, or mechanical shaking for proper contact between the reactant molecules and electricity. When chemical reactions occur there can be a great variety of rearrangements of atoms.

Both the passages present the same information, i.e., chemical reactions and the breaking of bonds. However, Passage A is personal and subjective while Passage B is impersonal and objective. Passage A uses personal pronouns and active voice, which gives subjectivity to the passage. However, the exclusion of personal elements and personal pronouns in Passage B produces a style consistent with objectivity and the use of the third person and passive voice places emphasis on the subject matter.

> Objectivity in communication can be achieved by using factual and impersonal language.

3.3.2 Linguistic Techniques

Several linguistic techniques or devices may be used in order to make the style objective and factual. These devices include the use of impersonal language, passive voice, and factual expressions.

Impersonal Language

Since technical communication is more concerned with 'what was done', 'what happened' or 'what was looked into', i.e., 'action' rather than 'who did what' i.e., 'actor', one should use impersonal language. The use of impersonal language involves the use of impersonal passive and the exclusion of personal elements and personal pronouns. The impersonal passive is the most important linguistic device used to make technical communication impersonal, objective, and formal. Impersonal passive may be used to describe scientific experiments, rules, procedures, and processes.

> The use of impersonal language involves the use of impersonal passive and the exclusion of personal elements and personal pronouns.

Note the use of impersonal passive forms (underlined) in the following description:

"Certain solids such as iron are strongly attracted to magnets. Such materials are called ferromagnetic. Other substances such as oxygen gas and copper sulfate are weakly attracted to magnets. They are called paramagnetic. Still other substances, such as sodium chloride, are very feebly repelled by magnets and are called diamagnetic. Ferromagnetism is exclusively a property of the solid state, but all three types of magnetic behaviour just described are believed to arise from electrons in atoms."

An impersonal passive construction contains the past participle form of the main verb preceded by the appropriate tense form of the verb 'to be'.

Thus, the structure of the impersonal passive sentence is:

Object + to be + Verb in past participle form

Table 3.5 contains a list of appropriate 'to be' verb forms according to tense forms.

TABLE 3.5 List of Appropriate 'to be' Verb Forms

'to be' Verb Forms	*Tense/Verb Form*
is/am/are	Simple present
is being/are being/am being	Present continuous
was/were	Simple past
was being/were being	Past continuous
has been/have been	Present perfect
had been	Past perfect
will be/shall be	Future
would be	Conditional
would have	Perfect conditional
to be	Present infinitive
to have been	Perfect infinitive
being	Present participle
having been	Past participle

Now, examine Table 3.6 containing the active tense forms of the verb 'supply' and their passive equivalents.

TABLE 3.6 Example of Active and Passive Forms

Active Voice	*Passive Form*	*Tense*
supplies	is supplied	Simple present
is supplying	is being supplied	Present continuous
supplied	was supplied	Simple past
was supplying	was being supplied	Past continuous
has supplied	has been supplied	Present perfect
had supplied	had been supplied	Past perfect
will supply	will be supplied	Future
would supply	would be supplied	Conditional
would have supplied	would have been supplied	Perfect conditional
to supply	to be supplied	Present infinitive
to have supplied	to have been supplied	Perfect infinitive
supplying	being supplied	Present participle
having supplied	being supplied	Perfect participle

You may use a passive infinitive to change the **auxiliary + infinitive** combination into a passive form:

Active: We must not allow water to come into contact with sodium.

Passive: Water should not be allowed to come into contact with sodium.

Active: We ought to place the metal on a dry surface.

Passive: The metal ought to be placed on a dry surface.

Active: We can see several particles of iron and sulfur.

Passive: Several particles of iron and sulfur can be seen.

Active: They should have submitted the project report.

Passive: The project report should have been submitted.

Personal pronouns used as subjects are generally removed in passive constructions. In fact, the doer of the action or the subject is generally not mentioned in the passive form. However, the subject of a sentence should be retained in passive form if it is a material used and not an agent. For example,

Active: Smoke filled the conference room.

Passive: The conference room was filled with smoke.

Now, examine the following examples of active sentences and their passive equivalents given in Table 3.7.

TABLE 3.7 Examples of Active and Passive Sentences

Active Sentences	*Passive Sentences*
Friction reduces the efficiency of machines.	The efficiency of machines is reduced by friction.
We use hot dipping as a common method to apply metallic coatings.	Hot dipping is a method commonly used to apply metallic coatings.
A computer performs fast and accurate calculations.	Fast and accurate calculations are performed by a computer.
We examined the mixture under a microscope.	The mixture was examined under a microscope
You must complete the assignment by the end of this week.	The assignment should be completed by the end of this week.
We may classify alloy steels as well as plain carbon steels according to their ability to harden.	Alloy steels as well as plain carbon steels may be classified according to their ability to harden.
We use the name quicklime for calcium oxide.	The name quicklime is used for calcium oxide.
We can change a solid into liquid by heating.	A solid can be changed into a liquid by heating.

Checklist for Achieving Objectivity

- Use appropriate passive constructions.
- Use active forms sparingly.
- Avoid personal pronouns and expressions.
- Use factual words.

Now study the following personal and subjective paragraphs and their impersonal and objective versions given in Table 3.8.

TABLE 3.8 Example of Subjective and Objective Sentences

Personal and Subjective	*Impersonal and Objective*
We know that microscopes and telescopes are devices that we can use to magnify something. We can use a microscope to magnify the size of objects that are very small and we really cannot see them by the naked eye, such as bacteria and cells. On the other hand, we can use a telescope to "bring nearer" very distant objects such as ships, or the moon, the planets, and the stars.	Microscopes and telescopes are magnifying devices. The microscope is used to magnify the size of objects that are too small to be seen by the naked eye, such as bacteria and cells. A telescope, on the other hand, is used to "bring nearer" very distant objects such as ships, or the moon, the planets, and the stars.
You may notice that sound sources are present almost everywhere in our environment, and this is why the control of sound is a major problem. There are several unwanted sounds, which we call noise. We cannot deny the fact that the control of noise is becoming an important factor in our everyday lives. We know that excessive noise produces drastic changes in our personalities, it is fatiguing and it may cause deafness and even a reduction in our life span.	Sound sources are present almost everywhere in our environment, and the control of sound is a major problem. Unwanted sounds are called noise. The control of noise is becoming an important consideration in our everyday lives. Excessive noise is known to produce drastic changes in our personalities, it is fatiguing and it may cause deafness and even a reduction in our life span.
We sometimes map magnetic fields with the aid of a small magnetic compass. We may notice that at each point, the direction that the north pole of the compass indicates is the direction of the magnetic field. We can also map magnetic fields by sprinkling iron filings on a sheet of paper that covers a magnet or system of magnets. We can observe that the filings become induced magnets and align themselves with the field.	Magnetic fields are often mapped with the aid of a small magnetic compass. At each point, the direction indicated by the north pole of the compass is the direction of the magnetic field. They can also be mapped by sprinkling iron filings on a sheet of paper that covers a magnet or system of magnets. The filings become induced magnets and align themselves with the field.
Metals are malleable. We can easily hammer them into very thin sheets. We know that gold and silver are among the best malleable metals. We can easily hammer them into foils that are much thinner than this paper. Another important feature of metals that we can mention is ductility. We should, however, remember that all metals are not equally ductile. We can draw a wire of about 200 metres from 100 milligram of a highly ductile metal like silver.	Metals are malleable. They can be hammered into very thin sheets. Gold and silver are among the most malleable metals. These can be hammered into foils much thinner than this paper. Ductility is yet another characteristic feature of metals. All metals are not equally ductile. One can draw a wire of about 200 metres from 100 milligram of a highly ductile metal like silver.

3.3.3 Objectivity in Professional Speaking

Although speaking is personal and the use of personal pronouns and references help speakers make a point clear, one should try to be as objective as possible during any professional speaking situation like a seminar, a workshop, a meeting, or a discussion. One may use personal language during oral interaction in professional situations if one thinks this will improve one's communicative effectiveness. However, it should be understood that technical communication involves transfer of information without any personal distortion.

Apart from using the linguistic devices discussed above, the following additional suggestions may be followed in order to achieve objectivity during oral communication.

Avoid Hasty Generalisations

Generalisations are general statements that cover a wide range of conditions, situations, events, and times. As they do not refer to a single situation or condition, but cover a wide range of situations, they are different from specific statements, which are true for specific situations, events, and times. In order to be objective, one should avoid making hasty generalisations because they reveal and reflect one's bias. Moreover, hasty generalisations may offend one's listeners.

Avoid Sexist Language

In order to be objective, sexist language should be avoided. Plural subjects may be used instead of singular to avoid being sexist in language. In addition, using sexist words, such as men, women, mankind, chairman, policeman, manmade, fireman, gunman, and so on may be avoided. Instead, people, human beings, chairperson, police personnel, handmade, firefighter, security personnel, and so on may be used.

Do not Refer to Irrelevant Differences

Reference to irrelevant differences based on caste, or religion may be avoided. By describing a person as a 'Muslim lawyer', a 'Black activist', a 'Bengali teacher', or a 'female journalist', one reflects an unconscious bias because the classification is based on irrelevant differences. This should be avoided.

Avoid Racist Language

In order to be objective, racist language should be avoided. One should be very particular while referring to a group of people. One should call them the way they like to be called and not the way one likes to call them. Racist language may hurt people. A professional has to reflect an attitude that does not hurt his/her listeners.

Progress Check 3

1. **Read the following paragraphs and write down the correct forms of the underlined verbs:**
   (a) In a telescope, the objective and the eyepiece are similarly (mount). The focal length of the objective of the telescope is comparatively larger than that of a microscope. The objective (form) a real, diminished-in-size and inverted image of a distant object. The position of the eyepiece is so adjust that this image form between the optical centre of the eyepiece and its focus. The eyepiece then form the final image, which is virtual, enlarged, and erect.
   (b) These substances are sometimes combine with other chemicals, such as chlorine. By means of pressure and heat, and often with the aid of catalysts, the monomer molecules of the gas or liquid react and, as they combine, form the polymer molecules of the raw plastics, which is generally in the form of a powder or of granules. By careful control of the polymerisation, the monomer molecules arrange and join in a number of ways. Thus, the properties of each of the many plastics materials modify to suit a wide range of products and applications.
   (c) Plastics have specific properties, which make them preferable to traditional materials. In comparison with metals, plastics have both advantages and disadvantages. Metals tend to corrode by inorganic acids, such as sulphuric acid and hydrochloric acid. Plastics tend to be resistant to these acids, but dissolve or deform by solvents, such as carbon tetrachloride, which have the same carbon base as plastics. Colours can be apply to the surface of metals, whereas it mix in with plastics. Metals are more rigid than plastics, while plastics are very light, with a specific gravity normally between 0.9 and

1.8. Most plastics do not readily conduct heat or electricity. Plastics soften slowly and easily shape while they are soft.

(d) The eyepiece that use in a microscope is a system of convex lenses. It fix in such a way that the image form by the objective lens lies between the eyepiece and its focus. This image acts as the object for the eyepiece, which forms a further magnify virtual image of the object. It is this image that we observe when we look into a slide through a microscope. The final image see remains invert with respect to the object.

(e) Natural laws, which may be qualitative statements or mathematical formulas, describe observed phenomena. They contrast with legislative laws that are require or prohibit, and which break. There is no room in science for the statement "the exception, that proves the rule". A familiar example of a natural law is the law of gravity. Less familiar examples of laws are those that describe the behaviour of gases. For example, all gases compress, and Boyle's law state that their volume is inversely proportional to the pressure exert on them. Boyle's law, like the law of gravity, give no reason for natural behaviour but simply state what the behaviour is.

(f) Nodes are points that displace from their rest positions by the standing wave. Therefore, nodes always occur at fixed points in vibrating strings, such as at the fixed ends. Antinodes, where the displacements vary between extreme amplitudes, occur midway between the nodes. Therefore, since the distance between two successive nodes be equal to one-half the wavelength, the distance between a successive node and antinode be one-quarter of a wavelength.

(g) Aluminium be strictly a modern-day metal. Despite the fact that the earth's crust contain an abundance of aluminium, wrest this metal from nature and separate it from the stubborn ores with which it associate not accomplish until about 1886 when a young American by the name of Hall and a Frenchman by the name of Heroult simultaneously discover a way to make aluminium cheaply. An interesting fact about these two young scientists be that they were born the same year, discover a method for obtain aluminium the same year, and both die the same year.

(h) One way in which nonferrous metals differ from iron is in the manner of their occurrence. Iron oxide occur in large and comparatively pure deposits; the other metals and compounds from which metals derive scatter through large volumes of rock, such as limestone or quartz. Since it would be difficult and costly smelt these large amounts of barren rock, recourse has to be taken to concentration or 'ore dressing', by which the metals or metallic compounds partially separate from the 'gangue', or worthless material, before smelt. As the methods of ore dressing are rather general, we consider them here, rather than under specific metals.

2. Read the following paragraphs and complete them by using the correct form of verbs from the boxes given before each paragraph:

(a) Force, wash out, give, shake, place, carry

The simplest method of ore dressing depends on the fact that in general the metallic compounds have a higher specific gravity than the gangue, and hence settle faster in a stream of water. Gold panning is the simplest illustration of the procedure. On a larger scale, it —1— on in jigs where the ore —2— on a screen and a pulsating stream of water —3— through the screen, causing the lighter gangue —4—. Another form of gravity concentrator is the 'table', consisting of a surface with longitudinal ridges, which —5— a jerking end-to-end motion while a stream of water flows across it laterally. By this means, the heavy ore —6— over the end while the gangue washes off the front.

(b) make, displace, release, lose, vibrate, produce, vibrate, depend, stretch, die out

When a string —1— under tension between two fixed points, we —2— it —3— by —4— it to one side and then —5— it. At most frequencies of vibration the energy —6— rapidly and the vibration

—7—. However, when the string —8— at certain natural (resonant) frequencies, standing waves —9— by the interference between the wave and its own reflection from the fixed ends. These resonant frequencies —10— on the length and mass of the string, and the tension in the string.

3. **Rewrite the following passages formally and objectively using impersonal passive and other devices:**
   (a) We know that the only aluminium ore that we use in this country is bauxite. Aluminium occurs in this ore in the form of aluminium hydroxide. We may find such ores in Arkansas, Georgia, Alabama, and in several other states. We produce aluminium from this ore. We also use this ore for manufacturing chemicals and high temperature insulating materials, and for grinding wheels and stones.
   (b) Plastics are organic materials, which at some stage we can shape or mould according to our need or as we require them. They are synthetic man made materials, not natural materials, and are composed of long chain-like molecules which we call polymers. We can form each of these polymer molecules by joining together many thousands of small molecules we call monomers. The monomer molecule is an arrangement of atoms, which we can make to react with similar monomer molecules to form a chain. We call the reaction polymerisation.
   (c) We know that nuclear reactions that go on in the interior of the sun liberate a large amount of energy. Nuclei of deuterium, which we know is the heavier isotope of hydrogen, collide in the sun's interior to produce helium. The energy that we find in these reactions fires the sun, which, in turn, emits lights of different wavelengths. Of these wavelengths, it is the infrared wavelengths, that heat up the earth.
   (d) In order to produce and hear a sound, we require a source of vibratory energy (such as a speaker or vibrating string), a material medium (usually air), and a receiver (the ear). Some of the energy from a vibrating source is sent as a longitudinal wave through the medium to the ear. We know that sound waves will not travel through a vacuum. The ear is sensitive to small pressure changes that the sound wave causes and is able to convert these small pressure variations into electrical impulses. These are sent by auditory nerves to the brain, where they produce the sensation of sound.
4. **Which of the following statements about objectivity in oral communication is false?**
   (a) While presenting a technical paper in a seminar, the speaker should try to be as subjective as possible.
   (b) Technical communication involves the transfer of information without any personal distortion.
   (c) In order to be objective, hasty generalisations should be avoided.
   (d) In order to avoid sexist language, plural subjects may be used instead of singular ones.
   (e) In order to be objective, irrelevant differences based on caste or religion should not be referred to.

3.4 FORMAL LANGUAGE

Formal language refers to the use of formal words, scientific vocabulary, specialised terminology, and formal phrases and expressions. The use of formal language is a specific feature of technical communication. Every field of science and technology has its own list of terms and phrases. One should be familiar with the jargon of one's professional field. The term 'jargon' refers to words or expressions used by a particular group or profession.

Formal language refers to the use of formal words, scientific vocabulary, special-ised terminology, and formal phrases and expressions.

Read the following passage and note the use of formal words and specialised terminology (underlined):

"Magma is the original source of most minerals. The constituent minerals, mostly rock-forming silicates and oxides are deposited at various stages as the magma cools down during its passage. Minerals having nearly similar fusion points segregate and concentrate together resulting in magmatic segregation. Important deposits of metallic oxides, such as magnetite and ilmenite, and sulphides, such as pyrrhotite and chalcopyrite, are formed in this way. Magmatic segregation may take place at different depths during the travel of magma and at different temperatures. Most of the ferro-magnesium silicates and other oxides are formed at great depths by magmatic segregation."

It is evident that the technical words and phrases used in the above passage are essential to convey the above information about magma.

Read the following passage and note the words and phrases in bold:

"The position that an element **has** in the periodic table **tells** its electronic **arrangement**. The electronic **arrangement tells** us how many shells of electron it **has**. The group, the atom is in, indicates the number of electrons in its **outermost shell**. This number **tells** about many **qualities** of the atom, such as valence, metallic character, the size of the atom, and so on."

Now read the following revised version of the passage:

"The position that an element **occupies** in the periodic table **defines** its electronic **configuration**. The electronic **configuration informs** us how many shells of electron it **occupies**. The group, the atom is in, indicates the number of electrons in its **valence shell**. This number **defines** many **properties** of the atom, such as valence, metallic character, the size of the atom, and so on."

You will agree that the revised passage is more formal and scientific.

Checklist for Using Formal Language

- Use formal words.
- Avoid colloquial and informal words and expressions.
- Use appropriate scientific phrases.
- Use appropriate technical terms.
- Use standard and formal sentence structures.
- Avoid conversational tone.

Writing Definitions of Engineering Terms

Writing definitions of technical terms is not uncommon in technical fields like Engineering. Given the complex nature of the definitions, it can be a daunting task. Though there is no substitute for memorizing the technical terms, there are some tips that can make the process of defining those terms easier.

Definitions of technical or engineering terms can be broadly classified into three types:

1. The first type is the easiest where the term can be explained using a few words, sometimes even one word. For example, Butterworth: filter. This can be alternatively defined in a sentence as 'Butterworth (filter)'. Note, the one-word definition is given in the bracket.
2. The second type requires a sentence to explain the term. For example, Accelerometer: A sensor or transducer for measuring acceleration.
3. The third category is the most difficult to remember because it requires extensive explanation that can run into a few sentences or a few paragraphs. For example, Alternator: An electromechanical device that converts mechanical power into AC electrical power. Typically, a magnet spins inside a coil, inducing alternating current in the windings. The magnet can be a permanent magnet, an iron rotor

in which a magnetic field is induced, or an electromagnet powered by an externally applied current. The best way is to understand the meaning of the terms, and then follow the abovementioned strategies. Over a period of time, one would be surprised with the results.

Progress Check 4

1. **Study the following statements about style in technical communication, and write True or False against each of them:**
   (a) Including personal elements and personal pronouns may help in achieving objectivity.
   (b) Precision in the use of words does not require the technical communicator to have an exact knowledge of the meaning of words.
   (c) Clarity may involve choosing the best words to express one's ideas and arranging those words to make one's readers understand these ideas.
   (d) The use of impersonal language makes writing objective and factual.
   (e) The term jargon refers to words or expressions used by poets to express their feelings.
   (f) Style is the distinctive mode or manner of expressing ideas in language.
   (g) The most effective style is the one that encodes the thought content of the message into pompous language.
   (h) Conciseness is the quality of being brief but comprehensive in expression.
   (i) Formal language refers to the use of colloquial and conversational words and expressions.
   (j) The use of concrete and specific words and phrases bring vividness and clarity.
2. **Which of the following is not an aspect of style in technical communication?**
   (a) Objectivity
   (b) Pompous language
   (c) Formal language
   (d) Use of imagery
   (e) Specialised terminology
   (f) Technical subject matter
   (g) Clarity
   (h) Precision
   (i) Conciseness
   (j) Directness
   (k) Vagueness

Exercise

1. **Discuss technical style briefly.**
2. **Write short notes on the following:**
   (a) Accuracy in technical communication
   (b) Precision in technical writing
   (c) Clarity of expression
   (d) Objectivity in oral communication
   (e) Formal language

3. **Read the following passage and rewrite it making the style direct and precise by removing ornamentation, repetitions, exaggeration, or figures of speech:**
We have before us an ordeal of the most grievous kind. We have before us many, many long months of struggle and of suffering. You ask, what is our policy? I will say : it is to wage war, by sea, land, and air, with all our might and with all the strength that God can give us. To wage war against a monstrous tyranny, never surpassed in the dark, lamentable catalogue of human crime. That is our policy. You ask, what is our aim? I can answer in one word: victory–victory at all costs, victory in spite of terror, victory however long and hard the road may be; for without victory, there is no survival. Let that be realised; no survival for the British Empire; no survival for the urge and impulse of the ages that mankind will move forward towards its goal. But I take up my task, with buoyancy and hope. I feel sure that our case will not be suffered to fail among men. At this time I feel entitled to claim the aid of all, and I say, "come, then let us go forward together with our united strength".
4. **Complete the following paragraph by using appropriate passive forms of the verbs given in the brackets:**
Hot dipping is a common method ——— (use) to apply metallic coatings. In this method, the structure ——— (dip) into a bath of molten coating metal. A good metallurgical bond ——— (formed) with the substance, owing to interfacial alloying. There is less control over the coating thickness in the dipping process: the coat tends to be uneven, thicker on lower surfaces and thinner on top. However, all surfaces ——— (expose) to the molten metal ——— (coat). The process —— (limit) to low melting point metals such as tin, zinc, and aluminium.
5. **Read the following paragraphs and fill in the blanks by using appropriate forms of the verbs given in the box. One verb may be used more than once.**

(a)

illustrate	discover	fall	make	balances
affect	accelerate	call	drop	

When an object is —1— near the surface of the earth, it increases its speed as it falls. Therefore, freely falling objects —2— toward the centre of the earth. By rolling balls down inclined planes, Galileo —3— that this acceleration, which—4— the acceleration due to gravity, is the same for all bodies, independent of their mass. This —5— by simultaneously dropping a book of many pages and single sheet of paper, —6— into a compact ball, from the same height; they both hit the ground at the same instant. Of course, the speed, density, and shape of the object —7— the result because of air resistance and buoyancy. Because of this effect, objects —8— freely may eventually reach a constant velocity —9— the terminal velocity. For example, a parachutist does not accelerate continually. Once the parachute is open the drag of the air eventually —10— the force of gravity and the acceleration becomes zero, producing a constant terminal velocity.

(b) transmit, produce, result, call, transfer

All sources of sound –1– vibratory energy at frequencies within the audible range of the ear. Some of the most common sound sources are vibrating strings (stringed musical instruments), vibrating air columns (wind musical instruments), vibrating membranes (speakers and drums), and vibrating rods. This vibratory energy –2– to the surrounding medium, normally air, where it –3– from particle to particle to the ear.

Many sound sources have several different natural frequencies or resonant frequencies of vibration. Each different vibratory state –4– a mode of vibration. At these resonant frequencies, a small energy input –5– in a large amplitude.

6. **Rewrite the following passages formally and objectively using impersonal passive and other devices:**
   (a) You can notice the fact that when you apply force on an object, the velocity of the object changes, i.e., it accelerates the object. You know that the resistance to this change in velocity is something, which depends on the mass of the object. What does that mean? Well, the answer is simple. That means that you can change the velocity of lighter objects more easily than you can change the velocity of heavier bodies.
   (b) We have seen that force produces accelerations and therefore we find changes in the motion of objects, but in some cases we may not find any acceleration, even though we notice that forces are present. We call this a state of no acceleration equilibrium; it arises because of the fact that the forces balance each other.
   (c) You must be aware that chemical reactions involve the breaking of bonds and the making of new ones. You often need to supply energy to get the reaction going. The energy that you supply may be in the form of heat, light, or mechanical shaking for proper contact between the reactant molecules and electricity. When chemical reactions occur, you may notice a great variety of rearrangements of atoms.
   (d) What does Newton's second law of motion tell us? It tells us that any unbalanced (net) force produces acceleration. However, acceleration is the time rate of change of velocity; therefore, you may find a rigid object stationary or moving at a constant velocity (speed and direction) only when there is no net force acting on it. Two or more forces are in equilibrium only if their vector sum is zero since this corresponds to a state of no acceleration.
7. **The following passages are full of wordy phrases, repetitions, trivial details, and vague words. Rewrite them making them clear and concise.**
   (a) We all know the fact that matter exists in different forms, which include solid, liquid, and gas. Infact, the existence of matter in different forms, such as solid, liquid, or gas, may be explained in terms of its dependence on energy. Two of them share a common characteristic. These two are higher energy-states of matter and they flow to take the shape and to occupy the total volume of any container. When the first of these two, i.e., gases and vapours, loses sufficient energy (in the form of heat or by doing work), it condenses to a liquid. The fact eminent here is that liquids are incompressible b they can flow. Liquid molecules are capable of moving and they flow past each other, but the point is that compared to that of gases, their motion is much slower.
   (b) There is no such thing as a perfectly smooth material; all known materials have some irregularities in their surfaces. What is the implication of these irregularities in the surface of a material? Frankly speaking, the implication is very significant. When two objects are in contact, these irregularities interlock, and the surfaces adhere to each other. If a force is applied in such a way that these objects slide over each other, the adhesion between the surfaces results in resistance to the relative motion of the objects. This resistance to the relative motion is called friction. The friction force always acts in the opposite direction to the motion, and it opposes any tendency of motion.
   (c) What is an ionic compound? We can define an ionic compound as a collection of an equal number of positive and negative ions kept in a certain way. In simple words, a collection of an equal number of positive and negative ions kept in a three-dimensional lattice is an ionic compound. An important fact is that we can dissociate ionic compounds into their constituent three-dimensional lattice. Infact, we can dissociate ionic compounds into their constituent ions with little effort. Further, we can electrolyse ion compounds to produce elements or covalent molecules of the respective atoms.

Key to Progress Check

Progress Check 1

1. (a) False (b) True (c) True (d) False (e) True
   (f) True

Progress Check 2

1. (a) When a material is subjected to repeated varying loads over a long period, it gradually loses its strength. This is known as fatigue. It occurs more rapidly if the material has a flaw. Fatigue is a common cause of failure in machinery.
   (b) Local Area Network (LAN) is a group of desktop computers located close to one another through a cabling system to enable them to share access to computing resources.
   (c) Manganese is a very hard metal added to various ferrous metals and alloys to render them more forgeable, which it does by combining with the sulphur present as an impurity. It is commercially available as manganese metal, prepared by reduction with aluminium, or as ferromanganese, which is prepared in the electric furnace.
   (d) In lead refining, gold, silver, and platinum are obtained in the zinc crust of the Parkes process. This crust is placed in a retort and the zinc is distilled off. The residue is an alloy containing gold, silver, and platinum, in addition to lead. This alloy is then heated in an oxidising atmosphere until the lead is oxidised, leaving an alloy of the precious metals.

Progress Check 3

1. (a) Mounted, forms, adjusted, is formed, forms
   (b) Combined, react, combine , may be arranged, joined, can be modified
   (c) Make, to be corroded, can be dissolved, deformed, applied, can be mixed, can easily be shaped
   (d) is used, is fixed, formed, magnified, seen, inverted
   (e) describe, contrast, required, prohibit, may be 'broken'. Describe, can be compressed, states, exerted, gives, states
   (f) are not displaced, must always occur, vary, occur, is, is
   (g) is, contains, wresting, separating, is associated, was not accomplished, discovered, is, discovered, obtaining, died
   (h) Differ, occurs, are derived, are scattered, to smelt, are partially separated, smelting, consider
2. (a) is carried, is placed, forced, to be washed out, is given, is shaken
   (b) is stretched, can make, vibrate, displacing, releasing, is lost, dies out, vibrates, are produced, depend
3. (a) The only aluminium ore used in this country is called bauxite. Aluminium occurs in this ore in the form of aluminium hydroxide. Such ores are found in Arkansas, Georgia, Alabama, and in several other states. Aside from producing aluminum, the ore is also used for manufacturing chemicals and high temperature insulating materials, and for grinding wheels and stones.
   (b) Plastics are organic materials, which at some stage can be moulded or shaped as required. They are synthetic man made materials, not natural materials, and are composed of long chain-like molecules called polymers. Each of these polymer molecules is formed by joining together many thousands

of small molecules called monomers. The monomer molecule is an arrangement of atoms, which can be made to react with similar monomer molecules to form a chain. The reaction is known as polymerisation.

(c) Nuclear reactions that go on in the interior of the sun liberate a large amount of energy. Nuclei of deuterium, which is the heavier isotope of hydrogen, collide in the sun's interior to produce helium. The energy liberated in this reaction fires the sun, which, in turn, emits lights of different wavelengths. Of these wavelengths, it is the infrared wavelengths that heat up the earth.

(d) For a sound to be produced and heard, a source of vibratory energy (such as a speaker or vibrating string), a material medium (usually air), and a receiver (the ear) are required. Some of the energy from a vibrating source is transmitted as a longitudinal wave through the medium to the ear. Sound waves will not travel through a vacuum. The ear is sensitive to the small pressure changes caused by the sound wave and is able to convert these small pressure variations into electrical impulses. These are transmitted by auditory nerves to the brain, where they produce the sensation of sound.

(e) Microscopes and telescopes use two lens systems. The first one, called the 'objective', forms the image of the object; the second lens system, called the 'eyepiece', takes this image and forms its image in turn. It is the latter that we see through the instrument. The objective is a lens or a system of lenses, which acts as a converging (convex) lens. In a microscope, the object to be viewed is kept at a distance slightly larger than the focal length of the objective. The objective forms an inverted, magnified, and real image of the object.

4. (a)

Progress Check 4

1. (a) False (b) False (c) True (d) True (e) False
   (f) True (g) False (h) True (i) False (j) True
2. (b), (d), and (k)

CHAPTER 4

Organisation in Technical Communication

Meaning is the key to effective communication and logical organisation is the key to meaning.

LEARNING OBJECTIVES

- Understanding organization in technical communication.
- Knowing and understanding logical techniques that help communication organize information effectively.
- Learning to use the seven basic patterns of logically organizing information in technical communication.

4.1 INTRODUCTION

Technical communication is always purposeful, and all technical compositions and presentations are organised and logically structured. For the technical communicator, it is the cohesive element that brings his/her perspective, knowledge, and ideas into focus for the audience. Many technical writers and presenters ignore the fact that the organisation, structure, order, or pattern that they use in their writing or speech will determine the effectiveness of their message.

> Organisation in technical communication refers to the process of arranging the information logically.

Organisation in technical communication refers to the process of arranging information logically. Unlike general communication, technical communication follows a linear logical pattern to organise information. Whether one has to write a technical report, make an oral presentation, write an email message, or take part in a professional discussion, one has to consider what kind of organisation one is going to use. One needs to organise the information that one presents in a systematic way.

Let us try to understand this with the help of an example. Read the following extract from a textbook on thermodynamics.

> "There are essentially three types of internal combustion (IC) engines:
>
> (i) Reciprocating engines
> (ii) Rotary gas turbine engines
> (iii) Jet and rocket engines
>
> In reciprocating engines, the fuel is burnt within the engine cylinder. In gas turbine engines, the fuel is burnt outside the turbine in a separate combustion chamber as in external combustion engines. But, since the products of combustion themselves form the working substance, these are named internal combustion engines.
>
> The petrol and diesel engines are reciprocating engines. Gas turbine engines used both in aircrafts and in stationary power plants form a category of rotary turbo engines. In jet and rocket propulsion engines, the thrust developed as a result of momentum change from low velocity entering air to high velocity. Exit jet is utilised for propulsion. In jet propulsion engines, gas turbines are used only to provide the work required for the compressor of the engine.
>
> All these are internal combustion engines. There is no direct heat transfer from the fuel to the working substance in them. As a result, very high internal temperatures are attained, and a high thermal efficiency can be obtained provided materials could be found to withstand high temperatures. Unfortunately, the metallurgical limit of most materials of construction falls much below the temperatures attained. Hence, it is common to resort to cooling of cylinders in reciprocating engines, and the use of excess air in gas turbine engines to bring down working temperatures."

It is apparent that the writer uses a particular logical pattern to organise information in the above passage. The logical pattern that the author uses involves the process of dividing internal combustion (IC) engines into three types on the basis of how they are arranged in space. By categorising internal combustion engines, he has simplified the text for the readers and is able to present a clear and logical picture of internal combustion (IC) engines. Here, the author has used *spatial logical organisation*, i.e. organisation by place.

Now, let us read the following short paragraph to find out how the author has organised information here:

> "The space age began on October 4, 1957, when Russia launched Sputnik 1 into orbit. This was followed a month later by Sputnik 2, which carried the dog Laika. However, the first US satellite, Explorer 1, did not follow until January 31, 1958, but its instruments made the first major discovery of the space age—the Van Allen radiation belts around the Earth, where electrons and protons from the Sun are trapped by the Earth's magnetic field. Soon after, probes were sent to explore the moon and the planets, and on the way, they detected a solar wind of sub-atomic particles streaming from the sun."

There are seven basic patterns of logically organising information in technical communication: spatial, chronological, general to specific, specific to general, increasing order of importance, decreasing order of importance, and emphatic organisation.

The author has narrated events related to launching of satellites in the order in which they occurred, beginning with the first launching of Sputnik 1 by Russia, going on to Sputnik 2, and then the first US satellite, and so on. The author has used *chronological organisation* here.

There are so many ways of constructing an idea to accomplish a specific communicative objective. There are seven basic patterns of logically organising information in technical communication, i.e., spatial, chronological, general to specific, specific to general, increasing order of importance, decreasing order of importance, and emphatic organisation. We may choose a logical organisation that suits the subject, helps our readers or listeners, and above all, helps us to develop the information that we want to convey in a natural and spontaneous way.

Many times, one single logical organisation or pattern may not fully answer all the requirements of a given technical discourse.

However, one single logical organisation or pattern may not fully answer all the requirements of a given technical discourse, and one may need to explore the possibilities of combining patterns to achieve the desired effect. We may organise one part of our document or presentation chronologically while we organise the remaining parts according to increasing order of importance.

Progress Check 1

1. **Study the following statements about logical organisation in technical communication, and write True or False against each of them.**
   (a) Those who write or speak illogically are always familiar with methods of organising ideas.
   (b) Every technical composition or presentation has to be logically structured in order to be meaningful.
   (c) Technical communicators need to bring their perspective, knowledge, and ideas into focus for the audience.
   (d) Organisation in technical communication refers to the process of arranging information logically.
   (e) Effective technical writers and presenters give very little consideration to the kind of logical organisation they are going to use.
   (f) Technical communicators choose the logical organisation that will help readers/listeners the most.
   (g) An effective logical organisation helps the writer or speaker.
   (h) One single logical organisation or pattern always fully answers all the requirements of a given technical discourse.

4.2 BASIC PATTERNS OF ORGANISATION IN TECHNICAL COMMUNICATION

4.2.1 Spatial Organisation

Spatial organisation, as summarised in Table 4.1, refers to organisation by place. It is also called *spatial order or order of place*. It is the simplest logical organisation that technical writers or speakers may use to structure information in a technical document or presentation. This logical pattern involves the process of dividing a subject or topic based on how they are arranged in space. This pattern can make a complex or difficult subject easy to understand by categorising its various elements spatially. Once broken into simple manageable parts, the reader or audience may find the subject easy to follow.

> Spatial organisation is the logical division of a subject or topic on the basis of how they are arranged in space.

Spatial organisation can be used both in writing and in speech. Technical reports, proposals, oral reports, or oral presentations may be organised spatially by simple divisions of the subject. Suppose a report or presentation has to be prepared about the functioning of a company or organisation. The report or presentation may be organised by simple divisions of the company: production department, administrative department, marketing division, and so on. Similarly you may organise a description from left to right, from large to small, from top to bottom, from near to distant, and so on.

Using spatial organisation is easy as you need not think about what will come next. You may concentrate on other aspects of writing/speech once you have decided to use spatial order because the order will be so obvious and natural. Moreover, such simple categorising may present a clear and logical picture of something and simplify a difficult subject for the reader or audience. However, spatial order may sometimes lead to monotony in longer texts or presentations. You should try to avoid the monotony by being creative and innovative.

TABLE 4.1 Spatial Organisation

Description	*Advantages*	*Disadvantages*
Logical division of a subject on the basis of how they are arranged in space	• Easy to use • Presents a clear and logical picture • Simplifies a difficult subject • Spatial words and phrases provide coherence	• Creates monotony in longer texts or presentations • May not provide proper emphasis

4.2.2 Chronological Organisation

Chronological organisation (Table 4.2) refers to the narration of events in the order in which they occur in time, beginning with the first event, going on to the next, and so on. This logical sequence may sometimes become essential for a particular piece of writing or speech simply because the information involves a simple chain of events—what did, could, can, or will happen—in the order of occurrence. In fact,

> Chronological organisation is the narration of events in the order in which they occur in time.

technical writers and speakers frequently use this organisation, as it is quite easy and natural to record events in the order of their happening.

Chronological sequence can be used in several technical and professional documents such as periodic reports, progress reports, accident reports, factory procedures, industrial processes, experimental descriptions, instruction manuals, and so on. It may also be used in several oral forms such as sales presentations, discussions of day-to-day reports on the progress of professional projects, oral reporting, oral instructions, and so forth.

It is very easy to use chronological order and one does not have to think about what will come next, because the order will be obvious. Moreover, it may be easy to use appropriate sequence words and time connectives such as first, then, later, after this, before, until, next, the next month, after that time, and so on. This provides coherence and clarity and the reader or the audience never gets confused. Finally, it is easy to check and review a chronological account for accuracy. However, chronological sequence might make a document or presentation quite boring and monotonous. In addition, it may not provide proper emphasis because of having assigned importance to unimportant material due to chronological compulsion. While using chronological sequence, you should use appropriate strategies to deal with such problems.

TABLE 4.2 Chronological Organisation

Description	*Advantages*	*Disadvantages*
Logical organisation of events in the order in which they occur in time	• Easy to use • Time connectives provide coherence • Readers or listeners do not get confused • Easy to check and review mistakes • Presents a clear and logical picture	• May create boredom • Can create monotony • May assign importance to unimportant material due to chronological compulsion

4.2.3 General to Specific Organisation

> In general to specific or deductive logical order, general information is followed by specific information.

General to specific or *deductive logical order*, as summarised in Table 4.3, is the most common logical organisation used in technical communication. This logical pattern involves the process of moving from a general statement, premise, principle, or law to specific details. Technical writers and speakers find this logical sequence quite helpful in organising short informative talks and presentations, technical descriptions of objects and processes, classificatory information, and so on.

A general statement covers a wide range of conditions, situations, events, and times while a specific statement refers to a single situation or condition.

Study the following statements:

1. Air pollution has been a major threat not only to the quality of environment but also to human health.
2. The highest personal exposures to combustion emissions occur not in urban smog but in homes with unvented combustion appliances.
3. Gases are high-energy states of matter.
4. The world is full of poisonous substances.

All the above statements are general as they do not refer to a single situation or condition but cover a wide range of situations. Thus, general statements are different from specific statements, which are true for specific situations, events, and times.

Now read the following passage about fuel cells:

> "Fuel cells convert the energy stored in the chemical bonds of fuels directly into electrical power. In these direct energy conversion devices, the intermediate steps of conversion of chemical energy to heat followed by conversion of heat to mechanical work are completely eliminated. High temperature, generated because of the combustion of fuels and subsequent processes, found in almost all indirect energy conversion devices, are non-existent in fuel cells. In these electrochemical devices, the chemical energy of the fuel is directly converted into low voltage direct current electrical energy. Because energy conversion can be carried out isothermally, fuel cell efficiency is not subject to the limitations of Carnot efficiency. In addition, since it is possible to bypass the processes of conversion of chemical energy to heat, and that of heat to mechanical energy in a fuel cell, its efficiency is very high."

The above paragraph is organised such that it begins with general information and is followed by specific information. The first sentence in the above paragraph is the most general statement of the paragraph as it conveys the most general information about fuel cells, i.e., function of fuel cells. On the other hand, the subsequent sentences of the paragraph are specific and give specific information about subsequent processes in fuel cells. In fact, the first statement is a generalisation while the other statements in the paragraph support the first statement with specific details.

General to specific organisation follows a direct approach. It leaves very little to the imagination of the readers or listeners because the writer/speaker makes everything clear in the beginning itself. Generalisations help readers/listeners to understand the details, examples, and illustrations quickly.

TABLE 4.3 General to Specific Organisation

Description	*Advantages*	*Disadvantages*
Logical organisation of moving from the general to the particulars	• Generalisations help readers/ listeners understand the details • Readers or listeners have clarity about the theme or thesis statement	• Retaining audience attention may become a problem • May create boredom

4.2.4 Specific to General Organisation

Specific to general organisation or inductive logical order (Table 4.4) is the direct opposite of the general to specific structure. It is an objective and scientific logical technique that scientists have been using over the years. In this logical organisation, specific details, examples, and illustrations come first. They are followed by a general statement or generalisation. The writer/speaker uses details to lead to a conclusion. Effective examples and illustrations may help readers/listeners understand the generalisation.

Read the following short paragraphs:

(i) Sodium chloride (NaCl), an ionic compound, upon melting or upon dissolving in water, produces Na^+ and Cl^- ions. Thus, ionic compounds can be dissociated into their constituent ions with little effort.

(ii) If you push a rubber ball under the surface of water in a container, you will feel an upward force against the bottom of the ball. Hence, it is evident that water exerts pressure upwards.

(iii) In sodium hydroxide (NaOH), the hydroxide ion is made of a covalent bond between the O and H atoms, while in hydrogencyanide (HCN) the cyanide ion has a triple bond connecting the C and N atoms. Thus, the same molecule can have both ionic and covalent bonds in it.

In specific to general or inductive logical order, specific information is followed by general information.

In each of the above paragraphs, conclusions or general statements follow specific observations.

TABLE 4.4 Specific to General Organisation

Description	*Advantages*	*Disadvantages*
Logical organisation of moving from particulars to the general	• Objective and scientific • More convincing • Effective examples and illustrations help readers/ listeners to understand the generalisation	• Getting audience attention in the beginning could be difficult

4.2.5 Order of Increasing Importance

Organising thoughts and ideas in the order of increasing importance (Table 4.5) is quite a popular logical organisation that technical and business writers and presenters use in several oral and written forms. The writer/speaker begins with unimportant details that attempt to appeal to the reader/listener and arouse his/her interest. The important details come later followed by the most important point. This technique is similar to the climatic order used by fiction and script writers to develop a climax in their stories.

In the logical order of increasing importance, unimportant details are followed by important details.

TABLE 4.5 Order of Increasing Importance

Description	*Advantages*	*Disadvantages*
Organising thoughts and ideas in the order of increasing importance	• Familiar logical sequence • Holds, builds, and retains audience attention • Easy to follow	• Too time consuming for busy technocrats or executives who are interested only in important points • Needs extra effort on the part of the reader/ listener who has to patiently wait for the main point to be discussed

The logical order of increasing importance is very relevant for different kinds of technical and business documents and presentations (Table 4.6). Technical articles, reports on experimental work, thesis, dissertations, and technical reports were traditionally organised in this way. The pattern has also been traditionally used to organise information in technical presentations, seminars, and workshops.

TABLE 4.6 Using Order of Increasing Importance

Report on Experimental Work/Thesis/Dissertation	*Scientific and Technical Articles*	*Technical Reports*	*Oral Presentations/ Seminars/Workshops*
• Background • Literature survey • Statement of problem • Methodology • Analysis of results • Discussion of results • Conclusions • Recommendations	• Introduction • Statement of problem • Materials • Methods • Results • Discussions • Conclusions	• Background • Introduction • Statement of problem • Analysis of problem • Discussions • Conclusions • Recommendations	• Introduction • Statement of problem • Analysis • Results • Discussions • Conclusions • Recommendations • Suggestions

Writers/speakers find it easy to use order of increasing importance in their writing and speech. The audience also finds it simple and easy to follow because it is a familiar and logical sequence traditionally used by scientists and researchers. The main advantage of this organisation is that it can build, hold, and retain audience attention. On the other hand, readers/listeners need to put in extra effort in waiting patiently for the main point to be introduced. So, this logical order might be slightly more time consuming for busy technocrats or executives who are more interested in the important points. In order to overcome this problem, all points must be made interesting for the audience.

4.2.6 Order of Decreasing Importance

Organising thoughts and ideas in the order of decreasing importance (Table 4.7) is quite the opposite of the order of increasing importance. In this kind of organisation, the logical sequence is reversed and important material is placed first. Less important or unimportant details follow. This logical order is more appropriate for busy technocrats or executives who do not have either the patience or time to wait till the most important point comes at the end.

In the logical order of decreasing importance, important details are followed by unimportant details

TABLE 4.7 Order of Decreasing Importance

Description	*Advantages*	*Disadvantages*
Organising thoughts and ideas in the order of decreasing importance	• Less time consuming for busy technocrats and executives who are more interested in important points • Readers/listeners need not wait for the main ideas • Easy to follow	• Audience interest gradually decreases • Retaining audience attention may become a problem • May create monotony and boredom

The logical order of decreasing importance could be relevant for different kinds of technical or business documents and presentations meant for busy professionals. As the busy reader need not wait for the main ideas, it could be less time consuming. However, the interest of the audience may gradually decrease and retaining their attention may become a problem. This order may create monotony and boredom for the reader because he/she has already received the important information and what is left is unimportant and uninteresting. To use this logical organisation, strategies should be adopted to make the entire document/ presentation interesting and relevant for the audience.

4.2.7 Emphatic Organisation

Emphatic organisation (Table 4.8) is a modified version of organisation using increasing order of importance. This order tries to avoid the disadvantages of organising by the increasing or decreasing order and retain their advantages. In emphatic organisation, an abstract or a short summary is added in the beginning of the technical document. Refer to Table 4.9 for exhibiting the use of emphatic organisation in technical articles and reports.

TABLE 4.8 Emphatic Organisation

Description	*Advantages*	*Disadvantages*
Organising thoughts and ideas in the order of increasing importance with an abstract or summary in the beginning	• A summary or abstract helps readers to get the gist of the matter in the beginning • Readers need not wait for the main ideas • Familiar logical sequence • Holds, builds, and retains audience attention • Easy to understand	• May create monotony • Difficult to use

This organisation is now quite popular among technical and business writers, as it has integrated the advantages of organising by the increasing as well as decreasing importance of subject matter. A summary or abstract in the beginning helps readers get the gist of the matter and they need not wait for the main points to come at the end. Apart from holding and retaining the interest of the audience, it provides easy reading and better comprehension. However, the summary or abstract should be drafted carefully because the success of this logical sequence depends on the effectiveness of the summary.

In emphatic organisation, ideas are presented in the order of increasing importance with an abstract or summary in the beginning.

TABLE 4.9 Using Emphatic Organisation

Report on Experimental Work/ Thesis/Dissertation	*Scientific and Technical Articles*	*Technical Reports*
• Abstract/Summary • Background • Literature survey • Statement of problem • Methodology • Analysis of results • Discussion of results • Conclusions • Recommendations	• Abstract/Summary • Introduction • Statement of problem • Materials • Methods • Results • Discussions • Conclusions	• Abstract/Summary • Background • Introduction • Statement of problem • Analysis of problem • Discussions • Conclusions • Recommendations

Progress Check 2

1. **Study the following table and match different logical structures (left column) with appropriate descriptions of the logical patterns (right column):**

	Different logical structures		Descriptions of the logical patterns
A.	Spatial organisation	1.	Organising thoughts and ideas in the order of increasing importance with an abstract or summary in the beginning
B.	Chronological organisation	2.	Organising thoughts and ideas in the order of increasing importance
C.	General to specific order	3.	Organising thoughts and ideas in the order of decreasing importance
D.	Specific to general order	4.	Logical organisation of events in the order in which they occur in time
E.	Increasing order of importance	5.	Logical organisation of moving from the particular, to the general
F.	Decreasing order of importance	6.	Logical division of a subject on the basis of how they are arranged in space
G.	Emphatic organisation	7.	Logical organisation of moving from the general to the particular

2. **Read the following sets of sentences. Each set forms a paragraph, but except for the first sentence all the remaining sentences in the set are in the wrong order. Organise them logically:**

(i) (a) Hot dipping is a common method used to apply metallic coatings.
(b) The process is limited to low melting point metals such as tin, zinc, and aluminium.
(c) There is less control over the coating thickness in the dipping process: the coat tends to be uneven, thicker on lower surfaces and thinner on top.
(d) In this method, the structure is dipped into a bath of molten coating metal.
(e) A good metallurgical bond is formed with the substance, owing to interfacial alloying.
(f) However, all surfaces exposed to the molten metal are coated.

(ii) (a) Crude oil is a mixture of different compounds that boil at different temperatures.
(b) The remaining and heaviest fraction is the residue, which supplies waxes, asphalts, and some fuel oils.
(c) The fraction obtained by boiling between about 140 degrees and 320 degrees C is termed kerosene.
(d) The next fraction, normally refined into gasoline, boils between about 30 degrees and 200 degrees C.
(e) The lightest fraction consists of gases that boil below atmospheric temperature.
(f) The fraction boiling above about 320 degrees C is commonly refined into heating, diesel, and lubricating oils.

(iii) (a) Aluminium is the lightest of the common metals, having a specific gravity of 2.70.
(b) Moreover, because of its lightness, the greatest single use of aluminium is in the field of transportation.

(c) Aluminium does not rust and strongly resists corrosion.
(d) Its use in the building industry is of no small importance.
(e) Aluminium is also used to a very great extent in electric cables, cooking utensils, and protective foil for wrapping foods and other products.
(f) Due to its high electrical and heat conductivity, as well as its chemical resistance, it finds many everyday uses.

3. Read the following sets of sentences. Each set forms a paragraph, but the sentences in the set are in the wrong order. Organise them according to the right logical order:

(i) (a) Consequently, the electron microscope has become an invaluable analytical tool, widely found in medical and industrial research establishments.
(b) Electron microscopes are microscopes that can magnify by up to one million times.
(c) By overcoming the severe limitations of traditional microscopes, electron microscopes can reveal some of the details of molecular structure.
(d) Developments have now widened their role to embrace specialised forms of chemical analysis.

(ii) (a) This resistance to the relative motion is called friction.
(b) Friction force always acts in the opposite direction to the motion, and it opposes any tendency of motion.
(c) Friction forces will slow moving objects.
(d) There is no such thing as a perfectly smooth material; all known materials have some irregularities in their surfaces.
(e) If a force is applied in such a way that these objects slide over each other, the adhesion between the surfaces results in resistance to the relative motion of the objects.
(f) Consequently, when two objects are in contact, these irregularities interlock, and the surfaces adhere to each other.

Exercise

1. Answer the following questions:
(a) What is the significance of logical structuring of ideas in technical communication?
(b) What are the advantages of using spatial organisation in technical presentations?
(c) Which logical structure would be appropriate for the annual report of a multinational company?
(d) When does the use of chronological organisation become essential?
(e) How does emphatic organisation differ from logical order of increasing importance?

2. Write brief notes on the following:
(a) Spatial organisation
(b) Chronological organisation
(c) General to specific order
(d) Specific to general order
(e) Increasing order of importance
(f) Decreasing order of importance
(g) Emphatic organisation

3. Identify the logical structure used in this chapter.

4. Analyse several passages, texts, technical articles, reports, seminar presentations and try to identify the logical organisation followed in them. Discuss your answer with your Communication teacher.

Key to Progress Check

Progress Check 1

1. (a) False (b) True (c) True (d) True (e) False
   (f) True (g) True (h) False

Progress Check 2

1. A – 6, B – 4, C – 7, D – 5, E – 2, F – 3, G – 1
2. (i) a, d, e, c, f, b (ii) a, e, d, c, f, b (iii) a, c, f, b, e, d
3. (i) b, c, d, a (ii) d, f, e, a, b, c

SECTION

2

Listening Comprehension

CHAPTERS

5 CHAPTER

The Listening Process

Listening is the process of creating meaning in the speaker.

—Michael Rost

LEARNING OBJECTIVES

- Understanding the process of listening
- Learning to differentiate between hearing and listening
- Analysing the differences between effective and ineffective listening
- Knowing how to differentiate between active and passive listening
- Identifying barriers to listening
- Understanding listening comprehension skills

5.1 THE LISTENING PROCESS

"You are not listening to me," says the teacher. "Sir, I am listening to you," the student replies. "No, you are not," the teacher emphatically says. The problem is simple. The student is not able to focus 100% on what the teacher is speaking, and the teacher is able to sense it. It is important to be a good listener and to be perceived as one.

> It is important to be a good listener and to be perceived as one.

> Effective listening involves not only recognising unit boundaries phonologically, but also the recognition of false starts, pauses, hesitations, stress, intonation, and rhythm patterns.

Listening is a process of receiving and interpreting the spoken word. It involves recognising what is said and comprehending the matter, i.e., understanding the main and subsidiary points as well as the links between the different parts of speech. This means that effective listening involves not only recognising unit boundaries phonologically, but also the recognition of false starts, pauses, hesitations, stress, intonation, and rhythm patterns. While receiving and interpreting the spoken word, the listener is concerned with four factors, i.e., sensing, message decoding or interpreting, evaluating and response, as illustrated in Fig. 5.1.

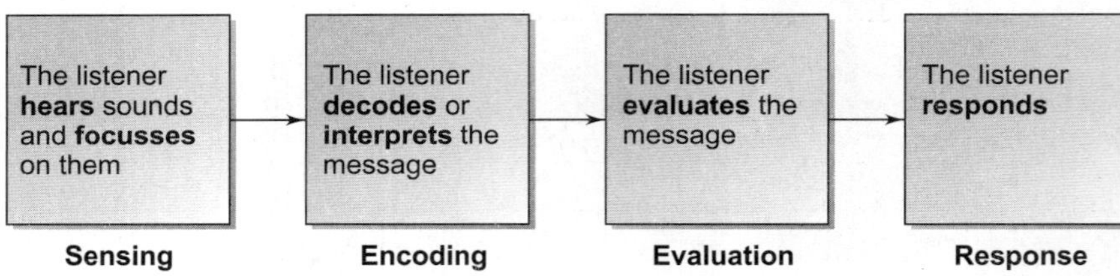

Fig. 5.1 The Listening Process

Listening begins with physical hearing of the message and taking note of it. Sensing is, thus, the first step of the listening process. You hear sounds and concentrate on them in order to receive the message. You recognise unit boundaries phonologically as it is important for you to recognise phonological differences. Once you are able to recognise the sound patterns, you have to decode and interpret the message.

> In order to evaluate a verbal message correctly, facts have to be separated from opinions, relevant information from irrelevant information, examples from ideas, and explicit information from implicit information.

Decoding or interpreting in listening refers to the process of changing the coded message into information. It involves understanding the spoken language. Although interpretation of a verbal message may be influenced by your social, cultural, educational, professional, and intellectual frames of reference, verbal messages use a common language code, which can be easily decoded because if the message cannot be decoded or understood, communication fails. For example, if you do not understand French, you can not decode a message encoded in French. The process of message decoding in listening also involves the recognition of false starts, pauses, hesitations, stress, intonation, and rhythm patterns.

> We should be aware of our own prejudices and biases so that we avoid making wrong conclusions.

After the message has been decoded and interpreted, its significance is evaluated and appropriate conclusions are drawn from it. In order to evaluate a verbal message correctly, facts have to be separated from opinions, relevant information from irrelevant information, examples from ideas, and explicit information from implicit information. The intention and attitude of the speaker also have to be analyzed and understood. When we listen, we have to construct a parallel message based on the sound clues received from the speaker. We should be aware of our own prejudices and biases so that we avoid making wrong conclusions.

Response is the action or reaction of the listener to the message. It is the last stage of listening. If the message has been analysed, interpreted, and evaluated correctly, the response will be appropriate. The response makes the communication more effective as it clarifies the message and helps the speaker to know whether the message has been understood or not.

The response makes the communication more effective as it clarifies the message and helps the speaker to know whether the message has been understood or not.

5.2 HEARING VERSUS LISTENING

A clear distinction should be made between listening and hearing. Hearing happens automatically as it is an involuntary physical act. It does not require the conscious involvement of the listener. When you move on a railway platform, you hear several voices. You do not listen to them. Suddenly there is an announcement on the public speaker and we listen to it. When we listen, we pay conscious attention to what is being said.

Table 5.1 summarises the differences between listening and hearing.

TABLE 5.1 Differences Between Listening and Hearing

Listening	*Hearing*
• Voluntary	• Involuntary
• Requires conscious efforts	• Happens automatically
• Active process	• Passive process
• The listener plays a very active part	• The listener plays a passive part
• A two-way interactive process engaging the speaker and the listener	• A one-way process

Progress Check 1

1. Which of the following statements about the process of listening are false?

(a) The process of decoding in listening takes place as soon as the message reaches the receiver.
(b) Listening refers to the accurate perception of what is being said.
(c) Listening requires no special effort by the listener.
(d) Effective listening involves only recognising unit boundaries phonologically.
(e) Response is the action or reaction of the listener to the message.
(f) Listening involves perceiving and interpreting the sounds correctly, and understanding the implied meaning.
(g) Hearing happens automatically as it is an involuntary physical act.
(h) Listening is a two-way interactive process engaging the speaker and the listener.
(i) While receiving and interpreting the spoken word, the listener is not concerned with message decoding.
(j) Decoding in listening refers to the process of changing the coded message into information.

5.3 TYPES OF LISTENING

As illustrated in Table 5.2, listening may be classified into the following six types on the basis of purpose and output:

1. Superficial listening
2. Appreciative listening
3. Focused listening
4. Evaluative listening
5. Attentive listening
6. Empathetic listening

TABLE 5.2 Types of Listening

Types	*Characteristics*
Superficial listening	The listener has little awareness of the content of the verbal message.
Appreciative listening	The purpose of listening is to derive pleasure.
Focused listening	The purpose is to get some specific information.
Evaluative listening	The purpose is to evaluate the oral message, commentary and develop a line of thought.
Attentive listening	It is interactive and productive, facilitating proper interaction and more effective listener-speaker relationships.
Empathetic listening	It involves listening to the speaker's feelings, emotions, and state of mind.

5.3.1 Superficial Listening

In this type of listening, the listener has little awareness of the content (what is being said). The output in this type of listening is zero because the listener tends to ignore the message, and is not able to concentrate on the theme, main points, and supporting details of the message.

5.3.2 Appreciative Listening

The main purpose of appreciative listening is to get enjoyment and pleasure. Examples include listening to recordings of songs, entertaining stories, jokes, anecdotes, and so on. The output may be taking part in the entertainment process. For example, a music lover may listen to the latest hit, pick up the chorus and tune, and try to sing along.

5.3.3 Focused Listening

Focused listening involves listening for specific information. The main purpose is to get some specific information that might be used to take a decision. This is the most common type of listening that we practice in non-formal oral communicative situations. Examples include listening to the radio, watching and listening to television programmes, listening to railway and airport announcements, and so on.

> Focused listening is the most common type of listening that we practice in non-formal oral communicative situations.

5.3.4 Evaluative Listening

Evaluative listening involves evaluation of the oral message or commentary and developing a line of thought. The listener interprets and analyses what he or she listens to in order to understand both the explicit as well as implicit meaning of the oral message. It may also involve matching topics against one's own interests, and making mental notes of the important points. Thus, the main purpose of evaluative listening is to evaluate the content of the oral message to select appropriate information. The output could be an oral response, or summarising and recalling information at a later stage. Examples include listening to structured talks, classroom lectures, workshops, seminars, and so forth.

> The listener interprets and analyses what he or she listens to in order to understand both the explicit as well as implicit meaning of the oral message.

5.3.5 Attentive Listening

Attentive listening demands the complete attention of the listener. It is basically active and intelligent listening in situations such as group discussions, meetings, job interviews, and so on. The listener pays attention to all parts of the message, i.e., the central idea, main points, supporting details, examples, and illustrations. There is no 'selective dismissal' of any part of the oral message.

> Attentive listening demands the complete attention of the listener.

As attentive listening is interactive and productive, facilitating proper interaction and more effective listener-speaker relationships, it requires conscious effort on the part of the listener and demands concentration, involvement, and responsibility. Some other examples of attentive listening include listening to administrative instructions, formal conversational interaction, suggestions, requests, important telephone calls, and so on.

5.3.6 Empathetic Listening

Empathetic listening is listening not only to what the speaker is saying but also to how he/she is saying, i.e., his/her feelings, emotions, and state of mind. The listener has to understand and respond to the affective signals that the speaker might make and has to be alert to the speaker's implied meaning, intention, and attitude. Moreover, he/she has to understand and interpret non-verbal clues and the body language of the speaker.

> Empathetic listening is listening not only to what the speaker is saying but also to how he/she is saying it.

Progress Check 2

1. Match List I with List II and select the correct answer from the given options:

LIST I	LIST II
(1) Superficial listening	(a) Listening to a musical programme
(2) Appreciative listening	(b) Listening to a frustrated colleague
(3) Focused listening	(c) Listening to a speaker during a group discussion
(4) Evaluative listening	(d) Listening to a business presentation
(5) Attentive listening	(e) Listening to a news report
(6) Empathetic listening	(f) listening to a radio programme while reading a newspaper

OPTIONS

(i) 1 – b, 2 – a, 3 – e, 4 – d, 5 – c, 6 – f
(ii) 1 – f, 2 – a, 3 – d, 4 – c, 5 – c, 6 – b
(iii) 1 – f, 2 – a, 3 – e, 4 – d, 5 – c, 6 – b
(iv) 1 – f, 2 – a, 3 – c, 4 – e, 5 – d, 6 – b

5.4 LISTENING WITH A PURPOSE

We listen to different kinds of oral messages for different purposes.

The above description of different types of listening clearly indicates that the most important thing to settle initially is simply why a particular oral message is being listened to. Listening to classical music is quite different from listening to a lecture. People may listen for relaxation or entertainment, for getting information, for solving problems, or for discussion at a later stage. They listen to different kinds of oral messages for different purposes. Is it serious listening or light listening? What matters most is the overall purpose of listening.

Although the basic purpose of listening is to receive information from various sources, there can be different purposes in listening. One may listen to:

- Get an introductory idea of an oral message
- Understand the main points of a lecture
- Discover the speaker's ideas during a conversation
- Understand differing viewpoints in order to contribute to a discussion
- Aim a broad understanding of the subject matter of a seminar
- Obtain specific information
- Understand new changes and developments in a particular field
- Broaden one's outlook and understanding
- Seek evidence for one's own points of view

In order to achieve the above listening purposes, one needs to understand the differences between effective and ineffective listening. Study Table 5.3 to understand these differences:

TABLE 5.3 Difference Between effective and Ineffective Listening

Effective Listening	*Ineffective Listening*
The listener is aware of a clear specific purpose of listening and he/she is motivated to listen.	The listener has no clear purpose and he/she has no motivation to listen to the speaker.
The listener understands the language of the speaker.	The listener finds it difficult to understand the language of the speaker.
The content of the oral message is accessible to the listener because of his/her familiarity with the content.	The content is unfamiliar and far removed from the listener's knowledge and experience.
The listener pays attention to a person's speech and concentrates on the theme, main points, and supporting details of the message.	The listener does not pay attention to a person's speech and is not able to concentrate on the theme, main points, and supporting details of the message.

(*Contd.*)

As the listener concentrates on the important parts of the message, he/she thinks ahead, hypothesises, and predicts.	The listener does not think ahead as he/she pays the same amount of attention to all parts of the message.
The listener asks questions for clarifications to ensure that he/she has understood the speaker.	The listener does not question the speaker regardless of whether he/she has heard accurately or not.
The listener has and uses background information to help understand the lecture or speech.	The listener does not have or does not use background information.
The listener interprets and analyses while he/she listens.	The listener does not interpret and analyse while he/she listens.
The listener is able to use different strategies for different kinds of oral discourses.	The listener is not able to use different strategies for different kinds of oral discourses.

Progress Check 3

1. **Which of the following is not a clear aspect of effective listening?**
   (a) predicting and hypothesising
   (b) lack of motivation to listen
   (c) use of background information
   (d) comprehensible language
   (e) interpreting and analysing the message
   (f) paying the same amount of attention to all parts of the verbal message
   (g) use of similar strategies for different kinds of oral discourses
   (h) asking clarifying questions
   (i) inaccessible and unfamiliar content
   (j) a clear specific purpose of listening
   (k) concentration on the core information
   (l) lack of interest in the verbal message
2. **Analyse the following situations and identify effective and ineffective listeners:**
   (a) Anita is taking part in a meeting. She is carefully listening to each member of the team. While listening to them, she is interpreting and analysing what they are speaking. She is trying to understand both explicit as well as implicit meaning of the verbal messages in order to respond to their views.
   Effective/Ineffective
   (b) John is listening to a lecture on software technology. As he is a student of English literature, he is not interested in the subject. Moreover, he is feeling sleepy and is listening in an unconscious manner without paying any attention to what he is listening.
   Effective/Ineffective
   (c) Rajesh is listening to a business presentation. However, his mind is busy thinking about the questions that he will ask. He wants to show the audience that he knows much more than the speaker. So, he is not able to pay attention to the content or the visual aids that the speaker is using.
   Effective/Ineffective
   (d) Serjesh is taking part in a group discussion on the topic "Implementation of flexitime in the banking sector". He is listening to the first speaker, who is a bit nervous. Serjesh is encouraging her to express her ideas clearly and is giving non-verbal signals to indicate comprehension. She stops to

find words and he gives her words by saying, "I hope you are trying to say that flexitime is not a good idea for the banking sector".

Effective/Ineffective

(e) Kavita is listening to the teacher, who is explaining different steps of computer programming. She is not taking any interest in the lecture as she is amused at the hair style of the teacher and is wondering how he will look without any hair.

Effective/Ineffective

(f) Mohan is listening to a talk on the Indian economy. Although he is a student of mechanical engineering, he is trying to understand the lecture by concentrating on the main points and supporting details. He finds the visuals used by the speaker very interesting and helpful.

Effective/Ineffective

(g) Neha is taking part in a selection G.D. She is listening to the second speaker, who is using abstract phrases and expressions. She tries to infer the meaning of unfamiliar words from contextual clues. She pays attention to the speaker's intention, and is trying to understand and interpret non-verbal clues and body language of the speaker.

Effective/Ineffective

5.5 BARRIERS TO LISTENING

As listening is a complex process, it is desirable to take care of the barriers that may hamper the smooth flow of oral communication. Awareness of these barriers can help the listener adopt effective strategies to avoid them. The barriers to the listening process may emanate from either the speaker, listener, or the circumstances of communication. In oral communicative situations, any interference or noise that interferes with the listening process can create misunderstanding and confusion and may sometimes lead to communication breakdown.

The barriers to the listening process may emanate either from the speaker, listener, or from the circumstances of communication.

Barriers to listening could be physical, psychological, linguistic, or cultural (Table 5.4).

TABLE 5.4 Barriers to Listening

Physical Barriers	*Psychological Barriers*	*Linguistic Barriers*	*Cultural Barriers*
• Noise • Physical discomfort • Physical distractions • distance	• Emotional disturbance • Anxiety • Over arousal of emotions	• Improper message decoding • Ambiguous language • Jargon	• Cultural differences • Different values • Different social norms

5.5.1 Physical Barriers

Physical distractions and disturbances can easily disrupt the process of listening. Barriers to listening could be noise, physical discomfort, or any physical factor. Physical noise refers to any sound that disrupts the listening process. For example, a person is talking on his/her mobile phone and a queer shrilling sound disturbs the transmission. When a person tries to talk to someone on a running train, bus, or in a crowded market, several distractions in the surroundings disrupt the listening process. In order to avoid physical noise during the process of listening, we have to ensure that all channels are free from noise during the time of communication.

Physical discomfort can also easily disrupt the listening process because one cannot be a good listener if one is feeling uncomfortable. For instance, if a person is listening to a business presentation in a conference room but the room temperature is very high and there is no air-conditioner, his/her discomfort due to high room temperature may distract his/her attention and he/she may not be able to focus on the presentation. This can lead to poor comprehension. It is, therefore, important that you avoid any discomfort before beginning to listen to someone.

In order to ensure a comfortable listening without physical disturbances, we should take care of the following points:

- Ensure that there is no distracting noise from outside. Close the door if there is some disturbing noise from outside.
- If it is a very important communicative situation like a meeting or conference, mobile phones should be switched off.
- Be sure that the infrastructure, such as seating arrangement, is comfortable.
- As distance can sometimes become a barrier to effective listening, we should sit at a proper place, maintaining appropriate distance.
- Be comfortable and at ease.

5.5.2 Psychological Barriers

Perhaps some of the most common barriers to listening result from the listener's disturbed state of mind, i.e., they are psychological in nature. As listening is a purposeful activity, any psychological or emotional turbulence or disturbance can prove to be a barrier to effective listening because it leads to lack of interest and concentration. Feelings of anger, frustration, sadness, anxiety, or fear influence our reception and receptivity to others' ideas. Over arousal of emotions may adversely affect the listeners ability to decode an oral message, and he or she may find it difficult to concentrate on what the speaker is saying.

> As listening is a purposeful activity, any psychological or emotional turbulence or disturbance can prove to be a barrier to effective listening because it leads to lack of interest and concentration.

Thus, one must ensure that one is in a normal state of mind before one takes part in a communicative interaction. The listener should be tension-free and should not upset himself/herself by too much thinking and speculation. For example, if a person has to face a job interview and he is too nervous, he/she should avoid such feelings of discomfort. Whatever may be the purpose of listening, the listener needs to concentrate on the content of the oral message if he/she wants to take an active part in the communication process.

5.5.3 Linguistic Barriers

> Improper message decoding during listening is the recurrent barrier in the process of oral communication.

Improper message decoding during listening is the recurrent barrier in the process of oral communication. Since the message is decoded incorrectly by the listener, it may lead to confusion and misunderstanding. While decoding an oral message, the listener should concentrate on the linguistic code. If he/she listens to something in a language or dialect that he/she is not able to follow, a communication breakdown will definitely occur. For example, if he/she does not understand French properly, he/she may not understand a lecture in French.

In order to avoid linguistic barriers, the following points should be noted:

- Ensure that the speaker is using a language that the listener understands.
- Sometimes, the speaker may use difficult words, jargon, technical terminology, or unclear phrases. The listener should feel free to ask for clarifications. No good speaker will mind it.
- If the speaker uses ambiguous language open to several interpretations, the listener should ask the speaker to clarify and explain.
- When the listener is in doubt, he/she should ask questions.

5.5.4 Cultural Barriers

If the speaker and listener belong to different cultures and share different values, listening could become a difficult process. In oral communication, it is the listener who assigns meaning to message cues and meanings are assigned in terms of the listener's frame of reference. This interpretation of meaning can create misunderstandings during intercultural communication due to differences in norms and values. Our values are our personal guides to thought and behaviour, and exert a strong influence on us.

In order to avoid cultural barriers during listening, a listener should be sensitive to cultural differences and take into account the values of the speaker while interpreting an oral message. The listener's weakness in viewing others within his/her own cultural frame of reference may lead to confusion and misunderstanding. The moment he/she interprets others' point of view from his/her angle, he/she allows his/her preconceived notions and prejudices to start working for him/her. His/her frame of reference is individual to him/her as it is based on his/her experiences, exposure, education, personality, and several other elements peculiar to him/her. In order to avoid communication failure, the listener has to be sensitive to this fact and try to put himself/herself in the other person's position.

> A listener should be sensitive to cultural differences and take into account the values of the speaker while interpreting an oral message.

Progress Check 4

1. Which of the following steps to overcome barriers to listening may not be effective:

(a) Avoiding any physical discomfort before listening to someone.

(b) Ensuring that all channels are free of noise during the time of communication.

(c) While listening to a lecture or talk, the listener sits at a proper place and maintains appropriate distance.

(d) If the speaker uses ambiguous language open to several interpretations, the listener does not ask the speaker to clarify and explain.

(e) The listener ensures that he is in a normal state of mind before taking part in a communicative interaction.

(f) The listener tries to be tension-free and avoids upsetting himself by too much thinking and speculation while listening to a presentation.

(g) Whatever may be the purpose of listening, the listener concentrates on the content of the oral message in order to take an active part in the communication process.

(h) If the speaker uses difficult words, jargon, technical terminology, or unclear phrases, the listener does not disturb the speaker by asking questions for clarifications.
(i) The listener is sensitive to cultural differences and takes into account the values of the speaker while interpreting an oral message in order to avoid cultural barriers during listening.
(j) The listener is sensitive to the fact that his/her frame of reference is individual to him/her as it is based on his/her experiences, exposure, education, personality, and several other elements peculiar to him/her.
(k) The listener is aware of his/her prejudices and biases.
(l) In order to avoid communication failure, the listener tries to put himself/herself in the other person's position.

Exercise

1. Answer the following questions briefly:

(a) What is listening?
(b) What are the different steps involved in the process of listening?
(c) How is hearing different from listening?
(d) How is effective listening different from ineffective listening?
(e) What are barriers to listening? What steps should you take to overcome them?
(f) What are the different types of listening?

2. Ask a friend to read the following speech and answer the questions that follow. Do not read yourself.

Ladies and gentlemen,

I would like to talk about something that may not sound very interesting but it is definitely very important. Well, I'll say something about forests. To be precise, I'd throw some light on two aspects of forests, i.e., significance of forests and their excessive exploitation.

Forests provide several products of daily use, such as food, timber, firewood, wood pulp, forage and fibre, apart from being a vast storehouse of medicinal plants that are yet to be fully explored and exploited. Forests are potent sources of many industrial raw materials. The greatest significance of forests, however, lies in their critical role in maintaining ecological processes and life support systems.

According to official records our country has an area of 633.4 lakh hectares notified as forests, which represents 19.27 per cent of the total geographic area. The National Forest Policy of 1952 recommends that 33 per cent of the land area of the country should be under forests. Contrary to this guideline, however, forests have been under increasing assault since independence. Excessive exploitation of forests and overgrazing have seriously decimated our forest resources.

QUESTIONS

1. What is the central idea of the speech?
2. What is the attitude of the speaker towards forests?
3. What do the forests provide?
4. What is their significance according to the speaker?
5. What percentage of the geographic area do our forests comprise?
6. What is the recommendation of the National Forest Policy of 1952?

7. What is the direct result of excessive exploitation of forests and overgrazing?
8. What conclusion can you draw from this speech?

Key to Progress Check

Progress Check 1

1. c, d and i

Progress Check 2

1. (iii) 1 – f, 2 – a, 3 – e, 4 – d, 5 – c, 6 – b

Progress Check 3

1. b, f, g, i, and l
2. **Effective listeners** Anita, Serjesh, Mohan, Neha
   Ineffective listeners John, Rajesh, Kavita

Progress Check 4

1. (d) and (h)

6 CHAPTER

Improving Listening Comprehension

The most important thing in communication is hearing what isn't said.

—Peter Drucker

LEARNING OBJECTIVES

- Acquiring listening skills
- Learning to identify different aspects of effective listening
- Knowing the 10 thumb rules for good listening
- Grasping techniques for active listening
- Knowing strategies for listening in conversational interaction
- Understanding techniques for listening to structured talks
- Knowing how to become an effective team listener
- Grasping techniques for note taking

6.1 LISTENING COMPREHENSION

Comprehension is the act of understanding or the power of the mind to understand. Listening comprehension is the act of understanding an oral message. As a professional, you have to achieve the ability to comprehend material delivered at relatively fast speed and understand spoken material in standard Indian English, British English or American English. You need intelligent listening skills in situations such as an interview in which you are a candidate, or a group discussion, or a meeting in which you are a participant.

> Listening comprehension is an act of understanding an oral message.

Being a complex process that involves perceiving and interpreting the sounds correctly as well as understanding the explicit and implied meaning of the oral message, listening comprehension includes several skills and sub-skills. These skills include scanning, prediction, speech decoding, comprehending, and oral discourse analysis. The first two skills are similar to scanning and prediction in reading comprehension. Scanning is the ability to locate specific information in a conversation, speech, or presentation whereas prediction is guessing information. The three other skills need some explanation.

> Scanning is the ability to locate specific information in a conversation, speech, or presentation whereas prediction is guessing information.

6.1.1 Speech Decoding

Speech decoding is integral to listening comprehension. It involves sound perception and recognition, word recognition, and accent recognition.

Sound Perception and Recognition

Decoding of verbal messages requires the ability to perceive and recognise speech sounds and sound patterns accurately as well as the ability to recognise the way sounds combine to form syllables and utterances. The listener has to be attentive to the sounds that he/she hears because any lapse or mistake may lead to miscommunication and misunderstanding. Moreover, a large number of competing sounds from the environment may interfere with concentration and if the listener is not careful, he/she may not perceive sounds accurately.

> The listener has to be attentive to the sounds that he/she hears because any lapse or mistake may lead to miscommunication and misunderstanding.

Word Recognition

Speech decoding during listening also involves the ability to recognise words accurately, understand definitions of the words and phrases being used, recognise the way words are used in context, and identify discourse markers and attention signals.

Accent Recognition

In order to decode a verbal message, the listener has to recognise stress and intonation patterns. In addition, he/she needs to identify pauses, false starts, hesitations, and turn-taking in a conversation, discussion, or other transactions involving more than one speaker.

6.1.2 Comprehending

Comprehending a verbal message involves the ability to:

- Identify the central theme, main ideas, and supporting details
- Concentrate and understand long speeches
- Identify the level of formality
- Deduce incomplete information
- Decode unfamiliar vocabulary

6.1.3 Oral Discourse Analysis

Oral discourse analysis is the process of identifying relationships among different units within the speech or oral message. It includes critical skills, attitude analysis, and inferential skills.

> Oral discourse analysis is the process of identifying relationships among different units within the speech or oral message.

Critical Skills

When you listen to a structured talk, speech, or presentation, you need to analyse it in order to distinguish between relevant and irrelevant information, factual and non-factual information, examples and ideas, and so on. Critical skills are, thus, essential to effective listening comprehension.

Attitude Analysis

You may have to analyse a verbal message in order to understand the speaker's attitude to you and the topic under discussion. This is more important in meetings, discussions, and conferences. Attitude analysis includes the following skills:

- Identifying a speaker's attitude
- Understanding the speaker's attitude
- Evaluating a speaker's attitude

Inferential Skills

Effective listening comprehension involves understanding not only the explicit meaning of a verbal message but also the implicit meaning because the speaker may not speak everything explicitly and clearly. Thus, the listener may have to analyse a verbal message in order to draw inferences and conclusions. This may involve interpreting the non-verbal clues and body language of the speaker.

Progress Check 1

1. Complete the following table in the light of the above discussion about listening comprehension skills:

Listening comprehension skills

Literal skills

.Sound recognition

- ____________________________
- ____________________________

Word recognition

- Recognising words accurately
- ______________________________
- ______________________________
- ______________________________

Accent recognition

- ______________________________

Scanning

- ______________________________

Prediction

- ______________________________

Comprehending

- Identifying theme or central idea
- ______________________________
- ______________________________

Critical and analytical skills

Critical skills

Distinguishing between

- Facts and opinions
- ______________________________
- ______________________________
- ______________________________

Attitude analysis

- ______________________________
- ______________________________
- ______________________________

Inferential skills

- ______________________________

6.2 EFFECTIVE LISTENING STRATEGIES

Complete comprehension of an oral message is more challenging than reading. A text can be reread if there is any problem in comprehension but there is no such scope in listening. As listening is a major aspect of academic and professional interaction, mastering the art of effective listening is essential. Moreover, listening is a communication opportunity and taking advantage of such opportunities makes a person a dedicated professional.

> Complete comprehension of an oral message is more challenging than reading.

> Most students who do not have a systematic approach to listening suffer from lack of concentration, boredom, ineffective listening, and poor comprehension.

Most students who do not have a systematic approach to listening face difficulties in understanding a lecture, a seminar, or a discussion. They suffer from lack of concentration, boredom, ineffective listening, and poor comprehension. As one has to ensure high degree of understanding and remembrance, one should follow a systematic approach to listening. For example, an eminent scholar has to deliver a lecture on a topic relevant to a particular person's studies and career and he/she wants to listen to the professor. In order to take full advantage of this opportunity, he/she needs to follow a systematic listening method and apply appropriate listening strategies for better comprehension.

In order to improve your listening comprehension, some basic tips on good listening need to be followed and active listening techniques should be adopted. In addition, listening strategies should be developed for specific listening tasks such as lecture comprehension, two-way interactions, group interaction, student-teacher consultations, student-student negotiation, seminars, discussion sessions, and so on.

6.2.1 Ten Thumb Rules for Good Listening

Remember the 10 thumb rules for good listening that are listed in Table 6.1. These suggestions can help improve listening effectiveness.

TABLE 6.1 Rules of Good Listening

1.	Talking	×
2.	Thinking	×
3.	Distractions	×
4.	Mind wandering	×
5.	Putting the speaker at ease	✓
6.	Pre-judgement	×
7.	Patience	✓
8.	Being angry	×
9.	Empathising with the speaker	✓
10.	Taking notes	✓

Stop Talking

Do not talk while listening. One cannot be a speaker and a listener at the same time. The listener should accept his/her role and allow the speaker to talk. He/she should forget about his/her response to the listener and concentrate on the speaker's words.

Stop Thinking

It is not enough for the listener to keep his mouth shut while he/she is listening. He/she has to stop thinking too. He/she cannot listen effectively while thinking. He/she will not be able to focus 100% on what the speaker is telling.

Remove Distractions

In order to focus 100% on the person speaking, the listener should avoid all kinds of distractions. He/she should not create any distractions for himself/herself and should not allow others to interrupt.

Do Not Let Your Mind Wander

One of the main causes of listening inefficiency is the slowness of speech. We can listen faster than the speaker can speak. This lag time may make the listener's mind wander or daydream. This can be avoided by concentrating on each word spoken by the speaker.

Put Speaker at Ease

A conducive environment should be provided to the speaker in order to enable him/her to be at ease. If the speaker is not comfortable, he/she will not be able to speak clearly.

Do not Pre-judge

Give the speaker a chance to complete what he/she has to say. Pre-judgement closes the mind and does not allow you to perceive the speaker impartially. You can make proper judgement only after you have fully comprehended the information.

Be Patient

The speaker should be allowed sufficient time and not interrupted until he/she takes a pause and invites the listener to do so. Patience is the key to good listening. The listener may be in a hurry as he/she has to go somewhere or do something, but good listening demands that he/she listens to the speaker patiently.

Do not be Angry

The listener should control his/her temper while listening. He/she may not like what the speaker is telling, or may completely disagree with his/her point of view but good listening demands that he/she listens to him/her calmly without making any fuss.

Empathise with the Speaker

In order to understand the speaker's perspective and appreciate his/her point of view, the listener should try to put him/her in the speaker's position.

Take Notes

The listener should take notes if he/she wants to keep a record of what was said, and wants to use it at a later stage.

6.2.2 Active Listening Practices

Listening can be passive or active. Passive listening is the process of just absorbing the message encoded in the spoken word without any involvement. In passive listening, the listener plays no role. On the other hand, active listening is a dynamic, interactive communicative process in which the listener:

> Passive listening is the process of just absorbing the message encoded in the spoken word without any involvement.

- Pays attention
- Shows interest in the speaker and speech
- Takes note of the speaker's body language
- Avoids distractions
- Responds non-verbally to encourage the speaker

As active listening is interactive and productive, it facilitates proper interaction and produces new understanding. It promotes more effective listener-speaker relationships, and helps us take advantage of opportunities we might miss by being a passive listener. That is why one needs to be an active listener rather than a passive one. Active listening requires conscious efforts on one's part and demands concentration, involvement and responsibility.

> Active listening demands concentration, involvement, and responsibility.

In order to become an active listener, we have to adopt a set of listening practices that may help us understand the meaning of an oral message. Listed below are some guidelines to be followed by an active listener.

Attentive Listening

Unlike a passive listener, the active listener should show interest in the speaker and the speech. He/she should show desire to listen and be interested in what the speaker is telling. He/she should not show non-verbal signals such as audible snoring or rolling eyes that indicate that he/she does not want to listen. His/her posture must reflect his/her interest and his/her body language should indicate his/her keenness to listen.

An active listener would listen to the speaker patiently and carefully and be alert and pay attention while listening. Passive listeners generally listen to others in an unconscious manner without paying attention. By paying attention to both content as well as presentation, we can understand the speaker better.

Using Non-verbal Skills

Appropriate non-verbal skills may be used to indicate interest and understanding. Eye contact should be maintained with the speaker. The speaker should be helped and encouraged by positive body signals such as an occasional nod or a smile. The listener may also send non-verbal signals to indicate comprehension. He/she should also pay attention to the body language of the speaker in order to understand and interpret non-verbal clues for signs of stress, anxiety, excitement, enthusiasm, or boredom. This will help the listener analyse the verbal message in the right perspective.

> Active listening includes using non-verbal skills, improving speaker's contribution, asking questions, making clarifications, and analysing an oral message.

Improving Speaker's Contribution

An active listener should take appropriate steps to improve the speaker's contribution. He/she should encourage the speaker to express his/her ideas clearly by indicating understanding and appreciation of his/her point of view.

Asking Questions

Asking questions forms an important part of the listening process as it leads to building up a good rapport between the speaker and the listener. By asking relevant questions we can get the maximum information from a speaker. Moreover, asking questions shows that one is listening and this encourages the speaker. The listener should not wait to be asked and must instead readily ask relevant clarifying questions.

He/she may ask open-ended or closed questions. Open-ended questions provide the speaker with an opportunity to elaborate a point whereas closed questions ask the speaker to be more exact and specific.

> Open-ended questions provide the speaker with an opportunity to elaborate a point whereas closed questions ask the speaker to be more exact and specific.

Examples of Open-ended Questions

1. What are the advantages of this deal?
2. What is your personal opinion about the problem?
3. What do you think about this proposal?

Examples of Closed Questions

1. Is this deal acceptable to the management?
2. Are we facing this problem for the first time?
3. Will you accept this proposal?

While asking questions, the listener should not argue or be rigid on a question. The listener should have the liberty to handle the question the way he/she wants. Here are some tips on how to ask questions:

- Questions should be asked at the appropriate points. The speaker should not be interrupted.
- Questions should be chosen carefully. The purpose of asking a question should be to get clarifications and indicate comprehension.
- Simple language should be used to phrase questions.
- Questions should be asked one at a time.
- The listener should wait for an answer patiently.
- The listener should listen carefully to the answer and not jump to conclusions.

Clarifying

Clarify what the speaker is saying by paraphrasing what has been said or summarising one's understanding of the key points. This way the listener can show that he/she is listening carefully and paying attention.

Analysing

As an active listener, one should interpret and analyse what one hears in order to:

- Understand both explicit as well as implicit meaning of an oral message
- Differentiate between ideas, opinions, feelings, and facts, as expressed by the speaker
- Infer the meaning of unfamiliar words from contextual or internal clues
- Draw inferences and conclusions from the speech

6.2.3 Listening in Conversational Interaction

We may have to listen during two-way interactions that may include informal conversations, academic interactions, student-teacher consultations, student-student negotiation, job interviews, and so on. Listening plays a key role in these communicative situations as the output of listening in all these situations is to make considered oral responses. We need to develop effective listening strategies for these communicative situations.

The following suggestions can help improve listening effectiveness during face-to-face conversational interactions:

Listen for Conversational Signals

During a conversation, discussion, or other transaction involving more than one speaker, every participant has to take his/her turn at the appropriate moment. Many a time nobody is there to indicate this turn, or prompt or invite the participant to do so. Each participant has to look out for conversational signals indicating the possibility of starting his/her turn so that he/she is able to take a turn at the appropriate moment.

> Listening in conversational interaction involves looking out for conversational signals, evaluating, labelling carefully, using attention signals, and adjusting the pace of listening.

Evaluate

While listening to professional and administrative requirements involving requests, suggestions or instructions, the listener should evaluate what he/she listens to in order to make a mental commentary and develop a line of thought. He/she has to determine necessary action as the output is to perform some physical activity, make an oral response, impart or solicit information, and so on.

Be Careful While Labelling

Whenever a listener hears someone for the first time, he/she starts forming impressions about him/her. These impressions about the background, nature, qualities, social standing, character of the speaker may be true or false. As these impressions lead to changes in the listener's behaviour towards the speaker, he/she should be careful while forming such impressions.

Use Attention Signals

In order to indicate that the listener is participating actively in a conversational interaction, he/she must use appropriate attention signals. These attention signals could be receptive expressions and utterances such as 'oh yes', 'yes', 'fine', 'of course', 'well', 'ok', 'that's fine', 'no problem', 'really', 'oh no', or just informal grunts such as 'uhuh's', 'mm's', 'un-hum', and so forth.

Adjust Your Pace of Listening

As mentioned before, the speed at which we listen is faster than the speed at which we can speak. This time lag may prove boring and lead to a lack of concentration, which may result in poor listening comprehension. So, we should adjust our pace of listening by reviewing what the speaker is saying during this lag time. Moreover, while the listener waits for the speaker's next idea, he/she should concentrate on the implications of what the speaker is talking about.

Work Hard at Listening

Most of us are really not good listeners. Thus, we have to work hard to become good listeners. Every chance to listen to someone provides us an opportunity to learn something. We must be actively involved in all communication and try to make every listening experience a memorable learning experience.

Progress Check 2

1. **Which of the following is not an effective listening strategy for two-way interactions?**
   (a) Labelling
   (b) Listening for conversational signals
   (c) Too many informal grunts
   (d) Making social judgements
   (e) Using attention signals
   (f) Carrying on mental commentary
   (g) Using receptive expressions and utterances
   (h) Increasing speed of listening

6.2.4 Listening to Structured Talks

In order to understand a structured talk (i.e., lectures, seminar talks, presentations, speeches, oral reports, and so on) or any other formal oral discourse, we require effective listening strategies that help us in comprehending the subject-content and language patterns of the oral message. These techniques include pre-listening analysis, predicting, use of background knowledge, intensive listening, and ability to understand the links between different parts of speech. In order to become an effective listener, we need to learn and polish these listening techniques.

Pre-listening Analysis

Pre-listening analysis includes determining the purpose of listening and knowing the speaker or presenter.

> Listening to structured talks involves determining the purpose of listening, knowing the speaker, guessing the expected information, using background information and intensive listening techniques, and comprehending the logical links between different parts of presentation.

Determining the Purpose

The most important aspect of pre-listening analysis is determining what needs to be achieved by listening to the speaker. Does the listener want to listen to the speaker to get a broad understanding of a topic of his/her interest? Does he/she intend to obtain specific information? Does he/she want to be aware of the opinions and reactions of the speaker to a specific situation or problem? Does he/she want to understand specific instructions? Whether his/her purpose is to get facts or opinions, understand attitude or perspective, he/she must have a clear idea of what he/she wants to remember at the end of the conversation/talk/lecture/speech/presentation/seminar/workshop.

Knowing Your Speaker

The second essential aspect in pre-listening analysis is analysing the speaker. If the listener knows the speaker well, he/she will be able to make appropriate adaptations for better understanding. Is the speaker an expert of the subject, or just a generalist? What are his/her background and specific qualifications that make him/her fit for the presentation? Has the listener ever heard him/her before? Is he/she a native speaker? Answers to these questions will give the listener a fairly good idea of the speaker and help him/her improve.

Predicting

Predicting is a listening strategy for lecture comprehension. It is the process of guessing the information that one expects to receive during a lecture or talk. The listener should be able to think ahead, hypothesise, and predict.

> Predicating is the process of guessing the information that one expects to receive during a lecture or talk.

Predicting includes various micro-skills, including the ability to:

- Guess the information that the lecture contains
- Use the title of the lecture/talk/presentation to roughly predict the central theme and the focus of the verbal message
- Scan the use of visual aids in the opening part of the lecture to predict the nature and scope of content
- Identify oral clues used by the speaker

The listener should try to guess the overall content of the speech, i.e. guessing the information that he/she expects to receive. The more he/she is familiar with the content, the more he/she understands the oral message. For example, if he/she is going to listen to a speech by the chief guest at the annual day programme of his/her college, the listener may ask himself/herself the following questions:

> The listener should also develop a positive attitude to the speaker and the topic.

1. What is he going to talk about?
2. Is he going to talk about our college?
3. Is he going to tell something that I already know?
4. Is he going to talk about the growth of the college?
5. How long is he going to talk?
6. Will he give academic suggestions to the students of the college?
7. Will he ask questions?

Answers to such questions will help develop the required interest and motivation that are essential for effective listening. The listener should also develop a positive attitude to the speaker and the topic.

Using Background Knowledge

Once the listener has guessed the information that he/she is likely to receive, he/she may recall related information. He/she can pool his/her 'background knowledge' to get a general idea of what he/she is going to listen to. A familiar topic will make him/her more interested in the talk and he/she will actively listen to it, resulting in total comprehension. For example, when going to listen to a lecture on "Information Technology and Communication" if one is using one's background knowledge about information technology, one would find it easy to understand the lecture. Even if the speaker introduces new ideas and concepts, one may not find them too difficult. Moreover, the whole exercise of using background information will provide the necessary motivation essential for an active listener.

> Once the listener has guessed the information that he/she is likely to receive, he/she may recall related information.

Intensive Listening

Once the listener has determined his/her purpose, analysed his/her speaker, and used prediction techniques and background knowledge, he/she is ready to listen to the lecture or talk. Most speakers organise the talk into three segments: introduction, body, and conclusion. The listener has to concentrate on each segment to understand the overall meaning, focus, and implication of the talk. The guidelines for this have been given below:

> Most speakers organise a talk into three segments: introduction, body, and conclusion.

Listening to the Introduction

- Listen to the opening or introduction of the talk to get answers to the following questions:
  - (a) What is the position, knowledge, background, experience of the speaker?
  - (b) What is his/her credibility?
  - (c) What is the overall purpose of the talk?
  - (d) What is the central idea or theme?
  - (e) What is the overall organisational structure?

(f) What does the speaker intend to do? (describe, instruct, report, narrate, explain, argue, persuade, illustrate, and so on)

(g) What are the main points of the talk?

- Concentrate on the visual aids, if used by the speaker.
- Identify the key words or phrases that the speaker might use to emphasise the main points.

Listening to the Body

- As the body of a talk or lecture contains the main message, you should pay attention to every part of the body carefully.
- Concentrate on the verbal signposts in order to recognise the organisation and main points of the oral message.
- Recognise main supporting details of the oral message.
- Concentrate on visual aids such as overhead transparencies, flipcharts, handouts, slides, multimedia visuals, and so on to get a clear idea of the important points of the talk.

Listening to the Conclusion

- Listen to the closing or conclusion of the talk to understand the main themes of the verbal message.
- Recognise the speaker's focus of the talk.
- Concentrate on what the speaker wants the listeners to do, or remember.

Understanding the Links between Different Parts of Speech

The most important aspect of lecture comprehension is identifying the key points of a lecture. In order to recognise key points, we have to understand the links between different parts of speech. This involves recognising listening cues used by the speaker. Every speaker uses various techniques to indicate the relative importance of different parts of information contained in the talk. These techniques include identifying prosodic and syntactic features, oral discourse markers, and transitions.

> Every speaker uses various techniques to indicate the relative importance of different parts of information contained in the talk.

Prosodic Features and Syntactic Features

> Prosodic features include pauses, stress, intonation, and rhythm patterns.

Prosodic features include pauses, stress, intonation, and rhythm patterns. A listener needs a proper understanding of English pronunciation and articulation in order to understand these features. The chapter on "Oral Communication and Speaking Techniques" in Part Three of this book contains a detailed discussion on these topics.

Syntactic features comprise grammatical structures such as subordinate clauses, noun complements, and so on. Comprehending these syntactic structures during listening demands a fairly good understanding of English grammar. Listeners should concentrate on these features to get the correct meaning of the message.

> Syntactic features comprise grammatical structures such as subordinate clauses, noun complements, and so on.

Oral Discourse Markers

Oral discourse markers include signal phrases, logical connectors, and transitional signals.

Signal Phrases

Lecturers and speakers use specific words and phrases to indicate major transitions and emphasis in their lectures. As illustrated in Table 6.2, they help the listener understand the links between different parts of the talk.

> Lecturers and speakers use specific words and phrases to indicate major transitions and emphasis in their lectures.

TABLE 6.2 Signal Phrases

Purpose of the Speaker	*Signal Phrases*
Introducing a topic	Today, I'd like to talk about…, What I'm going to discuss is…, The main point of the discussion today is…, To begin with.., In the first place.., My first point is …, At the start let me say that…, First I'd like to discuss.., Today I'd like to describe…'.
Developing an idea	If we critically examine the situation…, As you know that.., The most significant point is.., The best solution to the problem is…, It is significant to note that…, Let's try to understand it.., It's very interesting to note.., This means that.., As you are aware…, The crucial factor is.., The point to note is,
Emphasising a point	I am sure you'll agree with me.., No one can deny the fact that.., I'd like to emphasise.., The next point is crucial to my argument..,
Contrasting several ideas	In contrast, On the other hand.., If we make a comparative analysis.., On the contrary.
Showing transition of ideas	The next important point is.., The second significant aspect is.., Let's consider another factor .., My next point is..,
Concluding	Finally, At the end.., That's all I wanted to discuss.., I'd like to sum up.., I'd like to conclude.., In conclusion..,

Logical Connectors and Transitional Signals

As illustrated in Table 6.3, speakers use logical connectors to show logical organisation and rhetorical features of a talk.

TABLE 6.3 Logical Connectors and Transitional Signals

Purpose of the Speaker	*Logical Connectors and Transitional Signals*
Adding a point	Moreover, in addition, Next, Then, Furthermore, Second, Finally
Comparing	Similarly, Likewise, In the same way
Making a contrast	In contrast, By comparison, In comparison, However, Nevertheless, If we make a comparative analysis
Showing segmentation	Right, OK, Well, All right, And, Now, That's fine, That's all, etc.
Exemplifying	In other words, For example, For instance, Take for example
Temporal	Eventually, At that time, For the time being, As, After, Before, Since, Till, Until, When, As soon as, By the time
Explaining/Showing cause and effect	Therefore, Thus, So, That is why, As, Because, Hence, For that reason, As a result, As a consequence, Consequently
Showing emphasis	Obviously, As you can see, Infact, As you know, Actually, Naturally, Of course, You see

Other Transitions

Apart from oral discourse markers, speakers might use several other transitions to lead listeners from one idea to another. The following are some such transitions:

- **Visual transitions:** Some speakers may add a visual between regular visual aids in order to give a "visual" transition. Such visuals might be an important clue to understand that part of the talk or presentation.
- **Repetitions:** Speakers may use the same words, phrases, or ideas twice to initiate a transition.
- **Questions:** Speakers may ask a question to make a transition.
- **Sequence:** A speaker may use sequence or point-by-point description to indicate transition (for example, There are two important considerations...The first one is.. The second one is).
- **Flashback:** A speaker may use a flashback technique to start a new point (for example, Do you recall my first observation).
- **Pauses:** Some speakers effectively use pausing as a transition technique because they give the listeners time to think.

Progress Check 3

1. **Which of the following is not an effective listening strategy for lecture comprehension?**
   (a) Audience analysis
   (b) Predicting
   (c) Use of background knowledge
   (d) Recognising key phrases
   (e) Concentrating on speaker's appearance
   (f) Understanding the visual aids
   (g) Recognising minor points of the oral message
   (h) Analysing the situation
   (i) Speaker analysis
   (j) Understanding all the illustrations
   (k) Identifying the key points of a lecture
   (l) Concentrating on the verbal signposts in order to recognise the organisation
   (m) Determining the purpose of listening
   (n) Recognising the focus of the talk
   (o) Understanding the links between different parts of speech
   (p) Recognising listening cues

6.2.5 Team Listening

In view of the widespread use of oral communication in team management and decision making, there can be little doubt about the value of good listening skills in achieving group communicative goals. When we take part in a group communicative situation, we cannot contribute to the stated purposes of the communication unless we are listening properly. By participating as an active listener, we may meet a personal need to contribute to the accomplishments of the goals of a group activity. Moreover, active participation as a listener in a group and its discussions and deliberations serves the group-centered needs of an individual. Finally, active listening meets the ego-centered needs of listeners by enhancing their status as successful "communicators".

Listening in teams is more difficult than listening to structured talks and well-organised lectures. While we listen to a talk, we get information in an organised and structured form. Understanding the main points is not difficult because the speaker may repeat them several times during the talk. The use of signposts and visual aids also make comprehension easier. On the other hand, when we listen to deliberations during a group discussion, meeting, or team interactions, we get information in a disorganised and unclear form. There are no repetitions of points, no visual aids to clarify points and improve comprehension, no verbal signposts to indicate organisation and main points in an oral message. It is, therefore, important that we take extra precautions during team listening.

Active listening meets the ego-centered needs of listeners by enhancing their status as successful "communicators". Listening in teams is more difficult than listening to structured talks and well-organised lectures.

The following suggestions are designed to help improve team listening skills.

Avoid Distractions

There are two kinds of distractions that might disrupt the listening process—surrounding noise and physical disturbances, and disturbed state of mind.

There are two kinds of distractions that might disrupt the listening process. The first of these distractions result from surrounding noise and physical disturbances. In order to avoid these external distractions during the process of listening, you have to ensure that all channels are free of noise during the time of communication. The second type of distractions may result from your disturbed state of mind. The best way to control these distractions is to avoid team listening while you are emotionally disturbed. However, if you cannot avoid listening, you should focus 100% on what other members of the team are talking about.

Avoid Negative Non-verbal Signals

Using negative non-verbal signals during group communication is not only rude but also against team spirit as it may lead to misunderstanding and mistrust between team members. Do not use non-verbal signals to show disagreement, boredom, and lack of comprehension. It is better to express these feelings verbally. Avoid using fingers or negative head shaking to say 'no', or 'rolling eyes' to indicate that the speaker is a fool, or negative hand gestures to show that you disagree.

Do not use non-verbal signals to show disagreement, boredom, and lack of comprehension.

It is impolite to interrupt a person who is speaking as it shows lack of respect and creates misunderstanding.

Don't Interrupt

It is impolite to interrupt a person who is speaking as it shows lack of respect and creates misunderstanding. You may have something important to say or may be very eager to give a quick reply or opinion but it is not fair to interrupt the speaker. It makes you overeager and careless. Good team spirit demands better manners.

Be Involved

In order to be an effective team listener, do not just absorb the message encoded in the spoken word without any involvement but be alert and pay close attention while listening to your team members. Make conscious efforts with concentration, involvement and responsibility to improve your listening effectiveness as a team member.

Make conscious efforts with concentration, involvement and responsibility to improve your listening effectiveness as a team member.

Recognise Important Facts

It is important to recognize important facts during team listening because team members might express them informally in a casual manner. You have to obtain relevant information and identify the main ideas and supporting details. Although you have to listen carefully to everything that your team members say, you need to filter the information to identify the overall purpose, the central theme and the main focus of what they are saying.

It is important to recognize important facts during team listening because team members might express them informally in a casual manner.

Good team members avoid making subjective observations while listening to each other and avoid giving judgements on what they listen.

Be Objective

Good team members avoid making subjective observations while listening to each other. Being objective will help you as well as the team members in getting a clear picture of each other's ideas and feelings. Also, avoid giving judgements on what you listen. Expressions such as "I think your reasoning is inappropriate", or "I do not understand your attitude" are judgmental and should be avoided.

Make Notes

Make notes to retain and use the information that you receive during team listening. Do not rely on your memory. Refer to the next section for learning effective note taking techniques.

Progress Check 4

1. Which of the following listening practices will make you a better team listener?

(a) Using negative non-verbal signals
(b) Controlling external and internal distractions
(c) Becoming actively involved
(d) Listening between the lines
(e) Interrupting
(f) Asking questions
(g) Rephrasing
(h) Taking notes
(i) Being subjective
(j) Relaxing during lag time

6.2.6 Listening and Note Taking

While listening to a lecture or a talk, or to a team member during a group discussion or meeting, one needs to remember the information so that it can be used in some other form. It is better not to trust only one's memory, and one should take notes while listening. Taking notes helps one to understand the points clearly and keep a record for future reference. Even if the facts are easy to remember, they should be jotted down for clarity.

Note taking may be defined as the process of writing down quickly, briefly, and clearly the important points of a lecture, speech, presentation, or any structured verbal message. It involves summarising and paraphrasing the verbal message.

Techniques of Note Taking

Taking notes while listening to lectures and talks is an important academic activity. Learning effective note-taking techniques is essential because it is more challenging than making reading notes. While reading a text, you can reread several times for better comprehension and notes can be made leisurely. However, this is not possible in note taking because the speaker is not going to repeat his/her points for your convenience.

> The four steps of note taking include listening, filtering, paraphrasing, and noting.

It is important that you avoid writing down everything you hear. You have to carefully filter the information that you receive and adopt a strategy that enables you to understand the lecture quickly and make appropriate notes. Effective note-taking strategies are essential. Note taking includes four simple steps, i.e., listening, filtering, paraphrasing, and noting.

Listen

- Follow the 10 thumb rules for good listening and apply active listening techniques for better comprehension.
- Carefully listen to the verbal message in order to identify its purpose and scope.
- Identify different modes and styles of delivery (i.e., reading style, conversational style, informal style, rhetorical style, and so on).
- Deduce meanings of words and phrases from their context and infer relationships.
- Recognise key terms related to the subject/topic of the lecture.
- Recognise function of stress and intonation to signal information structure.
- Recognise function of non-verbal cues as markers of emphasis and attitude.
- Interpret the oral message with reference to oral conventions followed by the speaker.

Filter

- Do not try to write everything.
- Filter the information received.
- Concentrate on verbal signposts to recognise the organisation and main points in an oral message.
- Identify relationships among units within the speech (i.e., main points, supporting points, minor points, generalisations, hypotheses, illustrations, and so on).
- Look out for key phrases and signal words.
- Identify the role of discourse markers.
- Identify the main points.

Paraphrase

- After identifying the core information, rephrase suitably.
- Use appropriate words and phrases to express the central idea, main points, and main supporting details.
- Do not use full sentences.

Note

- After restructuring and rephrasing the core information, jot them down.
- Use appropriate reduction techniques such as abbreviations and symbols to save time.
- Use subordinating techniques and a suitable method of sequencing, i.e. numerals and numbers, decimalisation, and so on.
- Use note cards or notebooks to record notes.

Progress Check 5

1. **Study the following statements about note making, and mark True or False against each of them.**
   (a) Note taking refers to the process of making reading notes.
   (b) Note taking does not involve paraphrasing.
   (c) The act of decoding in note taking involves recognition of false starts, pauses, intonation, and rhythm patterns.
   (d) While taking notes, the listener should write everything that he/she hears in the lecture.
   (e) The listener must adopt a careful strategy that enables him/her to understand the lecture.
   (f) Every speaker follows certain oral conventions.
   (g) Identifying key points of a lecture does not involve recognising signal words and phrases.
   (h) Lecturers and speakers never try to indicate major transitions in their lectures.

Exercise

1. **Answer the following questions:**
   (a) What is listening comprehension?
   (b) Discuss some positive listening practices.
   (c) Differentiate between active and passive listening.
   (d) What are the different strategies for lecture comprehension?
   (e) What are the factors that make an effective team listener?
   (f) What is the process of taking notes while listening?
2. **Listen to the radio for half an hour. Evaluate and scan the information that you receive for topics of interest to you. Match topics against your own interest and make mental notes. Write a summary of what you have listened after one hour.**
3. **Listen to the weather report on television. Concentrate on the weather forecast about your area in order to decide appropriate clothes to wear during the day.**
4. **Listen to a panel discussion on television. Listen to what the speakers are saying, also how they are saying it (for example, is he or she surprised, annoyed, angry, upset, confused, relaxed, tense, pleased, confident, nervous, and so on). Prepare a brief report on the discussion mentioning the important points of discussion.**
5. **Listen to a 30-minute television news report. Use the listening techniques discussed in this chapter. Then, write a summary of the news highlighting significant events, incidents, and persons in the news.**

6. **Listen to a specific long dialogue in a television serial or film. Concentrate on the structural, syntactic, discourse, semantic, and phonological clues. Understand the explicit as well as implicit meaning of the expressions used in the dialogues. Reconstruct the dialogue.**
7. **Form a group of four or five students and conduct a group discussion on any of the topics mentioned below. You may elect a group leader to conduct the discussion. Listen to the views of each team member and write a summary of the discussion, adding your input to the discussion.**
   (a) Reducing IIM fees by the government was a retrograde step
   (b) Human cloning should be banned
   (c) Coalition politics is to stay in India
   (d) Unemployment problem
   (e) Controlling environmental pollution
8. **For one week concentrate on your listening practices in the following communicative situations:**
   (a) Informal conversations
   (b) Classroom interactions
   (c) Tutorials and practicals
   (d) Student-teacher consultations
   (e) Seminars and workshops
   (f) Technical presentations
   (g) Academic discussions
   Now identify some of your bad listening practices and discuss them with your English language teacher. Ask him/her to suggest ways to improve your listening habits.
9. **Listen to any lecture in your college. Take notes while you listen. Apply effective note taking strategies and rephrase your notes properly. After a few days, reconstruct the lecture on the basis of your notes. Show the reconstructed lecture to the teacher who gave the lecture, and request him to comment on it.**
10. **Listen to a 30-minute detective serial on TV along with a friend. Follow plot development, logical argument, and visual information about the content. Listen to the dialogues carefully, analyse the climax, and write brief notes on the following:**
    (a) the plot of the serial
    (b) the main characters of the serial
    (c) justification of the climax in the serial
    Discuss your notes with the friend and ask him/her to comment on the accuracy of your descriptions.

Key to Progress Check

Progress Check 1

1. **The following table summarises listening comprehension skills:**

Listening comprehension skills	
Literal skills	Sound recognition
	• Recognising sounds and sound patterns accurately • Recognising the way sounds combine to form syllables and utterances
	Word recognition

	• Recognising words accurately • Understanding the definitions of the words being used • Recognising the way words are used in context • Identifying discourse markers and attention signals Accent recognition • Recognising stress and intonation patterns Scanning • Locating specific information in a conversation or speech Prediction • Guessing information Comprehending • Identifying theme or central idea • Identifying main ideas • Identifying supporting details, illustrations, and examples
Critical and analytical skills	Critical skills Distinguishing between • facts and opinions • relevant and irrelevant information • explicit and implicit information • examples and ideas Attitude analysis • Understanding the speaker's intention • Identifying a speaker's attitude • Evaluating a speaker's attitude Inferential skills • Drawing inferences and conclusions

Progress Check 2

(a), (c), (d) and (h)

Progress Check 3

(e), (g) and (j)

Progress Check 4

(b), (c), (d), (f), (g) and (h)

Progress Check 5

1. (a) False (b) False (c) True (d) False (e) True
   (g) True (g) False (f) False

SECTION 3

Speaking Strategies

CHAPTERS

- Chapter 7: The Speech Process
- Chapter 8: Phonetics and Spoken English
- Chapter 9: Oral Communication and Speaking Techniques

7 CHAPTER

The Speech Process

Mend your speech a little,
Lest it may mar your fortune.

William Shakespeare

LEARNING OBJECTIVES

- Understanding the speech process
- Realizing the importance of conversation skills
- Knowing the two forms of conversation
- Grasping strategies for good conversation
- Knowing the four factors essential for improving fluency and self-expression
- Learning the use of body language to improve the effectiveness of the verbal message during an oral interaction

7.1 THE SPEECH PROCESS

Like listening, speaking is crucial to effective communication. Students need to interact orally with their teachers and classmates, make explanations during tutorials and practical sessions, take part in seminars and workshops, technical presentations, academic discussions, academic interactions, viva voce tests, and so on. On the other hand, professionals in different fields are required to take part in discussions, meetings, conferences, seminars, business presentations, telephonic conversations, teleconferences and videoconferences, and so forth. In fact, success in the highly competitive environment of today will depend not just on professional knowledge but also on the ability to present that knowledge in an appropriate oral form.

Speaking is the purposeful process by which people, using audible and visible symbols, communicate meaning in the minds of their listeners. It is flexible, changing, as well as complex and varied. Whether it is an informal conversation or a very formal business meeting, the function of oral communication is creating messages that stimulate in listeners meanings that bring about the desired change in their understanding or opinions. Let us look more closely at the speech process (Fig. 7.1).

Speaking is the purposeful process by which people using audible and visible symbols communicate meaning in the minds of their listeners.

Fig. 7.1 The Speech Process

As noted earlier, speaking is an interactive communicative process that involves speakers and listeners. While communicating a message orally, the speaker is concerned with five factors, i.e. message, audience, speech style, message encoding, and feedback.

7.1.1 The Message

The speech process begins with the selection of a message. The message includes everything that the speaker does or says, both verbally and non-verbally. Here, the speaker is concerned with the content of the specific message that he/she wants to convey. It consists of the 'what' of oral communication. The speaker's knowledge, experiences, abilities and the overall objectives of speaking generally determine the scope of 'the message'. The speaker should be clear about what message he/she wants to get across. In order to make a message have the desired impact, its content must be clear and relevant. In a professional situation, selecting a message might involve finding and selecting a subject or general topic, and deciding about the type, scope, and sources of information.

The speaker's knowledge, experiences, abilities and the overall objectives of speaking generally determine the scope of 'the message'.

7.1.2 The Audience

To be an effective speaker, familiarity with one's audience is necessary. The more formal the speaking situation, the more important it is for the speaker to know his/her listeners in order to decide how to present his/her ideas. Professional situations such as seminars, conferences, meetings, discussions, job interviews, and so on demand a careful audience analysis that might involve answering the following questions:

> To be an effective speaker, familiarity with one's audience is necessary.

- Who are the listeners?
- What is their age, sex, educational background, and so forth?
- Why will they listen to the speaker?
- What is their knowledge about the topic/subject under consideration?
- What are their personal and professional needs?
- What do they expect from the speaker?

7.1.3 The Speech Style

Speech style is the manner in which the content of the speech is presented. It is the manner of speaking. It could be very formal, as in a technical seminar, or very informal, as in a casual conversation. It depends on the purpose of speaking and the relation between the speaker and the listeners. A person discussing an academic topic with his class teacher would like to be polite and formal. On the other hand, he/she can afford to be informal if he/she is going to discuss the same topic with his/her friend. However, most of the time we may choose a style that falls between these two extremes. We should choose a style that is appropriate to the type and nature of our content, the audience, as well as the occasion and setting.

> We should choose a speech style that is appropriate to the type and nature of our content, the audience, as well as the occasion and setting.

7.1.4 Encoding

Encoding in oral communication involves selecting a language, an appropriate oral form, and positive non-verbal signals. Verbal messages need a common language code, which the listener may easily decode. If the listener cannot understand the message, communication fails. For example, the speaker cannot speak in Bengali with a person who does not understand Bengali. If the speaker and his listeners use the same language as L1, it may be used in informal situations. However, English should be used in formal situations.

> Encoding in oral communication involves selecting a language, an appropriate oral form, and positive non-verbal signals.

While communicating orally, we may have the option to choose an appropriate oral form. These options include face-to-face interpersonal communication (meetings, conferences, group discussions, panel discussions, interviews) or speaker-audience communication (speeches, debates, seminars, workshops, symposia), electronic communication (teleconferencing and videoconferencing) or telephonic communication.

Encoding in speaking also involves using non-verbal signals. Non-verbal communication includes gestures, facial expressions, body movement, and posture.

7.1.5 Feedback

Feedback is the process through which the speaker receives information about how his/her message has been received by the listeners, and his/her response to those cues. The feedback process is not complete until the speaker has responded to the listener.

> The feedback process is not complete until the speaker has responded to the listener.

Progress Check 1

1. **Which of the following statements about the speech process is True?**
   (a) Speaking is an interactive communicative process that involves speakers and listeners.
   (b) The function of oral communication is creating messages that stimulate in listeners' meanings and bring about the desired change in their understanding or opinion.
   (c) While communicating a message orally, the speaker is not concerned with the selection of a message.
   (d) Speech style depends on the purpose of speaking and the relation between the speaker/s and listener/s.
   (e) Professional situations such as seminars, conferences, meetings, discussions, and job interviews do not need an audience analysis.
   (f) Encoding in oral communication involves selecting a language, an appropriate oral form, and positive non-verbal signals.
   (g) Encoding in speaking does not involve using non-verbal signals.
   (h) Non-verbal communication includes gestures, facial expressions, body movement, and posture.

7.2 CONVERSATION AND ORAL SKILLS

Every one of us takes part in some kind of conversation, formal or informal. Conversation is an interactive process involving speakers and listeners. While talking to someone, we use audible and visible symbols in order to communicate meaning in the minds of our listeners. Conversation links people together, as it is probably the most important factor that makes social interaction possible. It establishes, maintains, improves, and consolidates social as well as professional relations.

> Conversation links people together, as it is probably the most important factor that makes social interaction possible.

Although the ability to converse well in social, academic, and professional situations is so important, we generally ignore it. We rarely plan or prepare ourselves for a conversation. Many of us are self-complacent or over-confident and believe that conversation is a natural process and that we need not prepare ourselves for this. On the other hand, there are some people who find themselves shying away from conversation because they feel inadequate in talking to others. The fact is that conversation provides us with opportunities to express ourselves, establish our individuality, and show the world what we are. If we fail to express our feelings, reactions, responses, or views properly to the other person, we would fail as individuals.

> Conversation skills include the ability to start a conversation, choose a topic for conversation, help others to start, keep a conversation going, move from one topic to another, and conclude a conversation naturally.

As conversation is a tool of social interaction, it is essential to be able to converse well in both informal as well as formal situations. One should have the ability to start a conversation, pick a topic for conversation, help others to start, keep a conversation going, move smoothly from one topic to another, and conclude a conversation naturally. One should also be able to understand, interlocute, create coherent discourse, and take appropriate turns in conversations, as well as have the ability to negotiate meanings with others through creating reciprocity of perspectives on what is said.

7.2.1 Types of Conversation: Formal and Informal

There are two types of conversation: formal and informal. As shown in Table 7.1, formal conversation differs from informal conversation in content, approach, style, attitude, and in language. Formal conversation is the type of conversation that we have in formal situations while informal conversation involves exchange of personal information with friends and relatives. Formal conversation may include making inquiries and exchanging information at public offices, and the transaction of academic, business, professional, and other official work. Informal conversation, on the other hand, includes greetings, simple social exchanges, and general inquiries during social interactions and everyday informal situations.

TABLE 7.1 Differences between Formal and Informal Conversation

Formal Conversation	*Informal Conversation*
• Formal content	• Personal and emotional content
• Always factual	• May be emotional or factual
• Formal words and expressions	• Colloquial words and expressions
• Accepted rules and customs	• No accepted rules
• Fixed norms of behaviour associated with the conduct of official matters	• No fixed norms
• Formal elements of conversational interaction	• No formal elements
• Structured transitions and turns	• Abrupt transitions
• Always formal in style	• Both formal and informal in style
• Objective approach	• Both objective and subjective
• Logically organised and structured	• Not always structured

7.2.2 Strategies for Good Conversation

> Good conversation could be both pleasure and power.

A good conversation with someone we like provides much-needed relaxation and peace of mind that recharges us and fills us with renewed energy and vigour. It makes time pass pleasantly. Moreover, if we can converse well, we can persuade people and get things done. It gives us power.

> Good conversation largely depends on our ability to adjust to other people and our good attitude.

Good conversation largely depends on our ability to adjust to other people and our good attitude. Most students cannot converse well and face difficulties in talking to their teachers, colleagues, and even friends. Conversation skills can be improved by following some basic tips regarding good conversation and learning effective conversation techniques. The following suggestions will help in this regard.

Be an Active Listener

A person can never be an effective conversationalist without being an effective listener.

One should learn to be an active and efficient listener. A person can never be an effective conversationalist without being an effective listener. When you talk to someone, whether in a formal or informal oral situation, you must listen to the person carefully and attentively. You cannot respond to the person unless you listen and understand. You should not interrupt the person while he or she is speaking. This is unacceptable and reflects bad manners.

Be a Subtle Speaker

One should be careful about what one tells and how it is told. A speaker should not just speak whatever comes to his/her mind and he/she should never tell things that he/she is not supposed to. A speaker should be pragmatic and always think in terms of the results of what he/she is telling. He/she should use an appropriate style of speaking because the way he/she speaks creates an image in the listener's mind.

Speak with Clarity

The speaker should be clear and effective, and should use effective speaking techniques. He/she should take care of articulation and pronunciation and speak distinctly, focusing attention on his/her message, while taking care of his/her voice quality, accent, and intonation.

Be Simple

It pays to be simple during a conversation. One cannot impress others by being difficult, vague, and abstract; you should in fact, use simple and familiar language while talking to people. You may use informal vocabulary during an informal and casual conversation but use only formal vocabulary during a formal situation.

Use Appropriate Pauses

Speaking too quickly may result in lack of comprehension on the part of the listener. This will result in confusion. So, it is essential to speak slowly with appropriate pauses.

Someone rightly said that good conversation is good manners.

Be Polite

Politeness is the key to good conversation. Someone rightly said that good conversation is good manners. Never be rude and impolite. Be courteous and use polite expressions and phrases during oral interaction.

Be Friendly

No one likes to talk to unfriendly people.

It is easy to talk to friendly people. If you are dogmatic and unfriendly during a conversation, the other person talking to you might find it difficult to continue the conversation. By the way, no one likes to talk to unfriendly people. So, be friendly. Be cheerful and smile. Make the other person feel comfortable. Avoid making a remark that might hurt the other person. It is important to understand the point of view of the other person. Do not jump to conclusions. Do not be in a hurry to make judgements. As a general rule, do not make generalizations such as 'All business people are cunning" or "Women are foolish". They might lead to arguments. Use moderate statements.

Be Positive

We should express positive feelings during a conversation and avoid criticising others. It is important to learn to appreciate the good and positive qualities of other people and express our appreciation.

Be Flexible

Effective conversation requires clarity, simplicity, politeness, flexibility, tact, good manners, and positive attitude.

It is essential to be flexible during a conversation. A good conversationalist is always flexible in approach, attitude and style. Rigidity goes against the spirit of good conversation. We may need to change our approach to a topic of conversation or even the topic itself if we are getting bored or if it is leading to a heated argument.

It is better to think before speaking than to suffer afterwards.

Be Tactful

It is necessary to be very tactful during conversation, especially when talking to one's teacher, boss, senior colleague, or someone who matters. It is better to think before speaking than to suffer afterwards. Choose the topics carefully and avoid controversial issues that may lead to unnecessary arguments.

Do not Argue

Most people argue for argument's sake.

Most people argue for argument's sake. They do so without realising what they intend to achieve by it and end up wasting their strength and time. However, a good conversationalist never argues during a conversation. We may disagree with the person we are talking to but there is no need to impose our point of view on the other person. Everyone has a right to express his/her views. So, it is important to respect the views expressed by other people and express our disagreements and reservations in a friendly way.

Be Interested

We should be interested in the conversation and our behaviour and attitude should reflect our interest. We should also take keen interest in the other person or persons talking to us. Maintain eye contact with each one of them and contribute to the conversation in a lively manner. Some people remain lifeless during a conversation. They just listen without contributing anything to the conversation. That might show a lack of interest and should be avoided at all costs. We should take active part in the conversation by contributing to it in a meaningful way.

Progress Check 2

1. Which of the following will make you an effective conversationalist?

(a) Good manners
(b) Negative attitude
(c) Pragmatic approach
(d) Clarity of expression
(e) Lack of confidence
(f) Passive listening
(g) Difficult and flowery language

(h) Friendly attitude
(i) Flexible approach
(j) Tact
(k) Ability to argue aggressively
(l) Rigid stand

7.2.3 Improving Fluency and Self-Expression

Fluency is the most important characteristic of effective speech. What does this term mean? What is fluency? Let us try to understand this term and the skills needed in order to achieve fluency in speech.

Fluency is the natural flow of words without any unnecessary pauses and repetition. This natural flow of words or smoothness of expression can come from the ability to compose and speak meaningful utterances by using appropriate vocabulary and grammar skills. Fluent and expressive speech normally depends on the range of vocabulary appropriately used, as poor vocabulary will cause lack of fluency. Fluency also depends on the appropriate use of macro-skills of grammar and pronunciation such as subject-verb agreement, tense formation, clause linkage, use of transitional words, basic intonation patterns, rhythm, and so on. Moreover, one should be confident of the content of one's speech in order to be fluent.

> Fluency is the natural flow of words without any unnecessary pauses and repetition.

In order to improve self-expression and achieve the desired clarity and fluency, articulation, pronunciation, voice quality, accent, and intonation need to be improved. These five important aspects are briefly described below.

Articulation

In order to speak English fluently, clearly, and confidently, articulation has to be improved. Articulation is a set of speech habits established over a long period. It is basically our ability to modify voice or breath with tongue, teeth, lips, and other organs of speech in order to produce speech sounds. Good articulation helps us to speak more distinctly and focus attention on our message. These are the two essential conditions of effective speaking.

> Good articulation helps us to speak more distinctly and focus attention on our message.

We should learn to produce English sounds correctly. Every language has a set of speech sounds. English has 44 speech sounds that include twelve pure vowels, eight diphthongs, and twenty four consonants. Some of these speech sounds might not be present in other languages and we may find it difficult to articulate them. Regular practice is required to be able to articulate them correctly. To be an effective speaker one must practice articulation of difficult English vowel and consonant sounds, change faulty speech patterns, and practice appropriate and correct speech patterns. Moreover, one needs proper ear-training to be sensitive to sounds. This aspect is dealt with in the next section on phonetics.

'Good' Pronunciation

> Pronunciation is the manner of uttering or speaking (words and sounds), and 'good' pronunciation is the way of speaking that ordinary people find easy to understand. One cannot classify pronunciation as 'correct' or 'incorrect'.

An important aspect of improving expression is learning 'good' pronunciation. Pronunciation is the manner of uttering or speaking (words and sounds), and 'good' pronunciation is the way of speaking that ordinary people find easy to understand. Daniel Jones defines 'bad' pronunciation as, "a way of talking which is difficult for most people to understand". However, one cannot classify pronunciation as 'correct' or 'incorrect'.

Any good dictionary would give acceptable English pronunciations of words. As dictionaries give the pronunciation of a word in phonemic symbols, it is essential to be familiar with phonemic transcription. In addition, one should learn effective pronunciation techniques.

Voice Quality

> Voice modulation gives variety to oral delivery.

It is essential to refine the quality of one's voice and learn to adjust or vary its tone or pitch (i.e. voice modulation). As voice modulation gives variety to oral delivery, it can improve expression during oral presentations, speeches, debates, conferences, group discussions, and meetings. An impressive voice may be a God gift but voice quality can be improved by proper voice training and regular practice.

We should first analyse the quality of our own voice by critically listening to our recorded voice, or asking someone to listen to us and comment on our voice. Then, we should identify the weak points of our voice, (for example, it is too low, or too harsh). These weaknesses can be improved upon with the help of friends, classmates, teachers, and by cultivating sensitivity to sounds and voices, getting proper ear-training, practising voice modulation according to meaning and intention of the message and learning to vocalise one's feelings.

Accent and Intonation

> Unlike most Indian languages, which are syllabic, English is a stressed language.

Unlike most Indian languages, which are syllabic, English is a stressed language. In syllabic languages, such as Hindi or Bengali, each syllable receives equal importance. However, English pronunciation focuses on specific stressed words while non-stressed words or syllables are spoken fast. This means that the stressed words/syllables stand out from the rest, are usually said more loudly, on a different pitch, and are held for a longer time than the other word/syllable or words/syllables.

> Intonation is the variation of the pitch of the voice.

Intonation is the variation of the pitch of the voice. When we speak, we can notice the variations in the level at which our voice is pitched. Sometimes the pitch of our voice rises, sometimes it falls, and at other times it remains level. We should learn correct intonation patterns. It is essential to improve self-expression.

Progress Check 3

1. Study the following table and match different aspects of improving self-expression (left column) with appropriate strategies (right column):

Aspects of improving self-expression	*Strategies*
A. Articulation	I. Consult a good dictionary to find acceptable English pronunciation of words.
B. Pronunciation	II. Learn phonemic transcription.
C. Voice quality	III. Improve the quality of your voice and learn to adjust or vary the tone or pitch of your voice.
D. Accent and intonation	IV. Correct faulty speech patterns and practice appropriate and correct speech patterns.
	V. Cultivate sensitivity to sounds and voices and undertake proper ear-training.
	VI. Speak more distinctly and focus attention on the message.
	VII. Learn correct intonation patterns.
	VIII. Learn effective pronunciation techniques.

7.2.4 Body Language

Body language (Table 7.2) is an integral part of oral communication. It includes facial expressions, gestures and body movements, eye contact, distance, space, time, and mannerisms. As non-verbal communication expresses individual emotions, social attitudes and feelings, it can convey more meaning than spoken words. When we are not able to find an exact word for something we want to say, we may use some kind of facial or physical gestures to convey our meaning.

Body language includes eye contact, facial expression, gestures, posture, body movements, distance, space, time and mannerisms.

As culture, social class, age, occupation, ethnic background, and communication contexts influence non-verbal forms of communication, we must be very careful while using non-verbal messages.

We should take care of the non-verbal cues that we pass on to our listeners or receive from our speaker during any formal situation because a wrong gesture or facial expression can lead to miscommunication and confusion. Different non-verbal cues may suggest different meanings (Table 7.3). We may annoy or displease a colleague, irritate a teacher or supervisor, or even lose a business deal. As culture, social class, age, occupation, ethnic background, and communication contexts influence non-verbal forms of communication, we must be very careful while using non-verbal messages.

TABLE 7.2 Body Language

Non-verbal Forms	*Description*
Eye contact	the way a person observes or looks at the audience while speaking or listening
Facial expression	use of eyes, eyebrows, forehead, and mouth for expression
Gestures	visible bodily action that may express implicit meaning
Posture and body movements	the way a person stands, walks, moves, or uses body movements

Eye Contact

Our eyes are usually a mirror of our truest and innermost feelings. That is why we normally distrust people who do not maintain eye contact while telling us something, whereas we believe those who look directly at us. Since the eyes are probably the most accurate predictor of our feelings and attitudes, we should know how to use good or positive eye contact.

> We normally distrust people who do not maintain eye contact while telling us something.

Although the frequency and duration of eye contact varies from culture to culture, we can learn to maintain positive eye contact with our listeners. Following are some suggestions in this regard:

> Good or positive eye contact improves the effectiveness of a verbal message during oral interaction.

- Maintain eye contact while listening to someone. This will indicate that you are paying attention to what the person is speaking.
- Use eye contact to show sincerity and confidence. Do not speak while looking at your feet. This will either mean that you are too shy or that you are telling a lie.
- Learn the cultural patterns of eye contact in order to understand the differences and to avoid misunderstandings.
- If there is more than one listener, as in the case of a meeting, group discussion, and oral presentation, the speaker should look at all the listeners giving each of them equal importance.
- If someone is avoiding eye contact, the speaker should not try to look continuously at the person and embarrass him/her.
- The speaker should not look at a person the way a doubtful police officer would look at a convict or a doctor looks at a patient. You should adopt a relaxed and confident approach rather than one of mistrust or worry.

Facial Expression

Facial expression is another dimension of body language. Facial expression normally shows how we feel. For example, if someone has offended a person, his/her face will express it. Normally our face easily reveals our emotions.

> Facial expression normally shows how we feel.

> Like a positive eye contact, positive and appropriate facial expression adds meaning and helps to improve the effectiveness of a verbal message.

Like a positive eye contact, positive and appropriate facial expression adds meaning and helps to improve the effectiveness of a verbal message. The following suggestions may be borne in mind in this regard:

- Facial expressions must be kept quite natural.
- Positive facial expressions should be used. A good smile gives very positive signals and helps to make the atmosphere friendly. Moreover, it indicates

goodwill and shows that the speaker is a positive and pleasant person. However, he/she should not smile constantly and the smile should not be totally unrelated to his/her content or contradict his/her message.

- Facial expression should be consistent with the verbal message, i.e., facial expression and content should match.
- The speaker should be his/her natural self and not try to hide his/her feelings.
- It is important to learn the cultural patterns of facial expression so that misunderstandings can be avoided.

Facial expression refers to the use of eyes, eyebrows, forehead, and mouth for expression.

TABLE 7.3 Examples of Non-verbal Cues*

Non-verbal Form	*Non-verbal Cue*	*What Does it Suggest?*
Eye contact	Sustained eye contact	Trust, admiration, confidence
	Brief eye contact	Stress, nervousness
	Avoiding eye contact	Fear, shyness, lack of sincerity, mark of respect in some cultures
	Eye squinting	Antagonism
Facial expression	Raising eyebrows	Surprise, question, curiosity
	Lowering eyebrows	Acceptance, submission
	Furrowed forehead	Anger, frustration, displeasure
	Wide open eyes	Surprise, astonishment
	Open mouth	Shock
	Swallowing	Nervousness
Gestures	Frowning	Anger, displeasure
Posture and body movements	Leaning towards a speaker/listener	interest
	Pulling away/leaning back	Fear, disgust, anger, distrust

* As non-verbal cues and the meaning they convey differ from culture to culture, the suggestions given here may not be relevant to all cultures.

Gestures

A gesture is a visible bodily action that may express implicit meaning. It refers to the use of fingers, hands, and arms for expression. It is an important dimension of body language. Gestures may reveal the mindset of the communicator and convey thoughts through voluntary or involuntary physical movements. For example, if a person is very upset and nervous, his/her hands may tremble. Although most of the gestures

Although most of the gestures that we make are voluntary, we may sometimes send out negative signals by making some inappropriate involuntary gestures.

that we make are voluntary, we may sometimes send out negative signals by making some inappropriate involuntary gestures.

Using positive physical gestures require conscious effort and practice but it will definitely be worth it. Positive and appropriate gestures can make us better oral communicators. The following suggestions may help us this regard:

- Gestures should be natural.
- Avoid using gestures to express negative feelings. Such feeling should be expressed verbally. For example, if we have to say 'no', we should not use fingers or shake our heads to express it. Such negative gestures could be very annoying for some people.
- Avoid confusing gestures or body movements (biting nails or scratching head).
- Use positive gestures.
- Do not reflect nervous mannerisms.
- Do not use fingers too often.
- Use hands and arms very carefully and effectively.
- While using gestures, be sure that they are consistent with the verbal message and there is no contradiction.
- Learn the cultural patterns of physical gestures to avoid cross-cultural misunderstandings.

> A gesture refers to the use of fingers, hands, and arms for expression.

Posture and Body Movements

Your posture talks about your personality. It may tell that you are a bold, confident, and dynamic person or a timid, submissive, and servile fellow. Similarly, your body movements give important signals about your personality. Use your posture and body movements to reflect self-confidence, maturity, alertness, and physical stamina. Read the following suggestions:

- Posture should be examined and corrected if it is not appropriate.
- Posture should be natural; standing, sitting and bowing in a natural way.
- Avoid making funny or confusing postures or body movements.
- While using body movements, ensure that they are consistent with the verbal message.
- Learn the cultural patterns of posture and body movements to avoid cross-cultural misunderstandings.

> Appropriate posture and body movements may reflect positive personality traits such as maturity, confidence, alertness, and physical stamina and fitness.

Progress Check 4

1. **Study the following statements about body language and mark True or False against each of them.**
   (a) Body language includes both intentional and unintentional messages.
   (b) Messages are easy to understand when verbal and non-verbal messages contradict each other.
   (c) When verbal and non-verbal messages contradict each other, listeners believe non-verbal cues.
   (d) Most of us look another person straight in the eye when we tell a lie.
   (e) Prolonged eye contact does not show respect in all the cultures.

(f) Everyone can control facial expressions.
(g) We are sometimes not aware that we are sending non-verbal messages.
(h) Facial expression can never show how we feel.
(i) Body movements give important signals about a person's personality.
(j) Non-verbal cues have different meanings in various cultures.

Exercise

1. **Write brief notes on the following:**
   (a) Oral communication skills
   (b) Articulation
   (c) Good pronunciation
   (d) Stress and intonation
   (e) Strategies for good conversation
   (f) Forms of conversation
2. **Answer the following questions:**
   (a) Describe the speech process.
   (b) Discuss the importance of conversational skills.
   (c) List four factors essential for improving fluency and self-expression.
   (d) Discuss how body language can be used to improve the effectiveness of a verbal message during an oral interaction.
3. **Analyse different patterns of eye contact, facial expression, gestures, posture, and body movements used in your culture, and describe how they differ from British or American cultures.**

Key to Progress Check

Progress Check 1

1. (a), (b), (d,) (f) and (h).

Progress Check 2

1. (a), (c), (d), (h), (i), (j)

Progress Check 3

1. (A) IV and VI
   (B) I, II, and VIII
   (C) III and V
   (D) VII

Progress Check 4

1. (a) True (b) False (c) True (d) False (e) True
   (f) False (g) True (h) False (i) True (j) True

8 CHAPTER

Phonetics and Spoken English

No two people pronounce exactly alike. The differences arise from a variety of causes, such as locality, early influences and social surroundings...

Daniel Jones

LEARNING OBJECTIVES

- Understanding the concept of 'acceptable English pronunciation'
- Knowing 'phonetic transcription' and phonemic symbols of English
- Understanding sound and spelling mismatch in English
- Identifying speech sounds of English
- Knowing pronunciation guidelines related to consonants, diphthongs, and vowels
- Understanding the concept of Mother Tongue Influence

8.1 ENGLISH PRONUNCIATION

As mentioned earlier, in order to speak correct English, correct English pronunciation should be used. By being careful in one's speech habits simple mistakes in speaking can be avoided. Learning appropriate pronunciation techniques gives one the confidence to avoid common lapses and errors in speaking.

> A truly acceptable pronunciation is one that allows the listener to understand the content of a message without being distracted by its form.

Interestingly, there is no such thing as a 'correct pronunciation' because there is no one right way of speaking. The pronunciation of English varies from one country to another and there are marked pronunciation features associated with English spoken in important English speaking countries like the United Kingdom, United States of America, Canada, and Australia. Even within the United Kingdom, there are variations between England, Scotland, Wales, and Northern Ireland. One particular accent, called Received Pronunciation (RP) has come to be accepted as the standard in the United Kingdom. Thus, it is better to consider pronunciation in terms of 'acceptable pronunciation' and 'unacceptable pronunciation' rather than correct or incorrect pronunciation. Acceptable pronunciation is, clearly intelligible to all ordinary people whereas 'unacceptable pronunciation' refers to a way of talking that is difficult for most people to understand.

It would be difficult for us to learn correct English pronunciation without learning the basics of phonetics. Phonetics is a branch of linguistic science that deals with pronunciation. However, here the word 'phonetics' refers to the study of English speech sounds.

8.2 BASICS IN PHONETICS

> Sounds are heard. Letters are seen. Letters provide a means of symbolising sounds. If they do so in a logical manner—in other words, if the essential sounds of any particular language or dialect are represented consistently—the writing is said to be phonetic.
>
> **Daniel Jones**

In order to speak correct English, one should have some idea of English phonetics.

As we all know there are twenty-six alphabets in English. However, the language has forty-four speech sounds. This means that there is no 'one-to-one correspondence' between letters and sounds in English as it is in many Indian languages. This is the reason why many Indians find it difficult to learn English pronunciation. The duality of English spelling and pronunciation may confuse a beginner and make English pronunciation difficult to master.

> Phonetics is the study of the sound system of a language.

Table 8.1 contains examples of words where different letters (underlined) represent the same sound.

TABLE 8.1 Examples of Words having Different Letters Representing the Same Sound

Sound	Examples
/S/	see, censor, miss,
/SH/	shoe, chef, mention, precious, tension, passion, anxious
/Z/	zoo, season
/K/	kill, chemistry, call, sick
/EE/	meet, key, deal, seize, physique, recast
/OO/	zoo, movie, soup, true, truth, juice
/AH/	market, fast, clerk, aunt, heart

There is duality of spelling and pronunciation in English: different letters may represent the same sound while the same letter could represent different sounds.

Now, study Table 8.2, which contains examples of words where the same letters (underlined) represent different sounds.

TABLE 8.2 Examples of Words having Same Letters Representing Different Sounds

Letter/s	Examples
/S/	sell, busy, pleasure, pension
/T/	tell, mention, culture
/CH/	chef, chemical, rich
/E/	pet, decent, decay

8.3 PHONETIC TRANSCRIPTION

Phonemic symbols of English are a reliable guide to the English pronunciation. It is, thus, the writing of a language by means of a separate symbol for every sound. A pronunciation symbol or a phonemic symbol represents each English sound. As the letters of the English alphabet can be a poor guide to pronunciation, it is advisable to learn the phonemic symbols of English because these symbols are a reliable guide to English pronunciation. Knowledge of these symbols is useful in referring to a dictionary to find out the pronunciation of any word. Every good dictionary contains a list of these pronunciation symbols. Phonetic transcription can be defined as a kind of alphabetical writing in which each letter represents one sound.

Phonemic symbols of English are a reliable guide to the English pronunciation.

8.3.1 Consonant Sounds

A consonant sound may be defined as a speech sound that is produced with stoppage of air. For example, to say the word 'paper' our lips try to stop air from passing through while producing the sound 'p'. Thus, the voice or breath in consonants is partially hindered by the tongue, teeth, lips, or other organs of articulation. There are twenty four consonant sounds in English. These consonant sounds are classified according to the nature of constriction as plosives, affricates, nasal consonants, lateral consonants, and fricatives.

Table 8.3 contains the phonemic symbols for consonants.

TABLE 8.3 Consonant Symbols

Phonemic Symbols		Examples
1	p	Paper, pipe, plastic, upper, accept, couple, cup, cap
2	b	Bulb, base, behave, absorb, carbon, cable, mob, cab
3	t	Table, start, top, pot, take, cattle, cot, cat
4	d	Design, data, develop, crude, tend, blend, doll, bad
5	k	Kick, cast, chemist, accurate, act, block, factor
6	g	Give, graphite, ago, against, diagram, organic, inorganic
7	tʃ	Chance, rich, beach, discharge, feature, launch, preach
8	dʒ	Judge, adjust, bridge, magic, charge, generator, cage
9	f	Fast, feature, filter, flash, draft, effect, graph
10	v	Very, variant, velocity, vertical, volatile, give, negative
11	θ	Theory, thermal, thrust, faith, both, earth, method
12	ð	Brother, gather, feather, further, mother, neither, bathe
13	s	Simple, sea, mass, ask, assembly, device, elastic, gas
14	z	Zero, design, physical, positive, result, busy, laser
15	ʃ	Shift, pressure, ash, nation, crush , emission, machine
16	ʒ	Vision, pleasure, treasurer, leisure, measure, extrusion
17	m	Machine, emission, automatic, column, compact, compare
18	n	New, number, anode, carbon, crane, drain, electron
19	ŋ	Evening, bearing, distinguish, building
20	h	Handle, hardware, heavy, height
21	l	Level, call, collect, realise
22	r	Role, red, correct, marriage
23	w	Water, weaver, wonder
24	j	Yes, you, year, your

A consonant sound is produced with stoppage of air.

There are twenty- four consonant sounds in English.

8.3.2 Vowel Sounds

Unlike a consonant sound, a vowel sound is unobstructed in articulation by the tongue, teeth, or lips. During the articulation of a vowel sound, the active articulator is raised towards the passive articulator in such a way that there is a sufficient gap between the two for air to escape through the mouth without friction. For example, when speaking the word 'art', air escapes freely and continuously without any friction while pronouncing the first sound 'AH'.

A vowel sound is produced without stoppage of air.

There are twenty vowel sounds. Vowel sounds are classified as pure vowels and diphthongs. There are twelve pure vowels and eight diphthongs. Pure vowels are further classified as long vowels and short vowels. Study Tables 8.4, 8.5 and 8.6, which contain phonemic symbols for vowel sounds.

There are twenty vowel sounds in English: twelve pure vowels and eight diphthongs.

TABLE 8.4 Long Vowel Symbols

Phonemic Symbols		*Examples*
25	iː	Easy, feel, free, seize, ceiling
26	uː	Shoe, fool, true, coup, truth
27	ɜː	Firm, birth, hurt, curl, burn
28	ɑː	Art, farm, part, fast, aunt
29	ɔː	Fought, port, sport, form, sought

TABLE 8.5 Short Vowel Symbols

Phonemic Symbols		*Examples*
30	e	Pet, said, led, men
31	ɒ	Hot, shot, pot
32	ʌ	Hut, shut, cut, blood
33	æ	Hat, cat, bat
34	ə	Ago, about, announce
35	ʊ	Wood, food, book
36	ɪ	Hit, sit, fill

Pure vowels include five long vowels and seven short vowels.

TABLE 8.6 Diphthong Symbols

Phonemic Symbols		*Examples*
37	ɪə	Fear, here, year
38	eə	Fair, hair, air
39	ʊə	Poor, truer
40	ɔɪ	Oil, boil, spoil
41	eɪ	Say, late, train
42	ɑɪ	Try, sight, bike
43	əʊ	Go, so, old, gold
44	aʊ	Now, how

A diphthong is a combination of two short vowels.

8.4 PRONUNCIATION GUIDELINES

8.4.1 Pronunciation Guidelines Related to Consonants

Following spellings too closely may result in mistakes while pronouncing consonant sounds. Remember the following simple guidelines:

1. The spelling **CH** may confuse you because it has three different sounds tʃ, k and ʃ. Study the following examples:

   CH Pronounced as tʃ

   Examples: Chain, chair, chairman, chalk, challenge, chamber, cherish, champion, preach, exchange, recharge, preacher, match, attachment, bench, beach

   CH pronounced as k

   Examples: Character, chasm, chimera, choreographer, chloral, choir, cholera, cholesterol, choral, chord, chorus, chromatic, chromatin, chrome, chromite, chromium, chromosome, chronic, chronicle, chronology, chronological, archives, archipelago, archangel, machinations, schizophrenic, archbishop, schism, mechanical

   CH pronounced as ʃ

   Examples: Chauffeur, chef, chagrin, chevron, chic, chiffon, chauvinism, chauvinist, chivalry, chivalrous, cache, chassis, chicanery, champagne, chaise, machine, sachet, brochure

2. The spelling **G** may also confuse you because it has three different sounds g, dʒ and ʒ. Study the following examples:

   G pronounced as g

   Examples: Gadget, gainful, galaxy, gallant, gallery, galvanise, gargle, garment, glossary, glue, gossip, govern, graceful, gradual, graphic, graphite, grease, grievance, against, regard, magnet, stagnant, regress

   G pronounced as dʒ (the letters in bold)

   Examples: Gauge, cage, gelatin, gelatinous, gem, gemstone, gender, gene, general, generate, generation, generous, genius, gentle, gentry, gesture, giraffe, gorgeous, gym, gymnast, gypsum, gypsy, gyroscope, manage, change, stranger, baggage, cleavage

   G pronounced as ʒ (the letters in bold)

   Examples: Garage, mirage, beige, regime, rouge, bourgeois, bourgeoisie

3. The spelling **S** has generally the sound s, but it may also have the sounds ʃ, z and ʒ. Study the following examples:

   S pronounced as ʃ

   Examples: Sugar, sugary, sure, surely, surety, pension, tension, expansion, mansion, dissension, ensure, insure, insurance, insured

S pronounced as z

Examples: Busy, these, rays, lease, noise, chase, cause, disease, because, arise, oppose, expose, pause, prose, praise, rose, tease, vase, transient, transit, transition, transitive, trousers

S pronounced as ʒ

Examples: Pleasure, measure, treasure, treasury, treasurer, vision, leisure, leisurely, lesion

4. The spelling **SS** may have the sounds s, ʃ and z Study the following examples:

SS pronounced as s

Examples: Aggressive, miss, kiss, asses, masses, classes, assent, assert, assertive, assertion, assign, assist, assimilate, assistance, associate, association, assumption, dissect, dissension, dissertation, dissident, dissimilar, vessel

SS pronounced as ʃ

Examples: Aggression, passion, assure, assurance, mission, session, assuredly

SS pronounced as z

Examples: Dissolve

5. The spelling **T** has generally the sound t, but it may also have the sounds tʃ and ʃ. Study the following examples:

T pronounced as tʃ

Examples: Nature, culture, future, fracture, puncture, mature, nurture, capture, lecture, picture, gesture, signature

T pronounced as ʃ

Examples: differential, differentiate, mention, edition, initiation, nation, national, relation, location, sanction

6. Sometimes consonants are not pronounced at all. They become silent. Study the following examples: (The letter/s in bold is/are silent.)
Examples: han**d**some, han**d**kerchief, gran**d**father, gran**d**mother, gran**d**son, fore**h**ead, cu**p**board, cou**p**, **p**sa**l**m, **p**sychology, a**d**just, a**d**justment, a**d**jective, a**d**join, a**d**joining, a**d**journ, of**t**en, **g**neiss, **g**nome, **g**nostic, bou**r**geoi**s**, su**b**tle, sache**t**, si**g**n, si**g**nboard, fa**r**m, pa**l**m, ca**l**m, a**r**tist, sta**r**te**r**, cha**r**te**r**, ma**r**ket, **k**not, **k**now, **k**nowle**d**ge, bouque**t**

Minimal Pairs

A minimal pair is a group of words that differ from each other only in one sound. However, this difference brings about a change in meaning. For example, the words 'fill' and 'till' differ only in the first consonant sound but they mean different things. They are minimal pairs. Read the following minimal pairs aloud:

> A minimal pair is a group of words that differ from each other only in one sound

Sip	ship	Said	shed	Face	phase	Rage	raise
So	show	Same	shame	Race	raise	Refuge	refuse
Sack	shack	Sank	shank	Seal	zeal	Region	reason
Sake	shake	Seat	sheet	Sip	zip	Major	measure
Sale	shale	Self	shelf	Sage	says	Ledger	leisure
Sell	shell	Sock	shock	Page	pays		

Progress Check 1

1. **Read the following statements and mark True or False in the light of the above discussion:**
   (a) The English pronunciation varies from one country to another.
   (b) Acceptable pronunciation refers to a way of talking, which is clearly intelligible and easy for most people to understand.
   (c) Phonetics does not deal with pronunciation.
   (d) There is one to one correspondence between letters and sounds in English.
   (e) The number of sounds and letters in English is not the same.
   (f) One letter or a combination of letters in English may represent different sounds at different places.
   (g) Different letters or combination of letters may represent the same sound.
2. **List three words each with different spellings for the consonant sound having:**
   (a) the same consonant sound as in **sh**oe
   (Examples: **sh**ip, so**c**ial, na**t**ion)
   (b) the same consonant sound as in **z**oo
   (c) the same consonant sound as in **ch**air
   (d) the same consonant sound as in **j**oy
   (e) the same consonant sound as in **s**ee
   (f) the same consonant sound as in **c**are
3. **List at least three words to show that the consonant letters 'C', 'G', 'S', and 'T' can have different sounds in different words.**

8.4.2 Pronunciation Guidelines Related to Vowels

As there is no one-to-one correspondence between vowel letters and sounds in English, vowel sounds may be pronounced wrongly if care is not taken.

Table 8.7 lists vowel sounds and corresponding words.

TABLE 8.7 Vowel Sounds and the Corresponding Words

Some Possible Letter/s Representing the Vowel	*Vowel Sounds*	*Examples*
ee/ea/i/e/ie/ey	iː	Free, meal, unique, legal, field, key
oo/u/ou/ui/ew/ue	uː	Zoo, truth, coup, juice, shrewd, true
ir/ur/er/ear	ɜː	Shirt, curl, stern, learn
a/ar/al/er/ear/au	ɑː	Cast, farm, calm, clerk, heart, aunt
a/ar/al/or/oa/our/oar/au/o /augh/ough/wor	ɔː	Water, warm, talk, port, coast, course, board, Cause, chlorine, taught, sought, sword
e/ea/ai	iː	Bed, head, said
o/e	ɒ	Socket, entrepreneur
u/ou/oo	ʌ	Fun, couple, enough, blood
a	æ	Man, apt, stand
a/e/er/or/eur/ure/o/ou	ə	Adult, entrance, anthem, farmer, factor, entrepreneur, nature, automatic, luminous
u/oo/oul	ʊ	Pull, look, should
i/e/y/a/ui	ɪ	Sit, behave, baby, accurate, circuit
ear/eer/iu/year	ɪə	Fear, peer, helium, year
a/ay/ai/au	eɪ	Made, say, train, gauge
oor/uer	ʊə	Poor, truer
ow/ou	aʊ	Now, how, founder
oi/oy	ɔI	Spoil, coil, joy, loyal
y/igh/ig/i/eigh	aɪ	Try, sight, sign, five, height
o/ow/oa	əʊ	So, low, coal
air/are/ae	eə	Chair, care, aerial

Read the following **minimal pairs** aloud:

Sit	seat	Cut	cart	Farm	firm	Red	raid	Tell	tail
Fill	feel	Hut	hurt	Heart	hurt	Men	main	Fate	fight
Hill	heal	Shut	shirt	Last	lust	Sent	saint	Set	sight
Hit	heat	Full	fool	Calm	come	Fed	fade	Let	light
Lid	lead	Pull	pool	Card	curd	Let	late	Fell	file
Mill	meal	Spot	sport	Hard	hurd	Met	mate	Plate	plight
Knit	neat	Pot	port	Fast	first	Sell	sale	Date	diet
Pick	peak	Cop	corp	Last	lost	Trend	trained	Fail	file
Slip	sleep	Shot	short	Part	pot	Pen	pain	Lay	lie
Ship	sheep	Sot	sort	Cast	cost	Edge	age	Tape	type
Live	leave	Cot	court	Bard	bird	Fell	fail	Tale	tile

Progress Check 2

1. **Read the following 105 words aloud and identify words that contain a long vowel sound and classify these words into five classes according to the five long vowels.**
abbreviate, absent, airfield, absurd, accident, accessory, accelerator, accompany, mortar, faulty, acetylene, achieve, acknowledge, actually, adamant, diesel, kerosene, technique, advance, aeroplane, aerospace, affiliate, water, frequency, absolute, alcohol, allergy, allergic, altogether, amateur, ambulance, analogous, decrease, frequent, announcer, anonymous, diverge, inertia, apparatus, lubricant, appearance, apprentice, architecture, assault, attractive, attribute, august, authentic, authority, automatic, automobile, barrack, bathe, biography, bouquet, chlorine, chronicle, coefficient, deficiency, delegate, differential, embarrass, encompass, female, finale, luminous, fluoride, forgive, forget, furniture, gymnastic, gynaecology, harmony, penal, hindrance, intermission, organic, intervene, motor, nuclear, natural, plutonium, overseas, overlook, outspread, outward, parlour, paramount, particular, alright, quadrant, repose, research, restoration, surface, survive, survey, translate, volatile, wooden, movie, magazine, police, garden
2. **Read the following sentences aloud, identify words containing long vowel sounds, and insert these words in the appropriate column in the table below.**
   (a) Good morning, sir.
   (b) Good evening, teacher.
   (c) Good to see you again.
   (d) I am glad to meet you.
   (e) Speak to me.
   (f) Excuse me.
   (g) Could you tell me your name, please?
   (h) Can you tell me where the canteen is, please?
   (i) I need a glass of water.
   (j) Thank you sir.

Phonemic symbol	*Examples*
iː	
uː	
ɜː	
ɑː	
ɔː	

3. **The most common English vowel sound is the start vowel ə. Most of the vowel sounds are reduced to this sound in continuous English. Read the following fifty words and identify words that begin with this short vowel.**
Examples: **a**bout, **a**dult, **a**nnounce
ability, abolish, above, absent, abrupt, abscond, academic, academy, access, accident, accessory, accompany, account, accuse, acid, acknowledge, achieve, acquaint, acquire, acre, action, addition, address, adjacent, adjunct, admire, advance, adversary, advise, advocate, aeronautics, aeroplane, affair, affect, afford, after, accept, accelerate, average, away, awkward, axis, assert, antique, analyse, analysis, anarchy, another, arrange, aspect

8.5 PROBLEM SOUNDS AND DIFFERENCES IN PRONUNCIATION

8.5.1 Sound and Spelling Mismatch

Look at the words below:

Chef, chemistry, movie, soup, true, character, busy, nature, handkerchief, sign

Now concentrate on the underlined part:

Chef, chemistry, movie, soup, true, character, busy, nature, handkerchief, sign

Notice some discrepancies in their spellings and sounds?

As discussed earlier, there are many words in the English language where the spellings may not match with their pronunciation. The reasons for this are galore.

The English language has evolved over centuries and has the influence of many different countries. Some words from other languages like French, Sanskrit, and Latin have made their way into the language.

> There are many words in the English language where the spellings may not match with their pronunciation.

Other reasons like adjacent sounds and stress patterns have already been discussed in detail in the earlier part of this chapter. Also, there is an additional factor of Mother Tongue Influence (MTI), which will be discussed in the next section.

As a result of a combination of these factors, the spellings and pronunciations or sounds of many words may not match. The guidelines given in this chapter will help one overcome this challenge.

8.5.2 Mother Tongue Influence

As we have learnt so far, there are several reasons for differences in pronunciation. One major factor is the influence of one's native language on another language like English. This is called the Mother Tongue Influence (MTI). A person is used to a language and its style since birth. When he/she is introduced to another language later on, there is usually some influence of the native language on the new one.

For example, people from Punjab who are not well conversant with English, usually find it difficult to pronounce words with the 'z' sound like 'pleasure' or 'measure'. They pronounce it as 'player' or 'mayer'. Similarly, they pronounce names of places like 'Noida' and 'Gurgaon' as 'Neeoda' or 'Gurganwa'. On the other hand, Bengalis find it difficult to pronounce words with the 'v' sound. They are heard pronouncing words like 'wicket' as 'bhicket'. Then, there are people with Hindi background. They pronounce words like 'school' as 'isskool'. People from South India too find it difficult to converse with people from other parts of the country. Sometimes, South Indians pronounce 'm' as 'yum' and 'n' as 'yen'.

> The influence of one's native language on another language is called the Mother Tongue Influence.

8.5.3 How to Pronounce Correctly

As mentioned earlier, there are no correct or incorrect pronunciations. They are only different due to a variety of factors. However, the more homogeneity there is, the better the communication would be. Also, each language has certain rules and guidelines to follow, and the English language is no exception. Therefore, it is advisable to learn the most commonly accepted ways of pronunciation.

To learn the right way to pronounce, the best place to start is school. If the teachers and parents teach the right way to pronounce and familiarise kids with commonly confusing words, the kids would overcome challenges like the MTI. Places where this is not possible, one can watch news channels or other programmes in English, and observe how they speak. Also, one should observe people who are conversant with the language as to how they speak. Above all, one should practice and not shy away from making mistakes or taking feedback. Over a period of time, one would be conversant with the English language, making one's communication more effective and universally accepted.

Exercise

1. **Answer the following questions:**
   (a) Explain what is 'acceptable English pronunciation'.
   (b) Describe 'phonetic transcription' and phonemic symbols of English.
   (c) Discuss English speech sounds.
   (d) Describe pronunciation guidelines related to consonants, diphthongs, and vowels.
2. **Write short notes on the following:**
   (a) Phonetic transcription
   (b) English consonants
   (c) Vowel sounds
   (d) Diphthongs
3. **Read the following 100 words aloud and identify words that contain a long vowel sound. Classify these words into five classes according to the five long vowels. Refer to a dictionary to check your answer.**
   Absentee, accident, accumulate, adamant, admission, affection, advance, adoption, ambulance, amusement, anarchy, attractive, apartment, analysis, arbitrate, believe, breadwinner, burglar, business, brought, capital, carpet, cartel, catalyst, conscientious, creative, cellulose, ceremonial, charge, chlorine, chronicle, clearance, correspondence, crescent, catalogued, coordinated, conceive, dependable, determined, debauch, demonstration, departmental, dilemma, disciple, disguise, displease, decreased, designate, document, engineered, earthquake, enterprising, enthusiastic, experienced, enlarged, examine, equitable, fatal, favourable, ferment, finalised, gardening, group, harnessed, hardly, heart, heated, harmonised, inhabitant, interpolate, introvert, inclination, launch, luxurious, localised, martial, manage, maintain, mechanised, processed, parallel, paralyse, programmed, redesigned, resignation, resource, recruitment, support, systematise, tested, trained, transaction, resourceful, self disciplined, sensitive, sincere, successful, tactful, trustworthy,

Key to Progress Check

Progress Check 1

1. (a) True (b) True (c) False (d) False (e) True
   (f) True (g) True

2. (a) Conscious, passion, tension
   (b) zip, busy, dissolve
   (c) cheap, lecture, catch
   (d) jug, bridge, gym
   (e) sick, kiss, society
   (f) pick, kill, camp
3. C camp, delicious, cell
   G good, gem, regime
   S soup, please, measure
   T tea, mature, patience

Progress Check 2

1. The following words do not contain any long vowel:
   absent, accident, accessory, accelerator, accompany, acknowledge, actually, adamant, aeroplane, aerospace, affiliate, alcohol, allergy, amateur, ambulance, analogous, announcer, anonymous, apparatus, appearance, apprentice, attractive, barrack, bathe, biography, chronicle, coefficient, deficiency, delegate, differential, embarrass, encompass, fluoride, forgive, forget, gymnastic, gynaecology, hindrance, intermission, natural, overlook, outspread, outward, paramount, particular, quadrant, repose, restoration, surface, survive, survey, translate, volatile, wooden
   The following table shows the words that contain long vowels:

Phonemic symbol	Examples
iː	abbreviate, airfield, acetylene, achieve, diesel, kerosene, technique, frequency, decrease, frequent, female, penal, overseas, magazine, police,
uː	absolute, lubricant, attribute, bouquet, luminous, nuclear, plutonium, movie,
ɜː	absurd, allergic, diverge, inertia, furniture, research
ɑː	advance, architecture, finale, harmony, parlour, garden
ɔː	mortar, faulty, water, altogether, assault, august, authentic, authority, automatic, automobile, chlorine, organic, alright,

2.

Phonemic symbol	Examples
iː	evening, teacher, see, meet, speak, me, please, canteen, need
uː	Excuse
ɜː	sir
ɑː	glass, water
ɔː	morning

3. Ability, abolish, above, abrupt, abscond, academy, accessory, accompany, account, accuse, acknowledge, achieve, acquaint, acquire, addition, address, adjacent, admire, advance, advise, advocate, affair, affect, afford, accept, accelerate, away, assert, analysis, another, arrange

CHAPTER 9

Oral Communication and Speaking Techniques

Self-expression and fluency can be improved by applying appropriate speaking techniques.

LEARNING OBJECTIVES

- Understanding the importance of oral communication
- Learning strategies for effective oral communication
- Knowing techniques to develop effective word accent
- Identifying weak forms in English speech
- Learning to develop voice quality
- Recognising rhythm in connected speech
- Understanding techniques to develop correct tone in fluent speech
- Understanding how to make various oral interactions effective

9.1 ORAL COMMUNICATION

As we have learnt in the Chapter 1, *Communication Today*, oral communication is communication done orally between people. It is communication done through speaking or the word-of-mouth. Therefore, it is also called verbal communication.

> Oral communication is done through speaking or the word-of-mouth.

The biggest advantage of oral communication is that it provides immediate feedback to the sender of the message. It also gives a personal touch to the communication. Certain aspects like gestures, facial expressions, voice modulation, and tone can all be done using oral communication. In fact, the sender can even modify his/her message based on the feedback he/she gets during the conversation.

This method of communication is given less preference over written communication in business scenarios because any mistake made during a conversation, is difficult to correct. Also, the latter leaves a proof of communication.

9.1.1 Strategies for Effective Oral Communication

Oral communication skills can go a long way in development of relationships and professional success. Some of the areas where oral communication is useful are:

- Greeting people
- Asking questions
- Answering questions
- Selling products or services or ideas
- Giving messages
- Making presentations or speeches
- Having discussions
- Telephonic conversations
- Video chats

In a nutshell, we can say that oral communication is omnipresent. It is a crucial part of both, personal and professional lives. Therefore, it becomes very important to be adept at it.

Improving Fluency and Self-Expression

Having effective oral communication skills means the ability to speak fluently and express oneself clearly. Two important ways to develop these are learning how to pronounce correctly and the right word accents. Pronunciation techniques have already been covered in the Chapter 8, *Phonetics and Spoken English*. Let us now learn about techniques for developing effective word accents that can help improve one's oral communication skills.

Word Accent

Any stress or relative emphasis given to a certain part of a word to make communication effective, is called a word accent.

> Learning how to pronounce correctly and the right word accents go a long way in making oral communication effective.

Techniques to Develop Effective Word Accent

Stress is an important feature of the English language. This feature of English needs some explanation. Stress is the degree of force with which we pronounce a sound. This degree of force is mainly pressure from the chest affecting the air-stream. However, the listener may perceive this degree of force as loudness. The stress system of English makes it different from Hindi and other Indian languages. In most Indian languages, we place the same amount of stress on all parts of a word. However, it is not so in English, where one part of a word may be more prominently pronounced than the others.

> Stress is the degree of force with which we pronounce a sound.

Word Stress Words are made up of one or more than one separately pronounced parts, which are called syllables. For example, the word 'teach' consists of one such part (syllable), whereas the word 'teacher' consists of two such parts (syllables). Thus, we define a syllable as a group of sounds with one vowel sound and one or more than one consonant sounds. Most of the words that we use may consist of one, two, or three syllables. Table 9.1 lists these syllables.

> A syllable is a group of sounds with one vowel sound and one or more than one consonant sounds.

TABLE 9.1 List of One, Two and Three Syllables

One Syllables	*Two Syllables*	*Three Syllables*
Read	Reader	Readership
Lead	Leader	Leadership
Sharp	Sharpen	Sharpener
Stand	Standard	Standardize
Part	Partake	Particle
Mark	Remark	Remarkable
Care	Careful	Carefully
Shame	Shameless	Shamelessly
Out	Outrage	Outrageous
Own	Owner	Ownership

Words having more than three syllables may also be used. Some examples of these are listed in Table 9.2.

TABLE 9.2 List of Words Having More than Three Syllables

Words having four syllables	Engineering, mechanical, electronics, electrical, decoration, introduction, ordinary, artificial, beneficial, architecture, entrepreneur, chronology, chronometer, entertainment, advertisement, advertiser, economist, economy, disappointment, absolutely, accessory, necessary, accidental, incidental, accompany, accordingly, bureaucracy, convocation, deficiency, departmental, benevolent, ceremony, certificate, discontinue, experiment
Words having five syllables	Opportunity, aboriginal, abnormality, communication, accelerator, deliberation, academician, civilisation, examination, international, multinational

In words of two or more syllables (actor, actress, singer, doctor, wonderful, interesting, punctuality, opportunity), one of the syllables stands out from the rest. The stressed syllable is relatively loud, long in duration, said clearly and distinctly, and made noticeable by the pitch of the voice. It is said to be accented. Thus, a stressed syllable has the following three features:

> Three features of a stressed syllable are loudness, duration, and a different pitch.

- It is said more loudly than the other syllable or syllables;
- It is said on a different pitch; and
- It is held for a longer time than the other syllable or syllables.

Let us try to understand this with the help of a few examples. In the word 'student', the first syllable 'stu' is more prominent than the second syllable 'dent', and thus the first syllable is accented. On the other hand, in the word 'include', the second syllable 'clude' is more prominent than the first syllable 'in', and thus the second syllable is accented. In the word 'physics', the first syllable 'phy' is more prominent than the second syllable 'sics'.

Table 9.3 contains few more examples of word stress.

TABLE 9.3 Additional Examples of Word Stress

Stress on the first syllable	absent, alkali, demonstrate, graduate, marriage, matrimony ordinance, progress, technocrat, weather
Stress on the second syllable	advantage, competitive, converge, credential, eccentric, impossible, necessity, position, reception, tremendous
Stress on the third syllable	accidental, inspiration, introductory, mathematics, panorama residential
Stress on the fourth syllable	affiliation, congratulation, responsibility

Primary Stress and Secondary Stress In longer English words, there may be more than one prominent syllable. In such words, one syllable may have the main strong stress called primary stress, whereas the other syllable may have a weak stress called secondary stress. For example, in the word 'introduction', the third syllable 'duc' is said with force and is held for a longer time, whereas the first syllable 'in' is held for lesser time and is said with a little less force. Thus, the first syllable has the secondary stress while the third syllable has the primary stress.

> In longer English words, there may be more than one prominent syllable.

Table 9.4 illustrates the stress system in some long English words.

TABLE 9.4 Primary and Secondary Stress in Words

Word	*Primary Stress*	*Secondary Stress*
Avalanche	1st syllable '**av**'	3rd syllable '**lanche**'
Beautify	1st syllable '**beau**'	3rd syllable '**fy**'
Photograph	1st syllable '**pho**'	3rd syllable '**graph**'
Stethoscope	1st syllable '**ste**'	3rd syllable '**scope**'
Antecedent	3rd syllable '**ce**'	1st syllable '**an**'
Chronological	3rd syllable '**lo**'	1st syllable '**chron**'
Information	3rd syllable '**ma**'	1st syllable '**in**'

(Contd.)

Instability	3rd syllable '**bi**'	1st syllable '**in**'
Departmental	3rd syllable '**ment**'	1st syllable '**de**'
Possibility	3rd syllable '**bi**'	1st syllable '**po**'

Most dictionaries use the mark / ' / to show the primary stress in a word. Notice the way stress is marked in the following words:

'summer, 'television, 'secular, 'reference de'ficiency, infor'mative, occu'pation.

Progress Check 1

1. **How many syllables do the following words have?**
   Controversy, demonstrate, entrance, foreign, forehead, jewellery, journey, knowledge, magistrate, mechanism, autonomous, combustion, conduction, curriculum, distinguish, empirical, impossible, impression, informative, involuntary, judicial, machine, manipulate, material, maternal, mechanic, memorial, mistake, municipal, necessity
2. **Speak the following words aloud and underline words that stress on the first syllable:**
   Neighbour, accent, catalogue, entrance, secondary, welcome, telephone, encounter, appropriate, ceremonial, philosophy, farmer, father, remark, transform, summarise, carbon, differential, reluctant, refuse

Using Correct Stress Patterns

In order to use correct stress patterns, the simple rules given below should be followed:

1. **Words with weak prefixes are accented on the root.**

Examples

a'broad,	in'clude	in'crease	a'bove	a'ffect
be'come	be'low	dis'able	dis'arm	dis'card
dis'own	dis'place	in'cur	pre'cast	pre'clude
pre'date	re'call	re'cast	re'cite	un'roll
un'safe	un'said	un'seat	un'sound	un'subtle

2. **In most two-syllabic words containing a long vowel, the stress is generally on the syllable with the long vowel sound.**

Examples

'artist	a'crue	'father	'farmer	'party
'partner	'starter	'faster	'carbon	'market
'teacher	a'chieve	can'teen	ma'chine	'colonel
'fortune,	'journey	'leader	'speaker	'army
'argue	'ardent	'armour	'curtain	'easy
e'ffuse	e'lude	em'bark	'fasten	'faulty
'female	'fertile	fif'teen	'harness	'harvest
'heathen	'hermit	i'mmune	im'part	im'port
im'prove	in'form	i'nert	in'sert	in'trude
'lawyer	'leaflet	'learned	le'gume	'margin
'master	'mercy	mon'soon	'nasty	'nurture
ob'serve	'orchid	'ordain	'organ	'parlour
re'mark	re'lease	re'search	re'trieve	'serpent
'service	'season	'thermal	'treason	'turban
'turbine	'water	'worthy	'carpet	'worship

3. Words ending in -ee are generally accented on the last syllable.

Examples

a'gree	de'cree	de'gree	refe'ree	trus'tee

4. Words ending in -tion have the stress on the syllable before it.

Examples

'action	a'ttention	a'ttraction	calcu'lation	'caption
appli'cation	'caution	co'llection	combi'nation	co'nnection
con'dition	con'ception	communi'cation	con'duction	confir'mation
co'rrection	congre'gation	con'vention	con'struction	conso'lation
'diction	congratu'lation	di'rection	du'ration	intro'duction
di'stinction	di'straction	do'nation	in'jection	in'tention
'function	'fiction	exami'nation	'friction	frus'tration
lo'cation	limi'tation	'mention	imi'tation	re'lation
re'jection	re'tention	'nation	'sanction	se'lection
'section	pro'duction	'station	esti'mation	infor'mation

5. Words ending in -sion, -ssion, -cion and -shion have the stress on the syllable before it.

Examples

'mansion	e'xpansion	'pension	'tension	di'ffusion
'passion	co'mmission	com'passion	'mission	con'cession
'fission	'session	po'ssession	pro'cession	pro'fession
e'ffusion	con'fusion	con'vulsion	suc'cession	sub'mission
persu'asion	supp'resion	elec'trician	su'spicion	mu'sician
phy'sician	oc'casion	pre'cision	de'cision	'fashion

6. Words ending in -ic, -ical, -ically, -ious, -ial, -ially, -ian, -ious, -logy, -nomy, -graphy have generally the stress on the syllable preceding the suffix.

Examples

aca'demic	spe'cific	aro'matic	ar'tistic	me'chanic
poly'technic	e'lectric	mag'netic	eco'nomic	'magic
elec'tronic	'magical	me'chanical	e'lectrical	eco'nomically
em'pirical	me'chanically	'partial	'partially	confi'dential
es'sential	es'sentially	prefe'rential	confi'dentially	li'brarian
'vicious	'cautious	'precious	de'licious	ma'licious
su'spicious	cere'monious	psy'cholcgy	e'conomy	physi'ology
e'cology	chro'nology	bi'ography	pho'tography	ty'pography

7. Words ending in -icy, -ify and -ity have the stress generally on the third syllable from the end.

Examples

'policy	'scarcity	'codify	i'dentify	'pacify
a'bility	a'trocity	actu'ality	ac'tivity	a'ffinity
fa'cility	'classify	elec'tricity	'purity	punctu'ality
'clarity	vi'cinity	mo'rality	to'tality	po'larity
le'gality	ca'pacity	lo'cality	'rectify	'charity

8. The suffixes -eer, -self, -ever, -ique, and -mental are accented on the first syllable.

Examples

ca'reer	her'self	my'self	him'self	your'self
how'ever	for'ever	what'ever	when'ever	phy'sique
u'nique	'mental	depart'mental	compart'mental	senti'mental

9. **The suffixes -ed, -ment, -es, -ing, -age, -ance, -en, -er, -ess, -ful, -hood, -ice, -ish, -ive, -less, -ly, -ness, -or, -ship, -ter, -ure, -y, and -zen do not affect the sress pattern of a word.**

Examples

a'ffect	a'ffected		
a'muse	a'mused		
re'source	re'sources		
e'ffort	e'ffortless		
'court	'courtship		
'friend	'friendship		
'tribute	'tributory		
'lazy	'lazily	'laziness	
'start	'starter	'starting	
e'ffect	e'ffective	e'ffectual	
a'ppoint	a'ppointed	a'ppointment	
a'ppear	a'ppeared	a'ppearing	a'ppearance

10. **The suffixes -al, -ible, -ial, and -ially generally affect the sress pattern.**

Examples

'accident	acci'dental
'origin	o'riginal
'sentiment	senti'mental
'access	ac'cessible
'president	presi'dential

11. **The stress pattern in the two-syllabic English words that function both as nouns/adjectives and as verbs generally depends upon the grammatical category of the word. The stress is on the first syllable if the word is used as a noun or adjective and on the second if it is a verb.**

Examples

Noun/Adjective	*Verb*
'convert	con'vert
'process	pro'cess
'transport	trans'port
'conduct	con'duct
'contrast	con'trast
'contact	con'tact
'object	ob'ject
'perfect	per'fect
'present	pre'sent
'produce	pro'duce
'project	pro'ject
'record	re'cord
'refund	re'fund
'report	re'port
'research	re'search
'subject	sub'ject

Practice

Practice 1: Stress on the First Syllable Speak the following words aloud, stressing the first syllable. Speak the first syllable loudly, distinctly, clearly, and hold for a longer time than the other syllables in the word.

Absence, accident, acid, active, actual, actually, adult, advertise, aeroplane, agent, agency, alcohol, allocate, ambulance, ancient, anecdote, animal, arbitrary, architect, aristocrat, aspirant, borax, borrow, bottom, brilliant, calcium, calendar, camera, capital, capsule, captain, capture, carriage, ceremony, chancellor, character, chemical, controversy, difference, difficult, discipline, evidence, extrovert, factory, family, fashion, favourite, foreign, forehead, formula, frequent, harmony, honorary, hostile, husband, illustrate, indicate, influence, interest, interview, jealous, jewellery, juvenile, laser, lawyer, leaflet, lethargy, living, local, lubricant, luggage, luxury, magistrate, magnet, magnify, manage, manifest, manner, manuscript, margin, market, mechanism, medicine, memory, mercury, message, microphone, microscope, mineral, miniature, minimum, mobile, modem, molecule, moment, mountain, multiple, mystery, national, narrow, nationalise, natural, necessary, negligence, negligible, neutral, neutron, nitrogen, nominal, nourish, nuclear, nucleus, nutrient, nature, obligate, ocean, ombudsman, opposite, optic, optimism, optimise, optimum, ordinary, organism, orient, ornament, origin, orthodox, oscillate, oxygen, ozone, packet, pageant, palace, panic, paper, parallel, paralyse, paramount, paramour, paraphrase, paragraph, parcel, pardon, parliament, parlour, partial, particle, partner, passage, passion, passive, pattern, patronise, penalty, penetrate, pension, perfect, permanent, person, personal, petrol, pharmacy, phosphorous, photocopier, photograph, physical, physics, picture, picnic, pilgrim, plagiarise, platform, pleasure, pocket, poison, policy, polish, popular, populate, portion, positive, possible, practice, precedence, precious, perfect, preference, pregnant, president, pressure, previous, primary, principal, principle, product, project, profile, profit, programme, promise, proper, proverb, punctual, puncture, qualify, quality, quantity, quarter, quotable, radical, radiator, rainbow, rampant, ransom, rapture, rational, reason, recognise, reconcile, rectangle, refuge, region, regular, relevant, reverse, rigorous, salient, sanction, scholar, second, seminar, sentiment, serious, session, shoulder, similar, singular, sovereign, spectacle, splendour, stadium, standard, summary, summit, supervise, sympathy, telegraph, temperature, tension, terminal, territory, travel, treasure, ultimate, ultrasound, vegetable, verify, vehicle, vibrant, victory, vicious, visible, vision, vital, volatile, voluntary, volume, vulnerable, vulgar, warrant, water, weapon, wisdom, woman, wonder, yesterday

Practice 2: Stress on the Second Syllable Speak the following words aloud stressing the second syllable. Speak the second syllable loudly, distinctly, clearly, and hold for a longer time than the other syllables in the word.

Believe, absorb, account, achieve, acquire, activity, address, adjust, admire, admit, adopt, advertisement, advice, advise, affiliate, agree, allow, alternative, amount, apologise, arithmetic, assemble, behaviour, cartoon, cashier, catalysis, certificate, chromatic, collect, combine, combustion, commission, committee, compartment, complexion, conception, condense, condition, conduction, confess, confirm, congratulate, conservative, contain, continuous, converse, corroborate, curriculum, deceive, decline, deliberate, departure, design, detergent, diffusion, direction, discover, distinguish, distributive, diversify, domestic, economy, electric, electrode, electron, embrace, embarrass, exhaust, exhaustion, explore, express, extraordinary, extreme, familiar, fraternity, frustrate, impression, improve, inform, involve, internal, investigate, judicial, machine, magnetic, magnificent, maintain, maternal, mechanic, memorial, mentality, mistake, municipal, neglect, negotiate, notorious, November, obligatory, oblige, observe, obstruct, occasion, offense, offend, opinion, opponent, oppose, optician, organic, original, originate, outrageous, pacific, paralysis, parameter, particular, particularly, peculiar, perfection, persuasive, pervert, phenomenon, phonetic, photography, photographer, physique, police, polite, political, politicise, pollute, potential, practitioner, precaution, prefer, prepare, preserve, prestige, procedure, proceed, production, productive, professor, profound, promote, propose, proposal, provide, psychosis, psychology, quotation, react, reaction, reactive, reactivate, reality, reciprocate, reflect, reflection, reform, refresh, reliable, reliance, relieve, religion, religious, resource, resort, responsible, return, reveal, revert, review, revoke, revolt, sophisticate, sophisticated, sincere, spectacular, surpass, suspense, suspicion, technique, technocracy, telegraphy, thermometer, transact, transaction, transcend, transcribe, transfer, transition, translate, transmit, unanimous, unchanging, unconscious, unfaithful, unnecessary, unsound, ultimatum, vernacular

Practice 3: Stress on the Third Syllable Speak the following words aloud stressing the third syllable. Speak the third syllable loudly, distinctly, clearly, and hold for a longer time than the other syllables in the word.

Aeronautics, affidavit, alcoholic, circulation, introduction, complication, corporation, counteract, departmental, derivation, designation, differentiate, distribution, electricity, electrician, independent, information, introduce, introduction, intervene, interrupt, interpose, international, intermission, intonation, irresponsible, mathematical, mineralogy, mountaineer, nationality, obligation, oceanography, operation, opportunity, opposition, oriental, overhead, overseas, personality, personnel, pioneer, population, productivity, radiation, recollect, recommend, represent, representative, situation, souvenir, telegraphic, territorial, ultrasonic, ultraviolet, vegetarian, volunteer

Practice 4: Stress on the Fourth Syllable Speak the following words aloud stressing the fourth syllable. Speak the fourth syllable loudly, distinctly, clearly, and hold for a longer time than the other syllables in the word.

Apologetic, characteristic, communication, configuration, degeneration, encyclopedia, entrepreneur, negotiation, qualification

Progress Check 2

1. **Speak the following words aloud and mark the correct stress:**

   Disappoint, employee, interrupt, precipitation, awkward, handsome, cinema, justice, kerosene, kitchen, knowledge, currency, designate, library, literacy, legislative, emphasise, generalise, adventure, autonomous, connect, concession, irrational, negotiable, manipulate, reproduction, recalculation, laureate, hundred, circumstance, consequence, compulsory, authorise, challenge, empirical, nicotine, merchant, minimise, modern, forgery, chronicle, encourage, excuse, involuntary, cigarette, decompose, perform, persuade, straightforward, supremacy, suspension, material, suspicious, progressive, afternoon, reprehend, seventeen, understand

Weak Forms Certain very common words, such as articles, personal and relative pronouns, auxiliary verb forms, prepositions, and conjunctions usually have two pronunciations, i.e., a strong pronunciation and a weak pronunciation. The weak pronunciation is generally used in connected speech whereas the strong pronunciation is used when the word is stressed or spoken in isolation, and also when the word comes at the end of a sentence. Study the following examples:

Weak forms are unstressed syllables that are weakened and reduced to give prominence to stressed syllables.

I am looking **for** my book.	(Weak pronunciation)	f + ə
What are you looking **for**?	(Strong pronunciation)	f + ɔ:

I am going **to** the party.	(Weak pronunciation)	t + ə
What are you up **to**?	(Strong pronunciation)	t + u:

He did not look **at** me.	(Weak pronunciation)	ə + t
What are you looking **at**?	(Strong pronunciation)	æ + t

The use of weak forms is integral to stress patterns in English because the unstressed words are reduced to give prominence to accented syllables. This weakening of unstressed syllables in a sentence is a characteristic feature of spoken English. Consider the following examples (the underlined words are in weak form):

'Look **<u>at</u>** 'these 'flowers.
I **<u>am</u>** **<u>from</u>** 'Bangalore.
They **<u>are</u>** 'coming **<u>to</u>** the 'party.
She **<u>was</u>** 'writing a 'letter.
They **<u>were</u>** 'present in the 'meeting.
I **<u>am</u>** 'waiting **<u>for</u>** my 'friend.
He **<u>has</u>** 'gone **<u>to</u>** the 'club.
She **<u>can</u>** 'join you.
<u>Can</u> you 'wait **<u>for</u>** me?
<u>That</u> is the spirit.

Study Table 9.5, which contains a list of words that generally appear in weak form in connected speech.

TABLE 9.5 List of Words Appearing in Weak Form

Prepositions	at, for, from, of, to
Articles	a, an, the
Conjunctions	and, as, than, that, but
Auxiliary verbs	is, am, are, was, were, does, can, has, have, had, shall, will, would, must

Progress Check 3

1. **Speak the following sentences aloud, identify the words that appear in weak form, and underline them.**
   (a) What can I do for you?
   (b) Can I help you?
   (c) I am coming from the library.
   (d) I want to send this parcel to New York.
   (e) What are you waiting for?
   (f) I am waiting for you.
   (g) Are you waiting for the train?
   (h) Was he present in the meeting?
   (i) When was the last announcement made?
   (j) They must be working very hard.
   (k) One atom differs from another in its atomic number and electronic configuration.
   (l) You can never see air moving but can only detect its motion.
   (m) You should try as hard as you can.
   (n) That is not really expensive.
   (o) You are welcome.
   (p) Thanks for coming to the party.
   (q) They have been waiting for you for half an hour.
   (r) Do not look at these papers.
   (s) Can you join me for a moment?
   (t) I would love to join you, but I am busy.

Voice Quality

Another important way to develop effective oral communication skills is through improving one's voice quality. Several paralinguistic features of speaking such as voice quality, rhythm, pitch, and tone have to be manipulated to achieve the desired fluency and confidence in speaking.

Developing Voice Quality

A person's voice reflects his/her personality. An impressive voice does reflect an impressive personality. It is, therefore, important that one should try to improve the quality of one's voice. Although the quality of a person's voice depends mainly on factors that are beyond his/her control, it can be improved if sincere efforts are made. A person's voice depends on several factors, which include his/her vocal habits formed since childhood, the structure and physical condition of his/her voice mechanism, the patterns of his/her oral interactions along with its influences on his/her speech habits, and his/her overall personality. Developing a person's voice might include making effective changes in his/her speech habits.

> You can improve the quality of your voice by analysing your voice and undertaking regular practice sessions to improve and control the pitch, volume, and depth of your voice.

As developing the quality of one's voice is desirable to become a confident speaker, a systematic plan needs to be followed. In order to develop the quality of your voice, you should first analyse your voice. Then, with regular practice specific features of your voice can be improved.

Analyse Your Voice Analysing one's voice is the first step in improving voice quality. One must listen to one's voice carefully to understand the following aspects of one's voice:

- Pitch (highness or lowness of the sounds produced)
- Volume (loudness of the sounds made)
- Quality (specific identifying feature of sounds that are produced)
- Rate of speaking (the duration of individual sounds, the length of the phrases, and the duration of the pauses between phrases)

A balanced pitch makes the voice pleasant, lively, and clear.

A recording of a person's voice made while talking to someone, reading something aloud, taking part in a discussion, or while giving an oral presentation should be listened to carefully and critically and the following questions should be answered:

(a) Is the pitch of the voice varied and flexible? (It is neither too high nor too low.)
(b) Does the voice vary to fit the content?
(c) Does the voice change with the person's mood?
(d) Does the voice reflect the speaker's personality?
(e) Does the person adjust the volume of his/her voice to suit his/her reading material?
(f) Is the rate of speaking fitting the occasion? (that is neither too slow nor too fast.)
(g) Does the voice fit the topic and the occasion?
(h) Does the speaker vary the rate of speaking according to the need of the content?
(i) What is the overall impression of his/her voice?

If these questions are answered honestly, a fairly good idea of the quality of the voice being studied can be formed.

Voice Practice Once we have determined the quality of our voice, we need to undertake regular practice to improve the specific features of our voice. We must follow a systematic routine for practice, and set aside regular practice periods. Practice sessions should be relaxed. Practice should focus on improving one feature of our voice at a time. The transition from practice to performance should be slow and gradual.

Although the quality of our voice depends on factors beyond our control, we can improve it if sincere efforts are made. English speech sounds should be practiced individually and in context. Fine distinctions must be made between long and short vowels, vowels and diphthongs, and different consonant sounds. We should practice speaking long stretches of conversation and concentrate on the production of sounds.

In order to improve the pitch of our voice, practice needs to be varied and flexible and monotony should be avoided. Pitch should be controlled if it is too high or too low. We may try to speak words, phrases and sentences in different ways by changing the pitch of our voice. A balanced pitch will make the voice pleasant, lively, and clear.

We should also practice how to adjust the volume of our voice to fit our topic and content. Notice how a good public speaker varies his/her voice to fit his/her material. Listen carefully to newsreaders to note how they vary their voice according to the content of the news. Reading different kinds of material should be practised making adjustments in the volume of one's voice. A friend can listen to the practice readings and give feedback. Regular practice will enable one to adjust one's voice according to the needs of the content.

We should also practice to control our rate of speaking. It is a general observation that students speak faster than they should. People often mistake fluency for speed of speaking. They are, however, not the same thing. Whether one should speak fast or slow depends on several factors, which include the type of audience, the nature of content, the occasion, and so on. What is important to remember is that the listener should have no difficulty in understanding the message. Therefore, the speaker should be neither too fast nor too slow. His/her rate of speaking should fit the content, the occasion, and the audience.

People often mistake fluency for speed of speaking.

Rhythm in Connected Speech

Rhythm is a pattern of successive accented and unaccented syllables in an utterance or a sentence. In connected speech in English, one sound is linked closely to the next in such a way that it is difficult to tell exactly where one word ends and the next begins. This linking of words and phrases affects our pronunciation in more than one way and helps to maintain rhythm in speech.

Rhythm is the result of the regular occurrence of stressed and unstressed syllables in connected speech.

Rhythm is an important characteristic feature of English speech. In an utterance or a sentence in connected speech, some syllables stand out from the rest and are stressed, while some syllables remain unstressed. In fact, stressed and unstressed syllables make a pattern in connected speech and this pattern is known as rhythm. Speak the following sentences aloud to understand this feature of English speech:

1. Can I 'help you?
2. 'What can I 'do for you?
3. I am 'pleased to 'meet you.
4. I am 'glad to 'meet you.

In the first sentence above, there is one stressed syllable and three unstressed syllables, while in each of the remaining sentences there are two stressed and four unstressed syllables. Thus, it is evident that in every sentence or utterance there are some syllables that stand out from the rest and are stressed. Stressed syllables occur at regular intervals of time, and it is this regularity of occurrence of stressed syllables that gives English its characteristic rhythm. The rhythm in English pronunciation is maintained by pronouncing the stressed syllables carefully while the unstressed syllables are crowded together between the stressed syllables.

It is the regularity of occurrence of stressed syllables that gives English its characteristic rhythm

Speak the following sentences aloud maintaining the stress patterns as marked, and note how unstressed syllables are crowded together between the stressed syllables:

1. 'What is your 'father?
2. My 'father is a 'singer.
3. I 'want a 'glass of 'water.
4. The 'pleasure is 'mine.
5. My 'sister 'wants to be a 'doctor.
6. It is 'nice to 'see you a'gain.
7. I 'wonder if you could 'find an 'English 'teacher for me.
8. Would you 'mind 'giving me your 'notebook for a 'day?
9. There is 'someone 'waiting for you in the 'living 'room.
10. She would 'like to be 'come a 'social 'worker.

Progress Check 4

1. **Identify the rhythm pattern of the following expressions. Read the solved example.**

   Sentence: Please call the doctor.

   Rhythm pattern: **SSUSU** (**S** stands for stressed syllable while **U** stands for unstressed syllable)

   (a) What can I do for you?
   (b) Can I help you?
   (c) I beg your pardon.
   (d) Please cancel the trip.
   (e) I don't know what to do.
   (f) I'd like to join your company at the earliest.
   (g) Could you please do me a favour?
   (h) When can you join?
   (i) My greatest strength is my ability to work under pressure.
   (j) I want to work as a systems manager in a leading company.

Developing a Correct Tone

In order to be fluent in English, we need to develop the correct tone or intonation. A tone refers to the modulation of the voice expressing a particular feeling or mood. It is an important feature of spoken English and plays an important role in verbal interaction. The tone of a voice shows the attitude of the speaker and reveals his/her intention. It gives implicit information by indicating the type of sentence spoken by the speaker.

> Tone is the modulation of the voice that shows the attitude, approach, and intention of the speaker.

In order to use and identify correct tone in spoken English, we should identify the tonic syllable, understand different types of tones, and divide an utterance into tone groups.

Tonic Syllable

Tonic syllable is the syllable on which the pitch change begins. Some people call it the 'nucleus'. Look at the following sentences:

> Tonic syllable is the syllable on which the pitch change begins.

'What's your 'father?

In this sentence, there is a high static tone on the syllable 'what's', i.e., the accented syllable is on a level pitch. However, the tone starts falling down on the last stressed syllable 'fa', i.e., the voice slides down from the original pitch, becoming softer and softer until it stops. Thus, 'fa' is the tonic syllable or the nucleus. A pitch change begins on the syllable, which we want to make the most important. Although there are exceptions, the last stressed syllable of a tone group is generally the tonic syllable.

> A pitch change begins on the syllable, which we want to make the most important.

Now consider the following examples:

1. She is a 'painter.
2. What is your 'problem?
3. I 'want a 'glass of 'water.
4. 'What do you 'want?
5. 'What a 'beautiful 'scene.

Types of Tones

There are several tones. However, we will discuss three of them, i.e., falling tone, rising tone, and falling-rising tone.

Falling Tone The pitch of our voice falls on the tonic syllable in a falling tone. We use the falling tone in ordinary statements (assertive sentences, including both affirmative and negative, without any implication), wh-questions (questions beginning with a wh-word, such as what, when, where, and so on), polite expressions, greetings, imperative sentences (commands, prohibitions, and so forth), and exclamatory sentences. Table 9.6 gives some examples (the symbol ` is used here to indicate a falling tone).

Falling tone is used in ordinary statements, wh-questions, polite expressions, greetings, and in imperative and exclamatory sentences.

TABLE 9.6 Examples of Falling Tone

Type of Sentence	*Examples*
Ordinary statements	I'm 'pleased to 'talk to you. I can 'drive a 'car. She's 'going to 'London. I'm at'tending the 'meeting.
Wh-questions	'What's the 'problem? 'Why are you 'late? 'What do you 'want?
Polite expressions	'Thanks for 'helping. 'So 'nice of you.
Greetings	'Good 'morning. 'Good 'evening. 'Good 'night.
Imperative sentences	'Pick up the 'phone. 'Close the 'door. 'Finish the 'job.
Exclamatory sentences	'What a 'fine 'morning! 'How 'wonderful!

Rising Tone The pitch of our voice rises on the tonic syllable in a rising tone. We use a rising tone in polite questions, conditional expressions, polite requests, direct questions (requiring yes/no answers), and incomplete utterances. Table 9.7 gives some examples (the symbol \ is used here to indicate a rise of tone).

TABLE 9.7 Examples of Rising Tone

Type of Sentence	*Examples*
Polite questions	'How is your \study?
	What's the \time?
	'Can I \help you?
Conditional expressions	If you 'work \hard, you 'may 'get the pro'motion.
	If you 'do 'what I \say, you will 'get 'what you 'want.
Polite requests	'Please 'give me your \pen?
	'Please 'sit \down.
	'Could you please 'tell me your \name?
Direct questions	'Do you 'like 'English \music?
	'Have you fi'nished the \job?
	Did you at'tend the \meeting?
Incomplete utterances	By the \way,
	I'm not at'tending the 'meeting.
	Fortunately,
	The 'car didn't 'hit the 'old 'man.

Falling-rising Tone There is a change in the pitch from high to low in a falling-rising tone. You use this tone when you are in doubt or want to convey some implicit or special meaning. Study the following examples (The symbol ∨ is used here to indicate a rise and fall of tone):

1. Her 'husband is ∨smart. (Implied meaning: Her husband is smart but not intelligent)
2. I don't 'want to 'go to the ∨party. (I don't want to go but I'll go because you want me to go.)
3. The 'place is ∨nice. (The place is nice but the people are not.)

Rising tone is used n polite and direct questions, polite requests, conditional expressions, and incomplete utterances.

Tone Group

An utterance or a sentence should be divided into tone groups. A sentence or an utterance in English may consist of a single tone group or several tone groups. For example, the sentence "Could you please tell me something about your career goals?" has one tone group while the shorter sentence "Well, I'm ready." consists of two tone groups. Although there are no fixed rules for the division of a sentence into tone groups, it should be borne in mind that a full stop or a new clause indicates the end of a tone group, whereas a comma may or may not indicate the end of a tone group.

Falling-rising tone is used to express doubt, uncertainty, and implicit meaning.

Examine the following examples carefully to understand tone group division. The use of a slant line/ indicates the end of a tone group.

1. I am sure you would like to meet the group members. (one tone group)
2. I have worked for six years as an assistant manager in Mumbai for Infosys. (one tone-group)
3. If I attend the meeting,/I shall put your point of view before the board. (two tone groups)
4. Luckily,/there was no one in the room/when the explosions started. (three tone groups)
5. Whatever may be the circumstances,/I always complete my projects on time. (two tone groups)

Progress Check 5

1. Divide the following utterances into tone groups by using an oblique bar/to indicate the end of a tone group.

(a) Good morning ladies and gentlemen, I am here to talk about the dangers of AIDS.
(b) For the last six years, I have been working as a sales engineer at Tata Steel.
(c) I always strive to be the best in whatever I do.
(d) I have strong communication and interpersonal skills.
(e) As a dynamic extrovert student, I took active interest and participated in extra-curricular activities in the college.
(f) With the qualifications and skills you are seeking, I am sure I would be able to get the desired results for your company.
(g) My academic record reflects my sincerity and strong determination.
(h) Working with such a growing organisation has been one of my career objectives since the very beginning.
(i) I have successfully completed several projects as a leader but at the same time I have worked in cross-functional teams as a member and have done well.
(j) I believe your company is one of them and I would like to be a part of such a company.
(k) Although I would prefer a full-time position, I can also consider a part-time position.
(l) Although I want to be part of your company, I am afraid I would not be able to accept a lower position.

Various Oral Interactions

We have already touched upon the types of oral communication in Chapter 1, *Communication Today*. To recap, communication can be classified as formal and informal communication, or internal and external communication. They can be further divided into sub-categories like face-to-face interactions, telephonic conversations, presentations, casual chats, etc. Given below are some strategies for developing effective oral communication skills related to some of the commonly used oral communication methods. These are in addition to the generic strategies discussed so far.

Communication can be classified into formal and informal communication, or internal and external communication.

Telephonic Conversations

Here are some tips for effective telephonic conversations in a professional setting:

- Always start a telephonic conversation with a greeting.
- Call at an appropriate time of the day that suits the receiver of the call.
- Set out the agenda of the call.
- Keep a positive tone.
- Speak clearly with a speed and volume that is comfortable to understand.
- Be an effective listener.
- Modify the message according to the feedback received during the conversation.
- End on a positive note with a clear plan of action.
- Thank the receiver for his/her time.

Debates and Discussions

Here are some tips for effective oral communication skills in debates and discussions in a professional set up:

- Set out the agenda at the start.
- Listen to other people's points of view.
- Disagree to another person's point of view, politely.
- Substantiate points with facts and examples.
- Keep the tone professional even if someone is cracking a joke.
- Summarize the discussion at the end.
- End on a positive note with a clear plan of action.

Speeches

Here are some tips for making effective speeches:

- Do a thorough homework and know the facts.
- Practice beforehand.
- Always keep the tone professional.
- Customise the style of speech according to the background of the audience.
- Keep a track of the feedback of the audience and adapt the speech accordingly.
- Summarize at the end.
- End on a positive note with a clear plan of action.

Presentations

Here are some tips for making effective presentations:

- Do a thorough homework and know the facts.
- Practice beforehand.
- Always keep the tone professional.
- Customise the style of presentation according to the background of the audience.
- Pause when nervous or when in the need to recollect something.
- Keep a track of the feedback of the audience and adapt accordingly.
- Summarize at the end.

- End on a positive note with a clear plan of action.
- Answer questions to the satisfaction of the audience.

Social Events

There are many types of social events that one may have to be a part of in both, personal and professional settings. Some examples are cultural events, office parties, and picnics. Here are some general tips for effective oral communication during such events in the professional setting:

- Start with a greeting.
- Do not get personal.
- Listen effectively.
- Speak clearly with a speed and volume that is comfortable to understand.
- Adapt to the audience feedback.
- Disagree to another person's point of view, politely.
- End on a positive note.

The tips given above are not exhaustive, but give an idea about the way to become effective speakers or listeners at various events that involve oral interactions.

Exercise

1. **Answer the following questions:**
   (a) What are the different techniques to develop word accent?
   (b) Discuss how to develop voice quality.
   (c) Explain rhythm in connected speech.
   (d) Discuss different techniques to develop correct tone in fluent speech.
2. **Write short notes on the following:**
   (a) Word stress
   (b) Primary and secondary stress
   (c) Weak forms
   (d) Rising tone
   (e) Falling tone
3. **Speak the following words aloud and mark the correct stress. Use a dictionary to check the answers.**
   Accomplishment, adamant, administered, allocation, application, approval, arrangement, attainment, classification, collaborated, comparison, complete, computerise, construction, contracted, controlled, cooperation, delegate, developed, discovery, encouragement, escalated, establish, estimate, evaluated, expansion, experienced, exploration, facilitate, formulation, functioning, government, guidance, identification, implement, innovative, improvement, index, initiate, inspection, institute, interesting, interpret, introduction, investigate, justified, locate, moderated, motivate, negotiate, organised, originated, overcome, permanent, perceive, performance, pioneer, planning, presentation, provocative, preside, promotion, purchaser, recommend, recorded, rectify, reasonable, repair, replacement, restore, reverse, select, sparked, specify, stimulate, strengthen, summarise, supervise, transcribe, transform, upgraded, validate, vitalised, active, competent, diplomatic, discreet, efficient, energetic, fair, firm, logical, mature, methodical, motivated, objective, pleasant, positive, practical, reliable

4. Speak the following sentences aloud, identify the words that appear in weak form and underline them.

(a) It is nice meeting you.
(b) I am pleased to meet you.
(c) It is a pleasure to talk to you.
(d) Thanks for coming.
(e) I would like to talk to you later.
(f) See you again.
(g) See you later.
(h) Can I do something for you?
(i) I will attend the party.
(j) I have been working in a department store for the last three years.
(k) You can contact me at my home address.
(l) I am interested in this job.
(m) Today I would like to inform you about a national problem in India–child marriages.
(n) It is a great pleasure to be here today.
(o) I am here today to talk about the dangers of AIDS.

5. Read the following conversation between two friends and identify words that appear in weak form. Underline them.

Ravi: Hello, Anil. How are you?
Anil: Fine. Thanks. And you?
Ravi: Pretty well. Thanks.
Anil: How about your parents?
Ravi: They are OK. How are your studies?
Anil: It is going on. And yours?
Ravi: Just fine. I have completed almost half the course.
Anil: I haven't seen you for sometime. Where have you been?
Ravi: Well, I have been very busy these days. I hardly got any time to move out.
Anil: It's good to see you again.
Ravi: Really. I am also glad to have met you again.
Anil: Thanks. By the way, what are you doing today evening?
Ravi: Nothing in particular.
Anil: I'll come to meet your parents.
Ravi: At what time will you come?
Anil: About 7 pm in the evening.
Ravi: I'll wait for you.
Anil: Well, see you in the evening.
Ravi: See you.

Key to Progress Check

Progress Check 1

1.		
	word having two syllables	entrance, foreign, forehead, journey, knowledge, machine, mistake
	word having three syllables	demonstrate, jewellery, magistrate, mechanism, combustion, conduction, distinguish, impossible, impression, judicial, material, maternal, mechanic, memorial,
	word having four syllables	controversy, autonomous, curriculum, empirical, informative, manipulate, municipal, necessity
	word having five syllables	involuntary

2. Neighbour, accent, catalogue, entrance, secondary, welcome, telephone, farmer, father, summarise, carbon

Progress Check 2

1. The following words have stress on the first syllable:
awkward, handsome, authorise, challenge, forgery, chronicle, laureate, hundred, circumstance, consequence, cinema, justice, kerosene, kitchen, knowledge, currency, designate, library, literacy, legislative, nicotine, merchant, minimise, modern, emphasise, generalise

   The following stress on the second syllable:
adventure, autonomous, connect, concession, compulsory, empirical, encourage, excuse, involuntary, irrational, negotiable, manipulate, material, perform, persuade, straightforward, supremacy, suspension, suspicious, progressive

   The following words stress on the third syllable:
afternoon, cigarette, decompose, disappoint, employee, interrupt, reprehend, seventeen, understand, reproduction

   The following words stress on the fourth syllable:
recalculation, precipitation

Progress Check 3

1. (a) What **can** I do **for** you?
   (b) **Can** I help you?
   (c) I **am** coming **from** the library.
   (d) I want **to** send this parcel **to** New York.
   (e) What **are** you waiting for?
   (f) I **am** waiting **for** you.
   (g) **Are** you waiting **for** the train?
   (h) **Was** he present in the meeting?

(i) When **was** the last announcement made?
(j) **They must** be working very hard.
(k) One atom differs **from** another in its atomic number **and** electronic configuration.
(l) You **can** never see air moving **but can** only detect its motion.
(m) You **should** try as hard as you can.
(n) **That** is **not** really expensive.
(o) You **are** welcome.
(p) Thanks **for** coming **to** the party.
(q) They **are** waiting **for** you **for** half **an** hour.
(r) Do **not** look **at** these papers.
(s) **Can** you join me **for** a moment?
(t) I **would** love **to** join you **but** I **am** busy.

Progress Check 4

1.

	Sentence	Rhythm pattern
(i)	What can I do for you?	SUUSUU
(ii)	Can I help you?	UUSU
(iii)	I beg your pardon.	USUSU
(iv)	Please cancel the trip.	SSUUS
(v)	I don't know what to do.	UUSSUS
(vi)	I'd like to join your company.	USUSUSUU
(vii)	Could you please do me a favour?	UUSUUUSU
(viii)	When can you join?	SUUS
(ix)	My greatest strength is my ability to work under pressure.	USUSUUUSUUUSSUSU
(x)	I want to work as a system manager in a leading company.	USUSUUSUSUUUUSUSUU

Progress Check 5

1. (a) Good morning ladies and gentlemen, /I am here to talk about the dangers of AIDS. (Two tone groups)
(b) For the last six years, I have been working as a sales engineer at Tata Steel. (One tone group)
(c) I always strive to be the best in whatever I do. (One tone group)
(d) I have strong communication and interpersonal skills. (One tone group)
(e) As a dynamic extrovert student, /I took active interest and participation in extra-curricular activities in the college. (Two tone groups)
(f) With the qualifications and skills you are seeking, /I am sure I would be able to get the desired results for your company. (Two tone groups)
(g) My academic record reflects my sincerity and strong determination. (One tone group)
(h) Working with such a growing organisation has been one of my career objectives since the very beginning. (One tone group)
(i) I have successfully completed several projects as a leader /but at the same time I have worked in cross-functional teams as a member and have done well. (Two tone groups)
(j) I believe your company is one of them /and I would like to be a part of such a company. (Two tone groups)

(k) Although I would prefer a full-time position, /I can also consider a part-time position. (Two tone groups)

(l) Although I want to be part of your company, /I am afraid I would not be able to accept a lower position. (Two tone groups)

SECTION 4

Professional Speaking

CHAPTERS

- Chapter 10: Job Interviews
- Chapter 11: Group Discussions
- Chapter 12: Presentation Skills

10 CHAPTER

Job Interviews

A job interview is a pre-arranged and planned conversation used for evaluating the suitability of a candidate for a particular position.

LEARNING OBJECTIVES

- Understanding the nature of the interviewing process
- Knowing the characteristics of job interviews
- Identifying pre-interview preparation techniques
- Knowing the different types of interview questions and how to answer frequently asked questions
- Understanding how to project a positive image during a job interview
- Knowing alternative interview formats

10.1 INTRODUCTION

Many people get nervous at the very idea of a job interview. For most job applicants, job interviews are frightening simply due to the fear of being rejected. Even if a person is self-confident, with a good grasp of the subject of his/her specialisation, he/she is most likely to be tense and nervous before and during the interview. However, we can overcome our fear of the interview process by understanding the process and making ourselves ready and prepared for it.

> Success in a job interview depends on knowledge, self-confidence, good speaking skills, thorough preparation, and use of appropriate interview strategies.

The interviewing process is a complex means of gathering relevant data about a candidate for a particular job position, promotion, or making a selection panel. It is a structured mechanism for professional evaluation for employment as well as promotion. Although interviewing may be practiced along with other screening methods such as group discussions and oral presentations, recruitment experts believe that a job interview provides the best opportunity to examine the relevance of an applicant's knowledge and experience and is an effective technique used for evaluating the suitability of a candidate for a particular position through a question-answer oral session. It could be either a face-to-face meeting or a formal conversation through telephone, or videoconferencing between a candidate and the members of the selection committee or representatives of the concerned employers.

> The interviewing process is a complex means of gathering relevant data about a candidate for a particular job position, promotion, or making a selection panel.

> An interview could be either a face-to-face meeting or a formal conversation through telephone, or videoconferencing.

Job interviews in today's technologically advanced world are more challenging than they used to be a few years ago. As the selection committee faces the challenge of getting the right person into the job, the members of the committee are interested in a correct evaluation of the candidate's personal qualities, qualifications, talents, traits, and suitability for the position to be filled in. However, it is not an easy task for any selection committee to judge a candidate's abilities and personal qualities on the basis of a half-hour conversation with the candidate. Therefore, new and more effective interviewing techniques have been devised for the correct evaluation of a candidate. Some organisations prefer to conduct preliminary and screening interviews before the final interview. In fact, there are several factors responsible for making job interviews more challenging today. They include:

> Some organisations prefer to conduct preliminary and screening interviews before the final interview.

- **Growing competition in the job market**
  There is more competition in the job market today due to the availability of more qualified and experienced candidates. The fast increase in population, the availability of sophisticated specialised education and training, the trend of 'hire and fire' by most organisations, and globalisation of the world economy have increased the number of job seekers. If there is one job, there are hundreds of applicants.
- **Changing demands of the job market**
  The job market is not the same. There are more opportunities but at the same time there are more challenges, more demands, and more expectations. There are more job positions but these are less stable than they used to be. Moreover, the positions are more demanding and often include a broader range of responsibilities than positions in the past.

- **Growing professionalism of the business world**
The business world has become more professional. With the expansion of multinational companies and worldwide business operations, the world has become a global village. As only the best can survive, most companies have to struggle to survive and grow. They need very efficient, competent, and highly dynamic personnel to run the show and achieve the desired success.
- **Increasing focus on the candidate's personal qualities**
There is an increasing focus on the candidate's personal qualities rather than on qualification, experience, and job skills. Most recruitment experts believe that proper training can easily develop these skills but it is not easy to develop personal motivations and qualities.
- **Changes in the interviewing techniques**
The interviewing process has become more complex. Most organisations have their own recruitment departments with highly competent people who receive appropriate training so that they can make valid selection decisions. Moreover, there are specialised recruitment agencies to help companies get the right people for the right jobs. These agencies have developed new and effective interviewing techniques for evaluating a candidate's suitability for a particular position.

> There are specialised recruitment agencies to help companies get the right people for the right jobs.

A candidate may have knowledge, confidence, and speaking skills to face a job interview but he/she still needs proper orientation and guidance to face a job interview effectively and confidently and improve his/her chances of success. The candidate should be familiar with the types of interviews, interview formats, and appropriate interviewing strategies. He/she should know how to plan and prepare for a job interview, how to develop the interview file, how to project success during the interview, how to reflect confidence while answering questions and how to uphold his/her personality and overcome interviewing hazards.

> The candidate should be familiar with the types of interviews, interview formats, and appropriate interviewing strategies.

Progress Check 1

1. Which of the following statements about job interview are True?

(a) There is less competition in the job market today due to the lack of availability of qualified and experienced candidates.

(b) A job interview is an important technique used for evaluating the suitability of a candidate for a particular position through an oral question-answer session.

(c) Interviewing can be practiced along with other screening methods such as group discussions and oral presentations.

(d) A job interview is always a face-to-face meeting between a candidate and the members of the selection committee or representatives of the concerned employers.

(e) Some organisations conduct preliminary and screening interviews before the final interview.

(f) Most recruitment experts believe that proper training can easily develop personal qualities and positive traits.

(g) Job interviews in today's technologically advanced world are more challenging than they used to be a few years ago.

(h) Job interviews are more challenging today because of the growing competition in the job market.
(i) There is an increasing focus on the candidate's qualification, experience, and job skills rather than on personal qualities.
(j) Most organisations have their own recruitment departments with highly competent people who receive appropriate training so that they can make valid selection decisions.

10.2 CHARACTERISTICS OF A JOB INTERVIEW

As noted earlier, a job interview is a pre-arranged and planned conversation characterised by a defined purpose and some level of informality. Let us discuss these aspects in some detail.

10.2.1 Planning

A job interview is pre-arranged and planned. Despite flexibility during an interview, the basic structure of most job interviews is planned for effective results. Several factors such as the time, the venue, the number of experts, the areas to be covered in the interview, the papers and materials needed, and so on are decided much before the interview. The interviewers may also consider the best ways of opening and concluding interviews. However, no job interview is just a mechanical process of asking and answering questions. The interviewer may plan and generate specific questions for each candidate with modifications in the planned interview design.

> Despite flexibility during an interview, the basic structure of most job interviews is planned for effective results.

10.2.2 Purpose

A job interview is purposefully designed to achieve certain objectives. Organisations invest both time and money on the job interviews to ensure correct selection. Thus, there may be HR interviews to test the personality traits of candidates, technical interviews to generate information in response to specific questions for testing subject knowledge, situational interviews to test problem-solving skills and assess how candidates will behave in certain situations, and criterion based interviews to judge knowledge and abilities in a tightly focused way to evaluate how well a candidate fits a particular position. Whatever may be the format of a job interview, the purpose is predefined so that the predictive capabilities of job interviews are enhanced.

10.2.3 Conversation

A job interview is a conversation between a job aspirant and the member/s of a selection committee or employer/s or their representatives. It is basically a question-answer session involving specific questions and appropriate answers. As it includes both listening and speaking, the candidate has to listen actively during a job interview and speak clearly and precisely using simple words, short sentences, correct articulation, and appropriate pronunciation. It also requires certain flexibility in the usage of tenses.

10.2.4 Two-Way Interaction

The job interview is a two-way interaction that may take place between the candidate and one interviewer (one-to-one interviews) or the candidate and more than one interviewer (panel interviews). In order to ensure uniformity, one-to-one interviews are generally structured and each candidate may be asked exactly the same kind of questions in the same style. Some one-to-one interviews may involve unstructured questions too. Panel interviews are more common. They may include two to twenty people but most selection committees normally consist of three to six people. Each member of the committee may focus on a particular aspect of evaluation to ensure effective decision making.

Panel interviews may include two to twenty people but most selection committees normally consist of three to six people.

10.2.5 Informality

Although a job interview is a planned conversation, it is less formal than many public speech situations. The success of any job interview depends on its informal and friendly atmosphere wherein the candidates get opportunities to reveal their potentiality and feel free to present their best. Not many people enjoy facing a job interview. So, an interview will not be able to achieve its goals if the tension is not reduced by developing a friendly relation between the candidate and the interviewer/s.

Although a job interview is a planned conversation, it is less formal than many public speech situations.

10.3 INTERVIEW PREPARATION TECHNIQUES

Preparing well is the key to success during an interview.

When a candidate has applied for a job and is getting ready for that important moment in his/her life, the job interview, he needs to prepare for it systematically, even if it is not the first job interview for the person. Preparing well is the key to success during an interview. Facing a job interview—whether a face-to-face personal interview, a telephone interview, or an interview through videoconferencing—is easier when one prepares for it in a systematic way.

A job interview is a formal, structured, and systematic interaction between the candidate and a group of people who want to hire him/her for a particular job position. He/she has to establish a relationship, impress the interviewer/interview panel and convince them that he/she is the best candidate for the job, for all of which he/she will get hardly more than thirty minutes. It sounds an impossible task but it is not if proper preparation is done in a planned and systematic way.

Pre-interview preparation techniques include self-analysis, skills assessment, company analysis, job analysis, subject revision, and developing the interview file.

Planned preparation for the job interview will help the candidate:

- Develop the needed confidence
- Enter the job interview with information and understanding
- Strongly support his/her candidature
- Deal with interview anxiety effectively
- Be sensitive to the needs and expectations of the interviewers
- Know his/her strengths and weaknesses
- Strike up a positive interaction with the interviewers
- Know his/her job and the organisation that he/she wants to join
- Adapt his background, knowledge, and skills to fit the job.

Thus, preparing for the job interview involves:

- Analysing yourself
- Identifying your skills

- Researching the organisation
- Analysing the job position
- Revising your subject knowledge and brushing up your general awareness
- Developing the interview file.

10.3.1 Analyse Yourself

We cannot project ourselves successfully unless we know our strengths and weaknesses properly. It may sound foolish but it is true that most of us really do not know ourselves. That is why a simple question like "Tell us something about yourself" unnerves many candidates during job interviews. Self-analysis is the first step towards effective planning for a job interview. It includes analysing our background, identifying our major accomplishments, achievements, our special interests and hobbies, and analysing our career goals in terms of the contribution we can make to the job we aspire for.

> Self-analysis is the first step towards effective planning for a job interview.

Analyse Your Background

We should begin self-analysis with a critical examination of our educational and professional background. Do we have the right background for the job? This is the first question that we should ask ourselves. Some of the questions that ask you to talk about your background include "Tell us something about yourself", "How would you describe yourself?", "If you had to live your life again, what would you change?", "Describe yourself in a few sentences", "Tell us something about your education and background", and so on. The purpose of these questions is to identify the match between the candidate's background and the requirements of the job.

The candidate may have impressive qualifications and experiences but the interviewers would be more interested in knowing whether he/she has the right background for the job in question. If a person has Bachelor of Technology degree in Electronics and he wants to join the sales and marketing division of an electronics company, he must be prepared to answer the question "What makes you fit for a sales position?" If a candidate has the right background, he/she should highlight this during the interview. He/she should be able to talk about his/her background briefly. In fact, he/she must always be ready with a two-minute bio, presenting his/her background in a positive manner.

Identify Your Accomplishments

An accomplishment can be defined as the completion of a particular task with the help of one's skills. It may be a successfully organised college trip or cultural programme, the completion of an academic project, or solving a difficult problem or situation. Each of these can be an accomplishment that the candidate may be proud of. You should identify and make a list of such accomplishments. You may start from your school life. Anything you did during your school life that showed a positive dimension of your personality could be the first entry in the list. Next, you may explore your college life to identify instances that you did well in despite constraints and problems. If you have professional experience, you should identify problem situations that you could handle effectively.

> An accomplishment can be defined as the completion of a particular task with the help of one's skills.

The list need not be very long. Four to eight accomplishments are more than sufficient to make one confident while answering questions related to this aspect of one's personality. Some questions that might ask you to reflect on your accomplishments include:

- What are your accomplishments?
- Describe a situation in which you were successful.
- Have you ever solved a problem?
- What makes you stand out from the rest of the applicants?
- Tell us about a problem you have faced and solved.

Identify Your Achievements

An achievement is different from an accomplishment. While accomplishments reflect special skills, achievements show our academic and professional success and distinguish a successful person from the non-achievers. They convince the employer that the candidate is an achiever and therefore worth hiring. You should make a list of scholarships, fellowships, awards, prizes, distinctions, commendations, certificates, or anything that shows achievement or recognition. The interviewers may ask you straight questions like "What are your achievements?", or "Have you ever done anything that has given you a sense of achievement?", "Do you consider yourself an achiever?", and so on.

> Accomplishments reflect special skills, achievements show our academic and professional success and distinguish a successful person from the non-achievers.

Identify Your Special Interests and Hobbies

The third aspect of self-analysis is identifying special interests and hobbies. A list of such activities should be made. As your *curriculum vitae* may also include your hobbies, interests, and activities, you should be ready to justify them during an interview. You should identify and list your extra-curricular, co-curricular, and professional activities as well as your hobbies and interests. As most organisations prefer dynamic and active employees, special interests and activities must show the candidate as a dynamic and energetic person who can accept all challenges.

> As most organisations prefer dynamic and active employees, special interests and activities must show the candidate as a dynamic and energetic person who can accept all challenges.

Analyse Your Career Goals

> It is important that you analyse your career goals in terms of the job position you have applied for.

You should analyse your career goals—what you want to do in life, your career objectives, your long-term goals in life, where you see yourself in five/ten years, your short-term career objectives. These are some aspects regarding which questions are frequently asked in job interviews. You should have a clarity about your objectives. If you are facing a job interview for the position of an executive in a multinational company and you mention that your career goal is to become a teacher, you will weaken your case. So, it is important that you analyse your career goals in terms of the job position you have applied for.

10.3.2 Analyse Your Skills

Every job has a set of functions and requires certain skills to perform it. The main purpose of a job interview is to find out whether the candidate possesses the skills and knowledge required to carry out the functions associated with the job. Thus, analysing skills is an integral part of preparation for an interview. You should assess the skills that you possess and try to find out techniques for adapting these skills to fit the job desired. Most employers would like to see the match between the candidate's skills and the requirements for the job and may ask you the following questions:

> Skills assessment is the process of analysing your skills in terms of the skills required for the position you are seeking.

- How will you rate yourself for this position on a scale of one to ten?
- Why should we hire you?
- What makes you suitable for this position?
- What are your strengths?
- What is your greatest strength?

A candidate may have impressive skills and abilities but the employers would be more interested in knowing whether he/she has the right skills and abilities. Relating skills to the needs of the organisation and requirements of the job is essential.

There are two types of skills that might be assessed during an interview, i.e., learned skills and intuitive skills. Learned skills are the ones that might have been taught or have been learned while intuitive skills are a part of one's personality. For example, we learn oral communication skills while we do not need to learn to be honest because honesty is innate. Study the following list of learned and intuitive skills given in Table 10.1.

> Learned skills are the ones that might have been taught or have been learned while intuitive skills are a part of one's personality.

TABLE 10.1 List of Learned and Intuitive Skills

Learned Skills	*Intuitive Skills*
• Computer programming	• Adaptability
• Data processing	• Analysis
• Marketing	• Assertiveness
• Driving	• Boldness
• Managing a product line	• Broad-mindedness
• Administration	• Courage
• Consulting	• Creativity
• Foreign languages	• Decision making
• Business writing	• Diplomacy
• Interpersonal skills	• Discretion
• Negotiation skills	• Efficiency
• Public relations	• Foresight
• Professional speaking	• Imagination
• Listening	• Initiative

(*Contd.*)

• Management • Planning • Coordinating • Public speaking • Selling • Supervising • Time management • Teaching • Training	• Leadership • Motivating • Objectivity • Patience • Perseverance • Resourcefulness • Sincerity • Stamina • Team building

In order to analyse your skills, a systematic approach should be adopted. First, a list of all skills should be made. Then, list the skills required for the job. Finally examine how many of your skills match with the job requirements. During the interview, you may use appropriate adjectives to describe your special skills, abilities, and aptitudes that are of significance and of direct relevance to the job applied for. In order to sell yourself at a right price tag, you should use precise words to make the best impression possible. These are examples of a few such adjectives:

> active, competent, conscientious, creative, dependable, determined, diplomatic, discreet, efficient, energetic, enterprising, enthusiastic, experienced, fair, firm, innovative, logical, mature, methodical, motivated, objective, pleasant, positive, practical, reliable, resourceful, self disciplined, sensitive, sincere, successful, tactful, trustworthy.

10.3.3 Research the Organisation

You must thoroughly research the organisation you want to join before the interview. Interviewers may ask a few questions to test your knowledge about the organisation and your interest in them. Some of these questions may include "Why do you want to join us?", "What do you know about our company?", "What made you interested in our organisation?", "How do you rate our company?", "Tell us why you are interested in our company?", "Our company was recently in the news. Can you tell why?," and so on. Unless you research the company you will not be able to answer any of these questions.

> Researching an organisation involves gathering basic information about the nature, operations, status, structure, growth rate, and activities of the organisation.

The candidate should have some basic information about the organisation, which may include:

- Major areas of operation
- Products/services of the organisation
- Focus of the activities of the organisation
- Growth rate
- Hierarchical structure of the organisation
- Work culture
- The financial standing and turnover of the organisation
- Corporate culture
- Recent developments in the organisation

- New products, services, and projects
- Factors making the organisation successful

There are many ways to research the organisation. The first and the most obvious is visiting the website of the organisation. Nowadays every organisation has its website with key information about it. You should note down important points that might help you during the interview. You may refer to company directories, quarterly publications, magazines, company reports, and relevant business and professional publications. You may also read the company's brochures and recent annual report. Finally, you may talk to concerned people to get first hand information about the organisation.

10.3.4 Analyse the Job Applied

You should know what the job is all about. You cannot adapt your skills to fit the job desired unless you know about the job. Moreover, without sufficient knowledge about the job position you may not be able to answer questions like "Why are you interested in this job?", "What makes you fit for this position?", "What do you know about this position?", "What makes you think you are fit for this job?", "How will you rate yourself for this position?". With a little preparation, you can answer these questions confidently.

> Job analysis will provide you broad information about the position.

You should have broad information about the position so that you can respond to the questions testing your suitability for the job. You should try to answer the following questions before you actually face the interview:

- What does this job involve?
- What are the responsibilities associated with this job?
- What are the special duties?
- How is this position different from similar positions at other organisations?
- What are the challenges of this position?
- What are the skills and abilities needed for this job?
- What is the level of professional knowledge needed?
- What are the areas of expertise/areas of specialisation or micro-specialisation related to the job?
- What are the prospects?
- What are the chances of career enhancement?

In order to research the job, you may use several available resources such as the internet, the library, the organisation's public relations office, people working in the organisation, particularly alumni of your institution.

10.3.5 Revise Your Subject Knowledge

A job interview is to assess the candidates' level of knowledge and technical expertise as it relates to the job at hand. Although a good grade is an indicator of one's command over the subject, many organisations focus on evaluating the subject competence of candidates. They may conduct special technical interviews where a group of subject experts might ask probing questions to judge the depth and scope of the candidates' subject knowledge. It is, therefore, advisable to revise one's subject knowledge before the interview. Subject basics must be clear because the experts might test your grasp

> Although a good grade is an indicator of one's command over the subject, many organisations focus on evaluating the subject competence of candidates.

of the subject. They may ask you a few exploring questions to find out your level of understanding. It is important to be thoroughly prepared and if there is time, revise the last course and read up on the latest developments in the subject. Discussing relevant topics with friends, classmates, or colleagues would also be helpful.

Revise your subject for clarity and confidence.

You should also brush up your general awareness. The interviewers may test your knowledge on a wide range of topics related to burning social, political, economic, scientific, and environmental issues, national and international affairs, controversial topics, key newsmakers, and much more. As an educated person, you are expected to be aware of such matters. Therefore, reading newspapers, watching news on television, and visiting informative websites to brush up your knowledge about recent developments in different areas are essential.

10.3.6 Develop the Interview File

Preparing for an interview demands a professional approach. Therefore, you should develop an interview file that may contain the following papers and documents:

1. Interview letter
2. Original degrees, certificates, and transcripts
3. Experience certificates
4. References and testimonials
5. Certificates of merit
6. Copies of your rèsumè
7. Your visiting cards
8. Other relevant papers that might be needed during the interview.

An index of all the papers and documents in the file makes for easy reference and location. You should also keep photocopies of essential papers like degrees and experience certificates, as you might be asked to submit these. Keeping everything ready in order will help in projecting yourself as an organised and systematic person.

You should also keep photocopies of essential papers like degrees and experience certificates, as you might be asked to submit these.

Progress Check 2

1. Study the following table and match different pre-interview preparation steps (left column) with appropriate stages of interview preparation (right column):

Pre-interview preparation steps	Stages of interview preparation
1. Identify your achievements.	A. Self-analysis
2. Assess the skills you possess.	B. Skills analysis
3. Keep your basics clear.	C. Company analysis
4. Keep photocopies of essential papers.	D. Job analysis
5. Relate your skills to the needs of the job.	E. Revision
6. Visit the website of the organisation you want to join.	F. Developing the interview file
7. File the reference letter.	
8. Identify your accomplishments.	

9. List the skills necessary for the job.
10. Keep your credentials ready.
11. Identify your special interests and hobbies.
12. Find out responsibilities associated with the job.
13. Analyse your career goals.
14. Brush up your general awareness.
15. Find out the financial standing and turnover of the company.
16. Revise your subject knowledge.
17. Keep your original degrees, certificates, and transcripts ready.
18. Make an index of all the papers and documents for easy reference and location.
19. Analyse your background.
20. Find out about the products/services of the organisation.

10.4 INTERVIEW QUESTIONS

As mentioned before, the suitability of a candidate for a particular position is evaluated during a job interview through an oral question-answer session. Thus, the interview contains specific questions and appropriate answers. The candidate should understand the nature of different types of interview questions, analyse expected questions in order to devise answering strategies, and practise these answers. Some tips on job interview questions and answers are discussed below.

10.4.1 Types of Interview Questions

You should be familiar with the nature and type of questions being asked during job interviews so that you are ready to answer them confidently. Usually, there are seven different types of questions that are asked to elicit certain responses from candidates. They include open, closed, probing, reflective, loaded, hypothetical, and leading questions.

Open Questions

An open question asks the candidates to "talk about" something. Its main purpose is to encourage the candidates to talk broadly about a topic or subject. It broadens the scope of the response by forcing the candidates to engage in deeper thinking. Following are some of the examples of open questions:

> An open question asks the candidates to "talk about" something.

- Tell us something about yourself.
- Talk about your interests and activities.
- Describe the most difficult situation that you recently faced.
- What are the advantages of a mixed economy?
- What do you think about the impact of multinational companies on the Indian economy?

Closed Questions

Unlike open questions, closed questions limit the scope of the response by asking the candidates to provide specific information or facts. It permits the candidate no freedom of selection as they are required to give very specific answers. Following are some such examples:

- When did you complete your graduation?
- What was your major subject in the college?
- Where did you receive your first professional training?
- Do you know data processing?

Unlike open questions, closed questions limit the scope of the response by asking the candidates to provide specific information or facts.

Probing Questions

The main purpose of a probing question is to probe more deeply or ask for an explanation or clarification of a statement just made.

The main purpose of a probing question is to probe more deeply or ask for an explanation or clarification of a statement just made. Probing questions encourage the candidate to talk in greater depth about a topic or subject. For example, after the response, "I believe that students should be allowed in academic decision making.", the interviewer might ask the probing question, "Do you think that this should include all academic decisions?".

Reflective Questions

Reflective questions are asked to confirm the statements given by the candidate. The purpose is to check that the interviewer understands what the candidate has said. Following are some examples of reflective questions:

- That means you want the public sector companies to be totally privatised?
- Am I right in thinking that you are against economic liberalisation in India?
- Does that mean that you favour a total ban on any type of violence in movies?

Reflective questions are asked to confirm the statements given by the candidate.

Loaded Questions

Loaded questions assess the candidate's response to a sensitive issue, subject or point. The main purpose of loaded questions is to judge the candidate's ability to handle difficult and sensitive situations. There may not be any right or wrong answer to a loaded question, rather, it would be a reasonable or unreasonable response. The following are some examples:

- You are too short. Don't you think this is going to be a handicap for you?
- Your GPA in the first semester of your B.Tech is too low. How do you justify that?
- Do you think that a Ram Temple should be constructed at the sight of Babri Masjid?

The main purpose of loaded questions is to judge the candidate's ability to handle difficult and sensitive situations.

Hypothetical Questions

A hypothetical question may involve a hypothetical situation. It may be asked to test the possible reactions of the candidate to a certain situation. The candidate may be asked the question, 'What would you do if…?', or the candidate may be given a situation and asked how he/she will deal with it. Some examples are given here:

> A hypothetical question may be asked to test the possible reactions of the candidate to a certain situation.

- What would you do if you face a group of angry employees who want to harm company vehicles because one of the workers has been hurt by a company lorry?
- One of your staff has been involved in activities detrimental to your organisation. He has been doing this for money that he needs for the treatment of his ailing mother. What would you do?

Leading Questions

> A leading question is asked to obtain a desired response.

A leading question is asked to obtain a desired response. It leads the candidate to a particular answer. Such questions generally suggest a point of view on the part of the interviewer and call for agreement with a 'yes' answer. Given below are some examples:

- Don't you agree that our company is a market leader in electronics products?
- Don't you think that MNCs have boosted the Indian economy?
- Don't you agree that our economy needs more privatisation?

Progress Check 3

1. Study the following table and match different interview questions (left column) with appropriate type of question (right column):

	Interview questions	Type of question
1.	Don't you think that the Indian economy is too closed?	A. Open
2.	What would you do if your company is facing financial losses due to the wrong policies of the Marketing Director who happens to be your immediate supervisor?	B. Closed C. Probing D. Reflective
3.	Do you have any marketing experience?	E. Loaded
4.	Tell us something about the effect of globalisation on India.	F. Hypothetical
5.	Why did you leave your first job?	G. Leading
6.	When did you work for TCS?	
7.	Am I right in thinking that you support the idea of uniform civil code for India?	
8.	Do your poor grades reflect your casual attitude to studies?	
9.	Tell us something about your achievements.	
10.	Do you think that religion and politics should not be mixed?	

10.4.2 Answering Strategies

Keys to Answering Questions

> How a question is answered is sometimes more important than the answer itself.

How a question is answered is sometimes more important than the answer itself. The way a question is answered reflects a person's communicative ability. The following suggestions will help in improving the quality of answers:

Attentiveness

> The candidate should listen to the interviewer attentively in order to understand the question and then respond to it.

When a person attends a job interview, he/she cannot answer the interview's questions correctly unless he/she is listening properly. Many candidates start answering before they have heard the complete question. This is wrong. The candidate should listen to the interviewer attentively in order to understand the question and then respond to it. Moreover, the interviewer should not be interrupted while he or she is speaking. This constitutes rude behaviour and is against the norms of any formal interaction.

Accuracy

> The candidate should not try to bluff the interviewer; it is better to accept that he/she does not know an answer rather than give an incorrect answer.

The candidate should give particular attention to dates, timelines, persons, places, and other details. If he/she cannot remember a date or time, it should not be mentioned. Giving an incorrect or incomplete answer will reduce the chances of success. The candidate should not try to bluff the interviewer; it is better to accept that he/she does not know an answer rather than give an incorrect answer. No one is expected to know everything and there is nothing wrong in accepting one's lack of knowledge.

Brevity

> A long answer does not necessarily mean a better answer.

The candidate should be brief and to the point particularly in open questions, where he/she has the scope to speak as much as he/she can. He/she should listen to the question carefully and answer only what is asked, not taking more than one minute to answer any question, irrespective of its nature and complexity. A long answer does not necessarily mean a better answer; it is usually otherwise.

Focus

> Trying to impress interviewers by giving information that is not asked for should be avoided.

The candidate should be focused and specific. Very often, candidates deviate from the question asked and do not answer specifically. Trying to impress interviewers by giving information that is not asked for should be avoided. The more specific the answer, the more convinced the interviewers are likely to be of a candidate's suitability for the position. Concrete and specific words and phrases should be used, and obscure, abstract, and vague words that may confuse the interviewers should be avoided.

> Clarity of expression generally reflects clarity of thought and professionalism.

Clarity

Candidates should answer directly and clearly. The candidate should not give the interviewers a chance to ask for an answer to be repeated or classified. Clarity of expression generally reflects clarity of thought and professionalism.

Positive Attitude

Interviewers may ask negative or sensitive questions to explore the negatives in the candidate's personality.

The candidates' answers should reflect a positive attitude. Interviewers may ask negative or sensitive questions to explore the negatives in the candidate's personality. Therefore, it is important to remain positive and answer even negative questions positively.

Logical Thinking

Logical arguments and illustrations should be used when answering questions that demand careful thinking.

The ability to think logically is always an asset during an interview. Answers should always be rational and logical because illogical answers reflect a disorganised personality. Logical arguments and illustrations should be used when answering questions that demand careful thinking (i.e., probing and hypothetical questions).

Frequently Asked Interview Questions

Candidates should analyse commonly asked interview questions so that an answering strategy may be devised in advance.

Several popular questions repeatedly appear in job interviews. Twenty basic interview questions with their possible answers are given here. Practising replies to these questions and rehearsing mock interviews to develop confidence will help in improving job interviewing skills.

Please note that the answers given here are only indicative and may need some tweaking depending on the type of job or company or industry one is applying for.

1. **Tell us something about yourself.**

   This may be the first question of an interview. Without focusing on any specific area, a brief description highlighting the relevance of one's background, education, skills, and experience may be given.

   Reply

   - I am a B.Tech. in Chemical Engineering from the Indian Institute of Technology, New Delhi. For the last six years I have been working as a sales and application engineer at the Filtration Division of TAPCOM Limited, Singapore. I have experience in selling filtration and fluid purification products and equipment, covering applications such as hydraulic fluids and process fluids. I enjoy travelling and visiting new places. I am resourceful, self-disciplined, and energetic. Sometimes, the interviewer may ask the candidate not to cover the aspects that are covered in the resume. In such a case, one can focus on hobbies, achievements, skills, etc.

2. **What are your career objectives?/ What type of position are you looking for?/ What do you want to do?/ What are your short-term and long-term career goals?**

   All these questions are similar as the interviewers would like to know whether working in their company falls within the candidate's objectives. A positive answer to this question would include a focused statement expressing the candidate's career goals in relation to the targeted position and conveying the candidate's motivation and interest in the job.

Reply

- I want to obtain a challenging position in a large software consulting organisation, where I should be able to use my specialised qualification, understanding and experience in business process modelling and organisational change management to suit customer needs.

3. **Tell us something about your interests and activities.**

   This is a direct question. The interviewers want to know if the candidate's interests and activities match the key components of the job. The candidate should mention his/her activities, projecting himself/herself as a dynamic and energetic person who accepts challenges.

   Reply

   - I am an extrovert and love to interact with all kinds of people. I am a member of the Institution of Engineers, New Delhi and the International Society of Mechanical Engineers, Mumbai. I am also the Secretary of the Delhi Chapter of the Society for Promotion of Science. I enjoy playing badminton and lawn tennis in my free time. I also like classical music and ghazals.

4. **Why should we hire you?/ What makes you fit for this position?**

   The interviewers want to know the candidate's interpretation of the job and his/her assessment of his/her suitability for the position. The candidate should be able to establish how well his/her qualification, knowledge, and skills match the needs of their organisation and job requirements.

   Reply

   - As you are looking for someone with experience in automobile sales, with a technical background, my specialised qualification and extensive experience in automobile sales in an expanding company makes me the best candidate for the job. My twelve years as sales manager in Topsel Toyota, Kolkata have provided me with sufficient experience in motivating and leading a dynamic sales team, planning and implementing sales promotion activities, and setting and achieving targets. With the qualifications and skills you are seeking, I am sure I would be able to get desired results for your company.

5. **Why do you want to join our company?/ What makes you interested in our organisation?/ Why are you interested in our company?**

   Interviewers would like to test the candidate's knowledge about their organisation and his/her interest and motivation to work with them. This question should be answered in the light of the company analysis that the candidate has done, projecting the strengths of the company.

   Reply

   - The professional excellence maintained and pursued by your company has impressed me. Your company's experience and innovation, combined with the user-friendliness, reliability, and quality of its products and solutions have made it a world leader in mobile communications. Working with such a growing organisation has been one of my career objectives since the very beginning.

6. **What according to you would be an ideal company to join?**

   This question is similar to question 5. The interviewers want to know the candidate's opinion of their company. The candidate should answer this question by conveying his/her interest and motivation to work with the organisation, which he/she feels is the ideal one for him/her.

Reply

- I think that the best companies create jobs and roles where employees feel they have some control over what they do, where professional relationships are valued, and where more than lip service is paid to the work-life balance. I believe your company is one of them and I would like to be a part of such a company.

7. **Tell us something about your work experience.**

This is a straight question asking the candidate to describe his experiences. The answer should be brief and specific, describing the candidate's experiences and mentioning how they improved his/her skills.

Reply

- During the past six years, I have gained valuable marketing experience as Manager (Sales and Marketing) at Dharampal Premchand Limited, Noida. At DPL, I was responsible for creating and building up a strong dealer/distribution network within the North-eastern Region and Eastern states of India, as well as Institutional sales on all-India basis. Before joining DPL, I worked in National Trade Corporation, New Delhi as a sales trainee. With excellent communication and presentation skills and the ability to understand and articulate key opportunities for maximising profitability, I have been able to prove myself as an outstanding sales professional.

8. **Tell us something about your academic achievements.**

This is a straight question asking the candidate to list his/her academic achievements. The candidate should give a direct answer mentioning his/her achievements and enlisting his/her skills and personal qualities.

Reply

- My academic record reflects my sincerity, strong determination, and ability to achieve excellence. In 2004, I graduated as a Bachelor of Technology in Electronics from IIT, Bombay, with an overall grade point average of 4.46. I won Best Student Award in 3rd year for getting a high GPA of 4.8. I also received the IIT Merit scholarship during 2002-2003 for my academic performance. As a dynamic, extroverted student, I took active interest and participation in extra-curricular as well as co-curricular activities in the college. I won first position in the Inter-University Debate Competition in March 2003, and second position in the IIT Elocution Competition, 2004. As a member of National Cadet Corps, I won the best IITB cadet award in 2002.

9. **Where do you see yourself in five years?**

Interviewers would like to know if the candidate's ambitions and career goals are realistic. The candidate should answer this question in the light of his/her self-analysis, explicitly express his/her intention to stay with the organisation for a long period.

Reply

- I would be working as a senior executive in your company.

10. **Why are you interested in this job?/ What interests you most about this position?**

Interviewers would like to assess the candidate's interest and motivation to join the position and see if his/her interest areas match the job. This question should be answered in the light of the job analysis, highlighting his/her interest in the job as well as his/her suitability for it.

Reply

- As a high calibre IT professional, I have been looking for an opening like this one, which provides a fast moving, dynamic work environment, and accelerated and challenging growth opportunities. I am sure in this position I will have opportunities to utilise my exposure and experience in software and functional and system level testing policies and procedures.

11. Can you tell us about your responsibilities at your present job?/ What are you doing right now?/ What are your duties at your present position?

This is a straight question asking the candidate to list his responsibilities at his/her present job. Be specific and tell what you do and how you do it.

Reply

- As a product specialist at Pfizer Limited, I develop market strategies and programmes to address key issues; analyse the market competition; and conduct market research to identify opportunities, threats, and key issues. Moreover, I develop marketing plans for new products, plan line extensions, and execute the launch.

12. What are your strengths?

Interviewers would like to know if the candidate's strengths match the needs of the job. This question should be answered in the light of the candidate's self-analysis highlighting his/her strong points as well as his/her suitability for the job.

Reply

- I have strong communication and interpersonal skills and the ability to get along with others. I have been able to achieve company targets and live up to commitments with a sense of urgency. Last year my company wanted me to convince the government authorities in the industry department to approve starting a new manufacturing unit in Gurgaon and I was successful in getting the project approved.

13. Tell us about a problem you have faced and the strategy you used to handle it?

Interviewers want to know how the candidate handles a problem. In order to illustrate one's problem solving skills, brief description of a problem situation and the strategy to solve it should be outlined.

Reply

- Last month, the work supervisors at our factory suddenly stopped working as the personnel manager misbehaved with one of them. They were demanding the removal of the personnel manager, who was very senior as well as very efficient. The General Manager was desperate and called me into get them back on work. I met the angry supervisors and convinced them that the personnel manager is very senior and the company needs his services, but that he would personally apologise to them for his behaviour. Then, I convinced the erring manager to apologise to the supervisors. Finally, I invited both the angry supervisors and the personnel manager to a meeting where we solved the problem together.

14. What is your greatest weakness?

Interviewers want to know how the candidate would handle a question like this. It is best to mention a mild weakness or a weakness that is actually a strength and also tell them how one attempts to improve the weakness.

Reply

- I aim at and call for nothing short of perfection, and become nervous when I am not able to do something up to my satisfaction. However, I know that this may sometimes delay a work and try to compensate with very hard work.

15. **How will you rate yourself on a scale from one to ten?**

Interviewers want to check the candidate's level of confidence. An indirect answer that shows the candidate's confidence and belief in himself would be the best approach.

Reply

- I always strive to be the best in whatever I do. I believe in being the best.

16. **Are you a leader or a follower?**

Interviewers want to know how the candidate handles a question like this. The best approach is to take a middle path, mentioning how one is capable of taking on both roles.

Reply

- I am both a leader and a follower. I have successfully completed several projects as a leader but at the same time I have worked in cross-functional teams as a member and have done well.

17. **How long do you want to stay with us?/ How long do you plan to work for us?**

This question should be answered directly by conveying the candidate's interest and motivation to work with the organisation for a long period.

Reply

- I would like to be a part of your organisation for a long period.

18. **Are you interested in a full-time or part-time position?**

Interviewers would like to check the candidate's willingness to work. The candidate should leave open as many possibilities as possible and express his/her willingness to accept any responsibility.

Reply

- Although I would prefer a full-time position, I can also consider a part-time position.

19. **Will you accept a lower position for the time being?**

Unless one is very desperate to join somewhere, this question should be answered with a polite refusal.

Reply

- Although I want to be part of your company, I am afraid I would not be able to accept a lower position.

20. **When can you join us?/ When can you begin?/ How long will you take to join us?**

Interviewers would like to check the candidate's willingness to work. The candidate should give a very positive response to this query.

Reply

- As soon as I am released from my present job.

10.4.3 Interview Practice

After analysing expected questions and planning how to answer them, the candidate is ready to face the interview. He/she should then practise the probable answers in order to develop the required confidence as well as to experience the actual interview. The main purpose of the practice is to help one learn how to answer questions with confidence in a natural and spontaneous way. The candidate should mimic the real interview and try to be his/her natural self while practising. Practice should be continued until one is sure of confidently answering all the questions. The following are some suggestions for practising.

> The main purpose of an interview practice is to help one learn how to answer questions with confidence in a natural and spontaneous way.

Mock Interviews

Mock interviews should be conducted with the help of friends, classmates, colleagues, or relatives. Two or three people may form a mock interview panel that poses the questions. The candidate can ask them for their feedback regarding the answers and comments on his/her self-confidence, accuracy, communicative effectiveness, assertiveness, and other personality traits. Although they may not give him/her very perfect comments, their views will help in making appropriate changes in the answers or in the ways of answering them.

Audio/video Practice

The candidate may record his/her answers to expected interview questions on an audio/video recorder and listen to them after sometime. He/she can judge the quality of answers in the light of prefixed parameters. He/she may also ask others to listen to the answers and suggest improvements. This will help the candidate in assessing his/her preparation and make appropriate modifications in his/her answers.

Rehearse Open Questions

The candidate should rehearse answers to open questions such as "Tell us something about yourself." before a group of friends, classmates, colleagues, or roommates. They should be invited to comment on his/her answers, gestures, body movements, and mannerisms, and point out weaknesses. Analysing their reactions, comments, and suggestions will help the candidate to improve the quality of his/her answers and his/her body language.

Progress Check 4

1. **Read the following answers to a few interview questions. Rewrite the answers, making them more appropriate by changing the language, style, tone, and attitude of the answer:**

   (a) **Question:** How are you?
   Answer: So so.

   (b) **Question:** Tell us something about yourself.
   Answer: I am a highly qualified engineer who was born and raised in the capital of the country. I was educated at premier institutions of the country. I am an extrovert and because of this, I am very popular among my friends. I believe in honesty and hard work. I am working as an assistant manager in Mumbai for Infosys. In fact, I have been working here since 1998. My first degree was B.Sc. in Physics, which I received in 1994. For this, I attended the University of Delhi. I also

completed B.Tech in Electronics from IIT, Kanpur in the year 1998. I have many hobbies like playing tennis, swimming etc.

(c) **Question:** What type of position are you looking for?
Answer: Well, I want the post of a senior product architect in a big software company because I have extensive experience in the areas of product and system architecture with expertise in enterprise applications.

(d) **Question:** Could you please tell us about your responsibilities at your last job?
Answer: My last job was with Hyquip Projects Private Limited, Hyderabad, as Manager (Sales and Marketing). It was a very responsible position that kept me very busy. In fact, I had to perform several extra responsibilities because of my lazy colleagues. My main duties included selling of flat steel products mainly CR/GP/GC products, and creating and building up a strong dealer/distribution network within the North-eastern Region and Eastern states of India. I was also responsible for institutional sales on an all-India basis.

(e) **Question:** What is your career goal?
Answer: It is difficult to say because I have several career objectives. Anyway, I want to work in a big IT company in a big post, which should give me respect, money, and recognition. In fact, I deserve them because I have lot of experience with VB, ASP, NET, XML and SQL Server.

(f) **Question:** What is your greatest strength?
Answer: Well, I have many strengths and to talk about one of them is a difficult task but I will try to answer this question. I think my greatest strength is that I can work under pressure. I do not care about circumstances and I do not believe in making excuses. I believe in completing my projects on time. I can give you one example. Last month the Director (Sales) of my company asked me to prepare the Annual Sales Report of our division of the company. They had to submit the report to the headquarters within three days. I did the job. In fact, my boss knew that only I could do this job.

(g) **Question:** Why do want to work in JBM?
Answer: It is a good question which I would like to answer. As you know that your company JBM is very big and has very fast growth. It is not like the company in which I am working. You see there is no growth in my company. But it is different in JBM, where the addition of new facilities and continuous expansion is a regular phenomenon. You can see that I am a seasoned professional with a proven track record in quality assurance systems. I need a better company than the one in which I am working, and JBM is a good option. It will give me a long-term career with immense opportunities to grow.

(h) **Question:** When can you join us?
Answer: It is difficult to tell now. I will inform you after I receive the offer from you.

10.5 IMPORTANT ASPECTS FOR A JOB INTERVIEW

10.5.1 Projecting a Positive Image

> Three factors that play an important role in positive projection during job interviews are the way the candidate looks, speaks, and behaves.

When a person has prepared for the job interview well, analysed expected questions, and devised answering strategies, he/she may feel confident to face the interview. However, it is not sufficient to merely answer questions correctly during an interview. The success of a job interview largely depends on a person's ability to project a positive professional image before the interviewers. Although one cannot develop such an image overnight as it takes time to groom one's personality, one can project success during the interview by following some basic tips.

A job interview provides the meeting place where the interviewers personally interact with the candidate to explore the relevance of his/her knowledge and experience by posing questions directly to him/her. Apart from assessing the candidate's knowledge and experience, the interviewers also examine his/her appearance, mannerisms, non-verbal communication skills, and personal traits. In order to ensure an impressive performance in a job interview, one has to take care of each of these factors. These are discussed below in detail.

> The success of a job interview largely depends on a person's ability to project a positive professional image before the interviewers.

Look Your Best

As visual impact plays an important role during a face-to-face interview, the candidate should strive hard to look his/her best by giving his/her outward appearance the needed polish and grooming. An impressive personality is always a positive factor. Some candidates ignore this aspect during interview and they are rejected just because they give a poor visual impact. In order to convey the image of a dynamic, energetic and well-groomed professional, the following points should be borne in mind.

> An impressive personality is always a positive factor.

Dress Formally

The interviewee should wear a formal dress and try to look presentable. Some organisations follow strict dress norms. Therefore, it may be a good idea to find out the dress norm of the organisation and appear at the interview dressed to conform to that norm. Alternatively, the candidate should choose a dress that fits his/her body and personality and gives him/her a polished look. It should be simple, sober, dignified, and conventional, and shoes should be well-polished.

Prepare Your Person

Although a job interview is not a fashion show or a date with the boy or girl one wants to marry, one should thoroughly prepare oneself because it is an important meeting. On the day of the interview, the interviewee should appear well groomed and smartly turned out.

Relax

The candidate should not overstress himself/herself on the interview day. He/she should be relaxed, eat a good but light breakfast or lunch, watch television, and participate in light conversations with family members. He/she should not read serious books or exercise rigorously. It is important that he/she keeps himself/herself mentally free so that he/she is able to appear fresh.

Speak Carefully

The candidate's style of speaking is very important because the way he/she speaks forms his/her image during a personal interview. Expert interviewers can read a person's personality by analysing his/her style of speaking.

> Expert interviewers can read a person's personality by analysing his/ her style of speaking.

Speak Clearly

The interviewee should speak clearly and effectively. He/she should use effective speaking techniques, be articulate and speak distinctly, focusing attention on his/her message. Care should be taken to regulate voice quality, accent, and intonation.

Speak Confidently

The interviewee should not be shaky and confused while he/she speaks and should instead speak confidently and with a smile.

Speak Slowly with Appropriate Pauses

Interviewees should not speak in a hurry. Inexperienced speakers may often try to control their nervousness by speaking too fast. This should be avoided as speaking too quickly exposes one's nervousness and the interviewers will not be able to follow properly what is being said. Effort should be made to speak slowly and take appropriate pauses.

10.5.2 Good Manners and Positive Behaviour

A major part of projecting oneself as a well-behaved dynamic professional is one's conduct during the interview. It is important that one takes care of one's mannerisms and behaviour patterns during the interview. The conduct of most candidates is not positive during an interview. Some interviewers might use a friendly tone and try to create an informal atmosphere to make the interviewee comfortable but the candidate should always remember that a job interview is a formal situation and he/she cannot behave the way he/she behaves when he/she is with friends. The interviewee must behave formally and try to impress the interviewers with good manners and a positive behaviour pattern.

> Some interviewers might use a friendly tone and try to create an informal atmosphere to make the interviewee comfortable but the candidate should always remember that a job interview is a formal situation.

Be Polite

Being polite, pleasant, and courteous is the key to a successful job interview. The candidate should never be rude and impolite, but should instead be courteous and use polite expressions and phrases. If he/she is dogmatic and unfriendly during interview, interviewers might find it difficult to continue the interview. By being cheerful he/she should put interviewers at ease. The candidate should also avoid making remarks that might show that he/she is a snob and should try honestly to understand the point of view of the interviewers.

> Being polite, pleasant, and courteous is the key to a successful job interview.

Be Flexible

The candidate should express flexibility during the interview and not be rigid on anything. An ideal employee is always flexible. One is likely to work in a team environment and should be a team player who can go along with people. Obstinate people are not successful team players because rigidity goes against team spirit. So, it is important to be flexible in approach, attitude, and style.

> An ideal employee is always flexible.

Be Tactful

It is important to be very tactful during a job interview. It is better to think before speaking than to suffer afterwards. Words and phrases should be chosen carefully, and controversial issues that may lead to unnecessary arguments should be avoided.

Do not Argue

The interviewee should never argue with the interviewers. He/she may disagree with the interviewers but should not press the point too hard. Expressing disagreements and reservations in a negative way that might offend the interviewers should be avoided, instead, he/she should express respect for the views expressed by them.

> The interviewee should never argue with the interviewers.

Be Interested

The candidate should express interest in the process of interviewing because interviewers are likely to prefer a more interested but less qualified candidate to a less interested and more qualified one. The interviewee should be interested in what the interviewer is asking and his/her behaviour and attitude should reflect this interest. The interviewee should maintain eye contact with each interviewer and respond to their questions in a lively manner. Some candidates remain lifeless during an interview. This shows a lack of interest and it may lead to rejection.

> Interviewers will prefer a more interested but less qualified candidate to a less interested and more qualified one.

Control Nervousness

Most people are scared of job interviews and feel nervous before and during the interview. It is quite natural because whenever faced with a difficult situation, the body responds by releasing extra energy to deal with the situation. As a result, the heartbeat quickens, breathing becomes more rapid, and the mouth becomes dry. It is important to control nervousness, be practical, and identify one's shortcomings. Candidates should never entertain negative thoughts such as "I can't face this interview", "I come from poor background", "I am going to be rejected", "I am not ready", and so on. Instead positive self-talk such as, "I am going to make it", "I am well-prepared and confident", "I am going to succeed", and so forth are more useful in creating a feeling of confidence about oneself.

Progress Check 5

1. You cannot project a positive professional image during a job interview by being:

(a) Simple
(b) Pleasant and courteous
(c) Alert and responsive
(d) Tense and nervous
(e) Well-dressed and presentable
(f) Confident
(g) Polite and friendly
(h) Cheerful
(i) Argumentative

(j) Rigid
(k) Tactless
(l) Interested

10.6 ALTERNATIVE INTERVIEW FORMATS

As mentioned above, job interviews have become more complex and sophisticated today. Gone are the days when a job interview was a simple exchange of information during a face-to-face conversation in a conventional office setting. Although face-to-face interviews are still the most common interview format, interviews also take place in non-conventional settings and there are several alternative interview formats, which include interviews through telephone, and videoconferencing.

10.6.1 Telephone Interviews

Telephone interviews have become very common today due to compelling reasons of time and distance. Unlike a face-to-face interview, which generally takes place in an office with the focus on a traditional structure of questions and answers in a conventional setting, a telephone interview takes place in a non-conventional setting. Although the telephone interview has certain inherent weaknesses as an interview format, its popularity is increasing. Moreover, it is less cumbersome for both the interviewers as well as the candidates.

The telephone interview generally has a fixed structure. The number of interviewers may vary from one to eight. The chairperson of the selection committee introduces the members of the committee to the candidate. Then, each expert introduces himself/herself and asks questions. This goes on till each member has talked to the candidate. Each of them may form an opinion about the candidate and then a final decision is made on the basis of consensus.

The following suggestions will help improve telephone interview skills:

- Candidates should plan and prepare for the interview in a manner similar to that for a face-to-face interview. All the relevant interview techniques and strategies discussed earlier can be applied here too. The interviewers may ask the candidate to give a date and time for the interview or may fix it themselves.
- The candidate should ensure that there are no distractions during the telephone interview.
- The names of all the members of the interview panel should be written down at the beginning of the call and they should be referred to by name throughout the interview. It is important for the candidate to know who is speaking in order to establish rapport with them. Each member of the panel should be greeted when he/she asks the first question.
- The interviewee must organise his/her papers and documents and keep them close so that he/she may easily refer to them.
- He/she must also keep a pen and paper to take notes.
- When an interviewer passes on the telephone to other members of the interview board, the candidate must thank him/her.
- As in a face-to-face interview it is best to answer briefly in telephone interviews too.

- The interviewee should speak clearly and distinctly, keeping his/her voice level up to reveal a high energy level.

10.6.2 Interview Through Videoconferencing

Interviews may also be held through videoconferencing. This is very similar to a face-to-face job interview because the interviewers can watch the candidate answering questions and can assess his/her bevaviour and non-verbal gestures. Some organisations might prefer to have a screening interview through videoconferencing. Situational interviews may also be conducted through videoconferencing.

The videoconferencing interview also has a fixed structure. The number of interviewers may vary from one to eight, as in a face-to-face or telephone interview. The chairperson of the selection committee may introduce the members of the committee to the candidate. Then, each expert may talk to the candidate asking him/her a few questions. This may go on till each member has talked to the candidate. As the form and structure of a videoconferencing interview is similar to a traditional face-to-face personal interview, candidates may apply the same techniques and strategies of interviewing here.

Exercise

1. **Describe the significance of job interviews today. Discuss the kinds of questions that may be asked during an interview. Describe in brief the strategies to deal with loaded and open questions.**
2. **Most employers and interviewers look for the following personal qualities and skills. Assuming you have to convince interviewers that you have these skills and traits, provide examples from your experience to prove that you have.**
    (a) Communication skills
    (b) Confidence
    (c) Positive attitude
    (d) Motivation
    (e) Ability to get along with people
    (f) Integrity
    (g) Ability to work under pressure
    (h) Interpersonal skills
    (i) Courage
    (j) Persuasiveness
3. **Write short notes (not more than 50 words) on the following:**
    (a) Pre-interview preparation techniques
    (b) Self-analysis
    (c) Job analysis
    (d) Company analysis
    (e) Interview questions
    (f) Telephone interviews

4. Study the following table and match the different interview questions (left column) with the appropriate type of question (right column):

Interview questions	*Type of question*
1. When did you work at Reliance India?	A. Open
2. What was the nature of your work at TCS?	B. Closed
3. How is Indian Standard Time measured?	C. Probing
4. What do you think about the US war against Iraq?	D. Reflective
5. Do you think that the US war against Iraq is justified?	E. Loaded
6. What would you do if you are not selected by us?	F. Hypothetical
7. Do you have any sales experience?	G. Leading
8. What according to you are the causes of India's poverty?	
9. What is your hobby?	
10. Why did you leave your last job?	
11. Am I right in thinking that you do not support the idea of reservation for women in parliament?	
12. What are the problems of the Indian public sector?	
13. Do you think that politicians encourage corruption at high places?	
14. What would you like to do after retirement?	
15. What is the full form of UNESCO?	

5. Suppose you are facing an interview for the position of an executive trainee in an MNC, and they ask you the following questions. Write your responses to these queries during the interview.

(a) Tell us something about your background and academic credentials.
(b) Why do you want to join our company?
(c) If you have the option to choose between a job in the public sector and the private sector, what would you choose, and why?
(d) Why should we hire you?
(e) What are your strengths for this position?
(f) What do you think about the role of multinational companies in the Indian economy?
(g) What is your greatest weakness?
(h) What do you consider your greatest achievement?
(i) Who is your ideal?
(j) How will you react if we reject you?

Key to Progress Check

Progress Check 1

1. Except 1, 4, 6, and 9, all the statements about job interview are True.

Progress Check 2

1. Identify your achievements. A
2. Assess the skills you possess. B

3. Keep your basics clear. E
4. Keep photocopies of essential papers. F
5. Relate your skills to the needs of the job. B
6. Visit the website of the organisation you want to join. C
7. File the reference letter. F
8. Identify your accomplishments. A
9. List the skills necessary for the job. B
10. Keep your credentials ready. F
11. Identify your special interests and hobbies. A
12. Find out responsibilities associated with the job. D
13. Analyse your career goals. A
14. Brush up your general awareness. E
15. Find out the financial standing and turnover of the company. C
16. Revise your subject knowledge. E
17. Keep your original degrees, certificates, and transcripts ready. F
18. Make an index of all the papers and documents for easy reference and location. F
19. Analyse your background. A
20. Try to know about the products/services of the organisation. C

Progress Check 3

1. Don't you think that the Indian economy is too closed? G
2. What would you do if your company is facing financial losses due to the wrong policies of the Marketing Director who happens to be your immediate supervisor? F
3. Do you have any marketing experience? B
4. Tell us something about the effect of globalisation on India. A
5. Why did you leave your first job? C
6. When did you work for TCS? B
7. Am I right in thinking that you support the idea of uniform civil code for India? D
8. Do your poor grades reflect your casual attitude to studies? E
9. Tell us something about your achievements. A
10. Do you think that religion and politics should not be mixed? E

Progress Check 4

1. (a) **Question:** How are you?
   Answer: I'm fine thank you, and you?

   (b) **Question:** Tell us something about yourself.
   Answer: I was born and raised in New Delhi. I attended the University of Delhi and received my B.Sc. degree in Physics in 1994. Then, I did B.Tech in Electrcnics from IIT, Kanpur in 1998. I have worked for 6 years as an assistant manager in Mumbai for Infosys. I enjoy playing tennis and swimming in my free time. I am an extrovert and believe in honesty and hard work.

   (c) **Question:** What type of position are you looking for?

Answer: I am looking for a suitable position in an innovative software company where I will be able to use my experience in the areas of product and system architecture with expertise in enterprise applications.

(d) **Question:** Could you please tell us about your responsibilities at your last job?
Answer: As Manager (Sales and Marketing) at Hyquip Projects Private Limited, Hyderabad, I was involved in the sales and marketing of flat steel products, mainly CR/GP/GC products. I was responsible for creating and building up a strong dealer/distribution network within the North Eastern Region and Eastern states of India, as well as institutional sales on all-India basis.

(e) **Question:** What is your career goal?
Answer: I want to work as a system manager in a leading IT company where I will have opportunities to use my experience with VB, ASP, NET, XML and SQL Server.

(f) **Question:** What is your greatest strength?
Answer: My greatest strength is my ability to work under pressure. Whatever may be the circumstances, I always complete my projects on time. Last month the Director (Sales) of my company asked me to prepare the Annual Sales Report of our division of the company. We had to submit the report to the headquarters within three days. I prepared the report in a record time of two days.

(g) **Question:** Why do want to work in JBM?
Answer: I have watched with interest the growth of JBM, a well-recognised name in sheet metal technologies. With the addition of new facilities and continuous expansion, I am convinced that JBM is becoming one of the market leaders and I would like to be a part of the team. Moreover, as a seasoned professional with a proven track record in quality assurance systems, I am sure JBM is the company that will give me a long-term career with immense opportunities to grow.

(h) **Question:** When can you join us?
Answer: Immediately.

Progress Check 5

1. You cannot project a positive professional image during a job interview by being
   (d) tense and nervous
   (i) argumentative
   (j) rigid
   (k) tactless

11 CHAPTER

Group Discussions

The ability to take effective part in group discussions is one of the most important skills that contribute to professional success.

LEARNING OBJECTIVES

- Knowing the nature and importance of group discussion
- Understanding the characteristics of successful group discussions
- Learning to identify areas of evaluation in selection group discussions
- Knowing how to participate in group discussions
- Chalking out strategies for making individual contributions in group discussion
- Knowing how to exchange opinions and suggestions in group discussions

11.1 WHAT IS A GROUP DISCUSSION?

We often find people discussing various social, economic, and political issues. These discussions might be both informal and formal. Informal private discussions can take place at a restaurant, at a recreation club, at a college canteen, at a bus stop, at a coffee shop, or even at home. On the other hand, formal discussions may take place at an office, at a meeting place, at a conference hall, or at a recruitment centre. Why do people discuss? The most obvious answer is that we involve in discussion in order to develop a better perspective on key issues by bringing out various view points. When we exchange differing views on an issue, we get a clear picture of the problem and are able to understand it. This understanding makes us better equipped to deal with the problem. This is precisely the main purpose of a discussion.

> Group discussion is a systematic and purposeful interactive oral process.

> One gets involved in a discussion in order to develop a better perspective on key issues by bringing out various viewpoints.

Let us now try to understand the term 'group discussion'. The literal meaning of the word 'discuss' is 'to talk about a subject in detail'. So, group discussion may refer to a communicative situation that allows its participants to express views and opinions to other participants. It is a systematic oral exchange of information, views, and opinions about a topic, issue, problem, or situation among members of a group who share certain common objectives.

Group discussion (GD) is basically an interactive oral process. Here, the exchange of ideas, thoughts, and feelings takes place through oral communication. Each member of the group listens to other members as well as gives his or her views orally. He or she has to use clear language, persuasive style, and has to use voice and gesture effectively. This means that participants need to be proficient in oral communication in order to take effective part in a group discussion.

> Participants need to be proficient in oral communication in order to take effective part in a group discussion.

GD is a group process, i.e., it involves both person-to-person as well as person-to-group interactions. Every group member has to develop goal-oriented or group-oriented interaction. Effective interactions in discussion should lead to unification between the activities of individuals as a work team, and towards the achievement of common group goals. A participant should be concerned with the ego needs of other participants, unity of the group, and the overall objectives of the discussion.

> A participant should be concerned with the ego needs of other participants, unity of the group, and the overall objectives of the discussion.

GD is systematic. Each participant knows the topic in advance and has the opportunity to use his/her experience and knowledge to understand and analyse the topic. The exchange of ideas in GD takes place in a systematic and structured way. The participants are seated face-to-face and each participant gets an opportunity to express his/her views and comment on the views expressed by other members of the group. A formal speech making or group procedure may follow in order to ensure optimal participation.

> GD is systematic. Each participant knows the topic in advance.

GD is a purposeful goal-oriented activity. The goals or objectives of a discussion are generally decided before the discussion takes place. This means that each participant is usually aware of the purpose or purposes of the discussion in advance. A GD may help achieve group goals as well as individual needs. Group goals are common and shared by each participant whereas individual needs may be the personal goals of the members of the group.

> The goals or objectives of a discussion are generally decided before the discussion takes place.

To conclude, we may define group discussion as a form of systematic and purposeful oral process characterised by the formal and structured exchange of views on a particular topic, issue, problem, or situation for developing information and understanding essential for decision-making or problem solving.

11.1.1 Group Discussion versus Debate

Group discussion differs from debate in nature, approach, and procedure. Debates are intended to advocate a particular point of view while GDs raise a particular issue for a positive exchange of views. Unlike debate, which is competitive in nature, GD is basically a cooperative group process. A debate follows a limited approach because the speaker must argue either in favour or against a given point of view. On the other hand, in GD the approach is not limited to the support of a single point of view.

> Debates are intended to advocate a particular point of view while GDs raise a particular issue for a positive exchange of views.

Although both debate and GD are formal situations, debate is more formal in procedure than GD. In order to ensure that all facts, viewpoints, suggestions, or solutions are considered before a decision is taken, a flexible procedure is followed in GD. Moreover, decision in a debate depends on voting while a GD is designed to reach group consensus.

11.2 IMPORTANCE OF GROUP DISCUSSION

The ability to take effective part in GD is one of the most important skills that contribute to professional success. Whether one is a student, a job seeker, a professional engineer, or a company executive, one needs effective GD skills. A student may have to take part in academic discussions, student meetings, group deliberation, interactive classroom sessions, or selection GDs for admission to professional courses. A job seeker may be required to face selection GDs as part of the selection process. Professionals in different fields also have to take part in professional meetings and discussions. All these situations require the ability to make a significant contribution to group deliberation and help the group in the process of decision-making.

> Group discussions aid in problem solving, decision-making, and personality assessment.

> A job seeker may be required to face selection GDs as part of the selection process.

The importance of GD has increased in recent times due to its increasing role as an effective tool in (a) problem solving, (b) decision-making, and (c) personality assessment. In most of the organisations, companies, and institutions, group discussion aids in problem solving and decision-making. When a problem situation arises, the concerned people discuss it. They exchange their perceptions about the problem and its possible solutions. The alternative solutions are discussed and analysed, and the best option is chosen by the group. Similarly, whenever there is a need to take a decision in a particular case, the matter is first discussed by a group of people and the different aspects are analysed, interpreted, and evaluated. This leads to effective decisions.

GD is also used as a technique for personality assessment of candidates for job selection or admission to professional courses. Groups of six to eight members are formed, and are given a topic to discuss within a limited time (generally 30 to 45 minutes). The given topic may be an opinion, a problem or a case. The members of the selection committee closely evaluate the different skills reflected by the candidates

> The members of the selection committee closely evaluate the different skills reflected by the candidates and those who reflect leadership qualities and emerge as natural group leaders are normally shortlisted for a personal interview.

and those who reflect leadership qualities and emerge as natural group leaders are normally shortlisted for a personal interview.

Thus, all of us need effective GD skills. It can do wonders for us and may ensure academic success, popularity and power in an organisation, a job offer that we always waited for, or admission to a course that is going to change our life. Therefore, it is important to be able to take part in a GD effectively and confidently. Participants should know how to persuade other group members, how to reflect confidence while speaking, how to reflect leadership qualities, and how to make the group achieve its goals. They should have the ability to take initiatives during a discussion, present their personal views in an effective way, develop their ideas logically, analyse and respond to the views expressed by other members, and emerge as the natural leader of the group.

Participants should know how to persuade their group members, how to reflect confidence while speaking, how to reflect leadership qualities, and how to make the group achieve its goals.

Progress Check 1

1. Which of the following statements about group discussions are False?

(a) We involve in discussion in order to develop a better perspective on key issues by bringing out various view points.
(b) Group discussion is an interactive oral process.
(c) Effective interactions in discussion never lead to unification between the activities of individuals as a work team and towards achievement of common group goals.
(d) The exchange of ideas in GD takes place in a systematic and structured way.
(e) The goals or objectives of a discussion are generally decided before the discussion takes place.
(f) Debates raise a particular issue for a positive exchange of views while GDs are intended to advocate a particular point of view.
(g) An effective GD begins with a purpose, which is shared and understood by all the group members.
(h) The participants of a successful GD develop procedures to guide them.
(i) Debate is a cooperative group process but GD is basically competitive in nature.
(j) The development of a cooperative, friendly, and cordial atmosphere is an important characteristic of successful GDs.
(k) An effective GD ensures an equitable distribution of participation by all.
(l) There is always an elected or formal leader in a GD and the leadership functions are performed by the elected leader.
(m) The ability to take effective part in GD is one of the most important skills that contribute to professional success.
(n) In most organisations, companies, and institutions, group discussion aids in problem solving and decision-making.
(o) GD is also used as for personality assessment of candidates for job selection or in admission to professional courses.

11.3 CHARACTERISTICS OF A SUCCESSFUL GROUP DISCUSSION

Effective group discussions achieve group goals and aid in decision-making. However, a large number of group discussions end without a group consensus. It is therefore, important to know the characteristics that make a group discussion successful. Successful group discussions share some or all of the following features:

11.3.1 Agreement on Group Goals

An effective GD begins with a purpose, which is shared and understood by all the group members. As the participants know why they are taking part in the discussion, they can concentrate better and can be more active in realising the group goals. They can smoothly work from a general purpose to specific goals. Moreover, the agreement on group goals brings clarity and provides direction to the group.

> Agreement on group goals brings clarity and provides direction to the group.

11.3.2 Goal Oriented Interaction

Successful discussions motivate group members to have goal-oriented interactions. Effective GD members are not only aware of the group goals but also work towards the attainment of these goals. As they are more interested in achieving these group goals than promoting their personal interests, they develop and promote meaningful interactions that aid in implementing the purpose of the discussion.

> Effective GD members are not only aware of the group goals but also work towards the attainment of these goals.

11.3.3 Agreement on Procedures

Participants of a successful GD develop procedures to guide them. They decide how they will organise the presentation of individual views, how an exchange of the views will take place, and how they will reach a group consensus. In order to ensure attainment of group goals, they may develop norms of interaction. If the participants of a GD fail to do so, there may be anarchy and the more assertive and aggressive members might dominate and monopolise the entire discussion. This may make the entire process meaningless.

> Participants of a successful GD develop procedures to guide them.

11.3.4 Cooperative and Friendly Atmosphere

> Members cooperate with each other as they understand and appreciate different points of views, different positions, opinions, ideas, and approaches enrich the process of discussion and broaden the horizon of the group.

An important characteristic of successful GDs is the development of a cooperative, friendly, and cordial atmosphere where disagreements do exist but they do not lead to serious conflicts. Members cooperate with each other as they understand and appreciate different points of views and try to pool them together in order to develop group consensus. There may be direct but goal-oriented confrontation as each member presents his/her points of view as well as reservations and differences. However, these different positions, opinions, ideas, and approaches enrich the process of discussion and broaden the horizon of the group.

11.3.5 Use of Effective Communication Techniques

The success of a GD depends on an effective use of communication techniques. Effective GD members keep the channels of communication open and speak clearly and precisely using simple words, short sentences, correct articulation, and appropriate pronunciation. They are direct, specific, and try to avoid and check barriers to group communication. Moreover, they use non-verbal communication tactfully and interpret the body language of other participants. As they are active team listeners, they encourage others to speak.

> Effective GD members keep the channels of communication open, speak clearly and use non-verbal communication tactfully.

11.3.6 Equitable Distribution of Participation

An effective GD ensures an equitable distribution of participation by all. Each member is important and no one is allowed to dominate or monopolise the discussion. As optimal participation by all is the group-goal, members encourage each other to participate. Reluctant and shy members are drawn into the discussion.

11.3.7 Shared Leadership

There is generally no elected or formal leader in a GD. The leadership functions are shared and performed by the various members of the group. As there is a willingness on the part of each participant to reach to a group consensus, they come forward to perform leadership tasks such as starting the discussion, keeping the discussion going, encouraging non-participants to speak, making periodic summaries, checking the group progress, and so on.

> Leadership functions are shared and performed by the various members of the group.

Progress Check 2

1. **Which of the following factors are not required for successful group discussions?**
   (a) Agreement on group procedures
   (b) Meaningful interactions
   (c) Designated leadership
   (d) Unfriendly atmosphere
   (e) Goal-oriented confrontation
   (f) Common group goals
   (g) Effective use of communication techniques
   (h) Goal-oriented interaction
   (i) Unequal distribution of participation
2. **Which of the following two situations is more conducive to a successful group discussion?**
   (a) A heterogeneous group of eight persons have to discuss the topic "Human cloning should be banned". The group discussion begins with an agreement on group objectives as well as on procedures to guide them. However, two members of the group start quarrelling between themselves as to who should start the discussion. They speak against each other. It is finally decided that the group will avoid conflicts between members and instead of openly showing differences the group members can criticise each other through cross-talk and in whispers. They also decide to develop and promote meaningful goal-oriented interactions.

(b) A heterogeneous group of nine persons have to discuss "There should be no reservation for women in parliament". The interactions began in a very friendly atmosphere and the members agreed on procedures to guide them. However, one member tried to dominate and monopolise the discussion. He could be finally convinced to allow others to speak. They decided how they would organise the presentation of individual views and how an exchange of views would take place. As they seemed to be more interested in achieving group goals than in promoting their personal interests, they tried to develop and promote meaningful interactions in a friendly atmosphere. There is an equitable distribution of participation among all the group members.

11.4 GROUP DISCUSSION AS A TOOL FOR SELECTION

Group discussion has emerged as an effective and potentially powerful technique for evaluating personality traits of candidates for job selection or admission to professional courses. The GD test occupies a major position in the employment procedure of nearly all industrial concerns, public limited organisations, and multinational companies. More than any other selection method, GD tests are relied upon for making hiring decisions. These selection GDs may vary from a brief discussion on a simple topic to an exhaustive interactive discussion of a controversial issue or an actual company problem. However, they all intend to evaluate the depth and range of the candidate's knowledge, his or her ability to orally present that knowledge in a convincing manner, and his/her effective group communication, leadership, and team management skills.

> There are four major areas of evaluation in selection of GDs: subject knowledge, oral communication skills, leadership skills, and team management.

> Selection GDs may vary from a brief discussion on a simple topic to an exhaustive interactive discussion of a controversial issue or an actual company problem.

11.4.1 Subject Knowledge

As all participants must possess a thorough understanding of the topic on which they are supposed to speak, subject knowledge is the first requirement of effective participation in a group discussion. Participants need to have a fair amount of knowledge on a wide range of subjects. They should know all about national and international affairs, burning social and economic topics, scientific and environmental issues, key newsmakers, controversial topics, and a lot more. Although a GD test is not designed to assess the ability of the candidate's general awareness of the environment around him/her or to test his/her knowledge of current events, he/she is expected to be aware of such matters of everyday observation or experience as may be expected of an educated person. People with depth and range of knowledge are always sought after in dynamic companies and organisations.

> Although a GD test is not designed to assess the ability of the candidate's general awareness of the environment around him/her or to test his/her knowledge of current events, he/she is expected to be aware of such matters of everyday observation or experience as may be expected of an educated person.

The topics for GD tests may include interesting and relevant ideas pertaining to society, culture, polity, economy, scientific and technical research; social, economic, political or environmental problems; controversial issues; or case studies. The best way to keep one abreast of latest events and national as well as international developments is to read daily newspapers, good magazines and periodicals, watch news bulletins and informative programmes on television. Moreover, we should use the Internet to improve our knowledge about recent developments in different areas. The World Wide Web is a vast database of current authentic materials that presents information in multimedia form and reacts instantly to a user's input.

Subject knowledge also implies the ability to analyse facts or information in a systematic way to correlate them with personal experiences and exposure. It is this ability to analyse existing knowledge and assimilate new ideas that can give birth to bright and brilliant ideas and schemes. In all group discussions, people with ideas carry the day. A person putting forward new ideas that may work, will be accepted as the natural leader of the group. During a selection GD, participants are supposed to analyse the topic and give their interpretation of it. Examiners will evaluate each person's contribution to the discussion or the ideas put forward by them based on its relevance to the topic, original approach, and wide perspective.

Subject knowledge also implies the ability to analyse facts or information in a systematic way to correlate them with personal experiences and exposure.

11.4.2 Oral Communication Skills

The participants in a group discussion must possess not only subject knowledge but also the ability to present that knowledge in an effective way. As the exchange of ideas in a group discussion takes place through speech, one of the prerequisites of success in group discussion is the ability to speak confidently and convincingly. In fact, a vital part of every successful group discussion is high quality oral communication. The members of the selection committee closely evaluate the oral communication skills of the candidates. They generally assess the oral competence of a candidate in terms of team listening, appropriate language, clarity of expression, positive speech attitudes and adjustments, clear articulation, and effective non-verbal communication.

Listening Skills

When a person takes part in a group discussion, he/she cannot contribute to the stated purposes of the communication unless he/she is listening properly.

As all comments during a group discussion must be heard and understood, listening skills are probably one of the most important communication skills that one needs in order to be successful in a GD. When a person takes part in a group discussion, he/she cannot contribute to the stated purposes of the communication unless he/she is listening properly. By participating as an active listener, he/she may contribute effectively to the groups deliberations. Moreover, active participation as a listener in a group and its discussions and deliberations make a person a successful leader because a good leader is a good listener.

Appropriateness of Language

During a GD, the selection panel judges a candidate's grasp of language and ability to use appropriate words and expressions. Appropriateness of language demands that there should be no errors of grammar, or usage and there is precision in the use of words, phrases, sentences, and paragraphs. Participants must be certain that they are expressing their ideas precisely and exactly so that their listener is able to understand them without confusion and misunderstanding. They should be simple and concise, avoiding difficult words, unfamiliar phrases, or flowery language.

Clarity of Expression

Clarity is the art of making your meaning clear to your audience. The secret of clear expression is clear thinking. Sloppy, illogical, or incomplete thinking may cause lack

Sloppy, illogical, or incomplete thinking may cause lack of clarity during a GD.

of clarity during a GD. A confused person is likely to confuse others. So, it is essential to think clearly and positively. In addition, direct, clear and specific language should be used during a GD, rather than roundabout constructions, indirect expressions, exaggeration, artificial eloquence, and ornamentation in speech.

Positive Speech Attitudes

The selection panel also evaluates speech attitudes and adjustments. Is the participant a responsible group communicator or a careless speaker? Is he/she mature and dignified or immature and apologetic? Is he/she positive towards his/her listeners or antagonistic to them? Is he/she a relaxed speaker or a tense one? Is he/she sincere to other speakers or just indifferent? The examiners closely watch these aspects. So, it is important to reflect positive speech attitudes and adjustments during a GD.

> So, it is important to reflect positive speech attitudes and adjustments during a GD.

Clear Articulation

The quality of a person's voice and articulation plays an important role during a GD. A participant can easily impress the other members of the discussion group as well as the selection panel if he/she has a cheerful voice with good articulation. Avoid a slow or weak voice, a monotonous tone, and indistinct articulation. Do not speak too fast. Be slow, clear, and distinct.

Non-verbal Cues

As non-verbal cues such as eye contact, body movements, gestures, facial expressions, and so on can speak louder than words, examiners closely watch the non-verbal behaviour of candidates. They generally evaluate the body language cues of candidates to determine personality factors such as nervousness, cooperation, frustration, weakness, insecurity, self-confidence, defensiveness, and so forth. So, it is important to be careful while using non-verbal messages. However, one should recognise the power of non-verbal messages and use them effectively. A person's body language must reflect his/her self-confidence, cooperation, positive attitude, openness of mind, and sincerity.

> A person's body language must reflect his/her self-confidence, cooperation, positive attitude, openness of mind, and sincerity.

Progress Check 3

1. Which of the following may not be a positive factor during a GD test?

(a) A deep and thorough understanding of the subject under discussion.
(b) Ability to correlate facts with your experiences.
(c) Negative speech attitudes.
(d) Confidence in oral communication.
(e) Passive listening.
(f) Ability to use appropriate words and expressions.
(g) Ornamental expression.
(h) Clear voice and articulation.
(i) Poor expression.
(j) Analytical skills.
(k) Effective use of body language.

11.4.3 Leadership Skills

A candidate's success in a GD test will depend not only on his/her subject knowledge and oral skills but also on his/her ability to provide leadership to the group. The examiners evaluate a candidate's unique set of personal skills, which allow him/her to prove himself/herself as a natural leader in a GD. Thus, it is necessary to reflect the qualities of leadership in order to create the right impression on one's examiners. Adaptability, analysis, assertiveness, composure, self-confidence, decision-making, discretion, initiative, objectivity, patience, and persuasiveness are some of the leadership skills that are tremendously useful in proving oneself as a natural leader in a GD.

> Leadership functions during a GD include initiative, analysis, assertiveness, self-confidence, objectivity, patience and composure, persuasiveness, and motivation.

> Although leadership functions are shared in GD, each participant should try to be the first one to perform the function whenever a need arises.

In every group discussion, there is an element of leadership. We can define leadership in GD on a functional basis. Thus, anything that contributes to goal achievement can be considered a leadership function. Although leadership functions are shared in GD, each participant should try to be the first one to perform the function whenever a need arises. Leadership functions during a GD include the following:

Initiative

Initiative is a vital element that forms the basis of leadership during a GD. As there is no formal leader to conduct the discussion, someone in the group has to take the initiative to perform the required leadership function. A person can display his/her ability to take appropriate initiative by performing the following leadership functions:

- initiate the proceedings of the discussion;
- create an atmosphere in which members feel free to participate;
- promote positive group interactions;
- point out areas of agreement and disagreement;
- clarify points when required;
- keep the discussion on the right track; and
- lead the discussion to a positive and successful conclusion within the time allotted.

Analysis

> Those who lack an analytical bent of mind and rational thinking cannot be successful in a GD.

The ability to analyse a situation, a problem, or a condition is the mark of a successful leader. Those who lack an analytical bent of mind and rational thinking cannot be successful in a GD. A leader should be able to analyse the given topic for discussion in order to develop his/her own point of view. His/her capacity to analyse the subject in a convincing manner and present all the facts logically can help in carrying the rest of the group with him/her. Moreover, the leader should listen carefully to each participant in order to analyse his or her opinions and views. A positive analysis of all the views, suggestions, proposals, and solutions exchanged during the discussion can lead to the identification of common elements that may form the basis of group consensus.

Assertiveness

A leader has to be bold and assertive without being offensive, aggressive, and rigid. If a person is mild and weak, he/she will be too eager to give up in the face of opposition and obstacles. In fact, a weak, submissive, and passive person can never be successful as a group leader. Assertiveness is a desirable leadership quality that can make a person successful during a GD. If one is assertive, one can tackle obstacles and handicaps effectively. Assertiveness can help in bringing order to a chaotic group, encourage balanced participation, deal with conflict effectively, and lead the discussion to a positive end. By taking a firm stand, an assertive leader can control members of the group who are more interested in sabotaging the discussion rather than contributing to its success. It is always desirable that the leader does not take a rigid stand but he/she must be able to assert himself during a GD.

> A leader has to be bold and assertive without being offensive, aggressive, and rigid.

Self-confidence

Self-confidence is the hallmark of a leader. Selection experts and examiners always look for a candidate with a strong but realistic level of confidence. So, it is important to remember to talk with confidence and self-assurance. A participant's confidence will not only impress the examiners but also help him/her lead the group and instill confidence in each of its members. A leader can tackle problems with confidence and find workable solutions with ease. However, he/she should avoid being boastful and pretending that he/she knows everything and has a solution for every problem. He/she should not forget that over-confidence causes failures whereas under-confidence leads to lack of productivity.

> Selection experts and examiners always look for a candidate with a strong but realistic level of confidence.

Objectivity

Objectivity is the quality of being impartial, rational, and factual. In order to be successful as a group leader, one needs to view a situation or a problem dispassionately and objectively. In other words the leader's approach should be systematic, scientific, and realistic. As group discussion is an exchange of views and opinions on a specific topic, there would be conflicting views and heated arguments. The leader should not become sentimental because if he/she gets emotional and excited, his/her ideas may get jumbled and arguments will become dogmatic and self-appointed. The leader can overcome opposition by adopting a logical, rational, and practical viewpoint, and utilising concrete and foolproof illustrations and examples. As he/she should be rational rather than emotional, irrational ideas and emotional bias should not influence him/her. A leader's ideas and arguments should be fully backed by relevant facts and figures, this will give validity and appeal to his/her arguments.

> In order to be successful as a group leader, one needs to view a situation or a problem dispassionately and objectively.

Patience and Composure

Patience is the key to successful leadership in GD. A successful leader never loses his cool and is not easily provoked. Even in the face of extreme provocation, the leader keeps a patient profile. So, during the GD it is essential to keep one's cool and not get provoked. Handling a group of heterogeneous elements requires a lot of patience and composure. It is always difficult to bring a group of people together to discuss an issue amicably because a few in the group would try to monopolise the group and create problems. In such a condition, if the leader wants to bring the discussion to a successful conclusion, he/she has to tackle the situation with tact and patience. His/her ability to keep cool and maintain his/her composure despite provocation will help bring together people with different temperaments and strike a consensus in the GD.

Persuasiveness

One of the vital prerequisites for success in group discussion is the ability to persuade other members of the group to accept and believe in what one says. Persuasion is an art that requires an ample amount of convincing power. This art can be acquired by consistent practice. In GD, participants can make a favourable and forceful impact on the group by being persuasive and convincing. In order to be persuasive, one has to advance strong, convincing, and logical arguments properly supported by factual data and forceful illustrations. A firm tone and a sober voice would also help in establishing superiority. Listeners should immediately realise that the speaker means business. A leader's ability to convince others and make them accept his/her views and suggestions will establish his/her credentials for leadership.

> In order to be persuasive, one has to advance strong, convincing, and logical arguments properly supported by factual data and forceful illustrations.

Motivation

Those determined to win are highly motivated and have the ability to motivate others. Motivation constitutes the base on which group leadership can grow. All organisations look for candidates who are motivated and can accept challenges. A person with motivation can work hard to do the best job possible and can achieve targets. Examiners can easily evaluate a participant's level of motivation during a GD. A leader can display the quality of motivation by being an active and positive contributor to the process of discussion. By clarifying the topic of the discussion, explaining its different aspects, and providing enough material for other members to follow and discuss, a leader can motivate them to take an active part in the group deliberations. Moreover, by encouraging the shy ones to speak and promoting optimal participation, he/she can involve everyone in the group to bring the discussion to a successful conclusion.

> Those determined to win are highly motivated and have the ability to motivate others.

11.4.4 Team Management

Apart from subject knowledge, oral communication, and leadership skills, every participant needs team management skills in order to be successful in a GD test. The leader in a group discussion should be able to manage the group despite differences of opinion and steer the discussion to a logical conclusion within the fixed time limit. The examiners will assess whether each participant is a team player who can get along with people or an individualist who is always fighting to save his/her ego. Employers today look for candidates who can work in a team-oriented environment. GD participants need a number of team management skills in order to function effectively in a team. Some of the skills needed to manage a group effectively include adaptability, positive attitude, cooperation, and coordination.

> The examiners will assess whether each participant is a team player who can get along with people or an individualist who is always fighting to save his/her ego.

> Team management skills include adaptability, positive attitude, cooperation, and coordination.

Adaptability

Adaptability refers to the ability to adjust with other members of the group and get along with them. It is an important leadership quality that one needs in order to be an effective team player. A person who lacks the ability to get along with others will not succeed as a group leader because an effective leader has to rise above his personal likes and dislikes in order to accommodate the larger interests of the group. In most group discussions there are several categories of participants who might differ from each other in temperament, IQ, social attitudes, personal preferences, points of view, and other aspects. In order to emerge as the natural leader of a group, one has to adjust oneself suitably with others in the group. In fact, by being adaptable and flexible the leader will be able to carry the entire group with him/her.

By being adaptable and flexible the leader will be able to carry the entire group with him/her.

Positive Attitude

A team player should have a positive attitude because no one would like to work with a person who always complains and is negative towards everything and everyone. In a GD, each participant should get an opportunity to offer his/her valuable viewpoint to the enrichment of the discussion. Therefore, every participant should encourage other members to contribute effectively to the group process. Sometimes one may have to face aggressive, rigid, authoritarian, obstinate, and quarrelsome people, but a cheerful approach and a positive attitude will help in dealing with them tactfully. If a team mate shows respect for their ideas and handles them with tact and understanding, they will automatically look up to him/her for help and support. Thus, if a person has a positive attitude, he/she can bind the team and get along well with his/her teammates, including the difficult ones.

If a person has a positive attitude, he/she can bind the team and get along well with his/her teammates, including the difficult ones.

Cooperation

The very idea of group discussion is based on the concept of cooperation, where all members are expected to work as a team. A team derives its success from the inherent factor of cooperation. Each member supports the other member because the success of each member depends on the success of the team. On the other hand, a hostile approach by any member will go against the spirit of cooperation and will result in either delaying or sabotaging the entire process of discussion. It is, therefore, very important that every group member subordinates his/her ego as well as his/her individual interest to the larger group interest of the group working together in order to achieve the group goal within the time allotted.

Coordination

Group discussion is a group activity wherein the success of the group depends on the involvement of each member of the group. It is important that each participant reflects team spirit by developing coordination during the discussion. As a group cannot function as an effective team and accomplish a task without a coordinator, an assertive team member should come forward to accept the leadership by coordinating its activities. A person can emerge on the natural leader and coordinator of a group with a positive approach, a tactful handling of difficult situations, resourcefulness, and objective behaviour.

A person can emerge as the natural leader and coordinator of a group with a positive approach, a tactful handling of difficult situations, resourcefulness, and objective behaviour.

Progress Check 4

1. **Study the following table and match the actions in GD (left column) with the appropriate leadership/team management skills that they reflect (right column):**

	Actions in a GD	Leadership/team management skills
1.	Keep a patient profile despite provocation	(a) Initiative
2.	Encourage other members to contribute effectively to the group process	(b) Analysis
3.	Convince others effectively	(c) Assertiveness
4.	Promote optimal participation	(d) Self-confidence
5.	Clarify points and point out areas of agreement and disagreement when needed	(e) Objectivity
6.	Coordinate the group activities	(f) Patience
7.	Bring order to a chaotic group	(g) Persuasiveness
8.	View a situation dispassionately	(h) Motivation
9.	Get along with other members of the group	(i) Adaptability
10.	Subordinates his/her individual interest to the larger group interest and supports other members of the group	(j) Positive attitude
11.	Talk with self-assurance	(k) Cooperation
12.	Analyse the given topic	(l) Coordination

11.5 GROUP DISCUSSION STRATEGIES

As group discussion is a systematic and purposeful oral process characterised by the formal and structured exchange of views on a particular topic, issue, problem, or situation, it should be well planned and well conducted. Seven strategies have been described here for participating in group discussions.

11.5.1 Getting the GD Started

As mentioned before, there is generally no elected or formal leader in a GD. So, there is no one to get the GD started. In a selection GD, the group, which may consist of six to ten persons, is given a topic to discuss within 30 to 45 minutes. After announcing the topic, the total GD time, and explaining the general guidelines and procedures governing the GD, the examiner withdraws to the background leaving the group completely free to carry on with the discussion on its own without any outside interference.

In the absence of a designated leader to initiate the proceedings of the discussion, the group is likely to waste time in cross talks, low-key conversations, cross-consultations, asides, and so on. The confusion may last until someone in the group takes an assertive position and restores the chaos into order. It could be you.

In order to get the GD started, the assertive, natural leader will have to remind the group of its goal and request them to start the discussion without wasting time. A few examples of the opening lines are given below:

> In order to get the GD started, the assertive, natural leader will have to remind the group of its goal and request them to start the discussion without wasting time.

- Well friends, may I request your kind attention? I am sure all of us are keen to begin the GD and complete it within the allotted time. Let me remind you that we have only thirty minutes to complete the task. So, let us get started.
- My dear friends, may I have your attention please? As you all know, we have to complete the discussion in 45 minutes and we have already used up five minutes. I think we should start the discussion now.
- Hello everybody. I am sorry to interrupt but I have something very important to say. We are here to discuss the topic — "Reduction of IIM fees is a retrograde step"—and the time given to us is just 30 minutes. Let us begin, shall we?
- Hello friends! May I have your kind attention for a few seconds, please? I am sure you will agree that we are here to exchange our views on the reservation policy of the government and we have to complete the discussion within 35 minutes. As we have already used up more than five minutes, we should begin the discussion now. Shall we start?

Once the GD has been successfully initiated, the leader should propose the procedures to be followed during the discussion. The procedures may include time management, order of speaking, length and nature of individual contributions, and nature of group interactions. It is very important to follow a plan that includes time for every individual speaker as well as for the exchange of views, suggestions, and solutions. All members of the group should be in agreement on these pertinent items. While trying to get the GD started, the leader should attempt to create an atmosphere in which all members feel free to participate.

> While trying to get the GD started, the leader should attempt to create an atmosphere in which all members feel free to participate.

11.5.2 Contributing Systematically

The success of a group discussion depends on systematic contribution by each member of the group. In order to make systematic contributions to the group deliberations, all the group members should understand the process of reflective thinking. They should be able to identify the stage of the discussion (i.e., individual stage, where each member has to systematically present his or her views without any disturbance; or group interaction stage, where members have to exchange views and opinions in order to reach to a group consensus) and contribute accordingly. When a participant makes a contribution, he/she should ensure that his/her contribution

> A group discussion has two stages: an individual stage and a group interaction stage. Individual stage, where each member has to systematically present his or her views without any disturbance; or group interaction stage, where members have to exchange views and opinions in order to reach to a group consensus).

- relates to what has previously been said by other members,
- focuses on the theme of the discussion,
- deals with the specific point under consideration,
- is directed towards the overall objective of the GD, and
- is as per the requirement of the particular stage of discussion.

Moreover, contributions must reflect the depth of understanding and knowledge of the subject as well as the participant's ability to analyse it. Each participant must see the topic from his/her perspective so that his/her background and personal experiences give it a new interpretation, which may prove valuable to the group for taking a decision.

Each participant must see the topic from his/her perspective so that his/her background and personal experiences give it a new interpretation, which may prove valuable to the group for taking a decision.

11.5.3 Creating a Friendly Cooperative Atmosphere

Creating an atmosphere conducive to positive discussion is the responsibility of each member of the group.

Creating an atmosphere conducive to positive discussion is the responsibility of each member of the group. A friendly, cooperative atmosphere encourages effective and positive deliberations that lead to successful conclusion. Although a GD is a serious and formal occasion, there is no need to make it too serious and boring. It is desirable to make it an enjoyable experience for all. Members of a group discussion can do much to create a conducive and friendly atmosphere. The following suggestions may be helpful in this regard:

- All participants should help the group to make the discussion lively and pleasurable.
- Participants should develop a consensus regarding group standards early in the discussion.
- In order to maintain friendly attitudes, participants should demonstrate a sense of fair play by treating others as they would like themselves to be treated.
- Participants must conduct themselves with decorum and dignity.
- All participants must show interest in what others say.
- Every participant should make sure that other members feel free to express their views, opinions, comments, and feelings.
- Members must be kept informed of their own progress and they should be appreciated for contributing effectively to the group goals.

11.5.4 Moving the Discussion Along

A GD without a leader may drift without a proper direction. A leader should ensure that the GD moves along the right direction so that it is able to complete the task within the fixed time limit. He/she should make sure that every member of the group gets some time to present his/her views and no one member monopolises the discussion. No one should be allowed to do all the talking because the purpose of a GD is to exchange views, and not to hear just one person. If someone tries to take too much time, the leader may politely thank the aggressive member but firmly ask him/her to give the next person a chance to speak.

If someone tries to take too much time, the leader may politely thank the aggressive member but firmly ask him/her to give the next person a chance to speak.

It is very important to avoid any digression that may sidetrack the group. The leader may volunteer to avoid digressions and bring order out of chaos by requesting the members to see reason and come to the point. The following are some examples of how to do this:

- I do understand your point but I think we should stick to the main subject at hand.
- I see what you mean but it would be better if we limit our discussion to the given subject.
- That is all well said but I do not find a link between what you want to say and the subject in hand. Could you please return to the main point?

- That is not the main point under discussion. Let us come to the main subject.

The leader may use other techniques to keep the GD on the right track. He/she can emphasise the point that everyone has to keep the objectives of the GD in mind and adhere to the time schedule. He/she may summarise or clarify the points already put forward by the group members and thereby focus their attention on the main objective of the GD and keep the discussion from slowing down.

> The leader may summarise or clarify the points already put forward by the group members and thereby focus their attention on the main objective of the GD and keep the discussion from slowing down.

11.5.5 Promoting Optimal Participation

As the success of a GD largely depends on the involvement of each member of the group, the leader should promote optimal participation. As every member has a resource potential that can be used to make the discussion successful, the leader should encourage non-participants to speak. With patience, restraint, and proper motivation, he/she can inspire even the shy and reluctant members to give their views on the given subject. It will not only reflect his/her leadership qualities but also lead the discussion to a successful conclusion. Leaders may find the following suggestions quite helpful in this regard:

- Make each member feel that his or her contribution is necessary to make the discussion successful.
- Encourage each member to make his or her maximum contribution.
- Recognise members of the group who have not talked and request them to express their views.
- When a member makes a contribution, the leader may request the non-participating members to comment on it.
- Direct some relevant questions related to the topic to reticent members.
- Try to control talkative members.
- Make talkative members take responsibility for getting non-participants to speak.
- Avoid pushing the GD too fast, and take care of slow speakers.

11.5.6 Handling Conflict

One important aspect of participating in any group discussion is dealing with conflict. As a group always tends to be heterogeneous, conflict is natural in any group activity and may sometimes be desirable for the success of a group process. Expect differences of opinions during a GD but do not let these conflicting opinions go against the basic purpose of a GD. Do not be a silent spectator when two or more people are in conflict. Although conflict resolution is a complex art, a leader needs to remember just a few simple tips in order to handle conflict during a GD. The following suggestions will help leaders deal with conflict during a GD:

- Maintain a friendly attitude and try to create an atmosphere in which people respect conflicting opinions as they feel free to express their opinions and expect others to talk freely. This will generate goodwill and take care of conflicts within the group.
- Strictly follow that has been decided earlier in the discussion.
- Avoid conflicts between persons and not conflict between ideas.
- Clarify conflicting statements given by group members so that they do not lead to personal differences.
- Provide positive guidance to the group by making occasional summaries.

- When two people are in conflict, they should both be encouraged to express themselves completely and then their views can be summarised. This will satisfy the egos of both the group members.
- Help establish an attitude of critical objectivity.

11.5.7 Effecting Closure

In the absence of a designated leader to close the discussion formally, the group is likely to continue until the examiner announces that the time is over. Every member has to see that the GD ends with positive conclusions within the given time limit. In order to complete the GD within the allotted time, the leader has to remind the group of its goal and request them to reach to a group consensus. He/she should do the following himself/herself or get them done by other group members in order to develop group consensus:

- Summarise the progress made by the group.
- Put forward the common points of agreement.
- Indicate the differences that need to be resolved.
- Review decisions/suggestions/views already decided.

Once the closure of a GD is successfully initiated, the leader may propose the consensus views, if any. It is not essential that every GD ends with a consensus but every GD must end with some positive conclusion. The leader must emphasise the points of agreement in order to indicate a common viewpoint regarding the topic.

> It is not essential that every GD ends with a consensus but every GD must end with some positive conclusion.

Progress Check 5

1. Read the following instructions about GD and classify them as do's and don'ts in group discussions:

(a) Initiate the proceedings of the group discussion.
(b) Get involved in cross talk, low-key conversations, cross-consultations, and asides.
(c) Force the group to start the discussion without wasting time.
(d) Propose the procedures to be followed during the discussion.
(e) Encourage personality conflicts.
(f) Create an atmosphere in which all members feel free to participate.
(g) Try to be the centre of attention all the time.
(h) Comment on everyone and everything.
(i) Keep members informed of their own progress.
(j) Monopolise the discussion.
(k) Avoid any digression that may sidetrack the group.
(l) Encourage non-participants to speak.
(m) Make each member feel that his or her contribution is important.
(n) Control talkative members.
(o) Push the GD too fast.
(p) Maintain a friendly attitude.
(q) Avoid conflicts between ideas.
(r) Provide positive guidance to the group by making occasional summaries.

(s) Help to establish the attitude of critical objectivity.
(t) Put forward the common points of agreement.

11.5.8 Techniques for Individual Contribution

As indicated before, every GD should have two distinct sections, an individual section where each member of the group presents his/her views and a group interaction section where members exchange their views and try to reach to a group consensus. Sometimes the two sections are mixed up and the group is not able to develop a procedure to conduct the discussion because no one emerges as the natural leader of the group. This is a very difficult situation, and might lead to confusion and chaos. Members of a group discussion should not let this happen. All participants should ensure that the group follows certain norms regarding individual contribution and group interaction.

> Techniques for individual contribution involve analysing and interpreting the given topic, which may include opinions, problems/ issues, or case studies.

> Sometimes a group is not able to develop a procedure to conduct the discussion because no one emerges as the natural leader of the group.

Topic Analysis

Speaking in a GD involves no planning, preparation, or practice. Participants have to speak on the spur of the moment. As they do not have any aids to help them know what to say, their presentation depends on their reading, knowledge, experience, and background. Participants should think about the topic with a cool and open mind in order to analyse what they know about the topic. All the aspects of the topic should be examined and related to their personal experiences; this will give them fresh ideas. In order to understand the topic and analyse it, participants need to ask themselves the following questions:

- What is this topic all about?
- What do I know about it?
- What do I personally think about it?
- Does it require a judgement from me?
- What should my point of view be?
- What should my approach to the topic be?

The first speaker has the extra responsibility of introducing the topic to the group members. The rest, however, should refer to the earlier speakers. It is generally a good idea to begin your presentation with an expression of gratitude to the earlier speakers for their ideas. Participants should express their agreement/disagreement with others politely.

> The first speaker has the extra responsibility of introducing the topic to the group members.

> It is generally a good idea to begin your presentation with an expression of gratitude to the earlier speakers for their ideas.

While analysing a given topic, participants should identify the nature of the discussions can be classified into three types, i.e., opinions, problems or issues, and case studies. Different strategies should be followed to express views on these different types of topics. The following suggestions will help participants make their contribution valuable to the group:

> Topics given in group discussions can be classified into three types, i.e., opinions, problems or issues, and case studies.

Discussing Opinions

The topic of a group discussion could be a one-sentence opinion. These opinions may relate to any of the following:

(a) Social issues (Example: There should be no reservation in jobs)
(b) Economic conditions (Example: Sick public sector companies should be privatised)
(c) Moral issues (Example: Human cloning should be banned)
(d) Political concepts (Example: Parliamentary democracy has failed in India)
(e) Ongoing issues and debates in society (Example: Uniform civil code is essential for social harmony in India)

When an opinion has to be discussed, the participants should begin his/her individual presentation by interpreting the opinion and making his/her stand clear. For example, if the topic is "Reduction of IIM fees is a retrograde step", the participant should begin by clearly stating his/her point of view, i.e., "I strongly feel that reduction of IIM fees is a retrograde step" or "The decision of the Government of India to reduce IIM fees is a positive step." Next, he/she must state why he/she thinks so, supporting his/her point of view with examples and illustrations. As every participant's purpose is to influence the group members' choices by shaping, reinforcing, or changing their responses to the idea being discussed, views must be presented in a logical and convincing manner. No member will accept a point of view if that is not supported with sufficient data. Finally, the talk should be concluded with a thesis statement that restates the point of view. One needs to be concise, to the point, and direct.

> The participant should begin by clearly stating his/her point of view.

> The talk should be concluded with a thesis statement that restates the point of view.

Discussing Problems

If the topic is a 'problem' or an 'issue', GD participants must try to understand the nature of the problem. There are three types of problems—problems of fact, problem of value, and problem of policy. In a problem of fact, one is concerned with the truth of a statement (Example: Inflation is inevitable in a developing country), or an explanation of a fact (Example: Glorification of violence and crimes in Indian films accounts for the high crime rate today). However, with a problem of value one is concerned with certain questions related to value judgements or the desirability of some actions, concepts, persons, processes, or things (Example: Has the American war against Iraq helped Iraqis?). Finally, a problem of policy is concerned with certain questions related to policy decisions (Example: What should the government do to control corruption at high places?). The participant may decide his/her approach as per the nature of the problem.

> There are three types of problems–problems of fact, problems of value, and problems of policy.

> Once the problem is defined, the next step is an analysis and examination of available facts, supporting the given conclusion, explanation, or statement about the problem.

If the topic is a 'problem of fact', participants should begin their presentation with a definition and interpretation of the 'problem'. It is important to see the problem from one's own point of view, which could be different from those of other group members because of one's unique background and experience. Once the problem is defined, the next step is an analysis and examination of available facts, supporting the given conclusion, explanation, or statement about the problem. The analysis may involve a brief review of its history or background, its causes, its effects, attempts to solve it, or the present state of the problem. The participant may decide the amount of information to be included and the focus of his/her contribution according to the particular statement to be discussed. Finally, one may conclude one's talk with a thesis statement that restates one's point of view. If the topic demands, the conclusion may reflect the speaker's understanding of the possible solutions to the problem.

While expressing an opinion on a 'problem of value' or a 'problem of policy', GD participants should begin their presentation with an interpretation of the given question from their point of view. Once the question is interpreted, the next step is an examination of the question according to their perceptions of what is desirable and proper in the given situation. The point of view may be supported with facts, examples, and illustrations. Finally, the presentation must be concluded by restating the point of view.

> Once the question is interpreted, the next step is an examination of the question according to their perceptions of what is desirable and proper in the given situation.

Discussing Case Studies

> We may define a 'case study' as an actual problem situation in an organisation, demanding immediate attention and solution.

Companies, big or small, face many challenges in order to survive in the competitive business environment. Similarly, institutions and government organisations have to face difficult situations due to the bitter reality of the 'survival of the fittest'. Thus, the recruitment process in many organisations may focus on evaluating the candidate's analytical and problem-solving skills and they can ask students to discuss a case study. We may define a 'case study' as an actual problem situation in an organisation, demanding immediate attention and solution.

To discuss a case study, GD participants need to follow an entirely different strategy. They should begin their presentation with a brief summary of the case and their interpretation of the situation, emphasising the need to solve the problem immediately. Next, they can suggest ways and means to solve the problem situation. They may propose and examine several possible solutions or alternative courses of action and then choose the most effective one, giving reasons for their choice. Participants may use persuasive language while making other members accept the solution/s proposed by them. Finally, they may conclude by summarising their plan to solve the case.

Progress Check 6

1. **Which of the following questions may not be helpful during a topic analysis?**
   (a) What is the focus of this topic?
   (b) Why has the examiner given this topic for discussion?
   (c) What is this topic all about?
   (d) What do I know about it?
   (e) What do other group members think about it?
   (f) What should be my point of view?
   (g) What are the other topics that the examiner might have given?
   (h) What should my approach to the topic be?
   (i) Does it require the judgement of other group members?
   (j) What should my strategy be to deal with this topic?

2. Study the following table and identify the strategies that may be effective in dealing with opinions/problems/case studies during a GD:

Opinions	Problems	Case Studies
1. Analyse and interpret the given opinion.	1. Interpret the given problem for discussion from your point of view.	1. Summarise and present the main facts of the case.
2. Always disagree with the given opinion.	2. Always evaluate the seriousness of the problem.	2. Suggest ways and means to solve the problem situation.
3. Make your stand clear in the beginning.	3. Always describe the history and background of the problem.	3. Begin your presentation with a solution to the problem situation.
4. Support your views with quotations by eminent people on the subject.	4. Never mention the causes of the problem.	4. Examine several alternative courses of action.
5. Illustrate and support your point of view.	5. Examine the statement/question about the problem objectively.	5. Propose the most effective solution, giving reasons for accepting it.
6. Repeat your point of view.	6. Support your point of view with facts, examples, and illustrations.	6. Use persuasive language.
7. Present both aspects of the opinion in detail.	7. Mention the solution/s to the problem as per the need of the topic.	7. Force other members to accept only your proposal.
8. Express your point of view only after listening to all the speakers.	8. Conclude by restating your point of view.	8. Conclude by summarising your plan to solve the case.

11.5.9 Group Interaction Strategies

Group discussion is a forum that provides opportunities for interaction. This interaction is possible only if every member of the group contributes and demonstrates his/her level of understanding on the given topic for discussion. However, there are several unpredictable factors involved in a GD. These include the setting, the examiners, other group discussion participants, the requirements of the selection procedure, etc. You hardly know anything about them. You need several skills and micro-skills in order to emerge successful in a GD test. In order to ensure an impressive performance in a GD test, you should know how to exchange opinions and suggestions in group discussions.

> There are several unpredictable factors involved in a GD such as setting, examiners, other group discussion participants, requirements of the selection procedure, etc.

Exchanging Opinions

GD is a cooperative exercise where opinions and views of each member of the group are important for developing consensus and reaching to a conclusion. So, you have to ask for opinions, give opinions, support opinions, balance points of view, or express agreements and disagreements.

Exchanging opinions during GDs include asking for opinions, giving opinions, supporting opinions, balancing points of view, agreeing, and disagreeing.

Asking for Opinions

You may ask one person to give his or her opinion on any point or your request might be directed at a group of people in general. Study the examples in Table 11.1.

TABLE 11.1 Examples of Obtaining Opinion During Group Discussion

Directed at One Person	*Directed at a Group of People*
What is your opinion about this?	What is the general view on this?
What do you feel about it?	What is the general feeling about this?
What do you think about that?	Any reaction to that?
Have you any strong view on this?	Does anyone have strong views on this?
Have you any strong feelings about that?	Does anyone have strong feelings about that?
Do you want to make any comments?	Does anybody have any comments to make?
Do you have anything to say?	Does anybody have anything to say?

Giving Opinions

During a GD you may have to give your opinions about the subject being discussed. You also have to react to the views given by other members. You may express an opinion in a strong way, neutral way, or in a tentative way. It is very important to make other members aware of the nature of your opinion. If the other members know that you have strong views on something, they may not like to argue with you or ask you to change your views whereas they might like to convince a person whose views are neutral or tentative (Table 11.2).

TABLE 11.2 Different Types of Opinions

Strong Opinions	*Neutral Opinions*	*Tentative Opinions*
• I have no doubt that ...	• I think that...	• It appears to me that...
• I'm pretty sure that...	• I feel that...	• It seems to me that ...
• I'm quite convinced that...	• I believe that...	• I'm inclined to think that...
• It's perfectly clear to me that...	• From a social point of view...	• I tend to favour the view that...
• I'm convinced that...	• The way I find it is that...	• As it appears to me, ...
• I'm sure that...	• As I see it...	• I can reconcile to the view that...
• There's no doubt that...	• As I find it...	• I might accept the view that...
• I strongly believe that...	• According to me...	
• As far as I am concerned...	• The way I see it is that...	
• I'm totally convinced that...	• Personally, I think...	

Supporting Your Opinions

In order to make your views acceptable to the other group members, you need to support them with facts, examples, illustrations, or arguments. Sometimes you may feel that giving one reason or consequence for your point of view is sufficient to convince the listeners. This is illustrated by the following examples:

> Sometimes you may feel that giving one reason or consequence for your point of view is sufficient to convince the listeners. However, in many cases during a discussion, more than one reason may be needed to support your opinions.

- I have no doubt that capital punishment should be abolished because it promotes barbarism, which is no longer valid to our modern ideas, times, and values.
- I'm convinced that our company must open new branches because our business has expanded.
- I think we should go ahead with the project as it will help us establish the name of our company in India.
- I'm pretty sure that reducing the prices will improve our sales.

However, in many cases during a discussion, more than one reason may be needed to support your opinions. In order to develop your opinions by giving a series of causes or consequences, you may have to use connectives or transitional words. Some examples are given below.

- I think implementing uniform civil code in India is out of question. First of all, it would be impossible to develop a civil code that is acceptable to all the religious groups in India, and what's more, forcing any civil code on an unwilling group would go against the democratic spirit and lead to social unrest.
- I think we should go ahead with the plan to reduce the price of our car. This will help us clear the old stock and apart from that it will pose tough competition to other cars in this segment and improve our sales.
- Capital punishment should not be abolished. First, if we abolish death sentence, there won't be fear in the minds of the criminals because it serves as a deterrent, and in addition, absence of the death sentence will encourage personal vendettas, as the relatives of the victim might take law in their hands to punish the killer.
- We must reduce our energy consumption. First, there's the high price of oil and electricity. Secondly, there's the long-term danger of using up oil stocks.

Balancing Points of View

In order to be reasonable and rational, GD participants may have to balance points of view by trying to look at both sides of a given opinion. They need to balance advantages and disadvantages. The following are some examples.

- The fall in interest rates is good for industry as it makes borrowing cheaper. However, it might adversely affect the balance of payments situation in India by affecting the exchange rates and making essential imports like oil more expensive.
- Of course, reducing the prices of our car will help us clear the old stock and improve our sales, but it will adversely affect the company profits and can damage the company's image in the long run.
- Although capital punishment serves as a deterrent by instilling fear of the law in the minds of the criminals, it promotes barbarism, which is no longer acceptable to our modern ideas, times, and values.

Agreeing and Disagreeing

Agreeing and disagreeing are the two aspects of interaction in a GD. When a participant agrees or disagrees to someone or accepts or rejects the suggestions and proposals given by other members, he/she should clearly express his/her agreement/ disagreement. When you agree with someone your expression of agreement should indicate to the listener the strength of your agreement, which might be strong or neutral. Look at the following examples given in Table 11.3.

> When you agree with someone your expression of agreement should indicate to the listener the strength of your agreement, which might be strong or neutral.

TABLE 11.3 Examples of Strong and Neutral Agreement

Strong Agreement	*Neutral Agreement*
• I strongly agree.	• I agree.
• I quite agree.	• Yes.
• I completely agree.	• Of course.
• I'm in complete agreement.	• Right.
• Of course, yes.	• That's true.
• Yes, certainly.	• You are right.
• Yes, definitely.	• OK
• Exactly.	• That's fine.
• Precisely.	• I think you are right.

Similarly, our expression of disagreement should indicate to the listener the strength of our disagreement. Read the examples in Table 11.4.

TABLE 11.4 Examples of Strong and Neutral Disagreement

Strong Disagreement	*Neutral Disagreement*
• I strongly disagree.	• I disagree.
• I disagree completely.	• I don't agree.
• This is totally unacceptable.	• No.
• That is out of question.	• That's not true.
• Definitely not.	• That's not right.
• Of course not	• I think you are mistaken.

Progress Check 7

1. **Give opinions on the following topics for discussion according to the directions in brackets. Support your opinion with some kind of justification. Begin by reading the first solved example.**

   Example

   Reduction of IIM fees is a retrograde step. (Neutral opinion supporting the point of view)

   I think that the reduction of IIM fees is a retrograde step because it will lead to a fall in academic standards at IIMs due to paucity of funds.

   (a) There should be reservation for women in the parliament. (Neutral opinion rejecting the point of view)

   (b) Coalition governments can never be strong. (Neutral opinion supporting the point of view)

   (c) IITs should be privatised. (Neutral opinion rejecting the point of view)

   (d) The public sector has failed in India. (Neutral opinion rejecting the point of view)

   (e) There should be no reservation in jobs. (Strong opinion supporting the point of view)

   (f) Indian Railways should be privatised. (Strong opinion supporting the point of view)

2. **Respond to the following opinions by agreeing or disagreeing. Justify your point of view.**

   (a) Religion and politics should not be mixed.

   (b) The key industries in India should be privatised.

   (c) President's rule should be imposed in states one month before election.

   (d) The present examination system in universities in India needs modification.

   (e) States should be given more autonomy for better governance.

3. **Study the following table. Combine the advantage/s and disadvantage/s to provide a balanced opinion.**

	Opinion	Advantages	Disadvantages
(i)	Sales tax should be increased.	• Create more revenue for the government	• Leads to inflation
(ii)	Foreign equity should be allowed in the Indian print media.	• Lower the prices of Indian newspapers and magazines • Improve the quality of print media	• involve foreigners in our democratic process
(iii)	Strikes should be banned in essential services like health and power.	• Improve the efficiency of these services	• Create employee dissatisfaction
(iv)	All government offices should be computerised.	• Promotes efficiency	• Increases unemployment
(v)	Interest rates in India should be reduced.	• Makes borrowing cheaper • Promotes industry	• Makes imports expensive • Adversely affects balance of payments

Exchanging Suggestions and Proposals

An opinion is what seems to be probably true while a suggestion is a proposal to do something.

During a group discussion, participants need to get the suggestions of other members of the group in order to conduct the discussion, and to explore possible solutions to actual problem situations. There is a difference between an opinion and a suggestion. An opinion is what seems to one to be probably true while a suggestion is a proposal to do something.

Exchanging suggestions and proposals include requesting and making suggestions/proposals, and accepting and rejecting suggestions/proposals.

Requesting Suggestions

Your request for suggestions might be directed at one person or it may be an open request for the group. Look at the following Table 11.5.

TABLE 11.5 Examples of Request for Suggestion

Directed at One Person	*Directed at a Group of People*
• What do you suggest?	• Any suggestions?
• What is your suggestion?	• Any recommendations?
• What would you suggest?	• Do any of you have any suggestions?
• What should we do?	• I'd like to have some of your recommendations.
• What do you recommend?	• Do any of you want to make any suggestion/recommendation?
• Do you think we should...?	

Making Suggestions

During a case study discussion, participants, particularly leaders, may have to make suggestions or present various alternatives to solve the problem situation. Like opinions, suggestions may also be strong, neutral, or tentative. Study the following examples in Table 11.6.

TABLE 11.6 Examples of Different Type of Suggestions

Strong Suggestions	*Neutral Suggestions*	*Tentative Suggestions*
• There's no way but to...	• I suggest that...	• One alternative could be...
• There's no alternative but to...	• I would suggest that...	• One way would be to...
• The only way is to...	• We should...	• One solution could be...
• The only alternative is to...	• My suggestion is that...	• How about ——ing ...
• The only solution is to...	• My recommendation is that...	• What about —— ing...

Several phrases may also be used to put forward alternatives. The following are some examples.

- There are at least three different ways to deal with this situation. The first solution is to... Another possibility could be... The third alternative can be...
- There appears to be at least two solutions to this problem. One solution could be to... Another alternative is to...

Accepting and Rejecting Proposals

While discussing a problem or a case, proposals put forward by other members of the group may need to be accepted or rejected. As the leader's acceptance will show his/her support to the concerned member, the expression he/she chooses should indicate the strength of his/her support. Strong phrases may be used to indicate a strong acceptance while the use of weak phrases or informal expressions might show neutral or weak support. Some examples are given in Table 11.7.

TABLE 11.7 Examples of Strong and Weak Support

Strong Support	*Weak Support*
• I'm sure that is the best option.	• Good idea.
• It is the best solution.	• It appears to be a good idea.
• It is an excellent idea	• It may be tried.
• I strongly favour this.	• Sounds OK.
• I'm strongly in favour of that.	• Sounds fine.
• That's a great idea.	• OK.
• I'm completely in favour of that.	• Fine.

Similarly, the expression of rejection of a proposal put forward by other members must indicate the strength of the rejection. Strong, standard or diplomatic rejections may be used according to the need of the situation. Table 11.8 gives some examples.

TABLE 11.8 Examples of Different Types of Rejections

Strong Rejections	*Standard Rejections*	*Diplomatic Rejections*
• It is not possible/feasible.	• I'm sorry, but that is not possible/ feasible.	• I appreciate your point of view but ...
• It's not possible to accept that.	• I'm sorry I can't accept that.	• That's a good idea but I still feel that...
• I can't accept it.	• I'm afraid I am against that.	• You have a point but...
• I'm strongly against that.	• I'm sorry, but that is not acceptable.	• I can see your point but...
• I'm completely against this.	• I'm afraid that is not practical.	• That sounds interesting but...
• I really find it unacceptable.		• That's a good point but I still think that...
• I'm absolutely against this proposal.		

When a leader supports or rejects proposals or solutions given by other members, he/she has to give reasons for doing so. Look at the following examples.

- I'm sure that is the best option. My first reason is that ... My second ...
- It is the best solution. Firstly because... Secondly....

- It is an excellent idea. First, due to … and secondly….
- I'm strongly in favour of this solution. One reason is … Another is…
- I'm sorry, but this is not practical. Firstly because… Secondly….
- I'm absolutely against this proposal. First, due to … and secondly….

Progress Check 8

1. **Study the following table that contains some problems (left column) and their proposed solutions (right column). Give suggestions in the light of these solutions. Read the solved example.**

Solved Example

Problems	Proposed solutions
One of the chemical products of the company have been found to be harmful.	(i) Stop production. (ii) Withdraw the stock from the market.

First of all, we must stop production of the chemical product. Then we should withdraw the stock from the market in order to save the name and reputation of our company.

Problems	Proposed solutions
(a) Your company is having problems with its production, which has been reducing for unknown reasons.	(i) Appoint a new production manager. (ii) Rationalise and modernize production methods.
(b) The company wants to recruit efficient executive trainees,	(i) Use a recruitment agency. (ii) Advertise in the press.
(c) Sales of a new electronic stabiliser have been very poor and stocks are high.	(i) Stop production. (ii) Cut prices.
(d) Due to increased competition, the new television model launched by the company has failed to make an impact on the market.	(i) Intensify publicity. (ii) Cut prices. (iii) Introduce attractive customer prizes.
(e) There have been problems in the delivery and distribution of goods.	(i) Improve distribution networking. (ii) Set up automated regional warehouses.

2. **Study the following table and accept or reject the proposals (left column) by giving reasons and choosing appropriate expressions as indicated in brackets (right column).**

Proposals	Reasons for accepting/rejecting
(a) We suggest that we should introduce five days of working instead of six days by working an extra hour everyday.	• Improve efficiency • Promote a better work culture (standard acceptance)
(b) What do you think of giving every officer in the company a laptop with internet facility?	• Burden on company exchequer • No obvious benefit (diplomatic rejection)
(c) I suggest that we introduce flexitime in the administrative departments of our company.	• Need lot of official adjustments and readjustments

	• Create dissatisfaction in other departments • Adverse affect on the motivation of staff in other departments (standard rejection)
(d) What about hiring a recruitment agency to recruit our sales staff?	• Expensive • Time consuming (diplomatic rejection)
(e) Why don't we consult a specialised security agency to take care of our security problems?	• More effective • Save time and money (strong support)
(f) I suggest we shift our headquarters from Kolkata to Mumbai.	• Expensive exercise • Time consuming (diplomatic rejection)

Exercise

1. **Answer the following questions:**
   (a) Which of the following statements about group discussion is false?
      (i) Group discussion is concerned with some form of outcome: reaching a decision, resolving a difference, solving a problem, understanding a situation, or achieving some other group goal.
      (ii) The purpose of GD is clearly defined and accepted by the group.
      (iii) GD involves person-to-person interactions but it does not involve person-to-group interactions.
      (iv) The leadership function is shared in GD and it is not the responsibility of one person.
      (v) GD is systematic and logical.
   (b) Which of the following are specific functions of group discussion? (Tick the correct ones)
      (i) Aiding in problem solving
      (ii) Advocating a particular point of view
      (iii) Getting group vote
      (iv) Resolving a difference
      (v) Training others in personal skills
      (vi) Securing commitment
   (c) Any effective problem-solving discussion relies on some basic principles of reflective thinking. Which of the following do not involve these principles?
      (i) Awareness of the problem
      (ii) Definition of the problem
      (iii) Analysis of the problem
      (iv) Establishing the criteria for solutions
      (v) Suggesting possible solutions
      (vi) Exploring possible solutions
      (vii) Sticking to one solution
      (viii) Selecting the best solution

2. **Write short notes on the following.**
   (i) Nature and importance of group discussion
   (ii) Selection group discussions
   (iii) Individual contribution in group discussion
   (iv) Group interaction in GD
   (v) Leadership functions in GD
3. **Give opinions on the following topics for discussion according to the directions in brackets. Support your opinion with some kind of justification.**
   (a) Public sector has contributed to India's poor economic growth. (Strong opinion accepting the point of view)
   (b) The policy of reservation in jobs goes against the concept of social equality. (Neutral opinion rejecting the point of view)
   (c) The coming of multinational companies to India has boosted the Indian economy. (Neutral opinion accepting the point of view)
   (d) All the banks in India should be privatised. (Strong opinion rejecting the point of view)
   (e) Terrorism should be controlled by force and not by negotiation. (Strong opinion accepting the point of view)
4. **Form a group of four persons and discuss the following topic. Write a report on each discussion and show it to your communication teacher for his comments and suggestions.**
   (i) Brain drain should be stopped.
   (ii) Technical and professional education should be completely privatised.
   (iii) Indian media needs to be more accountable.
   (iv) The structure and system of the civil services examination needs to be changed.
   (v) Multinational companies should not be allowed to invest in key industries.
   (vi) Human cloning should be banned.
   (vii) Sick public sector units should be sold to private companies.
   (viii) There should be reservation for women in police services to protect their interests.
5. **Suppose you discuss the following case in a GD. There are four possible solutions to the problem situation. You reject three of them and accept only one. Write as you will speak in the GD to comment on the effects of the proposals that you reject and give reasons for the one you accept.**
   This company is a reputed car manufacturer of Europe, manufacturer of the best selling car in the continent. It introduced their most basic model (a 999 cc petrol car) in India at a price of Rs 2,70,000 about six months ago. This is close to the Maruti Alto LX Model. However, the sales of the car is very discouraging. The company could sell only 1200 units against the 25000 units manufactured by the company for India this year. The stocks are lying unsold and the company dealers are very disappointed. What should the company management do?
   (i) The company should stop further production of the car.
   (ii) The company should reduce the price of the car.
   (iii) The company should send the remaining 13,800 units of the car to Europe.
   (iv) The company should intensify the publicity campaign for the car.
6. **Read the following description of a company problem and then discuss the list of proposals, giving reasons for your point of view.**
   A medium sized company, which produces electronic toys, is facing a strike by its sales representatives who are demanding a hike in their sales incentive. Background information to the case is given below.

Key facts

- Most of the sales representatives are very senior.
- Sales representatives work 40 hours week (9.00—18.00) with a lunch break of one hour.
- The salary structure of the sales representatives is linked to their sales performance.
- There has been no revision of scales for the sales staff for the last six years.
- The sales staff gets a sales linked incentive, which is 1 % of their annual sale.
- There has been more pressure on increasing sales due to the launch of several new products during the last six months.
- The sales figures have gone up and order books are full.
- Sales representatives have a strong union.

Key to Progress Check

Progress Check 1

1. (c), (f), (i) and (l).

Progress Check 2

1. (c), (d), (e), and (i)
2. The second situation is more conducive to a successful group discussion.

Progress Check 3

(c), (e), (g), and (i)

Progress Check 4

1. (f)	2. (j)	3. (g)	4. (h)	5. (a)
6. (l)	7. (c)	8. (e)	9. (i)	10. (k)
11. (d)	12. (b)			

Progress Check 5

Do's	Don'ts
1. Initiate the proceedings of the group discussion.	1. Get involved in cross talk, low-key conversations, cross-consultations, and asides.
2. Propose the procedures to be followed during the discussion.	2. Force the group to start the discussion without wasting time.
3. Create an atmosphere in which all members feel free to participate.	3. Encourage personality conflicts.
4. Keep members informed of their own progress.	4. Try to be the centre of attention all the time.
5. Avoid any digression that may sidetrack the group.	5. Comment on everyone and everything.
6. Encourage non-participants to speak.	6. Monopolise the discussion.
7. Make each member feel that his or her contribution is important.	7. Push the GD too fast

8. Control talkative members.
9. Maintain a friendly attitude.
10. Provide positive guidance to the group by making occasional summaries.
11. Help to establish the attitude of critical objectivity.
12. Put forward the common points of agreement.

8. Avoid conflicts between ideas.

Progress Check 6

1. (b), (e), (g), and (i)

2.

Opinions	Problems	Case Studies
1, 3, 5, 6	1, 5, 6, 7, 8	1, 2, 4, 5, 6, 8

Progress Check 7

1. (a) I do not think that reservation for women in parliament will serve any purpose. In fact, it will create social inequality and lead to illogical reservation demands.
   (b) I believe that a coalition government can never be strong because it cannot take bold and strong decisions due to so many pulls and pressures by the coalition parties for their narrow vested interests.
   (c) I think that IITs should not be privatised because their privatisation will lead to a rise in tuition fees and fall in academic standards.
   (d) I do not think that public sector has failed in India. On the contrary, it has contributed to India's economic growth.
   (e) I am firmly convinced that there should be no reservation in jobs because it leads to incompetence and inefficiency.
   (f) It is perfectly clear to me that privatisation of Indian Railways will increase its effectiveness and efficiency.
2. (a) I strongly agree. Mixing religion and politics will lead to communal differences and social divisions.
   (b) I do not agree. India is a socialistic country and the main objective of government control is the welfare of the masses. By privatising essential industries, the very objective of socialism will fail.
   (c) I do not agree with the idea of state elections under President's rule. This may develop mistrust between the state government and the central government. Moreover, it may lead to misuse of power on a large scale by the political party at the centre.
   (d) I agree. The present system of examination promotes learning by rote and discourages creativity and originality, which are so essential for personality development.
   (e) I do not agree with the idea of more autonomy for states because it will promote regionalism and lead to national disintegration.
3. (i) I do not agree with the idea of increasing sales tax. I accept that it can create more revenue for the government but I strongly feel that it pushes up inflation.
   (ii) I do not agree. Although allowing foreign equity in the print media may lower the prices of Indian newspapers and magazines and improve the quality of print media, it is against our national interests because it will involve foreigners in our democratic process.
   (iii) Personally I am in favour of a complete ban on strikes in essential services like health and power. I can accept that it creates employee dissatisfaction but I feel that it improves the efficiency of these services.

(iv) I do not agree that all the government offices should be computerised. Computerising government offices may promote efficiency but it increases unemployment.

(v) I do not agree that interest rates in India should be reduced. Although the fall in interest rates makes borrowing cheaper and promotes industry, it adversely affects the balance of payments situation by making imports expensive.

Progress Check 8

1. (a) As I see it, we have no alternative but to appoint a new production manager. In addition, I think that we should rationalise and modernise production methods.

   (b) I think there are two possible ways of dealing with this problem. We could either use a recruitment agency, or advertise in the press.

   (c) I strongly recommend that we stop production. In addition, I suggest that we should cut prices to clear stocks.

   (d) As I see it, there are three possible solutions. One solution is to intensify publicity to create market demand. Another possibility is to cut prices to face the competition. Finally, we could introduce attractive prizes for customers to promote sales.

   (e) I think that we should improve our distribution networking. In addition, we should set up automated regional warehouses in order to improve distribution of stock.

2. (a) That is a good idea. It will definitely improve efficiency and promote a better work culture.

   (b) I can see your point but I still feel that it will be burden on company exchequer with no obvious benefit.

   (c) I am afraid that is not practical. Firstly, because it will need lot of official adjustments and readjustments. Secondly, it will create dissatisfaction in other departments and adversely affect the motivation of staff in other departments.

   (d) That sounds interesting but I think it will be both expensive and time consuming.

   (e) I am sure that is the best option. My first reason is that it will be more effective than our security arrangements. My second reason is that it will save both time and money.

   (f) That is a good idea but I still feel that it will be an expensive exercise that will take up too much time.

12 CHAPTER

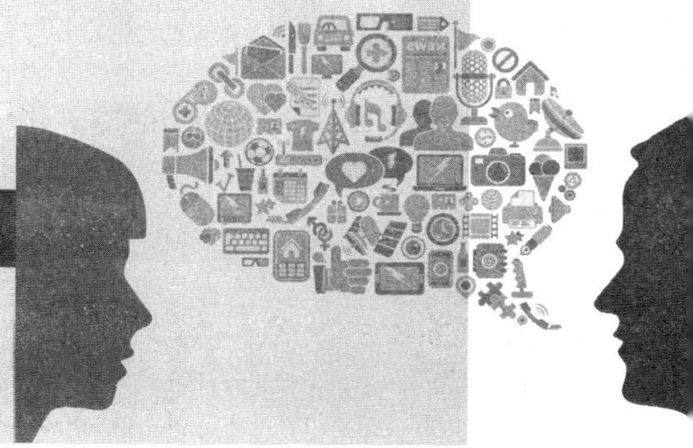

Presentation Skills

Half the world is composed of people who have something to say and can't; the other half have nothing to say and keep saying it.

—Lenny Laskowski

LEARNING OBJECTIVES

- Understanding the nature and importance of presentation skills
- Knowing different pre-presentation planning steps
- Identifying the four important steps in preparing an effective oral presentation
- Learning how to structure and organize a presentation.
- Understanding the major elements in the introduction, body, and conclusion of an oral presentation
- Knowing how to identify specific techniques for rehearsing a presentation
- Reviewing techniques for effective delivery
- Learning how to handle stage fright

12.1 ORAL PRESENTATION

An oral presentation is a form of oral communication. It is a participative two-way communication process characterised by the formal and structured presentation of a message using visual aids. It is purposeful and goal-oriented, and communicates a message to an audience in a way that brings about the desired change in their understanding or opinion. It is flexible, changing, as well as complex and varied. Thus, an oral presentation is:

> Oral presentations are purposeful, interactive, formal, and audience oriented.

- Purposeful—The presentation will be made with a definite purpose.
- Interactive—It involves both the speaker as well as the listeners.
- Formal—It is a formal situation.
- Audience oriented—The topic will have to be dealt with from the listeners' perspective.

There are several forms of oral presentation, such as seminars, workshops, symposia, student presentations, industry conferences, product launches, press conferences, team presentations, annual general meetings, departmental presentations, and company profile presentations. Whatever may be the form of presentation, they all seek to achieve certain objectives. These objectives may range from exploring a new area of information to introducing a new product by a company.

> Speeches are intended to celebrate an occasion, to felicitate a person, to welcome or bid farewell to someone, or to inaugurate a function, while oral presentations raise a particular issue for discussion.

Oral presentations differ from other forms of oral communication such as speeches and debates. Although speeches and presentations share several common features, there is a thin dividing line between the two. Speeches are intended to celebrate an occasion, to felicitate a person, to welcome or bid farewell to someone, or to inaugurate a function, while oral presentations raise a particular issue for discussion.

12.2 IMPORTANCE OF PRESENTATION SKILLS

We may not all be professional public speakers but we may have to make a presentation at some point of time or the other. Whether one is a student, a professional engineer, an academician, or a business executive, one may have to make oral presentations in front of one's colleagues or professional peers. A professional student may be required to make presentations in the form of progress reports, student seminars, research presentations, and so on. Professionals in different fields, including scientists and engineers, have also to make oral reports, present seminars, deliver project presentations, or present a proposal orally. Similarly, business executives may have to introduce a new product that their company has launched, to present a new sales plan that they want others to know about, or they may just have a brilliant idea that they would like to share with their colleagues.

Thus, of the many skills that contribute to professional success, none is more important than the ability to communicate orally in front of a group of people. Business people rank oral presentation skills among the most important factors responsible for their success. Oral presentation is a tool of professional and business interaction. In fact, in some organisations, institutions, or universities, recruitment is made on the basis of a selection process, which involves oral presentation in the form of seminar presentation, short lectures, business presentations or some other form of oral presentation.

> Business people rank oral presentation skills among the most important factors responsible for their success.

A good presentation can do wonders for a person; it may help in getting a lucrative job offer from the company he/she always wanted to join, he/she may get a big business deal or the promotion he/she had been waiting for. The list is long. On the other hand, a poor presentation of ideas not only reduces the professional image of the person presenting it, but may result in major business or personal loss.

Therefore, the ability to deliver an effective presentation is essential for all of us. We should know how to present our ideas in a persuasive way, how to make our audience interested in our presentation, how to use appropriate visuals during our presentation, and how to reflect confidence while speaking. A person making a presentation should have the ability to begin his presentation in an effective way, develop his/her ideas logically and conclude his/her presentation with something memorable. He/she needs to understand the basic elements of an effective presentation—the 4 Ps, i.e., Plan, Prepare, Practice, and Perform.

> The basic elements of an effective presentation are the 4 Ps, i.e. Plan, Prepare, Practice, and Perform.

Progress Check 1

1. Which of the following statements about oral presentations are false?

(a) Oral presentation is a form of address in which a speaker addresses an audience.
(b) Oral presentations are less formal than speeches.
(c) Oral presentations are more formal than conversation.
(d) An oral presentation is a one-way communication process characterised by the formal and structured presentation of a message.
(e) Oral presentations are purposeful and goal-oriented, and communicate a message to an audience in a way that brings about the desired change in their understanding or opinions.
(f) Workshops and industry conferences are the two forms of oral presentation.
(g) The objectives of oral presentations may range from exploring a new area of information to introducing a new product by a company.
(h) Oral presentations do not differ from other forms of oral communication such as speeches and debates.
(i) Oral presentations are intended to celebrate an occasion, felicitate a person, to welcome or bid farewell to someone, or to inaugurate a function.
(j) Business people rank oral presentation skills among the most important factors in their success.

12.3 STAGES OF A PRESENTATION

12.3.1 Planning the Presentation

An oral presentation is the formal, structured, and systematic presentation of a message to an audience and it involves conveying a lot of information in a limited time. It should, therefore, be planned well in advance so that the material is delivered effectively. Planning the presentation is, thus, the most important element. It helps the presenter to:

- Know the audience

> Planning a presentation involves defining the purpose, analysing the audience, analysing the occasion, and choosing a suitable title.

- Stimulate the interest of the audience
- Be sensitive to the needs and expectations of the audience
- Strike up interaction with his/her immediate audience in as many ways as possible
- Know his/her purpose
- Analyse the occasion
- Fit the material to the time at his/her disposal
- Select and narrow a topic for his/her presentation.

Planning an oral presentation, thus, involves purpose identification, audience analysis, analysing the occasion, and the process of selecting and narrowing the topic of presentation. The following suggestions will help in planning well:

Defining the Purpose

Planning a presentation should start by defining its purpose. What is the purpose of this presentation? This is the most important question that needs to be answered in order to make a presentation focused, with clear objectives. A general purpose as well as a specific purpose should be identified. General purposes include:

- To inform—to share information
- To persuade—to change behaviour, attitude, belief, values, and so on
- To demonstrate—to help listeners know how to do something

Identifying the specific purpose of a presentation involves identifying an observable measurable action that the audience should be able to take, and using one idea that matches audience needs, knowledge, expectations, and interests. It should focus on audience behaviour and restate the speech topic.

A presentation could be informative, persuasive or demonstrative depending on the purpose.

Study the following examples:

- At the end of my presentation, the audience will be able to describe three advantages of using HP PrecisionScan LT software.

  (Informative presentation)
- At the end of my presentation, the audience will believe that the HP PrecisionScan LT is the best scanning software.

  (Persuasive presentation)
- At the end of my presentation, the audience will be able to use HP PrecisionScan LT software.

  (Demonstrative presentation)

Analysing the Audience

The desired results cannot be achieved from a presentation unless the person making the presentation knows his/her audience well. Audience analysis is an integral part of the process of oral presentation. It includes identifying audience characteristics, analysing audience needs and expectations, and identifying factors for getting and maintaining audience attention.

> Lenny Laskowski, *an international professional speaker and an expert on presentation skills, has used the word A-U-D-I-E-N-C-E as an acronym, and has defined some general audience analysis categories that all surveys should include. The 'acronym' is reproduced below:*
>
> **A_udience**—*Who are the members? How many will be at the event?*
> **U_nderstanding**—*What is their knowledge about the topic I will be addressing?*
> **D_emographics**—*What is their age, sex, educational background, and so forth?*
> **I_nterest**—*Why will they be at this event? Who asked them to be there?*
> **E_nvironment**—*Where will I stand when I speak? Will everyone be able to see me?*
> **N_eeds**—*What are the listener's needs? What are my needs as a speaker? What are the needs of the person who wants me to speak?*
> **C_ustomised**—*How can I custom fit my message to this audience?*
> **E_xpectations**—*What do the listeners expect to learn from me?*

Identify Audience Characteristics

In order to know the audience, the presenter needs to identify their basic characteristics. He/she should try to gather as much background information about his/her listeners as he/she can—their age, gender, social, economic and educational background, religion, political affiliations, profession, attitudes (likes and dislikes), beliefs (true and false), and values (good and bad). If these audience characteristics are identified, he/she will be much better equipped to plan and prepare his/her presentation effectively.

Analyse Audience Needs and Expectations

Those who will attend and listen to the presentation have their needs and expectations. They will be there for a reason. If the presenter wants them to listen to him/her, he/she has to understand and respond to their needs and expectations. For this he/she should ask the following questions:

- Why will they listen to me?
- Who asked them to be there?
- Is their attendance compulsory?
- What are their interests?
- What ideas or experience do I have that the audience may like to hear?
- What are their needs?
- What do they expect?
- How do my objectives meet audience needs?

> The presentation must be audience oriented, dealing with the topic from their perspective. The presenter may not change his/her ideas and facts for his/her audience but he/she may change the way he/she conveys them.

Answers to these questions will help him/her make appropriate modification in his/her presentation to suit his/her audience. The presentation must be audience oriented, dealing with the topic from their perspective. The presenter may not change his/her ideas and facts for his/her audience but he/she may change the way he/she conveys them. He/she may tell them what he/she wants to tell but in a way that appeals to them.

Recognise Factors for Getting and Maintaining Audience Attention

> Listeners will be more interested in the presentation if it meets their requirements.

Once the characteristics, needs, and expectations of the audience have been identified, factors that meet the needs of the listeners should be determined. Listeners will be more interested in the presentation if it meets their requirements. As a result, they will listen more attentively, understand what is said, and remember the key points of the presentation. The presenter needs to consider the following specific questions in this context:

- How can I relate my presentation to the needs and expectations of my audience?
- What should I do to ensure that my audience remembers my main points?
- What style will appeal to my audience?
- What are the changes that I should make?
- Have I incorporated ways of encouraging my listeners to give feedback and share information that will make my presentation more effective?
- Have I planned strategies for dealing with listeners' communication apprehensions?
- How will I handle hostile listeners or those who are disruptive?

Moreover, more informed decisions can be made about how to best adapt to the varying moods of listeners and how to tap their curiosity, interest, and motivation. Perhaps the best rule to remember in identifying factors for getting and keeping audience attention is to remain flexible. A blend of methods and alternatives to accommodate listeners' perceptions may be the best approach to audience analysis.

Analysing the Occasion

The occasion on which the presentation is to be made should be analysed in order to understand the nature of the event or communicative situation. Several aspects of the event like its background, the people involved, the organisations or associations linked to the event, and so on need to be considered. Here are some relevant questions.

- Is my presentation part of a larger event like a national/international seminar with a central theme, or just an internal conference where I am supposed to present my views on a particular topic?
- Am I familiar with the procedures of the event?
- Who are the sponsors?
- Who are the other speakers?
- What is the venue?
- What is the duration of my presentation?

In fact, thinking through the answers to some of these questions ahead of time may ensure that the presentation is effective.

Choosing a Suitable Title

Generally, a title has to be chosen for the presentation. The title gives the audience the first glimpse of the presentation and they form their first impression. Therefore, it is essential that the title is appropriate and conveys the essence of the message. A vague, misleading, and fussy title may confuse the audience.

> The process of choosing a title may begin by first identifying a topic.

The process of choosing a title may begin by first identifying a topic. The choice of the topic depends on the occasion, the audience, the type, and purpose of the presentation. A list of topics may be compiled, including potential topics like social, economic, political, technological and environmental problems (for example, poverty, unemployment, overpopulation, corruption, crime, inflation, AIDS epidemic, and so on.); ideas regarding society, education, business and economy, government, technological systems, and so forth, and reactions to debatable issues (for example, universal civil code, Article 370, politics and religion, and abortion). When all the possible topics have been noted, the choices can be evaluated and an appropriate topic may be chosen.

After a suitable topic has been selected for the presentation, it should be narrowed down as per the focus of the presentation in order to phrase a clear, complete, specific, and focused title. In this process, the nature of the general and specific purposes of the presentation as well as audience expectations and rhetorical sensitivity may be considered. For example, if the selected topic is 'pollution', it may be narrowed to any of the following:

- Vehicular pollution hazards in New Delhi (local focus)
- Pollution of the Ganges (national focus)
- CFC's and ozone depletion (international focus)

Progress Check 1

1. **What is the problem in the following flow diagram representing planning a presentation?**

   Analyse the occasion. ⟶ Choose the **title.** ⟶ Analyse the **audience.** ⟶ Define the **purpose.**

2. **Study the following table and match different pre-presentation planning steps (left column) with appropriate stages of planning a presentation (right column):**

Pre-presentation planning steps	Stages of planning a presentation
1. Analyse the background.	A. Purpose analysis
2. Recognise factors for getting and maintaining audience attention.	B. Audience analysis
3. Identify an observable measurable action that the audience should be able to take.	C. Occasion analysis
4. Narrow the topic as per the focus of your presentation.	D. Choosing the title
5. Restate the speech topic and focus on audience behaviour.	
6. Identify audience characteristics.	
7. Identify a general purpose.	
8. Analyse audience needs and expectations.	
9. Determine factors meeting the needs of your listeners.	

12.3.2 Preparing the Presentation

> Preparing for a presentation involves developing the central idea and the main points, gathering supporting material, and planning visual aids.

Once the presentation has been planned, it is time to begin preparing for it. Preparing well is the key to success. Making an oral presentation—whether a seminar presentation, an oral report, a project presentation, or a business presentation—is easier when it is prepared it in a systematic manner. Being prepared helps the presenter

- deal with speech anxiety effectively;

- develop the required confidence;
- seek precise and relevant examples and illustrations; and
- check for accuracy, redundancies, and cliches.

Preparing for a presentation involves developing the central idea and main points, gathering relevant supporting material, and planning visual aids.

Developing the Central Idea

The central idea of the presentation is its core idea or thesis statement. It should be a complete declarative sentence that captures the essence of the message. The following are the characteristics of a central idea:

- It restates the presentation topic.
- It is a simple audience-centered idea.
- It is a one-sentence summary of the presentation.
- It focuses on the content of the speech.
- It uses specific language.

> The central idea of the presentation is a complete declarative sentence that captures the essence of the message.

Developing the Main Ideas

Develop the main ideas for the presentation. The presenter may make a logical division of the central idea, establish reasons for the idea being true, or support the central idea with a series of steps. Choosing one of these techniques will largely depend on the topic of the presentation as well as its objectives. Study the following examples:

- Logical division of the central idea
  Example: Central idea: Unemployment in India
  Logical divisions: A. Types B. Causes C. Solutions
- Establishing reasons for the central idea being true
  Example: Central idea: Education in India needs to be restructured
  Establishing reasons: A. Reason 1 B. Reason 2 C. Reason 3
- Supporting the central idea with a series of steps
  Example: Central idea: Indo-Pak Relations can be improved
  Series of steps: A. Strategy 1 B. Strategy 2 C. Strategy 3

> The presenter may make a logical division of the central idea, establish reasons for the idea being true, or support the central idea with a series of steps.

Gathering Supporting Material

One of the most difficult aspects of preparing a presentation is gathering relevant supporting information. Information that will be used in the presentation should be carefully selected. This will depend on the scope and length of the presentation.

While gathering supporting information a systematic approach should be adopted. First, the presenter should gather all his/her thoughts on the subject and then recall related information from his/her personal knowledge and experience. Thereafter, several research resources such as the Internet, library resources, personal interviews, and discussion with experts, colleagues, and special interest groups should be consulted. A list of material to be included in your presentation should be made. The supporting material gathered may include facts, examples, definitions, quotations, and so on.

> One of the most difficult aspects of preparing a presentation is gathering relevant supporting information.

An outline of the collected material is developed, and reworked until it is in good order. After that, the first draft is written and revised as required. It is important to check for accuracy, redundancies, and cliches.

Planning Visual Aids

Using appropriate visual aids will increase the effectiveness of presentations. Good visuals may serve the following purposes.

- ***They Serve as Speech Notes:*** Visual aids may be used as notes to emphasise and clarify the main points of the presentation. Each visual aid may contain a main idea. Effective titles may be used to convey the main message of the visual aid.
- ***They Give Confidence:*** Using good visuals might increase the presenter's self-confidence because they refresh his/her memory, establish his/her credibility, and show that he/she has planned, is well-prepared, and is professional.
- ***They Help Focus on the Theme of the Presentation:*** Visuals help the presenter to focus on the theme of the presentation and concentrate on the objectives of his/her presentation. He/she may use effective visuals to highlight the central idea of his/her presentation.
- ***They Increase Audience Interest:*** Interesting and relevant visual aids make the audience more interested in what is being said. They may force even a hostile and demotivated audience to pay attention.
- ***They Give Clarity and Precision:*** Visuals make the presentation easy to understand and remember.

Any of the following types of visual aids may be used.

A. *Three-Dimensional Visual Aids*

(a) Objects
(b) Models
(c) People

B. *Two-Dimensional Visual Aids*

(a) Drawings
(b) Photographs
(c) Slides
(d) Maps
(e) Graphs
  - Bar graphs
  - Pie graphs
  - Line graphs
  - Picture graphs

(f) Charts
(g) Overhead transparencies
(h) Computer generated presentations
(i) Chalkboard

The following suggestions will help in planning and using visual aids effectively:

- Relevant visual aids must be chosen. The visual aids should match the message. Using a visual that does not match with what is being said is distracting and may confuse the audience.
- The presenter must be familiar with his/her visual aids and rehearse his/her presentation with using the visual aids.
- Computer software programs such as PowerPoint and Corel Presentations may be used to enhance the effectiveness of the presentation. However, special care must be taken while designing electronic presentations or multimedia presentations because making the presentation overly dependent on electronic visuals may create certain handicaps.
- Handouts may be distributed, i.e., charts, presentation abstracts, summaries, brochures, pamphlets, outlines, and so on, in order to complement the presentation.
- While using overhead transparencies, eye contact should be maintained with the audience.
- Visual aids must be introduced before actually showing them.

Using a visual that does not match with what is being said is distracting and may confuse the audience.

Progress Check 3

1. Complete the following statements by choosing an appropriate option.

(a) Being prepared does not help you to:
  (i) deal with speech anxiety effectively.
  (ii) identify redundancies and cliches used during the presentation.
  (iii) develop the required confidence.
  (iv) seek precise and relevant examples and illustrations.

(b) Preparing an effective oral presentation does not involve:
  (i) developing the central idea and main points.
  (ii) gathering relevant supporting material.
  (iii) planning visual aids.
  (iv) organising the presentation.

(c) The central idea of the presentation does not:
  (i) restate the presentation topic.
  (ii) include all the supporting points.
  (iii) capture the essence of the message.
  (iv) focus on the content of the speech.

(d) In order to develop the main ideas of the presentation, you need not:
  (i) develop an outline of the supporting material.
  (ii) make a logical division of the central idea.
  (iii) establish reasons for the central idea being true.
  (iv) support the central idea with a series of steps.

(e) While gathering supporting information, the presenter need not:
  (i) gather all his thoughts on the subject of the presentation.
  (ii) recall related information from his personal knowledge and experience.
  (iii) consult several research resources.

(iv) analyse audience characteristics.

(f) Visual aids may not

(i) serve as speech notes to emphasise and clarify the main points of the presentation.

(ii) help focus on the theme of the presentation.

(iii) help recall related information from personal knowledge and experience.

(iv) make the audience more interested in what is being said.

12.3.3 Organising the Presentation

After the central idea as well as the main ideas have been developed, relevant supporting material has been gathered, and appropriate visual aids have been planned, the message has to be organised and structured. Good organisation is essential for effective presentation. The key to good organisation is the repetition of the main ideas of your message. Just remember the three Ts:

> Your presentation should be organised into three distinct parts: introduction, body, and conclusion.

Tell the audience what you are going to tell.
Tell it.
Tell them what you have told.

Divide the presentation into three distinct parts: the introduction, body, and conclusion.

Introduction

The opening of the presentation should convince the audience to listen to it. It has five functions:

> The opening of the presentation should convince the audience to listen to it.

- Get the audience's attention
- Introduce the subject
- Give the audience a reason to listen
- Establish the credibility
- Preview the main ideas

Get Audience Attention

The speaker needs to get the attention of his/her audience and hold it until the end of his/her talk. Listeners form their first impression of the presentation quickly, and first impressions matter. Therefore, the opening should capture their attention. Audience attention may be captured in several ways. These techniques include using any one of the following:

- ***Startling Statement/Statistics*** Say something surprising or unexpected, or give statistics that surprises the audience.
- ***Anecdote*** Tell a short entertaining account of an event, a short story.
- ***Questions*** Ask some interesting questions. The question should be rhetorical with an obvious answer.
- ***Quotations*** Start the presentation with a relevant quotation that throws light on the central idea of the presentation.
- ***Humour*** Start the presentation with a humorous reference.

Introduce the Subject

A statement of the central idea should be included in the introduction. In simple and direct language the audience has to know what the presentation is about.

Give the Audience a Reason to Listen

Audience attention should be drawn to the topic of the presentation by showing them how the topic affects them directly. Giving relevant statistics can motivate the audience.

Establish the Credibility

The speaker's credibility should be established early in a speech. He/she should be able to convince the audience that he/she is worth listening to. The speaker should be well prepared, appear confident, and strike a rapport with the audience by narrating personal experiences relevant to the topic.

Preview the Main Ideas

The audience should be told what they are going to listen to. The preview to the presentation should be given towards the end of the introduction. The preview should include a statement of the central idea and mention the main points of the presentation.

> *Remember the acronym*
>
> *KISS*
> *(KEEP IT SIMPLE AND SHORT)*
> *Your audience will understand a simple message easily.*
>
> *SHORT*
> *Your audience may concentrate better if your message is short.*

Body

The body contains the main content of the presentation. Most people fail to make an effective presentation simply because they try to convey so much information and include so many ideas. The speaker may be tempted to include so many points in his/her presentation but it is advisable to focus on a few main ideas, two to four. Each main point should be supported by appropriate details but not excessive data. This will spoil the presentation because it may confuse the audience. In short, the *mantra* (key) is to use a few main points with relevant supporting details. The speaker should concentrate on each main point and use appropriate transitions to indicate a change of point as the audience may not be able to differentiate between the main points and minor points. He/she should ensure that his/her information is accurate, complete, and relevant.

> Most people fail to make an effective presentation simply because they try to convey so much information and include so many ideas.

As the body of the presentation is structured, the speaker should choose the sequence he/she will follow from among any of the following organisational patterns:

- Sequential
- General to specific

- Specific to general
- More important to less important
- Less important to more important
- Categorical
- Problem and solution
- Contrast and comparison

In developing the sequence of a presentation, transitions between sections, illustrations that will be used, and points of emphasis should also be decided.

Conclusion

The conclusion of your presentation should accomplish the following five specific objectives:

(i) Summarise the presentation
(ii) Re-emphasise the central idea
(iii) Focus on a goal
(iv) Motivate the audience to respond
(v) Provide closure

Summarise Your Presentation

The conclusion gives the speaker the last chance to present his/her key ideas. The main ideas should be repeated.

Re-emphasise the Central Idea

The central idea of the presentation should be restated in a memorable way.

Focus on a Goal

The speaker should focus on the specific objective of the presentation and concentrate on what he/she wants his audience to do, think, change, remember, and so on.

Motivate the Audience to Respond

The audience should be motivated to give feedback. They may be encouraged to ask questions.

Provide Closure

Verbal techniques may be used to let the audience know that the speech has ended. Appropriate words and phrases such as "in conclusion", "lastly", "finally", and "as my last point" may be used. The speaker may thank the audience for their patient listening. Non-verbal cues may also be used to signal closure.

> The speaker may thank the audience for their patient listening. Non-verbal cues may also be used to signal closure.

Progress Check 4

1. **Answer the following questions:**

   (a) Which of the following is not one of the functions of 'introduction' in an oral presentation?

   (i) Introduce the subject
   (ii) Demotivate the audience

(iii) Establish the credibility
(iv) Preview the main ideas

(b) The techniques used to capture audience attention does not include the use of:
(i) a question
(ii) an anecdote
(iii) a joke
(iv) a poem

(c) In order to involve the audience with the topic of presentation, the speaker should:
(i) include a statement of his/her central idea in the introduction
(ii) tell the audience what he/she is going to talk about
(iii) show the audience how the topic affects them directly
(iv) use a diagram

(d) In order to establish credibility, the speaker should:
(i) show the audience how the topic affects them directly
(ii) tell the audience his/her personal experience with the topic
(iii) involve the audience with the topic of his/her presentation
(iv) motivate the audience by giving relevant statistics

(e) Which of the following is false?
(i) The speaker should include as many points in his presentation as he can.
(ii) The audience will understand a simple message easily.
(iii) The audience may concentrate better if the message is short.
(iv) The speaker should focus on a few main ideas.

(f) Which of the following organisational pattern may not be very effective for structuring your presentation?
(i) General to specific
(ii) Categorical
(iii) Problem and solution
(iv) Classification

(g) Which of the following is not one of the functions of the 'conclusion' in an oral presentation?
(i) Summarising the presentation
(ii) Establishing credibility
(iii) Re-emphasising the central idea
(iv) Focusing on a goal

(h) In order to provide closure, the speaker should:
(i) restate the central idea of the presentation in a memorable way
(ii) focus on the specific objective of the presentation
(iii) motivate the audience to give feedback
(iv) use verbal techniques to let the audience know that the speech has ended

2. Correct the following flow diagram.

Tell the audience what has been told. ⟶ **Tell** it. ⟶ **Tell** the audience what is going to be told.

3. Study the following table and match the introductions used during oral presentations (left column) with appropriate techniques to capture audience attention (right column):

	Introductions used during oral presentations	Techniques to capture audience attention
(i)	Francis Bacon once said, "Travel is a part of education in the younger sort and a part of experience in the older." This is exactly what I want to talk about today.	A. The Startling Statement
(ii)	In choosing a college, most young boys and girls today face a dilemma. They have to decide whether they want co-education or just education. Well, friends, I am here today to talk about the cultural impact of co-education in our society.	B. Anecdotes
(iii)	The man took the girl to a hotel room where they spent the night. In the morning he abandoned her and never saw her again. The girl was just fourteen years old. She was just a child—a child who got into the flesh trade to feed her ailing parents. Today I would like to inform you about a national problem in India—child prostitution.	C. Questions
(iv)	The sales of our company has gone down by more than 30 per cent during the last two years; several new products launched by us have not been successful in the market; our sales strategy has completely failed. Ladies and Gentlemen, I am here today to talk about a new sales strategy that will change the entire scenario.	D. Quotations
(v)	Would you like to save 400 per cent on your next purchase of diskettes for your computer class? Would you be willing to give just a few minutes to learn to format your own diskettes instead of paying 400 per cent more for preformatted ones? Today I want to talk about how to format a diskette.	E. Humour

12.3.4 Rehearsing the Presentation

The speaker, having planned, prepared, and organised a presentation well, may feel confident about delivering it without any rehearsal. However, it is important to rehearse the presentation properly because it will give him/her more confidence and avoid any distraction and deviation during actual presentation. Moreover, it will make him/her familiar with his/her message and will give sufficient time to make positive changes in the presentation. Therefore, before giving a presentation, it should be practised several times.

> Rehearsal should be planned and conducted properly and systematically.

Before rehearsing a presentation it is necessary to answer a few pertinent questions. Who will the audience be? How many rehearsals are necessary? What would the methods of rehearsal be? Where should rehearsals be held? Should delivery notes be used while rehearsing? What should the duration of each rehearsal be? The answers to these questions depend on the topic, the speaker's familiarity with the topic, his/her oral communication skills, and objectives.

Specific computer software designed to help with rehearsal of presentations may be used. The presentation graphics package will help concentrate on key points, which may be displayed on the screen. There would be timing and pacing indicators that would help in maintaining an appropriate delivery rate and pauses for effectiveness. However, using computer software for rehearsals may make one computer-dependent.

The following suggestions will help in rehearsing the presentation in a proper and planned way.

Plan the Rehearsal

Reharsals should be planned well in advance, leaving sufficient time between the rehearsal and the actual presentation so that there is enough time to make the required modifications in the presentation. A rehearsal is an opportunity to review and revise the presentation. Hearing oneself speak may also give some new ideas to make the presentation more effective.

> A rehearsal is an opportunity to review and revise the presentation.

Rehearse Before a Live Audience

If possible rehearsals should be held before a live audience, involving them in the presentation. This helps in analysing their reactions and responding to them appropriately, in preparation for the actual presentation. Friends, classmates, colleagues, or roommates can make up the audience. Their responses, comments, and suggestions on your presentation help point out weaknesses and improve the presentation.

Timing During Rehearsal

While rehearsing a presentation, particular attention should be paid to timing. Although the rate of delivering the presentation may vary according to the communicative situation, delivery technique and style of speaking, a rate that varies between 120 to 180 words per minute is ideal. The speaker may be tempted to talk too quickly in presentations. However, to be effective he/she should speak slowly and pause appropriately between important points. This speed should be maintained during rehearsal too.

Recreate the Presentation Environment

Rehearsal is essential in order to experience the actual presentation. The main purpose of rehearsals is to help learn to make the presentation with confidence in a natural and spontaneous way. The speaker should be his/her natural self while rehearsing, and keep practising until he/she is confident of delivering the presentation smoothly.

12.3.5 Improving the Delivery

Once the presentation has been planned, prepared, organised and rehearsed properly and systematically, it can be delivered. What is important is said in a presentation but how it is said is more important. It is essential to improve delivery in order to give effective presentations. Improving delivery involves understanding several delivery methods, choosing an appropriate method, and controlling and reducing stage fear.

> The way a presentation is delivered does influence the way listeners will respond to the message.

The way a presentation is delivered does influence the way listeners will respond to the message. Thus, the most important element of a presentation is the speaker's performance. It involves choosing an appropriate delivery technique, using speech notes, and deciding the non-verbal behaviour.

Choosing Delivery Methods

There are three basic methods of delivery: the memorising method, reading method, and the outlining method. A speaker may choose a method of delivery that suits his/her content, style, and objectives.

Memorising Method

Some people prefer the memorising method, i.e., they memorise the entire presentation and present it from memory. This method may be used if the speaker has stage fear and is very nervous about giving the presentation. Learning what one intends to say word for word may develop the required confidence in the person. However, this method has its disadvantages. First, the speaker may forget something in the middle of his/her talk preventing him/her from continuing his presentation. This could be disastrous. Moreover, if the entire presentation is memorised, it may not sound spontaneous and natural creating monotony in the presentation. Finally, if the speaker concentrates more on what he/she is saying, he/she may not be able to involve the audience in his/her presentation.

> Some people memorise the entire presentation and present it from memory.

The following are some suggestions to use the memorising method effectively:

- Plan, prepare, and write out the presentation.
- Do not memorise the entire presentation. Instead, the significant parts of the presentation, such as the opening part, the attention-catching statements, central idea, the main points, and important illustrations should be memorised.
- Rehearse thoroughly before giving the presentation and keep a set of notes ready for reference.
- Try to be flexible and spontaneous.

Reading Method

The reading method may be used to deliver presentations, i.e., the presentation is written out and delivered by reading from the manuscript. This method is useful while presenting a technical paper or report that may contain complex technical information or statistical data. This method of delivery helps control nervousness during presentation because there is no danger of forgetting anything in the middle of the talk. This gives the speaker confidence. However, specific techniques will have to be used to involve the audience and avoid monotony.

> In the reading method the presentation is written out and delivered by reading from the manuscript.

The following suggestions will be helpful in using the reading method effectively:

- Prepare a full script of the presentation. Use capitals, spacing, and underlining to break out important parts and highlight significant points.
- Before giving the presentation, rehearse it before a live audience. Learn to look at long stretches of your presentation so that you may establish eye contact with the audience.
- Use non-verbal signals (i.e., facial expressions, gestures, body movements, and so on) and voice modulation in order to maintain the interest of the audience.
- Adopt a conversational tone. Use personal expressions and short sentences.

Outlining Method

Presentations may also be given with the help of delivery notes. This is the most effective delivery method as the notes will make the speaker familiar with his/her message and give him/her confidence. He/she is able to establish eye contact with his/her audience because he/she only has to glance at his/her notes for a while and can then concentrate on his/her audience. Moreover, he/she can afford to be flexible and spontaneous. However, the notes should be prepared carefully because the success of the presentation largely depends on the quality and type of delivery notes.

> The outlining method is the most effective delivery method as the notes will make the speaker familiar with his/her message and give him/her confidence.

The following suggestions will help use the "notes" method effectively:

- Plan and prepare the presentation carefully and write notes or outlines that contain all the important points, transitions, and illustrations. Use capitals, spacing, and underlining to show important transitions.
- Rehearse the presentation using the outlines. Systematic practice helps develop the required confidence.
- While delivering the presentation notes, the speaker should glance down at each main point, look up at his/her audience, maintain eye contact with them, pause for a moment and then explain the point.
- The speaker should try to be comfortable with the way he/she phrases his/her ideas. He/she may look at the examples and illustrations, but should not pick up the words from his/her notes and just repeat them.
- In order to sound spontaneous and natural, he/she should use the notes just as starting points.

Progress Check 5

1. Which of the following statements about delivery techniques are True?

(a) In the memorising method, the presentation is written out and delivered by reading from the manuscript.

(b) If the entire presentation is memorised, it may not sound spontaneous.

(c) While using the reading method to deliver the presentation, the entire presentation should be memorised and then should be presented from memory.

(d) The reading method of delivery helps control nervousness during presentation because the speaker knows what he/she is going to speak.

(e) The outlining method is the most effective delivery method as the notes will make the speaker familiar with his/her message, give him/her confidence, and enable him/her to establish eye contact with his/her audience.

Handling Stage Fright

Everyone who has faced an audience and has made a speech or presentation must have experienced stage fright. Perhaps one of the most difficult things that need to be handled during a presentation is one's first encounter with stage fright. Whenever we are faced with a frightening situation we find difficult to handle, our body responds. This response is in terms of extra energy to deal with the situation. As a result, the heartbeat quickens, breathing becomes more rapid, the mouth becomes dry, blushing occurs, palms sweat, and several other physiological changes occur. We become nervous or anxious and suffer from stage fright. In fact, even very good speakers experience some degree of stage fright when they have to give a presentation before an audience. So, some degree of stage fright is quite normal. However, it is important to learn to handle stage fright and use the extra energy positively to improve presentation delivery.

> Even very good speakers experience some degree of stage fright when they have to give a presentation before an audience.

> Do you know that
> - *You feel more nervous than you appear.*
> - *The more you think that you are nervous, the more nervous you will feel.*
> - *Your audience cannot easily detect your stage fright.*
> - *Even the most experienced presenters get nervous before an important presentation.*
> - *Even great speakers like Kennedy and Churchill were extremely fearful of speaking in public.*

The following strategies can be used to control and reduce stage fright:

Concentrate on the Three Ps: Planning, Preparation and Practice

As discussed earlier, presentations should be well-planned, thoroughly prepared, and rehearsed repeatedly. Knowing the purpose, audience, and occasion helps to reduce speech anxiety. Effective preparation familiarises the speaker with his/her message and thus reduces stage fear. Knowing the introduction, body and conclusion well in advance gives the speaker the confidence to control his/her speech anxiety. Finally, practice makes one perfect, if the presentation is well rehearsed. There is nothing to fear and there may be little or no stage fright at the time of presentation because the speaker is familiar with the situation.

Set Realistic Goals

Set objectives that are realistic. If the goals are unrealistic and beyond one's capabilities, it will unnecessarily create nervousness. In fact, the normal stress of the speaking situation is heightened by unrealistic ambitions. The speaker should be practical and identify his/her shortcomings. If he/she is not a very effective oral communicator, he/she should set humble goals. Moreover, he/she may set himself up to feel nervous by putting undue emphasis on a presentation.

Avoid Negative Thoughts

Entertaining negative thoughts may sometimes create more anxiety. Avoid thoughts such as "I am going to fail", "I can't speak", "My topic is boring", "I didn't prepare well", "I am not ready", "My audience don't like me", "I'm not fluent", and so on. Instead, positive self-talk such as, "I really know this presentation and believe in what I'm saying", "The topic is very interesting", "I am well-planned and confident", and so on.

The speaker should feel confident about his/her planning and preparation, have faith in himself/herself, tell himself/herself that everything is fine and that his/her listeners are positively disposed towards him/her.

Begin the Presentation with a Pause

Beginning presentations is accompanied by feelings of excitement and nervousness. This can be controlled by taking a few moments to make oneself comfortable. The speaker should not be in a hurry to start rather he should approach his/her audience calmly with a smile, adjusting his/her delivery notes, establish eye contact with the audience, and then begin his/her presentation.

> The speaker should not be in a hurry to start; rather he should approach his/her audience calmly with a smile, adjusting his/her delivery notes, establish eye contact with the audience, and then begin his/her presentation.

Speak Slowly

> Speaking too quickly exposes one's nervousness.

Inexperienced speakers often try to control their nervousness and stage fright by speaking too fast. This should be avoided as speaking too quickly exposes one's nervousness. The audience will recognise this and they will moreover find it difficult to understand the talk. Therefore, it is important to speak slowly and take appropriate pauses.

Learn and Practise Stress Reduction Techniques

Learn effective stress reduction techniques, such as deep breathing, isometrics, progressive relaxation, mental relaxation, and so on. They are useful in reducing stage fright. Usually stage fear is expressed by discomfort, which may range from mild embarrassment to outright panic. The key in dealing with stage fear is to maximise one's performance by coping with the obstacles that prevent positive performance.

Progress Check 6

1. **Analyse the following statements and mark True/False against each of them in the light of the above discussion and your personal experience and knowledge:**
   (a) Stage fright is quite normal.
   (b) Good speakers do not feel nervous while giving a presentation.
   (c) Speech anxiety can be useful.
   (d) Knowing your audience helps to control stage fear.
   (e) Planning and practice reduce stage fear.
   (f) Knowing your introduction and conclusion well in advance may, in fact, increase stage fright.
   (g) Nervous speakers tend to take slow deep breaths.
   (h) The more experience you gain as a public speaker, the less nervous you will feel.
   (i) Rehearsing aloud reduces speech anxiety.
   (j) Inexperienced speakers often try to control their nervousness and stage fright by speaking too slowly.

12.3.6 Checklist for Making a Presentation

Start With Confidence

A startling statement/quotation/anecdote/question/joke are good options for starting a presentation. The speaker must make sure that the technique used to start the presentation helps emphasise or support his/her point. It must match his/her message. Examples from personal and professional life can be used to stress points. The speaker must be willing to give of himself/herself by sharing his/her experiences and insights with the audience. It is useful to practise the opening of one's speech and plan exactly how it should be said.

> It is useful to practise the opening of one's speech and plan exactly how it should be said.

Be Organised

Presentations should be organised properly with an introduction, body, and conclusion. The introduction should provide an overview of the main points of the presentation. The speaker should make the purpose of the presentation clear, use transitions and signposts to clarify its organisation, and incorporate credible and interesting supporting material.

Stay Relaxed

Advance planning and preparation help in staying relaxed and tension-free during the presentation. Focussing on the message rather than the audience also helps in staying calm and confident.

Pay Attention to Body Language

Effective gestures, body movements, and walking patterns make an impression on the audience. The speaker should, at all times, maintain eye contact with the audience. These aspects should be borne in mind while rehearsing the presentation.

Use Appropriate Visual Aids

Visuals should be chosen with a view to creating maximum effect. They should focus on the main points of the presentation and help in retaining audience attention.

Pay Attention to all Details

The speaker should pay attention to even the smallest details, making sure to organise all his/her papers, speaking notes, handouts, and visual aids, before starting the presentation.

> The speaker should pay attention to even the smallest details, making sure to organise all his/her papers, speaking notes, handouts, and visual aids, before starting the presentation.

Close in a Memorable Way

The presentation should be concluded in a memorable way, with a summary of the keypoints. The audience should leave with a positive impression of the speaker and his/her presentation.

Exercise

1. **Write short notes on the following:**
   (a) Nature and importance of oral presentations
   (b) Audience analysis
   (c) Visual aids in presentations
   (d) Organising an oral presentation
   (e) Delivery methods
2. **Answer the following questions:**
   (a) Write as many reasons as you can to state that why oral presentation skills could be useful to you now or in the future.
   (b) Why is systematic planning important for making effective presentations?
   (c) What are the important steps taken in preparing an effective oral presentation?
   (d) What are the essential elements in the introduction, body, and conclusion of an oral presentation?
   (e) Why should you practise and rehearse a presentation?
   (f) Why is it essential to control stage fear?
3. **STEP 1**
   Form a pair of two persons and ask each other the following questions:
   - What is your name?
   - Where are you from?
   - What does your father do?
   - How many brothers or sisters do you have? (Give names and ages)
   - Who do you live with?
   - Where do you study?
   - What are you studying?
   - What do you like to do in your free time?
   - What hobbies or special interests do you have?
   - What are some of your future plans and goals?

   STEP 2
   Now concentrate on the answers that each of you give. Prepare a short talk of self-introduction. Present it before each other.
4. **Select an oral presentation topic and prepare an outline for your presentation using the following oral presentation matrix (OPM). This matrix provides the core of your presentation. Fill in the blanks in the matrix.**
   As you know, you must first develop an **introduction** to get the audience's attention and to reveal what you're going to present. Next, you must mention the main points in the **body** of the presentation. Finally, you must develop a **conclusion** that restates your points and pulls the presentation together. You may use the OPM to shape your presentation.

   Oral Presentation Matrix

   (a) *Title of the Presentation*______________________________
   (b) *Audience*____________________________________
   (c) *Type of audience:* Captive/Voluntary/Interested/Uninterested/Neutral
   (d) *Audience attitude to you:* Positive/Negative/Neutral
   (e) *Purpose*

General Purpose

To inform ________________________

To persuade _____________________________

To entertain _____________________________

Specific Purpose

At the end of my speech, the audience will be able to ____

____

____

(f) Central idea

____

____

(g) Main ideas

____

____

____

(h) Supporting material

____

____

____

(i) Organisation

Introduction

Attention-catching opening line: ____

____

Introduce the subject. ____

____

Give the audience a reason to listen. ____

____

Preview your main ideas: Today I'd like to ______________________________________

Body

Main idea + Supporting detail

Main idea + Supporting detail

Main idea + Supporting detail

Conclusion

Today I've ____

____

4. **Use the internet to find out more about making oral presentations. Check at least three to four websites and make appropriate notes. Discuss the material with your communication teacher and your friends.**

Key to Progress Check

Progress Check 1

1. The statements (b), (d), (h) and (i) are false.

Progress Check 2

1. The order is incorrect. The correct diagram about planning a presentation is given below:

   Define your purpose. ⟶ Analyse your audience. ⟶ Analyse the occasion. ⟶ Choose the title.

2. 1-C, 2-B, 3-A, 4-D, 5-A, 6-B, 7-A, 8-B, 9-B

Progress Check 3

1. (a) (ii) (b) (iv) (c) (ii) (d) (i) (e) (iv)
   (f) (iii)

Progress Check 4

1. (a) (ii) (b) (iv) (c) (iii) (d) (ii) (e) (i)
   (f) (iv) (g) (ii) (h) (iv)
2. **Tell** the audience what is going to be told. ⟶ **Tell** it. ⟶ **Tell** them what has been told.
3. (i) D (ii) E (iii) B (iv) A (v) C

Progress Check 5

1. Statements (b), (d), and (e) are correct.

Progress Check 6

1. (a) True (b) False (c) True (d) True (e) True
   (f) False (g) False (h) True (i) True (j) False

SECTION

5

Reading and Language Comprehension

CHAPTERS

13 CHAPTER

The Reading Process

Reading makes a man complete.

—Francis Bacon

LEARNING OBJECTIVES

- Understanding the reading process
- Identifying the purposes of reading
- Understanding strategies for reading different kinds of texts
- Knowing how to differentiate between efficient and inefficient reading
- Identifying the differences between active and passive reading
- Grasping techniques to improve reading speed

13.1 INTRODUCTION

13.1.1 Reading—A Communicative Process

What Bacon said years ago is still very relevant. Reading is an important communicative process and reading skills are probably the most important language skills required for academic and professional purposes. Quick, efficient, and imaginative reading techniques are essential in order to achieve academic success, because academic performance depends on the quantity and quality of reading.

Academic performance depends on the quantity and quality of reading.

Reading is a complex communicative process of receiving and interpreting the written word. It involves recognising what is written and comprehending the matter, i.e., understanding the main and subsidiary points as well as links between different parts of the written material. While receiving and interpreting the written word, the reader is concerned with four factors, i.e., decoding, comprehending, text analysis, and response, as illustrated in Fig. 13.1.

Reading is concerned with four factors: decoding, comprehending, text analysis, and response.

Decoding or interpreting in reading refers to the process of changing the coded message into information. As it involves understanding the written language, it requires the ability to recognise words accurately, understand the definitions of the words being used, and the manner in which words are used in varying contexts. A written message can be decoded, only if we know the language in which the message is encoded. As in the case of decoding in listening, the decoding and interpretation of a written message may be influenced by our social, cultural, educational, professional, and intellectual frames of reference.

Interpretation of a written message may be influenced by our social, cultural, educational, professional, and intellectual frames of reference.

Comprehension in reading refers to the identification of the central theme, main ideas, supporting details, and writing patterns. In order to comprehend a technical message, we need to think critically and analytically about what we are reading so that we are able to respond to the lexical meaning of words and the relationships between them, understand the specific details, and recognise the meaning and function of sentence patterns accurately as well as their logical and thematic coherence.

After decoding and comprehending the literal meaning of a written message, its significance is evaluated and appropriate conclusions are drawn from it. Text analysis is essential for critical and evaluative understanding of a text. Text analysis refers to the process of identifying relationships among different units within the text in order to distinguish between relevant and irrelevant information, explicit and implicit information, facts and opinions, examples and ideas, and draw inferences and conclusions.

Text analysis refers to the process of identifying relationships among different units within the text in order to distinguish between relevant and irrelevant information, explicit and implicit information, facts and opinions, and examples and ideas and draw inferences and conclusions.

Response is our action or reaction to the written message. It completes the reading process as it is the last step of reading. Our response to a text depends largely on our correct understanding and evaluation of the text. We may immediately respond to the message, as in the case of reading a letter, a memo, an e-mail message, or a fax message. Alternatively, we may need to remember the information so that we are able to use it in some other form later.

Response is our action or reaction to the written message.

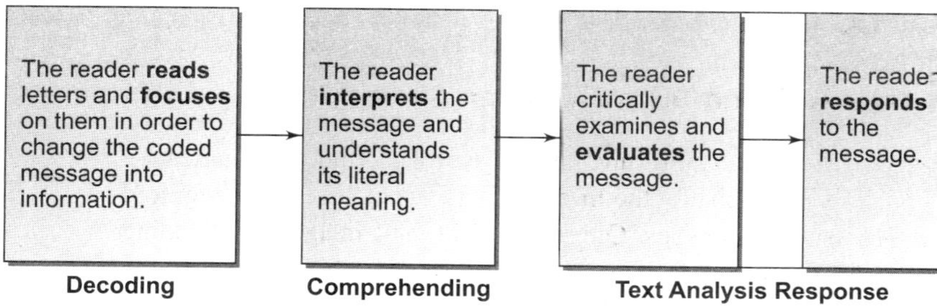

Fig. 13.1 The Reading Process

13.1.2 Reading with a Purpose

The most important thing to settle initially is simply why a particular message is being read. Is it for relaxation, for getting information, or for discussion at a later stage? Is it serious reading or light reading? Different kinds of texts are read for different purposes. What matters most is the overall purpose of reading.

> The most important thing to settle initially is simply why a particular message is being read.

An engineering student has to read and interpret textbooks, research papers, and articles in technical journals, teaching notes, notices, web materials, directories, encyclopedias, laboratory instruction sheets, safety manuals and regulations, technical reports, and reference materials. Although the basic purpose of reading is to extract information from various sources, it may primarily be to:

- Get an introductory idea of a text
- Get a broad understanding of the subject matter
- Understand scientific ideas, theories, and principles
- Obtain specific information
- Understand new changes and developments in a particular field
- Broaden one's outlook and understanding
- Discover the author's viewpoints
- To seek evidence for one's own point of view.

In order to achieve the above reading purposes, we need to understand the differences between efficient and inefficient reading (Table 13.1).

TABLE 13.1 Differences between Efficient and Inefficient Reading

Efficient Reading	*Inefficient Reading*
• The language of the text is comprehensible.	• The language of the text is not comprehensible.
• The content is accessible because of the reader's familiarity with the content.	• The content is unfamiliar and far removed from the reader's knowledge and experience.
• The reader has background information to help understand the text.	• The reader does not have or use background information.
• The reader concentrates on the important parts of the text, think ahead, hypothesise, and predict.	• The reader pays the same amount of attention to all parts of the text. He/she does not think ahead but deals with the text as it comes.

(Contd.)

• The reader has a clear specific purpose which motivates him/her to read.	• The reader has no clear purpose and uses the same strategy for all texts.
• The reader is able to use different strategies for different kinds of reading.	• The reader is not able to use different strategies for different kinds of reading.
• The reading is fast.	• The reading is slow.

Progress Check 1

1. **Study the following statements about the process of reading, and mark True or False against each of them:**
   (a) Reading is a complex communicative process of receiving and interpreting the written word.
   (b) While receiving and interpreting the written word, the reader is not concerned with comprehending.
   (c) Decoding or interpreting in reading refers to the process of changing the coded message into information.
   (d) Text analysis refers to the process of identifying the central theme, main ideas, supporting details, and writing patterns.
   (e) The reader's response to a text depends on his/her subject knowledge.
   (f) Efficient reading does not involve the use of background information to help understand a text.
   (g) An efficient reader pays the same amount of attention to all parts of a text.
   (h) An inefficient reader is not able to use different strategies for different kinds of reading.
   (i) An efficient reader is aware of a clear specific purpose in reading and is motivated to read.
   (j) The basic purpose of academic reading is to extract information from various sources.
2. **Which of the following may not result in efficient reading?**
   (a) Unfamiliar content
   (b) Clear language
   (c) Background information
   (d) Clear purpose
   (e) Lack of motivation
   (f) Use of effective reading strategies

13.2 READING DIFFERENT KINDS OF TEXTS

As determining the overall purpose of reading is very important, the reader should analyse the kind of text that he/she has to read. This will help him/her identify appropriate reading strategies. He/she may have to read different kinds of texts with different purposes and varying levels of reading comprehension. The text or the written message that he/she reads may vary from a light entertaining short story to a serious discussion about the latest developments in nuclear physics. Some of the aspects related to different reading activities are discussed next.

Reading different kinds of texts requires different kinds of reading strategies.

13.2.1 Reading Entertaining Messages/Texts

We may read entertaining messages or texts for relaxation. This is the most common form of reading and it is casual as we are not paying attention about what we are reading. For example, when we read a short story or a gossip about a film actress, the purpose is not to receive serious information but to be entertained. Similarly, we may read a novel, an entertaining write-up, or a joke for pleasure and enjoyment. Although the output in this type of reading may be some entertaining information, the reader need not concentrate on the theme, main points, and supporting details of the message.

13.2.2 Reading General Messages/Texts

We may read general messages or texts, such as newspapers, magazine articles, encyclopaedias, and so on, to improve our general awareness or knowledge about various areas of general interest. The main purpose of such reading is to broaden our outlook and widen our intellectual understanding and appreciation of things around us. Although this kind of reading is generally broad and extensive, the reader has to concentrate on the theme, main points, and supporting details of the text or message.

13.2.3 Reading Reference Materials

The main purpose of reading or scanning reference materials is to obtain specific information that might be used in various academic and professional activities. It involves focused reading to quickly identify a specific listing, an entry, or any other relevant piece of information. This kind of reading requires effective scanning skills.

13.2.4 Reading Business Documents

Reading different kinds of business documents such as business and project reports, letters, memos, e-mail messages, and so forth, requires our complete attention. The reader must pay attention to all parts of the document. As this kind of reading is interactive and productive, facilitating proper interaction and more effective reader-writer relationships, it requires conscious efforts on the part of the reader and demands concentration, involvement, and responsibility. Some other examples of this kind of reading include reading administrative instructions, business proposals, company profiles, and so on.

13.2.5 Reading Scientific and Technical Texts

Reading scientific and technical texts is a complex and multifaceted process. As we are concerned with the subject-content of what we read as well as the language in which it is expressed, we should try to understand not only linguistic and semantic patterns, but also discipline-specific information. Comprehension of linguistic and semantic patterns involves visual skills, perceptual skills, vocabulary skills, skimming skills, critical reading skills, and knowledge of how linguistic symbols combine to convey meaning. However, the comprehension of discipline-specific information transfer entails a basic understanding of the subject and familiarity with the material.

> Comprehension of linguistic and semantic patterns involves visual skills, perceptual skills, vocabulary skills, skimming skills, critical reading skills, and knowledge of how linguistic symbols combine to convey meaning.

Progress Check 2

1. **Which of the following reading activities require a basic understanding of the subject and familiarity with the material?**
   (a) Reading entertaining messages
   (b) Reading general texts
   (c) Reading reference materials
   (d) Reading business documents
   (e) Reading scientific and technical texts

13.3 TYPES OF READING

13.3.1 Active and Passive Reading

Reading is not merely a passive process of absorbing the message encoded in the printed word, but a dynamic communicative process in which the reader approaches the text for a particular reason. You need to be an active reader rather than a passive one. Active reading refers to a set of reading practices you may use to help understand the meaning of a written message.

Study Table 13.2 to understand some of the differences between active and passive reading.

TABLE 13.2 Differences between Active and Passive Reading

Active Reading	*Passive Reading*
• The reader pays attention to both content as well as style	• The reader pays attention to either content or style
• The reader interprets and analyses what he or she reads in order to understand both explicit as well as implicit meaning of a written message	• The reader does not analyse what he or she reads
• The reader predicts and responds to context	• The reader does not predict and respond to context
• The reader pays attention to the writer's intention	• The reader does not pay attention to the writer's intention
• The reader differentiates between ideas, opinions, feelings, and facts	• The reader does not distinguish between factual and non-factual information
• The reader infers the meaning of unfamiliar words from contextual or internal clues	• The reader does not infer the meaning of unfamiliar words from contextual or internal clues
• The reader identifies and evaluates a writer's attitude	• The reader does not identify or evaluate a writer's attitude
• The reader understands and interprets graphic information	• The reader does not interpret graphics
• The reader draws inferences and conclusions	• The reader is only concerned with the literal meaning of a written message

Thus, active reading is interactive and productive. It facilitates proper interaction and enhances understanding. It promotes more effective encoder-decoder relationships, and helps us take advantage of opportunities we might miss by being passive readers.

Progress Check 3

1. **Study the following statements about active and passive reading, and mark True or False against each of them:**
   (a) Reading is a passive process of absorbing the message encoded in the printed word.
   (b) An active reader draws inferences and conclusions.
   (c) In active reading, the reader approaches the text for a particular reason.
   (d) An active reader interprets and analyses what he or she reads in order to understand both the explicit as well as the implicit meaning of a written message.
   (e) A passive reader differentiates between ideas, opinions, feelings, and facts.
   (f) Active reading produces new understanding.

13.4 DEVELOPING A GOOD READING SPEED

As we have to read both extensively as well as intensively, we cannot afford to read slowly. Extensive reading is a must to broaden our general understanding of a subject while intensive reading is required to get an in-depth knowledge and understanding of the finer details of a subject. Most productive examinations demand selective intensive reading of some topics. On the other hand, recognition type examinations such as objective tests (true/false, multiple choice) demand wide extensive reading of a large number of topics. The reading needs may vary but in order to improve reading efficiency reading speed has to be increased.

Extensive reading is a must to broaden our general understanding of a subject while intensive reading is required to get an in-depth knowledge and understanding of the finer details of a subject.

Reading speed is measured in words per minute (wpm). Casual or general reading such as reading novels, poems, stories, and humorous articles do not require much concentration and, therefore, the reading speed is faster than that of serious reading. However, academic or professional reading such as reading technical texts, articles, and proposals require more concentration and reading speed cannot be increased at the cost of reading efficiency. Table 13.3 gives a general idea of reading speed for different purposes.

TABLE 13.3 Reading Speed Indicators for Different Purposes

Reading Speed	*Casual Reading*	*Academic and Professional Reading*
Very fast	+400 wpm	+350 wpm
Fast	300–400 wpm	250–350 wpm
Average	200–300 wpm	150–250 wpm
Slow	Less than 200 wpm	Less than 150 wpm

13.4.1 Check Your Reading Speed

Read the following passage:

People travelling long distances frequently have to decide whether they would prefer to go by land, sea, or air. Hardly anyone enjoys sitting in a train for more than a few hours. Train compartments soon get cramped and stuffy. It is almost impossible to take your mind off the journey. Reading is only a partial solution, for the monotonous rhythm of the wheels clicking on the rails soon lulls you to sleep. During the day, sleep comes in snatches. At night when you really wish to go to sleep, you rarely manage to do so. Inevitably, you arrive at your destination almost exhausted.

Long car journeys are even less pleasant, for it is quite impossible even to read. On motorways, you can at least travel safely at high speeds, but more often than not, the greater part of the journey is spent on narrow bumpy roads that are crowded with traffic. By comparison, trips by sea offer a great variety of comforts. You can stretch your legs on the spacious decks, play games, swim, meet interesting people, and enjoy good food, assuming the sea is calm. If it is not, and you are likely to get sea-sick, no form of transport could be worse. Even if you travel in ideal weather, sea journeys take a long time. Relatively few people are prepared to sacrifice up to a third of their holidays for the pleasure of travelling on a ship.

Aeroplanes have the reputation of being dangerous and even hardened travellers are intimidated by them. They also have the grave disadvantage of being the most expensive form of transport. But nothing can match them for speed and comfort. Travelling at a height of 30,000 feet, far above the clouds, and at over 500 miles an hour is an exhilarating experience. You do not have to devise ways of taking your mind off the journey, for an aeroplane gets you to your destination rapidly. For a few hours, you settle back in a deep armchair to enjoy the flight. The journey is so smooth that there is nothing to prevent you from reading or sleeping. However, you decide to spend your time, one thing is certain; you will arrive at your destination fresh and uncrumpled. You will not have to spend the next few days recovering from a long and arduous journey.

Now study the following statements in the light of the above passage and mark True or False against each of them:

1. Everyone enjoys sitting in a train for more than a few hours.
2. You can easily take your mind off a train journey.
3. A train journey is so smooth that there is nothing to prevent you from reading or sleeping.
4. The monotonous rhythm of the wheels clicking on the rails lulls you to sleep.
5. You find it difficult to sleep at night in a ship.
6. Long car journeys are more pleasant than train journeys.
7. Trips by sea offer a great variety of comforts.
8. People prefer to travel on a ship during holidays.
9. Travelling by air is an exhilarating experience.
10. A journey by air makes you arrive at your destination fresh and uncrumpled.

Check your answers with those given by us at the end of this chapter, and analyse your reading speed by referring to the following:

13.4.2 Clue to Check Your Reading Speed

1. False	2. False	3. False	4. True	5. False
6. False	7. True	8. False	9. True	10. True

TABLE 13.4 Example of Reading Speed

Time Taken to Read the Passage	*Reading Speed*	*Comments*
One minute or less	Very fast	You are an extremely efficient reader.
90 seconds or less	Fast	You are an above average reader.
Two minutes or less	Average	You are an average reader.
More than two minutes	Slow	Your are a poor reader.

13.4.3 Score: 60 or less

A score of 60 or less indicates inefficient reading with very poor comprehension and the reading speed hardly matters.

Increasing reading speed will definitely improve reading efficiency. By improving reading speed, with each fixation of the eyes, the reader will able to see longer stretches of language and thus more easily contextualise unknown vocabulary and be able to achieve general understanding.

Progress Check 4

1. **Which of the following statements about reading speed are not True?**
   (a) Intensive reading broadens general understanding of a subject while extensive reading is required to get an in-depth knowledge of a subject.
   (b) A motivated reader is rarely a slow reader.
   (c) It is not possible to increase reading speed.
   (d) Faster eye fixation helps perceive word groups and thought units quickly.
   (e) Serious reading is faster than casual reading.
   (f) Reading speed depends upon the nature of the reading material.
   (g) Extensive reading is required to get an in-depth knowledge and understanding of the finer details of a subject.
   (h) Increasing reading speed improves reading efficiency.

Exercise

1. **Write brief notes on the following:**
   (a) Efficient reading
   (b) Active and passive reading
   (c) Reading methods
   (d) Reading speed
2. **Expand the following statements in one paragraph each:**
   (a) Reading is a complex communicative process of receiving and interpreting the written word.
   (b) Decoding or interpreting in reading refers to the process of changing the coded message into information.
   (c) Determining the overall purpose of reading is essential for effective reading.

(d) We may have to read different kinds of texts with different purposes and varying levels of reading comprehension.
(e) Professional reading requires better concentration.
(f) Text analysis is essential for critical and evaluative understanding of a text.

3. Analyse the following reading materials and identify the reading practices that you may use to ensure reading effectiveness:
(a) An e-mail message
(b) An inquiry letter
(c) A technical report
(d) A proposal
(e) A chapter in a text book
(f) A journal article
(g) A short story
(h) A trip report

Key to Progress Check

Progress Check 1

1. (a) True (b) False (c) True (d) False (e) False
   (f) False (g) False (h) False (i) True (j) True
2. (a) and (e)

Progress Check 2

1. Reading scientific and technical texts will require a basic understanding of the subject and familiarity with the material.

Progress Check 3

1. (a) False (b) True (c) True (d) True (e) False
   (f) True

Progress Check 4

1. (a), (c), (e), and (g)

14 CHAPTER

Reading Strategies

LEARNING OBJECTIVES

- Understanding different reading skills
- Knowing vocabulary skills
- Analysing eye reading and discussing how to develop visual perception skills
- Knowing how to identify prediction techniques
- Identifying scanning skills
- Knowing skimming skills
- Analysing intensive reading strategies and discussing how to distinguish between facts and opinions, and draw inferences

14.1 READING SKILLS

As a complex process of decoding and comprehending the written message, reading could be quite a challenging activity because the act of understanding is not always simple. Depending on the purpose of reading, the reader will require different reading strategies and skills in order to understand the subject-content and language patterns of a message. These skills include vocabulary skills, visual perceptual skills, rapid reading skills, and intensive reading skills. Rapid reading skills include prediction, scanning and skimming skills while intensive reading involves detailed reading, critical reading, and inferential skills.

Rapid reading skills include prediction, scanning and skimming skills while intensive reading involves detailed reading, critical reading, and inferential skills.

We need to learn and polish these reading skills in order to become efficient and active readers. In this chapter, we will discuss these skills. Table 14.1 summarises these skills.

TABLE 14.1 Reading Skills

Vocabulary skills	• Recognising the definitions of the words being used • Guessing the meaning of words from the structure • Inferring the meaning of words from their context
Visual perceptual skills	• Accurate visual perception of words and phrases • Quick eye fixations
Prediction techniques	• Using index or chapter headings to predict the theme of the text • Guessing to predict information • Scanning graphic or non-verbal context such as graphs, diagrams, charts, and so on to predict the nature and scope of content • Using discourse and linguistic clues
Scanning skills	• Locating specific information
Skimming skills	• Identifying a theme or central idea • Identifying main ideas • Identifying organisational patterns of writing
Intensive reading skills	• Reading for details • Critically reading a text to – distinguish fact from opinion, – identify and evaluate a writer's attitude, and – understand the author's intention. • Drawing inferences and conclusions

14.1.1 Vocabulary Skills

A good vocabulary is essential for effective reading skills. In order to understand what we read, we need to recognise the meaning of words as well as guess the meaning from word structure and infer the meaning from the contexts. We need to learn and practice these vocabulary skills.

A good vocabulary is essential for effective reading skills.

Word Meaning Recognition

Word meaning recognition is the first step towards understanding a written message. We are supposed to perceive the words and phrases used, and recognise their definitions to follow what we read. We may find it difficult to understand a message if we do not know the meaning of the words and phrases used. The following suggestions will help in developing word meaning recognition skills:

> Word meaning recognition is the first step towards understanding a written message.

- The reader should develop appropriate sight recognition skills so that he/she is able to recognise a word or phrase in a fraction of a second.
- The reader should be able to quickly recall the meaning of the word.
- The reader should not stop reading if he/she is not able to recall the meaning of a certain word or phrase. He/she should continue reading till he/she completes a reasonable portion of the message.
- The reader should not immediately consult the dictionary because it will be time-consuming and will disrupt the reading flow.
- The reader should be able to guess the meaning of an unfamiliar word/phrase from the contextual clues.

Guessing the Meaning from Word Structure and Context

While reading textbooks, professional journals, reports, and technical manuals, we may frequently find unknown and difficult words. We may find it difficult to understand the message and this leads to poor comprehension. In such cases, the reader should apply various strategies that will help him find out the meaning of an unfamiliar word/phrase and newly introduced specialist vocabulary. These strategies include analysis of the word structure to guess its meaning and the identification of context clues and signal words to understand the meaning of unknown words.

Analysis of Word Structure

One of the word meaning recognition strategies is to guess the meaning of a word from its structure. The use of prefixes, suffixes, and word roots give clues to the meaning of uncommon words. For example, suppose the reader comes across the word 'interurban' and he/she has never heard the word before but knows the meaning of the word 'urban'. He/she can easily make out the meaning of this word if he/she knows that 'inter' is a prefix that means 'between'. Table 14.2 contains the meaning of some of the most common prefixes and suffixes.

> The use of prefixes, suffixes, and word roots give clues to the meaning of uncommon words.

TABLE 14.2 Common Prefixes and Suffixes

Common Prefixes			*Common Suffixes*		
Prefix	***Meaning***	***Examples***	***Suffix***	***Meaning***	***Examples***
a/an/il/in/dis/ im/un	not	illogical, disorder, unfair	able, ible	able to, can be done	readable, loveable
anti	against	antisocial	ance, ence, tion	state of being	residence
auto	self	autograph	ant, ent	person	resident
bi	two, twice	bi-monthly	al, ly	similar to, related to	legal, mental

(Contd.)

de	away	deflate	cy, cracy	condition	diplomacy
ex	former	ex-student	er, or	person, degree	writer, hotter
hetero	different	heterogeneous	ess	feminine	waitress
homo	similar	homogeneous	ify	make, do	beautify
inter	between	internet	ful	full of	useful
intra	within	intravenous	less	not	harmless
mis	wrong	misunderstand	ship	being	friendship
micro	small	microcomputer			
mono	one	monologue			
multi	many	multinational			
over	more	overeat			
post	after	postgraduate			
pseudo	false	pseudo-secular			
pro	in support of	pro-party			
re	repeat	redo			
semi	half	semi-final			
sub	under	submarine			
super	above	superpower			
trans	across	transverse			

Analysis of Context Clues

The context can also give a clue to the meaning of a word. The reader needs to look for the contextual signal words, examples, illustrations, and linguistic clues that indirectly help define an unknown word or phrase. He/she should analyse these context clues in order to guess the meaning of an unfamiliar word or phrase. For example, notice the signal clue in the following sentence:

> The reader needs to look for the contextual signal words, examples, illustrations, and linguistic clues that indirectly help define an unknown word or phrase.

He is down-to-earth and you will find his approach to life very practical.

In this example, the words 'you will find his approach to life very practical' help in inferring the meaning of the phrase 'down-to-earth'. Notice the signal clue in the next example:

Although she is very loquacious, she remains silent before her father.

The word 'although' contrasts the word 'loquacious' with the words 'remains silent' and the reader can guess that the word 'loquacious' means someone 'who talks' and does not remain silent.

Thus, the reader can guess the meaning of an unknown or unfamiliar word by analysing its structure or analysing the contextual clues.

Progress Check 1

1. **Guess the meaning of the following words with the help of prefixes/suffixes used:**
   Autonomous, auto-pilot, cloudless, pro-government, anti-war, inefficient, multipurpose, bicameral, biannual, interpersonal, intermix, interpose, bisect, semicircle, semiconscious, microchip, microclimate, monoplane, monolith, overtired, pseudo-intellectual, misjudge, misplace, misprint, subscript, submerge, plentiful, replant, reiterate, reinterpret
2. **Read the following sentences and guess the meaning of each of the underlined words with the help of context clues:**
   (a) He is very <u>discourteous</u> and you will never find him polite to other people.
   (b) He is very smart, elegant and well-dressed whereas his wife is very <u>scruffy</u>.
   (c) My sister is very <u>sensitive</u> and feels things very intensely.
   (d) The earthquake was such a big <u>catastrophe</u>; thousands of people were killed.
   (e) He is so <u>thrifty</u> that he will not spend even a single rupee for you.
   (f) I do not think he will be offended by your remark. You know he is so <u>broadminded.</u>
   (g) There should be <u>equitable</u> distribution of participation in group discussion. Each member of the group should contribute to the discussion.
   (h) There was only one <u>survivor</u>. All the other members of the family were killed in the accident.
   (i) I really did not expect such a <u>turnout</u> in the meeting; there were more than sixty people.
   (j) The high salary and perks <u>make up for</u> the late night duties and extra hours of work.

14.1.2 Eye Reading and Visual Perception

In order to be an efficient reader, one needs to develop visual perception skills. Visual perception is a basic requirement for reading effectiveness because we recognise a word through sight. Inaccurate visual perception may lead to visual misreading and lack of comprehension. It may also lead to confusion and misunderstanding. Many people are inefficient readers only because they suffer from poor visual perception.

> Visual perception is a basic requirement for reading effectiveness because we recognise a word through sight.

In fact, efficient reading involves reading with fast eye movements. If we read by saying words loudly or silently to ourself, our reading will be very slow. It may reduce our reading speed much more than we think it can. Eye reading makes reading fast, efficient, and result oriented. We need to improve our visual perception skills and ability to identify words and phrases. The following suggestions will help us improving eye reading skills.

> Effective eye reading requires accurate visual perception of words and phrases, faster eye fixations, and complete elimination of vocalisation.

Develop Faster Eye Fixations

Eye fixation is the resting of the reader's eyes on a particular word, phrase, word group, or thought unit. Faster eye fixation will help in perceiving the word groups and thought units quickly.

Read in Word Groups/Thought Units Instead of Word-by-word

The reader should try to read in word groups instead of word-by-word. The focus should not be on single words, instead, it should be on thought units comprising several words.

Improve Accurate Visual Perception of Words and Phrases

The reader needs to improve accurate visual perception of words in order to read fast. This requires better concentration and motivation for reading. A motivated reader is always a faster reader.

> A motivated reader is always a faster reader.

Avoid Vocalisation and Sub-vocalisation

Vocalisation is saying words loudly while sub-vocalisation is saying words silently to oneself. Both these habits make reading slow. They should be avoided and reading should be with fast eye movements.

Rapidly Recognize Word Meaning

The reader should try to recognise the meaning of a word quickly. This requires a good stock of perceptive vocabulary. He/she should try to infer and guess the meaning of words from contexts.

Concentrate While Reading

The reader needs to concentrate while reading a text. He/she must have the urge to read and understand. If he/she is motivated to read, he/she will concentrate and read efficiently.

14.1.3 Rapid Reading Skills

Prediction

To be an efficient reader one needs to learn and practice prediction techniques. Prediction is a rapid reading skill. It refers to the process of reading quickly in order to guess the information that a passage or text contains. An efficient reader is able to think ahead, hypothesise, and predict. Predictions about the content of a passage are generally based on headings, sub-headings, one's background knowledge of the subject, graphic or non-verbal context such as graphs, diagrams, charts, and so on as well as linguistic clues.

> An efficient reader is able to think ahead, hypothesise, and predict.

Prediction includes various micro-skills including the ability to:

- Guess the information that the text contains
- Use the index or chapter headings to roughly predict the central theme of the text
- Scan graphic or non-verbal context such as graphs, diagrams, charts and so forth to predict the nature and scope of content
- Use discourse and linguistic clues.

> Prediction involves the use of index, headings, sub-headings, non-verbal context, and linguistic clues to guess the information that a text contains.

Prediction involves a pre-reading survey of a text. The techniques of prediction involve:

(a) Glancing rapidly through the text, before reading any part of it, in order to familiarise oneself with the subject

(b) Guessing the information that the text contains
(c) Recalling related information
(d) Analysing the aids in the text that might make reading faster and easier.

Prediction involves a pre-reading survey of a text.

Thus, in order to predict and respond to the content of a text, the reader should run his/her eyes through the text as fast he/she can in order to predict the information that the text contains. He/she should pay particular attention to the heading, the sub-headings, the first paragraph, the first sentence of each paragraph, and the topic sentence in each paragraph. He/she should also use his background information to get an idea about the content of the text, and interpret aids in the text that might make reading faster and easier.

Progress Check 2

1. **Run your eyes through Passage 1, as fast as you can (no more than 30 seconds), in order to predict the information that the text contains and answer the questions given at the beginning of the passage. You should pay particular attention to the heading, the sub-headings, the first paragraph, the first sentence of each paragraph, and the topic sentence in each paragraph.**

Questions

1. Which of the following topics and sub-topics does the passage discuss? Tick the right ones.
   (a) Definition of a covalent bond
   (b) Several aspects of the process of electrolysis
   (c) Characteristics of ionic compounds
   (d) Characteristics of covalent compounds
   (e) Electrolysis of covalent bonds
   (f) Comparison of ionic and covalent bonds
2. Which of the following questions cannot be answered by reading the following passage?
   (a) How do the properties of covalent compounds differ from those of ionic compounds?
   (b) What are the different chemical processes in nature?
   (c) What are the characteristics of compounds having ionic bonds?
   (d) What is an ionic bond?
   (e) Why does water dissolve many but not all substances?
   (f) What do we mean by understanding an observation?

PASSAGE 1

Ionic and Covalent Bonds

Ionic Bond An ionic bond is non-directional in nature. A cation and an anion are considered charged spheres. These ions, thus, attract each other. This electrical charge is responsible for their force of attraction and repulsion. These ions have a uniform field of force around them and will, thus, attract oppositely charged ions from all directions. Hence, ionic bond is non-directional.

Characteristics of Ionic Compounds There are many important characteristics of compounds having ionic bonds. An ionic compound is a collection of an equal number of positive and negative ions arranged in a three-dimensional lattice. Ionic compounds can be dissociated into their constituent ions with little effort. Further, they can be electrolysed to produce elements or covalent molecules of the constituent atoms. NaCl upon melting or upon dissolving in water produces Na+ and Cl– ions. Electrolysis of molten NaCl gives Na and Cl_2. Water also weakens the attraction between the ions in an ionic compound. This is why many ionic compounds dissolve well in water. Moreover, ionic compounds can conduct electricity. Most ionic compounds are made of metals.

Covalent Bond A covalent bond is the force of attraction, which arises due to the mutual sharing of electrons between the two atoms. This type of bond is formed between two similar non-metallic elements or dissimilar atoms.

Characteristics of Covalent Compounds There are many important characteristics of covalent compounds. The properties of covalent compounds are quite different from those of ionic compounds. They do not ionise or conduct electricity. Electrolysis of covalent bonds is, thus, not possible. Many covalent bonds are not soluble in water. Covalent bonds dissolve much easier in organic liquids. Since the bonding in covalent bonds is by electron sharing and not by electron attraction, the number of atoms in covalent molecules is not indefinitely large. They have lower melting and boiling points than ionic compounds. Many covalent molecules exist in the gas phase or liquid state (Cl_2, H_2O).

2. **Glance rapidly through Passage 2 (take no more than 30 seconds) in order to predict the information that the text contains. After you have read the text, you should answer the questions at the beginning of the passage.**

   Questions

   1. Which of the following questions cannot be answered by reading the text?
      (a) How are the non-ferrous metals refined?
      (b) How do non-ferrous metals differ from iron?
      (c) What are the methods of ore dressing?
      (d) What is gold panning?
      (e) How are slags formed?
      (f) What is gravity concentrator?
      (g) What is oil flotation?

PASSAGE 2

Producing Non-Ferrous Metals

One way in which non-ferrous metals differ from iron is in the manner of their occurrence. Iron oxide occurs in large and comparatively pure deposits; other metals and compounds from which metals are derived are scattered through large volumes of rock, such as limestone or quartz. Since it would be difficult and costly to smelt these large amounts of barren rock, recourse is taken in concentration or ore dressing, by which metals or metallic compounds are partially separated from the 'gangue,' or worthless material, before smelting. As the methods of ore dressing are rather general, we consider them here, rather than under the specific metals.

Methods of Ore Dressing

Gravity The simplest method of ore dressing depends on the fact that, in general, metallic compounds have a higher specific gravity than gangue, and hence settle faster in a stream of water. Gold panning is the simplest illustration of the procedure. On a larger scale, it is carried on in jigs where the ore is placed on a screen and a pulsating stream of water is forced through the screen, causing the lighter gangue to be washed out. Another form of gravity concentrator is the 'table', consisting of a surface with longitudinal ridges, which is given a jerking end-to-end motion while a stream of water flows across it laterally. By this means the heavy ore is shaken over the end while the gangue washes off the front.

Oil Flotation Oil flotation is a method ore separation method that is gaining popularity. This process is based on the following: if a finely ground mixture of ore minerals and gangue is mixed with water, a little of certain oils added, and the whole stirred violently to produce a froth, the metallic mineral will be found in the froth. This method is capable of removing the last traces of mineral from the gangue, and is hence used to supplement the gravity process.

While discussing the metallurgical treatment of non-ferrous ore, it should be understood that the reference is to metallic mineral that has been concentrated by one of these methods. We shall also consider briefly the kinds of furnaces used for non-ferrous smelting.

Scanning

Scanning refers to the ability to locate specific information or facts as quickly as possible. While trying to look for the meaning of a word in a dictionary or looking for a telephone number in the telephone directory, we scan and try to look for specific information. Scanning is an important rapid reading technique, which provides better comprehension while reading a scientific or technical text. It may serve several purposes, which include looking for:

> Scanning refers to the ability to locate specific information or facts as quickly as possible.

(a) A specific point or fact in a text
(b) Relevant graphic details
(c) A formulae in a text
(d) A word in a dictionary
(e) Train or television schedules
(f) Any references or bibliographical listings
(g) Examination results
(h) Any notes/questions/remarks at the end of the text.

We may know how to scan a newspaper or a dictionary but may do it slowly with less accuracy. What is important is to increase scanning speed with accuracy. The following suggestions will help increase proficiency at scanning.

Know What You Want to Find

In order to scan any reading material, the reader needs to know what he/she wants to find. If he/she does not know what he/she is looking for, he/she will not be able to scan well. So, the purpose of scanning should be determined and the reader should not be confused about the information that he/she requires.

Do Not Read Everything

As the reader knows what he/she is looking for before he/she begins to read, he/she should not read everything. He/she should concentrate on the information that he/she needs with his/her eyes only on the particular word, phrase, and word group or thought unit that he/she is looking for. The attempt should be to perceive word groups and thought units quickly.

Use Guides and Aids

Every reading material contains certain guides and aids, which should be used to find what the reader wants.

Know the Organisation of the Material to be Read

The reader needs to know the organisation of the reading material to scan it with speed and accuracy. Practise scanning different kinds of reading materials, such as newspaper listings, dictionaries, telephone directories, and analyse the way information is structured in these materials.

Concentrate While Scanning

The reader needs to concentrate while scanning a reading material. He/she must have the urge to read and scan the material. This will improve his visual perception and help him identify the required information quickly.

Progress Check 3

1. **Scan Passage 3 in order to answer the questions given below. Do not take more than 30 seconds.**

   Question

   1. How many times does the term 'iron' appear in the passage?

PASSAGE 3

Iron

The element iron has an industrial importance, which exceeds that of any other metallic element. It is very abundant, ranking fourth in the earth's crust (after O, Si, and Al); it is very common, being an essential constituent of several hundred minerals; it is easy to make by simply heating some of its minerals with carbon; and it has many desirable properties, especially when impure. For all these reasons, iron has become such a distinctive feature of civilisation that it gives its name to one of the ages in archaeological chronology.

About 5 per cent by weight of the crust of the earth is iron. Some of this iron is meteoric in origin and occurs in an uncombined, metallic state. However, most of it is combined with oxygen, silicon, or sulphur. The important source minerals are hematite (Fe_2O_3), limonite ($Fe_2O_3.H_2O$), magnetite (Fe_3O_4), and siderite ($FeCO_3$), usually contaminated with complex iron silicates from which these minerals are produced by weathering. Iron sulphides, such as iron pyrites (FeS_2) or fool's gold, are also quite abundant, but they cannot be used as sources of iron because sulphur, an objectionable impurity in the final product, is hard to remove.

Besides the earth's crust, there is a possibility that the centre of the earth may be iron. Indirect evidence based on the study of earthquake waves and tidal action indicates that the core of the earth is liquid and has a density corresponding to that of liquid iron at high pressure.

Iron is practically never produced in a pure state, since it is difficult to make and is too expensive for most purposes. Furthermore, impure iron (steel) has desirable properties, especially when the specific impurity is carbon in carefully controlled amounts. The industrial production of impure iron is carried out on a massive scale in a blast furnace, in which complicated high-temperature reactions occur involving iron ore, limestone, and carbon. The blast furnace is designed for continuous operation. Iron ore, limestone, and coke are added at the top; preheated air or oxygen is blown in at the bottom. As the molten iron forms, it trickles down to a pit at the bottom, from which it is periodically drawn off. All told, it takes about 12 h for material to pass through the furnace. The actual chemical processes, which occur in such a furnace, are still obscure. It is generally agreed, however, that the active reducing agent is not carbon but carbon monoxide. As the charge settles through the furnace, the coke is oxidised by the incoming oxygen by the reaction $2C(s) + O_2(g) \rightarrow 2CO\ (g)$, thus, forming the reducing agent CO and liberating large amounts of heat. As the carbon monoxide moves up the furnace, it encounters oxides of iron in various stages of reduction, depending on the temperature of the particular zone.

Skimming Skills

> Skimming is a rapid reading technique that prepares the reader for detailed reading.

Skimming is a more sophisticated skill than scanning. It refers to the process of reading a text or passage in order to get a rough idea of what the text or passage is all about. It is a rapid reading technique that prepares the reader for detailed reading. As the main objective of skimming is to understand the central idea and the main points of a text, the reader needs to use a reading strategy that involves fast reading and quick analysis.

Skimming also involves discovering the purpose and organisation of a text. One of the most important purposes of reading for academic and professional purposes is obtaining relevant information for various purposes. This involves not only the ability to recognise the main ideas and supporting details but also the ability to identify different writing patterns used to develop these ideas. Authors use a variety of discourse patterns in scientific writing.

> Skimming involves three main skills: identifying the central idea, recognising main ideas, and identifying the writing patterns of the passage/text.

Skimming is essential for better understanding of a text. Skimming should answer the following questions about a text.

1. What is the overall purpose of the text?
2. What is the central idea or theme?
3. What is the logical organisation? (general to specific, specific to general, chronological, more important to less important, less important to more important, and so on.)
4. What does the author intend to do? (describe, instruct, report, narrate, explain, argue, persuade, illustrate, and so on.)
5. What are the main points of the text?

Identifying the Central Idea

> Every essay, article, passage, or textbook chapter deals with a theme or central idea or thesis.

The first step of skimming is to identify the central idea. Every essay, article, passage, or textbook chapter deals with a theme or central idea. All the other ideas, points, examples, illustrations in the text support and expand this central idea. This central idea is also called *thesis*. The *thesis* answers the following three questions:

- What is the subject?

- What does the author want to say about the subject?
- What is the author's point of view?

In order to understand the central idea of a text, the reader should carefully read the following:

- the title or the main heading
- the sub-headings
- the opening paragraph
- the last paragraph

The title or the main heading of a text can give a clue to the content. Similarly, the sub-headings can also help in identifying the central idea. The opening and the last paragraphs generally sum up the subject and the author's point of view. The reader should also glance over the beginning of the text to identify its logical organisation. Identify the discourse technique used in the text, i.e., definition, description, explanation, comparison and contrast, narration, classification, and so on.

> The opening and the last paragraphs generally sum up the subject and the author's point of view.

Let us try to understand this with the help of an example.

Progress Check 4

1. Read the following passage and try to identify the central idea of the passage by quickly reading the title and the sub-headings.

PASSAGE 4

Physical Properties of Metals

Malleability and Ductility Metals are malleable. They can be hammered into very thin sheets. Gold and silver are among the most malleable metals. These can be hammered into foils much thinner than this paper. Ductility is yet another characteristic feature of metals. All metals are not equally ductile. One can draw a wire of about 200 metres from 100 mg of a highly ductile metal like silver.

Thermal and Electrical Conductivity All metals are conductors of heat. Silver is the best conductor of heat. The poorest conductor among metals is lead (Pb). Electrical conductivity is yet another common property of metals. They offer little resistance to the flow of current and, thus, display high electrical conductivity. The best conductors of electrical current are silver and copper. They are followed by gold, aluminium, and tungsten. Mercury and iron offer greater resistance to the flow of current.

Chemical Properties Metals form positive ions by losing electrons. Hence, they are electropositive elements. This ionization behaviour gives rise to certain characteristic chemical properties of metals.

Reaction with Oxygen All metals combine with oxygen and form metal oxides. The atoms of the metal give away loosely bound electrons, forming positive metal ions. The atoms of oxygen, on the other hand, receive electrons, forming negative oxide ions.

$$Mg \rightarrow Mg_2+ + 2e-$$
$$O + 2e- \rightarrow O_2$$
$$\overline{Mg + O \rightarrow MgO}$$

Metal oxides are basic in nature. Some of them dissolve in water forming alkalies.

$$Na_2O + H_2O \rightarrow 2NaOH$$

Although all metals react with oxygen, their reactivity is different. Some metals, such as sodium and potassium, react vigorously with oxygen. They catch fire even if kept open in the air. Magnesium needs to be heated before it combines with oxygen. Once heated to ignition temperature, magnesium ribbon burns, producing intense heat and light. The reaction of oxygen with copper is, however, slow. A lot of heat is to be provided to carry out this reaction. Copper, thus, shows low reactivity towards oxygen.

The title of the passage is "physical properties of metals". This tells us the subject of the passage. The sub-titles of the passage are, 'Malleability and Ductility', 'Thermal and Electrical Conductivity', 'Chemical Properties' and 'Reaction with Oxygen'. These sub-titles tell us what these properties are. Now, the reader can easily make out the central idea.

Recognising Main Ideas

Once the central idea of the text has been identified, the reader can easily recognise the main ideas that support and expand the central idea. Most writers structure the main ideas in a logical way and it may not be difficult to identify them. In order to do this, the reader first needs to identify the topic sentence in each paragraph of the text, understand discourse coherence, and text organisation, recognise the meaning and function of sentence patterns accurately, and recognise discourse/semantic markers and their function.

> The reader first needs to identify the topic sentence in each paragraph of the text, understand discourse coherence, and text organisation, recognise the meaning and function of sentence patterns accurately, and recognise discourse/semantic markers and their function.

Each paragraph may deal with one main idea. This idea is generally expressed in a topic sentence, which is usually placed at the beginning of a paragraph. This topic sentence summarises the paragraph by stating the gist of the idea to be developed in the paragraph. It may be a statement, a generalisation, a description, or a problem. The other sentences of the paragraph develop, support, exemplify, and explain the central theme.

> A topic sentence summarises the paragraph by stating the gist of the idea to be developed in the paragraph.

Read the following paragraph about crude oil:

Crude oil is a mixture of different compounds that boil at different temperatures. The lightest fraction consists of gases that boil below atmospheric temperature. The next fraction, normally refined into gasoline, boils between about 30 degrees and 200 degrees centigrade. The fraction boiling between about 140 degrees and 320 degrees centigrade is termed kerosene. The fraction boiling above about 320 degrees centigrade is commonly refined into heating diesel and lubricating oils. The remaining, and heaviest, fraction is the residue, which supplies waxes, asphalts, and some fuel oils.

The information in the above paragraph is organised in the form of a description. Sentence 1 introduces the topic, which is "the composition of crude oil". Each of the sentences 2, 3, 4, 5, and 6 describes the boiling points of gases, gasoline, kerosene, and other fractions of crude oil.

If the topic sentence is placed at the beginning of a paragraph, its organisation would be as shown in Fig. 14.1.

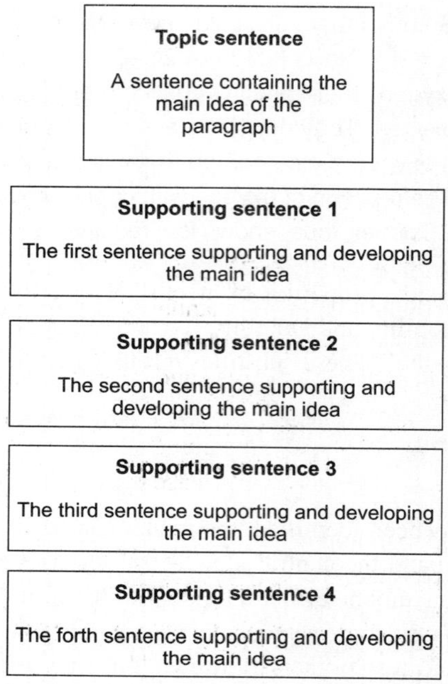

Fig. 14.1 Organisation of a Paragraph having Topic Sentence at the Beginning

However, if the topic sentence appears at the end of a paragraph, the organisation of this paragraph would be as shown in Fig. 14.2.

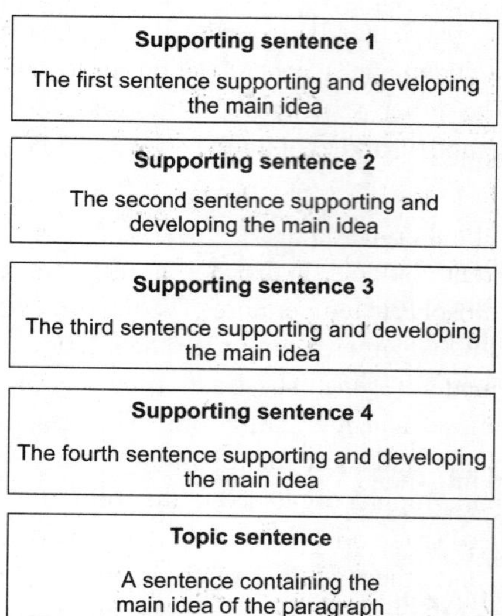

Fig. 14.2 Organisation of a Paragraph having Topic Sentence at the End

Read the following paragraph about vehicular pollution:

Dangerous pollutants such as ozone, aldehydes, and ketones are the result of a complex chain reaction caused by carbon monoxide, nitrogen oxides, and hydrocarbons emitted by motor vehicles. Moreover, the prolonged inhalation of carbon monoxide present in the toxic fumes reduces the carbon carrying capacity of the blood, and may cause headache, sickness, and even death. Likewise, unburned fragments of hydrocarbons help to form smog and thicken the atmosphere with elements that may cause cancer. *Thus, vehicular pollution causes serious health problems.*

Sometimes the writer does not include a topic sentence, expressing the main idea through details only and the reader has to infer the main idea.

The topic sentence in the above paragraph is given at the end. Sometimes the writer does not include a topic sentence, expressing the main idea through details only and the reader has to infer the main idea.

Identifying Writing Patterns

Skimming involves discovering the purpose and organisation of a text. While skimming a passage or text, the reader should be able to identify the specific writing pattern used by the writer in the passage. Technical writers use different writing patterns or techniques of exposition to develop ideas. A writer may use a writing pattern according to the nature and type of message to be communicated. Generally, authors use the following writing patterns:

Skimming involves discovering the purpose and organisation of a text.

- Definition
- Description
- Sequence of events
- Generalisation
- Classification
- Illustration example
- Cause and effect
- Comparison and contrast

Read the following two paragraphs:

Paragraph 1

When sunlight (or white light of bulb) is passed through a prism, a spectrum is obtained. This spectrum consists of seven colours—violet, indigo, blue, yellow, orange, and red. The different colour bands are diffused, i.e., the second colour starts before the first ends. As there is no separation between different colours, the solar spectrum (spectrum of sunlight) is a continuous spectrum.

Paragraph 2

Ionic compounds can be dissociated into their constituent ions, and can be elctrolysed to produce elements of the constituent atoms. In contrast, electrolysis of covalent molecules is not possible. Many ionic compounds dissolve well in water whereas many covalent compounds are not soluble in water. Ionic compounds can conduct electricity while covalent compounds neither ionise nor conduct electricity. Most ionic compounds are made of metal. However, many covalent compounds are in the gas phase or in liquid state. Moreover, ionic compounds have higher melting and boiling points than covalent compounds.

In the first paragraph the author uses the writing technique of description while the author of the second paragraph uses the technique of comparison and contrast.

Progress Check 5

1. **Study the following statements about the rapid reading strategies, and mark True or False against each of them:**
   (a) Prediction does not involve guessing the information that a passage contains.
   (b) The reader can use his background information to get an idea about the content of a text.
   (c) Skimming refers to the process of reading a text or passage in order to get a rough idea of what the text or passage is all about.
   (d) The main objective of skimming is to look for specific information.
   (e) Scanning refers to the ability to identify the main points in a passage.
2. **Read the following passage about properties of liquids and identify the topic sentence in each paragraph:**

PASSAGE 5

Liquids are practically incompressible. Unlike gases, but like solids, a liquid does not change much in volume when the pressure on it is changed, even when the pressure of thousands of atmospheres are involved. The kinetic theory accounts for this by saying that the amount of free space between the molecules of a liquid has been reduced almost to a minimum. Any attempt to compress the liquid meets with resistance as the electron cloud of one molecule repels the electron cloud of the adjacent molecule.

Liquids maintain their volume. No matter what the shape or size of the container, a 10 ml sample of liquid occupies 10 ml volume, whether it is placed in a small beaker or in a large flask, whereas a gas spreads out to fill the whole volume accessible to it. Gases do not conserve their volume, because the molecules are essentially independent of each other and can move into any space available. In liquids, the molecules are closed, and mutual attraction is strong. Consequently, the molecules are clustered together.

Liquids have no characteristic shape. A liquid sample assumes the shape of the bottom of its container. The kinetic theory explains this property by saying that there are no fixed positions for molecules. Molecules are free to slide over each other in order to occupy positions of the lowest possible potential energy. On earth, gravity pulls the liquid specimen to the bottom of its container, in an orbiting satellite, intermolecular forces pull the specimen into a spherical glob.

Liquids diffuse slowly. When a drop of ink is carefully released in water, at first, there is a rather sharp boundary between the ink cloud and the water. Eventually the color diffuses throughout the rest of the liquid. In gases, diffusion is much more rapid. Diffusion occurs because molecules have kinetic energy and move from one place to another. In a liquid, molecules do not move very far before they collide with neighbouring molecules. Eventually, each molecule of a liquid does migrate from one side of its container to the other, but it undergoes many billions of collisions in doing so. In contrast, a gas is mostly empty space, and the molecules of one gas can quickly mix with those of another.

Liquids evaporate. Although there are attractive forces, which hold the molecules together in a clump, it is evidently possible for molecules to escape from open containers. Molecules with kinetic energy great enough to overcome the attractive forces can escape into the gas phase. In any collection, a given molecule does not have the same energy all the time. There is continual exchange of energy in collisions.

3. **Run your eyes through the following passage, as fast as you can (no more than 30 seconds), in order to skim the passage. Read the heading, the sub-heading, the first sentence of each paragraph, and skimming everything in between.**

PASSAGE 6

Microscopes and Telescopes

Microscopes and telescopes are magnifying devices. The microscope is used to magnify the size of objects that are too small to be seen by the naked eye, such as bacteria and cells. A telescope, on the other hand, is used to "bring nearer" very distant objects, such as ships, the moon, the planets, and the stars.

Lens Systems Microscopes and telescopes use two lens systems. The first one, called the objective, forms the image of the object; the second lens system, called the eyepiece, takes this image and forms its image in turn. It is the latter that we see through the instrument. The 'objective' is a lens or a system of lenses, that acts as a converging (convex) lens. In a microscope, the object to be viewed is kept at a distance slightly larger than the focal length of the objective, which forms an inverted, magnified, and real image of the object.

The eyepiece is also a system of convex lenses. It is fixed in such a way that the image formed by the objective lens lies between the eyepiece and its focus. This image acts as the object for the eyepiece, which forms a further magnified but virtual image of the object. It is this image that we observe when we look into a slide through a microscope. The final image seen remains inverted with respect to the object.

The objective and the eyepiece of a microscope are mounted at the ends of a tube. The mounting is done in such a way that their axes are common. The power of magnification of the microscope is the ratio of the size of the image to that of the object.

In a telescope, the objective and the eyepiece are similarly mounted. The focal length of the objective of the telescope is comparatively larger than that of a microscope. The objective forms a real, diminished-in-size, and inverted image of a distant object. The position of the eyepiece is so adjusted that this image is formed between the optical centre of the eyepiece and its focus. The eyepiece then forms the final image, which is virtual, enlarged, and erect.

Now that you have skimmed the passage, mark **True** or **False** against each of the following statements:

(a) The passage is about the significance of microscopes and telescopes in medical sciences.
(b) In a telescope, the objective and the eyepiece are similarly mounted.
(c) The objective and the eyepiece of a microscope are mounted at the ends of a tube.
(d) The eyepiece is a system of concave lenses.
(e) Microscopes and telescopes are magnifying devices.
(f) Telescopes use two lens systems but the microscope uses three lens systems.

14.1.4 Intensive Reading Skills

In comparison to rapid reading skills, intensive reading is detailed reading that demands better concentration and motivation. The three rapid reading techniques of prediction, scanning, and skimming prepare the reader for intensive reading. If these techniques are used correctly and effectively, it will prepare the reader for the contents and provide better comprehension and retention of the information. Using prediction/scan/skim method gives the reader a correct beginning. It helps in concentrating and focusing on the reading assignment, which is essential for academic and professional reading.

> The three rapid reading techniques of prediction, scanning, and skimming prepare the reader for intensive reading.

Moreover, intensive reading requires text analysis for critical and evaluative understanding of a text. Text analysis is the process of identifying relationships among different units within the text in order to distinguish between:

- Relevant and irrelevant information,
- Facts and opinions,
- Explicit and implicit information,
- Examples and ideas, and
- Draw inferences and conclusions.

In nutshell, we need the following micro-skills of reading for intensive reading of a technical text:

(a) understanding major and minor details
(b) distinguishing between factual and non-factual information
(c) understanding the characteristics of a writer's use of language
(d) understanding and interpreting graphic information
(e) identifying and evaluating a writer's attitude
(f) understanding the author's intention
(g) responding to more than the plain sense of the words
(h) distinguishing between explicit and implicit information
(i) drawing inferences and conclusions

> Intensive reading skills include distinguishing between facts and opinions, and drawing inferences and conclusions.

Thus, in order to develop intensive reading skills, thorough reading practice is required. It also demands that an appropriate reading method be used. Moreover, the reader should develop his/her critical reading and inferential skills as well as his/her ability to receive and interpret graphic information. Here two of these skills are discussed—i.e., distinguishing between facts and opinions, and drawing conclusions and inferences. In the next chapter, we will discuss strategies for reading technical texts, reading methods, receiving and interpreting graphic information and detailed reading of technical materials.

Distinguishing between Facts and Opinions

A reader should be able to distinguish facts from opinions and ideas. Distinguishing between facts and opinions requires the ability to read with critical response and analyse the information in a text. It requires contributions by, both, the author and the reader and involves critical and analytical skills. So, it involves the reader's understanding of a text as well as his/her response to it.

> A fact is a truth that can be objectively verified by observation or experimentation. On the other hand, an opinion is something subjective, which cannot be objectively verified.

A fact is a truth that can be objectively verified by observation or experimentation. On the contrary, an opinion is something subjective, which cannot be objectively verified. Although science is mainly concerned with facts, opinions are also important. A discerning reader must make a distinction between the two to avoid confusion and misunderstanding. Table 14.3 differentiates between facts and opinions.

TABLE 4.3 Differences Between Facts and Opinions

Facts	*Opinions*
India is an agricultural country.	India is a great country.
Nearly two-thirds of India's population depends directly on agriculture for its livelihood.	Indian farmers are the best in the world.
Several multinational companies have opened their offices in India.	The coming of multinational companies to India has boosted the Indian economy.
The Government of India has reduced IIM fees.	Reduction of IIM fees by the government is a retrograde step.

It is obvious that a fact is universal in nature whereas opinions are quite personal and may differ from person-to-person.

Drawing Inferences and Conclusions

An inference can be defined as a statement that is based on some situations, observations, facts, or specific details. Drawing inferences is the process of knowing the unknown from the known. As science is a process of reasoning, scientists and technocrats have to draw inferences and conclusions based on observations. All the theories and laws of science have gone through the process of induction, which is an important method of drawing inferences. Induction is a reasoning process of drawing general statements from specific observations. All of us draw inferences from situations, statements, and observations.

> An inference can be defined as a statement that is based on some situations, observations, facts, or specific details.

> Induction is a reasoning process of drawing general statements from specific observations.

Inferences and conclusions can be drawn from the following:

(a) Facts
(b) Specific details
(c) Examples and illustrations
(d) Factual observations
(e) Contextual clues

The following are some examples of drawing inferences (inferences are printed in bold):

(a) We may find that it is easier to pull down than to pull up on a rope, and it may be easier to push rather than to pull objects. We also find it easier to do a certain amount of work by exerting small forces through large distances, rather than large forces through small distances. **We can, therefore, perform certain tasks more easily in some ways than in others**.

(b) When an object is allowed to fall freely to the earth from some height, it accelerates as it falls. This acceleration is directed toward the centre of the earth, and its magnitude varies with the distance from the earth. However, if air is neglected, it has the same magnitude for all objects at any location. Near the surface of the earth, the acceleration due to gravity has a magnitude of 9.81 m/s^2 or 32.2 ft/s^2.

This implies that **there is some net external force due to the attraction between the object and the earth.**

Progress Check 6

1. **Study the following statements about intensive reading strategies, and mark True or False against each of them:**
   (a) Intensive reading demands the total concentration and complete attention of the reader.
   (b) The three rapid reading techniques of prediction, scanning, and skimming prepare the reader for intensive reading.
   (c) Academic or professional reading involves detailed and thorough reading and the reader needs intensive reading skills.
   (d) To retain important information, the reader needs to think critically and analytically about what he/she is reading.
   (e) Drawing inferences and conclusions is a rapid reading technique.
   (f) Critical reading requires a contribution by both the author and the reader, and involves critical and analytical skills.
   (g) Critical reading skills do not entail the ability to distinguish between facts and opinions.
   (h) Making inferences is an inductive process.

Exercise

1. **Write brief notes on the following:**
   (a) Prediction techniques
   (b) Guessing the meaning from the context
   (c) Scanning
   (d) Skimming
   (e) Critical reading
   (f) Inferential skills
2. **Read the following paragraphs and underline the sentence that contains the main idea (topic sentence).**
   (a) Fuels may be classified according to the phases–solid, liquid or gas–in which they are available. A gaseous fuel is most convenient to burn, and it is easy to control its combustion. A liquid fuel requires initial heating to vaporise it before combustion begins. A solid fuel requires much more initial heating to ignite. In addition, it requires special equipment to handle it and to dispose the ash that is formed.
   (b) Vehicular pollution causes serious health problems. Carbon monoxide, nitrogen oxides, and hydrocarbons emitted by motor vehicles trigger off a complex chain reaction resulting in dangerous pollutants such as ozone, aldehydes, and ketones. The prolonged inhalation of carbon monoxide present in the toxic fumes reduces the carbon carrying capacity of the blood, and may cause headache, sickness, and even death. Likewise, unburned fragments of hydrocarbons form smog and thicken the atmosphere with elements that may cause cancer.

(c) Tungsten has a number of uses. Principal among these is an incandescent lamp filament. Its value here is due to its very high melting point, about 3600 degree centigrade, and its ability to be drawn into fine wire. It is used also for phonograph needles and as heating elements in very high temperature furnaces. However, its chief use, from a tonnage standpoint, is as a constituent of high-speed steel. It is available in the market as tungsten powder, wire, and as ferrotungsten.

3. **Run your eyes quickly through Passage 7 (take no longer than one minute) in order to answer the following questions:**
   (a) What is the central idea of the text?
   (b) What are the main points of the passage?
   (c) What are the different uses of friction?
   (d) Why is friction sometimes undesirable?
   (e) What are the properties of friction forces?

PASSAGE 7

Friction

There is no such thing as a perfectly smooth material; all known materials have some irregularities in their surfaces. Consequently, when two objects are in contact, these irregularities interlock, and the surfaces adhere to each other. If a force is applied in such a way that these objects slide over each other, the adhesion between the surfaces results in a resistance to the relative motion of the objects. This resistance to the relative motion is called friction. The friction force always acts in the opposite direction to the motion, opposes any tendency of motion, and slows down moving objects.

Friction is normally used to start fires, allows us to move and to stop, holds nails in wood, and can even be used to weld two surfaces together. However, friction is often undesirable, since it produces unwanted heat, causes wear, and reduces the efficiency of machines. Its effects can usually be minimised by lubrication, by smoothing the surfaces, and by the use of bearings and rollers. Since friction tends to oppose any motion, friction forces always act in the opposite direction to any tendency of motion.

Friction forces have the following properties:

1. They act parallel to the surfaces in contact, and in the opposite direction to any relative motion or tended motion.
2. Larger forces are required to start objects sliding than to keep them sliding at a constant speed. Therefore, starting friction forces are larger than sliding friction forces. However, once one surface is sliding over another, friction forces do not depend on the sliding speed.
3. Friction forces are proportional to the forces pushing the surfaces together (the normal force N). The normal force always acts perpendicular to the surfaces. Therefore,

$$F \text{ x } N \text{ or } F = \mu N$$

The constant μ is called the co-efficient of friction; it depends on the nature of the two surfaces in contact. Some typical values are listed in Exhibit 1. Note that these co-efficients have no units since they are the ratio of two forces. That is,

$$\mu = F/N$$

The co-efficient of friction corresponding to the maximum friction force before an object begins to slide is called the co-efficient of static friction. The co-efficient of sliding or kinetic friction is used when the object is sliding. Note that the co-efficients of static friction are larger than those of sliding friction.

Exhibit 1: Typical Values of Friction Coefficients between Two Surfaces

Surface	μS	μK
Glass on glass	0.95	0.80
Steel on steel	0.58	0.25
Wood on wood	0.35	0.30
Wood on metal	0.40	0.20
Wood on brick	0.60	0.25
Steel on wood	0.55	0.40
Steel on concrete	0.50	0.33
Rubber tyre on dry concrete	0.95	0.71
Rubber tyre on wet concrete	0.72	0.52
Wood on concrete	0.55	0.35

4. Skim the following passage and answer the questions given at the end.

PASSAGE 8

The sun is the most direct source of energy. It powers the flow of wind and water cycles and sustains all life. Plants use this energy to synthesise carbohydrates from simple substances like carbon dioxide and water. All the food is derived from the process of photosynthesis. In fact, the energy by which all the animals including human beings live is generated by the oxidation of the food produced by the plants.

The sun contains in its core hydrogen nuclei moving at very great speeds. Whenever these nuclei collide and fuse to form a nucleus of a heavier element, it results in nuclear reactions. These reactions generate tremendous amount of energy. It is this energy that powers the sun.

The sun emits lights of different wavelengths. If sunlight is passed through a prism each of these wavelengths is refracted by a different amount. Violet has the shortest wavelength, and red has the longest. The wavelength of green is midway between that of violet and red. Light with wavelength shorter than that of violet is called ultraviolet light. Light with wavelength longer than that of red light is called infrared light. About one-third of the light from the sun is infrared.

We know that nuclear reactions that go on in the interior of the sun liberate a large amount of energy. Nuclei of deuterium, which is the heavier isotope of hydrogen, collide in the sun's interior to produce helium. The energy liberated in these reaction fires the sun, which, in turn, emits lights of different wavelengths. Of these wavelengths, it is the infrared wavelengths that heat up the earth. The reaction in which the hydrogen in the sun is converted into helium is called a fusion reaction.

Questions

(a) What is fusion reaction?
(b) What is the central idea of the passage?
(c) What is the main idea of the first paragraph?
(d) What is photosynthesis?
(e) What is the main idea of the last paragraph?

5. Read the following passage and answer the questions given at the end:

PASSAGE 9

Matter and Energy

The physical universe (which includes living organisms) is composed entirely of matter and energy, which together are the basis of all objective phenomena. Matter is usually defined as anything that has mass and occupies space. The term mass describes the tendency of an object to remain at rest if it is stationary or to continue in motion if it is already moving. (For example, a boulder is harder to move than a pebble, and harder to stop; it has more mass). The mass of an object can be determined, for example, by measuring its weight, the force with which it is attracted to the earth. Because the force of gravity is not the same at every point of the earth's surface, the weight of an object is not constant. Consequently, the mass of an object can be determined from a direct measurement of its weight. A familiar example of a natural law is the law of gravity. Less familiar examples of laws are those that describe the behaviour of gases. For example, all gases can be compressed, and Boyle's law states that their volume is inversely proportional to the pressure exerted on them. Boyle's law, like the law of gravity, gives no reason for natural behaviour but simply states what the behaviour is.

Having observed nature, and summarised the observations as laws, scientists then further their understanding by asking: Why are things the way they are? Why, for example, are all gases compressible? At this point, scientists depart from observations and begin to make guesses. In accounting for the compressibility of gases, they postulate that all gases consist of sub-microscopic particles (called molecules) with relatively large spaces between them. When a gas is compressed, the molecules are pushed closer together. Such a model for a gas is an example of a 'theory'. In general, any theory is an 'explanation of observed behaviour' in terms of a simple model that has familiar properties. The observed facts are thus 'explained,' but only in the sense that they are made plausible by being related to simpler or more familiar phenomena. Since it is a product of the mind, theory is not infallible. It may have to be modified or even completely discarded in the light of further experiments.

Once a model has been proposed to account for some observations, it may be possible to predict from the model behaviour that has not been previously investigated. New experiments can be performed to test the validity of the model and incidentally uncover new facts. Thus, theories serve as a stimulus for the growth of science.

Questions

1. Which of the following statements are not facts in the light of the above text:
   (a) Theories serve as a stimulus for the growth of science.
   (b) Matter has mass and occupies space.
   (c) Scientists sometimes depart from observations and begin to make guesses.
   (d) Any theory is an explanation of observed behaviour in terms of a simple model that has familiar properties.
   (e) The mass of an object can be determined.
   (f) Since it is a product of the mind, it may have to be modified or even completely discarded in the light of further experiments.
   (g) The force of gravity is not the same at every point of the earth's surface.
   (h) The mass of an object can be determined from a direct measurement of its weight.
   (i) All gases can be compressed.
   (j) The exception proves the rule.

(k) Boyle's law is very important.
(l) The weight of an object is not constant.
(m) Scientists explore the natural world.

2. Which of the following cannot be inferred from the passage?
   (a) The physical universe includes non-living organisms.
   (b) Matter has the tendency to remain at rest if it is stationary or to continue in motion if it is already moving.
   (c) Matter and energy can be objectively examined.
   (d) There are laws that describe the behaviour of gases.
   (e) Scientific theories are infallible.
   (f) Experiments test the validity of any experiment.

Key to Progress Check

Progress Check 1

1. having self-government, automatic pilot, without clouds, in favour of government, against war, not efficient, having many purposes, having two chambers, occurring twice a year, between persons, mix together, insert (a thing) between others, divide into two, half of a circle, half conscious, small piece of semiconductor, small localised climate, aeroplane with one set of wings, single block of stone, very tired, not a genuine intellectual, judge wrongly, put in the wrong place, print wrongly, written or printed below the line, go under water, abundant, plant again, say or do again, interpret again
2. (a) lacking courtesy, (b) shabby and untidy, (c) easily offended or hurt, (d) grief or sudden misfortune, (e) economical, (f) tolerant, (g) fair, (h) one who remains alive, (i) number of people attending a meeting, (j) compensate for

Progress Check 2

Passage 1

1. (a), (c), (d), (f)
2. (b), (e), (f)

Passage 2

(a), (e)

Progress Check 3

Fifteen times

Progress Check 5

1. (a) False (b) True (c) True (d) False (e) False
2. Paragraph 1: Liquids are practically incompressible.
   Paragraph 2: Liquids maintain their volume.
   Paragraph 3: Liquids have no characteristic shape.
   Paragraph 4: Liquids diffuse slowly.
   Paragraph 5: Liquids evaporate.

3. (a) False
   The passage is about the lens systems of microscopes and telescopes.
   (b) True
   (c) True
   (d) False
   The eyepiece is a system of convex lenses.
   (e) Microscopes and telescopes are magnifying devices. True
   (f) False.
   Both microscopes and telescopes use two lens systems.

Progress Check 6

1. (a) True (b) True (c) True (d) True (e) False
   (f) True (g) False (h) True

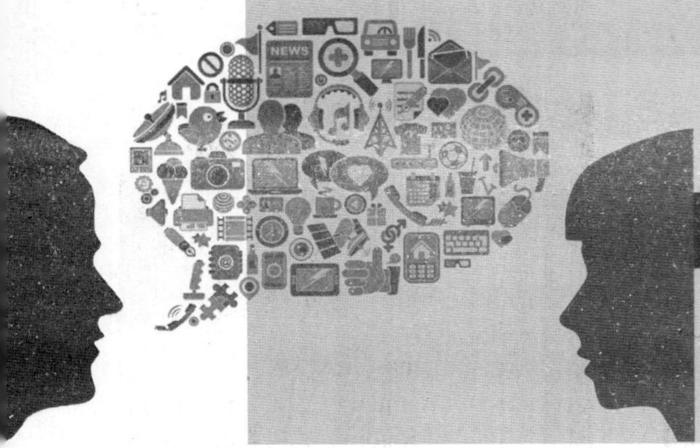

CHAPTER 15

Comprehension of Technical Materials

Reading technical materials involves a complex process of obtaining discipline-specific information, and retaining this information for future use and reference.

LEARNING OBJECTIVES

- Knowing techniques for reading scientific and technical texts
- Understanding two reading methods
- Knowing how to read and understand instructions and technical manuals
- Understanding how to read and interpret graphic information
- Learning to read and comprehend technical material
- Learning how to summarize complex text
- Developing effective analytical skills

15.1 COMPREHENSION

Comprehension is the ability to understand something. In the context of this chapter, comprehension is the ability to understand technical materials like scientific texts and instructional manuals.

Comprehension is the ability to understand something.

For students in the scientific and technical fields, effective comprehension skills can give them an edge. The following sections discuss how to develop effective comprehension skills by improving one's reading, memorizing, summarizing, and analytical skills.

Students of professional courses who do not have a systematic approach to reading and face difficulties in understanding a scientific text.

Reading is crucial to academic/professional success. We need excellent reading skills because we may be required to read different kinds of reading materials, which include scientific texts, instruction manuals, and technical materials in different forms. Students of professional courses who do not have a systematic approach to reading and do not apply appropriate reading strategies, face difficulties in understanding a scientific text. They suffer from lack of concentration, boredom, slow reading speed, and poor comprehension. It is important for such students to be able to read and understand scientific and technical material.

15.1.1 Reading Scientific and Technical Texts

Reading scientific and technical texts involves a complex process of obtaining discipline-specific information, and retaining this information for future use and reference. The comprehension of discipline-specific information transfer entails a basic understanding of the subject and familiarity with the material. The reader is concerned with the subject-content of what he/she reads as well as the specific language in which it is presented. He/she needs to use all the techniques and strategies of reading discussed in the previous chapter. The following simple guidelines may improve reading effectiveness and help in reading and comprehending technical materials.

Prepare for Reading

Reading technical texts is entirely different from reading general material. When we have to read a newspaper, we may simply open the newspaper and start reading it. However, we may not do so while reading technical materials. We need to prepare our mind to receive the information because we have to receive as well as retain important information. In order to ensure a high degree of understanding and remembrance, the reader should focus on the subject so that he/she can concentrate better. The reader should use appropriate prediction techniques to guess the overall content of the text and predict the information that he/she expects to receive. Moreover, the reader should recall related information that he/she already knows. He/she will also have to determine the time that he/she will need to complete the reading assignment. This pre-reading stage may not take much time. It is helpful in preparing the reader for detailed reading and he/she will be motivated to read the material.

Reading technical texts is entirely different from reading general material.

Scan the Text

Scanning the text before reading provides the reader with some key information about the text that will make reading faster and more effective.

Scanning the text before reading provides the reader with some key information about the text that will make reading faster and more effective. Scanning techniques are useful to discover graphic information, look for any references or bibliography listings, and look for any notes/questions/remarks at the end of the text. Identifying non-verbal signs and other aids in the reading text make reading easier.

Skim the Text

Skimming a technical text before detailed reading provides better comprehension.

Skimming a technical text before detailed reading provides better comprehension and ensures a high degree of remembrance. The reader should take a few minutes to skim the text before detailed reading in order to understand its gist. The reader should discover the purpose and organisation of the text, understand the subject of the text, and the author's central idea or point of view about the subject. He/she should be able to identify the main points of the text.

Read the Text Thoroughly

A technical text needs to be read thoroughly and slowly to understand all the details.

Academic or professional reading involves detailed and thorough reading. A technical text needs to be read thoroughly and slowly to understand all the details. While reading technical materials, the reader needs to concentrate on the way in which the writer has structured the information, and he/she should analyse graphic information. He/she also needs to respond to the lexical meaning of words and the relationships between them, understand the specific details, recognise the meaning and function of sentence patterns accurately, and recognise their logical and thematic coherence. In addition, he/she needs to think critically and analytically about what he/she is reading in order to interpret and analyse the text. The following points should be noted:

- Read silently with quick eye movements. A line of print can be read with three eye fixations.
- Respond to the lexical meaning of words and the relationships between them, and consult the glossary, if any, in order to know the meanings of unfamiliar words and scientific/technical terms. In addition, look for the contextual signal words as well as examples that indirectly help define an unknown word or phrase.
- Recognise discourse/semantic markers and try to understand the function of each discourse marker.
- Recognise the meaning and function of sentence patterns accurately.
- If necessary, turn back some pages to ensure understanding.

Make Notes

You may have to develop some technique that helps you in the process of remembering what you have read.

While reading a technical text, the reader needs to remember the information that he/she has received so that he/she is able to use it in some other form later. This information transfer is the most important function of academic reading, i.e., reading for academic purposes. However, this is not an easy task. It may not be possible for the reader to remember everything because the process of forgetting is very fast. He/she may read and understand something today but find it difficult to retain it in his/her memory for more than a few weeks. You may have to develop some technique that helps you in the process of remembering what you have read. Note-making is one such technique. Note-making strategies have been discussed in the later chapters.

Review What You Have Read

Once the reading assignment has been completed, the reader should try to recall and remember the content of the text. The accuracy of recall may be checked by a quick survey of the text.

Reading Methods

The ability to read scientific and technical texts effectively largely depends on an efficient method of reading. As a high degree of understanding and remembrance is required, a systematic approach to reading should be followed. Here two reading methods are described, the ERRQ reading technique, and the SQ3R reading method. Either of these methods may be used while reading a technical text.

Two reading methods that can be used effectively for reading scientific and technical texts are ERRQ and SQ3R techniques.

ERRQ Reading Technique

The ERRQ reading technique was developed by Dorothy Watson in 1985. It has four stages, namely, Estimate, Read, Respond, Question (Table 15.1). The basic purpose of this strategy is to get the reader to link what he/she has with new information. This technique might be useful for reading any kind of text.

TABLE 15.1 ERRQ Technique

Stage	*Description*
Estimate	Estimate what the text will be like. Rapid reading techniques may be used for this purpose.
Read	Read the text carefully and thoroughly.
Respond	Respond to the text.
Question	Question things about the text and analyse responses to it.

SQ3R Reading Technique

SQ3R is a well-tried and widely used reading technique. This reading technique was developed by F.P. Robinson in 1946 in his book *Effective Study*. It has been recommended by a number of communication experts and ESL researchers as it ensures a high degree of understanding and remembrance.

SQ3R has five stages, namely Survey, Question, Read, Recall, and Revise. Table 15.2 summarises the SQ3R technique.

TABLE 15.2 SQ3R Technique

Stage	*Description*
Survey	Glancing rapidly through the text before reading any part of it to discover its purpose, and identify its organisation.
Question	Asking appropriate questions for each part of the text in order to give a purpose to the reading.
Read	Reading carefully and thoroughly, and making notes at the end of each section.
Recall	Recalling the content at the end of each part of the text and checking and amending notes.
Revise	Checking the accuracy of reading recall, and reviewing notes.

Progress Check 1

1. **Examine the following statements in the light of the above discussion about reading scientific and technical texts and reading methods, and mark True or False against each of them:**
   (a) Reading a technical text does not involve recalling related information that is already known.
   (b) The ERRQ reading technique is less elaborate than SQ3R reading method.
   (c) The ability to read scientific and technical texts effectively largely depends on an efficient method of reading.
   (d) Reading of academic texts may require a high degree of understanding and remembrance.
   (e) The ERRQ reading technique is more difficult to use than the SQ3R reading method.
   (f) The first step of the SQ3R method is asking appropriate questions for each part of the text in order to give a purpose to the reading.
   (g) The pre-reading survey does not include guessing the information that is expected to be received.
   (h) Detailed reading involves reading a text or passage carefully and thoroughly to get all the details.
   (i) Silent reading with quick eye movements can help a reader to concentrate on the reading assignment.
   (j) A line of print can be easily read with a single eye fixation.

15.1.2 Reading Instructions and Technical Manuals

Reading Instructions

Students may have to read different kinds of instructions, such as laboratory instruction sheets; simple instructions in the classroom or workshop; instructions to use and operate instruments, machines or devices; instructions related to project work and so on. In order to understand these instruction materials, appropriate reading strategies are required.

> Reading instructions and technical manuals requires effective reading strategies such as prediction, scanning, skimming, and intensive reading skills.

Instructions are directives to carry out certain actions. They may consist of a single word or a set of instructions to tell a user how to start, use, operate, and maintain a highly complex and sophisticated system or machine. Reading isolated instructions may involve scanning and skimming skills while reading complex and lengthy instruction materials would also require intensive reading skills.

The following reading technique may be adopted in order to increase efficiency in reading and understanding instructions:

> Reading isolated instructions may involve scanning and skimming skills while reading complex and lengthy instruction materials would also require intensive reading skills.

1. Glance rapidly through the sets of instructions in order to identify the nature and purpose of instructions.
2. Scan any graphic information.
3. Recognise distribution of emphasis and focus point.
4. Skim the instructions to:
   - Identify sequence words to understand the coherence and logical structure of instructions
   - Identify the number of steps or tasks involved in the procedure
   - Identify the main instructions

- Recognise transition points in the instructions
- Understand the ordering of instructions

5. After scanning and skimming, read the instructions carefully and thoroughly to get all the details.
6. Note the following:
   - Concentrate on precautions
   - Understand the safety points

Reading Technical Manuals

Students also have to read various kinds of technical manuals. Technical manuals are detailed guidelines to use, operate, and maintain complex systems. This may include instruction manuals, safety manuals and regulations, and user manuals. Reading technical manuals requires various reading strategies such as scanning, skimming, intensive reading skills, and critical and inferential comprehension.

> Technical manuals are detailed guidelines to use, operate, and maintain complex systems.

The following steps may be adopted in order to increase reading efficiency while reading technical manuals:

1. Glance rapidly through the manual before reading any part of it in order to get focus on the subject, guess the information that the text contains, and become aware of the aids in the text that might make reading faster and easier.
2. Take a few minutes to skim the manual before detailed reading to discover the purpose and organisation of the manual, and identify the main points in it.
3. Scan the manual to discover graphic information, pictures, or diagrams.
4. Finally, read the manual carefully and thoroughly to get all the details. Note the following:
   - Concentrate on the safety part
   - Identify the precautions to be taken
   - Consult the glossary, if any, in order to know the meanings of unfamiliar words and scientific/technical terms
   - Look for contextual signal words as well as examples that indirectly help define an unknown word or phrase
   - At the end of detailed reading, try to recall and remember the content of the text.

Progress Check 2

1. Examine the following statements about reading instructions and technical manuals, and mark True or False against each of them.

(a) Instructions may consist of a single word or may include a set of instructions to tell a user how to start, use, operate, and maintain a highly complex and sophisticated system or machine.

(b) Reading isolated instructions may not involve scanning and skimming.

(c) Reading complex and lengthy instruction materials would require intensive reading skills.

(d) In order to understand the coherence and logical structure of instructions, the sequence words should be identified.

(e) Skimming the instructions does not involve recognising transition points in the instructions.

(f) Technical manuals are detailed guidelines to use, operate, and maintain complex systems.

(g) Scanning a technical manual does not involve discovering graphic information, pictures, or diagrams.

15.1.3 Reading and Interpreting Graphic Information

As technical writers use several graphic techniques to present technical information, readers should be able to understand and interpret these graphic elements (Table 15.3).

There are four types of graphic aids generally used in technical documents: tables, diagrams, charts, and graphs.

A table is a very simple graphic aid that organises data into groups and shows quantitative data and related information. It may show several variables for a number of items and convey maximum data in minimum space. In order to interpret and analyse a table, the reader should concentrate on the information given in the columns and rows.

TABLE 15.3 Graphic Techniques

Graphic Aids	*Functions*
Tables	Organise data into groups and show quantitative data and related information.
Bar charts/diagrams	Show comparative or contrastive information
Tree diagrams/organisational charts	Show classificatory data
Graphs/line charts/ line diagrams	Show the trend or relationship between two dimensions
Flow diagrams	Show the steps of a process
Pie charts/diagrams	Show information related to proportions or percentages.
Flow charts	Present complex processes

Diagrams and charts are frequently used by technical writers to simplify complex information. They are used to present comparative, contrastive, or classificatory information. In order to interpret them, the reader should understand their nature and functions. Diagrams include bar diagrams, tree diagrams, line diagrams, flow diagrams, and pie diagrams while charts include bar charts, organisational charts, line charts, pie charts, and flow charts.

Bar diagrams and charts show comparative or contrastive information, convey relative magnitude, provide comparative analysis, and illustrate information classified into different groups. Tree diagrams or organisational charts show classificatory data and provide classificatory analysis. Flow diagrams show the steps of a simple process whereas flow charts present complex processes. Pie diagrams and charts show the relative size of the parts of a whole and show information related to proportions or percentages.

A graph is another important technique to simplify and present complex information. Graphs as well as line diagrams and line charts show the trend or relationship between two dimensions, reveal the distribution of data points in a certain dimension, and show trends in data. Moreover, they focus on the change in quantity.

Progress Check 3

1. **Study the following table and use the information given in the table in order to answer the question that follows:**

Components of a Microscope		*Functions of Each Component*
Optical parts	Eyepiece	Serves as a magnifying glass and limits the field seen by the eye
	Body tube	Refracts the light
	Objectives	Magnifies the image
Mechanical parts	Coarse and fine-adjustment dials	Provide clear image
	Nose-piece	Holds the objectives
	Metal plate	The specimen is placed on it
Illuminating parts	Illumination source	Provides the necessary light
	Condenser	Intensifies the light.

Question

Read the following statements and mark True or False in the light of the above table.

(a) A microscope is an optical instrument for magnifying micro-organisms.
(b) A microscope does not consist of any mechanical part.
(c) The body tube serves as a magnifying glass and limits the field seen by the eye.
(d) The condenser provides the necessary light.
(e) The coarse and fine adjustment dials provide a clear image.
(f) The eyepiece refracts light.
(g) The nose-piece holds the objective.
(h) We place the specimen on a metal plate.
(i) The objective magnifies the image.
(j) The illumination source intensifies the light.

2. **Study the following flow diagram about coal-based thermal plants, and answer the questions that follow:**

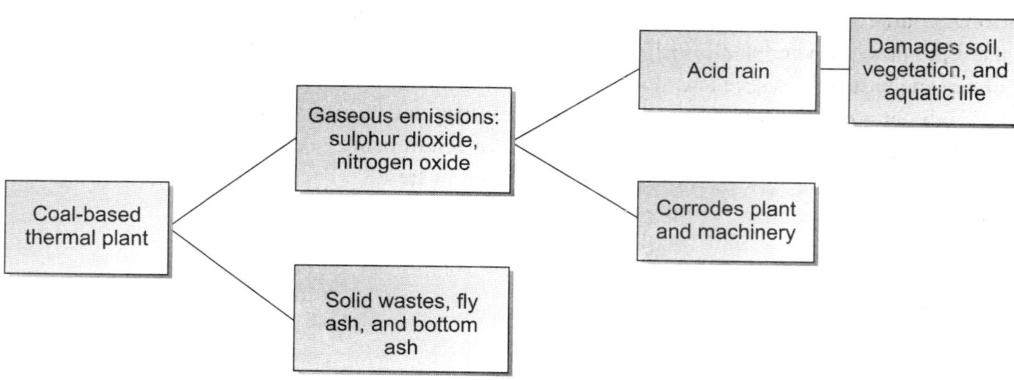

(a) What does acid rain do?
(b) Which of the following statements are True?
   (i) A coal-based thermal plant produces a tremendous amount of solid wastes.
   (ii) Gaseous emissions corrode plant and machinery.
   (iii) A coal-based thermal plant does not produce fly ash and bottom ash.
   (iv) Sulphur dioxide and nitrogen oxide may cause acid rain.

15.1.4 Reading Practice

The following reading practice exercises will help in dealing with technical materials. Answers to these exercises are given at the end of the chapter.

Reading Practice 1

First, the text should be scanned quickly in order to predict the information that it contains. Then, it should be read again thoroughly. Read slowly and think critically and analytically about the content, concentrate on the way in which the writer has structured the information. Look for the contextual signal words as well as examples that indirectly help define an unknown word or phrase. After reading and understanding the text, all the questions given at the end of the passage should be answered.

Electron Microscope

An electron microscope is a sophisticated microscope that can magnify objects up to one million times their original size. Unlike a traditional microscope, an electron microscope can reveal some details of molecular structure and can be effectively used for chemical analysis. It has become an invaluable analytical tool, widely used in medical and industrial research establishments.

There are two types of electron microscopes: the transmission electron microscopes (TEM) and the scanning electron microscope (SEM). Transmission electron microscopes have extremely high resolution and can provide detailed information about the structure of organisms most of which are far too small to be seen at all with a normal optical microscope. TEMs can also be used for studying the arrangement of atoms and molecules in metal and other materials. In fact, they are effectively used, both, to give information about the microstructure of new materials as they are being designed and also to help in the analysis of failures of materials. Most TEMs operate at accelerating voltages in the range of 50–100,000V.

On the other hand, SEM have very different uses as they are very useful for looking at the surfaces of objects and can provide a completely different range of information. They may produce an extremely fine beam of electrons, which is swept to-and-fro across the specimen. They are extremely useful in studying the details and contours of different surfaces. They provide many other striking views of plant and animal cells that cannot be obtained by other means. In the microelectronics industry, scanning electron microscopes have proved to be an equally great asset. It is possible to use them to look in detail at the microcircuits that are now constructed on tiny silicon chips, the microscope is also used as an instrument to fabricate circuits by using the electron beam as a 'writing' tool, controlling it by a computer so that the required circuit is produced on a special surface.

Questions

1. Answer the following questions:
   (a) Do transmission electron microscopes (TEM) and scanning electron microscopes (SEM) serve different functions?
   (b) What is the most remarkable feature of transmission electron microscopes?
   (c) Can TEM help in achieving improved diagnosis of ailments? How?
   (d) What are the two important uses of electron microscopes in materials science?
   (e) Can SEM aid cancer research? How?
   (f) Can electron microscopes accurately describe the nature of the material under examination?
2. Read the following statements and mark True or False based on the text. Make appropriate inferences.
   (a) TEM has high resolving power.
   (b) SEM cannot be used in the microelectronics industry.
   (c) SEM can provide striking views of animal cells.
   (d) In TEM the electron beam is scanned to-and-fro across a specimen.
   (e) Electron microscopes are more useful than optical microscopes.
   (f) TEM can provide detailed information about viruses.
   (g) Electron microscopes help in the analysis of failure of materials.
   (h) Electron microscopes cannot give information about the microstructure of new materials as they are being designed.
   (i) Optical microscopes can study different forms of DNA.
   (j) SEM cannot be used in biological sciences.
3. Answer the following questions by choosing the best alternative under each. (Tick the correct answer.)
   (a) Some of the finest details of molecular structure can be revealed by
      (i) traditional microscopes
      (ii) optical microscopes
      (iii) electron microscopes
   (b) Infact, they are effectively used both to give information about the microstructure of new materials as they are being designed. What is being designed?
      (i) electron microscopes
      (ii) TEMs
      (iii) new materials
   (c) TEMs allow us to see very fine details of specimens because
      (i) electrons pass right through the specimens
      (ii) they have extremely high resolving power
      (iii) the electron beam is scanned to-and-fro across the specimen
   (d) TEMs can be used to
      (i) study details and contours of different surfaces
      (ii) study the arrangement of atoms and molecules in metal
      (iii) look in detail at the microcircuits that are now constructed
   (e) SEMs are very good for
      (i) looking at the surfaces of objects

(ii) helping in the analysis of failure of materials
(iii) providing detailed information about viruses

(f) SEMs can be used to look in detail at
(i) microcircuits that are now constructed on a tiny silicon chip
(ii) the normal outer surfaces of cells
(iii) both of these

Reading Practice 2

First, the text should be scanned quickly (no more than one minute), in order to predict the information that it contains. Particular attention should be paid to the heading, the sub-headings, the first paragraph, and the topic sentence in each paragraph. Then, solve the pre-reading exercise.

The text should be read again thoroughly. Read slowly and think critically and analytically about the content, concentrate on the way in which the writer has structured the information. Look for the contextual signal words as well as examples that indirectly help define an unknown word or phrase. After reading and understanding the text, all the questions in the exercises should be answered.

Pre-reading Exercise

Which of the following topics is not discussed in the following passage:

(a) Operation of electrical devices
(b) Relation between electricity and magnetism
(c) Operation of electric cars
(d) Artificial magnets
(e) Electromagnetic induction
(f) Measurement of magnetic fields
(g) Magnetic poles
(h) Motion of a magnetic pole near a conductor
(i) Magnetic properties
(j) Inducted magnetism

Magnetism

Electricity and magnetism are directly related because both types of phenomena are due to interactions between electric charges. However, while electric forces are always exerted between charges, whether they are at rest or in motion, magnetic forces only occur between moving charges. In fact, most magnetic properties of materials originate from the motions of the orbital electrons in atoms.

The operation of many devices, such as ammeters, voltmeters, electric motors, particle accelerators, and television sets, depends on magnetic forces that are exerted on charges that move through a magnetic field. In addition, since magnetic fields originate from moving charges, electric currents are surrounded by magnetic fields. The operation of electromagnets, magnetic relays and switches, and many other devices depends on the magnetic fields of electric currents.

Magnetic Properties Centuries ago it was noticed that pieces of a special kind of rock attracted each other. This type of rock is called magnetite or lodestone; it is a compound of iron and oxygen that is found in many parts of the world. This name originated from the discovery that it would align in a north-south direction; it was therefore called leading stone or lodestone. A sample of lodestone is a natural magnet.

Inducted Magnetism Some materials, such as iron, cobalt, and nickel, are attracted by magnets even when they are not magnets themselves. This is known as induced magnetism. By themselves, if they are not magnetised, these materials do not attract each other (except by the weaker force of gravity). However, when they are attracted to a magnet, they also act as magnets. They then have the ability to attract other pieces of similar materials. We can, for example, suspend many paper clips end to end from a single magnet. The paper clips may not be magnetised permanently themselves, but they act as magnets to attract other objects.

Artificial Magnets Pieces of iron, cobalt, and nickel can also become magnetised when they are either stroked many times in the same direction along their length with one end of a magnet, or if they are placed in the magnetic field of a current. These magnets are then artificial magnets, but they possess magnetic properties that are the same as those of natural magnets.

Magnetic Compass Magnets may be made in many different shapes, but they all have similar properties. A simple magnetic compass can be made by freely suspending a bar magnet on a pivot or from a string, so that the long axis of the magnet is horizontal. If there are no other magnetic materials nearby, the suspended magnet eventually aligns with the magnetic field of the earth in an approximately north-south direction. The same magnetic pole of the magnet always indicates a northerly direction; therefore, it is called a north-seeking pole or simply a north pole. The other magnetic pole is called a south-seeking pole or south pole.

When the north pole of one magnet is brought close to the south pole of another, the two magnets attract each other. However, if a north pole of one magnet is moved close to the north pole of another, the magnets repel each other. Therefore, like magnetic poles repel and unlike magnetic poles attract each other.

Magnetic poles occur naturally in unlike pairs. Even if a magnet is cut into two or more pieces, each piece will contain two unlike poles.

A magnetic pole may attract other dissimilar magnetic poles and even pieces of some unmagnetised materials. However, magnetic repulsion can only occur between like magnetic poles. We can use this fact to determine whether a material is magnetised.

Magnetic Fields We say that a magnetic field exists in any region where a magnetic pole experiences a magnetic force. Since magnetic forces occur between magnetic poles, magnetic fields are produced by magnetic poles. These magnetic fields are represented by lines of magnetic force, which indicate the direction of the force on a north magnetic pole. For example, exterior to the magnet, the lines of magnetic force are directed away from a north pole because it would repel any other north pole. They are also directed towards a south pole because a south pole attracts north poles.

Magnetic fields are often mapped with the aid of a small magnetic compass. At each point, the direction indicated by the north pole of the compass is the direction of the magnetic field. They can also be mapped by sprinkling iron filings on a sheet of paper that covers a magnet or system of magnets. The filings become induced magnets and align themselves with the field.

The earth itself behaves like a very large magnet with magnetic poles close to the geographical north and south poles. However, the earth's magnetic pole that is close to the geographic north pole is a south-seeking or south magnetic pole because it attracts the north poles of compasses and magnets. Similarly, the earth's north magnetic pole is located near the geographic south pole.

Questions

1. Study the following statements and mark True or False based on the text:
   (a) Artificial magnets possess magnetic properties similar to those of natural magnets.
   (b) The shapes of magnets may be similar but their properties are different.
   (c) Magnetite is a compound of iron and oxygen.
   (d) Electricity and magnetism are the result of interactions between electric charges.
   (e) Electric forces are rarely exerted between charges.
   (f) Magnetic fields originate from moving charges.
   (g) Electric currents are surrounded by magnetic fields.
   (h) A magnetic compass can be made by freely suspending a bar magnet on a pivot.
   (i) A magnetic pole attracts other similar magnetic poles.
   (j) Magnetic attraction can only occur between like magnetic poles.
   (k) Magnetic forces only occur between moving charges.
   (l) Magnetic fields may not be mapped with the aid of a magnetic compass.
2. Answer the following:
   (a) Where does a magnetic field exist?
   (b) Where are the magnetic fields of electric currents used?
   (c) Mention three materials that are attracted by magnets even when they are not magnets?
   (d) Does the earth behave like a big magnet?
   (e) How are magnetic fields produced by magnetic poles?
3. Which of the following cannot be inferred from the passage?
   (a) The motions of the orbital electrons in atoms play an important role in the magnetic properties of materials.
   (b) Natural magnets are different from artificial magnets.
   (c) This is known as induced magnetism.
   (d) Current carrying conductors experience magnetic forces in magnetic fields.
   (e) Moving charges experience magnetic forces, and electric currents are moving charges.
   (f) Induced magnetism has industrial relevance.
   (g) Magnetism can be temporary.
   (h) Magnetic poles do not occur in like pairs.
   (i) Nickel can become magnetised when it is placed in the magnetic field of a current.
   (j) A suspended magnet always aligns with the magnetic field of the earth.

Reading Practice 3

First, the text should be scanned quickly (no more than thirty seconds), in order to predict the information that it contains. Particular attention should be paid to the heading, the sub-headings, the figure used in the text, the first paragraph, and the topic sentence in each paragraph. Now solve the pre-reading exercise.

The text should be read again thoroughly. Read slowly and think critically and analytically about the content, concentrate on the way in which the writer has structured the information. Look for the contextual signal words as well as examples that indirectly help define an unknown word or phrase. After reading and understanding the text, all the questions in the exercises should be answered.

Pre-reading Exercise

Which of the following has been discussed/described in the passage?

(a) Major parts of a supercomputer
(b) Main components of a micro-computer
(c) Functioning of I/O section of a micro-computer
(d) Importance of micro-computer
(e) RAM and ROM
(f) Control bus signals
(g) A/D converter
(h) Central Processing Unit

Microcomputer*

The major parts of a microcomputer (Fig. 15.1) are the central processing unit or CPU, memory, and the input and output circuitry or I/O. Connecting these parts are three sets of parallel lines called buses. The three buses are the address bus, the **data bus** and the control bus. Fig. 15.1 illustrates these parts.

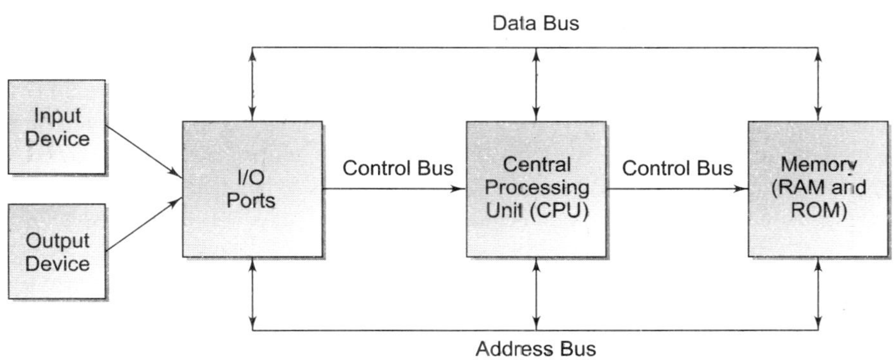

Fig. 15.1 Block diagram of a Simple Microcomputer

Memory The memory section usually consists of a mixture of RAM and ROM. It may also have magnetic floppy disks, magnetic hard disks, or optical disks. Memory has two purposes. The first is to store the binary codes for the sequences of instructions the computer has to carry out. While writing a computer programme, what we really do is write a sequential list of instructions for the computer. The second purpose of the memory is to store the binary-coded data with which the computer is going to be working. This data might be, for example, the inventory records of a supermarket.

Input/Output The input/output or I/O section allows the computer to take in data from the outside world or send data to the outside world. Peripherals such as keyboards, video display terminals, printers, and modems are connected to the I/O section. These allow the user and the computer to communicate with each other. The actual physical devices used to interface the computer buses to external systems are called **ports**. Ports in a computer function just as shipping ports do for a country. An input port allows data from a keyboard, an

* Adapted from: Hall, Douglas V, *Microprocessors and Interfacing: Programming and Hardware,* (New Delhi: Tata McGraw-Hill Publishing Company Limited) (1999)

A/D converter, or some other source to be read into the computer controlled by the CPU. An output port is used to send data from the computer to some peripheral, such as a video display terminal, a printer, or a D/A converter. Physically, the simplest type of input or output port is just a set of parallel D flip-flops. If they are being used as an input port, the D inputs are connected to the external device, and the Q outputs are connected to the data bus, which runs to the CPU. Data will then be transferred through the latches when they are enabled by a control signal from the CPU. In a system where they are being used as an output port, the D inputs of the latches are connected to the data bus, and the Q outputs are connected to some external device. Data sent out on the data bus by the CPU will be transferred to the external device when the latches are enabled by a control signal from the CPU.

Central Processing Unit The central processing unit or CPU controls the operation of the computer. In a microcomputer the CPU is a microprocessor. The CPU fetches binary-coded instructions from its memory, decodes the instructions into a series of simple actions, and carries out these actions in a sequence of steps.

The CPU also contains an address counter or instruction pointer register, which holds the address of the next instruction or data item to be fetched from memory; general-purpose registers, which are used for temporary storage of binary data; and circuitry, which generates the control bus signals.

Address Bus The address bus consists of 16, 20, 24, or 32 parallel signal lines. On these lines, the CPU sends out the address of the memory location that is to be written to or read from. The number of memory locations that the CPU can address is determined by the number of address lines. If the CPU has N address lines, then it can directly address 2^N memory locations. For example, a CPU with 16 address lines can address 2^{16} or 65,536 memory locations, a CPU with 20 address lines can address 2^{20} or 1,048,576 locations, and a CPU with 24 address lines can address 2^{24} or 1,67,77,216 locations. When the CPU reads data from or writes data to a port, it sends the port address out on the address bus.

Data Bus The data bus consists of 8, 16, or 32 parallel signal lines. As indicated by the double-ended arrows on the data bus line in Figure 15.1, the data bus lines are **bidirectional**. This means that the CPU can read data in' from memory or from a port on these lines, or it can send data out to memory or to a port on these lines. Many devices in a system will have their outputs connected to the data bus, but only one device at a time will have its outputs enabled. Any device connected on the data bus must have **three-state outputs** so that its outputs can be disabled when it is not being used to put data on the bus.

Control Bus The control bus consists of 4 to 10 parallel signal lines. The CPU sends out signals on the control bus to enable the outputs of addressed memory devices or port devices. Typical control bus signals are **Memory Read, Memory Write, I/O Read, and I/O Write**. To read a byte of data from a memory location, for example, the CPU sends out the memory address of the desired byte on the address bus and then sends out a Memory Read signal on the control bus. The Memory Read signal enables the addressed memory device to output a data word onto the data bus. The data word from memory travels along the data bus to the CPU.

Thus, we see that a microcomputer consists of memory, a CPU, and some input/output circuitry. These three parts are connected by the address bus, the data bus, and the control bus.

Questions

1. Study the following statements and write True or False based on the text:
   - (a) The memory section of a microcomputer stores binary codes for the sequences of instructions the computer has to carry out.
   - (b) An output port is used to send data from the computer to some peripheral, such as a video display terminal, a printer, or a D/A converter.
   - (c) Peripherals such as keyboards, video display terminals, printers, and modems are not connected to the I/O section.
   - (d) The actual physical devices used to interface the computer buses to external systems are called RAM and ROM.
   - (e) The central processing unit or CPU is a microprocessor in a microcomputer and controls the operation of the latter.
   - (f) The CPU fetches binary-coded instructions from its memory, decodes the instructions into a series of simple actions, and carries out these actions in a sequence of steps.
   - (g) The CPU does not contain an address counter or instruction pointer register.
   - (h) As indicated by the double-ended arrows on the data bus line in Figure 15.1, the data bus lines are bidirectional.
   - (i) No device connected on the data bus should have three-state outputs as there is no need to disable its outputs when it is not being used to put data on the bus.
   - (j) The Memory Read signal enables the addressed memory device to output a data word onto the data bus.
2. Complete the following table based on the above description of a microcomputer:

Components of a microcomputer	Functions of each component
Central Processing Unit	❑ controls --
	❑ ----------------- binary-coded instructions from ----------------- memory
	❑ ----------------- the instructions into --
-----------------------------------	❑ stores the ----------------- --.
	❑ stores the binary-coded data with which the computer is going to be working.
Input devices	❑ allow --.
Output devices	❑ send data from the computer to --

3. Answer the following questions:
   (a) What are the purposes of the memory section of a microcomputer?
   (b) What is the main function of the input/output section?
   (c) What are the main functions of the CPU?
   (d) What does the address bus consist of?
   (e) How is the number of memory locations that the CPU can address determined?
   (f) Why does the CPU send out signals on the control bus?

Reading Practice 4

First, the following portion of a technical manual for a Computer Uninterrupted Power Supply should be scanned quickly (no more than thirty seconds) in order to predict the information that it contains. Then, the instructions should be read thoroughly. Read slowly and think critically and analytically about the content, concentrate on the way in which the information has been structured. After reading and understanding the instructions, all the questions in the exercises should be answered.

15.1.5 User Manual Startups Lite

Installation

Inspection Inspect the UPS upon receipt. Notify the carrier and dealer if there is any damage. The packaging is recycleable; save it for reuse or dispose it off properly.

Placement Install the UPS in a protected area with adequate air flow and free from excessive dust. Do not operate the UPS if the temperature and humidity are not within the specified limits. In colder territories allow the UPS to come to room temperature before operating.

Connect to Utility Plug the UPS into a two-pole, three-wire, grounded receptacle only. Avoid using extension cords and adapter plugs.

Charging the Battery The UPS charges its battery whenever it is connected to utility power. For best results, charge the battery for 10 hours before use. It is acceptable to use the UPS without first charging the battery, but its run time may be reduced.

Connect the Loads Plug the loads into the output connectors of the UPS. To use the UPS as a master on-off switch, make sure that all the loads are switched on.

Caution: Do not connect a laser printer to the UPS. A laser printer periodically draws significantly more power than when idle, and will overload the UPS.

Caution: The UPS output can be used only for electronic loads such computers and telecommunications equipment.

Operation

To Reset the UPS Microprocessor, in Case of an Unknown Situation With the UPS unplugged from the wall outlet, press the OFF button for 2 seconds. This will reset the internal microprocessor.

Turn off the UPS Output Power To turn off the UPS's output power, press the OFF button for longer than 2 seconds.

Turn on UPS Output Power Press the ON button for 2 seconds to switch the UPS on and to supply power to the loads.

Note: The UPS is always on (CPU is operating) whenever it is plugged in and the mains are present. Even when the UPS is off, it maintains the battery and will respond to commands received through the computer interface port.

UPS Self-test Use the self-test to verify, both, the operation of the UPS and the condition of the battery. With the UPS plugged in to normal mains voltage, activate the self-test by pressing the ON button.

Auto Voltage Regulation The UPS automatically corrects high and low utility voltages so that the loads receive voltage within the normal range.

DC (Cold) Start When the UPS is off and there is no utility power, use the cold start feature to apply power to the loads from the UPS's battery. Press the ON button until the red BAT -Led illuminates. Release the button when the loads are powered within 4 seconds.

Questions

1. Read the following statements and mark True or False based on the above instructions related to installation and operation of STARTUPS LITE:
   (a) You need to inspect the UPS upon receipt.
   (b) You can operate the UPS even if the temperature and humidity are not within the specified limits.
   (c) For best results, charge the battery for two hours before use.
   (d) To use the UPS as a master on-off switch, you should ensure that all of the loads are switched on.
   (e) When the UPS is off, it does not maintain the battery and will not respond to commands received through the computer interface port.
   (f) You need to press the OFF button longer than two seconds in order to turn off the UPS's output power.
2. Complete the following statements by choosing the most appropriate option:
   (a) Install the UPS in:
      (i) a closed room
      (ii) an open field
      (iii) a protected area with adequate air flow
   (b) If there is a damage, you need to:
      (i) notify the carrier
      (ii) get the system repaired
      (iii) send the system back

(c) The UPS output can be used:
  (i) for all kinds of loads
  (ii) only for electronic loads
  (iii) only for a microcomputer
(d) The packaging:
  (i) can be saved for reuse
  (ii) can be disposed off
  (iii) both (a) and (b)
(e) With the UPS plugged in to normal mains voltage, activate the self-test by:
  (i) pressing the OFF button
  (ii) pressing the ON button
  (iii) pressing both OFF and ON button together

3. Answer the following questions:
  (a) What should be done in colder countries?
  (b) How does the UPS charge its battery?
  (c) What will happen if you use the UPS without first charging the battery?
  (d) Why should a laser printer not be connected to the UPS?
  (e) How will you set the UPS microprocessor?
  (f) When is the UPS operating?
  (g) Why is the self-test used?
  (h) Why does the UPS automatically correct high and low utility voltages?
  (i) What should you do when the UPS is off and there is no utility power?

15.2 SUMMARIZATION TECHNIQUES

Making a summary or a shorter version of a long text helps one recollect the main points. It acts as a ready reckoner for students to refresh their memories.

> A summary helps one recollect the main points.

The following are some tips for summarizing text:

- Take notes while reading.
- Highlight or underline important text while reading.
- Make tables or diagrams or flow charts to group similar text.
- Details that are not directly related to the central theme can be skipped.
- Illustrations, case studies, and examples can be skipped unless they are of significance to the central theme.
- Quotations, news clippings, and other such add-ons can be skipped unless they are of significance to the central theme.
- Do not copy-paste text; instead use crisp and short words and sentences.
- Do not introduce any new text or add one's own opinion.

15.3 DEVELOPING EFFECTIVE ANALYTICAL SKILLS

Analytical skills refer to the ability to visualise, understand, and solve problems based on the given data. The problems could be simple or complex and general or technical.

> Analytical skills refer to the ability to visualise, understand, and solve simple and complex problems.

The following are some ways that can help one develop effective analytical skills:

- Increase knowledge by reading and learning about new things.
- Study the text in detail.
- Do not rush at conclusions.
- Take time to think about the alternatives.
- Ask questions—why, when, what, where, how?
- Find connections between the data.
- Developing mathematical skills can help.
- Solve analytical puzzles, and play analytical games.

Developing analytical skills is not a choice but a necessary requirement in today's times of cut-throat competition, especially for people in the technical field.

Exercise

1. **Write brief notes on the following:**
   (a) Strategies for reading technical materials
   (b) ERRQ reading technique
   (c) SQ3R reading method
   (d) Interpreting graphic information
   (e) Strategies for reading instructions and manuals
2. **Choose a few passages from your textbooks and read them to answer the following questions. Check the accuracy of your answers by rereading the passages or showing your answers to your language teacher.**
   (a) What is the overall purpose of the text?
   (b) What is the central idea or theme?
   (c) What does the author intend to do? (describe, instruct, report, narrate, explain, argue, persuade, illustrate, and so on)
   (d) What are the main points of the text?
   (e) What are the main supporting details?
   (f) What are some of the conclusions that can be drawn from the passage?
3. **Read the user manuals of your television, computer, UPS system, scanner, and so on and frame appropriate questions that can be answered by reading these manuals.**

Key to Progress Check

Progress Check 1

(a) False (b) True (c) True (d) True (e) False

(f) False (g) False (h) True (i) True (j) False

Progress Check 2

(a) True (b) False (c) True (d) True (e) False
(f) True (g) False

Progress Check 3

1. (a) True (b) False (c) False (d) False (e) True
   (f) False (g) True (h) True (i) True (j) False
2. (a) Acid rain damages soil, vegetation and aquatic life.
   (b) (i) True (ii) True (iii) False (iv) True

Key to Reading Practice 1

1. (a) Yes
   (b) Extremely high resolving power.
   (c) Yes, by more effective pathological examinations.
   (d) The two important uses are : (i) giving information about the microstructure of new materials as they are being designed, and (ii) helping in the analysis of failure of materials
   (e) Yes, by allowing detailed pictures of the surfaces of cancer cells and its neighbours
   (f) Yes, by analysing the products of electron interaction with matter
2. (a) True (b) False (c) True (d) False (e) True
   (f) True (g) True (h) False (i) False (j) False
3. (a) iii (b) iii (c) ii (d) ii (e) i
   (f) iii

Key to Reading Practice 2

Pre-reading Exercise:

a, c, e, h,

1. (a) True (b) False (c) True (d) True (e) False
   (f) True (g) True (h) True (i) False (j) False
   (k) True (l) False
2. (a) A magnetic field exists in any region where a magnetic pole experiences a magnetic force.
   (b) The operation of many devices, such as ammeters, voltmeters, electric motors, particle accelerators, and television sets, depends on magnetic forces that are exerted on charges that move through a magnetic field. Moreover, the operation of electromagnets, magnetic relays and switches, and many other devices depends on the magnetic fields of electric currents.
   (c) Iron, cobalt, and nickel, are some of the materials that are attracted by magnets even when they are not magnets themselves.
   (d) Yes, the earth behaves like a very large magnet with magnetic poles close to the geographical north and south poles.
   (e) Magnetic fields are produced by magnetic poles because magnetic forces occur between magnetic poles.
3. (a) True (b) True (c) True (d) False (e) False
   (f) True (g) True (h) True (i) True (j) False

Key to Reading Practice 3

Pre-reading Exercise:
(b), (c), (e), (f), (h)

1. (a) True (b) True (c) False (d) False (e) True
   (f) True (g) False (h) True (i) False (j) True
2. The complete diagram is given below:

Components of a microcomputer	Functions of each component
Central Processing Unit	❑ controls the operation of the computer ❑ fetches binary-coded instructions from its memory ❑ decodes the instructions into a series of simple actions ❑ carries out these actions in a sequence of steps
Memory Unit	❑ stores the binary codes for the sequences of instructions the computer is programmed to carry out ❑ stores the binary-coded data with which the computer is going to be working.
Input devices	❑ allows data from a keyboard, an A/D converter, or some other source to be read into the computer under control of the CPU.
Output devices	❑ sends data from the computer to some peripheral, such as a video display terminal, a printer, or a D/A converter.

3. (a) There are two purposes of the memory section in a micro-computer. The first purpose is to store the binary codes for the sequences of instructions that you want, the computer needs to carry out while the second purpose is to store the binary-coded data with which the computer will be working.
   (b) The input/output section allows the computer to take in data from the outside world or send data to the outside world.
   (c) The central processing unit or CPU controls the operation of the computer. It fetches binary-coded instructions from memory, decodes the instructions into a series of simple actions, and carries out these actions in a sequence of steps.
   (d) The address bus consists of 16, 20, 24, or 32 parallel signal lines.
   (e) The number of memory locations that the CPU can address is determined by the number of address lines.
   (f) The CPU sends out signals on the control bus to enable the outputs of addressed memory devices or port devices.

Key to Reading Practice 4

1. (a) True (b) False (c) False (d) True (e) False
   (f) True
2. (a) iii (b) i (c) ii (d) iii (e) ii
3. (a) In colder territories allow the UPS to come to room temperature before operating.
   (b) The UPS charges its battery whenever it is connected to utility power.
   (c) If the UPS is used without first charging the battery, run time may be reduced.

(d) A laser printer periodically draws significantly more power than when idle, and will overload the UPS.
(e) With the UPS unplugged from the wall outlet, press the OFF button for two seconds in order to reset the internal microprocessor.
(f) The UPS is operating whenever it is plugged in and mains are on.
(g) The self-test can be used to verify, both, the operation of the UPS and the condition of the battery.
(h) The UPS automatically corrects high and low utility voltages so that the loads receive voltage within the normal range.
(i) When the UPS is off and there is no utility power, the cold start is used to apply power to the loads from the UPS's battery.

SECTION 6

Study Skills

CHAPTERS

16 CHAPTER

Note Making

Note making is an important study skill that is required for various academic and professional purposes.

LEARNING OBJECTIVES

- Knowing the essential features of note making and discuss the mechanics of note making
- Learning to adopt a reading strategy for effective note making
- Understanding two note-writing techniques—topicalising and schematising
- Knowing reduction devices for note making
- Grasping techniques for organising and sequencing notes

16.1 INTRODUCTION

The meaning of the word 'note' is 'brief written record as an aid to memory'. There are different types of notes, depending upon the purpose. These include concept ordering notes, revision notes, research notes, comparative notes, and analytical notes. However, this chapter deals with notes that students have to make as part of their study. Such notes generally summarise the reading done by students. Students prepare notes in order to help them remember the information that they have received while reading a textbook. Note making acts as a mechanism for gathering resources from many sources and pooling them towards a common objective.

> There are different types of notes, such as concept ordering notes, revision notes, research notes, comparative notes, and analytical notes.

We can define note making as a systematic method of writing down quickly, briefly, and clearly the important points of a reading text. There are several functions of note making. It is used to:

> Note making is a systematic method of writing down quickly, briefly, and clearly the important points of a reading text.

- Keep a record of the main points of a reading text for future use and reference
- Revise for an examination or a writing assignment
- Update information
- Reinforce or compare information contained in different textbooks/the textbooks and lecture
- To analyse a text.

Note making is a productive skill, which integrates both reading and writing skills. It involves the following:

- Reading strategy: a careful reading plan to identify the central idea, the main points, and important supporting details
- Note-writing techniques: topicalising, copying, transcribing and schematising
- Reduction devices: using abbreviations and symbols
- Organisation techniques
- Methods of sequencing: numerals and letters, decimalisation

16.2 STRATEGIES FOR EFFECTIVE NOTE MAKING

16.2.1 Reading Strategy

Students must adopt a careful reading strategy that enables them to understand the text quickly and make appropriate notes. The following strategy can be used:

- Read the text quickly in order to identify its purpose, scope, central idea, logical organisation, and different writing techniques, for example, description, narration, explanation, and so on.
- Read the text again in order to identify the main points and important details that support the main ideas. Ignore subordinate points or minor supporting details and examples.
- Recognise key lexical items related to the topic.

- Identify relationships among units within the text (for example, main points, generalisations, hypotheses, supporting points, illustrations).
- Read for key points and signal words.
- Recognise markers of cohesion.
- Ignore irrelevant matter and concentrate on the important points.
- Deduce meanings of words and phrases from their context and infer relationships.
- Recognise key terms related to the subject/topic of the text.
- Interpret graphic aids used in the text.

Progress Check 1

1. Study the following statements about note writing, and mark True or False against each of them.

(a) Note making is the creation of one's own notes.
(b) Note making does not involve paraphrasing.
(c) While making notes, everything that is read should be written.
(d) A careful strategy must be adopted to enable understanding the text.
(e) Note making acts as a mechanism for gathering resources from many sources and pooling them towards a common objective.

16.2.2 Note Writing Techniques

There are four different techniques of writing notes, i.e., topicalising, copying, transcribing, and schematising. Topicalising refers to writing down a word or phrase to represent a section of the text whereas 'copying' refers to writing down verbatim what is written, and 'transcribing' is writing down verbatim what is said. Schematising is the method of using graphics to organise notes. Two note writing techniques are discussed here, that is, topicalising, and schematising.

> Note writing techniques include topicalising, copying, transcribing, and schematising.

> Copying refers to writing down verbatim what is written, and 'transcribing' is writing down verbatim what is said.

Topicalising

After reading a passage carefully and identifying the central idea, the main points, and important supporting details, these should be rephrased. The topic, the main points or the main supporting details should be written as they appear in the text. In the text, these ideas appear in full sentences, but while making notes a word or phrase is used to represent an entire section of the text. While rephrasing a section of the text or a sentence, unnecessary or redundant words/phrases should be removed.

> Topicalising refers to writing down a word or phrase to represent a section of the text.

Table 16.1 contains examples of sections of a text/sentences rephrased in the form of words/phrases:

TABLE 16.1 Examples of Sections of a Text/Sentences Rephrased in the Form of Words/Phrases

A Section of a Text/Sentence	*Topicalising*
Petroleum is enormously important from an economic standpoint.	Economic importance of petroleum
Petroleum occurs widely in the sedimentary rocks of the Earth's crust and may occur as a gas, liquid, semi-solid, or solid.	Occurrence of petroleum as a gas, liquid, semi-solid, or solid
Forms of petroleum include crude oil, natural gas, asphalt, and gilsonite.	Forms of petroleum: crude oil, natural gas, asphalt, and gilsonite
Petroleum products are used in the manufacture of synthetic fibres, and in plastics and paints.	Use of petroleum products in the manufacture of synthetic fibres, plastics and paints.
An acid is a compound containing hydrogen.	Acid, a hydrogen containing compound
The fractions of crude oil include gases, gasoline, kerosene, diesel, and lubricating oils.	Fractions of crude oil: gases, gasoline, kerosene, diesel, and lubricating oils.
Fuel oil and natural gas are used to heat homes and commercial buildings.	Use of fuel oil and natural gas for heating homes and commercial buildings.

Progress Check 2

1. **Read the following sections of texts/sentences and topicalise/rephrase them in the form of words and phrases:**
   (a) The discovery of the electron spin completes the set of four characteristics required to describe an electron in an atom.
   (b) Petroleum is found in sedimentary rocks of the Earth's crust.
   (c) Elementary phosphorus can be made by the reduction of calcium phosphate with coke.
   (d) We can classify acids into two groups.
   (e) We call them organic acids.
   (f) There are two kinds of organic acids—citric acid and acetic acid.
   (g) We find citric acid in lemons and oranges and other citrus fruits.
   (h) There are three types of chemical reactions. These are decomposition reaction, combination reaction, and displacement reaction.
   (i) There are two elementary forms of carbon. They are diamond and graphite.
   (j) The input devices of a computer include keyboard and floppy disk drives.

Schematising

Scientific and technical texts may contain information in the form of figures, classifications, contrasts, processes, and so on. Hence, it is sometimes more convenient to schematise notes, i.e., organise notes in the form of tables and diagrams for accurate and easy read-back.

> Schematising refers to organising notes in the form of tables and diagrams for accurate and easy read-back.

The choice of a non-verbal method largely depends on the nature and kind of text. Table 16.2 contains some guidelines for schematising in note making.

TABLE 16.2 Guidelines for Schematising in Note Making

Nature of Information in the Text/Kind of Text	*The Diagrammatic Form in Which Notes can be Organised*
Description of a substance	Table
Description of processes	Flow diagram/Flow chart
Narrative description	Table
Classificatory information	Tree diagram
Comparative description	Table/List
Contrastive description	Table/List
Figurative information	Table/List

Study the following examples:

Example 1

Read the following paragraph about plastics and note how it is schematised in the form of a tree diagram:

The behaviour of plastics when heated provides the basis for the distinction between the two main classes of plastics available today. These two groups of plastics include thermoplastics and thermosetting plastics. The first group consists of plastics that soften when heated and become rigid when cooled again. In fact, with further heating and cooling these plastics can be made to change their shape repeatedly. This is due to the fact that only weak bonding is present between neighbouring molecules, and when warm, the molecules slide very easily past one another. Polythene, PVC, nylon, and perspex are examples of thermoplastics.

Thermosetting plastics, on the hand, become rigid on further heating and cannot be softened again. These plastics consist of polymer chains that react with one another at points of contact so that they become strongly linked together in three-dimensions. Intermolecular bonds prevent the relative movement of the original chains. Examples of thermosetting plastics are bakelite and melamine.

Notes

(Schematised in the form of a tree diagram)

Classification of Plastics

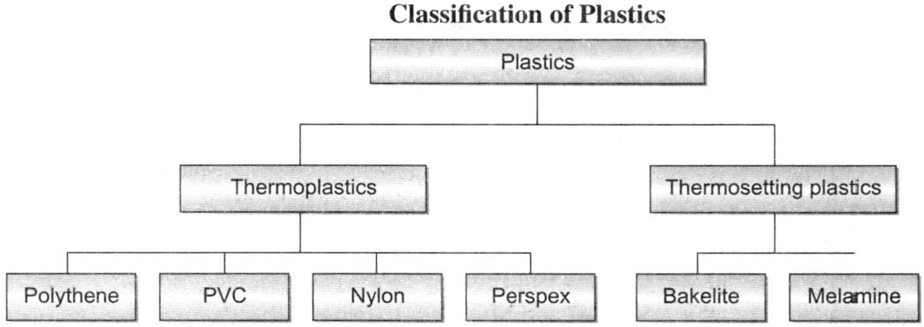

Example 2

An easy way to find out which fuel is better, is to compare the heat produced by them. Heat liberated in joules on complete burning of one gram of a fuel is expressed as its calorific value. The calorific value of fuels is usually determined by completely burning a known mass of the given fuel. All the heat produced by the fuel is utilised to heat a known quantity of a liquid in a container of known mass. The calorific value of the fuel is expressed in units of joule per gram or J/g.

Hydrogen has the highest calorific value amongst all the given fuels, i.e., 150 kJ/g. Most of the other fuels are compounds of hydrogen and carbon. Among hydrocarbons, methane has the highest calorific value, i.e., 55 kJ/g while butane (LPG) has the same calorific value. The calorific value of biogas is 35–40 kJ/g.

With 48 kJ/g, kerosene has the highest calorific value amongst all the gases followed by fuel oil (45 kJ/g) and ethanol (30 kJ/g). Charcoal has the highest calorific value amongst all solid fuels. Its calorific value is 33 kJ/g, whereas the calorific value of coal is 25–33 kJ/g. Wood is largely a mixture of carbohydrates. Its calorific value is 17 kJ/g. Animal dung is another example of this type of fuel. The calorific value of cow dung cake is 7–8 kJ/g.

Notes

(Schematised in the form of Table 16.3)

TABLE 16.3 Calorific Values of Some Common Fuels

State of the Fuel	*Name of the Fuel*	*Calorific Value (kJ/g)*
Solids	Charcoal	33
	Coal	25–33
	Wood	17
	Cow dung cake	7–8
Liquids	Kerosene	48
	Fuel oil	45
	Ethanol (alcohol)	30
Gases	Hydrogen	150
	Methane	55
	Butane	55
	Biogas	35–40

16.2.3 Reduction Devices

Reduction devices refer to the techniques used to shorten expressions in order to save time while making notes. They help give an organised picture of a passage by excluding repetitive and unnecessary information. Appropriate abbreviations and symbols may be used. However, it must be remembered that the notes have to be reread and the abbreviations and symbols have to be understood even at a later date. Therefore, standard abbreviations and symbols should be used so that there is no scope for confusion and misunderstanding.

Reduction devices involve the effective use of abbreviations and symbols.

Use of Abbreviations

There are standard abbreviations used in science and technology. Moreover, you may abbreviate words and phrases by using the following simple methods:

1. Use the First Letters of the Words Words may be abbreviated by just using their first letters. This method is applied to abbreviate several English words. Study the following examples:

Word	Abbreviation
Sulphur	S
East	E
West	W
North	N
South	S
Joule	J
That is	i.e.
Gram	g
Page	p.
Oxygen	O
Carbon	C
Phosphorous	P

2. Use the First Letters of the Phrases A phrase or a group of words may be abbreviated by just using the first letters of the words used in the phrase. This method is applied to abbreviate several English and Latin phrases. Study the following examples:

Word/Phrase	Abbreviation
Kilogram	kg
Centilitre	cl
Cubic centimeter	cc
Central nervous system	CNS
With effect from	wef
Atomic mass unit	amu
Specific gravity	sg
Electrostatic unit	esu
Take note that	N.B
Per annum	pa
Centigrade	C
Curriculum vitae	cv

3. Use the First Few Letters of Words/Phrases A phrase or a group of words may be abbreviated by just using the first few letters. This is a very common method of abbreviation.

Word/Phrase	Abbreviation
Approximately	approx
Difference	diff
Edition	ed
Professor	Prof
Especially	esp

Subject	sub
Second	sec
Minute	min
Computer	comp
Temperature	temp

4. Use the First Few Letters of Words/Phrases A phrase or a group of words may be abbreviated by just using the first letter and one and more other letters of words/phrases. This is a very common method of abbreviation. Study the following examples:

Word/Phrase	**Abbreviation**
Magnesium	Mg
Hour	hr
Month	mth
Year	yr
Strontium	Sr

5. Use Special Techniques to Abbreviate A phrase or a group of words may be abbreviated by using some special techniques, i.e., taking any letter/letters of the word or phrase to be abbreviated. Study the following examples:

Word/phrase	**Abbreviation**
Compare	cf
That is	ie
Et cetera, and others	etc
For example	eg
Mentioned earlier in the book	op cit

Use of Symbols While making notes, you may use appropriate signs and symbols. Study the following examples:

@	At the rate of
$	Dollar
%	Percentage
&	And
+	In addition, moreover, plus, and, furthermore
–	Reduce, minus
←	Result from, come from, develop from, caused by, made from
→	Leads to, causes, result in, move forwards
	Up, upward, go up, increase
>	Greater than, more than, over
<	Less than
≠	Is different from, is not, does not consist of, does not equal
=	Consist of, is equal to, is the same as
≡	Is equivalent to

$\downarrow$	Decrease, down, downward
$\propto$	Proportional to
$\therefore$	Thus, therefore, as a result, then, consequently, so, so that

16.2.4 Organisation Techniques

The nature and organisation of notes depends largely on the type and length of a text. When the text is small, the notes may contain just a few phrases. However, when the text contains a lot of information, the notes have to be organised in terms of headings and subordinate points. As the notes have to be read and understood at a later stage, it is very important to organise them in such a manner that the essence of the text can be recalled whenever required. Study the following guidelines:

When the text contains a lot of information, the notes have to be organised in terms of headings and subordinate points.

Providing a Suitable Title

Providing the notes with a suitable title will help in recalling the main subject and central idea of the passage. The topic or the central idea of a text generally forms the title. It is a good idea to underline the title in order to make the notes clearer.

Providing Headings and Sub-headings

The notes may be organised in terms of headings, sub-headings, and so on. An appropriate heading should be provided for every main point. Similarly, appropriate sub-headings may be given to important supporting details. Supporting details or subordinate points are placed under the heading with the indentation in order to indicate that they are dependent on the main topic. Subordinate points may be independent of each other or related to each other.

The following notes show how headings and subheadings provide logical coherence to the notes:

Supporting details or subordinate points are placed under the heading with the indentation in order to indicate that they are dependent on the main topic.

Electrochemistry

I. Introduction
II. Some important terms
  A. Conductors
  1. Types of conductors
    (a) Metallic conductors
    (b) Electrolytes
  B. Non-conductors
III. Electrolysis
  A. Definition
  B. Applications of Electrolysis
  1. Electroplating
    (a) Aim of electroplating
      (i) Decoration
      (ii) Repairs
      (iii) Protection

(b) Procedure
(c) Theory of electroplating
2. Electrochemical preparations

Progress Check 3

1. Read the following passage, and write (a) a title for it, (b) headings, and (c) sub-headings:
Carbon is a solid non-metallic chemical element occurring in the pure crystalline form as diamond and graphite. It is also found in the combined form as a constituent of all organic materials, including coal and petroleum. In addition, it is found as a constituent of inorganic compounds such as limestone and baking powder. However, carbon constitutes only 0.19 per cent of the earth's crust. Carbon's symbol is C.

The two elementary forms of carbon, diamond and graphite, have very different properties. In diamond the atoms are so tightly bound one to another that this makes it the hardest known substance. In contrast, graphite is a soft black substance with atoms hexagonally arranged in parallel sheets. Each sheet is only loosely bound one to another. Another important difference between diamond and graphite is that of electrical conductivity. Diamond is a non-conductor, while graphite conducts in the direction parallel to the hexagonal sheets. Both have high melting and boiling points.

16.2.5 Methods of Sequencing

Sequencing refers to the process of making a clear layout for fast and accurate interpretation of notes. It is an important part of note making, as it is used for the visual organisation of notes. In fact, sequencing provides coherence to the notes and helps in accurate and easy read-back. The sequencing of headings and subordinate points can follow any of the standard practices, which include use of numerals and letters and decimalisation.

Sequencing refers to the process of making a clear layout for fast and accurate interpretation of notes.

Numerals and Letters

The letters and numerals in a formal pattern of notes show the writer's analysis of the theme. Several patterns of listing may be used, modifying the system of numerals and letters that are used according to the nature and scope of information in the text (Table 16.4).

Two standard practices for sequencing notes include the use of numerals and letters, and decimalisation.

TABLE 16.4 Analysis of Numerals and Letters

Numerals/Letters	*Use*
I II III IV V VI	Roman numerals may indicate the main ideas or divisions of the text.
A B C D E F G	Capital letters, together with proper indentation, indicate the main subdivisions of the main ideas of the text.
1 2 3 4 5 6 7	Arabic numerals, together with proper indentation, indicate the minor divisions of the main subdivisions.
a b c d e f g	Small letters, together with proper indentation, indicate further subdivisions.
i ii iii iv v vi vii	Small Roman numerals may be used for further subdivisions of the minor points, or to indicate examples, illustrations, and so on.

Example:

Study the following notes and notice the method of sequencing used:

Types of Rocks

I. Igneous rocks = Solidification or crystallisation of magma.
   A. Fine-grained Extrusive
      1. Basalt
      2. Obsidian
   B. Coarse-grained intrusive
      1. Granite
      2. Gabbro
II. Sedimentary rocks = Compaction and cementation of sediments into a solid rock.
   A. Elastic or fragmental
      1. Sandstone
   B. Chemical
      1. Gypsum
III. Metamorphic rocks = change of solid state in mineralogy or texture resulting due to changes in physical conditions.
   A. Dynamo-thermal
      1. Schist
      2. Gneiss
      3. Marble
   B. Thermal
      1. Hornfelsic
      2. Rocks
      3. Marble
   C. Dynamic
      1. Mylonite
      2. Augen

Sequencing

- I—The first Roman numeral indicates the first main division of the text.
- II—The second Roman numeral indicates the second main division of the text.
- III—The third Roman numeral indicates the third main division of the text.
- A—The first capital letter, together with the indentation, indicates the first main subdivision of points I/II/III.
- B—The second capital letter, together with the indentation indicates the second main subdivision of points I/II/III.
- C—The third capital letter, together with the indentation, indicates the third main subdivision of point III.
- 1—The first Arabic numeral, together with the indentation, indicates the first subdivision of the points A/B/C in I/II/III.
- 2—The second Arabic numeral, together with the indentation, indicates the second subdivision of the points A/B/C in I/III.

- 3—The third Arabic numeral, together with the indentation, indicates the third subdivision of the point A/B in III.

Decimalisation Decimalisation may also be used as an effective technique for sequencing in note making. Study the following example. Here, decimalisation has been used to organise the notes on types of rocks given in the above example.

Types of Rocks

1. Igneous rocks = Solidification or crystallisation of magma.
   1.1 Fine-grained extrusive
      1.1.1 Basalt
      1.1.2 Obsidian
   1.2 Coarse-grained intrusive
      1.2.1 Granite
      1.2.2 Gabbro
2. Sedimentary rocks = Compaction and cementation of sediments into a solid rock.
   2.1 Elastic or fragmental
      2.1.1 Sandstone
   2.2 Chemical
      2.2.1 Gypsum
3. Metamorphic rocks = Change of solid state in mineralogy or texture resulting due to changes in physical conditions.
   3.1 Dynamo-thermal
      3.1.1 Schist
      3.1.2 Gneiss
      3.1.3 Marble
   3.2 Thermal
      3.2.1 Hornfelsic
      3.2.2 Rocks
      3.2.3 Marble
   3.3 Dynamic
      3.3.1 Mylonite
      3.3.2 Augen

16.3 NOTE MAKING PRACTICE

The following are examples of passages and their transformations in note forms.

Passage 1

The energy transmitted from one body to another in the form of rays or radiations is called radiant energy. Cosmic rays, gamma rays, X-rays, ultra-violet rays, visible rays, infrared rays, radio waves, and heat are examples of radiant energy. These waves are associated with electric as well as magnetic fields. Thus, these radiations are called electromagnetic radiation. The radiation important to us, is that from the sun, the earth and the atmosphere lying within the ultraviolet, visible and infrared spectral regions.

There are five important characteristics associated with each wave. These include wavelength, frequency, velocity, wave number, and amplitude. Wavelength is the distance between two adjacent crests or troughs in a particular wave. It is denoted by Greek letter lambda (λ). Frequency is defined as the number of waves or cycles that pass through a given point in one second. It is denoted by the Greek letter nu (ν). Velocity is the distance travelled by a wave in one second. It is denoted by the letter 'c'. Wave number is the reciprocal of wavelength and is defined as the number of waves per centimetre, it is denoted by '$\bar{\nu}$'. Finally, amplitude is the height of crest or depth of trough of a wave. It is denoted by the letter α.

Notes

Radiant Energy

I. Electromagnetic radiation
   A. Radiant energy = energy transmitted from one body to another in the form of rays.
   B. Examples: Cosmic rays, gamma rays, X-rays, ultra-violet rays, visible rays, infra-red rays, radio waves and heat
   C. Associated with elec and magnetic fields ∴ called electromagnetic radiation
II. Characteristics
   A. Wavelength = dist. bet. 2 adjacent crests or troughs in a part. wave symb. λ.
   B. Frequency = no. of waves or cycles passing through a given point in one sec. Symb. ♥ν.
   C. Velocity = dist. trav. by a wave in 1 sec. symb.c.
   D. Wave number = no. of waves per sec. symb. $\bar{\nu}$
   E. Amplitude = ht of crest or depth of trough of a wave. symb. α.

Passage 2

Coal is a natural resource, which constitutes approximately 85 per cent of the total fossil fuel reserves in the world. The coal deposits of India occur in two distinct stratigraphic horizons—Gondwana and the Territories. Gondwana coal contributes about 99 per cent of the country's coal resources. These mines are located in peninsular India, in the South Eastern quadrant, bound by the 78°E longitude and the 24°N latitude, thus, leaving a major part of the country devoid of any coal deposits. The major Gondwana coalfields are represented by isolated basins, which occur along prominent present day rivers such as Damodar, Koel, Sone, Mahanadi, PenchKanhan, Pranhita and Godavari. The relatively minor resource of tertiary coal is located on the either extremities of peninsular India.

Coal can be broadly classified in two categories—coking and non-coking. Coking coal are that which has caking property and which is used in metallurgical industries. Again depending on the quality of coke produced by this coal, it is sub-divided into prime coking coal, medium coking coal, and semi-coking coal. Similarly, non-coking coal is also categorised in seven grades (Grade A to G), depending on its caloric value.

Notes

Coal Deposits in India

1. Coal = natural resource
   Constitutes approx. 85%—total fossil fuel reserves in the world
2. Coal deposits of India—Two distinct zones
   2.1 Gondwana
      2.1.1 99% of the country's coal resources
      2.1.2 Located in peninsular India—S East. quadrant,

2.1.3 Bound by 78°E Long. & 24°N Lat.

2.1.4 Repr. by isolated basins along prom. rivers e.g. Damodar, Koel, Sone, Mahanadi, PenchKanhan, Pranhita and Godavari.

2.2 Tertiaries

Loc. on the either extremities of the peninsular India.

3. Types of coal

3.1 Coking coal = cooking properties + used in metal. Industries

3.1.1 Prime coking coal

3.1.2 Medium coking coal

3.1.3 Semi-coking coal

3.2 Non-coking coal 7 types = A to G

Passage 3

Matter may exist as a solid, liquid, or gas, depending on its energy. Gases and vapours are higher-energy states of matter; they flow to take the shape and to occupy the total volume of any container. When a gas loses sufficient energy (in the form of heat or by doing work), it condenses to a liquid. Liquids are also able to flow, but they are virtually incompressible. Matter that flows (i.e., a gas or liquid) is called a fluid. Liquid molecules are able to move and they flow past each other, but their motion is much slower than that of gases.

Solids are the lowest-energy states of matter. They usually possess rigid structures, they do not flow, and they are relatively difficult to compress. The atoms in a solid cannot move from one place to another, but they do vibrate about fixed positions in the structure. These vibrations are due to thermal energy.

When a solid is heated, the magnitude of these thermal vibrations increases until they 'shake apart' the solid structure and the solid melts, becoming a liquid. If heat is applied to the liquid, molecules increase their energy, and eventually have sufficient energy to escape through the liquid surface, becoming a vapour or gas. When a liquid boils, vapour molecules form inside the body of the liquid and then bubble to the surface, where they escape. Some molecules escape from a liquid even at temperatures below the boiling point, because one molecule may obtain energy from several others, so that its energy is sufficient to enable it to escape through the surface. This process is called evaporation, and since it leaves the other molecules with less average energy, the remaining liquid is cooled.

Notes

Forms of Matter

I. Gases and Vapours

A. Nature

1. Gases = higher-energy states of matter
2. flow to take the shape and to occupy the total volume of any container

B. Loss of energy by a gas → condenses to a liquid.

II. Liquids

A. matter that flows — virtually incompressible

B. Heating of liquid → the molecules increase their energy → energy escape through the liquid surface → a vapour or gas.

C. Boiling of a liquid → formation of vapour molecules

Evaporation = molecules escaping from a liquid even at temperatures below the boiling point

III. Solids
  A. Solids = the lowest-energy states of matter, rigid structures, vibrate about fixed positions due to thermal energy
  B. Heating of solid → increase in the magnitude of thermal vibrations → 'shake apart' the solid structure → the solid melts → becomes a liquid

Passage 4

The art of metallurgy includes the deriving of metals from their ores, or the condition in which they are found in nature; their purification, or their admixture with other metals; and finally their manufacture into shapes and forms usable in industry. The science of metallurgy includes the study of these processes with a view to their control and improvement, and the development of new metal mixtures or alloys and of new test methods.

Because of its wide scope, the field of metallurgy may be divided into two parts. The first part deals with the melting and refining of metals, and has been designated as Process or Chemical Metallurgy. The second deals with the physical and chemical behaviour of metals during shaping and treating operations, and their behaviour in the service of man. This phase is termed Physical Metallurgy.

Notes

Metallurgy

I. Metallurgy
  A. Art of metallurgy
    1. Deriving of metals from their ores
    2. Purification of metals
    3. Manufacture of metals into shapes and forms
  B. Science of metallurgy
    1. Study, control and improvement of the above processes
    2. Development of new metal mixtures or alloys
    3. Development of new test methods
II. Types of metallurgy
  A. Process or chemical metallurgy
    1. Melting of metals
    2. Refining of metals
  B. Physical metallurgy
    1. Physical and chemical behaviour of metals during shaping & treating operations

Exercise

1. Write short notes on the following:
  (a) Essential features of note making
  (b) Topicalising
  (c) Schematising
  (d) Reduction devices for note making
  (e) Organisation techniques
  (f) Sequencing notes.

2. Read the following passages, and make notes:

I. Internal combustion engines form the second largest application of thermodynamics, falling in the category of work producing plants. The majority of these engines are:

(a) Petrol engines used in automobiles

(b) Diesel engines used in heavy vehicles

The diesel engines are common in cars also. Some diesel engines are also stationary engines used in agriculture to power irrigation pumps, and in diesel generating sets, usually, for standby electric power generation. These engines comprise of a reciprocating piston and cylinder mechanism with suction and exhaust valves. In these engines, the reciprocating motion of the piston is converted to the rotary motion of the crankshaft via a connecting rod and crank mechanism.

In petrol engines, a mixture of atmospheric air and gasoline is sucked into the engine cylinder through the suction valve during an outward stroke of the piston. The mixture is compressed by an inward stroke of the piston. After compression, the mixture is ignited by an electric spark. Because of this method of ignition, petrol engines are also referred to as spark ignition engines. After ignition, the gases push the piston in another outward stroke. Finally, during the fourth inward stroke of the piston, the gases are exhausted to the atmosphere through the exhaust valve. Thus, the cycle is completed in four strokes of the piston. Two-stroke operation of the four processes of intake, compression, combustion, expansion, and exhaust is quite common in small petrol engines for two wheeled vehicles.

Diesel engines too, usually require four strokes (two strokes in marine diesel engines) of the piston. However, herein, air alone is sucked into the engine cylinder and compressed. The fuel is then injected. It gets ignited by itself as it comes in contact with hot compressed air. In the remaining two strokes, the gases push the piston during an outward stroke, and are then exhausted during the fourth inward stroke. Because of the self ignition of the fuel as a result of coming in contact with compressed air, which is hot, these engines are also referred to as compression ignition engines.

In both petrol and diesel engines, the combustion of fuel with air takes place inside the engine cylinder and the opening and closing of both suction and exhaust valves is timed according to the requirement of the cycle of operation.

Gas turbines form another major category of internal combustion engines. These have rotating blades housed in a casing, as in the case of steam turbines. The combustion of fuel is carried out with compressed air in a separate combustion chamber. The products of combustion enter the turbine and impart their momentum to the turbine blades before being exhausted. There are no suction and exhaust valves in turbines.

Gas turbine engines are used in very small aircrafts for propulsion through a propeller. In larger aircrafts, it is much more useful to use the jet exhaust for propulsion, the gas turbine is used only to run the compressor. These engines are also used as stationary gas turbine plants for power generation.

II. Silicon is like carbon in having four outer electrons it can use for bonding purposes, moreover, there is considerable similarity in the chemical properties of the two elements. Like carbon, silicon forms a tetrahedral molecule and a few higher hydrosilicons, which contain chains of silicon atoms. However, since SiO bonds are formed preferentially to Si-H or Si-Si bonds, the chemistry of silicon is primarily concerned with oxygen compounds rather than with hydrosilicons. Furthermore, whereas the smaller carbon atom often forms multiple bonds (i.e., double or triple), silicon invariably forms single bonds. As a result, oxygen-silicon compounds contain Si-O-Si bridges in which oxygen is bonded by single bonds to each of the two silicon atoms instead of being bonded by a double bond to one silicon atom. This is quite unlike the case of carbon, where oxygen is frequently found bonded to a single carbon atom.

The preparation of pure silicon is quite difficult. It can be accomplished by the reduction of SiO_2 with Mg or by the reduction of the chloride with Na. Since it is mainly used for addition to steel, it is usually prepared as ferrosilicon by the reduction of mixtures of SiO_2 and iron oxides with coke. The element is a semi-metal with a crystal structure like that of diamond. At room temperature it is inert to most reagents but will dissolve in basic solutions to liberate H_2. At elevated temperatures it reacts with many metals such as magnesium to form silicides (such as Mg_2Si).

III. The molecules of a solid are closer together than those of a fluid. The attractive forces between the molecules of a solid are so large that a solid tends to retain its shape. This is not the case for a fluid, where the attractive forces between molecules are smaller. There are plastic solids that flow under proper circumstances, and even metals may flow under high pressure. On the other hand, there are certain very viscous liquids that do not flow readily, and it is easy to confuse them with plastic solids. The distinction is that any fluid, no matter how viscous, will yield in time to the slightest stress. But a solid, no matter how plastic, requires a certain magnitude of stress to be exerted before it will flow.

Also, when the shape of a solid is altered by external forces, the tangential stresses between adjacent particles tend to restore the body to its original configuration. With a fluid, these tangential stresses depend on the velocity of deformation and vanish as the velocity approaches zero. When motion ceases, the tangential stresses disappear and the fluid does not tend to regain its original shape.

IV. A fluid may be either a gas or a liquid. The molecules of a gas are much farther apart than those of a liquid. Hence a gas is very compressible, and when all external pressure is removed, it tends to expand indefinitely. A gas is therefore in equilibrium only when it is completely enclosed. A liquid is relatively incompressible, and if all pressure, except that of its own vapour pressure, is removed, the cohesion between molecules holds them together, so that the liquid does not expand indefinitely. Therefore, a liquid may have a free surface, that is, a surface from which all pressure is removed, except that of its own vapour.

A vapour is a gas whose temperature and pressure are such that it is very near the liquid phase. Thus, steam is considered a vapour because its state is normally not far from that of water. A gas may be defined as a highly superheated vapour; that is, its state is far removed from the liquid phase. Thus, air is considered a gas because its state is normally very far from that of liquid air.

The volume of a gas or vapour is greatly affected by changes in pressure or temperature or both. It is usually necessary, therefore, to take account of changes in volume and temperature in dealing with gases and vapours. Whenever significant temperature or phase changes are involved in dealing with vapours and gases, the subject is largely dependent on heat phenomena (thermodynamics). Thus, fluid mechanics and thermodynamics are interrelated.

V. The revolution in computer technology has been going on for about forty years. In the first generation, during the Second World War, computers employed vacuum tubes and relays as switching devices. The collection of switches routed electrical currents in a manner that produced calculated results. As a matter of fact, all digital computers today still perform calculations using switching techniques.

In the second generation, which started in the late 1950s, tubes and relays were replaced by transistors. Transistors were faster, cheaper, smaller, required less energy, and produced less heat than tubes.

The third generation, born in 1964, replaced transistors with integrated circuits. An integrated circuit arranges thousands of switches on circuit boards small enough to be completely hidden by the tip of a finger. These became known as chips. Chips, too, were cheaper, cooler, and faster than their transistor forbears.

Starting in early 1970 a fourth generation of computers saw the shrinkage of computer components to microscopic dimensions. Chips contained a very large number of components on a very small chip. Once again, computer switches became smaller, less expensive, cooler, and faster.

Key to Progress Check

Progress Check 1

1. (a) T (b) F (c) F (d) T (e) T

Progress Check 2

1. (a) Four characteristics of an electron in an atom.
   (b) Occurrence of petroleum in sedimentary rocks.
   (c) Making of elementary phosphorus by reduction of calcium phosphate with coke.
   (d) Classification of acids into two groups.
   (e) Organic acids.
   (f) Two kinds of organic acids: citric acid and acetic acid.
   (g) Presence of citric acid in citrus fruits.
   (h) Types of chemical reactions: Decomposition reaction, Combination reaction, Displacement reaction.
   (i) Forms of carbon: Diamond and graphite.
   (j) Computer input devices: keyboard and floppy disk drives.

Progress Check 3

Forms of carbon: Diamond and graphite

1. Forms and Occurrence of carbon
   (a) Definition
   (b) Forms
   (c) Occurrence
2. Properties of diamond and graphite
   (a) Arrangement of atoms
   (b) Electrical conductivity
   (c) Melting and boiling points

17 CHAPTER

Summarising and Paraphrasing

Summarising and paraphrasing are productive skills integrating both reading and writing skills

LEARNING OBJECTIVES

- Knowing the essential features and mechanics of summarising
- Learning to adopt a reading strategy for effective summarising
- Understanding three summarising techniques—selection, rejection, and substitution
- Grasping techniques for outlining and paraphrasing core information to write a summary

17.1 INTRODUCTION TO SUMMARISING

Since technical language is concise, it is essential to know how to write summaries. Writing a summary is one of the most important study skills needed by students. It also helps in reading as it forces us to focus on what we read. It encourages active reading and helps remember the material better. Summarising also improves our ability to write concisely by making us aware of the kind of details or expressions that can be avoided to achieve precision in writing.

> There are different types of notes, such as concept ordering notes, revision notes, research notes, comparative notes, and analytical notes.

The meaning of the word summary is 'summed up', or 'condensed'. Summarising is an essential study skill required for study purposes. Students need summarising skills for various purposes. Then may have to write an abstract, a synopsis, a precis, or an outline. They need to understand these terms before becoming familiar with the concept of summarising.

An **abstract** is a very short version of a long text or passage. Every research article or paper contains an abstract, which very briefly tells the reader what the article is all about. A **synopsis** is generally a brief account of a research plan, which a researcher is supposed to submit before he or she starts the research work. **Precis**, which is synonymous with summary, is a brief account of something without details or formalities. An **outline** is a sketch in phrases or sentences that professional writers make before they start writing a professional document like a proposal or a report.

> Summarising is a process of condensing information without changing the original meaning and focus of a passage.

All the above forms of writing involve the process of summarising. Now we can define summarising as a process of condensing information without changing the original meaning and focus of a passage. This requires language competence and regular practice.

Summarising like note making is a productive skill integrating both reading and writing skills. It involves the following:

- ***Reading Strategy:*** a careful reading plan to identify the central idea, the main points and important supporting details
- ***Summarising Techniques:*** Rejection, selection, substitution
- ***Outlining and Paraphrasing***

17.1.1 Reading Strategy

In order to summarise a text or a passage, a careful reading plan should be adopted to ensure complete comprehension. The following reading method may be used:

- Glance through the text quickly in order to understand its central idea and main points. Concentrate on the topic, headings, and sub-headings.
- Then, read the text again carefully in order to understand the details. You should be able to make a distinction between:
  - — Main verses secondary points
  - — Facts verses opinions
  - — Ideas verses examples and opinions
  - — Important verses less important points
  - — Relevant verses irrelevant information

> In order to summarise a text or a passage, a careful reading plan should be adopted to ensure complete comprehension.

— Explicit verses implicit information

- While making a detailed reading of the text, you should analyse it in order to:
  — recognise key lexical items and markers of cohesion to identify relationships among different units within the text;
  — identify all examples, repetitions, restatements, and unnecessary details in order to remove them;
  — note phrases and expressions that can be replaced by words or shorter phrases; and
  — note the logical organisation of the passage (the logical order may be changed without disturbing the meaning).

Progress Check 1

1. Read the following paragraph and
  (a) write the central idea in one sentence, and
  (b) identify relevant and irrelevant information.

While Dalton's atomic theory explained many things and enabled us to interpret several observations, it could not explain everything. It was Dalton who gave us the idea of an atom. Dalton assumed that all matter was made of very tiny particles, which could not be broken down further. He called these tiny particles atoms. He assumed that the atom was not divisible, i.e., it was not composed of simpler constituents. Dalton's atoms were considered to be like marbles; hard, spherical particles that differed in mass, and in size, but were otherwise very similar. Moreover, Dalton considered atoms to be structureless. However, this picture changed dramatically at the turn of the 19th century. The twenty year period from 1895 to 1915 changed so many basic concepts related to atoms and revealed so many new phenomena that man's understanding of the natural world underwent a radical change. Scientists conducted many experiments and the evidence from these experiments made it clear that the idea of an indivisible atom must be abandoned. An atom is divisible and has a complex structure. It is composed of still smaller particles such as electrons, protons, and neutrons.

17.1.2 Summarising Techniques

Mainly three techniques are used in summarising, i.e., selection, rejection, and substitution.

Selection

In order to summarise a passage, the reader may select what is important. This process of choosing the information that is essential to the meaning of the passage is known as 'selection'. In order to select the core information, the reader need to concentrate on the central idea or theme of a passage, main points, and major supporting points. He/she may select the following in a text or passage:

(a) the theme, as expressed in the main heading or title;
(b) the main ideas of each paragraph and a few key phrases that support the main idea; and
(c) special terms or new phrases essential to understand the theme.

> This process of choosing the information that is essential to the meaning of the passage is known as 'selection'.

In the following passage, the important points have been marked (underlined) for writing a summary.

> There are three summarising techniques: selection, rejection, and substitution.

Air pollution has been a major threat not only to the quality of environment but also to human health. It has been a major concern of environmental scientists and people who are concerned with the protection of the natural environment. They are particularly worried about the potential of air pollution to threaten human health and environmental quality. In fact, air pollution, if not controlled, can cause serious problems for human beings. It was precisely this reason that made scientists and policy makers think seriously about the different ways in which to deal with the problem.

During recent years scientists and policy makers have paid substantial attention to airborne substances that have the potential to threaten human health and environmental quality. There have been a large number of studies of these pollutants, which have provided enough evidence to show that these pollutants may cause serious problems for human beings. This has resulted in better understanding of health hazards due to airborne substances and has led to the enactment of measures to control them. For example, there have been controls on emissions from automobiles and this has resulted in the control of vehicular pollution. Moreover, controls on industries that burn gasoline, kerosene, or coal have noticeably improved the quality of the air. Growing effort is being devoted to the isolation of industrial activities and waste dumps that can release complex chemicals into the air and water. In addition, a substantial and relatively effective regulatory structure is in place to control releases of radioactivity into the general environment.

However, in terms of human health, scientists may have missed the main point: that people typically spend 80 to 90 percent of their time indoors. Recent research in air pollution clearly shows that concentrations of many air pollutants can be higher indoors than out. Furthermore, efforts to control outdoor pollution do not check indoor pollution for the simple reason that the factors contributing to indoor pollution are virtually unaffected by controls on outdoor pollution. This perspective is not new just to the public or government officials; even environmental scientists and engineers specialising in air pollution have been startled to discover that the highest personal exposures to combustion emissions occur not in urban smog but in homes with unvented combustion appliances. Finally, concentrations of organic chemicals in homes and offices are often a hundred or a thousand times higher than they are outdoors and airborne radioactivity in homes is more significant by far than that released from nuclear power plants.

Number of words: 411

The underlined sentences, phrases, and words contained the core information that the passage conveys. The selected information may be reconstructed and a summary of the above passage written. The following summary illustrates how the process of selection can help us write effective summaries:

Summary

Air Pollution:
A Threat To Human Health & Environmental Quality

During recent years, scientists and policy makers have paid substantial attention to airborne substances that threaten human health or environmental quality. Controls on emissions from automobiles or industries that burn gasoline, kerosene, or coal have noticeably improved the quality of the air. However, recent research has revealed that concentrations of many pollutants can be higher indoors than out and that the factors contributing to indoor pollution are virtually unaffected by controls on outdoor pollution. The highest personal exposures to combustion emissions occur not in urban smog but in homes with unvented combustion appliances.

Concentrations of organic chemicals in homes and offices are higher than they are outdoors and airborne radioactivity in homes is more significant than that released from nuclear power plants.

Number of words: 122

Progress Check 2

1. **Read the following passage, and underline the sentences, phrases, or words that you would like to select to write a summary of the passage.**
   - All matter possesses the basic property of inertia, which is an opposition to any change in motion. This property is described by the quantity or 'mass' of an object. The more massive an object, the greater its inertia. An object has the same mass at any location; for example, its mass is the same on the earth, on the moon, and in free space.
   - A force is an action (such as a push or a pull) that tends to make a stationary object move, or changes the speed or direction of motion of a moving object. One type of force is due to the natural physical phenomenon of every particle of matter attracting all other particles of matter in the universe. This attraction between masses is called the force of gravity. The magnitude of the force of gravity between any two objects depends on their separation and their masses. The weight of an object is actually due mainly to its gravitational attraction toward a celestial body (such as the earth). Therefore, the weight of an object depends on its location. For example, the weight of an object on Earth's surface is not the same as its weight on the moon because the masses and the diameters of the earth and moon are quite different. Objects actually weigh less on the moon than on Earth. This is why astronauts can carry such large masses on the moon's surface.
   - In mechanics, some objects are considered rigid bodies, but in reality, rigid bodies do not exist. All known materials are deformed to some extent by the application of a force. To avoid structural failures, engineers must know the limitations of the materials they use, and they must be able to calculate the magnitudes of any deformations.
   - A deformation depends on the type of material used and on the nature (magnitude and orientation) of the applied loads. Materials are usually utilised according to their properties and cost. For example, steel girders are relatively strong; therefore, they are often used as the main supports in large structures. Wooden beams are used in smaller structures because they have sufficient strength and are lighter and less expensive than steel girders.
   - When a material is subjected to repeated varying loads over a long period, it gradually loses its strength. This is known as fatigue. It occurs more rapidly if the material has a flaw. Fatigue is a common cause of failure in machinery.

Rejection

Rejection is the process of removing all that is not important. The reader may reject all information that is unnecessary or redundant. The following are generally not included in a summary:

> Rejection is the process of removing all that is not important.

(a) repetitions
(b) examples and illustrations
(c) redundant expressions
(d) minor supporting details

The following is an example of a passage in which unimportant points have been marked (underlined):

Several devices are used for the protection of electric circuits. As these devices play an important role in protecting electric circuits, they are very commonly used. In fact, their absence might lead to several problems created by overloading or short circuiting. Sometimes a very high current may flow through the circuit due to overloading or a short circuit, and may damage the electrical machines and appliances being used.

The most important safety device used for protection of electric circuits is the fuse. We can define a fuse as a piece of wire of a material with a very low melting point. The low melting point of this wire is the key element in the functioning of the fuse. When a high current flows through the circuit the fuse wire gets heated and melts. As a result, the circuit is broken and current stops flowing. The fuse wire is normally made of pure tin or an alloy of a tin and copper. Both pure tin or an alloy of a tin and copper have low melting points.

Number of words: 180

The underlined sentences, phrases or words are unimportant as they are either repetitions, illustrations, or unnecessary details. The following summary of the paragraph illustrates how the process of rejection can help in writing effective summaries:

Summary

A fuse is an important safety device used for protection of electric circuits. It is a piece of wire of a material with a very low melting point. When a high current flows through the circuit the fuse wire gets heated and melts. Consequently, the circuit is broken and current stops flowing.

Number of words: 52

In the following example, the unimportant points are marked (underlined) for rejection in order to write a summary of the passage:

In order to computerise a factory, we need to develop a timesharing system. By computerising a factory, we mean that we want to make computer use available to as many people in the factory as possible, as cheaply as possible. However, there are two potential problems of a simple time sharing system. The first potential problem is, "What happens if the computer is not working?" The answer to this question is that everything grinds to a halt. In a situation where people have become dependent on computer, not much gets done until the computer is up and running again. The old saying about putting all your eggs in one basket comes to ones mind here.

The second potential problem of the simple timesharing system is saturation. Saturation is the result of an increase in the number of users. As the number of users increases, the time it takes the computer to do each user's task also increases. Eventually, the computer's response time to each user becomes unreasonably long. People get very upset about the time they have to wait.

A partial solution for the two potential problems of a simple timesharing system is to use a distributed processing system. The system has a powerful central computer with a large memory and a high-speed printer. Moreover, each user has a micro-computer instead of simply a video display terminal. In other words, each user station is an independently functioning micro-computer with a CPU, ROM, RAM, and probably magnetic or optical disc memory. This means that a person can do many tasks locally on the micro-computer without having to use the large computer at all. Since micro-computers are connected to the large computer through a network, a user can access the computing power, memory, or other resources of the large computer when needed.

Distributing the processing to multiple computers or processors in a system has several advantages. First, if the large computer goes down, the local micro-computers can continue working until they need to access the large computer for something. Second, the burden on the large computer is reduced greatly, because much of the computing is done by the local micro-computers. Finally, the distributed processing approach allows the system designer to use a local microcomputer that is best suited to the task it has do. Thus, a distributed processing seems to be the best way to go about computerising a factory.

Number of words: 398

By removing the underlined sentences, phrases and words, which are either repetitions, illustrations, or unnecessary details, a summary of the passage may be written. Given below is summary:

Summary

Computerising a factory requires a timesharing system. However, there are two potential problems of a simple time sharing system. The first is, "What happens if the computer is not working?". The second is that of saturation. As the number of users increases, the computer's response time to each user becomes long. Using a distributed processing system provides a solution. The system has a powerful central computer and each user has a micro-computer. Even if the large computer goes down, the local micro-computers can continue working. Second, the burden on the large computer is reduced greatly. Finally, the distributed processing approach allows the system designer to use a local micro-computer that is best suited to the task it has to do.

Number of words: 120

Progress Check 3

1. **Read the following passage and underline the sentences, phrases, or words that you think are repetitions, examples, illustrations, or unnecessary details. Now, remove the underlined sentences, phrases or words, and write a summary of the passage.**

   Photosynthesis is a very important process. It plays a significant role in maintaining ecological balance. In fact, photosynthesis maintains the proper balance of CO_2 in the atmosphere and purifies the air by liberating oxygen, which is a by-product of the process. Photosynthesis can be defined as a building process in which carbohydrates are synthesised from simple substances like carbon dioxide and water by the chlorophyll containing cells of the plant in the presence of light; oxygen being liberated as a by-product. All the food is derived from the process of photosynthesis, either directly by eating the plants, their various parts or their numerous products, or indirectly by eating plant-fed animals. In fact, the energy by which all animals including human beings live is generated by the oxidation of the food produced by plants.

   The oxidation of organic compounds during respiration liberates carbon dioxide in the atmosphere and, thus, helps in maintaining the proper balance of CO_2. The combustion of coal, oil, and other fuels causes enormous production of CO_2 yet the percentage of CO_2 has remained nearly constant since it was measured first. It is, therefore, obvious that the total rate of CO_2 consumption during photosynthesis just equals the CO_2 production on a global basis. It is this balance that maintains Earth's atmosphere.

If CO_2 is not utilised during photosynthesis, its proportion in the atmosphere will definitely rise greatly. Since CO_2 absorbs infrared radiation, there will be an appreciable rise in temperature. This may melt the polar ice caps and, hence, result in floods and consequently there will be a variation in the level of the oceans.

The process of photosynthesis purifies the air by liberating oxygen, which is a by-product of the process. The oxygen is used for respiration by all living organisms except the anaerobes, which can sustain life, by anaerobic respiration and fermentation. This interdependence of plants and animals is important in understanding the carbon cycle in nature.

Number of words: 328

Substitution

In order to summarise a passage, the technique of substitution may have to be used. It may involve synthesis (combining several sentences into one sentence), sentence substitution (substituting short sentences for long and clumsy sentences), and one word substitution (substituting one precise word for several words or phrases).

Synthesis

Synthesis, which is a grammar strategy of combining several sentences into one sentence, may be effectively used in summarising. Table 17.1 gives some examples.

> Synthesis, which is a grammar strategy of combining several sentences into one sentence, may be effectively used in summarising.

TABLE 17.1 Examples of Synthesis in Summarising

Sentences	*One Sentence Substitution*
The fact that light travels in straight lines is an important principle of physics. Scientists use a technical term to express this principle. This technical terminology is the rectilinear propagation of light. **Number of words: 32**	The rectilinear propagation of light is the technical terminology applied to the principle that "light travels in straight lines". **Number of words: 19**
As the name implies, mini-computers are small computers. Unlike a mainframe computer, which may fill an entire room, a minicomputer may fit in a single rack or box. In fact, it is a scaled-down version of a mainframe computer. **Number of words: 38**	Scaled-down versions of mainframe computers are called mini-computers. **Number of words: 08**
In order to computerise a factory, we may have to use an effective processing system. We may use distributed processing as an effective method. Frankly speaking, this seems to be the best way to go about computerising a factory. **Number of words: 39**	Distributed processing is the best way to go about computerising a factory. **Number of words: 12**

Sentence Substitution

Short sentences may be used to substitute long sentences. Table 17.2 gives some examples. It may be effectively used in summarising.

Short sentences may be used to substitute long sentences.

TABLE 17.2 Examples of Substitution in Summarising

Long Sentences	*Short Sentences*
Photosynthesis is a building process in which carbohydrates are synthesised from simple substances like carbon dioxide and water by the chlorophyll containing cells of plants in presence of light. **Number of words: 30**	In photosynthesis, chlorophyll-containing organisms capture energy in the presence of light to synthesise carbohydrates. **Number of words: 13**
In order to computerise a factory, what is needed most is an effective timesharing system. **Number of words: 15**	Computerising a factory requires a timesharing system. **Number of words: 07**
Corrosion engineering is not only the application of science to prevent or control corrosion damage safely but it is also the application of art to control corrosion damage economically. **Number of words: 29**	Corrosion engineering is the application of science and art to prevent or control corrosion damage economically and safely. **Number of words: 18**

One Word Substitution

One word should be used to substitute several words or phrases. A list of such words is given in Appendix C.

17.1.3 Outlining and Paraphrasing

An outline of the core information given in a passage should be prepared while writing a summary of it. An 'outline' is defined as a general statement without details. An outline of a passage or a text is a sketch containing only the main ideas. Once an outline of the core information has been prepared, the passage should be reconstructed by paraphrasing the core information.

An outline of a passage or a text is a sketch containing only the main ideas.

Paraphrasing refers to the process of rewriting a passage or text in different words without changing or distorting its original meaning. It involves changes in lexis, structure, and the logical organisation of the core information in a passage without changing its meaning.

Paraphrasing refers to the process of rewriting a passage or text in different words without changing or distorting its original meaning.

Phrasing requires various linguistic skills, which include using appropriate synonyms, replacing sentence patterns by appropriate equivalents, simplifying difficult terms and expressions for clarity, and modifying paragraph structure and organisation without altering the basic meaning. Paraphrasing has its uses in several writing activities. As technical writing involves selection of relevant material, evaluating evidence, and drawing appropriate conclusions, the ability to rephrase technical material in one's own words is essential. Rewriting and rephrasing are essential components of effective presentation.

Do's and Dont's of Paraphrasing

- Note down the essential/core information.
- Read the core information for identifying all the words and phrases that can be replaced without distorting the meaning of the passage.
- Restructure the outlines by using different words, phrases, sentence structures, sentence types and organisation.
- Note expressions that can be replaced by changing sentence structure/sentence type.
- Do not replace scientific and technical terms, or standard formal phrases.
- Note the logical structure of the passage. (Micro-structure = the ordering of phrases and sentences in a paragraph and Macro-structure = the ordering of main points/main supporting details in a passage.) The logical order can be changed without disturbing the original meaning.
- All the words and expressions changed.
- A final draft should be prepared.

Techniques of Paraphrasing

> Paraphrasing involves techniques for rewriting or replacing words, phrases, sentences, paragraph structures, and logical organization.

The following techniques may be used for paraphrasing the core information in a passage:

(A) Replacement of words and phrases
- Use of synonyms

(B) Change of sentence structure
- Gerund to clause
- Clause to gerund
- Active to passive
- Subordinate clauses to gerund constructions
- Complex/compound sentence to simple sentence
- Direct to indirect sentence

(C) Change of paragraph structure

(D) Change of logical organisation

In the following example the core information (underlined) is paraphrased to write a summary of the passage:

There has been a continuous growth in the number of vehicles all over the world. Millions of vehicles ply the world's roads, and everyday the number goes up. In fact, the growth of these vehicles has consistently outpaced that of the human population. <u>About half of the world's oil is consumed by a fleet of 500 million vehicles</u>. These vehicles account for most of the energy used in the carriage of people and freight. <u>Since 1970 the annual increase in the number of cars has averaged 4.7 per cent, whereas the annual increase in the number of buses and trucks has averaged 5.1 per cent. As per a rough estimate, a billion vehicles will ply the world's roads by the year 2030 if this increasing trend continues.</u> <u>Such rapid growth poses many problems</u>. It would be very difficult to handle some of these problems, which might lead to severe oil crises in all parts of the world, particularly in developing and underdeveloped countries. In the long run, <u>it causes oil consumption to rise faster than oil production, resulting in the squeezing of oil supplies</u>. Indeed, the ongoing rise in oil prices appears to be putting an end to the buyer's market, which emerged in the early 1980's (when an economic showdown and conservation efforts temporarily reduced world demand).

Number of words: 200

Table 17.3 that contains the core information and its paraphrased version.

TABLE 17.3 Examples of Paraphrasing

Core Information	*Paraphrasing*
About half of the world's oil is consumed by a fleet of 500 million vehicles.	A fleet of 500 million plus vehicles consumes about half of the world's oil.
Since 1970 the annual increase in the number of cars has averaged 4.7 per cent, whereas the annual increase in the number of buses and trucks has averaged 5.1 per cent.	Since 1970 the fleet's annual increase has averaged 4.7 per cent for cars and 5.1 per cent for buses and trucks.
As per a rough estimate a billion vehicles will ply the world's roads by the year 2030 if this increasing trend continues.	If the trend continues, a billion vehicles will ply the world's roads by the year 2030.
Such rapid growth poses many problems. In the long run, it causes oil consumption to rise faster than oil production, resulting in the squeezing of oil supplies.	In the long run, such rapid growth causes oil consumption to rise faster than oil production, which results in the reduction of supplies.

The following is the summary of the passage:

Summary

A fleet of 500 million plus vehicles consumes about half of the world's oil. Since 1970 the fleet's annual increase has averaged 4.7 per cent for cars and 5.1 per cent for buses and trucks. If the trend continues, a billion vehicles will ply the world's roads by the year 2030. In the long run, such rapid growth causes oil consumption to rise faster than oil production, which results in the reduction of supplies.

Number of words: 72

Summary Writing Practice

Read the following passages and write a summary for each one of them. Check answers with those given at the end of each passage:

Passage 1

The process of metamorphism which results in the formation of metamorphic rocks, may generate enough heat and pressure to alter existing mineral deposits of impure or low-grade ores into comparatively more pure and valuable minerals. Some banded hematite formations have changed to banded magnetite-quartzite rocks in Salem and Tiruchirapalli districts by metamorphism. Another example of heat changing pre-existing minerals into more pure minerals is offered by the conversion of bituminous coal into anthracite in the vicinity of dykes and sills in some cases. Sillimanite in Assam and Eastern Maharashtra (Bhandara district) and kyanite are formed by metamorphism. Talc, or hydrated magnesium silicate, is also a product of metamorphism of magnesium bearing rocks like dolomite, as seen near Jaipur in Rajasthan.

Some mineral deposits are of sedimentary origin and the deposits of sediment may be formed organically as in the case of coal deposits, or chemically, as in the case of some limestone or chalk deposits. Such deposits are always bedded and stratified.

Alluvial, detrital, or placer deposits are formed by breaking up of the parent rock and subsequent transportation of mineral particles by stream or wave action. The minerals are found in sizeable concentrations where the velocity, and hence the carrying power of the currents, is decreased. In such deposits, the minerals are concentrated into fractions according to their specific gravities and two or more minerals of similar specific gravities may be found together. Examples of such placer deposits are gold placers with the gold being associated with magnetite, chromite, and so on. Alluvial, gem deposits, platinum, tin, and wolfram are some other examples of alluvial or placer deposits.

Number of words: 269

Summary

Metamorphism generates enough heat and pressure to alter low-grade ores into valuable minerals. Banded magnetite-quartzite rocks in Salem and Tiruchirapalli districts, sillimanite in Assam and Eastern Maharashtra, and anthracite near dykes and sills are all formed by metamorphism. Some mineral deposits such as coal or chalk deposits are of sedimentary origin. Alluvial, or placer deposits are formed by the breaking up of the parent rock and subsequent transportation of the mineral particles by stream or wave action. Gold placers, chromite, alluvial, gem deposits, platinum, tin, and wolfram are some examples of alluvial or placer deposits.

Number of words: 93

Passage 2

Alloy steels as well as plain carbon steels may be classified according to their ability to harden. This is probably the most significant basis of classifying alloy and plain carbon steels. The ability to harden has been defined as the 'hardenability' of steel. The role played by the hardenability of steels is one of great importance, and any test that can be made to check this characteristic of steel will prove of value in the selection and qualification of any steel for a given application. In fact, hardenability is an important criterion of selecting or rejecting steel for a particular purpose.

It has been determined that the hardenability of steels is dependent upon several factors and these factors do not include the chemical composition or alloy content of the steel. What are the factors that influence the hardenability of steels? Such factors as methods of manufacture, practice in shaping, and variables in treating all influence the hardenability of steels. Because these variables will influence the hardenability, the usual methods of testing, without carrying out a test for hardenability, may not reveal the complete story about the steel. This being true, several methods have been designed to measure the ability of the steel to harden. There is one principle behind all hardenability tests. The principle behind all hardenability tests is to measure the maximum section or thickness of steel that can be made hard. The Jominy end-quench test is recommended as a hardenability test for alloy structural and tool steels. This test can be used for both shallow- and deep-hardening

Number of words: 263

Summary

Both alloy steels and plain carbon steels are classified according to their ability to harden, which is termed as the hardenability of steel. Hardenability of steel is dependent upon methods of manufacture, practice in shaping, and variables in treating. The usual methods of testing without a test for hardenability may not reveal everything about the steel. Hardenability tests play an important role in the selection of any steel for a given application. The principle behind all such tests is to measure the maximum section or thickness of steel that can be made hard.

Number of words: 93

Passage 3

The 21st century is witnessing an information revolution in which information processing and retrieval are being reliably done at incredible speeds. Advances in information technology has provided us with a wide range of effective communication tools, which has made communication easier, faster, and more reliable than it used to be. The computer is the most effective communication tool. Today computers can be found everywhere, in offices, banks, universities, shops, and even in homes—to mention just a few of their uses. In fact, we live in a computer-oriented society, and we are constantly exposed to computers with its potential to change our lives.

There are several factors that have made computers so popular today. Firstly, computers are able to store a large amount of data due to their storing capacity. A computer has memory to store data and it is the ability of a computer to store a large amount of data that has made it popular in offices and universities. Secondly, computers can process data into meaningful information. That means that computers cannot only store data, they can process them too. Finally, computers have also the ability to perform fast and accurate calculations. Computers can always function are powerful calculating machines.

Number of words: 202

Summary

Advances in information technology has provided us with a wide range of effective communication tools, which has made communication easier, faster, and more reliable than it used to be. The computer is the most effective communication tool. The computer, with its ability to store and process data and perform fast and accurate calculations, has revolutionised the modern age.

Number of words: 57

Exercise

1. **Read the following passages and summarise each one of them:**

PASSAGE 1

An ionic compound is a collection of an equal number of positive and negative ions arranged in a three-dimensional lattice. Ionic compounds can be dissociated into their constituent ions with little effort. Further, they can be electrolysed to produce elements of constituent atoms. Water also weakens the attraction between the ions in an ionic compound. This is why many ionic compounds dissolve well in water. Moreover, ionic compounds can conduct electricity. Most ionic compounds are made of metals.

In comparison, covalent bonds have quite different properties. They do not ionise or conduct electricity. Electrolysis of covalent bonds is, thus, not possible. Many covalent bounds are not soluble in water. Covalent bonds dissolve much easier in organic liquids. Since the bonding here is by electron sharing and not by electron attraction, the number of atoms in covalent molecules is not indefinitely large. They have lower melting and boiling points than ionic compounds. Many covalent molecules are in the gas phase or liquid state (CL_2, H_2O).

Number of words: 166

PASSAGE 2

Hydrocarbons are compounds of carbon and hydrogen. The unique property of carbon atoms to form long chains results in the possibility of a large number of hydrocarbons being formed. The natural source of hydrocarbons is petroleum (crude oil), which is preserved by nature in some reservoirs of porous rocks in the earth. Petroleum is withdrawn from such reservoirs through wells driven in them by puncturing the cap of protective impervious rocks that prevented it from seeping away.

The simplest hydrocarbon is methane. The simplicity of methane is clear from the fact that a molecule of methane has four hydrogen atoms linked to one central atom of carbon. This is simply expressed by its molecular formula CH_4.

The carbon atom has four electrons in its outermost orbit. However, quantum laws allow it to have another four to complete the set, which means that the valency of carbon is 4 (tetravalent). The carbon atom, therefore, forms a chemical bond with 4 atoms of hydrogen by sharing an electron with each of them. The valency of hydrogen is 1 (monovalent) and each of the four hydrogen atoms also shares an electron with the carbon atom. A methane molecule thus formed by 4 hydrogen atoms surrounding a carbon atom in a chemical bond makes for a very stable arrangement.

Number of words: 214

PASSAGE 3

In chemical cells, electricity is produced by chemical reactions between the components. These cells consist of two different conductors called electrodes that are located in a fluid conductor called an electrolyte, containing ions. Cells have emfs that are characteristics of the materials that are used. There are two classes of chemical cells.

If the switch is opened, the current in coil 1 decreases rapidly to zero, and a transient current is induced in coil 2, which tries to maintain the magnetic field. A current is induced in the secondary coil only when the current in the primary is changing, or when the two coils are moved relative to each other. This is called mutual induction. Faraday determined that the magnitude of the induced emf depends on the number of turns in the coils and the time rate of change of the magnetic field which is called as Self-induction.

While a changing electric current induces emfs in neighbouring circuits, it also induces an emf in its own circuit. As the current varies in a single isolated circuit, its magnetic field changes, and there is a corresponding change in the magnetic field surrounding that circuit. This changing magnetic field induces an emf that opposes the original change of the current in the same circuit. This is called self-induction. The self-induced emf is known as the counter or back emf. The self-induction unit for inductance is called the henry (H). In a circuit that has a self-inductance of 1 H, a time rate of change of current equal to 1 A/s induces a counter emf of 1 V.

Number of words: 262

PASSAGE 4

The resistance of a conductor may be defined in terms of current passing through it and the potential difference across its ends. Therefore, we can define the resistance (symbol R) as the ratio of potential differences across its ends and the current that flows through it. The symbol for ratio of potential differences across its ends is V and that of the current flowing through it is I. That is, resistance

$$R = V/I$$

Since the unit of potential difference is the volt and that of current is ampere, the unit of resistance is volt/ampere. The unit of resistance is called the ohm, named after George Simon Ohm. Ohm's law states that the current in a circuit is proportional to the voltage across it. It also states that the resistance in a circuit is the ratio of the voltage to its current.

The resistance of a material plays an important role in electric circuits. The parts or components of the circuit, which are to provide a path for the movement of charges, are made from materials with low resistance. These are usually referred to as conductors. Often some parts or components of the circuit are intentionally designed to offer high resistance. These are made from materials with a high resistance, which are called resistors. A substance that has infinitely high resistance will not allow electricity to flow through. It is called an 'insulator'. Rubber is an excellent insulator.

Number of words: 235

PASSAGE 5

Distributed processing seems to be the best way to go about computerising a factory. Engineers can have personal computers or engineering work stations on their desks. With these, they can use the programme available to design and test circuits. They can access the large computer if they need data from its memory. Through the telephone lines, the engineer, with a personal computer, can access data in the memory of other computers all over the world. The draughtsmen can have personal computers for simple work, or large computer-aided design systems for more complex work. Completed work can be stored in the memory of the large computer. The production department can have networked computers to keep track of product flow and control the machines that actually mount components on circuit boards, and so on. The accounting department can use personal computers with spreadsheet programmes to work with financial data kept in the memory of the large computer. The warehouse supervisor can likewise use a personal computer with an inventory programme to keep personal records, and those in the large computer's memory updated. Corporate officers can have personal computers tied into the network. They can then interact with any of the other systems on the network. Salespeople can have portable personal computers that they can carry with them in the field. They can communicate with the main computer over the telephone lines, using a modem. Secretaries doing word processing can use individual word processing units or personal computers. Users can also send messages to one another over the network. The specifics of a computer system such as this will obviously depend on the needs of the individual company for which the system is designed.

Number of words: 279

PASSAGE 6

One of the most important and interesting characteristics of Pascal is its ability to support many different types of data. These include simple data types, string data types, structured data types and pointer data types.

Simple type data are single items (numbers, characters, and so on) that are associated with single identities on a one-to-one basis. Actually, there are several simple data types. These include the four standard data types–integer, real, char and Boolean–and the user-defined simple types, which include subrange types and enumerated types.

String-type data represent strings of characters. Each single string type data item will represent one entire string. This data type is not found in all versions of Pascal, though it is included in Turbo Pascal.

Structured type data consists of multiple data items that are related to one another in some specified manner. Each group of data items is associated with a particular identifier. The individual data items within each group can also be associated with corresponding individual identifiers. There are four types of structured data in Pascal arrays, records, sets and files.

Pointer type data are used to construct dynamic structured data types. Description of their characteristics and use is beyond the scope of the present discussion.

Number of words: 199

Key to Progress Check

Progress Check 1

1. (a) Dalton's atomic theory that assumed that all matter is composed of extremely small particles called atoms has been challenged by modern researches.

(b)

Relevant information	**Irrelevant information**
It was Dalton who gave us the idea of an atom.	While Dalton's atomic theory explained many things and enabled us to interpret several observations, it could not explain everything.
Dalton assumed that all matter was made of very tiny particles, which could not be broken down further. He called these tiny particles atoms. He assumed that the atom was not divisible, i.e., it was not composed of simpler constituents. Moreover, Dalton considered atoms to be structureless.	Dalton's atoms were considered to be like marbles; hard, spherical particles, which differed in mass and in size, but were otherwise very similar.
However, this picture changed dramatically at the turn of the 19th century. Scientists conducted many experiments and the evidence from these experiments made it clear that the idea of an indivisible atom must be abandoned. An atom is divisible and has a complex structure. It is composed of still smaller particles, such as electrons, protons, and neutrons.	The twenty year period from 1895 to 1915 changed so many basic concepts related to atoms and revealed so many new phenomena that man's understanding of the natural world underwent a radical change.

Progress Check 2

1. All matter possesses the basic property of inertia, which is an opposition to any change in motion. this property is described by the quantity or mass. of an object. Is an indication of the quantity of matter that it possesses. The more massive an object, the greater its inertia. An object has the same mass at any location; for example, its mass is the same on the earth, on the moon, and in free space.

   A force is an action (such as a push or a pull) that tends to make a stationary object move, or changes the speed or direction of motion of a moving object. One type of force is due to the natural physical phenomenon of every particle of matter attracting all other particles of matter in the universe. This attraction between masses is called the force of gravity. The magnitude of the force of gravity between any two objects depends on their separation and their masses. The weight of an object is actually due mainly to its gravitational attraction toward a celestial body (such as the earth). Therefore, the weight of an object depends on its location. For example, the weight of an object on Earth's surface is not the same as its weight on the moon because the masses and the diameters of the Earth and moon are quite different. Objects actually weighless on the moon than on the earth. This is why astronauts can carry such large masses on the moon's surface.

   In mechanics, some objects are considered rigid bodies, but in reality, rigid bodies do not exist. All known materials are deformed to some extent by the application of a force. To avoid structural failures, engineers must know the limitations of the materials they use, and they must be able to calculate the magnitudes of any deformations.

   A deformation depends on the type of material used and on the nature (magnitude and orientation) of the applied loads. Materials are usually utilised according to their properties and cost. For example, steel girders are relatively strong; therefore, they are often used as the main supports in large structures. Wooden beams are used in smaller structures because they have sufficient strength and are lighter and less expensive than steel girders.

   When a material is subjected to repeated varying loads over a long period, it gradually loses its strength. This is known as fatigue. It occurs more rapidly if the material has a flaw. Fatigue is a common cause of failure in machinery.

Progress Check 3

1. Photosynthesis is a very important process. It plays a significant role in maintaining the ecological balance. Infact, photosynthesis maintains the proper balance of CO_2 in the atmosphere and purifies the air by liberating oxygen, which is a by-product of the process. Photosynthesis can be defined as a building process in which carbohydrates are synthesised from simple substances like carbon dioxide and water by the chlorophyll containing cells of the plant in the presence of light; oxygen being liberated as a by-product. All the food is derived from the process of photosynthesis, either directly by eating the plants, their various parts, or their numerous products or indirectly by eating plant-fed animals. In fact, the energy by which all the animals including the human beings live is generated by the oxidation of the food produced by plants.

   The oxidation of organic compounds during respiration liberates carbon dioxide in the atmosphere and, thus, helps in maintaining the proper balance of CO_2. The combustion of coal, oil, and other fuels causes enormous production of CO_2 yet the percentage of CO_2 has remained nearly constant since it was measured first. It is, therefore, obvious that the total rate of CO_2 consumption during photosynthesis just equals the CO_2 production on a global basis. It is this balance that maintains the Earth's atmosphere. If CO_2 is not utilised during photosynthesis, its proportion in the atmosphere will definitely rise to a greatly. Since CO_2

absorbs infrared radiation, there will be an appreciable rise in temperature. This may melt the polar ice caps and, hence, result in floods and consequently there will be a variation in the level of the oceans.

The process of photosynthesis purifies the air by liberating oxygen, which is a by-product of the process. The oxygen is used for respiration by all living organisms except the anaerobes, which can sustain life, by anaerobic respiration and fermentation. This interdependence of plants and animals is important in understanding the carbon cycle in nature.

Number of words: 328

Summary

Photosynthesis maintains the proper balance of CO_2 in the atmosphere and purifies the air by liberating oxygen. In photosynthesis, chlorophyll-containing organisms capture energy in presence of light to synthesise carbohydrates. All the food is derived from the process of photosynthesis, either directly by eating the plants, their various part or their numerous products or indirectly by eating plant-fed animals. The oxidation of organic compounds during respiration liberates carbon dioxide in the atmosphere, maintaining the proper balance of CO_2. The proportion of CO_2 in the atmosphere will definitely rise to a great extent if it is not utilised during photosynthesis.

Number of words: 99

18 CHAPTER

Referencing

Referencing is required for several academic purposes.

LEARNING OBJECTIVES

- Understanding the use and importance of referencing or documenting sources in technical writing
- Identifying methods of organising references from books, manuals, journals, reports, Internet, and so on
- Knowing the uses and methods of writing footnotes
- Grasping the techniques for preparing a working bibliography

18.1 INTRODUCTION

Reference skills are essential for study purposes. While writing a report, a proposal, an essay, or an article for the in-house college journals, students need to consult several sources to gather all the necessary data. Books, dictionaries, journals, published or unpublished reports, magazines, dissertations or websites may be referred. Credit should be given for all the material used from other sources. Whether it is quotations, details, or ideas, the source should be acknowledged by using a proper method of referencing. It is important to identify each source referred to so that the reader is able to find the original information if he or she wants to do so.

> Credit should be given for all the material used from other sources.

> Referencing is a systematic method of documenting or citing sources used in a passage or text.

Referencing is a useful skill that is required for several academic purposes. The meaning of the word reference is 'direction to a book, journal, newspaper and so on (or a passage in it) where information may be found' or 'book or passage so cited'.

There are several functions of referencing. It is used to:

- Keep a record of the sources of information that has been used
- Reinforce the authenticity of a source of information
- Inform the reader about the source being used so that the reader is able to find the original information if he or she wants to do so
- Avoid being guilty of plagiarism
- Reinforce or compare information contained in different sources.

There are different acceptable forms of references, depending upon accepted conventions in the discipline, the nature and volume of material borrowed, the frequency of borrowing, and the documentation style being followed. These referencing forms include parentheses, footnotes, endnotes, references, or bibliography. The term 'bibliography' refers to a "a list of books on a specific subject", whereas 'references' or 'footnotes' refer to the information related to the sources used in a document.

> There are different acceptable forms of references, depending upon accepted conventions in the discipline, the nature and volume of material borrowed, the frequency of borrowing, and the documentation style being followed.

> The term 'bibliography' refers to a "a list of books on a specific subject", whereas 'references' or 'footnotes' refer to the information related to the sources used in a document.

18.2 METHODS OF REFERENCING

It is important to use a standard form of documenting sources of information. Preferably we should follow the style acceptable in particular disciplines. Sometimes the organisation or institution may provide guidelines for arranging references in a scientific article, report, proposal, or other technical documents.

Whatever form of referencing is used, the writer has to provide complete information about the sources he/she has used or referred to in his/her writing. There are several acceptable methods of organising references. To organise references according to the conventions followed in one's area of specialisation, a style manual may be consulted or else the advice of colleagues and teachers may be taken.

> Different methods of referencing are used for books, user guides, reports, journals, magazines, newspapers, independent publications, unpublished sources, and web sources.

> To organise references according to the conventions followed in one's area of specialisation a style manual may be consulted or else the advice of colleagues and teachers may be taken.

The form of referencing depends on the type and nature of source used, i.e., books, journals, magazines, the World Wide Web, encyclopaedia articles, published reports, thesis, newspapers, published interviews, or unpublished material. The following are guidelines to organise references.

18.2.1 Books

The bibliographic information for a book contains three distinct parts, i.e., author, title, and publication information. Each part is separated from each other by an appropriate punctuation mark. This punctuation mark could be a full stop, a semi colon, or even a comma.

> The bibliographic information for a book contains three distinct parts, i.e., author, title, and publication information.

The first section of a bibliographic entry for a book includes the name of the author or names of authors. The name of the author begins with the last name or surname. For example, if the author of a book is Douglas V Hall, the entry would be: Hall, Douglas V. In case of multiple author books, the entry begins with last name of the first author.

The next section includes the title of the book. The title should be in italics. Publication information includes the place of publication, the name of the publisher, the year of publication, and the page number.

The following examples of book references represent several acceptable ways of organising bibliographic information for a book:

Single Author

Seippel, Robert G, *Transducers, Sensors and Detectors*, Reston, Va: Reston Publishing Company, Inc., 1983.

Dorf, Richard C, *Robotics and Automated Manufacturing*, Reston, Va: Reston Publishing Company Inc., 1983.

Slabaugh, WH, *Mechanism of Filiform Corrosion*, Ind. Eng.Chem., 46:1014 (1954).

Southall, J P C, *Mirrors, Prisms, and Lenses*, 3d ed. New York: The Macmillan Company, 1936.

Multiple Authors

Mick, John and Jim Brick, *Bit-Slice Microprocessor Design*, New York: McGraw-Hill Inc., 1980.

Auslander, David M and Paul Sagues, *Microprocessors for Measurement and Control*, California: Osborne/McGraw-Hill, Berkeley, 1981.

Later edition/Reprints

Wood, R W, *Physical Optics*, 3d ed. The Macmillan Company, 1934; reprinted (paperback) Dover Publications, Inc., New York, 1968.

Conrady, A E, *Applied Optics and Optical Design*, vol.1. New York: Oxford University Press, 1929; reprint (paperback) vol. 1 and 2, New York: Dover Publications, Inc., 1960.

Progress Check 1

1. **Suppose you have referred to the following books in a report. Read the information about each book and write appropriate book references.**
   (a) Dale Carnegie's bestselling book entitled "How to Develop Self Confidence and Influence People By Public Speaking", which has been published by Cedar Self Help of United Kingdom in the year 1926. You have referred to page 39 of the book.

(b) Douglas V. Hall's book entitled "Digital Circuits and Systems" published in 1989 by McGraw-Hill, Inc., New York.
(c) H.C. Perkin's book entitled "Air Pollution" published in 1974 by McGraw-Hill, New York. You have referred to pages 42 to 69.
(d) The book entitled "Style: Towards Clarity and Grace" written by Joseph M Williams and published by the University of Chicago Press, Chicago in 1991.
(e) The latest edition of the book "Process Control Instrumentation Technology" written by Curtis D. Johnson and published by John Wiley & Sons, New York.
(f) The book "Effective Business Writing" by V. Piotrowski Maryann published in 1996 by Harper Perenniel. You referred to page number 62.
(g) The third edition of the book "Business Communication" jointly authored by Raymond A. Dumont and John Lannon and published by Scot, Foresman, Little, Brown, Glenview in 1990. You referred to page number 38.
(h) The book "Local Networks, an Introduction" by William D. Stallings. It was published in 1984 by Macmillan, New York.

18.2.2 User Guides

The bibliographic information for a user guide or manual includes the name of the user guide, the name of the publisher, year of publication, and so on. A comma is used to separate each detail of the entry. The name of the guide is in italics (or underlined).

> The bibliographic information for a user guide or manual includes the name of the user guide, the name of the publisher, year of publication, and so on.

The following are some examples:

Macro Assembler User's Guide, Microsoft Corp., Bellingham, Washington, 1989.
SDK-86 MCS-86 System Design Kit User's Guide, Intel Corporation, Santa Clara, California, 1981.
Texas Instruments, Inc. *Third Generation TMS320 User's Guide*, Dallas, Tex., latest edition.
IBM PC/AT Technical Reference Manual, IBM Corporation, Florida, 1984.
DOS Technical Reference Manual, Microsoft Corp., Bellingham, Washington, latest edition.

18.2.3 Reports

The bibliographic entry for a published report includes name of the report writer/writers, title of the report, place of publication, the name of the publisher, and the year of publication. Study the examples given below:

> The bibliographic entry for a published report includes name of the report writer/writers, title of the report, place of publication, the name of the publisher, and the year of publication.

Raina, A K, *Final Report on Evaluation of Human Response to Vibration and Air-overpressure due to Blasting in Opencast Non-Coal Mines in India*, Nagpur: Central Mining Research Institute, January 2003.
Srivastava, BK and SK Sharma. *A Project Proposal on A Study of Quantification and their Weightages for Parameters of Environmental Impact Assessment*, Varanasi: Institute of Technology, Banaras Hindu University, May 2000.

Tiwary, RK, *Report on Assessment and Prediction of Ground Water Contamination in and around Chromite Mine Dump and its Management*, Dhanbad: EMG, Central Mining Research Institute, May 2003.

18.2.4 Journals

The bibliographic information for a journal includes the name of the author, name of the article/paper, name of the journal, volume number and issue number, page number, and date of the issue. A comma is used to separate each detail of the entry. The name of the article is within inverted commas while the name of the journal is in italics (or underlined).

> The bibliographic information for a journal includes the name of the author, name of the article/paper, name of the journal, volume number and issue number, page number, and date of the issue.

The following are some examples of journal references.

Hal Lancaster, "Learning to Manage in a Global Workplace", *The Wall Street Journal*, 2 (June 1998).

E.C. Winegartner, "Recording Electrical Resistance Corrosion", *Corrosion*, 16: 99-104, (June 1960).

Mitch Betts and Tim Quellette, "Taming the E-mail Shrew", *Computerworld,*6 (November 1995): 1, 32.

David Stewart, "Deception , Materiality, and Survey Research: Some Lessons from Craft", *Journal of Public Policy and Marketing*, (spring 1995): 15-28.

18.2.5 Magazines and Newspapers

The bibliographic information for a magazine or a newspaper includes the name of the author, name of the article/paper, name of the newspaper, and date of publication. As in a journal reference, a comma is used to separate each detail of the entry. The name of the article is within inverted commas while the name of the magazine or newspaper is in italics (or underlined).

> The bibliographic information for a magazine or a newspaper includes the name of the author, name of the article/paper, name of the newspaper, and date of publication.

The following are some examples:

Magazine references

Barbara DePompa, "Start Your Engines", *Success*, (December 1990): 24.
Rajlaxmi Bhattacharya, "Mission Impossible", *The Telegraph Magazine*, 26 (April 1998).
Howard Gleckman, "A Rich Stew in the Melting Pot", *Business Week*, 31 (August, 1998): 76.

Newspaper article

N Vidyasagar, "Roadband Goes Boom: Prices Crash", *The Times of India*, March 25, 2004.
Kirk Johnson, "Limits on the Work-at-home life", *The New York Times*, 17 December 1997, A 20.
Martha Groves, "Ethics at Work: Honor System", *Los Angles Times*, 3 November 1997.

18.2.6 Independent Publications

Apart from books, user manuals, journals, periodicals, magazines, and newspapers number of other sources such as pamphlets, theses, dissertations, brochures, conference proceedings, and other forms of published data are used. The bibliographic entry for these sources should resemble that provided for books. However, unpublished documents and conference proceedings are not italicised.

Unpublished documents and conference proceedings are not italicised.

The following are some examples:

Conference paper

Komp M J, F E Donald, M S Thomas, and R M Mickey, "Comparison of two air quality models (CDM and ISC) predicted concentrations for surface mining". Paper No. 84-15.5, presented at the 77th Annual Meeting of the Air Pollution Control Association, San Francisco, June 24-29, 1984.

V M S R Murthy, JL Jethwa, and A K Ghosh, "Planning for faster drivage rate with roadheaders in Indian Longwall mines: A field investigation". Proc. of the 6th International Symposium on Mine Planning and Equipment Selection, Ostrava, Czech Republic, September 3-6, 1997, 46-467.

18.2.7 Unpublished Sources

Unpublished sources such as class lectures, handouts, speeches, and so on may be used. Although the bibliographic entries for these sources may vary, sufficient information should be given so that the reader is able to evaluate the quality of the source and can obtain it for reference. It may be noted that unpublished titles are not italicised.

The following are some examples:

Class lectures or handouts

David Kirk Vaughan, "Public Speaking for Business", Class Handout-12, College of Commerce and Economics, Sultan Qaboos University, Muscat, January 2002.

Rizvi, MA, "Public Speaking for Business", Class assignment, College of Commerce and Economics, Sultan Qaboos University, Muscat, March 2002.

Singh, RK, HSS I —English for Science & Technology, Class handout, Indian School of Mines, Dhanbad, October 2003.

Rizvi, MA "HSS 351- English For Professional Communication", Class assignment, Indian School of Mines, Dhanbad, February 2004.

Asma Bhatti, "Business Communication", Class Handout, National Accounting Diploma Programme, College of Commerce and Economics, Sultan Qaboos University, Muscat, March 2002.

Speech

Rao, U R, XXI Annual Convocation, Indian School of Mines, Dhanbad, January 22, 1999.

18.2.8 Internet

The World Wide Web and other electronic databases now provide major sources of information. The bibliographical entries for Internet sources may include the author's name (if any), the title of the document, location of the information, and the web address.

> The bibliographical entries for Internet sources may include the author's name (if any), the title of the document, location of the information, and the web address.

The following are some examples:

Tikvart J A., "Particulate matter from surface coal mining", 1991 (http://www.epa.gov/ttn/scram/guidance/mch/cfym48.txt).

"Factor Information Retrieval, version 6.23", October 2000 (http:/www.epa.gov/ttn/chief/software/fire).

Progress Check 2

1. Study the following list of references, organize them correctly and rewrite:

(a) "Body Language: Actions Speak Louder Than Words," May 1995, 18-19, *National Underwriter*, Dorothy Leeds.
(b) IBM Corporation, Boca Raton, Fla., *IBM PC Technical Reference Manual*, 1983.
(c) Mitra, Sumit, and Ansari, Javed, M *India Today*, May 15, 1997, 22-29, "Challenges of Consensus."
(d) *Atlantic Monthly Magazine*, "Arts and Politics in America in the 1990s," Updike, John, October 2000, 50-55.
(e) Washington D.C: United States Environmental Protection Agency, Volume1: User's instructions, EPA–910/9-88-202R, 1992, pp.89-97, User's guide for the Fugitive Dust Model (FDM) (Revised),
(f) Industrial Research Laboratory, 1982, p.28, Research Triangle Park, Cowherd D. Jr. *Fugitive Emission Factor Update for AP-42 Final Report*. NC: US Environmental Protection Agency,
(g) London: IPM, 1989, Heriot, Peter, *Recruitment in the 90s*
(h) The Macmillan Company Morgan, JH, New York, 1960, *Cathodic Protection.*
(i) *Fortune*, Michael H. Martin, "Kinko's," 8 July 1996, 102.
(j) "The Writing Process," Kimberly Paterson, April 1998, *Rough Notes*, 59-60.

18.2.9 Footnotes

A footnote, as the term suggests, is a note of reference or comment written at the foot of a page. It is a kind of citation within the body of a text. A mark or a number is put at the last word, or phrase, of the point, which is elucidated in the footnote, and additional information is mentioned at the bottom of the page. Although the main purpose of footnotes is to indicate the source of a fact, opinion, quotation, a diagram, figure, or a picture in order to make acknowledgements, they are more commonly used to provide additional data, introduce persons, theories and ideas, explain unfamiliar or difficult terms and elucidate, elaborate, or validate an idea or a point.

Footnotes should be used if additional information about a term, idea, or fact needs to be given. A mark may be put (for example, word* / word? / word† / word‡ /) or a number (word[1] / word[2] / word[3]) at the last word, or phrase, of the point that needs to be elucidated in the footnote, and the additional information is mentioned at the bottom of the page. Following are some examples of footnotes are used.

> Footnotes should be used if additional information about a term, idea, or fact needs to be given.

Indicating the Source of a Quotation or a Diagram

A footnote may be used primarily to indicate the source of a fact, opinion, quotation, diagram, figure, or picture. Some examples are given here

Example 1*

> The Detroit Edison Co. uses units illustrated in Fig. 4-17 for determining the erosion-corrosion resistance of metals and alloys to high-velocity boiler feed-water at temperatures up to about 100*F*. The water impinges on the face of the plain disk specimen and escapes at right angles through the slot in the face of...
>
> *H.A. Wagner, J.M. Decker, and J.C. Marsh, Corrosion-erosion of Boiler Feed Pumps and Regulating Valves, Trans. ASME, 60: 389-97 (1946).

Source*: Mars G. Fontana and Norbert D. Greene. 1984. *Corrosion Engineering.* Singapore: McGraw-Hill. p.139.

Example 2*

> ...lines get in and out of step. The number of fringes between two successive positions of maximum visibility is about 1000, indicating that the wavelengths of the components differ by approximately 1 part in 1000. In more complicated cases, the separation and intensities of the components could be determined by a Fourier analysis of the visibility curves.* Since this method of inferring the structure of lines has now been superseded by more direct methods, to be described in the following chapter, it will not be discussed in any detail here.
>
> An alternative way of interpreting the eventual vanishing of interference at large path differences is instructive to consider at this point. In Sec. 12.6 it was indicated that a finite spread of wavelengths corresponds to wave packets of limited length, this length decreasing as the spread becomes greater. Thus, when the two beams in the interferometer traverse distances that differ by more than the length of the individual packets, these can no longer overlap and no interference is possible. The situation upon complete disappearance of the fringes is shown schematically in Fig. 13S. The original wave packet P has its amplitude divided at G_1 so that two similar packets are produced, P_1 travelling to M_1 and P_2 to M_2. When the beams are reunited, P_2 lags a distance $2d$ behind P_1. Evidently a measurement of this limiting path difference gives a direct determination of the length of the wave packets. This...
>
> * A.A. Michelson, "Studies in Optics," chap. 4, University of Chicago Press, Chicago, 1927.

Source*: Francis A Jenkins and Harvey E. White. 1981. *Fundamentals of Optics.* Singapore: McGraw-Hill p 278

Example 3*

Table 3.4 Effect of Humidity on Filiform Corrosion of Enameled Steel

Relative humidity, %	*Appearance*
0–65	No corrosion
65–80	Very thin filaments
80–90	Wide corrosion filaments
93	Very wide filaments
95	Mostly blisters, scatered filiform
100	Blisters

Source: M. Van Loo, D.D. Laiderman, and R.R. Bruhn, *Corrosion*, 9:2 (1953).

Source*: Mars G Fontana & Norbert D Greene. 1984. Corrosion Engineering. Singapore: McGraw-Hill p 47

Example 4*

3-28 High Temperatures The senior author's early work on high-temperature oxidation of stainless steels showed selective oxidation of chromium when exposed to low-oxygen atmospheres at high temperatures (1800°F). When there is competition for oxygen, the elements with higher free energies for their oxide formation (higher affinity for oxygen) are oxidized to a greater degree. In the case of stainless steels, this results in a more protective scale. However, the remaining or substrate metal will be deficient in chromium. This phenomenon was clearly demonstrated by Trax and Holzwarth.* Pitting of type 430 (17% Cr) trim on automobiles was attributed to depletion of chromium during bright-annealing operations. Chromium contents as low as 11% were determined at and near the surface of the steel. Another unusual case† showed the selective corrosion of chromium and iron from Inconel (75% Ni, 15% Cr, 9% Fe) by...

*R.V. Trax and J.C. Holzwarth, *Corrosion*, 16: 105–108 (1960).
†R. Bakish and F. Kern, *ibid.*, 89–90.

Source*: Mars G Fontana and Norbert D Greene. 1984. *Corrosion Engineering*. Singapore: McGraw-Hill. p 71

Providing Additional Data

A footnote may be used in order to provide additional information about people, concepts, ideas, theories, facts, or to give hints on how to get further details related to the topic being discussed. The following are some examples:

Example 5*

...wavelengths, increases rapidly with the absolute temperature. Calling W_B the total energy emitted from the surface of a blackbody per square meter per second and T the absolute temperature in kelvins, the *Stefan-Boltzmann** law states that

$$W_B = \sigma T^4 \qquad (21c)$$

The constant s has the value 1.3567×10^{-11} kcal/m^2 s K^4 or 5.670×10^{-8} J/m^2 s K^4. The wavelength of the maximum of each curve λ_{max} depends on the temperature according to *Wien's† displacement law*, which states that

$$\lambda_{max}\, T = \text{const} = 2.8970 \times 10^{-3} \text{ m K} \qquad (21d)$$

where λ_{max} is in meters. The shape of the curve itself is given by *Planck's‡ law*, which...

* Ludwig Boltzmann (1844–1906). From 1895 to his death by suicide in 1906, professor of physics at Vienna. The law was originally stated by Josef Stefan (1835–1983) and was independently demonstrated theoretically by Boltzmann. The latter is chiefly known for his contributions to the kinetic theory and the second law of thermodynamics.

† Wilhelm Wien (1986–1928). German physicist, awarded the Nobel prize in 1911 for his work in optics and radiation. He also made important discoveries about cathode rays and canal rays.

‡ Max Planck (1858–1947). Professor at the University of Berlin. He was awarded the Nobel prize in 1918 for his derivation of the law of blackbody radiation and other work in thermodynamics.

Source*: Francis A. Jenkins and Harvey E White. 1981. *Fundamentals of Optics*. Singapore: McGraw-Hill, p 448.

Example 6*

MECHANISM* The mechanism of filiform corrosion is not completely understood. The basic mechanism appears to be a special case of crevice corrosion as is illustrated in Fig. 3-13. During growth, the head of the filament is supplied with water from the surrounding atmosphere by osmotic action due to the high concentration of dissolved ferrous ions. Osmosis tends to remove water from the inactive tail, because of the low concentration of soluble salts (iron has precipitated as ferric hydroxide). Thus, as shown in Fig. 3-13, atmospheric water continuously diffuses into the active head and out of the inactive tail. Although oxygen diffuses through the film at all points, the concentration of oxygen at the interface between the tail and the head is high because of lateral diffusion. Corrosion is restricted to the head where hydrolysis of the corrosion products produces an acidic environment. Thus, filiform corrosion can be viewed as a self-propagating crevice. Although Fig. 3-13 adequartely explains the basic corrosion mechanism, the unusual growth characteristics (i.e., lack of spreading) and interactions between filaments are not understood.

* For further details see W.H. Slabaugh and M. Grotheer, Mechanism of Filiform Corrosion, *Ind. Eng. Chem.*, 46:1014 (1954).

Source*: Mars G Fontana and Norbert D Greene 1984. *Corrosion Engineering* Singapore: McGraw-Hill p 47.

Example 7*

A more important type of grating called the *echelle*,* which is intermediate between the echelette and the echelon, has a relatively coarse spacing of the grooves, some 80 to the centimeter. These are shaped as in Fig. 17K(*a*), but with a rather steeper slope. These are numbers for which concentration occurs are in the hundreds, whereas for an echelon they are in the tens of thousands. An echelle must be used in conjunction with another dispersing instrument, usually a prism spectrograph, to separate the various orders. If the dispersion of the echelle is in a direction perpendicular to that of the prism, an extended spectrum is displayed as a series of short strips representing adjacent orders, as shown in Fig. 17L.† This is part of a more extensive...

*George R. Harrison, *J. Opt. Soc. Am.*, 39: 522 (1949); 43: 853 (1953).

†The separation of orders, in taking the chellegram of Fig. 17L, was accomplished not by a prism but by an ordinary grating. This accounts for the weaker spectra between the orders marked, which occur in the second order and have echelle orders twice as great.

Source: Francis A. Jenkins and Harvey E White. 1981. *Fundamentals of Optics*. (Singapore: McGraw-Hill) p 372.

Explaining or Elucidating

A footnote may be used to explain unfamiliar or difficult terms or to elucidate, elaborate, and validate an idea or a point. The following are some examples:

Example 8*

...brightness curve* in Fig 9Y occurs not far from the yellow D line. It is for this reason that the index n_D has been chosen by optical designers as the basic index for ray tracing and for the specification of focal lengths. Two other indices, one on either side of n_D, are then chosen for purposes of achromatization. As indicated in the table, the ones most often used are n_C for the red end of the spectrum and n_F or n_G for the blue end.

For two thin lenses in contact, the resultant focal length f_D or power P_D of the combination for the D line is given by Eqs. (4h) and (4i):

$$\frac{1}{f_D} = \frac{1}{f'_D} + \frac{1}{f''_D} \qquad \text{or} \qquad P_D = P'_D + P''_D \tag{9t}$$

where the index D indicates that the quantity depends on n_D, f'_D and P'_D refer to the focal length and power of the crown-glass component, and f''_D and P''_D to the focal length and power of the flint-glass component. In terms of indices of refraction and radii of curvature, the power form of the equation becomes:

$$P_D = (n'_D - 1)\left(\frac{1}{r'_1} + \frac{1}{r'_2}\right) + (n''_v - 1)\left(\frac{1}{r''_1} - \frac{1}{r''_2}\right) \tag{9u}$$

*Brightness is a sensory magnitude in light just as loudness is sensory magnitude in sound. Over a considerable range both vary approximately as the logarithm of the energy. The curve shown represents the logarithms of the standard luminosity curve.

Source: Francis A Jenkins and Harvey E White. 1981. *Fundamentals of Optics*. (Singapore: McGraw-Hill). p 178.

Example 9*

> To verify this statement, we note that according to the discussion of Sec. 18.8 a vector drawn from O to Z gives the amplitude due to the upper half of the wave. Similarly, one from Z' to O gives that due to the lower half. Each of these has a magnitude $1/\sqrt{2}$, so that when they are added and the sum is squared to obtain the intensity due to the whole wave, we find that $I_0 = 2$, with the conventional scale of coordinates used in Fig. 18N.*
>
> **18.11 THE STRAIGHT EDGE**
>
> The investigation of the diffraction by a single screen with a straight edge is perhaps the simplest application of Cornu's spiral. Figure 18O(*a*) represents a section of such a screen, having its edge parallel to the slit *S*. In this figure the half-period strips corresponding to the point *P* being situated on the edge of the geometrical shadow are marked off on the wave front. To find the intensity at *P*, we note that since the upper half of the wave is effective, the amplitude is a straight line joining *O* and *Z*.
>
> * It will be noticed that the phase of resultant wave is 45°, or one-eight period behind that of the wave coming from the center of the zone system the Huygens' wavelet reaching *P* from M_o in Fig. 18K. A similar phase discrepancy, this time of one-quarter period, occurs in the treatment of circular zones in Sec. 18.6. For a discussion of the phase discrepancy in Cornu's spiral, see R.W. Ditchburn, "Light" p, 214. Interscience Publishers, Inc., New York, 1953; 2d ed (paperback), 1963.

Source: Francis A Jenkins and Harvey E White. 1981. *Fundamentals of Optics*. (Singapore: McGraw-Hill). p 393

18.2.10 Bibliography

The literal meaning of the term bibliography is "a list of books on a specific subject". Broadly, it refers to a descriptive list of all the sources that may provide further information on the subject. You may have to prepare a bibliography in order to give the major sources of further information on the topics discussed by you. While preparing a working bibliography, you should take care of the following points:

- Place the bibliography at the end of your document.
- Use an appropriate method of organizing references in the bibliography.
- Follow an appropriate logical order to list the sources in the bibliography.
- Use correct punctuation marks.
- Follow the conventions of your discipline.
- Refer to a style manual.

> Bibliography refers to a descriptive list of all the sources that may provide further information on the subject.

For example:

Bibliography

Source*: Hall, Douglas V., *Microprocessors and Interfacing: Programming and Hardware*, New Delhi: Tata McGraw-Hill Company Limited, 1999.

Exercise

1. **Read the following statements about referencing and write True and False against each of them:**
   (a) Referencing is used to keep a record of the sources of information that has been used in a document.
   (b) There are different acceptable forms of references and each discipline has its own preferred style of referencing.
   (c) The form of referencing does not depend on the type and nature of source used.
   (d) The bibliographic information for a book does not include the affiliation of the author.
   (e) Publication information for a journal includes the place of publication, the name of the publisher, the year of publication, and the page number.
   (f) The bibliographic information for a manual does not include the year of publication.
   (g) The bibliographic information for a published report is similar to that of a book.
   (h) You cannot refer to an unpublished report.
   (i) The World Wide Web and other electronic databases provide major sources of information.
   (j) A footnote is only used to indicate the source of a fact, opinion, quotation, a diagram, figure, or a picture in order to make acknowledgements.
2. **Study the footnotes given in one of your textbooks and classify them according to their functions.**
3. **Study a standard bibliography and classify the references according to the nature of sources, i.e., books, journals, Internet, etc.**

Key to Progress Check

Progress Check 1

1. (a) Carnegie, Dale. *How to Develop Self Confidence and Influence People By Public Speaking.* UK: Cedar Self Help, 1926, p.39.
   (b) Hall, Douglas V., *Digital Circuits and Systems*, New York: McGraw-Hill, Inc., 1989.
   (c) Perkin, H.C. *Air Pollution.* New York: McGraw-Hill, 1974, pp. 42-69.
   (d) Williams, Joseph M., Style: *Towards Clarity and Grace.* Chicago: The University of Chicago Press, 1991.
   (e) Johnson, Curtis D., *Process Control Instrumentation Technology*, John Wiley & Sons, New York, latest edition.
   (f) Maryann V. Piotrowski, *Effective Business Writing*, New York:: Harper Perenniel, 1996, p. 62.
   (g) Dumont, Raymond A. and John Lannon, *Business Communication*, Glenview: Scot, Foresman, Little, Brown, 1990, p. 38.
   (h) Stallings, William D., Local Networks, *an Introduction*, Macmillan, New York, NY, 1984

Progress Check 2

1. (a) Dorothy Leeds, "Body Language: Actions Speak Louder Than Words," *National Underwriter*, May 1995, 18-19.
   (b) *IBM PC Technical Reference Manual*, IBM Corporation, Boca Raton, Fla., 1983
   (c) Mitra, Sumit and Ansari, Javed M, "*Challenges of Consensus*," India Today, May 15, 1997, 22-29.
   (d) Updike, John, "*Arts and Politics in America in the 1990s*," Atlantic Monthly Magazine, October 2000, 50-55.
   (e) USER's guide for the Fugitive Dust Model (FDM) (Revised), Volume1: User's instructions, EPA–910/9-88-202R, Washington D.C: United States Environmental Protection Agency, 1992, pp.89-97.
   (f) Cowherd D. Jr., *Fugitive Emission Factor Update for AP-42 Final Report. Research* Triangle Park, NC: US Environmental Protection Agency, Industrial Research Laboratory, 1982, p.28.
   (g) Heriot, Peter, *Recruitment in the 90s*, London: IPM, 1989.
   (h) Morgan, J.H., Cathodic Protection, New York: The Macmillan Company, 1960.
   (i) Michael H.Martin, "Kinko's," Fortune, 8 July 1996, 102.
   (j) Kimberly Paterson, "*The Writing Process*," Rough Notes, April 1998, 59-60.

SECTION 7

Writing Strategies

CHAPTERS

19 CHAPTER

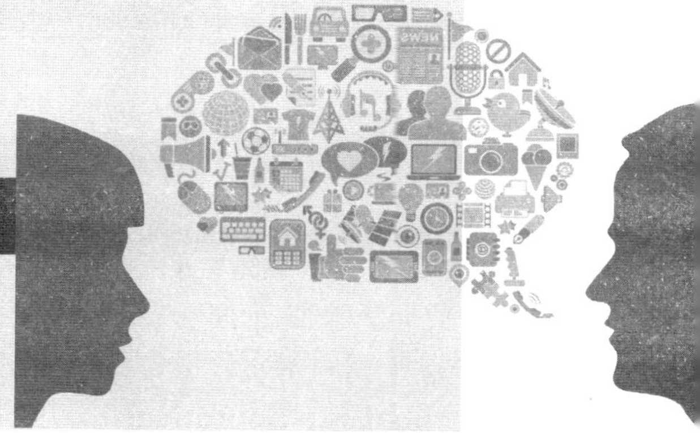

Writing Effective Sentences

In order to be an effective writer, one needs to use effective sentences.

LEARNING OBJECTIVES

- Knowing the essential features of a sentence
- Knowing the use of sentence structure effectively
- Understanding how to connect ideas logically within a sentence
- Deciding on sentence lengths in technical writing
- Grasping the concept of sentence emphasis and discuss techniques of emphasis

19.1 INTRODUCTION

The ability to write effective sentences is essential for success in technical communication because writing anything primarily involves writing sentences. Whether it is a long technical report or a brief e-mail message, sentences have to be written and the effectiveness of the writing will depend on the effectiveness of the sentences. Inappropriate, sloppy, loose, and awkward sentences can never make effective writing. It is important to learn to write correct and effective sentences before learning to compose serious messages.

19.1.1 What is a Sentence?

A sentence is a group of words that gives a complete meaning. As it is a systematic and meaningful arrangement of words and phrases, it gives a complete sense. A basic sentence structure may consist of two parts: the subject and the predicate. Read the following sentence and examine its structure:

There are two parts in a sentence: subject and predicate.

I like English movies.

Subject	Predicate
I	like English movies.

The subject of a sentence refers to the doer or the main part of the sentence that introduces the doer of the action. The subject could be a noun or pronoun that interacts with the verb. It may consist of one or more than one word. For example, the sentence given above contains only one word 'I'. Now, look at the following sentence:

The subject of a sentence refers to the doer or the main part of the sentence that introduces the doer of the action.

People travelling long distances frequently have to decide whether they would prefer to go by land, sea, or air.

In this sentence, 'people travelling long distances' is the subject of the sentence.

The predicate of a sentence refers to the remaining part of a sentence. In the first example given above, 'like English movies' is the predicate, whereas the predicate in the second example is 'frequently have to decide whether they would prefer to go by land, sea, or air'. As can be seen, the predicate of a sentence may consist of the verb, object, complement, and other elements.

Descriptive sentences depict a situation or condition in words, describe an object or a process, or provide a critical review of something. On the other hand, narrative sentences provide an account of events in sequence or time.

The kind of sentences used in a particular piece of writing will depend on the type and nature of the message. It may be descriptive, narrative, expository, or argumentative sentences depending on the purpose of the communication. Descriptive sentences depict a situation or condition in words, describe an object or a process, or provide a critical review of something. On the other hand, narrative sentences provide an account of events in sequence or time. Expository sentences expound and explain ideas while argumentative sentences attempt to persuade or convince.

Expository sentences expound and explain ideas while argumentative sentences attempt to persuade or convince.

19.2 WRITING EFFECTIVE SENTENCES

19.2.1 Sentence Structures

While constructing a sentence, particular attention should be paid to its structure. Faulty or inappropriate sentence structure will confuse readers and communication will not be effective. Edit sentences for structural errors. The following simple guidelines about sentence structure will effectively help you to improve your sentences.

Choose Appropriate Sentence Patterns

Sentence patterns should be used appropriately to the needs of the information to be conveyed. Any structure that suits the message may be used but the structure used should present ideas in a concrete and specific way. Concrete and specific sentences focus on meaning and clarity. Abstract sentences should be avoided. Two sentences should not be connected using a comma. To ensure easy readability, each sentence should include only one to two ideas.

> Concrete and specific sentences focus on meaning and clarity.

Avoid Awkward Sentence Structures

One of the most serious writing errors is constructing sentences with an awkward structure. This might be the result of using wrong word order, confusing phrases, and dangling clauses or modifiers. All written matter should be carefully edited for these sentence structure errors. Table 19.1 contains a few examples of awkward sentence structure and their improved versions.

TABLE 19.1 Examples of Awkward Sentence Structure and their Improved Versions

Awkward Sentence Structure	*Improved Versions*
The student finds it exhaustive and appropriate and has gone through the structure of the Artificial Intelligence module.	The student has gone through the structure of the Artificial Intelligence module and finds it exhaustive and appropriate.
I discussed the problem with the manager, who informed me that the payment was made manually because their computer did not show the payment.	I discussed the problem with the manager, who informed me that their computer did not show the payment because the payment was made manually.
Gold and silver are malleable metals among the best.	Gold and silver are among the best malleable metals.

Avoid Sentence Fragments

Ideas should be expressed in complete sentences and sentence fragments should be avoided. A fragmented sentence does not convey the complete meaning and can be quite confusing for the reader. Fragments generally begin with linking words such as since, although, because, as, and so on. These linkers are used to introduce dependent clauses and cannot be used to introduce independent clauses.

Table 19.2 contains examples of fragments and their improved versions.

> Fragments generally begin with linking words such as since, although, because, as, and so on, and do not convey the complete meaning.

TABLE 19.2 Examples of Fragments and their Improved Versions

Fragments	*Improved Version*
A covalent bond is the force of attraction. Which arises due to the mutual sharing of electrons between the two atoms.	A covalent bond is the force of attraction that arises due to the mutual sharing of electrons between the two atoms.
Since the bonding here is by electron sharing and not by electron attraction. The number of atoms in covalent molecules is not indefinitely large.	Since the bonding here is by electron sharing and not by electron attraction, the number of atoms in covalent molecules is not indefinitely large.
The industrial production of impure iron is carried out on a massive scale in the well known blast furnace. In which complicated high-temperature reactions occur involving iron ore, limestone, and carbon.	The industrial production of impure iron is carried out on a massive scale in the well known blast furnace, in which complicated high-temperature reactions occur involving iron ore, limestone, and carbon.

Avoid Fused Sentences

A fused sentence is basically an incorrect combination of two independent sentences. A fused sentence may be the result of the writer's intention to express a complete thought in a sentence. Overemphasising on expressing a 'complete thought' in a sentence should be avoided. More than one sentence may be used to express a single thought if it makes the point clearer. However, two independent clauses may be joined into one sentence by using appropriate connectives. If a conjunction or a semicolon is not used, a fused sentence will be produced. Like a sentence fragment, a fused sentence confuses the reader. Table 19.3 contains examples of fused sentences and their improved versions.

A fused sentence is basically an incorrect combination of two independent sentences.

TABLE 19.3 Examples of Fused Sentences and their Improved Versions

Fused Sentences	*Improved Versions*
We want to equip our corporate office with modern facilities, we would like to buy this product.	We want to equip our corporate office with modern facilities, and we would like to buy this product.
We would appreciate it if you could send the item immediately we are starting the new branch of our company on March 10, 2005.	We would appreciate it if you could send the item immediately as we are starting the new branch of our company on March 10, 2005.
The simplest method of ore dressing depends on the fact that in general metallic compounds have a higher specific gravity than the gangue they settle faster in a stream of water.	The simplest method of ore dressing depends on the fact that in general metallic compounds have a higher specific gravity than the gangue, and hence they settle faster in a stream of water.

Progress Check 1

1. **Revise the following sentences to correct awkward sentence structures, fragments, and fused sentences:**
   (a) Although all metals react yet their reactivity is different with oxygen.
   (b) Besides the earth's crust. There is a possibility that the centre of the earth may be iron.
   (c) Metals are malleable they can be hammered into very thin sheets.

(d) A thermometer consists of a capillary tube. Which is sealed at one end.
(e) Our company is interested in buying sixty scanners for our corporate office we would be glad if you could send us more information about the product.
(f) Micro-computers are small computers as the name implies.
(g) One distinguishing feature of a micro-computer is that. The CPU is usually a single integrated circuit called a microprocessor.
(h) I am writing to request a refund air tickets from New Delhi to Port Blair of my deposit on three round trip.

2. In each of the following sentences, the blank can be filled by one of the three alternatives given under it. Select the most appropriate alternative to fill the blank.

(a) When a car speeds up, we say that ________.
  (i) it will accelerate
  (ii) it accelerates
  (iii) it might accelerate
(b) Micro-computers ________ that work directly with 4-bit words to larger units that work directly with 32-bit words.
  (i) range with small controllers
  (ii) range in small controllers
  (iii) range from small controllers
(c) When I came to the conference hall, ________.
  (i) the delegates still did not come
  (ii) the delegates still had not come
  (iii) the delegates still could not come
(d) Newtons's second law of motion can be applied to situations where ________.
  (i) the acceleration could be zero
  (ii) the acceleration is zero
  (iii) the acceleration will be zero
(e) The information that ________ by the user using input cevices can be viewed on the VDU of a computer.
  (i) could be entered
  (ii) was entered
  (iii) has been entered
(f) When you ________, what you are really doing is writing a sequential list of instructions for the computer.
  (i) write a computer programme
  (ii) might write a computer programme
  (iii) are writing a computer programme
(g) When an organic compound is present in an aqueous medium, it ________ by shaking it with an organic solvent in which it is more soluble than in water.
  (i) is separated
  (ii) was separated
  (iii) has been separated

(h) If the organic compound is less soluble in the organic solvent, a very large quantity of solvent ———————————— to extract even a very small quantity of the compound.
   (i) would have been required
   (ii) would be required
   (iii) is being required

(i) Any device connected on the data bus ——————————— three-state outputs so that its outputs can be disabled when it is not being used to put data on the bus.
   (i) would have
   (ii) must have
   (iii) could have

(j) Metallurgy involves three main stages: concentration of ore, extraction of crude metal from the concentrated ore, and ————————————————.
   (i) a refining of the crude metal
   (ii) the refining of the crude metal
   (iii) refining of the crude metal

19.2.2 Sentence Coherence

The techniques of synthesis and combination may be used to make sentences logical and effective.

Sentence coherence is integral to sentence effectiveness. Appropriate connectives should be used to connect words, phrases, and clauses in a sentence.

Connectives

Overt devices are direct and explicitly stated while covert devices are indirect and implicit.

In order to achieve coherence, technical writers and speakers use several linking devices or connectives. There are two types of linking devices, overt and covert. Overt devices are direct and explicitly stated while covert devices are indirect and implicit. Covert devices include techniques such as repetition of the key word, the use of articles (a, an, the), pro-nominal forms (he/she/it/they, and so on), and the use of synonyms. However, technical communication largely uses overt linking devices or connectives to indicate the logical progression of ideas in oral discourse or writing.

Following are some examples, in which connectives (underlined) have been used:

Technical communication largely uses overt linking devices or connectives to indicate the logical progression of ideas in oral discourse or writing.

(a) When an object is placed on one side or the other of a converging lens and beyond the focal plane, an image is formed on the opposite side.
(b) If the object is moved closer to the primary focal plane, the image will be formed farther away from the secondary focal plane and will be larger.
(c) Land pollution is due to solid wastes.
(d) Fresh water is a renewable source, but its distribution is uneven.
(e) Asbestosis is caused by asbestos, which is used in making ceilings.
(f) As ethanol is an important industrial chemical, it is subjected to very small excise duty.
(g) Metals are known as electropositive elements because they can form positive ions by the loss of electrons.
(h) Sulphur dioxide is formed when sulphur or fuels containing sulphur are burnt in air.

(i) Cement is a white grey powder <u>that</u> sets after a few hours <u>when</u> mixed with water, <u>and</u> then hardens in a few days into a solid and strong material.

These connectives includes subordinators and coordinators. They can also be classified according to their functions. Table 19.4 lists the most common connectives and their functions:

Connectives include subordinators and coordinators.

TABLE 19.4 Common Connectives and their Functions

Connectives	*Function*
Before, prior to, before that, previously, earlier, while, as, just as, during, throughout, at that time, at that very moment, at the very time, the very moment, as soon as, when, on that occasion, till then, since then, by the time	Indicating time relation
if, in case, unless, on condition that, so long as, provided that, supposing, whichever, no matter, under any circumstances	Expressing condition
as, since, because, owing to, due to, caused by, bring about, arise out of, hence, thus	Expressing cause
as a result, as a consequence, result in, cause	Expressing result
except, though, although, not even	Expression of concession
as, like, as if, as though	Expression of comparison
while, where as, but, however	Expression of contrast
and so on, further, besides, alongside, along with, and, or	Expression of addition
namely, such as, like	Exemplifies

Now, read the following paragraph, and note the use of connectives (underlined):

Plastics have specific properties, <u>which</u> may make them preferable to traditional materials for certain uses. <u>In comparison with</u> metals, for example, plastics have <u>both</u> advantages and disadvantages. Metals tend to be corroded by inorganic acids, <u>such as</u> sulphuric acid <u>and</u> hydrochloric acid. Plastics tend to be resistant to these acids, <u>but</u> can be dissolved or deformed by solvents, <u>such as</u> carbon tetrachloride, <u>which</u> have the same carbon base as plastics. Colour must be applied to the surface of metals, <u>whereas</u> it can be mixed in with plastics. Metals are more rigid than most plastics, <u>while</u> plastics are very light, with a specific gravity normally between 0.9 and 1.8. Most plastics do not readily conduct heat or electricity. Plastics soften slowly <u>and</u> can easily be shaped <u>while</u> they are soft.

Progress Check 2

1. Read the following paragraphs and fill in the blanks with appropriate connectives:

(a) — 1— hydrogen gas escapes from a cylinder into the air, no change is visible. However, — 2 — the escaping hydrogen is directed at finely divided platinum, it is observed —3— the platinum glows —4— soon ignites the hydrogen. In the absence of platinum the H_2—O_2 reaction is too slow to observe. In contact with platinum, hydrogen reacts with oxygen from the air to form water. —5 — they react, they give off energy, —6— heats the platinum. —7— the platinum gets hotter, it heats the hydrogen and oxygen, —-8— their rate of reaction increases, —9— eventually ignition occurs —10— the reaction of hydrogen with oxygen becomes self-sustaining.

(b) —1— most metals, magnesium is seldom used in the pure form for metal parts. It is most commonly alloyed with aluminum, —2— several other alloys are produced. Magnesium can be forged, rolled, —3— extruded. It displays its best mechanical properties in the extruded form, —4— it attains a tensile strength of more than 25,000 pounds per square inch. As a cast material, its tensile strength is about half this amount. Cold working —5— a rapid increase in hardness; —6—, it is advisable to carry on such operations at temperatures ranging between 500° to 650° F. Magnesium can be heat treated —7—, —8—a substantial increase in mechanical properties.

(c) A force is an action —1— tends to make a stationary object move, —2— changes the speed or direction of motion of a moving object. One type of force is —3— the natural physical phenomenon —4— every particle of matter attracts all other particles of matter in the universe. This attraction between masses is called the force of gravity. The magnitude of the force of gravity between any two objects depends on their separation —5— and their masses. The weight of an object is actually —6— its gravitational attraction toward a celestial body. Therefore, the weight of an object depends on its location. For example, the weight of an object at the earth's surface is not the same —7— its weight on the moon —8— the masses and the diameters of Earth and moon are quite different. Objects actually weigh less on the moon than on Earth. That is why astronauts can carry such large masses on the moon's surface.

(d) The most important use of metallic copper is in the form of wire —1— bars in electrical conductors. It is —2— used in tubes and boilers —3— its property of heat conduction. Copper is one of the comparatively few metals, —4— are found in nature in its free state. Native copper is found mainly in the mines of Upper Michigan. It occurs elsewhere —5—, —6— the Michigan mines are the only ones —7— the ore is obtained in commercially viceble amounts. Native copper now being mined yields about 0.5 per cent copper. Copper ores have been found —8— yield as much as 40 per cent copper, —9— the average is around 2 per cent.

(e) Magma is the original source of most minerals. The magma —1— is chemically very reactive —2— its pressure, temperature, and composition of various minerals dissolves adjacent rocks through which it travels, —3— to new minerals. The constituent minerals, mostly rock-forming silicates —4— oxides, are deposited at various stages —5— the magma cools down during its passage. Minerals having nearly similar fusion points segregate and concentrate together —6— magmatic segregation. Important deposits of metallic oxides, —7— magnetite and ilmenite, and sulphides, such as pyrrhotite and chalcopyrite are formed in this way. Magmatic segregation may take place at different depths during the travel of the magma —8— at different temperatures. Most ferro-magnesium silicates and other oxides are formed great depths by magmatic segregation.

(f) Iron is practically never produced in a pure state, —1— it is difficult to make and is too expensive for most purposes. Furthermore, impure iron (steel) has desirable properties, especially —2— the specific impurity is carbon in carefully controlled amounts. The industrial production of impure iron is carried out on a massive scale in the well known blast furnace, —3— complicated high-temperature reactions occur involving iron ore, limestone, and carbon. The blast furnace is designed for continuous operation. Iron ore, limestone, and coke are added at the top; preheated air or oxygen is blown in at the bottom. —4— the molten iron forms, it trickles down to a pit at the bottom, from which it is periodically drawn off. All told, it takes about 12 hour for material to pass through the furnace. The actual chemical processes —5— occur in such a furnace are still obscure. It is generally agreed, however, that the active reducing agent is not carbon —6— carbon monoxide. —7— the charge settles through the furnace, the coke is oxidised by the incoming oxygen by the reaction 2C(s) + °2(g) —2CO(g) —8— forming the reducing agent CO and liberating large amounts of heat. —9— the carbon monoxide moves up the furnace, it encounters oxides of iron in various stages of reduction, depending on the temperature of the particular zone.

19.2.3 Length of Sentence

What should the standard length of a sentence be in technical writing? This question worries both students and professionals alike. Examine the first paragraph of this chapter. It consists of five sentences. The first sentence contains twenty words while the second one contains only thirteen words. On the other hand, the third sentence contains thirty-one words whereas the fourth and the fifth sentences include eleven and nineteen words respectively. What does this mean? Is any sentence length correct? Let us try to find out.

> The number of advocates of short sentences has been increasing because the growing complexity of technical information demands simplicity of language.

Although there is no hard and fast rule about the length of sentences in technical writing, there has been an increasing emphasis on writing 'short sentences'. Most language experts say that short sentences are better as they are readable. The number of advocates of short sentences has been increasing because the growing complexity of technical information demands simplicity of language. There is no doubt that long and clumsy sentences may be difficult to understand while shorter sentences are easier to understand. As it is always easier to understand facts in small bits, short sentences can communicate information more effectively.

However, the problem is that the terms 'short' and 'readable' are both relative and their interpretation may vary from person to person and profession to profession. What may appear to be a short and readable sentence to a professional researcher might seem to be a long and difficult sentence to a college student. Thus, sentences of various lengths may be used as per the needs of the writing assignment. The following suggestions may help in making appropriate decisions about the length of sentence while writing:

Use all Types of Sentences

The length of a sentence does not necessarily depend on the grammatical category of a sentence. For example, a simple sentence may be long and complicated while a complex or compound sentence can be short and simple. So, all types of sentences should be used (i.e., simple, complex, compound, and compound-complex) in order to bring variety to writing. Table 19.5 given examples of all types of sentences.

TABLE 19.5 Types of Sentences

Type	*Description*	*Examples*
Simple	a sentence with one main clause and no dependent clauses	• Liquids diffuse slowly. • The sun is the most direct source of energy. • We have to cancel our vacation due to a very urgent company seminar from January 17 to January 24.
Complex	a sentence with one main clause and one or more subordinate clauses	• When a drop of ink is carefully released in water, there is at first a rather sharp boundary between the ink cloud and the water.

(*Contd.*)

Compound	a sentence with two or more main clauses and no subordinate clauses	• We were to depart January 15 for Port Blair island and return to New Delhi on January 26. • The friction force always acts in the opposite direction to the motion, and it opposes any tendency of motion. • The sun powers the flow of wind and water cycles and sustains all life.
Compound-Complex	a sentence with two or more main clauses and one or more subordinate clauses	• The sun contains in its core hydrogen nuclei moving at very great speeds, and whenever these nuclei collide and fuse to form a nucleus of a heavier element, it results in nuclear reactions.

Adjust Sentence Lengths to Your Readers

Sentence lengths need to be adjusted according to the readers, who may vary from young students to seasoned professionals. It is quite possible that often a sentence that the writer thinks is 'short and readable' seems 'lengthy and difficult' to readers. Thus, a writer should anticipate his/her readers, their needs, and their level of language competence. Visualising one's readers will give a clear idea of the length of sentences that will be easy and comprehendible for them. The writer should be able to adapt to his/her readers, and create a message in a style that suits them.

> Sentence lengths need to be adjusted according to the readers, who may vary from young students to seasoned professionals.

> Simple ideas may be expressed in short sentences whereas expressing complex or sophisticated ideas may require comparatively longer sentences.

Adjust Sentence Lengths to Your Subject Matter

Apart from adjusting sentence lengths to suit one's readers, they should also suit the subject matter or the ideas that are being conveyed. Simple ideas may be expressed in short sentences whereas expressing complex or sophisticated ideas may require comparatively longer sentences. Thus, shorter sentences may be used in letters, memos, or e-mails as they convey simple ideas. However, comparatively longer sentences may be used in technical reports, proposals, or articles because they may contain complex scientific and technical information.

Adjust Sentence Lengths to the Demands of Style

Sentence lengths should also be adjusted to the demands of the writing style that the writer uses. A short sentence may be used as an effective opening or, for effective contrast, after a number of long sentences; while a long sentence may be used to bring a number of related thoughts together. Thus, if the style demands presentation of related details, long sentences may be used. However, short sentences may be preferred if the style of writing demands small divisions of thoughts.

> If the style demands presentation of related details, long sentences may be used. However, short sentences may be preferred if the style of writing demands small divisions of thoughts.

Progress Check 3

1. **Read the following two short paragraphs about a simple AC generator carefully and identify the grammatical category of each sentence in the paragraph:**

   The structure of a simple AC generator or alternator is simple. A closely wound coil is mounted in a magnetic field of a permanent magnet or an electromagnet so that it is free to rotate about an axis that is perpendicular to the magnetic lines of force. The coil is usually wound on a laminated iron core to increase the magnetic field.

   Circular metal conductors called slip rings are attached to the terminals of the coil, and graphite brushes make electrical contact as they slide over the slip rings. In operation, the coil is rotated by the application of mechanical energy, and the induced electric current is delivered through the slip rings and brushes to the external load. As the coil is rotated, its sides move in opposite directions through the magnetic field, but the induced currents combine in the coil itself.

19.2.4 Sentence Emphasis

Sentence emphasis refers to idiomatic stress in writing. It is essential to know how to place important words in the emphatic positions in a sentence in order to make your sentences effective. Effective writers never ignore the principles of sentence emphasis. Some of the techniques of sentence emphasis include placing the theme correctly, using parallel construction, and using correct subordination.

> Sentence emphasis refers to idiomatic stress in writing.

Placing the Sentence Theme

Every sentence has a theme or the main idea. The theme of the sentence can be expressed in a single word, a phrase or a clause depending on the nature and type of information. Some examples of themes (underlined) are given below.

> Techniques of sentence emphasis include placing the sentence theme correctly, and using parallel construction and correct subordination.

1. Acid rain causes water pollution.
2. Water pollution is caused by acid rain.
3. Plastics can be classified into two groups, according to their behaviour when heated.
4. The bevaviour of plastics when heated can be the basis of classifying them into two groups.
5. Iodine deficiency accounts for the largest number of mental retardation cases in India.
6. The largest number of mental retardation cases in India are the due to iodine deficiency.
7. Differences in the properties of liquids and gases result from the difference in their molecular structure.
8. The difference in the molecular structure of liquids and gases causes differences in their properties.

The theme has to be placed correctly in the sentence to have proper emphasis. If the main idea is not put in an important position in a sentence, the sentence may lack emphasis. Readers may be confused about the theme of the sentence and may not be able to understand its focus.

> If the main idea is not put in an important position in a sentence, the sentence may lack emphasis.

Parallel Construction

Parallel construction refers to the repetition of structure in a sentence. It is an important technique of sentence emphasis. It also improves the readability of a sentence. Once parallel construction is used, it should be maintained throughout. Single words, phrases, or subordinate clauses may be used in a series in parallel construction. The following are some examples:

> Parallel construction refers to the repetition of structure in a sentence.

Single Words in Parallel Construction

- The salary, perks, and posting of the job are excellent.
- The qualifications, experiences, and skills of the candidate were suitable for the job.
- Teaching, consultancy, and research are some of my important professional activities.

Phrases in Parallel Construction

- She is interested in the offer because of the good salary, reasonable perquisites, and comfortable posting.
- The selection committee recommended the candidate for selection on the basis of his high qualifications, relevant experiences, and appropriate skills.
- Teaching electronics to undergraduate and post-graduate technical students, providing consultancy to corporate sector, and doing research in microelectronics are some of my important professional activities.

Subordinate Clauses in Parallel Construction

- She is interested in the offer because the salary is good, the perks are reasonable, and the posting is comfortable.
- The selection committee recommended the candidate for selection because he has high qualifications, he has relevant experiences, and he has appropriate skills.
- I teach electronics to undergraduate and post-graduate technical students, I provide consultancy to the corporate sector, and I do research in microelectronics.

Correct Subordination

The principle idea should be placed in the main clause of the sentence while the subordinate ideas may be put in dependent clauses. The sentence will lack emphasis if the principle idea is placed in the subordinate clauses. Table 19.6 gives some examples.

> The principle idea should be placed in the main clause of the sentence while the subordinate ideas may be put in dependent clauses.

TABLE 19.6 Correct Subordination Examples

Incorrect Emphasis	*Improved*
The ozone (O_3) layer of the atmosphere absorbs most of the deleterious ultraviolet rays from the sun as it protects living organisms from extinction.	The ozone (O_3) layer of the atmosphere protects living organisms from extinction as it absorbs most of the deleterious ultraviolet rays from the sun.

(Contd.)

Although he is eager to change and join the new company, he is getting better salary and perks in the present position.	Although he is getting a better salary and perks in the present position, he is eager to change and join the new company.
The chairman used his authority when he controlled the misuse of company funds by the officials.	Using his authority, the chairman controlled the misuse of company funds by the officials.

Progress Check 4

1. **Revise each of the following sentences and correct parallel construction or incorrect subordination to make appropriate emphasis:**
   (a) The candidate that they selected for the post of manager was both qualified and he was experienced.
   (b) Although he wants to marry the girl, she is neither beautiful nor rich.
   (c) The article that he submitted for publication was both accurate and it was readable.
   (d) As she cannot understand and articulate key opportunities for maximising profitability, she does not have good communication and presentation skills.
   (e) The building is not only old and damaged, but also very costly to buy.
   (f) The police officer used his intelligence and common sense when he caught the criminal who was trying to escape after committing the crime.
   (g) With strong consulting, communication and interpersonal skills and being competent in working in cross-functional teams, I have been able live upto commitments with a sense of urgency.
   (h) Developing market strategies and programme to address key issues, to analyse the market, to identify opportunities, and developing marketing plans for introducing new products are some of my key duties as a product specialist at Pfizer Limited.
   (i) As he will be able to set and achieve stretch targets in a highly competitive marketplace, he has excellent client relationship and management skills and an ability to relate and interface easily at the top executive levels.
   (j) The memory section of a micro-computer may have magnetic floppy disks, magnetic hard disks, or it has optical disks.

Exercise

1. **Write brief notes on the following:**
   (a) Sentence structure
   (b) Grammatical types of sentences
   (c) Sentence coherence
   (d) Sentence emphasis
   (e) Sentence lengths in technical writing
2. **Improve the following sentences:**
   (a) If a change is made in any of the factors influencing a system at equilibrium. The reaction will occur in the direction that tends to undo the change made.
   (b) Boron is the first member of group 13 of the Periodic Table is the only non-metal of this group.

(c) When an organic compound is present in an aqueous medium, it is separated by shaking it with an organic solvent. In which it is more soluble than in water.
(d) Supporting software applications, analysing new systems requirements, and to manage projects within Flight Operations Department are some of the functions associated with her present position.
(e) I work in a multi-culture team environment at Air Deccan, and it has sharpened my cross-cultural and professional interaction skills.
(f) As the candidate would like to put his professional and academic experience to work for Air Sahara, working in a fast growing airline with an expanding route network has been one of his main career objectives.
(g) The solid mixture containing the compound is taken in a porous tube A fitted with a thick filter paper the solvent is taken in flask B.
(h) When the level of the liquid in tube A reaches up to the top in tube C. It gets siphoned and is collected in the flask which is being heated continuously.

Key to Progress Check

Progress Check 1

1. (a) Although all metals react with oxygen yet their reactivity is different.
   (b) Besides the earth's crust, there is a possibility that the centre of the earth may be iron.
   (c) Metals are malleable, and they can be hammered into very thin sheets.
   (d) A thermometer consists of a capillary tube, which is sealed at one end.
   (e) Our company is interested in buying sixty scanners for our corporate office, and we would be glad if you could send us more information about the product.
   (f) As the name implies, micro-computers are small computers.
   (g) One distinguishing feature of the micro-computer is that the CPU is usually a single integrated circuit called a microprocessor.
   (h) I am writing to request a refund of my deposit on three round trip air tickets from New Delhi to Port Blair.
2. (a) When a car speeds up, we say that <u>it accelerates</u>.
   (b) Microcomputers <u>range from small controllers</u> that work directly with 4-bit words to larger units that work directly with 32-bit words.
   (c) When I came to the conference hall, <u>the delegates still had not come</u>.
   (d) Newtons's second law of motion can be applied to situations where the <u>acceleration is zero.</u>
   (e) The information that <u>has been entered</u> by the user using input devices can be viewed on the VDU of a computer.
   (f) When you <u>write a computer programme</u>, what you are really doing is writing a sequential list of instructions for the computer.
   (g) When an organic compound is present in an aqueous medium, it <u>is separated</u> by shaking it with an organic solvent in which it is more soluble than in water.
   (h) If the organic compound is less soluble in the organic solvent, a very large quantity of solvent <u>would be required</u> to extract even a very small quantity of the compound.

(i) Any device connected on the data bus must have three-state outputs so that its outputs can be disabled when it is not being used to put data on the bus.

(j) Metallurgy involves three main stages: concentration of ore, extraction of crude metal from the concentrated ore, and refining the crude metal.

Progress Check 2

1. (a) when, if, that, and, as, which, as, so that, until, and
   (b) like, although, and, where, results in, therefore, thus, resulting in
   (c) that, or, due to, that, and, due to, as, because
   (d) and, also, because of, which, also, but, where, which, but
   (e) which, due to, giving rise, and, as, resulting in, such as, and
   (f) since, when, in which, as, which, but, as, thus, as

Progress Check 3

1. Simple
2. Complex
3. Simple
4. Compound-Complex
5. Compound
6. Compound-Complex

Progress Check 4

1. (a) The candidate that they selected for the post of manager was both qualified and experienced.
   (b) Although the girl is neither beautiful nor rich, he wants to marry her.
   (c) The article that he submitted for publication was both accurate and readable.
   (d) As she does not have good communication and presentation skills, she cannot understand and articulate key opportunities for maximising profitability.
   (e) The building is not only old and damaged, but also very costly.
   (f) Using his intelligence and common sense, the police officer caught the criminal who was trying to escape after committing the crime.
   (g) With strong consulting, communication and interpersonal skills and an ability to work in cross-functional teams, I have been able live upto commitments with a sense of urgency.
   (h) Developing market strategies and programme to address key issues, analysing the market to identify opportunities, and developing marketing plans to introduce new products are some of my key duties as a product specialist at Pfizer Limited.
   (i) As he has excellent client relationship and management skills and an ability to relate and interface easily at the top executive levels, he will be able to set and achieve stretch targets in highly competitive marketplace.
   (j) The memory section of a micro-computer may have magnetic floppy disks, magnetic hard disks, or optical disks.

CHAPTER 20

Paragraph Writing

Developing the ability to write effective paragraphs is essential because all technical documents contain a series of related paragraphs.

LEARNING OBJECTIVES

- Understanding paragraph structure
- Knowing the principles of paragraph writing
- Learning how to adjust paragraph lengths to your readers, to your content, and to the considerations of variety and emphasis
- Understanding the concept of unity in a paragraph and discuss how to write and develop topic sentences
- Knowing how to connect ideas logically within a paragraph
- Understanding the logical development of a paragraph

20.1 INTRODUCTION

A paragraph can be defined as a distinct section of a piece of writing. It consists of several related sentences and deals with one controlling idea. This controlling idea is called the topic or the theme of the paragraph. The main function of a paragraph is to develop, support, exemplify, or explain this theme.

> A paragraph can be defined as a distinct section of a piece of writing that deals with one controlling idea.

20.2 PARAGRAPH STRUCTURE

Read the following paragraph and examine its structure:

"*There are many important characteristics of compounds having ionic bonds. An ionic compound is a collection of an equal number of positive and negative ions arranged in a three-dimensional lattice. Ionic compounds can be dissociated into their constituent ions with little effort. Further, they can be electrolysed to produce elements or covalent molecules of the constituent atoms. NaCL upon melting or upon dissolving in water produces Na+ and CL– ions. Electrolysis of molten NaCL gives Na and CL_2. Water also weakens the attraction between the ions in an ionic compound. This is why many ionic compounds dissolve well in water. Moreover, ionic compounds can conduct electricity. Most ionic compounds are made of metals.*"

As is evident, the theme of the above paragraph is "there are several characteristics of ionic compounds". Each sentence of the paragraph helps to develop and support this theme. Table 20.1 explains the 'structure' of this paragraph.

TABLE 20.1 Example of a Structure of a Paragraph

Theme	*Supporting Details*	*Examples*
Characteristics of ionic compounds.	• An ionic compound is a collection of an equal number of positive and negative ions arranged in a three-dimensional lattice. • Ionic compounds can be dissociated into their constituent ions. • Ionic compounds can be electrolysed to produce elements or covalent molecules. • Ionic compounds can conduct electricity. • Water weakens the attraction between the ions in an ionic compound. • Most ionic compounds are made of metals.	• NaCL upon melting or upon dissolving in water produces Na+ and CL^- ions. • Electrolysis of molten NaCL gives Na and CL_2.

Thus, in technical and professional writing, a paragraph may consist of the following three kinds of sentences:

(a) **Main sentence**, which expresses the main idea of the paragraph.

(b) **Major supporting sentences**, which expand, illustrate, explain, support, or strengthen the main idea with secondary points and major supporting details.

(c) **Minor supporting sentences**, which further exemplify and support the main idea with minor points, minor supporting details.

These sentences may be arranged logically by taking care of the proper distribution of emphasis in a paragraph. It is important that the space devoted to each sentence should be in proportion to the importance of the idea it expresses. While phrasing sentences, appropriate keywords or lexical items, markers of cohesion, and linkers should be chosen.

It is important that the space devoted to each sentence should be in proportion to the importance of the idea it expresses.

20.3 PRINCIPLES OF PARAGRAPH WRITING

It is essential to develop the ability to write effective paragraphs as all longer pieces of technical composition contain a series of related paragraphs. In longer pieces of writing such as reports and proposals, paragraphs help to develop the core idea of the document. In fact, writing any technical message involves writing paragraphs. As the writing needs to be purposeful, precise and reader oriented, it is important to compose paragraphs that are clear, cohesive, concise, and result-oriented.

Writing an effective paragraph involves adopting a careful writing plan that ensures proper length, unity, coherence, and logical development of ideas.

Paragraph writing is a significant productive skill, integrating both composing and organising skills. In order to write an effective paragraph, a careful writing plan should be adopted to ensure proper length, unity, coherence, logical development, and organisation of ideas.

20.3.1 Paragraph Length

There is no definite rule about the length of paragraphs. The length of a paragraph may vary according to the nature and type of document. A paragraph may consist of one or two sentences, or may include more than ten sentences. Some examples are given here:

Paragraph 1

Thank you for submitting specifications and a cost estimate for the Pentium 4 HP Laptop. Your references and list of companies where you have supplied the system are quite impressive.

Paragraphs of various lengths may be used as per the needs of the writing assignment.

Paragraph 2

Distributed processing seems to be the best way to go about computerising our electronics factory. Engineers can have personal computers or engineering workstations on their desks. With these, they can use available programmes to design and test circuits. They can access the large computer if they need data from its memory. Through the telephone lines, the engineer with a personal computer can access data in the memory of other computers all over the world. The draughtsman people can have personal computers for simple work, or large computer-aided design systems for more complex work. Completed work can be stored in the memory of the large computer. The production department can have networked computers to keep track of product flow and to control the machines that actually mount components on circuit boards, and so on. The accounting department can use personal computers with spreadsheet programmes to work with financial data stored in the memory of the large computer. The warehouse supervisor can, likewise, use a personal computer with an inventory programme to keep personal records, and those in the large computer's memory, updated. Corporate officers can have personal computers tied to the network. They then can interact with any of the other systems on the network. Salespeople can have portable personal computers that they can carry with them in the field. They can communicate with the main computer over the telephone lines using a modem. Secretaries doing word processing can use individual word processing units or personal computers. Users can also send messages to one another over the network. The specifics of a computer system such as this will obviously depend on the needs of the individual company for which the system is designed.

The first paragraph, which has been taken from a business letter, consists of only two sentences and contains twenty nine words. In contrast, the second paragraph, which has been taken from a technical textbook on computer science, consists of seventeen sentences and contains two hundred and eighty one words. Both the paragraphs are appropriate so far the length is concerned.

Therefore, paragraphs of various lengths may be used as per the needs of the writing assignment. The following suggestions might help in making decisions about appropriate paragraph length while writing:

Adjust Paragraph Length to Readers

The reader is a very important element in technical and professional writing because they have to read, understand, and respond to the piece of writing. A writer does not write for himself/herself, he writes for the readers. It is, therefore, important that he/she adjusts paragraph lengths for his/her readers. If he/she does not expect his/her readers to grasp too much at one time, he/she may write short paragraphs dividing the subject into small manageable parts for easy understanding. However, when the readers are professionals and can read and understand longer pieces of information comfortably, comparatively longer paragraphs may be written. However, one should avoid very lengthy and clumsy paragraphs for any group of readers because they make difficult reading even for competent readers.

> One should avoid very lengthy and clumsy paragraphs for any group of readers because they make difficult reading even for competent readers.

Adjust Paragraph Lengths to Subject Matter

Most subjects have natural logical divisions that cannot be ignored while writing about them. As a paragraph marks a logical division of a thought, logical demands of the subject matter have to be followed. A thought in the middle cannot be broken and an incomplete thought cannot be presented in a paragraph just to make it short. In order to do justice to the content, paragraph lengths have to be adjusted to the subject matter or the information that is being conveyed. A complex subject should not be broken into small segments that are difficult for readers to perceive as a whole. Similarly, several unrelated thoughts should not be combined into a paragraph, this will confuse readers about the logical relationships within the paragraph.

> As a paragraph marks a logical division of a thought, logical demands of the subject matter have to be followed.

Adjust Paragraph Lengths to the Demands of Variety and Emphasis

Your natural adjustment of paragraph lengths should be made to ensure variety and emphasis. An important aspect in achieving effective paragraph length is to ensure avoiding monotony. Using paragraphs of the same length might make the writing very monotonous. A short paragraph may be used for effective contrast after a number of long paragraphs or a long paragraph after several short paragraphs.

> An important aspect in achieving effective paragraph length is to ensure avoiding monotony.

Progress Check 1

1. Read the following paragraph, and rewrite as two short paragraphs.

When we live in the environment and use the environmental resources, knowingly or unknowingly we put pressure on the environment. This pressure may lead to environmental problems if it exceeds a certain limit. The limit is of natural repair or replacement. For example, we use groundwater. If we use it with prudence, it will continue to serve us indefinitely as nature has an inherent capacity to replenish. If we exploit this resource beyond its limit of replenishment, we may lose it forever. The same is true of any other environmental resource. Environmental resources are those that are present in our environment and which we use in our day-to-day life. These resources are both renewable and non-renewable. Renewable resources are those that are automatically renewed through natural processes and, hence, they may be considered to be available indefinitely. Non-renewable resources are those that are present in limited quantities and, hence, if these are consumed injudiciously, we may not find them again. Obviously non-renewable resources are more prone to depletion.

20.3.2 Unity

Unity of Thought

Unity is the principle of oneness. Unity in communication means that the components, as well as the whole, deal with one main idea, thought, or thesis. Any writing, which does not have unity, distracts the reader and ceases to be purposeful. An important way of ensuring unity is to make sure that the composition is about a single theme. This enables the writer to examine an aspect of a topic in some detail. In fact, focusing on a single aspect of the topic helps the writer unfold the theme logically. Thus, any effective and purposeful composition should have one controlling idea or theme.

A paragraph is a logical division of the central theme of a longer piece of writing. As a unit that marks divisions of thought, a paragraph deals with one aspect of the central theme of the document and no paragraph should be allowed to lead the reader away from the controlling idea. That is, each paragraph should strengthen the main idea by contributing only to that aspect of the topic.

> A paragraph deals with one aspect of the central theme of the document and no paragraph should be allowed to lead the reader away from the controlling idea.

Thus, a paragraph develops a single idea related to the central theme. Each sentence in the paragraph is directly related to that idea and contributes to its development. In order to maintain the unity of a paragraph, only 'one main thought' should be expressed in a paragraph. The related ideas should be subordinated. There should be no digression and the main idea of the paragraph should not be sidelined or forgotten.

Topic Sentence

The 'main idea' or the 'theme' of a paragraph is sometimes expressed by one sentence called a 'topic sentence'. As discussed in an earlier chapter, a topic sentence states the gist of the idea to be developed in the paragraph. The other sentences of the paragraph develop, support, exemplify, and explain the central theme.

The topic sentence may be placed either in the beginning or at the end of a paragraph, depending on the logical organisation of the paragraph. If general to specific or deductive logical order is used, the topic sentence should be placed at the beginning. However, if specific to general or inductive logical order is used, the topic sentence may be placed at the end of the paragraph. Sometimes a topic sentence may not be included and the main idea is expressed through details only.

As the topic sentence plays a significant role in paragraph structure, it is advisable that it is phrased with utmost care and includes all the relevant information in it. The topic sentence should introduce the paragraph and give the reader a clear idea about the content of the paragraph. The topic sentence should summarise the paragraph. It may be written in the form of a simple, complex, or compound sentence, depending on the need and scope of the paragraph. In order to write an appropriate topic sentence, the writer should concentrate on the theme of the paragraph. Let us see an example. The following paragraph does not contain a topic sentence:

> The topic sentence should introduce the paragraph and give the reader a clear idea about the content of the paragraph.

"In fuel cells, the intermediate steps of conversion of chemical energy to heat followed by conversion of heat to mechanical work are completely eliminated. High temperatures generated because of combustion of fuels, and subsequent processes found in almost all indirect energy conversion devices are non-existent in fuel cells. In these electrochemical devices, the chemical energy of the fuel is directly converted into low voltage direct current electrical energy. Because energy conversion can be carried out isothermally, the fuel cell efficiency is not subject to the limitations of Carnot efficiency. In addition, since it is possible to bypass the processes of conversion of chemical energy to heat, and that of heat to mechanical energy in a fuel cell, its efficiency is very high."

The theme of the above paragraph is the **direct nature of energy conversion in fuel cells**. So the topic sentence must present this fact. Let us study the following suggested topic sentences for the paragraph:

1. Fuel cells are direct energy conversion devices.
2. A fuel cell is not an indirect energy conversion device.
3. Fuel cells convert the energy stored in the chemical bonds of fuels directly into electrical power.
4. Fuel cells are direct energy conversion devices, which convert the energy stored in the chemical bonds of fuels directly into electrical power.

As is evident, sentence number 1 is too general to be the topic sentence of the paragraph while the second sentence is indirect and inappropriate. Sentence 3 could be used as the topic sentence but the fourth sentence seems to be the most appropriate topic sentence for the paragraph.

Progress Check 2

1. Read the following paragraphs and write an appropriate topic sentence for each one of them:

(a) The lightest fraction of crude oil consists of gases that boil below atmospheric temperature. The next fraction, normally refined into gasoline, boils between about 30 degrees and 200 degrees Centigrade. The fraction boiling between about 140 degrees and 320 degrees Centigrade is termed kerosene. The fraction boiling above about 320 degrees Centigrade is commonly refined into heating diesel, and lubricating oils. The remaining and heaviest fraction is the residue, which supplies waxes, asphalts, and some fuel oils.

(b) The attractive forces between the molecules of a solid are so large that a solid tends to retain its shape. This is not the case for a fluid, where the attractive forces between the molecules are smaller. There are plastic solids, which flow under proper circumstances, and even metals may flow under high pressure. On the other hand, there are certain very viscous liquids that do not flow readily, and it is easy to confuse them with plastic solids. The distinction is that any fluid, no matter how viscous, will yield in time to the slightest stress. But a solid, no matter how plastic, requires a certain magnitude of stress to be exerted before it will flow.

(c) The image on the retina is not permanent but fades away after 1/20th of a second and overlaps the next image. This gives the impression of continuity. There is of course no film in the eye that records the images permanently as a photo film does. More importantly, the focal length of the eye lens is changed when its attached cilial muscles change their tension. When they are relaxed, the lens is thin and distant objects can be seen clearly. While looking at nearby-objects, the muscles compress the lens so as to the brain through the optic nerves. The brain interprets these signals as the sense of light.

(d) Dangerous pollutants such as ozone, aldehydes, and ketones are the result of a complex chain reaction caused by carbon monoxide, nitrogen oxides, and hydrocarbons emitted by motor vehicles. Moreover, the prolonged inhalation of carbon monoxide present in the toxic fumes reduces the carbon carrying capacity of blood, and may cause headache, sickness, and even death. Likewise, unburned fragments of hydrocarbons help to form smog and thicken the atmosphere with elements that may cause cancer.

20.3.3 Coherence

Coherence is very important in paragraph writing. In cohesive paragraphs, ideas are linked, and one idea logically leads to the next. As one word in a sentence naturally leads to another, one sentence in a paragraph leads to another. In order to achieve coherence in a paragraph, you need to use appropriate cohesive devices that may include covert linkers such as pronouns and overt transitional expressions such as sentence linkers and sequence words and phrases.

> In cohesive paragraphs, ideas are linked, and one idea logically leads to the next.

Pronouns

You may use common pronouns such as they, we, it or demonstrative pronouns such as this, that, these, and those in order to achieve coherence in a paragraph. In the following paragraph pronouns are used to maintain continuity:

The largest and most powerful computers are often called mainframes. Mainframe computers may fill an entire room. **They** are designed to work at a very high speed with large data words, typically 64 bits or greater, and **they** have massive amounts of memory. **They** are used for military defense control, for business data processing (in an insurance company, for example), and for creating computer graphics displays for science fiction movies. Examples of **this** type of computer are the IBM 4381, the Honeywell DPS8, and the Cray Y-MP/832. The fastest and most powerful of **these** computers are called supercomputers.

However, pronouns should be used carefully. The pronouns should used do not confuse the readers and they should naturally maintain continuity. It should, however, be noted that the demonstrative pronouns usually need a noun with them, for example, **this** type of computer, **these** computers.

Sentence Linkers

A sentence linker connects two sentences in a paragraph. It may consist of a single word or a phrase. The following paragraph demonstrates the use of sentence linkers (underlined):

Air pollution has been a major threat not only to the quality of environment but also to human health. **Moreover**, it was this reason that made scientists and policy makers think seriously about different ways to deal with the problem. **In fact**, during recent years scientists and policy makers have paid substantial attention to airborne substances that have the potential to threaten human health or environmental quality. There have been a large number of studies of these pollutants, which have provided enough evidence to show that these pollutants may cause serious problems for human beings. This has resulted in a better understanding of health hazards due to airborne substances and has led to the enactment of measures to control them. **For example**, there have been controls on emissions from automobiles and it has tried to control vehicular pollution. **Moreover**, controls on industries that burn gasoline, kerosene, or coal have noticeably improved the quality of the air. A growing effort is being devoted to isolation of industrial activities and waste dumps that can release complex chemicals into the air and water. **In addition**, a substantial and relatively effective regulatory structure is in place to control releases of radioactivity to the general environment.

The sentence linkers/transitional signals (moreover, in fact, for example, in addition) used in the above paragraph connect the phrases and sentences together and show the logical relation between them, thus, ensuring coherence, order and continuity of thought.

Table 20.2 gives a description of the most common sentence linkers and their functions.

TABLE 20.2 Most Common Sentence Linkers and their Functions

Sentence Linkers	*Function*
As an example, for example, as an illustration, for instance, in other words	Exemplifies
In addition, furthermore, moreover, likewise	Expresses addition or shows additive relation
At that time, at that very moment, at the very time, in the meantime, meanwhile, afterward	Indicates time relation
Thus, hence, therefore, as a result, it follows, consequently, accordingly, owing to, as a consequence, this results in, so	Indicates cause/result/effect
Similarly, also, likewise, too	Expresses comparison
On the other hand, in contrast, on the contrary, by comparison, however, nevertheless, conversely, in comparison	Expresses contrast
To conclude, in conclusion, in summary, to sum up, to summarise, in a nutshell	Indicates conclusion or expresses summary

Use of Sequence Words

The following words/phrases are generally used as sequence words: first, firstly, second, secondly, then, next, after that, now, later, finally, lastly, afterwards, following, and so on.

Following are some examples:

1. After I shut down the computer, I went to sleep.
2. First, take a form. Then, fill in the form and submit it to the chief manager of the bank.
3. Take a beaker half-filled with water and drop a piece of limestone (calcium carbonate) into it. You will not see any reaction. Now take another piece of limestone, hold it with a pair of tongs and heat it over a flame for 5–10 minutes. After it has cooled, drop it in water and observe. The water will have warmed up.
4. First, take about 200 gram of crushed ice in a glass beaker of 500 millilitre. Next, use a centigrade thermometer, dip it in the ice and measure the temperature. Using a spirit lamp, start heating the

ice on a constant and slow flame. Note the temperature every few minutes and plot the temperature against the time taken.

Progress Check 3

1. **Read the following paragraph and fill in the blanks with appropriate sentence linkers to complete it.**

   It is a well-known fact that when an object is dropped near the surface of the earth, it increases its speed as it falls. —1—, freely falling objects must be accelerated toward the center of the earth. By rolling balls down inclined planes, Galileo discovered that this acceleration, which is called the acceleration due to gravity, is the same for all bodies, independent of their mass. This may be illustrated by simultaneously dropping a book of many pages and single sheet of paper, made into a compact ball, from the same height; they both hit the ground at the same instant. —2—, the speed, density, and shape of the object may affect this result because of air resistance and buoyancy. —3—, objects falling freely may eventually reach a constant velocity called the terminal velocity. —4—, a parachutist does not accelerate continually. Once the parachute is open the drag of the air eventually balances the force of gravity and the acceleration becomes zero, producing a constant terminal velocity.

   The magnitude 9 of the acceleration due to gravity is approximately 9.81 rn/sec. or 32.2 ft/sec. at the surface of the earth. —5— the acceleration due to gravity changes with the distance from the centre of the earth, it is usually considered to be constant for small changes in height near the earth's surface. —6—, the equations of uniformly accelerated motion may be used for objects falling through distances, which are small compared with the radius of the earth.

2. **Read the following paragraphs and fill in the blanks with appropriate sequence words/ connectives:**

   (a) Take a torch, transparent glass sheet, cellophane sheets or paper of green, blue and red colours. —1—torch is lit behind these coloured sheets, these will produce green, blue, or red lights. —2—, produce green light and place a green coloured object in the path of light. The object appears green. —3—, produce red or blue light and illuminate the same green coloured object with it. It will appear black. Examine a red coloured object in green light, and —4— in blue light. Similarly, examine a blue coloured ojebt in red light and —5— in green light.

   (b) —1— you scan, place the item to be scanned face down on the scanner glass. —2—, click the start button in Windows and choose: Programs > HP PrecisionScan LT Software> HP PrecisionScan LT. —3—, click Start a New Scan. The HP scanner will scan the document and the scan will appear on the scanning software screen. Select from the drop-down list where you want to go. All supported programmes on your computer and your printer appear on the drop-down list. For a list of supported programmes, click the start button in Windows and choose: Programs > HP PrecisionScan LT Software> HP ScanJet Read me. Make any adjustment to the output type. Select text, black and white drawing, black and white photo, or colour photo. Make any optional adjustments to the selection borders. If you do not make any changes, the entire scan is selected. —4—, make any optional adjustments to the output size using inches, centimetres, pixels, or a percentage. —5—Finally, depending on what you selected in the second step, click to:

   - Send the scan to an application
   - Save the scan to a file
   - Print the scan to a printer

20.3.4 Developing a Paragraph

Unlike general communication, technical communication follows a linear logical pattern to organise information. As discussed above, a paragraph has a logical structure where the central theme contained in the topic sentence is expanded. As one word in a sentence leads to another word, one sentence in a paragraph leads to another. As a sentence cannot be meaningful without the correct arrangement of words, a paragraph cannot be meaningful without the correct arrangement of sentences. This organisation of sentences in a paragraph is determined by the nature of information and style of presentation.

The following example helps in understanding the relevance of logical arrangement and development of ideas in a paragraph with the help of an example. The following two paragraphs deal with the same theme.

Paragraph 1

In solids the molecular interactions are very strong. Molecular interactions lead to intermolecular attractive and repulsive forces. Thermal energy is the energy possessed by matter by virtue of its temperature and is also a measure of thermal motion or movement of molecules. In liquids the arrangement is in between these two extremes. In gases, the molecules have almost no molecular interaction and their thermal motions are manifested as random translatory movements of molecules. The molecules in solids have no translatory movement and only oscillate with respect to their equilibrium position.

Paragraph 2

Thermal energy is the energy possessed by matter by virtue of its temperature and is also a measure of thermal motion or movement of molecules. Molecular interactions lead to intermolecular attractive and repulsive forces. In gases, the molecules have almost no molecular interactions and their thermal motions are manifested as random translatory movements of molecules. In solids the molecular interactions are very strong. The molecules in solids have no translatory movement and only oscillate with respect to their equilibrium position. In liquids the arrangement is between these two extremes.

> A paragraph may be developed by employing an appropriate logica pattern, depending on the theme of the paragraph and the nature of information that it contains.

It is evident that paragraph 1 is difficult to understand because sentences are not organised logically while paragraph 2 is easy to understand as it is logically structured.

A paragraph may be developed by employing an appropriate logical pattern, depending on the theme of the paragraph and the nature of information that it contains.

Read the following paragraph and note the way it is developed:

Crude oil is a mixture of different compounds that boil at different temperatures. The lightest fraction consists of gases that boil below atmospheric temperature. The next fraction, normally refined into gasoline, boils between about 30 degrees and 200 degrees centigrade. The fraction boiling between about 140 degrees and 320 degrees centigrade is termed kerosene. The fraction boiling above about 320 degrees centigrade is commonly refined into heating, diesel, and lubricating oils. The remaining and heaviest fraction is the residue, which supplies waxes, asphalts, and some fuel oils.

There are six sentences in this paragraph. The first sentence presents the main idea of the paragraph, i.e., the definition of crude oil followed by the expansion of the definition with more specific information like the boiling range of different fractions of crude oil. This is deductive logical ordering. Deduction is the act of drawing particular facts from a general statement or principle.

You may recollect that we have already discussed the techniques of logical organisation in detail in *Organisation in Technical Communication.*

Exercise

1. **Read the following paragraph and fill in the blanks with appropriate sentence linkers and/or sequence words:**
   As the name implies, micro-computers are small computers. –1–, they range from small controllers that work directly with 4-bit words and can address a few thousand bytes of memory to larger units that work directly with 32-bit words and can address billions of bytes of memory. Some of the more powerful micro-computers have all or most of the features of earlier minicomputers. –2–, it has become very hard to draw a sharp line between these two types. –3–, one distinguishing feature of a micro-computer is that the CPU is usually a single integrated circuit called a microprocessor. The microprocessor is the CPU to which you add ROM, RAM, and ports to make a micro-computer. –4–, older books often used the terms microprocessor and micro-computer interchangeably. Micro-computers are used in everything from smart sewing machines to computer-aided design systems. –5–, the Intel 8051 single-chip controller; the SDK-86, a single-board computer design kit; the IBM Personal Computer (PC); and the Apple Macintosh computer are all micro-computers.
2. **Read the paragraphs in Part A and analyse the topic sentences given in Part B in order to choose an appropriate topic sentence for each paragraph.**

Part A

(a) It includes all non-living and living objects, happenings and forces, both natural and man-made, which influence the life of an organism; the relationship of organism (including man) to the environment. The environment is a continuum extending from the medium (air or water) in which one lives to distant objects such as the sun or moon, and possibly even beyond. All aspects of this continuum influence an organism and *vice versa.*

(b) Some natural occurrences can create, alter, destroy an environment. Humans, through their understanding, can modify the environment but cannot change natural laws. It should be realised that man's present concern for the environment has not arisen merely from a romantic love for nature. Instead, it has grown from a wise realisation and concern for the survival of humans and other organisms.

(c) Every species of plant and animal that exists today is the result of millions of years of biological evolution. Thus, once a form of life is lost from the earth, it cannot be created again. These aspects have profound ethical implications in environmental education.

(d) It is necessary for the development and progress of humankind. But at the same time, they are conscious of scientific studies that suggest that too drastic a change, natural or man-made, is harmful. Present threats to the environment are the result of too rapid technological developments and the injudicious use of resources.

Part B

(a) Environmentalists recognise change as a universal process.

(b) The environment is a part and product of nature and is governed by natural laws and principles.

(c) The term environment in the present context does not mean merely 'surroundings'.
(d) All life forms, including human beings, are related to one another either closely or remotely through common ancestry.

3. **Develop the following ideas/themes into paragraphs. Use the themes as topic sentences of the paragraphs:**
   (a) All matter occupies space.
   (b) Air pollution is a health hazard.
   (c) Computers have revolutionised information technology.
   (d) Matter exists in solid, liquid, and gaseous states.
   (e) The new millennium has brought new challenges.
   (f) Petroleum is an important source of energy.
   (g) Controlling vehicular pollution is essential for the survival of mankind.
   (h) Digital computers are counting machines.
   (i) A telescope is an optical instrument used for magnifying distant objects.
   (j) Accidents in factories result from ignorance of safety regulations.

Key to Progress Check

Progress Check 1

1. When we live in the environment and use the environmental resources, knowingly or unknowingly we put pressure on the environment. This pressure may lead to environmental problems if it exceeds a certain limit. The limit is of natural repair or replacement. For example, we use groundwater. If we use it with prudence, it will continue to serve us indefinitely as nature has an inherent capacity to replenish. If we exploit this resource beyond its limit of replenishment, we may lose it forever. The same is true for any other environmental resource.

   Environmental resources are those that are present in our environment and which we use in our day-to-day life. These resources are renewable and non-renewable. Renewable resources are those that are automatically renewed through natural process and, hence, they may be considered to be available indefinitely. Non-renewable resources are those that are present in limited quantities and, hence, if these are consumed injudiciously, we may not find them again. Obviously non-renewable resources are more prone to depletion.

Progress Check 2

1. (a) Crude oil is a mixture of different compounds that boil at different temperatures.
   (b) The molecules of a solid are closer than those of a fluid.
   (c) There are important differences between our eye and a camera.
   (d) Vehicular pollution causes serious health problems.

Progress Check 3

1. Therefore, of course, as a result, for example, even though, therefore
2. (a) when, first, now, then
   (b) before, now, then, moreover, finally

SECTION 8

Professional Writing

CHAPTERS

21 CHAPTER

Letter Writing

Business correspondence is a link between people.

LEARNING OBJECTIVES

- Understanding the differences between personal and business letters and discuss the letter writing process
- Knowing the form and structure of business letters
- Learning to use appropriate style and tone in a business letter
- Identifying five characteristics of good business letters
- Knowing how to write inquiry letters requesting information or seeking clarifications and write replies to inquiry letters
- Knowing how to write letters placing orders
- Knowing how to write instruction letters
- Knowing how to write letters urging action
- Knowing how to write complaint and adjustment letters

21.1 IMPORTANCE OF LETTER WRITING

Business correspondence is an instrument of decision making in the business world.

Business correspondence is an instrument of decision making in the business world. Its significance has increased with growing changes in modern life. In fact, a letter is an important channel of communication used to send information outside an organisation. As it helps to reinforce professional and business relations, it is a positive instrument of professional exchange of ideas, opinions, and information. Everyday business dealings and the ordinary activities of business would not be possible without letters. These days, emails have replaced letters in many areas; however, letters still have their own significance.

Letters reinforce personal and business relations.

In order to succeed in today's competitive environment, we need effective letter writing skills because we may have to write different kinds of business letters, such as a letter to request for services or information, give information, request for action, give instructions or guidelines, express an opinion, reinforce business relations, maintain good public relations, or motivate and persuade people.

21.2 TYPES OF LETTERS

A personal letter is an informal letter in the form of a private dialogue.

A personal letter is an informal letter in the form of a private dialogue, where the writer wants to say something and expects a response to the message. It may follow the norms of private conversation but it normally does not follow any set pattern of writing and the writer is free to choose any style or pattern that suits his/her mood and content. Thus, personal letters are varied in their language, style, tone, presentation and content. Read the letters of Nehru, Ambedkar and Ghalib on the internet, and you will notice a personal touch in each of them, which make them different from each other.

A business letter is a formal written message, written in a conventional form for a specific audience to meet a specific need.

A business letter, on the other hand, is a formal written message, written in a conventional form for a specific audience to meet a specific need. It is also a form of dialogue, where the writer wants to say something and expects a response to the message. However, it is more structured as it follows a set pattern in form and style.

21.3 WRITING EFFECTIVE BUSINESS LETTERS

21.3.1 Process of Letter Writing

It is easier to write an effective business letter while following a systematic writing plan. Letter writing is a typical composition process that involves pre-writing, writing, and post-writing.

Pre-writing

Pre-writing involves **audience analysis, purpose identification, scope determination,** and an **analysis of the action desired**. The writer should bear in mind the keyword APSA i.e., Audience, Purpose, Scope, and Action. The process should begin with the writer asking himself/herself the following questions:

1. Who is/are my reader/s? (Audience analysis)
2. Why am I writing? (Purpose identification)
3. How much should I write? (Scope determination)
4. What do I want the readers to do? (An analysis of the action desired)

Letter writing involves three steps: pre-writing, writing and post-writing.

Once these four questions are answered, half the work is done and the wirter is ready to write. Now, he/she may do background research, collect relevant information, make a list of the points that he/she wants to cover, or organise his/her thoughts to help him/her write.

Writing

Writing involves organising the matter, outlining what needs to be written and writing the first draft. Several writing strategies may be used, which includes **brainstorming, freewriting**, and **mind mapping**.

- **Brainstorming** is a planning technique in which you list ideas as they come to your mind.
- **Freewriting** is a process that allows you to express your ideas without worrying about spelling, grammatical mistakes, or organizational problems.
- **Mind mapping** is a clustering technique that takes advantage of your mind's natural ability to organise information.

Post-writing

Once the first draft has been written, it should be revised, edited and evaluated. Revising is the process of improving the content, the layout, and the sentence structure of the letter while editing involves correcting its grammar, spelling, punctuation, format, and structure. Evaluating, on the other hand, refers to the process of critically examining the letter to ensure that it can achieve its purpose.

21.3.2 Form and Structure

While writing a business letter, attention must be paid to, both, the parts of a business letter and to the choice of format. As a letter with a poor and loose structure cannot get the attention that it may seek, correct format and standard writing conventions should be followed while designing the letter. In order to ensure clarity of presentation, the letter should be divided into sections and sub-sections, each with a clear purpose and place in the body of the letter.

Parts of a Business Letter

A business letter includes ten elements, namely, sender's address, date, reference, inside address, subject, salutation, body, complimentary close, signature, and enclosures. Figure 21.1 shows the structure of a business letter.

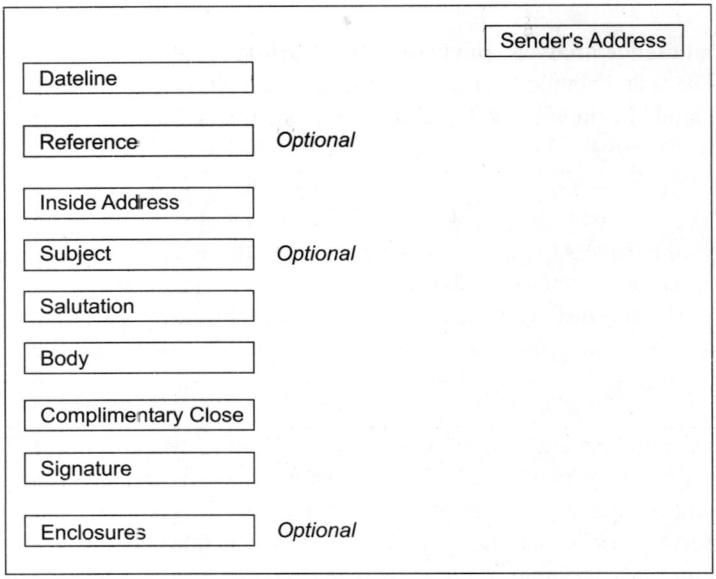

Fig. 21.1 Structure of a Business Letter

Sender's Address

The writer's address should be put in the top right hand corner. The street address, city and pin code, telephone, fax, and e-mail address should be mentioned. The writer should not include his/her name or title, as it is included in the letter's closing. If a printed letterhead is used, the address should not be written again.

> If a printed letterhead is used, the sender's address should not be written again.

Examples:

205 Barrackpore Trunk Road
Kolkata-700108

Nalco Bhawan
P-1 Nayapalli
Bhubaneshwar-750013

B-3/16, Janakpuri
New Delhi-110058

Date

The date line is used to indicate the date the letter was written. The month, day, and year should be written two inches from the top of the page.

Examples:

May 4, 2016

May 4, 2016

Reference

This is an optional element and may be placed below the dateline. The writer's reference number as well as the reference number of the recipient should be mentioned. (Your Reference/Our Reference).

Examples:

Reference: AVS/SP/04/329

Your Ref: AVS/SP/04/329 Our Ref: ATC/RS/127

Inside Address

The inside address is the receiver's address. Include a personal title such as Ms, Mrs, Mr, or Dr. The inside address begins one inch below the date. It should be left justified, no matter which format is used.

Examples:

Mr Nicholas Parker
Managing Director
Nicholas Parker UK Ltd
Royal Mint, Tower Bridge
London EC3N 4HJ, UK

Prof Pran Nath Pandit
Director, School of Humanities
Indira Gandhi National Open University
Maidan Garhi, New Delhi – 110068

The Executive Assistant
British Council
16 Camac Street, 1st Floor
Kolkata 700 017

Subject

This is also an optional element. It may be placed either before or below the salutation. The topic of the letter should be written in phrase form.

Examples:

SUBJECT: Purchase of Sixty Scanners

Dear Mr. Chopra,

Dear Mr. Chopra,

SUBJECT: Purchase of Sixty Scanners

Salutation

As salutation is a greeting used to address the receiver of the letter, it should be the same as that used in the inside address, including the personal title. Use the personal title and the surname should be followed by either a comma or a colon. Formal phrases such as "Dear Sir/Dear Madam/Dear Customer" may also be used if the name of the recipient is not known.

Examples:

Mr Nicholas Parker
Managing Director
Nicholas Parker UK Ltd
Royal Mint, Tower Bridge
London EC3N 4HJ, UK

Dear Mr Parker:

Prof Pran Nath Pandit
Director, School of Humanities
Indira Gandhi National Open University
Maidan Garhi, New Delhi – 110068
Dear Prof Pandit,

Ms Lara David
Personnel Manager
International Consultants Pvt. Ltd.
G-13/6, South Extension, Part-2
New Delhi – 110049
Dear Ms. David,

Body

As the body of a business letter contains the message of the letter, it must be organised carefully. It should be divided into three distinct parts, i.e., the opening segment, the middle segment, and the closing segment. In the first segment, which may consist of one or more than one paragraph, a friendly opening can be made and then a statement of the main point. The purpose of a business letter is generally found in the opening segment. The middle segment is the part in which all the details that support ideas are included as the main points. It may begin justifying the importance of the main point,

> The body of a letter contains an opening stating the main idea, a middle with details, and an action closing.

and the next few paragraphs may contain more information and supporting details. The closing segment of a letter usually restates the purpose of the letter and states what action the writer wants the reader to take.

Complimentary Close

The complimentary close begins one line after the last body paragraph. The first word should be capitalised and four lines should be left between the closing and the sender's name for a signature. The complimentary close can be very formal (Sincerely/Respectfully) or somewhat less formal (Yours sincerely/Yours truly/Best regards).

Signature

The signature contains the writer's name and title and, in some cases, the name of the organisation or company.

Enclosures

This is an optional element, which may be included in the letter. If any documents are enclosed along with the letter, they should be listed at the end of the letter.

Attention

Attention line is an optional element, which can be included when the letter is addressed to a company. The objective is to indicate the intended recipient of the letter. This line goes two lines below the recipient's address.

Attention: Human Resources Manager

Courtesy Copies

Courtesy copy is an optional element, which can be used when copies of the letter are being sent to more than one person. Each person's name is listed in alphabetical order, with each name being on a separate line. This element goes three lines below the last element of the letter.

cc: Abhinav Jain Sneha Gupta Yash Arora

Business Letter Formats

There are four popular styles of business letter formatting, namely, block, modified block, semi-block, and simplified. Although any of them may be used according to the writer's convenience and the need of the reader, consistency should be maintained and styles should not be mixed.

Block Format

Bussiness letter formats include block, modified block, semi-block, and simplified.

The block style shown in Fig. 21.2 is a popular letter format as it is very simple and easy to use. In this style all parts of a letter, that is, date line, inside address, salutation, body, and so on, begin at left. The paragraphs are not indented. It is better not to justify line endings for better readability. Fig. 21.2 illustrates block style formatting.

June 15, 2016

Mr D K Paul
Personnel Manager
Alpha Petrochemical Limited
621, Ahuja Chambers, Nariman Point
Mumbai-400 021

Dear Mr Paul:

It is with pleasure that I accept your offer of an Executive Trainee position at the production division of your company. I assure you that I will put all my skills and experience to work for APL.

As desired, I can join you by the end of September, 2016. I am grateful to you for giving me this opportunity to work with you. I look forward to meeting you in September.

Yours sincerely,

Sd/-*
Ravi Kapoor

*Sd/- refers to signature/signed by

Fig. 21.2 Block Format

Modified Block Format

The modified block style, shown in Fig. 21.3, is a modified version of the block style. In this style, the date line, the complimentary close, and the signature block begin at the centre of the page. The paragraphs are not indented and the line endings are unjustified. Study Fig. 21.3 to understand modified block style formatting.

June 15, 2016

Mr D K Paul
Personnel Manager
Alpha Petrochemical Limited
621, Ahuja Chambers, Nariman Point
Mumbai-400 021

Dear Mr Paul

It is with pleasure that I accept your offer of an Executive Trainee position at the production division of your company. I assure you that I will put all my skills and experience to work for APL.

As desired, I can join you by the end of September, 2016. I am grateful to you for giving me this opportunity to work with you. I look forward to meeting you in September.

Yours sincerely,
Sd/-
Ravi Kapoor

Fig. 21.3 Modified Block Format

Semi-Block Format

The semi-block style shown in Fig. 21.4 is similar to modified block format except that each paragraph is indented. The line endings are unjustified.

June 15, 2016

Mr D K Paul

Personnel Manager
Alpha Petrochemical Limited
621, Ahuja Chambers, Nariman Point
Mumbai-400 021

Dear Mr.Paul:

It is with pleasure that I accept your offer of an Executive Trainee position at the production division of your company. I assure you that I will put all my skills and experience to work for APL.

As desired, I can join you by the end of September, 2016. I am grateful to you for giving me this opportunity to work with you. I look forward to meeting you in September.

Yours sincerely,
Sd/-
Ravi Kapoor

Fig. 21.4 Semi-block Format

Simplified Format

The simplified format resembles the block style except that the salutation and complimentary close are omitted. It may also include a subject line in capital letters. This informal style of formatting is gaining popularity. Study Fig. 21.5.

June 15, 2016

Mr D K Paul

Personnel Manager
Alpha Petrochemical Limited
621, Ahuja Chambers, Nariman Point
Mumbai-400 021

ACCEPTING JOB OFFER

It is with pleasure that I accept your offer of an Executive Trainee position at the production division of your company. I assure you that I will put all my skills and experience to work for APL.

As desired, I can join you by the end of September, 2016. I am grateful to you for giving me this opportunity to work with you. I look forward to meeting you in September.

Ravi Kapoor

Fig. 21.5 Simplified Format

Progress Check 1

1. **Study the following layout of a business letter. The format is not correct. Rewrite the letter, making the needed changes in the structure and the format. You may use any of the four acceptable letter formats.**

May 16, 2016

31 C, Lake Temple Road
Kolkata-700 029

The Public Relations Manager
STCI LIMITED
Krishna Chambers, 59, Sir Vithaldas Thackersey Marg
New Marine Lanes, Mumbai-400 020

Dear Sir,
Please refer to your letter dated May 7 ...

Sincerely,

Sd/-
Avinash Goel

21.3.3 Style and Tone

> A good business letter can get you a job interview, get you off the hook, or get you money.
>
> **Malcolm Forbes**

A good business letter can increase your chances of acheiving whatever you want whereas a bad business letter may go unnoticed. What makes a letter effective? This can be understood by comparing the following two letters about the same topic. Read the direct request letter as shown in Fig. 21.6:

AVY TRADING CORPORATION

Court Lane, Civil Lines, Delhi
Web: www.avytrad.com
Phone: (011) 2547325
Fax: (011) 2547326
April 24, 2016

Mr Ravi Malhotra
Sales Manager, Reva Computers, Dealers in HP
Ajmer Road, Jaipur-302006

Dear Mr Malhotra,

We saw your advertisement in *The Times of India* about one of your important products. The advertisement caught our attention because we are interested in this product. In fact, we want to equip our corporate office with modern facilities and we would like to buy this product.

However, we cannot send the purchase order unless we know more about this product. Send us more information about the product as soon as possible. We want to know many things, which include product specification and special features of this model of the product, details of discount for bulk purchase, an estimate for the cost of the product, and details regarding terms of business and delivery dates.
Respond to this letter as early as possible.

Yours sincerely,

Rakesh Mathur
Purchase Manager

Fig. 21.6 Direct Request Letter

It is evident that this is not a good business letter for many reasons. First, it is not clearly written as the language used is not specific and concrete and the references are not clear. We do not know "which advertisement" or "what product" the writer is talking about. Second, the letter lacks courtesy and a tone of goodwill is missing. The tone is inappropriate and the attitude is negative. Look at the following sentences used in the letter:

(a) ... we cannot send the purchase order unless we know more about this product.

(b) Send us more information about the product as soon as possible.

(c) Respond to this letter as early as possible.

It seems the reader is under obligation to respond to the letter and to send the desired information. Finally, the letter is not concise. Now, read the following revised version of the letter (Fig. 21.7) which is more specific, precise and courteous:

AVY TRADING CORPORATION

Court Lane, Civil Lines, Delhi
Web: www.avytrad.com
Phone: (011) 2547325
Fax: (011) 2547326

April 24, 2016

Mr Ravi Malhotra
Sales Manager, Reva Computers, Dealers in HP
Ajmer Road, Jaipur-302006

Dear Mr Malhotra,

Please refer to your advertisement in the April 22, 2016 issue of *The Times of India* (New Delhi edition) about the HP ScanJet 3200C scanner.

Our company is interested in buying sixty scanners for our corporate office. We would be glad if you could send us more information about the product.

Specifically, we need the following information:

- product specification and special features of HP ScanJet 3200C model;
- details of discount for bulk purchase;
- an estimate for the cost of sixty units; and
- terms of business and delivery dates.

We look forward to hearing from you.

Sincerely,

Sd/-

Rakesh Mathur
Purchase Manager

Fig. 21.7 Revised Direct Request Letter

As is evident, this letter is clearer, more precise, and courteous. How is this achieved? Note that the second revised letter:

- Uses clear and specific words, expressions, and references

  Examples:

  (a) … your advertisement in the **<u>April 22, 2016 issue</u>** of The Times of India **<u>(New Delhi edition</u>**) about the **<u>HP ScanJet 3200C scanner</u>**.

  (b) Our company is interested in buying **<u>sixty scanners</u>** for our corporate office.

  (c) … product specification and special features of **<u>HP ScanJet 3200C model</u>**

  (d) an estimate for the cost of **<u>sixty units</u>**

- Uses polite, positive, and encouraging phrases

  Examples:

  (a) **<u>Please refer</u>** to your advertisement…

  (b) We **<u>would be glad</u>** if **<u>you could send</u>** us more information about the product.

- Emphasises the "You attitude" instead of the "We attitude" of the previous letter,

  Examples:

First letter (We attitude)	*Second letter (You attitude)*
We saw your advertisement… …we are interested in this product…	Please refer to your advertisement… …you could send us more information…

- Uses direct and concise language

  Examples:

First letter (Indirect language)	*Second letter (Concise and direct)*
The advertisement caught our attention because we are interested in this product. As a matter of fact, we want to equip our corporate office with modern facilities and we would like to buy this product.	Our company is interested in buying sixty scanners for its corporate office.

- Uses positive attitude

  Examples:

First letter (Negative attitude)	*Second letter (Positive attitude)*
…we cannot send the purchase order unless we know more about this product.	We would be glad if you could send us more information about the product.

- Closes with an expression of goodwill .

  Example:

First letter	*Second letter*
Respond to this letter as early as possible.	We look forward to hearing from you.

From the above examples it is clear that good business letters are characterised by appropriate style and tone. An effective style involves clear content, courtesy and consideration, conciseness, correct tone and correct attitude. In short, the five C's of business letters should always be remembered:

C—Clarity
C—Courtesy
C—Conciseness

C—Correct tone
C—Correct attitude

Clarity

A clearly written letter is one that is immediately understood by the reader. In order to be clear, simple, familiar and specific words and expressions and clear references should be used. Vague and unclear words and expressions should be avoided. It is important that the message is simple and clear so that the readers are able to understand and respond to it accordingly. In addition, short sentences and paragraphs should be used and the letter should separate ideas into paragraphs and guide the reader through the ideas with appropriate linkers and connectives. Table 21.1 shows how this can be done.

Five characteristics distinguish good business letters: clarity, courtesy, conciseness, correct tone, and correct attitude.

Simple, familiar and specific words and expressions and clear references should be used.

TABLE 21.1 Example of Clarity in Letter Writing

Original Version	*Revised Version*
Kindly be advised to make us aware of a few important points such as your service charges, methods of payment, concession schemes, and so on.	Please send us details regarding your service charges, methods of payment, concession schemes, and so on.
With reference to your inquiry last week, we would like to inform you that the information that you want can be sent within a week.	Thank you for your April 14, 2016 letter, asking about our 2005 training schedule. We would send you the schedule by April 28, 2016.
It may kindly be noted that there was a serious blunder in my last month's bank statement as there was a transfer of Rs 25,000 from my current account to my loan account, causing me much embarrassment due to the fact that several checks were bounced.	I would like to point out an error in my August bank statement. In July, the bank transferred Rs 25,000 from my current account to my loan account. As a result, several checks were bounced.
It may be requested that a refund of my deposit on the round trip air tickets bought last week from your firm is what we really need because we will neither be able to depart as scheduled for the island nor will be able to return as planned due to a very urgent company seminar during the same period.	I am writing to request a refund of my deposit on three round trip air tickets from New Delhi to Port Blair. We were to depart January 15, 2016 for the island and return to New Delhi on January 26, 2016. However, we have to cancel our vacation due to a very urgent company seminar from January 17, 2016 to January 24, 2016.

Courtesy

A good business letter must be courteous as the basic principle of business interaction is mutual understanding and respect. The letter must reflect courtesy and consideration, as the reader is under no obligation to do what the writer requests. Positive and encouraging phrases should be used and irritating phrases and expressions should be avoided. Moreover, it is important to try to build goodwill by using goodwill expressions that might help establish a long-term business relationship. Table 21.2 gives a few examples:

The letter must reflect courtesy and consideration, as the reader is under no obligation to do what the writer requests.

TABLE 21.2 Example of Courtesy in Letter Writing

Original version	*Revised version*
You must send the refund to me at the address below.	Please send the refund to me at the address below.
We want you to send us more information about your Executive Development courses.	We would be glad if you could send us more information about your Executive Development courses.
You have no other option but to talk to your accounts manager about the problem in my accounts.	Please talk to your accounts manager about the problem in my accounts. I look forward to hearing from you.
Please be advised that you are supposed to make the adjustment to my bill so that I can pay the other charges.	Please make the adjustment to my bill. I will be happy to pay the other charges. I appreciate your assistance in this matter.
You should not forget that I have been your customer for several years and always did business with you.	I have been your customer for over ten years and always enjoyed good business relations with you.
Under the circumstances it is your moral duty to see that we come to a satisfactory agreement on this matter.	In light of our long business association, I trust we can come to a satisfactory agreement on this matter.

Conciseness

Business letters should be concise and direct. The writer has to ensure that the letter makes its point in the fewest words possible. Unnecessary words, wordy expressions, empty words, wordy compound prepositions, repetitions, and redundancies must be avoided. In order to attain exact correspondence between the message and one's written expression, words should be used appropriately. Moreover, direct language should be used in order to avoid misunderstanding and confusion. Indirect expressions, rhetoric, ornamentation, or exaggeration should be avoided. Table 21.3 gives some examples:

> Unnecessary words, wordy expressions, empty words, wordy compound prepositions, repetitions, and redundancies must be avoided.

TABLE 21.3 Examples of Concise and Direct Text in Letter Writing

Original Version	*Revised Version*
It should be clear to everyone and there should be no doubt about the fact that the company would never be the one that encourages incompetence and lethargy. (28)	The company does not encourage incompetence and lethargy. (8)
I would like to express my gratitude to you for sending our consultancy fee. We have received your cheque No. 233632 dated 12 March 2016 for Rs. 75,000/- on April 15, 2016. (32)	Thank you for the cheque No. 233632 dated March 12, 2016 for Rs 75,000/- towards consultancy fee. (17)
I am very happy to inform you that the report on student involvement in academic decision-making completed for your research department is being sent to you along with this letter. (31)	Enclosed is the report on student involvement in academic decision-making, completed for your research department. (16)

(*Contd.*)

It was a great pleasure for us to know that you have started Oriental Credit and Finance services at Bangalore. As desired by you, we are pleased to send the items you request. (33)	We are delighted to hear that Oriental Credit and Finance Services are at Bangalore and are pleased to send the items you requested. (24)
We are happy to inform you that IDBI bank is a completely professional investment organisation as you will find a competent team of qualified and trained investment advisors who are waiting to guide and fulfill your investment needs. (38)	At IDBI bank, a team of qualified investment advisors is waiting to guide and fulfill your investment needs. (18)

Correct Tone

Tone in a business letter refers to the manner or mood of expression. It helps establish the relationship that the writer wishes to establish with the reader. A change of tone leads to a change in the emotional effect of an expression. For example, the sentence "Your application for the post of Assistant Manager has been received" will have a dull effect on the reader due its tactless tone while the revised statement "Thank you for your application for the post of Assistant Manager" will have a positive effect on the reader due to its tactful tone.

A change of tone leads to a change in the emotional effect of an expression.

It is important to use a tone appropriate to the situation in order to adapt one's expression to the demands of the situation and the needs of the readers. A tactless or negative tone can lead to misunderstanding, resulting in a negative response from the reader. Therefore, the tone should be formal, tactful, personal, and positive. Moreover, a conversational tone gives a personal touch to letters. Table 21.4 gives some examples.

The tone should be formal, tactful, personal, and positive.

TABLE 21.4 Example of Correct Tone in Letter Writing

Original Version	*Revised Version*
As we have given the job to another candidate, we cannot entertain your application.	Thank you for your application for a sales position in our company. However, the position has already been filled. Nevertheless, we have kept your resume for future use.
Send your consultant on Friday morning at 10.30 to discuss the training schedule for our company executives.	We would be glad if your consultant could meet us on Friday morning at 10.30 to discuss the training schedule for our company executives.
In light of the report of your current credit record, your application for a MSM credit account has been rejected. We are sorry to say that credit cannot be extended, at this time.	We genuinely appreciate your application of March 16, 2016 for an MSM credit account. After receiving a report of your current credit record, we find that credit cannot be extended at this time.
We need more time to complete the project report.	To complete the project report to the best of your satisfaction, please give us an extension of ten days.

Correct Attitude

Attitude in a business letter refers to the reflection of the opinion of the writer on the reader. Using the correct attitude involves proper understanding of the role of positive thinking in business interaction. The writer has to analyse the communicative context. The following guidelines can help in using correct attitude in business letters:

> The tone should be formal, tactful, personal, and positive.

- In order to establish goodwill and a long-term relationship with the reader, avoid a poor and negative language. This is more important in bad newsletters, rejections, refusals, denials and complaints.
- Tailor the letter to the needs of the reader.
- Use the "You attitude" instead of "I attitude" or "We attitude".

Table 21.5 gives some examples:

TABLE 21.5 Example of Correct Attitude in Letter Writing

Original Version	*Revised Version*
As you do not have a current account in our bank, we cannot process your request.	Please open a current account in our bank so that we are able to process your request.
As you have not given any attention to our request for a detailed report on your business activities, we will not be able to finalise the deal by the end of July 2016.	We would appreciate your immediate attention to our request for a detailed report on your business activities because we are planning to finalise the deal by the end of July 2016.
We will not be able to process your order because your business terms are too vague and are unacceptable to us.	Please send us your specific and clear business terms so that we can process your order.

Progress Check 2

1. **Read the following business letter and rewrite it making the needed changes in the language, style, tone, and attitude of the letter:**

> Dear Mr Chopra,
>
> I have gone through the letter sent by your office last week. Please be advised that our company can accept the offer to which the letter refers because it would be beneficial for our company in several ways. In fact, we have been looking for such innovative programmes for our junior executives for a long time but no training and consultancy company came forward with such a proposal. You are the first company to send us this interesting proposal.
>
> I have gone through the structure of the workshop and find it exhaustive and appropriate. However, the workshop may not be effective unless it includes some project work relating to some important areas of artificial intelligence. Moreover, our company may not be able to upgrade the knowledge level in this regard on a continuous basis unless project work is included.

(Contd.)

There is no doubt that you have worked hard to design the structure of the programme so that it is suited to our needs. Nevertheless, we would not be able to take any action unless we receive your final proposal. Send this positively by the end of May, 2016.

With regards,

Yours sincerely

(RS Prasad)

21.3.4 Types of Business Letters and Samples

Letters of Inquiry

Everyday business transaction consist of writing inquiry letters that request information or seek clarifications. We may need to write inquiry letters to individuals, firms, organisations, or institutions because we need some information. A letter of inquiry (Fig. 21.8) should be organised into three parts:

> Inquiry letters maintain a courteous tone, mention and explain the request clearly, and close with a goodwill expression.

Opening

The letter should open with a clear statement that tells the reader why the letter is being written. It is important to make the purpose of the letter clear in the very first paragraph. Questions or information needed should be listed in a clear and specific way.

Body

The body gives details that explain the request. The writer may tell the reader what he/she is working on, and why he/she needs the requested information. He/She may also provide necessary details that the reader needs to know in order to respond to the inquiry. If the request involves more than one question they should be listed.

Closing

The letter should be closed with a goodwill expression seeking an action-oriented response, and specifying the action that the reader is requested to take.

NATIONAL TOURS AND TRAVELS PVT LTD.
M-15/6, South Extension, New Delhi-110 049
www.nationaltours.com

May 18, 2016

Ms Savitha Kumar
Training Manager
Sarna Corporate Training Pvt. Ltd.
D-28/15, Ring Road, Delhi-110 052

Dear Ms Kumar:

Please provide information regarding training courses for field staff involved in aggressive selling of tour packages.

We presently have 24 sales trainees who need intensive training in sales and marketing skills. Kindly send us the following information to enable us to choose the right course for them:

1. List of the courses best suitable for our sales staff
2. Duration of each course
3. Course content
4. Fee structure

We would be glad if you could send us the information before May 25, 2016. We look forward to hearing from you.

Sincerely,

Sd/-
P R Mehta
General Manager

Fig. 21.8 Letter of Inquiry

Replies to Inquiry Letters

Two kinds of replies may be written to letters of inquiry, that is, letters giving the information asked for and letters of regret.

Letters Complying with Requests

A direct approach should be used in such letters. A positive response to an inquiry may be organized into three parts as shown in Fig. 21.9.

- **Opening:** Purpose of the letter.
- **Body:** The requested information and other relevant details.
- **Closing:** A goodwill expression.

Opening	⟶	Mention the purpose of the letter, telling the reader that the requested information is being provided.
Body	⟶	Give the requested information and other relevant details that the reader may be interested in.
Close	⟶	Close the letter with a goodwill expression.

Fig. 21.9 Positive Response To Inquiry

Now read the following sample letter in Fig. 21.10.

REVA COMPUTERS
Dealers in HP
Ajmer Road, Jaipur-302006

May 8, 2016

Rakesh Mathur
Purchase Manager
Avy Trading Corporation
Court Lane, Civil Lines, Delhi

Dear Mr. Mathur,

As you requested, we are sending you detailed information about the HP ScanJet 3200C model and our business terms, in the enclosed booklet.

We are the main dealers of HP scanners in North India and would be privileged to do business with reputed companies like yours. You could also visit our website www.revacomputer.com to receive more information about our company and a list of our customers.

We hope that the enclosed information will help you make your decision. Just send us an e-mail at info@revacomputer.com if you need any other information. We look forward to receiving a purchase order from you.

Sincerely,
Sd/-
Mr. Ravi Malhotra
Sales Manager

Fig. 21.10 Positive Response to Inquiry

Letters not Complying with Requests

An indirect plan should be used in such letters. Fig. 21.11 illustrates the three parts:

- **Opening:** Buffer statement
- **Body:** Explanation
- **Closing:** Goodwill expression.

Opening ⟶ A negative response letter should be opened with a buffer statement, which could be an expression of appreciation, a compliment, agreement, or understanding. The buffer statement will prepare the reader to receive the message without ill feeling.

Body ⟶ The reason for not being able to give the information asked for should be explained.

Closing ⟶ The letter should be closed with a goodwill expression.

Fig. 21.11 Negative Response to Inquiry

A sample negative response letter is presented in Fig. 21.12:

SF Consultants

906/845, Excel
Nariman Point, Mumbai-400 021

May 10, 2016

Ms Lily Thomas
26-B, Rana Pratap Marg
Lucknow

Dear Ms Thomas,

We appreciate your efforts to improve the professional knowledge and skills of your sales staff, and would be privileged to arrange training courses for reputed companies like yours.

We receive a large number of requests from big companies to organise training programmes for their sales staff. However, we conduct only ten sales training courses in a year. We have already finalised the list of the companies for whom we are going to conduct the courses during 2016-2017. Therefore, we are not in a position to give you the course details, and other related information for this year.

We thank you for your interest in our organisation and its training packages. If you wish, we would be glad to include your name in the list of companies for 2017-2018 training year.

With best wishes,

Yours sincerely,
Sd/-
S. Asfar Iqbal
Training Manager

Fig. 21.12 Negative Response to a Letter of Inquiry

Progress Check 3

1. **Rewrite the following inquiry letter by making the needed changes in its organisation:**

> 251, Park Street
> Kolkata-700 016
>
> June 16, 2016
> The Manager (Sales)
> Lexus Motors Ltd.
> 209, AJC Bose Road, Kolkata-700 017
>
> Dear Sir,
>
> I am a interested in buying the new Indica V2 from your company. However, I would like to take a car loan from HDFC bank through your company.
>
> We look forward to hearing from you.
>
> Please send me more information about car loans. Please refer to your advertisement in the June 14 issue of *The Times of India* about the new Indica V2.
>
> Sincerely,
>
> Sd/-
> Vikrant Vishal

Letters Placing Orders

A letter placing an order is a straight forward written message that orders supplies, services, or merchandise. To order items by letter, the direct pattern may be used, as shown in Fig. 21.13.

> ----------------------------------
> ----------------------------------
> ----------------------------------
> ----------------------------------
>
> Opening ⟶ The letter should begin by making it clear that it is a supply/purchase order.
>
> Body ⟶ The order items should be listed and specific data such as detailed description of the item/items, catalogue reference, quantity/number, price, insurance instructions, clear address, and such other information that might be necessary to execute the supply order should be included.
>
> Closing ⟶ The time-period for the delivery of the item/items must be mentioned and mode of payment must be stated. The letter should be closed with an expression of appreciation and goodwill.
>
> ----------------------------------
> ----------------------------------
> ----------------------------------

Fig. 21.13 Placing an Order

A sample order letter is given Fig. 21.14:

AVT TRADING CORPORATION

Court Lane, Civil Lines, Delhi

May 23, 2016

Mr Ravi Malhotra
Sales Manager
Reva Computers
Ajmer Road, Jaipur-302006

Dear Mr Malhotra,

Please send the following items on the business terms agreed upon:

Catalogue No.	Item Description	Quantity
128	HP Pavilion T2501 Desktop	05
236	HP ScanJet 3200C	05

We would be grateful if you could send the items duly insured. The insurance charges may be included in the bill.

We would appreciate receiving the items by June 15, 2016. As desired, we would make the payment by crossed bank draft two days after receiving the items.

Sincerely,

Sd/-
Rakesh Mathur
Purchase Manager

Fig. 21.14 Order Letter

Letters giving Instructions

Instruction letters specify the instructions with specific details, and focus on the required action.

A letter of instruction is a simple routine letter that consists of directions for the reader. A letter of instruction should be organised, as shown in Fig. 21.15, into three parts:

- **Opening:** Purpose and instruction/instructions
- **Body:** Details
- **Closing:** Focus on action and a courteous close

Opening	⟶	The letter should be opened with a clear statement of purpose followed by the instruction/instructions. If the letter includes several instructions, they could be numbered or the sequence of actions can be logically connected in instructions by using sequence words, that is, First, Second, Then, Next, After that, Later, Finally, and so on.
Body	⟶	The reader should be given necessary details regarding what action he/she should take.
Closing	⟶	Focusing on the required action, the letter should be closed with a courteous conclusion.

Fig. 21.15 Letter Giving Instructions

A sample instruction letter is given in Fig. 21.16:

April 21, 2016

Mr. Girjashankar
Chief Manager, State Bank of India
ISM Branch, Dhanbad

Dear Mr. Girjashankar:

I am writing to inform you that I have lost my cheque book number 233601. Please issue me a new cheque book. Also, please stop any payment against any cheque bearing the number 233601 to 233650.

I have signed the cheque requisition slip and handed over the same to my office peon. I am sending him to collect the cheque book. I would be obliged If you could give him the cheque book.

Thank you.

Sincerely,

A K Mishra
Dept of Mining Engineering
Indian School of Mines, Dhanbad

Fig. 21.16 Letter of Instruction

Letters Urging Action

Letters urging action open with an attention-catching statements, spellout what needs to be done, and motivate the reader to act.

Letters urging action are persuasive messages that urge the readers to do what the writer wants. Motivating someone to do what we want is not simple. It needs a tactful beginning, a reasonable approach and a well-presented argument. A tactful beginning can gain the reader's attention while a reasonable approach is required to convince the audience that a request/project/proposal is worthy. A well-presented argument is essential to motivate the reader to act. A letter urging action may be organised, as shown in Fig. 21.17, into three parts:

- **Opening:** Gains the reader's attention
- **Body:** Details that build the reader's interest and reduces resistance
- **Closing:** Motivates action

Opening ⟶ The letter should be opened with a brief statement that gains the reader's attention. It may be opened with a compliment, a question, a startling fact, a problem description, or a surprising statement. The purpose is to capture the attention of the reader.

Body ⟶ Related information should be given to build the interest of the reader and convince him/her that the request is reasonable. Direct and indirect reader benefits, specific details, statistics, and/or supporting examples may be included here.

Closing ⟶ The reader has to be motivated to act. The writer must be as specific as possible. The letter may be closed with a goodwill expression.

Fig. 21.17 A Letter Urging Action

The letter in Fig. 21.18 illustrates how the writer urges the audience to act:

SMART COUNSELLING SERVICES
C-26, Qutab Institutional Area, New Delhi-110016

April 16, 2016

S K Chatterjee
HR Consultant
Allen Management Consultants, Noida

Dear Mr Chatterjee,

Our organisation admires your consultancy's expertise in conducting training programmes in marketing management.

The success of your training programme in Export Management has revolutionised the very idea of corporate training. We are now organising our XIIIth Training Programme on 'Export Marketing' from 24th–28th May, 2016, at our office. I have been asked by the members of the Training Organising Committee to invite you to give a talk on "New Trencs in Export Marketing". By sharing your experiences with a big audience of enthusiastic marketing professionals, you can provide a new dimension to the whole programme.

We will offer you a standarc honorarium of Rs 5000 and the normal travelling expenses by air or train (AC I).

I am sending you the list of participants and other programme details. I am sure your presence will make the programme a great success. Please call me at 98xxxxxxxx by April 25, 2016 to give your approval so that we can make necessary arrangements.

Sincerely,

V S Sood

General Manager

Fig. 21.18 A Letter Urging Action

Progress Check 4

1. **Analyse the following order letter, and revise it making it more direct and effective:**

> July 4, 2016
>
> The Sales Manager
> PCS Industries Ltd.
> 113, Park Street
> Flat 2C, Poddar Point,
> Kolkata–16
>
> Dear Sir,
>
> We are opening a new branch of our company on July 10, 2016, and we would need six PCs for this branch. I was lucky to see your company's advertisement in the Times of India and was really impressed by your company's long IT experience, large service network, and effective after sales service. We are interested in your Orilion Silver Magic PC model. This model has a Pentium 4 and Processor 2.0 GHs with 43.1 centimetre colour monitor, 128 MB DDR RAM, and 40 GB HDD with 7200 RPM. The catalogue number of this product is PC/21. It costs Rs 23,400. However, there is an extra charge of Rs 2500 for freight, delivery and installation. As mentioned above we are interested in six PCs. We would also pay the extra charge for freight, delivery, and installation. The total amount for six PCs will be Rs 1,55,400. So, we are sending you a crossed cheque for Rs 1,55,400 drawn on State Bank of India.
>
> Please send us the above mentioned item as soon as possible.
>
> Best regards,
>
> Sincerely,
> P K Chakarvarthy

Complaint Letters

A complaint letter is an expression of dissatisfaction. The writer complains about something that went wrong, such as, a defective product, bad service, misbehaviour, mistaken billing, guarantee/warrantee problems, and so on. As anger can spoil a business message, complaint letters should not vent anger. They should be logical and persuasive based on solid facts and not on personal opinions or emotions.

> Complaint letters open with a clear problem statement, support the complaint with data, and close with an expression of goodwill.

As the basic objective of every complaint letter is to motivate change, persuasive language has to be used. The key elements in a complaint letter are (1) mentioning the purpose of the letter, (2) explaining what happened, (3) convincing the reader that your complaint is genuine, and (4) motivating the reader to act. A letter of complaint may be organised into three parts, as shown in Fig. 21.19.

Opening ⟶ The letter should be opened with a direct statement, which makes it clear that the writer is complaining to the reader about something.

Body ⟶ A direct, factual and plain explanation should be given along with relevant information supported by appropriate documents that convinces the reader that the complaint is genuine and the claim is legitimate. The tone of the letter should be polite but firm and not apologetic.

Closing ⟶ The writer should request the reader to take appropriate action and close the letter with an expression of goodwill.

Fig. 21.19 Parts of a Complaint Letter

The letter of complaint in Fig. 21.20 illustrates the organisation of ideas:

July 5, 2016

The General Manager
Dhanbad Telecom District
Bharat Sanchar Nigam Ltd.
Dhanbad

Dear Sir,

I would like to point out a billing error in my May, 2016 and July, 2016 telephone bills.

According to the May bill (see copy attached), I had to pay an arrear of Rs. 4391/-for January and March bills. As these bills were already paid in April 2016, I pointed out the error to the Accounts officer (TR), Dhanbad, and he assured me that the error would be corrected.

However, in my July bill (copy attached), the same arrear has appeared again. Moreover, my telephone number 2203821 has been disconnected because your computer claims that I have not paid the telephone bills for more than three months.

Please correct this error and instruct the concerned department to reconnect my telephone without any reconnection charge. I have enclosed the receipts for all the bills paid by me since April 2016. I would appreciate your cooperation in this matter.

Sincerely,

Dulal Chakarvarthy
14, Luby Circular Road
Dhanbad-826004

Fig. 21.20 Complaint Letter Illustrating the Organisation of Ideas

Adjustment Letters

An adjustment letter is an attempt to satisfy an aggrieved customer, who has the potential to damage the goodwill of the company in the market. In order to save the reputation of the company, the letter writer has to express clear understanding of the problem conveyed by the customer and offer reasonable solutions. The key elements in an adjustment letter are (1) appreciation and understanding, (2) apology and explanation, (3) investigation and action, and (4) expression of goodwill. An adjustment letter may be organized into three parts, as shown in Fig. 21.21.

> Adjustment letters open with an appreciation of the problem, explain the situation, promise positive action, and close with a statement of goodwill.

Opening ⟶ The letter should be opened with an appreciation of the problem and by thanking the customer for calling attention to the problem.

Body ⟶ Apology should be expressed for the inconvenience caused. A precise explanation should be given mentioning how the problem was caused along with relevant information that convinces the customer that the complaint has been understood and that a positive action will be taken to solve it. Results of the investigation into the complaint/claim should be described and reasonable settlement should be offered.

Closing ⟶ The letter should be closed with an expression of goodwill.

Fig. 21.21 Adjustment Letter

The following sample letter of complaint in Fig. 21.22 illustrates the organisation of ideas:

BHARAT SANCHAR NIGAM LTD.
Dhanbad Telecom District

July 12, 2016

Mr. Dulal Chakarvarthy
14, Luby Circular Road
Dhanbad-826004

Dear Mr. Chakarvarthy,

Thank you for your letter dated July 5, 2016 pointing out a billing error on your May, 2016 and July, 2016 telephone bills.

We are sorry for the inconvenience caused to you. I discussed the problem with our Accounts Officer, who informed me that our computer did not show your payment because you made the payment manually. As the list of manual payments reached the accounts department after the July bills had been finalised, your telephone was disconnected.

The errors have been corrected and you will receive the corrected bills within a week. In the meantime, your telephone line has been reconnected, and you do not have to pay any reconnection charge.

(Contd.)

Thank you for your cooperation.

Sincerely,

General Manager
Dhanbad Telecom District
Bharat Sanchar Nigam Ltd.
Dhanbad

Fig. 21.22 Adjustment Letter

Letters Calling for Quotations

The objective of a *Letter Calling* for a *Quotation* is to understand the terms of agreement and payment before actually entering into a monetary transaction.

A common practice in business transactions is to write a letter asking for the price of a service or a product from potential service providers or vendors. Such a letter is called a *Letter Calling for a Quotation* or *a Request for Quote Letter*. It is intended to understand the terms of agreement and payment before actually entering into a monetary transaction.

A letter calling for a quotation can be organised into three parts:

- **Opening:** Purpose of the letter.
- **Body:** The requested information along with other details.
- **Closing:** A goodwill expression.

National Tours and Travels Pvt. Ltd.
G-15, Lajpat Nagar, New Delhi- 110 050

May 08, 2016

Ms. Geeta Kumar
Store Manager
Divay Furniture
D-28/ 15, Ring Road, Delhi 110 052

Dear Ms. Kumar,

I am writing this letter requesting a price quotation for buying twenty computer chairs.

This is for our office, which is 3,000 square feet in size. We already have computer tables. Given your market specialisation in computer chairs, we would like to source the chairs from you. We would like to go in for a high-end model.

Please provide the following information:

- Model type
- Price per unit
- Applicable taxes
- Additional charges, if any
- Date by when you can deliver

(Contd.)

Kindly respond latest by May 20, 2016 as we have new employees joining immediately thereafter.

I would look forward to hearing from you.

Sincerely,

Sd/-
D R Saxena

General Manager

Fig. 21.23 Letter Calling for a Quotation

The format and guidelines for a response letter to a letter calling for a quotation, are the same as those for letters of inquiry, which were discussed earlier.

Tenders

When government organisations or financial institutions or other such big organisations invite bids from potential service providers for large projects, they usually follow a process called the tender process. This process has pre-defined deadlines.

Government organisations invite bids for large projects through the tender process.

The following is a sample advertisement inviting tenders by one such organisation.

Sealed tenders are invited from reputed contractors for repair work at Rose Apartments, Sec-14, Noida, for painting of the building and replacement of pipes. Last date for downloading tender documents from www.rsap.in is July 30, 2016.

Tender forms are usually very long in length, running over several pages. Therefore, a sample has not been included here. Students are recommended to search for some samples on the internet.

Exercise

1. **The following statements taken from business letters are wordy, indirect, imprecise, vague or discourteous. Rewrite them so as to make them more effective.**
   (a) It is with great pleasure that we acknowledge with thanks the receipt of your letter, which you sent on 20/6/2016 and we received on 06/06/2016.
   (b) We would like to make it very clear to you that our company has already done all it could to repair your PC and that we shall not be able to entertain any further communication in this regard from you, or from anyone on your behalf.
   (c) It is strange that you took four months to write to us about a billing error on your credit card statements. In view of this delay on your part it would not be possible for us to entertain your request of correcting the error within a week. You took four months to point out the error and we will take at least one month to correct the error.
   (d) I am sorry to tell you that I have had nothing but trouble with both my new Maruti Alto and your firm since I bought my new car from your firm in February 2016.

(e) I am directed to advise you that your arrangements for your journey to Singapore and back have been made. So, I would like to advise you that you should not at all feel anxious about this matter. You should just relax.

(f) We sincerely hope you will be good enough to permit us to inform you that we are not in a position to execute your order because we have yet not received your cheque as promised by you in our last meeting. Remember we will not send you your items unless we get the payment in full.

(g) This is to lodge a strong protest against the indifference of your company to my complaints about the defects in the air conditioner bought from your agency. At this point, I have just about given up on repairing the AC, and I am tired of writing to you. Unless you take prompt action to correct the AC's defects or refund the purchase price in full, I will be forced to go to the consumer's court.

(h) In response to your letter dated May 4, 2016, we are pleased to inform you that consequent to the receipt of your cheque for Rs. 51,990/- we are sending you your HP Pavilion t530i Desktop. As promised, we are also sending you several free gifts, which include a HP Digital Camera P5435, a Britannica Encyclopedia 2016 DVD, and Photo lab software.

(i) I am forced to write against the indifference of your bank to customer complaints. I would like to point out an error in my January bank statement that was supposed to be corrected but was not despite several reminders to your office.

(j) We are constrained to inform you that we would not be able to give you any discount this year. Although you have made an attempt to make out a case for claiming 20 per cent special discount on all supplies during this year, we are not convinced about what you say in support of your claim.

2. Read the following statements about different types of letters and tick Yes or No against each statement:

(a) An inquiry letter is a straightforward written message that asks someone for information.
Yes/No

(b) Letters placing order may not specify items or services, quantities, dates, prices, and payment method.
Yes/No

(c) The opening part of a negative response letter contains a buffer statement, which could be an expression of appreciation, compliment, agreement, or understanding.
Yes/No

(d) The buffer statement prepares the audience to receive a negative message without ill feeling.
Yes/No

(e) A letter of instruction is a persuasive letter that contains a sales message.
Yes/No

(f) Letters urging action are persuasive messages that urge the readers to do what the writer wants.
Yes/No

(g) A complaint letter seeks action-oriented response.
Yes/No

(h) A letter of adjustment begins with a clear statement of the problem or action requested.
Yes/No

3. Assume that you are Prateek Raj, a Fellow doing research in marketing management at Indian Institute of Mangaement, Ahmedabad. Write a letter to Ashok Ranjan, the Marketing Manager of Petronet LNG Limited, World Trade Centre, Babar Road, Barakhambha Lane, New Delhi-

110001. Request him to send you information about the company's marketing activities. Tell him that you need the information for market research purposes.

4. Assume that you are Ashok Ranjan, the Marketing Manager of Petronet LNG Limited, World Trade Centre, Babar Road, Barakhambha Lane, New Delhi-110001. You have received a letter of inquiry from Prateek Raj, a Fellow doing research in marketing management at Indian Institute of Mangaement, Ahmedabad. Mr. Raj has requested you to send information about the company's marketing activities. He needs the information for market research purposes. Write him a tactful reply politely saying that you are unable to send him the information because your company does not want to make its marketing activities and strategies public.
5. You are Manish Agarwal, Purchase Manager, Career Consultants, Camac Street, Kolkata. Write an order letter to the Sales Manager of Balaji Solutions, GC Avenue, Kolkata. You want four Travel Mate Acer notebooks, Model TM 244 FX-P26A, at the quoted price of ₹49,999/- each. You are ready to pay ₹4000/- for freight and handling. You want four carrybags at an extra cost of ₹4000/-. You are sending a crossed bank draft for ₹207996/- in favour of Bajaj Solutions, Kolkata. You want the delivery within a week.
6. Assume that you are Anil Saxena, the Purchase Manager of Alpha Engineering Company, Salt Lake City, Calcutta. Your company sent an order for 15 HP scanners (Model: ScanJet 3200C) to National Systems Limited, Electronics City, Hosur Road, Bangalore-560 100 on July 3, 2016, but you received only 12 scanners. Write a letter to Suresh Gautam, the GM (Sales and Marketing) of NSL making a complaint and asking him to send the remaining 3 scanners.
7. Suppose you want to take a car loan from State Bank of India. Write a letter to the Chief Manager, SBI branch of your locality requesting him/her to send you all the information related to SBI car loans.

Key to Progress Check

Progress Check 1

1.

31 C, Lake Temple Road
Kolkata-700 029

May 16, 2016

The Public Relations Manager
STCI LIMITED
Krishna Chambers, 59,
Sir Vithaldas Thackersey Marg
New Marine Lanes, Mumbai-400 020

Dear Sir,
Please refer to your letter dated May 7 …

Sincerely,

Sd/-
Avinash Goel

Progress Check 2

1.

Dear Mr Chopra,

Please refer to your letter no. HD (ELE)/176, dated March 29, 2016, containing the proposal to conduct a special workshop on Artificial Intelligence for the junior executives of our company. We are pleased to inform you that we are interested in the workshop.

I have gone through the structure of the Artificial Intelligence module and find it exhaustive and appropriate. However, you may consider including the initiation of some specific project work relating to artificial intelligence. This may help us in continuing our efforts to upgrade the knowledge level of our executives in this regard on a continuous basis.

It gives me immense pleasure in acknowledging the effort that you have put in to design the structure of the module, which is appropriately suited to our needs. I would appreciate if you could send us the final proposal by the end of May, 2016.

We look forward to hearing from you.

Sincerely

(R S Prasad)

Progress Check 3

1.

251, Park Street
Kolkata-700 016

June 16, 2016

The Manager (Sales)
Lexus Motors Ltd.
209, AJC Bose Road, Kolkata-700 017

Dear Sir,

Please refer to your advertisement in the June 14, 2016 issue of *The Times of India* about new Indica V2.
I am interested in buying the new Indica V2 from your company. However, I would like to take car loan from HDFC bank through your company. Please send me more information about car loans.

I would look forward to hearing from you.

Sincerely,

Vikrant Vishal

Progress Check 4

1.

July 4, 2016

The Sales Manager
PCS Industries Ltd. 113, Park Street
Poddar Point, Flat 2C, Kolkata–16

Dear Sir,

Please send me the following item/s:

Cat. No.	Item Description	Quantity	Price
PC/21.	The Orilion Silver Magic with Intel Pentium 4 Processor 2.0 GHs 43.1 cm colour monitor, 128 MB DDR RAM 40 GB HDD with 7200 RPM	06	1,40,400/-
	Freight, Delivery and Installation Charges		015,000/-
	Total		1,55,400/-

We would appreciate if you could send the item/s immediately as we are starting a new branch of our company on July 10, 2016. A crossed cheque for Rs 1,55,400 drawn on State Bank of India is enclosed.

Sincerely,

P K Chakarvarthy

CHAPTER 22

Writing Sales Letters

Sales letters are sale promotion instruments used by business houses to boost their sales.

LEARNING OBJECTIVES

- Understanding the nature of sales letters
- Knowing the structure of an effective sales letter
- Knowing the components of a persuasive sales letter
- Knowing how to write successful sales letters

22.1 INTRODUCTION

Sales letters are persuasive messages that persuade the readers to believe what the sender wants them to believe. Although expensive and time-consuming, sales letters are very effective as result-oriented business publicity. By penetrating a limited but important consumer market, they play an important role in mail marketing, involving the sale of goods and services.

Sales letters are persuasive messages that persuade the readers to believe what the sender wants them to believe.

Although the basic objective of every sales letter is to promote sales, they serve many purposes. They may intend to:

- Make new customers
- Promote a business idea
- Introduce new products in the market
- Generate new demand for an old product
- Promote goodwill
- Launch a sophisticated marketing campaign aimed at a target audience.

So, writing a sales letter may involve a careful analysis of the product, service, or idea that needs to be promoted through the letter. The 'central selling points' must be identified to make the letter innovative, fresh, and persuasive. The specific purpose of the sales letter must also be indentified. An audience analysis may be required to adapt the letter to a specific audience.

Writing a sales letter involves a careful analysis of the product, service, or idea that needs to be promoted through the letter.

Note: It is advisable to be adept at the concepts discussed in Chapter 21 on *Letter Writing* because this chapter discusses one type of letter writing in detail. The basic concepts of letter writing remain the same. Also, as mentioned in Chapter 21, the broad-level concepts discussed here will hold true even for writing sales emails.

22.2 STRUCTURE OF A SALES LETTER

A sales letter should be organised very tactfully because the reader is under no obligation to read the letter. The writer must ensure that the reader gives the attention that is needed to understand the message and act accordingly. Thus, the key elements in a sales letter are (1) gaining the reader's attention; (2) building the reader's interest in the product, service, or idea; (3) convincing the reader that the product or service is the best; and (4) motivating him/her to act.

A sales letter should be organised very tactfully because the reader is under no obligation to read the letter.

Like other business letters, sales letters may be organised into three distinct parts: opening, body, and closing.

22.2.1 Opening

The letter should open with an attention catching statement. Any of the following may be suitable:

> A sales letter opens with an attention catching statement, builds the interest of the reader, shows the worth of the product/ service, focuses on reader benefits, and motivates action.

Special Offers

- Videocon brings to you a special celebratory offer. Now, you can get a Videocon 74 cm Pure Flat TV, a DVD Player, and an 80 Litre Refrigerator just for Rs. 28,990/-. Hurry! rush to your nearest dealer to avail of this exclusive offer.
- If you do not get it within half an hour, you will get it free.
- Most cars give you a free audio system. We will give you a car FREE with our audio system.
- May this Baisakhi add speed to your life. Rush to your nearest Santro dealer to avail of a special offer of free insurance and a free car audio system for the Santro Xing.

Product Feature

- Oxyrich Shirts have been designed to release energy giving oxygen ions in high pressure situations like meetings, traffic jams, and crowded places. To keep you charged and focused. All day.
- 528 litres of boot space unfolds into 1328 litres of bedroom space, with self-activating door locks for added privacy! Call it the biggest boot on the roads. Or call it Skoda Octavia.

Stimulating Questions

- Wondering which way to go after the exams? NIIT invites you to Career Space.
- Are you with the (**right**) agency?
- Who says you have to select from what we have got?
- How many monsoon-ravaged roads does your car cover with every litre?

Startling Statements

- Shirts that are a breath of fresh air. Literally.
- If you are young, energetic, and enthusiastic, act differently.
- Making cars that last longer is care for our customers. Making the world last forever is care for our children. Our cars are better built so that our world stays well-built.
- Keep an eye on your money. At IDBI Bank, a team of qualified investment advisors is waiting to guide and fulfill your investment needs.

Facts

- Panasonic makes your life a little more colourful. Panasonic presents the world's smallest colour phone.
- Power energises India's entire economy. Invest in Reliance Diversified Power Sector Fund.

Special Appeals

- Be a proud owner of a Hilkon air conditioner designed for your room on your budget.
- A great Gold and Diamond collection for the greatest moments of your life.

Prizes

- Buy any LG product. Win prizes worth over ₹ 50 crores.

Promises

- No tension. No problem. Just enjoy every day, every season.
- Now look up to global education standards and turn your vision into reality.

Quotations/Proverbs

- "God created man to be immortal and made him to be an image of his own eternity." (Bible, The Wisdom of Solomon)
- Good health is not just felt, it shows.

Persuasive Suggestions

- Ensure that you get a job in a multinational company. Your job is well paid. You get an excellent work environment.
- Enhance your career in Software Engineering with a Masters Degree from Carnegie Mellon University, USA.
- Change your Career Path with our FAST TRACK courses which give the innermost power to boost up your confidence.
- Do what you want to do—freedom to learn, freedom to earn.
- Get fishy. Swirl, splash, and create some ripples on your mobile.

Mixed

- Don't pay for your obsession with music. Let us! Over 1 lakh m-xtasy world members! Are you a part of this music?

Progress Check 1

1. Study the strategies to capture the reader's attention in sales letters (Part A) and match them with the openings of a few sales letters (Part B):

PART A: Strategies to Capture the Reader's Attention in Sales Letters

1. Special Offers
2. Product Features
3. Questions
4. Startling Statements
5. Facts
6. Special Appeals
7. Prize Announcements
8. Promises
9. Quotations/Proverbs
10. Persuasive Suggestions

PART B: Some Openings of Sales Letters

(a) Think smart. Buy now. Buying a Maruti Suzuki right now makes more sense than ever.
(b) Today, our happy family of over 24 lakh policy holders is enjoying the unmatched benefits offered by PLI schemes.
(c) Get a free LG microwave with LG Health Zone air conditioners. Add to that a range of attractive offers, and you have a great opportunity to make your home a complete health zone.
(d) It does what no other car can. **It talks.**
(e) Are you thinking of a career in Business Management? IIBS has the answers.
(f) No matter where you are in India, JVC is close to you. Looking for a place to service your JVC product? Look no further than the 171 JVC Service points across India. These include 26 Authorised Service Centres which are equipped to service all JVC products, and 145 collection centres which arrange for your system to be repaired as soon as possible. Either way, we're there wherever you need us.
(g) Our expert loan counsellors have a unique way of giving you advice. **They listen**.
(h) You shop for perfect ingredients. But do you cook in perfect conditions?
(i) Every cloud has a silver lining.
(j) When it comes to protecting you and your family, few cars in the world match the Corsa's superior European safety standards.

22.2.2 Body

The body of a sales letter should contain information that builds the interest of the reader in the product/service and convinces him/her that the product is worth buying. Key features of the product may be included and the selling points emphasised. Convincing the customer that the product is worth buying could be a difficult task due to the presence of competing products in the market. Therefore, all claims have to be substantiated by facts, figures, testimonials, guarantees, and logic. The following strategies may be used to prove your point:

Statistics

All claims should be substantiated by facts, figures, testimonials, guarantees, and logic.

- PCS Computers are available at over 350 outlets across the country. And PCS has India's 2nd largest service network.
- For over 30 years, we've helped people with asthma live normal active lives. We pioneered inhalation therapy in India. And today, we manufacture the world's largest range of asthma inhalers. Not just that, we export millions of asthma inhalers across the globe. All in all, when it come to asthma, we've always been at the forefront.
- An IDBI bank International Debit cum ATM Card lets you access your savings account anywhere in India and abroad. Withdraw cash from your savings account at over 6000 ATMs in India. You can also withdraw cash in the local currency at 8.5 lakh ATMs abroad. Shop and dine at over 55,000 outlets in India and 1 crore worldwide.

Testimonials

- My 2 close relatives were very serious, treated successfully in Neeraj Clinic.

  Justice D. Shagir, Former Judge Supreme Court of India

- NIPS helped me to realise my dreams. As a premier institute in the field of hospitality education where learning extends beyond books and classrooms, it offers its students ample opportunities to train, learn and realise their dreams.

  Anurag Srivastava, an alumnus of NIPS

- ...Written in a conversational style, the book is fully capable of teaching spoken English.... The intricacies of English grammar are easy to understand when you read this book.

  ***Navbharat Times,* New Delhi**

Guarantees

- We do not give you a warranty for five years. Kejian is India's only handset with a lifetime warranty.
- Our courses are designed for the best jobs in IT with 100 per cent job guarantee.
- We give you not only an AC with extra cooling but also a six years warranty with it.

Customer Lists

- We are sending you a list of companies that are our permanent customers.
- Enclosed is a list of doctors who strongly believe in our inhalation therapy and recommend only Cipla asthma inhalers.
- Please find enclosed the names of institutes that have been using our security systems for more than five years.

Free Trials

- Try our new MINDPOWER absolutely free for 15 days. If you are not satisfied with it, just send it back to us. We know you will never do it because MINDPOWER will change the way you think.

Free Samples

- We are sending you two asthma inhalers as free samples. We are sure you will find the product more effective than the ones in the market.
- Enclosed are some free samples for your assessment. We believe you will find the product better than our claim.

22.2.3 Closing

This is the most important part of the sales letter because it motivates the reader to act. It should tell the reader what he should do, giving specific instructions and providing some special inducements to get a quick response. Any one of the following examples may be appropriate:

> The closing of a sales letter should tell the reader what he should do, giving specific instructions and providing some special inducements to get a quick response.

Incentives for early birds

- The first 200 subscribers will get three special gifts.
- There is a rebate of 25 per cent for the first 100 customers.

Limited offers

- This is a limited offer for professionals like you.
- The offer is valid till stocks last.

Deadline

- Initial offer closes on April 7, 2004.
- You must book your flat before July 1 to get the special rebate of 05 per cent.

Special bargain offers

- If you respond by June 20, you will be eligible for a special bonus from the company.
- Send the order within a week and get a special gift package.
- If you send your order before July 15, you will get six months extra warranty on the air conditioner.
- Act immediately and take part in our special summer bonanza.

The letter should be closed with a goodwill expression.

Figure 22.1 summarises the three parts of effective sales letters.

Opening	⟶	The letter should open with an attention catching statement that could be a special offer, a unique product feature, a stimulating question, a startling statement, a fact, a prize announcement, a promise, a remarkable quotation/proverb, or a persuasive suggestion. Its purpose is to get the reader to devote a few moments of attention to the letter.
Body	⟶	Related information that builds the interest of the reader in the product and convinces him/her that the product is worth buying, should be given. The selling points should be emphasized and claims should be substantiated by facts, figures, testimonials, guarantees, and logic.
Closing	⟶	The reader should be motivated to act and add special inducements to get a quick response. The letter should be closed with a goodwill expression.

Fig. 22.1 Sales Letter

22.3 SAMPLE SALES LETTER

The following sample sales letter in Fig. 22.2 shows how the writer persuades the audience:

HDFC
Salt Lake City, Kolkata- 700 064
www.hdfc.com

July 5, 2014

Mr. Somnath Pan
Chartered Accountant
9, Camac Street, Kolkata

Dear Mr. Pan:

Opening ⟶ Want to own your dream house? Need a Loan for it? Usually when you visit a bank, the loan officer tells you about the loan formalities, preconditions, payment modules, and so on. You have so many questions, doubts, queries but the man goes on talking. Well, visit our office. Our expert loan counsellors have a unique way of giving you advice. **They listen.**

Body ⟶ At HDFC, before we offer you advice, we listen to your concerns. After all, we understand that buying a home is the single largest investment for you. Our counsellors offer you expert advice on all your home loan issues. Our Personalised Loan Counselling includes:

- Advice on property related queries and title of documents
- Structuring EMIs for tax benefits
- A choice between smaller and larger EMIs for the first few years
- Guidance on your entitlements for larger loan amounts
- Options for moving to a larger home.

Closing ⟶ Talk to us today. Call HDFC toll-free Home Line at 2321 5060.

We are here for you.

Sincerely,

Vivek Srivastava
Manager, PLD

Fig. 22.2 Sample Sales Letter

Progress Check 2

1. **Read the following statements about sales letters and mark True or False against each statement:**
   (a) A sales letter is a straightforward written message that asks an individual to buy something. T/ F

(b) The opening part of a sales letter contains a brief, relevant, and engaging statement that does not reveal the request.
T/ F

(c) Techniques for motivating action in a sales letter may include offering an incentive.
T/ F

(d) Sales letters start with specific details about the product being marketed.
T/ F

(e) The middle of a sales letter provides the additional details that readers need in order to take action.
T/ F

(f) The closing part of a sales letter contains an engaging statement that encourages the reader to act.
T/ F

2. **Assume you are Avinash Gautam, sales manager at Thomas Cook (I) Ltd., 1st Floor, 19B, Shakespeare Sarani, Kolkata. Thomas Cook (I) Ltd sells holiday packages in Asia, Australia, Europe, Africa, and America. You have learned that Alpha Software is looking for a tour operator as it is going to offer its employees free holiday tours in Asia. You have to write an effective sales letter that convinces the company that Thomas Cook holidays are the best because choosing a Thomas Cook Holiday means choosing the finest airlines, the best hotels, professional tour managers, and much more. Emphasise the point that most tour operators either charge extra for all the must-see sights later, or won't bother to include them in the itinerary but on a Thomas Cook holiday, there are no such rude surprises. There are no extra charges, surcharges, or supplements. The advertised price includes airfare on the finest international airlines, accommodation in conveniently located hotels, ticket taxes, medical insurance, visa costs, all must-see sightseeing and more, and meals.**

   There are three options for Asia, Oriental Ecstasy (Thailand, Malaysia, Singapore) — 12 days, Oriental Fantasy (Malaysia, Singapore) — 07 days, and Exotic China with Japan (Beijing, Xian, Shanghai, Tokyo, Osaka, Bangkok) — 12 days. Prices start from Rs 39,024.

   Write an effective sales letter to Binu Mathews, Managing Director, Alpha Software, 16, Park Street, Kolkata. As a special incentive, offer a 10% rebate if there are more than 10 persons for a holiday.

Exercise

1. **Study a comprehensive newspaper advertisement of a product. Now assume that you are the Sales Manager of the company that has advertised the product. Draft a sales letter for the potential customers of the product.**
2. **Imagine that you are starting a Web Café with scanning, printing, and word processing facilities. It is going to be the only web café of its kind in the area. Moreover, you are providing 25 per cent rebate to the first 200 customers. As the General Manager of the cafe, write a sales letter to be distributed to your prospective customers.**

3. **Assume that you are Arun Singh, the local Director of NIIT, Kolkata chapter. Draft a sales letter for prospective students. Mention the value of NIIT training and the relevance of its courses. Refer to any newspaper advertisement of NIIT.**
4. **Assume that you are Sheela Khare, the Sales Promotion officer of LG. Write a sales letter promoting the sale of LG air conditioners to be distributed to prospective LG customers. Include the following offers in your letter:**

   Buy an LG air conditioner and get gifts worth ₹ 6,990/-.
   - Microwave worth ₹ 5,990/-
   - Microwave Cookware worth ₹ 1000/-
   - 0% finance

   +

   Scratch the LG Cup card and win guaranteed free gifts worth over ₹ 50 crore + 7 years warranty
5. **Assume that you are the Chief Manager of Corporation Bank, Bangalore branch. Write a sales letter for potential customers. Your letter should promote the housing, education, and personal loans of the bank.**
6. **Assume that you are Anil Saxena, the Purchase Manager of Alpha Engineering Company, Salt Lake City, Kolkata. Your company sent an order for 15 HP scanners (Model: ScanJet 3200C) to National Systems Limited, Electronics City, Hosur Road, Bangalore-560 100 on July 3, 2004, but you received only 12 scanners. Write a letter to Suresh Gautam, the GM (Sales & Marketing) of NSL making a complaint and asking him to send the remaining 3 scanners.**
7. **Suppose you want to take a car loan from State Bank of India. Write a letter to the Chief Manager, SBI branch of your locality requesting him/her to send you all the information related to car loans by SBI.**

Key to Progress Check

Progress Check 1

1. (a) Persuasive suggestion (b) Fact (c) Special Offer
   (d) Startling Statement (e) Question (f) Facts
   (g) Startling Statement (h) Question (i) Proverb
   (j) Special appeal

Progress Check 2

1. (a) False (b) True (c) True (d) False (e) True
   (f) True

2.

Thomas Cook (I) Ltd.
1st Floor, 19B, Shakespeare Sarani, Kolkata

July 10, 2014

Mr Binu Mathews

Managing Director, Alpha Software
16, Park Street, Kolkata

Dear Mr Mathews:

Discover how much more you can get for your money. Choose a Thomas Cook holiday.

I am sure you would like to offer your employees a holiday that provides them the experience of a lifetime. Unfortunately, most tour operators either charge extra for all the must-see sights later, or won't bother to include them in the itinerary.

On a Thomas Cook holiday, there are no such rude surprises. You can see the best of the world, without paying anything extra. Which means, no supplements and no surcharges, just a single all-inclusive price. We take care of everything from air tickets, accommodation, ticket taxes, and medical insurance to visa costs. When you see the world with us, you'll never need to compromise. You'll fly the finest airlines, stay at the best hotels, and enjoy delicious Indian cuisine. We know holidaying abroad is a special experience. Shouldn't the memories last a lifetime?

Enclosed is our brochure that contains several options within Asia. You may want to choose Oriental Ecstasy (Thailand, Malaysia, Singapore) — 12 days, or Oriental Fantasy (Malaysia, Singapore) — 7 days, or Exotic China with Japan (Beijing, Xian, Shanghai, Tokyo, Osaka, Bangkok) — 12 days. Prices start from ₹ 39,024/-. However, we will offer you a special 10% rebate if there are more than 10 persons for a holiday.

Compare our holiday with any other. We're confident you will choose Thomas Cook. Feel free to call our Kolkata office at 22824711/4712 (8 am to 8 pm, 365 days a year) or e-mail us at holiday@in.thomascook.com. You could also visit us at *www.thomascook.co.in*.

We look forward to hearing from you.

Sincerely,

Avinash Gautam
Sales Manager

23 CHAPTER

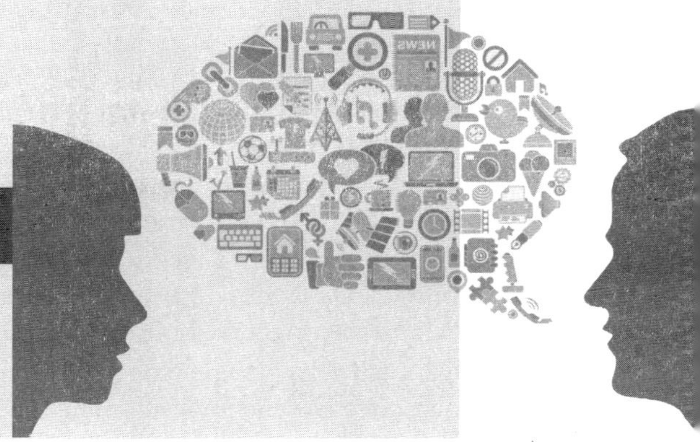

Résumés and Job Applications

The success of employment search largely depends on a candidate's ability to design a persuasive résumé and an effective job application

LEARNING OBJECTIVES

- Understanding the nature and importance of employment communication
- Knowing about résumé design and describe three acceptable résumé styles: chronological, functional, and combination
- Knowing how to write a persuasive resume
- Identifying the components of a job application letter
- Knowing how to write effective job applications

23.1 EMPLOYMENT COMMUNICATION AND ITS IMPORTANCE

Finding a job involves writing résumés and job applications.

Getting the job one wants depends on many factors, some of which one cannot control. For example, one has no control over other applicants who might be more qualified, more experienced, and better suited to the job at hand. But there is one factor that one does control, and that is, how well one communicates. Effective communication skills are the most important factor in helping job applicants find employment.

Although a job search begins long before really starting to communicate for a job, the applicant must learn to be an effective employment communicator. He/She may be the most qualified and experienced candidate for a job, but if he/she is not able to communicate effectively, he/she will not get the job. It is not enough to be the right candidate, one must be able to tell this persuasively to the people on the other side of the table.

An applicant may be the most qualified and experienced candidate for a job, but if he/she is not able to communicate effectively, he/she will not get the job.

Employment communication involves a complex process that includes writing employment letters, applications, and résumés. In fact, the success of employment search depends a lot on the candidate's ability to design a persuasive résumé and an effective cover letter. An employer has to read a large number of applications and résumés before he/she takes a decision to invite a candidate for a personal interview. No employer is under any obligation or compulsion to invite prospective candidates for a personal interview. In fact, the process of short listing candidates for an interview might result in the rejection of a large number of applicants. The screening committee tries to get to know the candidates through their application and résumé by evaluating their education, skills, and experience. Therefore, learning the art of writing applications that highlight one's strengths, and designing resumes that package one's skills and assets into a convincing advertisement is essential.

23.2 WRITING RÉSUMÉS

> A résumé packages your assets into a convincing advertisement that sells you for a specific job.
>
> **Mary Ellen Guffey**

A résumé is a selective record of an individual's background. It is basically a professional employment-seeking document that presents a summary of an individual's education, professional training, experience, skills, abilities, achievements, and references. It introduces the individual to a potential employer. A resume is sent to prospective employers when an applicant is seeking job interviews. So, the main objective of a résumé is winning a job interview by highlighting the applicant's fitness for a particular position.

A resume should have an effective design with a focus on readability and adaptation to audience expectations.

Writing an effective résumé that represents one's current skills, abilities, and background is a challenge faced by all candidates. As a well-written persuasive résumé tailored to a specific job position immediately grabs the attention of an employer, it should therefore, be made as persuasive as possible. The following section presents several techniques and suggestions for creating persuasive résumés.

23.2.1 Résumé Design

The design of a résumé largely depends on a person's background, employment needs, career goals, and professional conventions in the area of specialisation.

There is no one right design for a résumé. The design of a résumé largely depends on a person's background, employment needs, career goals, and professional conventions in the area of specialisation. For best results, a résumé must be designed to reflect the candidate's personality, employment goals, and his/her career aspirations. A résumé should be original. Although résumé-writing software may be used to design a résumé or it may be written by a professional résumé writer/résumé-writing services, it should be designed according to individual needs.

Résumés may have to be rewritten for every new job application because every job has its own requirements.

Résumés may have to be rewritten for every new job application because every job has its own requirements. Keeping a résumé job-specific gives it the required focus and makes it more effective. The contents of the different résumés prepared by a candidate might be roughly the same, but the organisation, format, structure, and emphases could be quite different.

However, whatever the résumé design, the résumé must answer the following questions:

(a) How can the employer contact the candidate?
(b) What are his/her career objectives?
(c) Which institutions have been attended?
(d) What courses (academic or professional) have been completed?
(e) What is his/her work experience?
(f) What are his/her career achievements?
(g) What are his/her special skills or capabilities?
(h) What are his/her awards or honors that he/she has received?
(i) What are his/her activities/special interests/hobbies?
(j) Who are his/her references?

Answers to these questions will provide the employer with all the relevant information needed to assess an applicant's suitability for a particular position.

Parts of a Résumé

The standard parts of a résumé include the heading, position sought, career objective, education, work experience, specific skills, achievements, activities, interests, and references.

Heading

The heading of a résumé includes contact information, which contains the applicant's name, full postal address with pin code, telephone number with area code, fax number, and e-mail address.

A résumé contains the heading, position sought, career objective, education, work experience, skills, achievements, activities, interests and references.

Position Sought

If applying for a solicited job position, the position sought should be mentioned so that the employer is able to distinguish the application from those who might have applied for other positions available in the company/organisation. However, it is not necessary to include this part in the résumé if the application is for an unsolicited job position.

Career Objective

Career objective is a special part in a résumé. It occurs just above the main experience and education parts. If responding to an advertised job position, the résumé should include the applicant's career objective, which should be tailored to the position he/she is seeking. Thus, it should be a specific one-sentence focused statement expressing his career goals in relation to the targeted position. It should convey his/her motivation and interest in the job he/she is seeking. The following are some examples:

1. To work as a system manager in a leading IT company where I will have opportunities to use my experience with VB, ASP, NET, XML, and SQL Server.
2. To obtain a challenging position in a large software consulting organisation providing business consulting, application development, and product engineering services, where understanding and experience of business process modelling and organisational change management to suit customer needs can be used to achieve set targets.
3. To contribute to the growth of a high technology materials engineering enterprise by working in a position where I will have opportunities to utilise my exposure and experience in modelling and designing steel structures, and my hands-on experience in using FEM/FEA software.
4. To work as a product architect in an innovative software company where I will be able to use my experience in the areas of product and system architecture with expertise in enterprise applications.

If you are just exploring a job position by sending an all-purpose résumé, you may use a general statement as your career objective. It would just express your general career goals and tell the potential employer the sort of work you are hoping to do. Study the following examples:

1. Seeking a suitable position in design/project management.
2. Challenging position in maintenance of computer printers and peripherals.
3. Position in academic administration.
4. Faculty position in Computer Aided Design.
5. Sales position in electrical products.

Professional Summary

> Professional summary should be included in the résumé if the applicant wishes to highlight the relevance of his/her qualifications, special skills, and key work experience to the position he/she is applying for.

Some résumés may include a professional summary in place of career objective. It is a one-sentence statement listing the applicant's most important qualifications, his/her essential skills, and his/her key work experience. This part should be included in the résumé if the applicant wishes to highlight the relevance of his/her qualifications, special skills, and key work experience to the position he/she is applying for. The following are some examples:

1. Six years experience in providing customer support to users of the industry's leading network routing, switching, security, and VOIP technology as a CCNA professional at CONVERGYS.
2. Four years of experience as production engineer with thorough understanding of weld technology and design and sound knowledge about trouble-shooting, fool proofing of processes, cost saving through process improvement, and low cost automation.
3. Over eight years of training and experience in testing, commissioning and integration of the GSM & CMDA nodes like IN, GPRS, EDGE, MMS with expertise in IP products and networking.
4. Five years of experience in sales of spare parts for central air conditioning equipment with extensive knowledge of spare parts of Carrier for Bahwan Engineering Group, Muscat.

Education

In this part of the résumé, specific details regarding the applicant's education and professional training must be included. The name and location of the school/college/university/institute attended, dates of attendance, major areas of study, degrees/certificates received should be mentioned. The applicant's grade point average/class/division if it is on the higher side may also be mentioned. Relevant training programmes, special courses, seminars and workshops that the applicant might have completed, attended, or conducted should also be included. Reverse chronological order is used to list educational information, that is, starting from the most recent educational information.

> Reverse chronological order is used to list educational information.

Work Experience

This part of the résumé should provide a brief and specific overview of the applicant's work and professional experience. As prior work experience is a vital part of any hiring decision, the applicant must draft this part of the résumé very carefully. If he/she has impressive work experience relevant to the position he/she is seeking, it makes more sense to mention it before providing the educational information.

Work experience should be given in reverse chronological order, by listing the most recent employment first. Title of the position, employer's name or name of the organisation/company, location of work (town, state), dates of employment, and important Job responsibilities, activities, and accomplishments should be included. Emphasis should be placed on those aspects of the applicant's experience and employment achievements that illustrate his/her capabilities and positive personality traits such as motivation, willingness to learn, positive attitude, confidence, ability to get along with others, and communication and interpersonal skills.

> Work experience should be given in reverse chronological order.

Special Skills, Abilities, and Aptitudes

In this part of the résumé, the applicant's special skills, abilities and aptitudes that are of significance and of direct relevance to the job applied for are listed. Examples of learned skills include computer programming, computer processing, data processing, foreign languages, machinery operation, consulting, drafting, technical writing, and so on. It is necessary to be selective and specific, highlighting only those skills and talents that are relevant to the targeted job.

> It is necessary to be selective and specific, highlighting only those skills and talents that are relevant to the targeted job.

> Activities and interests must show that the applicant is a dynamic and energetic person who can accept challenges.

Activities and Interests

Extra-curricular, co-curricular, professional activities, and hobbies and interests must be mentioned. These activities must show that the applicant is a dynamic and energetic person who can accept challenges. Companies prefer such people.

Achievements/Accomplishments/Honours

The applicant's achievements, accomplishments, and awards distinguish him from the rest. They convince the employer that he/she is an achiever and therefore worth hiring. This part should include scholarships, fellowships, awards, distinctions, commendations, certificates, or anything that shows achievement or recognition.

References

Some employers need references from persons who know the applicant's work or professional competence through formal and professional interaction with him/her. When applying for a solicited position where the employer wants references, the names of three persons who can give letters of recommendations or references should be mentioned. These persons may include the applicant's previous employer, teacher, immediate supervisor, research guide, colleague, subordinate, and so on. The name of the reference must be mentioned, his or her designation, and full contact address with telephone number, fax number, and e-mail address should be given.

It is important to note that the above-mentioned sections of a resume are only indicative. Some of them like education, experience, and contact details are necessarily to be included. However, the others depend on the country, or industry, or organisation, or even the strength of a candidate's experience or education. The following are some sections that may not always be included:

- A **career objective** can be skipped for more experienced candidates.
- Personal information like religion, age, etc., can be skipped.
- Do not add activities or interests or achievements or skills that are not directly related to the job being applied for. If there are none related to the job, best to skip these sections.
- Many companies do not need **references** at the resume stage. They will ask for them later. Also, adding a line like 'references would be provided on request', just wastes space. It is obvious.
- The situations where the section, **position sought**, can be skipped have already been discussed. Nowadays, including this information only in the email cover letter is common.

Therefore, a candidate should always research about the commonly accepted practices in the company or industry being targeted. No one resume format can fit all. It needs to be customised for getting the desired response.

Progress Check 1

1. **Study the following statements about résumés, and mark True or False against each of them.**
   (a) A résumé is a written summary of your education, experience, skills, special traits, and achievements.
   (b) Résumés de-emphasise skills and achievements aimed at a particular position.
   (c) Your résumé should begin with a statement expressing your career objective.
   (d) You may send your résumé to potential employers when you are exploring suitable openings.
   (e) The main objective of a résumé is requesting a job interview by highlighting your fitness for a particular position.
   (f) A well-written persuasive résumé tailored to a specific job position immediately grabs the attention of an employer.
   (g) Your resume should have an effective design with the focus on readability and adaptation to audience expectations.
   (h) The design of a résumé does not depend on a person's background and employment needs.
   (i) You may have to rewrite your résumé for every new job you apply for because every job has its own requirements.
   (j) The standard parts of a résumé include the heading, position sought, career objective, education, work experience, specific skills, achievements, activities, interests, and references.

23.2.2 Résumé Styles

Choosing an appropriate résumé style largely depends on the applicant's qualifications, career goals, and personal preferences.

> Chronological resume lists work experience items or educational/professional qualifications starting with the current or most recent and works backwards in time.

Chronological Résumé

This is the most common résumé style. It focuses on education and experience. It organises past employment record or education in reverse chronological order. It lists work experience items or educational/professional qualifications starting with the current or most recent and works backwards in time. An example is given in Fig. 23.1.

VIBHOR SAXENA
A-25/31, Sector-60, Noida- 201 301
E-mail: vibhor_saxena@dppc.com

POSITION SOUGHT	**Manager-Project**
OBJECTIVE	To contribute to the growth of a leading project management company by working in a challenging position where I will have opportunities to utilise my exposure to project management methodologies and experience as project leader in construction activities of large scale heavy engineering projects.
EXPERIENCE	**Project Leader,** Dharampal Premchand Ltd., Sector-60, Noida-201 301 December 2001 to present • Complete civil projects within or ahead of the schedule through strict planning, monitoring, and control while maintaining the best construction standards • Supervise erection of auxiliary facilities like water treatment, ETP, cabling, piping and other utilities • Maintain customer relations through effective presentation of technical expertise **Assistant Project Manager (Civil),** Subhash Projects and Marketing Ltd, Park Street, Kolkata December 1998 to November 2001 • Assist in the project management of various civil works being executed at site • Coordinate with Head Office, sites, various departments and sub-contractors • Maintain close liaison with clients
EDUCATION	**Pondicherry Engineering College,** Pondicherry B.Tech in Civil Engineering, July 1998 **Institute of Information Technology**, Mumbai Certificate in Computer Programming, December, 1994
SPECIAL SKILLS	• Proficient in MS-DOS, Microsoft Windows, Excel, and Word 98 and 2000 • Good problem-solving skills • Excellent communication and interpersonal skills • Competent in speaking French
ACTIVITIES	• Member, Institution of Engineers, New Delhi • Member, National Cadet Corps, 1994–1996 • Secretary, Society for Promotion of Science, New Delhi
INTERESTS	• Badminton, Football, Cycling • Classical Music, Movies, Fiction

Fig. 23.1 Chronological Résumé

Functional Résumé

Unlike chronological résumés that focus on education and work experience, functional résumés highlight accomplishments and emphasise skills. Some employers are more interested in the applicant's ability to handle the position they are applying for, and they would prefer a functional résumé rather than a chronological one. A functional résumé provides examples of experiences that demonstrate the skills needed for the targeted position. The example in Fig. 23.2 shows the chronological résumé in Fig. 23.1 reorganised as a functional résumé.

A functional résumé provides examples of experiences that demonstrate the skills needed for the targeted position.

VIBHOR SAXENA
A-25/31, Sector-60, Noida- 201 301
E-mail: vibhor_saxena@dppc.com

POSITION SOUGHT
Manager-Project

OBJECTIVE
To contribute to the growth of a leading project management company by working in a challenging position where I will have opportunities to utilise my exposure to project management methodologies and experience as project leader in construction activities of large scale heavy engineering projects.

PROJECT MANAGEMENT
- Assisted in the project management of various civil works being executed at site at Subhash Projects and Marketing Ltd
- Completed civil projects within or ahead of the schedule at Dharampal Premchand Ltd
- Maintained strict planning, monitoring and control while maintaining the best construction standards
- Supervised erection of auxiliary facilities like water treatment, ETP, cabling, piping, and other utilities

COORDINATION AND CUSTOMER RELATIONS
- Coordinated with Head Office, sites, various departments, and sub-contractors
- Maintained customer relations through effective presentation of technical expertise
- Maintained close liaison with clients

SPECIAL SKILLS
- Proficient in MS-DOS, Microsoft Windows, Excel, and Word 98 and 2000
- Good problem-solving skills
- Excellent communication and interpersonal skill
- Competent in speaking French

EDUCATION
Pondicherry Engineering College, Pondicherry
BTech in Civil Engineering, July 1998
Institute of Information Technology, Mumbai
Certificate in Computer Programming, December, 1994

EMPLOYMENT RECORD
2001/present **Project Leader**, Dharampal Premchand Ltd., Sector-60, Noida-201 301
1998/2001 **Assistant Project Manager (Civil),** Subhash Projects and Marketing Ltd, Park Street, Kolkata

ACTIVITIES
- Member, Institution of Engineers, New Delhi
- Member, National Cadet Corps, 1994-1996
- Secretary, Society for Promotion of Science. New Delhi

INTERESTS
- Badminton, Football, Cycling
- Classical Music, Movies, Fiction

Fig. 23.2 Functional Résumé

Combination Résumé

As the name suggests, a combination résumé follows a mixed style, drawing on the best characteristics of the chronological and functional résumés. It highlight skills but includes detailed information about the candidate's education and work experience. Study the example in Fig. 23.3.

VIBHOR SAXENA
A-25/31, Sector-60, Noida- 201 301
E-mail: vibhor_saxena@dppc.com

SKILLS

- Conversant in structural steel design and fabrication
- Have sufficient exposure to project management methodologies
- Competent in managing construction activities of large scale Heavy Engineering Projects
- Proficient in MS-DOS Microsoft Windows, Excel, and Word 98 and 2000
- Good problem-solving skills
- Excellent communication and interpersonal skills
- Competent in speaking French

EXPERIENCE

Project Leader, Dharampal Premchand Ltd, Sector-60, Noida-201 301
December 2001 to present

- Complete civil projects within or ahead of the schedule through strict planning, monitoring and control while maintaining the best construction standards
- Supervise erection of auxiliary facilities like water treatment, ETP, cabling, piping and other utilities
- Maintain customer relations through effective presentation of technical expertise

Assistant Project Manager (Civil), Subhash Projects and Marketing Ltd, Park Street, Kolkata

December 1998 to November 2001

- Assist in the project management of various civil works being executed at site
- Coordinate with Head Office, sites, various departments, and sub-contractors.
- Maintain close liaison with clients

EDUCATION

Pondicherry Eng College, Pondicherry
B.Tech in Civil Engineering, July 1998
Institute of Information Technology, Mumbai
Certificate in Computer Programming, December, 1994

ACTIVITIES

- Member, Institution of Engineers, New Delhi
- Member, National Cadet Corps, 1994-1996
- Secretary, Society for Promotion of Science, New Delhi

INTERESTS

- Badminton, Football, Cycling
- Classical Music, Movies, Fiction

Fig. 23.3 Combination Résumé

Note: Please note that the samples are indicative only. As mentioned earlier, the format needs to be customised according to the industry, company, etc., being targeted.

Progress Check 2

1. **Analyse the following chronological résumé of Adeeb Mallick, and reorganize it as a combination résumé:**

ADEEB MALLICK
209, 4th Floor, Ganpati Plaza, M I Road
Jaipur- 302 001, Tel: 0141-2564897
E-mail: adeeb@global.com.sg

OBJECTIVE

To be a part of a fast-growing multinational company in a position that offers the opportunity to work in a core R & D environment where I will be able to use my knowledge and experience in automation design, scanner design, tooling, plastic, and sheet-metal and rubber parts design.

EXPERIENCE

R & D Engineer (Mechanical), Global Group of Companies, Singapore

August 2000 to present

- Responsible for the development and delivery of a wide range of state- of-the-art products for the global market, from invention to mass production
- Design of electro-mechanical sub-systems, micro mechanisms, and transmission systems
- Work with the manufacturing team and parts suppliers throughout the product cycle in a fast-paced environment

EDUCATION

Indian Institute of Technology, New Delhi
M Tech in Mechanical Engineering, July 1998
MNR Engineering College, Allahabad
B Tech in Mechanical Engineering, July 2000

TECHNICAL SKILLS

- Knowledge of CAD tools such as Pro Engineer and Solid Designer
- Experience with analysis tools like MoldFlow and FEA
- Proficiency in MS-DOS, Microsoft Windows, Pagemaker, and Word 2000.
- Technical Writing Skills

ACTIVITIES

- Member, Institution of Engineers, New Delhi
- Member, International Society of Mechanical Engineers, Mumbai
- Member, Indian Yoga Club, Singapore
- Member, National Social Service

REFERENCES

TONY PARSONS
Director (Human Resources)
Global Group of Companies
Engineering
Blk 5234 #01-12, Ang Mo Kio Ave
TECHplace, Singapore-569873

A N SINHA
Professor of Mechanical
Birla Institute of
Technology
Ranchi, Jharkhand

23.2.3 Additional Tips

Like a job application, a résumé is an important employment-seeking document. Thus, it should be as persuasive as possible. As a résumé is created, reviewed, or revised, the following simple points should be borne in mind:

- ***Give the résumé a Professional Look*** In order to produce a clean, professional looking document, an appropriate résumé style should be chosen according to the background of the applicant, his/her employment needs, and the requirements that the prospective employers may have. To improve the readability of a résumé, it should be designed and formatted so that the main sections are noticeable and the individual components of experience or education are distinct and separate from each other. Well-defined headings and white space may be used to achieve this. The résumé should be computer friendly, avoiding overly decorative design and typography.

> The résumé should be computer friendly, avoiding overly decorative design and typography.

> All facts and academic and professional data should be verified for accuracy.

- ***Be Factual, Complete and Objective*** Facts should be used to demonstrate the applicant's skills and capabilities. All facts and academic and professional data should be verified for accuracy. Correct numbers, dates, names, and references should be used. Postal address, e-mail address, and telephone number should be included.

- ***Use Appropriate Writing Style*** Principles of business writing should be applied and the writing style should be carefully chosen. Consistency of phrasing should be maintained by using the same style of phrasing for similar information in the résumé. Punctuation style should also be consistent.
As so much information has to be included in a résumé, a terse writing style may be used selectively. For example, "Responsible for the development and delivery of a wide range of state-of-the-art products for global market" may be used instead of "I am responsible for the development and delivery of a wide range of state-of-the-art products for global market", or "Performed design of electro-mechanical sub-systems, micro mechanisms and transmission systems" is acceptable in place of "I performed design of electro-mechanical sub-systems, micro mechanisms and transmission systems".

> Principles of business writing should be applied and the writing style should be carefully chosen.

- ***Use Specific Details*** Specific details of the applicant's education, training, experience, references, and skills should be mentioned. Action verbs should be used to strengthen the résumé. Keywords that describe skills, personality traits, and job requirements should be emphasised.

> Keywords that describe skills, personality traits, and job requirements should be emphasised.

- ***Organise the résumé properly.***
- ***Take Care of Grammar, Usage, Vocabulary, Spelling and Punctuation.***

Progress Check 3

1. Look at the following resumes and identify their format types.

(a)

AYUSHI CHAUHAN
52/6, Raja Rammohan Sarani
Kolkata-700 009, 033-2365 5489
E-mail: ayushich@yahoo.co.uk.

POSITION SOUGHT — **Research Associate**

OBJECTIVE — To obtain a challenging academic position in a leading national institution of higher learning, where I can use my qualifications and skills in Marketing Management to prove my abilities

EXPERIENCE — **Lecturer in Marketing Management**, ICFAI Business School, Kolkata

August 2002 to present

- Teach several Marketing Management courses including International Marketing to undergraduate and postgraduate management students
- Improve course structure and teaching materials of several Marketing Management courses
- Foster a cooperative learning environment, ensuring students are given responsibility for their learning — including pair/group work, presentations, and classroom discussions
- Work as paper setter and examiner for undergraduate university examinations

EDUCATION — **Indian Institute of Management**, Indore
MBA in Marketing Management, July 2002

Lady Sri Ram College, New Delhi
BA Honours in Economics, June 1999

SPECIAL SKILLS

- Computer skills with proficiency in Word 2000, Excel, and Power Point
- Flair for research and writing
- Good written and oral skills in English
- Extremely detail-oriented and organised

ACTIVITIES

- Member, Indian Management Association, Kolkata
- Joint Secretary, Society for Marketing Innovations, Kolkata
- Secretary, Debating Society, Lady Sri Ram College, 1996-1998

(b)

RAKESH NARAYANA
3/7-C, Bharat Nagar, New Friends Colony
New Delhi-110065, (0091) 11-26729382,
E-mail: rakeshn@yahoo.co.uk.

POSITION SOUGHT — **Senior Flight Operations IT Officer**

OBJECTIVE — To work as a flight operations IT officer in a fast growing airline system where I will have opportunities to use my experience in systems analysis, implementations, and management within the Flight Operations Department.

EDUCATION

Delhi College of Engineering, New Delhi
B Tech in Computer Engineering, 2000
GPA 4.25/5.0

Patna Science College, Patna
B Sc Honours in Physics, 1995
First Class with distinction

EXPERIENCE

Flight Operations IT Officer, Air Deccan, Vasanthnagar, Bangalore
August 2000 to present

- Support software applications, analyse new systems requirements, and manage projects within Flight Operations Department.
- Selection/development of suitable IT packages, including basic systems design/concepts, evaluation, customisation, and integration of existing systems.

SPECIAL SKILLS

- Ability to discuss IT related issues and make recommendations to the management
- Excellent communication skills
- Ability to work in multi-cultural and multi-functional team environment
- Interpersonal skills

ACTIVITIES & INTERESTS

- Member, Lion's Club
- Member, ISIT
- Member, CAD Society, Delhi College of Engineering, 1998-2000
- Cricket, Basketball, Badminton

ACHIEVEMENTS

- National Talent Search Scholarship, 1990-1995
- DCE Merit Scholarship, 1998

REFERENCES

Prof D N Jha
Professor of Physics
Patna Science College
Patna
Tel: (091) 612-2265984
E-mail: jhadn@rediffmail.com

Dr S K Paul
Professor, Computer Engineering
Delhi College of Engineering, New Delhi
Tel: 9835646475
E-mail:skpaul@dce.ac.in

23.3 WRITING EFFECTIVE JOB APPLICATION LETTERS OR COVER LETTERS

A job application letter, also called a "cover letter", is written to apply for a specific position. It is a persuasive message that sells the applicant's talents to a prospective employer. It persuades the reader to believe in his/her suitability for a particular position. It is basically a self-promotion instrument used by the applicant to boost his/her professional value and career prospects. Although the basic objective of every job application is to draw a clear connection between the job one is seeking and one's qualifications, it serves several specific purposes. It:

> A job application letter is basically a self-promotion instrument used by the applicant to boost his/her professional value and career prospects.

- Introduces the applicant to the hiring organisation
- Introduces the applicant's resume
- Highlights the applicants positive personal traits and achievements
- Shows how the applicants special talents will benefit the organisation
- Emphasises how the applicant is right for the job by matching the requirements of the job with his/her qualifications
- Asks for an opportunity to be interviewed by the organisation.

So, writing a job application letter may involve a careful self-analysis. The applicant should evaluate his/her academic and professional qualifications, learned and intuitive skills, special traits and strengths, experiences, and career goals and interests. Moreover, he/she will have to research the company or organisation to know their needs so that he can match his personal strengths to employers' needs and job requirements.

> The key components of a job application letter are gaining attention, building interest, showing the worth of the applicant, and motivating action.

A letter of application is similar to a sales letter and it should be organised very tactfully because the reader is under no obligation to call the applicant for an interview. The applicant must ensure that the employer gives the attention that is needed to positively evaluate his/her credentials and is able to see the match between his/her qualifications and the requirements for the job. Thus, the key elements in an application letter are (1) gaining the reader's attention, (2) building the reader's interest in the applicant's candidature, (3) convincing the reader that the applicant is the best candidate, and (4) motivating the reader to act. As summarised in Fig. 23.4, these four elements should be included in three parts of the letter: an **opening** that gains the reader's attention, a **body** that builds the reader's interest and convinces the reader that the applicant is the best candidate, and a **closing** that motivates the reader to act.

> A letter of application is similar to a sales letter and it should be organised very tactfully because the reader is under no obligation to call the applicant for an interview.

Opening ⟶ The job application letter should open with an attention catching statement that could be a reference to the source of information, the applicant's credentials, a reference to a particular person for a solicited job, a startling statement, a stimulating question, or an expression of appreciation for unsolicited jobs. The purpose is to get the reader to devote a few moments of attention to the letter.

Body ⟶ Significant information about the applicant's qualifications should be given to build the interest of the reader in the applicant and to convince him/her that the applicant is worth hiring. A summary of the applicant's qualifications, professional training, and experiences, highlighting his/her strengths, assets, and skills should be presented. The applicant should relate his/her qualifications and experiences to the needs of the employer.

Closing ⟶ After supporting his/her candidature, the applicant has to conclude the letter by motivating the reader to contact him/her. The reader should be told how he/she can get in touch with the applicant and a formal interview should be requested. In order to persuade the reader to act, key career points should be emphasised and all claims should be substantiated by facts, figures, testimonials, guarantees, and logic.

Fig. 23.4 Job Application Letter

These days, cover letters through e-mails are more common. The basic principles remain the same as that of the offline job application letter. However, there are some differences in format. For example, an e-mail cover letter is usually shorter in length unlike its offline counterpart.

23.3.1 Job Application Letter Design

Parts of a Job Application Letter

Opening

The opening of an application letter is the most important part of a "job application package" because it sets the tone and focus of the application. The way an application letter opens depends on whether the applicant is writing in response to job advertisements/announcements (solicited) or he/she is exploring possible openings in a firm, company, department, or institution (unsolicited).

> The opening of an application letter is the most important part of a "job application package" because it sets the tone and focus of the application.

Solicited Application Letters In order to open a letter of application for a job that has been advertised, any of the following strategies may be tried to catch the attention of the reader:

Mentioning Source of Information The letter may open by mentioning the source of the information about the job clearly—newspaper advertisement, website vacancy notice, company circular.

- Your advertisement for a Materials Manger in the May 5, 2015 issue of *The Times of India* (New Delhi edition) caught my attention because with a Diploma in Materials Management and four years experience in the procurement of raw materials, I could serve JBM well.
- I am writing in response to your advertisement in the Opportunities section of your company's website, for software professionals for your development centre at Kolkata. As a software engineer having more than six years of experience in an IT organisation, with extensive exposure to design, development, and testing, I would be able to contribute to the growth and development of your company.

Matching Credentials to Employer Needs An important strategy to open a solicited letter of application could be to focus on the applicant's qualifications that meet the needs of the prospective employer.

- My 15 years' experience in export of automobile components, with thorough knowledge of the international market and export documentation, has given me well-rounded skills in Export Marketing to meet the challenges of Head, Export marketing, the position that your company advertised in the March 6, 2015 issue of *The Hindu*.
- As I am a B.Tech. in Chemical Engineering from the Indian Institute of Technology, New Delhi, with six years experience in selling Filtration and Fluid Purification Products and Equipment covering applications such as Hydraulic Fluids and Process Fluids, I have the qualifications described in your advertisement for a Sales and Application Engineer at the Filtration Division of your company.

Using References Making use of references is a popular strategy to open solicited application letters. It strengthens the application because most of the employers prefer to hire known people rather than strangers.

- Ms Seema Bhardwaj, a career counsellor at your business school, told me that ICFAI is looking for research associates. As an MBA from IIM Bangalore with two years academic experience, I am particularly interested in being a part of your institute's Centre for Management Research.
- I have been told by Mr Ravi Mehta, a member of your Technical Support Team and an alumnus of our institute, that you need sales engineers with experience in cement machinery and spare parts for your engineering centre in Chennai. I am a first class degree holder in Mechanical Engineering and have been assistant sales manager with F.L. Smidth Limited for four years. I believe I have the qualifications and skills that you need.

Unsolicited Application Letters When a job is not advertised and the applicant is writing to explore possible openings, more persuasive strategies should be used to open a letter of application. One of the following strategies may catch the attention of the reader:

Using Stimulating Questions that Highlight your Strengths Using stimulating questions that highlight the applicant's qualifications and strengths is an effective strategy to open unsolicited application letters. It attracts the attention of the reader by raising his/her curiosity to continue.

- Is your well-diversified infrastructure industrial conglomerate on the look out for professionals with relevant experience in the maintenance of large size cement plants and a high degree of commitment to lead your company's growth plans?

- Are you looking for professionals who have sufficient experience in installation/commissioning and operations of thermal plants with hands-on experience on various processes and controls for efficient and trouble-free operations of the power plant with optimal utilisation of resources?
- Will your fast growing company be able to utilise the services of a software developer with knowledge of and experience in J2EE EJB, Servlets, JSP, JDBC, HTML, and RDMBS?

Using Facts that Show Understanding of the Employer's Business Using facts that reflect an appreciation, understanding, or knowledge of the employer's business could be an effective opening for unsolicited application letters.

- Since Zafin Labs is a global leader in product innovation solutions targeted towards revenue recognition and revenue generation, it may need high calibre IT professionals who can efficiently handle both offshore and onsite projects in coordination with its global clients. As a quality engineer with eight years of experience in software functional and system level testing policies and procedures, I would be able to contribute to the growth of Zafin's Offshore Development Centre at Kolkata.
- I have watched with interest the growth of JBM, a well recognised synonym for sheet metal technologies. With the addition of new facilities and continuous expansion, the growth of human assets—horizontally and vertically—seems to be a regular phenomenon at JBM. Do you have an opening for a seasoned professional with a proven track record in quality assurance systems?

Using Startling Statements An unsolicited letter of application may open by using a startling statement. Surprising or unexpected statements, or statistics that surprise can be used. Sometimes, this could be very effective in capturing the attention of the reader.

- Delivering value: Two words that unequivocally express what it is to be a part of a company like yours. The Enterprise Solutions at your company has established leadership in *delivering value* to global corporations by leveraging business and IT expertise. Can you use the services of a talented professional who is capable of working with your global partners in CRM, SCM, EAI, ERP, and Business Intelligence in the role of a consultant?
- Your company has a tradition of providing excellent channels for personal development, working with international teams and possibilities to work across borders. Yes, it is the one thing that attracts me to Ericsson – the worldwide leader in communication. As I always wanted to work for a company where I would be a part of a worldwide team, I would like to know if you have any opening for a high profile professional in telecom management.

Progress Check 4

1. **Rewrite the following opening paragraphs of job application letters to make them more appropriate and effective according to the prompts given in the brackets:**
   (a) Refer to your advertisement for various faculty positions in January 16 issue of *The Hindustan Times*. This is a response to that advertisement. Treat this as an application for the post of Lecturer in Information Technology. I would like to inform you that I have a brilliant academic record. I also possess three years experience of teaching IT at NIIT, New Delhi.
   (Use reference to the job notification as a strategy to attract the attention of the reader.)
   (b) Your company has advertised the position of Chief Manger (Sales) in the April 24 issue of *The Times of India*. There are several skills that you are looking for in this position. These skills include

motivating and leading a dynamic sales team, planning and implementing sales promotion activities, and setting and achieving targets.
(Match your credentials to employer needs as a strategy to get the attention of the employer.)

(c) Please note that Mr Kushal Anurag works in your Public Relations Office. He advised me to apply for the position of production manger in your firm. I would like to add that I have relevant qualifications and experience that match your needs.
(Make use of reference to a person as a strategy to get audience attention.)

(d) I am looking for a job opening in your leading IT organisation. I have seven years of experience in software implementation, and developing or managing enterprise applications for financial service providers, including strong expertise in business analysis and process mapping.
(Make use of question as a technique to get the reader's attention.)

(e) I am a design engineer with ten years experience in testing, evaluating, and analysing software for CDMA mobile phones and designing, implementing, and executing test cases for Java J2ME API's as per internal-external customer requirements. I am looking for a suitable opening in your company. I know your company maintains professional excellence. It is true that your company is a world leader in mobile communications due to its experience and innovation, combined with the user-friendliness, reliability, and quality of its products and solutions.
(Make use of appreciation as a strategy to get audience attention.)

(f) This is to inform you that I am a young and competent graduate in Computer Science with 4 years hand-on implementation and maintenance experience on MS Clusters, Unix Clusters (AIX), Cisco series of Routers, Security Devices, Layer 3-2 switches, Internet and Internet Technologies, TCP/IP, LAN and VAN protocols and high speed leased line in a large network environment. I am interested in your company. I am sure your company is one of the companies that create jobs and roles where employees feel they have some control over what they do, where professional relationships are valued, and where more than lip service is paid to the work-life balance.
(Use a startling statement as a technique to attract the attention of the reader.)

Body

After capturing the attention of the employer, a persuasive letter of application must retain that attention and convince him/her that the applicant is worth hiring. As convincing the employer of his/her worthiness could be a difficult task due to the presence of competing candidates, the applicant has to substantiate his/her claims with facts, figures, testimonials, and examples. A few paragraphs of explanation may be given in support of his/her case. However, it is important to be brief, direct and specific.

In order to make a job application letter persuasive and convincing, the following steps should be followed:

Qualifications and Experience A summary of the applicant's qualifications, professional training, and experiences should be presented. If the applicant has sufficient experience in the field of employment, he/she should emphasise his/her experiences. However, if he/she is a fresher with little or no experience, he/she should emphasise his/her qualifications, special training, professional development programmes, or any refresher/orientation courses that he/she might have done.

Highlight Your Strengths The applicants should describe his/her strong points and special assets. He/She should also mention his/her intuitive and learned skills, special traits, and positive qualities that are normally not included in the resume.

Describe Capabilities Most employers would like to know what the applicant is capable of doing as well as what he/she can actually do for their organisations. They would like to see the match between his/her qualifications and the requirements of the job. The applicant may have impressive qualifications and experiences but the employers would be more interested in knowing whether he/she has the right qualifications and experiences. If the application is writing a solicited letter of application, he/she should explain how his/her qualifications and experience fill the stated requirements. If he/she is writing an unsolicited letter of application, he/she should research the company or organisation well in order to know their needs. He/she should relate his/her qualifications and experiences to the needs of the employer and requirements of the job. Showing how his/her qualifications and skills fit the job he/she is seeking is a key factor in persuasive job applications.

> Showing how one's qualifications and skills fit the job is a key factor in persuasive job applications.

The following are some examples:

(a) Your job notification indicated that you are looking for someone with experience in network planning and design. Designing Radio/Transmission networks and systems is a major focus of my present position as Network Planning Engineer at ERICSSON. Working in a 650 strong enterprise with high profile and result-oriented professionals has provided me with extensive experience and exposure in Transmission design, Digital Cross Connect, and frequency planning of Microwave Network. With good understanding of cell planning principles/RF Engineering/RBS(BSS), CME 20 products, and ITU recommendations, I have been able to use, Tems Cell Planner, Tems Investigation/Classic, OCS and other planning and optimisation tools.
My strong understanding of the telecommunication business and technologies has given me the ability to operate with end customer perspective and with high efficiency. With strong consulting, communication, and interpersonal skills, and an ability to work in cross-functional teams, I have been able live up-to commitments with a sense of urgency. With the qualifications and skills you are seeking, I believe I would be able to get the desired results for your company.

(b) I have the following qualifications to my credit:
- Five years of formal professional training that includes B Tech in Electronics from Delhi College of Engineering and a Post Graduate Diploma in Engineering Management from the Indian Institute for Production Management, Rourkela.
- Two years of experience as a Sales Engineer at Micro Systems and Controls, Kolkata.
- Strong in consulting and communication skills with the ability to interact with clients at all levels, demonstrated through strong influencing and negotiation skills.

(c) Developing market strategies and programme is to address key issues; analysing the market competition; conducting market research to identify opportunities, threats, and key issues; and developing marketing plans for new products and line extensions and executing their launch are some of my key duties as a Product Specialist at Pfizer Limited.
Working in a leading company like Pfizer with high profile professionals has provided me with extensive experience in product management that your Product Manager position requires. With a sound understanding of business and management principles in selling premium products, excellent analytical skills, and the ability to assess and interpret key market trends and patterns, I would be able to serve your company well.

(d) My education includes a BSc in Physics, and a Post Graduate Diploma in Sales Management. During the past three years, I have gained hands-on experience in brand sales as Sales Manager at Times Internet Limited, a reputed media organisation. My track record reflects outstanding success in building and maintaining relationship is with corporate decision-makers, and establishing large-volume, high-profit accounts. With excellent client relationship and management skills and an ability to relate and interface easily at the top executive levels, I have been able to set and achieve stretch targets in a highly competitive marketplace and would like to put my professional knowledge and experience to work for you.

Progress Check 5

1. Analyse the following middle paragraphs of job application letters in the light of the above discussion and rewrite them making them more effective:

(a) This is to inform you that I am highly qualified and experienced, and I have been able to prove myself as an outstanding sales professional. Just go on reading in order to believe what I am saying. I completed BE in Mechanical Engineering from Regional Engineering College, Durgapur, and MBA with specialisation in Marketing Management from Indira Gandhi National Open University, New Delhi. During my MBA, I worked as an assistant sales manager at Hyquip Projects Pvt Ltd. I was involved in sales and marketing of flat steel products mainly CR/GP/GC products. I have been working as Manager (Sales and Marketing) at Dharampal Premchand Ltd, Noida for the past four years. I am responsible for creating and building up a strong dealer/distribution network within the North Eastern Region and Eastern states of India, as well as Institutional sales on an All-India basis. I have excellent communication and presentation skills. Also, I have the ability to understand and articulate key opportunities for maximising profitability.

(b) I would like to tell you that I have been able to prove myself as a successful technical solutions professional. I have the ability to interact with clients at all levels. This is demonstrated through strong influencing and negotiation skills. I am also able to operate with end customer perspective and with high efficiency. I have in-depth domain knowledge of GSM/CMDA and Broadband/Soft Switch (MSN) technologies. I have been providing optimised technical solutions to customers at NOKIA for the last eight years. Also, I have been coordinating with the global design and product units for GSM/EDGE/CMDA technology products on Switching, IN Systems, and Prepaid and related solutions in the SS and BSS areas and Broadband/Soft Switch Networks.

(c) I am a fresh graduate because I have recently graduated from Indian School of Mines, Dhanbad. I did Bachelor of Technology in Electronics. My overall grade point average is excellent. I got very high GPA in third year. I got best student award for this. Also, I also received the ISM Merit scholarship. I got first position in Inter-University Debate Competition in March 2003, and second position in ISM Elocution Competition, 2004. I took active interest and participation in extra-curricular as well as co-curricular activities in the college. I had been a member of National Cadet Corps for three years. I learned many things. These included the value of self-discipline and commitment. I have a sound academic background, good verbal and written communications skills, proficiency in computers, and a high degree of commitment.

Closing

After supporting his/her candidature, the applicant has to conclude the letter by motivating the reader to act. He/She should tell the reader how he/she can get in touch with him/her and request a formal interview. In order to persuade the reader to act, the following steps may be followed:

Refer to the Résumé Refer the employer to the attached résumé for getting additional information regarding education, training, experiences, skills, and achievements.

- Enclosed is my résumé, which provides additional information regarding my education, training, experiences, skills, achievements, and references.
- The details of my education, training, and experiences are outlined in the enclosed resume.
- Please find enclosed my résumé for your kind consideration.

Restate Interest in the Company or Reinforce Suitability for the Position While closing a solicited letter of application, the applicant may restate his/her interest in the company or reinforce his/her suitability for the position.

- I am excited by an opportunity such as the one you advertised, and I believe I would be an asset to Reach Management Consultants Private Limited.
- I have been looking for an opening like this one, which provides a fast moving, dynamic work environment, and accelerated and challenging growth opportunities.
- I believe I do possess all the qualifications and skills needed to meet the challenges of a System Administrator in your firm.
- I am confident that I possess all the necessary qualifications for the position and would be able to contribute to the growth of your company.

Express Eagerness to Meet the Employer or Directly Ask for an Interview

- I look forward to having the opportunity to talk with you at your convenience, about the Project Execution Engineer position.
- Could you please arrange an interview at your convenience so that I may discuss my qualifications in detail?
- I would appreciate meeting with you to discuss how my experience in design of electro-mechanical equipment for hydropower stations/EHV Switchgear/DCS system could contribute to Jaiprakash Associates Limited.
- I would welcome any opportunity to further discuss my qualifications for the position of a Planning Engineer at your firm.
- I am eager to talk further with you about the Software Specialist position at your Dubai office. May I request you to fix a date for a meeting?
- I would like to talk with you about how I can put my qualifications and skills to work for Wisetech Solutions Pvt Ltd.

Include Contact Information such as Phone Numbers, e-mail, Date, and Time

- You can reach me at (91 33) 233822788 between 8:00 a.m. and 6:00 p.m, or contact me via e-mail: anurags@yahoo.co.uk.
- You can reach me through telephone between 8:00 a.m. and 6:00 p.m. at 9835212288.

- I can be contacted at (011) 28463971.
- You can reach me at (020) 22175983 after 6.00 pm.

Progress Check 6

1. **Revise the following closing paragraphs of job application letters to make them more appropriate and effective:**
   (a) I want to talk further with you about the position you want to fill. Refer to my attached résumé to get more detail about my education, professional background, and experience. You can meet me anyday that suits both of us. By the way, my telephone number is (011) 26555179.
   (b) I know that you would be interested in getting more information about my education, experiences, skills, achievements, and references. Here is my résumé that gives all that you need to know about me. Well, it is essential for you to know that I am interested in the Project Manager position at your engineering centre in Mumbai. What I like about this opening in your organisation is the fact that it combines professional training and personal development with practical experience in project management. It would be OK if you fix a date for meeting. My telephone number is (033) 265343788 and my e-mail address is rinajohn@rediffmail.com.
   (c) This is to request you to arrange an interview. I would discuss my qualifications in detail during the interview. For the time being, I am enclosing my résumé that contains the details of my education, training, and experiences. I have no doubt about the fact that I am quite fit for this position because I possess all the qualifications and skills that are essential for the service engineer position in your firm. Contact me by telephone at 9835825643 between 8:00 a.m. and 10:00 p.m.
   (d) If you want additional information regarding my education, experience, and references, you should refer to my enclosed résumé. I would like to restate that I want to join your organisation. You can talk to me if you want to discuss my suitability for this position. My telephone number is (0326) 2301589 and my mobile number is 9835412475. Do not call me before 6:00 p.m. You can contact me via e-mail also. My email address is prateekr@yahoo.co.uk.

23.3.2 Additional Tips

A letter of job application or a cover letter is an important employment-seeking document and it should be made as persuasive as possible. The following aspects should be taken care of:

Give the Letter a Professional Look

A standard business-letter format should be used. The letter should be easily read. One-inch to 1.5-inch margins should be provided all the way around the letter, leaving adequate spacing between paragraphs and between the components of the letter. Moreover, the layout of the letter should also be pleasing.

Use a Positive Tone

The tone of the letter should be consistently positive.

Show Confidence

The letter must reflect the applicant's confidence in his/her capabilities. However, sounding over-confident or complacent should be avoided.

Show Genuine Interest

Showing interest and concern is important. Care should be taken to avoid sounding indifferent, stiff, or too reserved.

Use Specific Details

Specific details of the applicant's education, training, experience, references, and skills should be emphasised.

Be Factual and Objective

Facts that demonstrate the applicant's skills and capabilities should be stressed. Care should be taken to use correct numbers, dates, names, and references.

Organise the Letter Well

Care should be taken to organise the letter properly.

Follow Consistent Style

Utmost care should be taken to ensure that grammar, usage, vocabulary, spelling and punctuation, are correct.

It is important to note that the format and guidelines discussed above are only indicative. The candidate must always adhere to the common practices followed in the country or industry being targeted.

Some sample application letters are given below.

Figure 23.5 shows a solicited application letter. The writer is attempting to get an interview for the position of a flight operations IT officer. In the opening paragraph of the letter, the writer indicates the source of the information, cites the specific job title, and draws a clear connection between the job and his/her qualifications. In the body of the letter, the writer summarises relevant experience. The closing of the application letter contains information about contacting the applicant and an implicit request for a personal interview.

3/7-C, Bharat Nagar
New Friends Colony
New Delhi-110065

April 23, 2015

The Manager
Human Resources Department
Qatar Airways, P O Box 22550
Doha, State of Qatar

Dear Sir/Madam

Your advertisement for a Senior Flight Operations IT Officer in **Times Ascent EAST** of the April 21, 2015 issue of *The Times of India* caught my attention because my four years as IT Officer in Air Deccan has provided me with the experience in systems analysis, implementations, and management within the Flight Operations Department that this challenging position requires.

Supporting software applications, analysing new systems requirements, and managing projects within the Flight Operations Department are some of the functions associated with my present position. Moreover, I have been involved in the selection/development of suitable IT packages, including basic systems design/concepts, evaluation, customisation, and integration of existing systems.

Working in a multi-culture team environment at Air Deccan has sharpened my cross-cultural and professional interaction skills. With excellent communication skills and the ability to discuss IT related issues and make recommendations to the Management, I have been able to prove myself as a successful Flight Operation IT professional. As working in a fast growing airline with an expanding route network has been one of my main career objectives, I would like to put my professional and academic experience to work for you.

The details of my education, training, and experiences are outlined in the enclosed resume. I look forward to having an opportunity to talk with you, at your convenience about the Senior Flight Operations IT Officer position. You can reach me at 0091-11-26729382 or by e-mail at rakeshn@yahoo.co.uk.

Sincerely,

RAKESH NARAYANA

Enclosure: resume

Fig. 23.5 Solicited Application Letter

Figure 23.6 contains an unsolicited application letter. The writer is exploring possible openings in Jackson Associates Limited, New Delhi. He opens the letter with a stimulating question that implicitly shows appreciation for the company. The body of the letter presents a summary of his qualifications and experience. The closing express eagerness to meet the employer.

208/III, Harikunj Tower

98 Nehru Place, New Delhi-110 019

March 29, 2015

Ms Rowena Paul

The Head, HR & Administration

Jackson Associates Limited

Jackson House, Basant Lok

Vasant Vihar, New Delhi 110 057

Dear Ms Paul,

Are you looking for dynamic, high caliber professionals to be part of your expansion and share the resulting success and satisfaction? As an experienced electrical engineer with a desire to work in an empowered work environment that offers unmatched opportunities through continuous training and career progression, I would like to be a part of your expanding multi-business company with linkages to technology leaders around the world.

After completing BTech in Electrical Engineering from IITD, I did a specialised course in Auto CAD. Since 2011 I have been working as an electrical engineer in F L Smidth Limited, a member of F L Smidth Group, engaged in design and manufacture of cement plants and machinery. In this position, I am involved in designing power system for large process industries and have considerable knowledge regarding International Codes and Standards. Moreover, I have gained hands-on experience in Switch Yard Design, Short Circuit Calculation, Relay Coordination, Harmonic Analysis, and the selection of LV and MV Motor, Distribution Transformers, and LV and MV Switch Board.

My enclosed résumé provides additional information regarding my education, training, experience, skills, achievements, and references. I would appreciate meeting with you to discuss how my experience in designing a power system for large process industries could contribute to Jackson Associates Limited. You can reach me at (011) 23658788 between 8:00 am and 6:00 pm or contact me via e-mail at shashiranjan@rediffmail.com.

Sincerely,

Shashi Ranjan

Enclosure: résumé

Fig. 23.6 Unsolicited Application Letter

Progress Check 7

1. **Study the following statements about job application letters, and mark True or False against each of them.**
   - (a) The basic objective of every job application is to draw a clear connection between the job you are seeking and your qualifications.
   - (b) Your letter of application stresses what you can do for the organisation by explaining how your education, experience, and special skills fill the stated job requirements.
   - (c) How you open your letter of application does not depend on whether the application is solicited or not.
   - (d) It is not proper to open a letter of application by referring to the name of an employee working in the company/organisation.
   - (e) You may use facts that reflect appreciation, understanding, or knowledge of the employer's business to open an unsolicited application letter.
   - (f) Using stimulating questions that highlight your qualifications and strengths is not an effective strategy to open unsolicited application letters.
   - (g) In the body of your letter of application, you present a summary of your qualifications, professional training, experiences, skills, and personal traits.
   - (h) Showing how your qualifications and skills fit the job you are seeking is a key factor in persuasive job applications.
   - (i) If you are responding to an advertised position, you should never include the exact position advertised and the name and date of the publication.
   - (j) Your letter of application introduces your résumé, relates your strengths to the reader's benefits, and seeks an interview.
2. **Analyse the following letter of application written by an Electronics Engineer seeking an R&D position in a multinational company providing electronic and product design services. Rewrite the application letter making it more focused and persuasive so that it looks professional and suggests quality.**

   Tips

   - Try to persuade the General Manager, Human Resources, of Sandvik Asia Ltd to call the applicant for an interview for the position of a planning engineer.
   - Explain the main part of the letter in two paragraphs, one for experience and the other for education.
   - Draw a clear connection between the education of the applicant and the job of a planning engineer.
   - Relate the experience to the requirements of the job.
   - Make the closing of the letter persuasive by restating the writer's interest in the company, and reinforcing her suitability for the position.
   - Explicitly request an interview.

480, H2, II Avenue

Anna Nagar, Chennai-600 040

January 21, 2014

The General Manager

Human Resources, Sandvik Asia Ltd.

Mumbai-Pune Road, Pune-411012

Dear Sir or Madam,

I would like to apply for the post of planning engineer in your company. I saw your advertisement in the January 19, 2014 issue of *The Times of India*.

I have the appropriate education and experience. I have a BTech in Electrical Engineering from MNR Engineering College, Allahabad, and a Post Graduate Diploma in Planning Management from IIPM, New Delhi. Presently I am a Manager (Planning) at Alfa Laval (India) Limited. I am involved in planning and controlling multi-disciplinary Mechanical and Electrical Building construction projects. I also interact with international clients and consultants. I have strong techno-commercial acumen, effective communication skills, and the ability to lead and manage a multi-disciplinary team of engineers.

I want to talk further with you about the position you want to fill. If you want to get more information about my education, professional background, and experience, you may refer to my attached résumé. You can meet me any day that suits both of us. By the way, my mobile number is 9835356498.

Sincerely,

Anita Agarwal

Enclosure: resume

Exercise

1. **Write letters of applications in response to the following advertisements. Assume that you have the requisite qualifications and experience.**
   (a) Wanted a service advisor at our Kolkata office. You should preferably be an automobile engineer with 2 to 4 years of relevant experience. A pleasant personality and good communication skills are essential. Please send your detailed résumé with a covering letter to Topsel Toyota, 25, Ganesh Chandra Avenue, Kolkata-700 013. E-mail: topcal@vsnl.com.

(b) We are a reputed IT company looking for software professionals for our development centre at Mumbai. As a Software Engineer you must have 1 to 4 years of experience in IT organisations. MCA/Engineering graduates with extensive exposure to design, development, and testing will be preferred. Proven expertise in any one of the following is essential:

Web Technologies

Java, EJB, J2EE, JSP, Web services, SOAP, CORBA, XML, J2ME, MQ Series, Websphere, Weblogic, Netscape server.

Microsoft Technologies

VB, ASP, IIS, MTS, Crystal Reports, VC++, NET, PL/SQL, Oracle 81/91, SQL Server, Windows C/C++.

Multimedia

Photoshop, Illustrator, Flash, 3D Max, Premiere, Director, After Effects, Elastic Reality, Sound Forge, Dreamweaver, HTML

Please mail your résumé within ten days, stating Role and Technology in the subject line, to: *career@wisetechsolutions.com.*

(c) Following position is open at our Avaya Pune Development Centre:

Senior Consulting Engineer

- BE in Information Technology
- 3+ years of IT industry experience
- Strong skills in either Database, Networking, or C++/Java
- Experience in Call Center Technologies/CTI desirable
- Exposure to Avaya products is a big plus
- Strong analytical and troubleshooting skills

Send your résumé to: Bigates Software Pvt Ltd, Wing A, Level 2, Tower 1. Cybercity, Megarpatta, Pune. Ph: (020) 2680 2782.

(d) Wanted a Quality Assurance Manager at our manufacturung unit in Mumbai. Applicants should have a degree in Mechanical Engineering, and should have worked in an engineering organisation, preferably with exposure to sheet metal components. Knowledge of SPC, Six Sigma, Deep Analysis, Pareto Analysis, MSA, with thorough understanding of the TS 16949 system and implementation thereof, is a prerequisite for the job. Please e-mail your résumé within seven days to: *excitingfuture@jbm.co.in.*, or send it to: Corporate HRD, JBM GROUP, Neel House, Lado Sarai, New Delhi-110 030.

2. Assume that you are Ayushi Chauhan (Refer to chronological résumé in Progress Check 3). You wish to explore faculty opening in Marketing Management at the Institute of Management Studies, New Delhi. Draft a persuasive unsolicited letter of application.

3. Assume that you are Manish Mehta. You completed your BTech in Chemical Engineering from IIT, Delhi in July 2001. Since then you have been working as a chemical engineer at Haldia

Petrochemicals Limited, Haldia. You are a dynamic professional with excellent communication, interpersonal and negotiation skills. You are proficient in MS-DOS, Microsoft Windows, Excel and Word 2000. Design a combination résumé for the position of chemical engineer in an expanding multinational petrochemical company based in Mumbai.

4. **Read the chronological résumé of Ayushi Chauhan for the research associate position in Figure 21.6, and redesign it as a functional resume.**
5. **Read the chronological résumé of Rakesh Narayana in Progress Check 3, and redesign it as a combination resume.**
6. **Evaluate your education, professional training, skills, accomplishments or achievements, activities/ interests, and experience (if any) and write a résumé.**
7. **Read the following information about how to prepare an effective resume and fill in the blanks with appropriate words/phrases/expressions from the ones given in the boxes.**

Address, extra-curricular activities, nicknames, e-mail address, degree, work experience, telephone number, skills, recent, grade point average (GPA), telephone, abilities, name, permanent address, academic, specific, objective, institution

Résumé Essentials

Before you write, take time to do a self-assessment on paper. Outline your –1——and ——2—— as well as your ——3—— and ———4———. This will make it easier to prepare a thorough resume.

The Content of Your Resume

——5——, ———6———, ——7————, ———8——— all your contact information should go at the top of your resume.

- Avoid ——9——-
- Use a ——10—— ———-
- Use a permanent ——11——— and include the area code
- Add your——12————-

Objective or Summary

An objective tells potential employers the sort of work you're hoping to do.

- Be ——13——— about the job you want
- Tailor your ——14—— to each employer you target/every job you seek

Education

New graduates without a lot of work experience should list their educational information first.

- Your most ——15——— educational information is listed first
- § Include your ——16—— (AS, BS, BA, and so on), major, ———— attended, minor/concentration
- Add your ——17—— if it is higher than 3.0
- Mention ——18—— honors.

responsibilities, achievements, academic, sports, professional, organisation, employment, position, work specific skills, references, skills, experience

Briefly give the employer an overview of work that has taught you skills. Use action words to describe your job duties. Include your work experience in reverse chronological order; that is, put your last job first and work backward to your first, relevant job. Include:

- Title of ——19——
- Name of ———20———
- Location of ——21——— (town, state)
- Dates of ————22————
- Describe your work ——23——— with emphasis on ——24——— ———— and ——25———

Other information

You may want to add:

- Key or special ——26—— or competencies
- Leadership ———27——— in volunteer organisations
- Participation in ——28———
- Computer skills
- Proficiency in different languages

Achievements

- ———— achievements in school/college
- ———— achievements

References

Ask people if they are willing to serve as ————29——— before you give their names to a potential employer. Do not include your reference information on your resume. You may note at the bottom of your resume: "References furnished on request".

Key to Progress Check

Progress Check 1

1. (a) True (b) False (c) False (d) True (e) True
   (f) True (g) True (h) False (i) True (j) True

Progress Check 2

1.

ADEEB MALLICK

209, 4th Floor, Ganpati Plaza, MI Road
Jaipur- 302 001, Tel: 0141-2564897
E-mail: adeeb@global.com.sg

SKILLS

- Knowledge and experience in automation design
- Knowledge of printer and scanner design
- Experience in tooling, plastic, sheet-metal, and rubber parts design
- Familiarity with CAD tools such as Pro Engineer and Solid Designer
- Experience with analysis tools like MoldFlow and FEA
- Proficiency in MS-DOS, Microsoft Windows, Pagemaker and Word 2000
- Team management skills
- Strong passion for design
- Expert in crises management with good problem-solving skills

EXPERIENCE

R&D Engineer (Mechanical), Global Group of Companies, Singapore, August 2000 to present

- Responsible for the development and delivery of a wide range of state-of-the-art products for the global market, from invention to mass production
- Perform design of electro-mechanical sub-systems, micro-mechanisms, and transmission systems
- Work with the manufacturing team and part suppliers throughout the product cycle in a fast-paced environment.

EDUCATION

Indian Institute of Technology, New Delhi
M Tech in Mechanical Engineering, July 2000
MNR Engineering College, Allahabad
B Tech in Mechanical Engineering, July 1998

ACTIVITIES

- Member, Institution of Engineers, New Delhi
- Member, International Society of Mechanical Engineers, Mumbai
- Member, Indian Yoga Club, Singapore
- Member, National Social Service, 1996–1997

REFERENCES	TONY PARSONS	A N SINHA
	Director (Human Resources)	Professor of Mechanical
	Global Group of Companies Engineering	Birla Institute of
	Blk 5234 #01-12, Ang Mo Kio Ave	Technology
	TECHplace, Singapore-569873	Ranchi, Jharkhand

Progress Check 3

1. and 2. are both chronological resumes.

Progress Check 4

1. (a) In response to your advertisement for various faculty positions in January 16 issue of *The Hindustan Times*, I would like to apply for the post of Lecturer in Information Technology. My brilliant academic record and three years experience of teaching IT at NIIT, New Delhi would allow me to contribute to the academic growth of your expanding university.
   (b) My twelve years as sales manager in Topsel Toyota, Kolkata have provided me with sufficient experience in motivating and leading a dynamic sales team, planning and implementing sales promotion activities, and setting and achieving targets. These are the skills that you are looking for in your new Chief Manager (Sales), the position that your company advertised in the April 24 issue of *The Times of India.*
   (c) As advised by Mr Kushal Anurag of your Public Relations Office, I apply for the position of production manager in your firm. I am sure my qualifications and experience would match your needs.
   (d) Can your leading IT organisation use the services of an IT professional with 7 years of experience in software implementation, developing or managing enterprise applications for financial service providers, including strong expertise in business analysis and process mapping?
   (e) The professional excellence maintained and pursued by your company has impressed me. Your company's experience and innovation, combined with the user-friendliness, reliability, and quality of its products and solutions have made it a world leader in mobile communications. Can you use the services of a design engineer with ten years experience in testing, evaluating, and analysing software for CDMA mobile phones and designing, implementing, and executing test cases for Java J2ME API's as per internal external customer requirements?
   (f) The best companies create jobs and roles where employees feel they have some control over what they do, where professional relationships are valued, and where more than lip service is paid to the work-life balance. I believe your company is one of them and I would like to be a part of such a company. I am sure you will be able to use the services of a young and competent graduate in Computer Science with 4 years hands on implementation and maintenance experience in MS Clusters, Unix Clusters (AIX), Cisco series of Routers, Security Devices, Layer 3-2 switches, Internet and Internet Technologies, TCP/IP, LAN and VAN protocols and high speed leased line in a large network environment.

Progress Check 5

1. (a) My education includes a BE in Mechanical Engineering from Regional Engineering College, Durgapur and MBA from Indira Gandhi National Open University, New Delhi. As I was interested in sales and

marketing, I specialised in marketing management. While obtaining my MBA, I worked as an assistant sales manager at Hyquip Projects Private Limited, Hyderabad. In that position, I was involved in sales and marketing of flat steel products, mainly CR/GP/GC products.

During the past four years, I have gained valuable marketing experience as Manager (Sales and Marketing) at Dharampal Premchand Limited, Noida. At DPL, I am responsible for creating and building up a strong dealer/distribution network within the North Eastern Region and Eastern states of India, as well as Institutional sales on an all-India basis. With excellent communication and presentation skills and the ability to understand and articulate key opportunities for maximising profitability, I have been able to prove myself as an outstanding sales professional. I am sure my experience gives me the special skills that you are seeking.

(b) With an in-depth domain knowledge of GSM/CMDA and Broadband/Soft Switch (MSN) technologies, I have been providing optimised technical solutions to customers at NOKIA for the last eight years. Moreover, I have been coordinating with the global design and product units for GSM/EDGE/CMDA technology products on Switching, IN Systems, prepaid and related solutions in the SS and BSS areas and broadband/Soft Switch Networks.

Because of my ability to interact with clients at all levels, as demonstrated through strong influencing and negotiation skills, and my ability to operate with end customer perspective and with high efficiency, I have been able to prove myself as a successful technical solutions professional. I believe my work experience and professional exposure gives me the skills you are seeking.

(c) My academic record reflects my sincerity and strong determination. In 2004, I graduated with a Bachelor of Technology in Electronics from the Indian School of Mines, Dhanbad with an overall grade point average of 4.48. I got best student award in third year for achievement. I also received the ISM Merit Scholarship during 2002–2003 for my academic performance. As a dynamic, extroverted student, I took active interest and participation in extra-curricular as well as co-curricular activities in the college. I won first position in the Inter-University Debate Competition in March 2003, and second position in the ISM Elocution Competition, 2004. As a member of the National Cadet Corps for three years, I learned the value of self-discipline and commitment, and prepared myself to become a member of a committed, workforce like yours.

As I have a sound academic background, good verbal and written communication skills, proficienc in computers, and a high degree of commitment, I would be able to contribute to the growth and expansion of your company.

Progress Check 6

1. (a) Please refer to my attached résumé for more detail about my education, professional background, and experience. I would welcome a chance to talk further with you about the position you are seeking to fill. I am ready to meet with you at your convenience. I can be contacted at (011) 26555179.

(b) Please find enclosed my résumé, which provides additional information regarding my education, experiences, skills, achievements, and references. As I have been looking for an opening like this, which combines professional training and personal development with practical experience in project management, I am eager to talk with you further about the project manager position at your engineering centre in Mumbai. May I request you to fix a date for a meeting? You can reach me at (033) 265343788 after 7:00 pm, or contact me via e-mail at rinajohn@rediffmail.com.

(c) The details of my education, training, and experience are outlined in the enclosed résumé. I believe I do possess all the qualifications and skills needed to meet the challenges of a service engineer in your firm. Could you please arrange an interview at your convenience so that I may discuss my qualifications in detail? I can be reached by telephone between 8:00 am and 10:00 pm at 9835825643.

(d) Please refer to my enclosed résumé, providing additional information regarding my education, experience, and references. As I am keen to be a part of your fast growing organisation, I would like to talk with you about how I can put my qualifications and skills to work for you. You can reach me at (0326) 2301589 or 9835412475 after 6:00 pm, or contact me via e-mail at prateekr@yahoo.co.uk.

Progress Check 7

1. (a) True (b) True (c) False (d) False (e) True
   (f) False (g) True (h) True (i) False (j) True

2. 480, H2, II Avenue
   Anna Nagar, Chennai-600 040

   January 21, 2014

   The General Manager, Human Resources
   Sandvik Asia Ltd
   Mumbai-Pune Road, Pune-411012

   Dear Sir or Madam:

   Your advertisement for the position of a planning engineer in the January 19, 2014 issue of *The Times of India* immediately caught my attention because my professional qualifications and training with a proven track record in reputed companies make me an excellent candidate for this position.

   Apart from doing B Tech in Electrical Engineering from MNR Engineering College, Allahabad, I have a Post Graduate Diploma in Planning Management from IIPM, New Delhi. Through these studies, I have gained in-depth knowledge of all aspects of planning electrical building construction projects.

   I have been Manager (Planning) at Alfa Laval (India) Limited for the last eight years. At Alfa Laval, I have gained valuable experience in planning and controlling multi-disciplinary mechanical and electrical building construction projects. Moreover, I have had the opportunity to interact with international clients and consultants. With strong techno-commercial acumen, effective communication skills, and the ability to lead and manage a multi-disciplinary team of engineers, I have been able to prove myself as a successful planning engineer. I would like to put my professional knowledge and experience to work for you.

My enclosed resume provides detailed information on my background. I am excited by an cpportunity such as the one you advertised, and I believe I would be an asset to Sandvik Asia Ltd. Could you please arrange an interview at your convenience so that I may discuss my qualifications in detail? I can be reached by telephone at 9835356498.

Sincerely,

Anita Agarwal

Enclosure: résumé

CHAPTER 24

Writing Business Memos

Business memos solve problems and act as means of decision making.

LEARNING OBJECTIVES

- Understanding the nature and importance of business memos
- Learning to distinguish between business letters and memos
- Identifying four characteristics of good business memos
- Knowing the different parts of a business memo
- Learning to write effective memos

24.1 INTRODUCTION AND IMPORTANCE OF BUSINESS MEMOS

The two widely recognised categories of communication in the business world are external communications and internal communications. Internal communication is essential for the internal functioning of any organisation. It integrates the managerial functions and serves to influence the behaviour and attitude of the people through persuasion and encouragement to contribute in achieving organisational objectives. Typical internal communications include business memos.

> Business memos describe problems, inform employees, request information, explain actions and policies, provide directions, and give feedback.

A business memo is a formal written message, written in a conventional form for someone within the organisation to meet a specific need. It is a form of dialogue, where the writer wants to say something and expects a response to the message. It is an important means of internal communication used to send information inside an organisation. Whether a person is a managing director in a multinational company, a sales manager in a small firm, or a junior executive in a government department, all have to write memos.

As business memos solve problems and act as a means of decision-making, they serve many purposes. They may:

> A business memo is a formal written message, written in a conventional form for someone within the organisation to meet a specific need.

- Describe problems
- Request for information or additional resources
- Contain proposals or requests for proposals
- Explain policy statements
- Contain office instructions or guidelines
- Persuade the reader to take an action
- Invite the reader to business meetings/conferences
- Give feedback, suggestions, or recommendations
- Seek explanations or clarifications
- Be just polite reminders.

As a link between people within an organisation, business memos help members of the organisation communicate without the need for time-consuming oral discussions, meetings, and conferences. Memos can move in all directions as they may involve any of the three channels of communication: downward, upward, and horizontal. **Downward memos** are used to communicate to the subordinates in the hierarchy of the organisation. They are primarily used to:

> Memos can move in all directions as they may involve any of the three channels of communication: downward, upward, and horizontal.

- Convey routine information such as new products or services being introduced, new policy changes, introduction of new procedures, new market strategies being followed, and so on
- Discuss matters relating to personnel practices such as transfers, official instructions, promotions, and so on
- Seek explanations or clarifications
- Send feedback
- Give instructions.

In contrast, **upward memos** are sent by subordinates to their superiors. They might convey grievances, complaints, suggestions, findings and recommendations, new ideas, problems, proposals, and so on. Unlike downward and upward memos, **horizontal memos** are sent to peer groups or to people who are hierarchically equivalent in the organisation. Although the main purpose of horizontal memos is to develop cooperation and coordination through peer interaction between different individuals working in an organisation, they may be used to persuade the reader to take an action, such as attend a meeting, give a presentation, and so forth.

Students too are required to write memos. In order to be successful at the workplace effective memo writing skills are essential. As we advance in our chosen career, we are called upon to communicate with others in the organisation more often and more effectively. We may have to write memos for different purposes. We may need to write a memo to introduce new information to the reader like new products or services being introduced, new policy changes, or new market strategies being followed; or to persuade the reader to take an action, such as attend a meeting, give a presentation or follow guidelines.

It is important to note that these days e-mail memos are more common than hardcopy memos. The basic principles remain the same though their formats would be different. The above-mentioned guidelines hold true for the e-mail memos too.

Some organisations even use the hybrid format where a business memo is typed on a hardcopy which is scanned and sent as an attachment through e-mail.

24.1.1 Letters Versus Memos

Like a business letter, a business memo is a positive functional instrument of professional exchange of business ideas, opinions, decisions, policies, and information. As both letters and memos are forms of business writing, they follow similar writing principles and strategies. Memos like letter are written to inform and make requests. However, a business memo differs from a business letter in several important ways:

- Unlike letters, which are used as a means to reach out to people outside an organisation, memos are used to send information inside an organisation.
- A memo is written in a specific format, which is different from the letter format.
- Memos are less formal than letters.
- Memos are less structured than letters.
- The tone of memo is more conversational than that of a letter.
- Memos contain less background explanation and information than letters.

24.2 WRITING EFFECTIVE BUSINESS MEMOS

24.2.1 Characteristics of Effective Memos

Memos play an important role in the decision-making process in an organisation by facilitating the flow of information within its various parts and units. Good memos share certain characteristics, which include the following:

> Four characteristics distinguish effective memos: clarity, conciseness, unity of theme, and informal tone.

Clarity

Clarity is the first characteristic of a good memo. A memo must be clearly written because an unclear and vague memo will confuse the reader, leading to delay and inaction. Read the following extract from memo that shows how the lack of clarity leads to confusion:

"There is going to be a one-day programme on a relevant topic related to value education for some of our staff. The programme will be organised by IIM, Kolkata in the last week of July. We need your support and involvement in order to make the programme successful."

As can be seen, the language used here is not specific and concrete and the references are not clear. The reader is not provided with the answers to the following questions:

1. What is the exact topic of the programme?
2. What is the exact date of the programme?
3. Who are the participants?
4. What kind of support does the reader need?

The following is a revised version of the same memo:

"On Saturday, July 24, 2014, the Value Education Cell of IIM, Kolkata will be organising a one-day programme on "Business Values and Corporate Management" for the Management Trainees of the Marketing Division. Kindly arrange accommodation for three persons in the Guest House from July 23, to July 25, 2014."

In order to maintain clarity in memos, the following points must be remembered:

- Clear references should be used.
- Simple, familiar, and specific words and expressions should be used.
- Cliches and overused proverbs and phrases should be avoided.
- Short sentences and paragraphs should be used. Ideas should be separated into paragraphs.
- Appropriate linkers and transitional signals should be used.

Conciseness

Concise and direct memos are more effective. A memo should contain only essential information. Unnecessary explanations, repetitions, wordy expressions, and exaggeration must be avoided in order to ensure that the memo makes its point with the fewest words possible.

Unity of Theme

A memo, which does not have unity of theme, distracts the reader and ceases to be purposeful. An important way of ensuring unity in a memo is to make sure that it deals with only one topic. A single topic is developed, and related ideas are subordinated. Focusing on a single topic helps the writer unfold the theme logically.

Informal Tone

Although a memo is a formal business document, its tone is usually informal and conversational. As the writer is likely to be familiar with the reader, personal tone may be used in memos. A very formal tone might sound intimidating.

Progress Check 1

1. **Read the following statements about business memos and mark True or False against each statement in the light of the above discussion:**
   (a) Internal communication is essential for the internal functioning of any organisation.
   (b) A memo is an efficient and effective way to convey information within an organisation.

(c) Memos never provide a summary of important information and do not suggest actions that should be taken.
(d) Memos never contain proposals or requests for proposals.
(e) Downward memos are used to communicate to the superiors in the hierarchy of the organisation.
(f) The main purpose of horizontal memos is to develop cooperation and coordination through peer interaction between different individuals working in an organisation.
(g) Good memos usually discuss only one topic.
(h) The tone of memos is generally conversational because communicators are unfamiliar with one another.
(i) Memos usually contain less background explanation and information than letters.
(j) An important way of ensuring unity in a memo is to make sure that it deals with only one topic.

24.2.2 Form and Structure

Writing memos is a professional activity that demands effort and sincerity. In order to write a memo that works, the correct format should be used and standard writing conventions followed. The memo should be divided into four segments to organise the information and to help achieve its purpose.

Parts of a Memo

Standards memos contain four parts: (1) Heading, (2) Opening, (3) Body, and (4) Closing.

> Business memos contain the heading (date, from, subject), an opening that states the main idea, a body with description and explanation, and an action closing.

Heading

The heading segment of a memo includes four elements, that is, date, the recipient's name and designation, the sender's name and designation, and the subject.

Date: (Complete and current)
To: (Name and designation of the recipient)
From: (Name and designation of the sender)
Subject: (Topic of the memo)

As the date line is used to indicate the date the memo was written, it should include the current date mentioning the month, day and year. The date given should be placed two inches from the top of the page.

Some experts suggest that it is enough if the designations of the recipient and the sender are mentioned against TO and FROM in the layout. However, the sender may also mention his/her name and the name of the recipient, but care should be taken to address the reader by her/his correct name.

The subject line should mention the topic of the memo. In long memos, it may include the summary of the central idea of the memo. A complete sentence should not be used for the subject line, it should be written in a phrase form. For example, "Executive Board meeting to discuss the recruitment policy" may be written instead of "Please attend the Executive Board meeting to discuss the recruitment policy". Being specific is important. For example, "leave" could refer to any leave because there could be different kinds of leave for different periods. Therefore, "Extra-ordinary Leave from March 16, 2014 to May 14, 2014" may be written instead of "Extra-ordinary Leave" or just "Leave".

Following are some examples:

SUBJECT: Summer Training Course for Marketing Executives

SUBJECT: Non-Plan Budget allocation for 2013–2014

SUBJECT: Your June 6, 2015 Memo about Summer Training Course for Marketing Executives

SUBJECT: Seminar on Tele Marketing Strategies

SUBJECT: Purchase of 50 Laptops for Sales Division

Fig. 24.1(a) to Fig. 24.1(d) contain examples of heading segments:

DATE:	March 29, 2014
TO:	Avinash Gautam Sales Manager
FROM:	S R Malhotra Director (Sales)
SUBJECT:	Sales Target for the year 2013–2014

Fig. 24.1(a) Sample 1 of Heading Segment

DATE:	March 23, 2014
TO:	All Sales Managers
FROM:	Director (Sales)
SUBJECT:	Sales Target for the year 2013–2014

Fig. 24.1(b) Sample 2 of Heading Segment

DATE:	June 16, 2014
TO:	Assistant Registrar (Accounts)
FROM:	Finance Officer
SUBJECT:	Audit of Project Accounts

Fig. 24.1(c) Sample 3 of Heading Segment

DATE:	July 4, 2014
TO:	Rakesh Soni, System Administrator
FROM:	Lopamudra Roy, Tele Marketing Executive
SUBJECT:	**Seminar on Telemarketing Strategies**

Fig. 24.1(d) Sample 4 of Heading Segment

Opening

Most memos begin with a short paragraph describing the problem that led to the need for the memo and the basic 'purpose' of the memo. The opening segment, thus, mentions the 'central idea', which may include the context, the specific assignment or task, and the purpose of the memo. These aspects are incapsulated in the word CAP (C for context, A for assignment, and P for purpose). While the context is the circumstance, or background of the problem, the assignment describes the efforts to solve the problem. The purpose gives the reason for writing the memo.

Most memos begin with a short paragraph describing the problem that led to the need for the memo and the basic 'purpose' of the memo.

The opening of a memo must answer the following questions:

- What is the problem?
- What led to the need for the memo?
- What is the purpose of the memo?

Following are some examples:

- I am happy to report that our new product "ACT Energiser 2", launched in January this year, has been highly successful in the first six months of its launch. I am sending you the sales report for the last six months.
- As you requested, here is a copy of the annual sales report for our new product "ACT Energiser 2", launched in January this year.
- Please answer the following questions about the use of existing computer and Internet facilities in your department.
- On April 16, 2014 the department is conducting a special induction programme for the sales trainees who joined the company in 2014.
- Here is a summary of the measures the Campus Security Department is taking to ensure that only authorised people are allowed into the administrative offices.

Body

The body of a business memo contains the message of the memo. It describes, explains, and discusses the central idea of the memo, and includes all the details that support the senders' ideas. It may begin justifying the importance of the main point, and the next few paragraphs may contain more information and supporting details. The body may also contain a brief statement of the key recommendations the sender has reached. Appropriate graphic techniques and non-verbal data may be used in order to highlight the main parts of the memo.

Closing

Memos should be closed with a courteous ending, stating what action the reader is required to take. The sender can tell the readers how they will benefit from the desired actions. If a problem is being discussed in the memo, it may be closed by assuming up analysis of the problem and key recommendations. Thus, the closing segment of a routine memo may contain action information seeking action-oriented response specifying the action that the reader is required to take, while complex and long memos may also contain a summary of the main ideas.

Following are some examples:

1. Please send your recommendations to me by March 5, 2015 so that we are able to complete the project by the end of April, 2015.

2. We urge all the staff members to follow the above guidelines with effect from August 5, 2015. If we all work together, we can easily implement a uniform health scheme for all employees.
3. Could you please discuss the problems with the marketing staff and send me a brief report by July 31, 2015?
4. We have streamlined the activities of the advertising section and made the needed changes. I am sure with your cooperation and active involvement we would be able to achieve results within three months.
5. Please submit a brief summary of the accounting problems being faced by your department so that we can take immediate steps to solve these problems.
6. Please submit your report by June 30, 2014. If you have any doubts or questions, please call me at 011-23654875.
7. I am sure the new promotion scheme would motivate our employees to work hard to achieve targets. I would welcome your comments and observations on the features of the new scheme. Your cooperation in this matter is greatly appreciated.
8. The seminar will throw new light on the use of effective telemarketing strategies in promoting our products. Please attend the seminar and send us your observations by June 25, 2014.

Optional Elements

A few optional elements may be used in memos, as per requirements. These elements include references, attachments, and distribution lists. It may be necessary to provide references to other memos, letters, notices, circulars, reports, and other documents. The standard practice is to list the references at the top of the memo. Attachments provide supporting material for the subject of the memo and may include lists, graphs, diagrams, pictographs, photographs, tables, and other sources of data. A list of attachments may either be given at the top of the memo or at the end. Distribution lists include the names of persons who might be receiving copies of the memo.

Figure 24.2 shows the structure of a business memo.

Interoffice Memorandum

DATE: (Complete and Current)

TO: (Name and designation of the recipient)

FROM: (Name and designation of the sender)

SUBJECT: (Topic of the memo)

OPENING

(Contd.)

Fig. 24.2 Structure of a Business Memo

Progress Check 2

1. **Study the following layout of a business memo. The memo format is not correct. Reorganise the memo, making the needed changes in the structure and the format.**

NATIONAL TOURS AND TRAVELS PVT. LTD.
M-15/6, South Extension, New Delhi-110 049
www.nationaltours.com

DATE: June 15, 2014

SUBJECT: SPECIAL TRAINING COURSES IN SALES AND MARKETING

Preeti Biswas

Training Organiser

P R Mehta
General Manager

24.2.3 Writing Strategies

As business memos are systematic attempts to solve problems and stimulate thinking or action in individuals and groups, a systematic writing plan needs to be followed. However, a memo may have to be written at short notice and there may not be time for detailed planning. That is why it is important to learn writing strategies that help in writing effective memos.

The following steps will help in organising and presenting a memo systematically.

- **Step 1:** Analyse the problem and purpose
- **Step 2:** Determine the needs of the reader
- **Step 3:** Determine the scope of your message
- **Step 4:** Organise your message
- **Step 5:** Write the first draft.
- **Step 6:** Revise, review, and edit
- **Step 7:** Write the final draft

Analysing the Problem and Purpose

Understanding/identifying the problem or context for writing the memo is the first step in composing an effective memo. The purpose of the memo should also be noted down in one or two sentences. In order to analyse the problem and purpose, the following questions should be answered:

1. What is the problem?
2. Why is it necessary to write this memo?
3. How should the reader respond or act?

By answering these questions briefly, it will be possible to determine what should be covered in the memo. Therefore, appropriate background information and supporting data should be gathered.

Determining the Needs of the Reader

A memo will be effective if the sender is able to connect his/her purpose with the interests and needs of the reader. When planning a memo, the sender should think about it from the reader's perspective. Answers to the following questions should be known:

1. Who is the reader?
2. How is this relevant to the reader?
3. What is in it for the reader?

Determining the Scope of the Message

In order to keep the memo precise and to the point, the sender has to select what he/she will include in his/her memo from a wide range of supporting data. Determining the scope and meaning of the message may involve using several prewriting strategies such as brainstorming, mind-mapping, and free-writing. Brainstorming is a planning technique in which ideas are listed as they come to mind, while mind-mapping is a visual technique for grouping ideas into categories. Freewriting is a prewriting process that allows us to express ideas without worrying about spelling, grammatical mistakes, or organisational problems. These techniques will help in selecting the necessary information to support the central idea of the memo.

Brainstorming is a planning technique in which ideas are listed as they come to mind, while mind-mapping is a visual technique for grouping ideas into categories. Freewriting is a prewriting process that allows us to express ideas without worrying about spelling, grammatical mistakes, or organisational problems.

Organising the Message

After determining what should be covered in the memo, the message needs to be organised by selecting an appropriate organisational pattern. There are two widely recognised patterns to organise a memo—direct pattern and indirect pattern.

Direct Pattern

In direct organisational pattern, which is the most common, the sender starts out by stating the most important points first and then move to supporting details. Most memos contain routine information and the writer can begin the memo in a straightforward manner by telling the reader what he or she has in mind.

In direct pattern, inductive reasoning is used. Thus,

In direct pattern, inductive reasoning is used.

- answers come before explanations;
- requests come before reasons;
- summaries come before details;
- conclusions come before discussions; and
- general statements come before specifics.

This plan is useful for routine memos where the reader might be more receptive. Thus, we can organise a routine memo, as shown in Fig. 24.3, according to direct organisational pattern:

DATE: ....

TO: ....

FROM: ....

SUBJECT: ....

Opening ⟶ State the main idea of the memo. Focus the reader's attention on it.

Body ⟶ Explain, support, and develop the main point more fully.

Closing ⟶ Specify the action that you want the reader should take.

SIGNATURE

Fig. 24.3 Direct Organizational Pattern

Figure 24.4 shows an example of a memo using direct pattern:

Syndicate

Consultancy Services Pvt. Ltd.

Nayadeep, Andheri (W), Mumbai-53

DATE: June 16, 2014

TO: All Employees

FROM: Arunabh Bhattacharya
Director (Sales & Marketing)

SUBJECT: New Health Scheme

Opening states the main point ⟶

The company is introducing a new health scheme called SCS Health Plan. You will receive your new medical card and a booklet outlining the terms and conditions of the scheme by June 30, 2014.

The main features of the SCS Health Plan include:

- Medical reimbursement for treatment at private hospitals and clinics.
- Direct payment of medical expenses to AIIMS and other important national hospitals.
- Medical facilities for retired staff.
- Token system at SCS Hospital.

Body explains and supports the main point ⟶

SCS Health Plan is compulsory for all the employees of the company. The use of the medical card is mandatory.

Closing ⟶

I am sure the new health scheme will improve the existing medical facilities and would benefit our employees. We encourage you to use your new medical card whenever you visit the health centre or the SCS hospital and follow the guidelines contained in the brochure. Your cooperation in this matter will be greatly appreciated.

Arunabh Bhattacharya

Fig. 24.4 Direct Pattern

Indirect Pattern

The indirect pattern makes an appeal or spews out evidence first and arrives at a conclusion based on these facts. This plan is best used when it is necessary to arouse the reader's interest before describing some action that should be taken. It is also appropriate to use while saying 'No' to something. In indirect structure:

> The indirect pattern makes an appeal or spews out evidence first and arrives at a conclusion based on these facts.

- Reasons come before requests
- Details come before summaries
- Background comes before conclusions
- Explanations come before refusals.

This plan is useful for negative messages or for memos that contain sensitive information, which cannot be handled in a straightforward manner. Such messages can be organised, as shown in Fig. 24.5, according to indirect organisational pattern:

		DATE: ....
		TO: ....
		FROM: ....
		SUBJECT: ....
Opening	⟶	Begin with a meaningful statement that prepares the reader for the message. Explain and clarify the message.
Body	⟶	State the main point of the memo.
Closing	⟶	Close the memo with a courteous ending and state what action the reader should take.
		SIGNATURE

Fig. 24.5 Indirect Pattern

Figure 24.6 shows an example of a memo using indirect pattern:

Syndicate

Consultancy Services Pvt. Ltd.
Nayadeep, Andheri (W), Mumbai-53

	DATE: June 16, 2014
	TO: All Employees
	FROM: Arunabh Bhattacharya Director (Sales & Marketing)
	SUBJECT: New Health Scheme
Opening includes ⟶ a meaningful statement that prepares the reader for the message.	For the past one year the company has been receiving a number of complaints about problems regarding payment of medical reimbursement. In fact, employees have been facing difficulties due to several provisions of the existing health scheme of the company. Keeping in view the genuine grievances of the employees, the company is introducing a new health scheme called SCS Health Plan. You will receive your new medical card and a booklet outlining the terms and conditions of the scheme by June 30, 2014.
Body states ⟶ the main point and explains and supports the main point further.	The main features of the SCS Health Plan include: • Medical reimbursement for treatment at private hospitals and clinics. • Direct payment of medical expenses to AIIMS and other important national hospitals.

	• Medical facilities for retired staff. • Token system at SCS Hospital.
	SCS Health Plan is compulsory for all the employees of the company. The use of the medical card is mandatory.
Closing ⟶ that states the action, courteously	I am sure the new health scheme will improve the existing medical facilities and would benefit our employees. We encourage you to use your new medical card whenever you visit the health centre or the SCS hospital and follow the guidelines contained in the brochure. Your cooperation in this matter will be greatly appreciated.
	Arunabh Bhattacharya

Fig. 24.6 Indirect Pattern

Writing the First Draft

Once the problem and purpose have been analysed, the needs of the readers and the scope of the message determined, and an appropriate organisational pattern has been selected, the first draft can be written. While writing the first working draft, the following points should be remembered:

- Write quickly
- Keep the audience in mind
- Focus on the purpose of the memo
- Do not give too much thought to perfect expression

Reviewing and Revising

Once the rough draft has been written, it needs to be reviewed, edited, and revised in order to improve the quality of its content and presentation. While reviewing is the process of analysing whether the memo achieved its purpose, editing involves correcting its format, mechanics, grammar, spelling, and punctuation. Revising focuses on improving the content and sentence structure of the memo.

While reviewing is the process of analysing whether the memo achieved its purpose, editing involves correcting its format, mechanics, grammar, spelling, and punctuation. Revising focuses on improving the content and sentence structure of the memo.

Writing the Final Draft

Once the rough draft has been revised, the final draft of the memo can be composed. While writing the final draft, the following points should be taken care of:

- Keep the memo simple, clear, concise, direct, and readable.
- Good sentence structure and clear, concise communication should be used.
- Appropriate words, short sentences and meaningful paragraphs should be used.
- Appropriate linking devices should be used.
- Graphic highlighting techniques should be applied to improve readability and comprehension.
- Important points should be emphasised.

Progress Check 3

1. **Read the following statements about business memos and mark True or False against each statement in the light of the above discussion:**
   (a) The purpose of a memo, the response you want, and a general profile of the audience may not help in determining what should be included in it.
   (b) Determining the scope of a memo involves selecting what should be included in it from a wide range of facts and figures.
   (c) Brainstorming is a planning technique in which you list ideas as they come to mind while free-writing is an effective technique to generate ideas.
   (d) In direct organisational pattern, discussions come before conclusions.
   (e) The key to the direct organisational pattern is the principle of deductive reasoning.
   (f) The indirect organisational pattern makes an appeal first and arrives at a conclusion based on these facts.
   (g) Direct organisational pattern is useful for negative messages or for memos that contain sensitive information.
   (h) Reviewing is the process of analysing whether a memo achieved its purpose.
   (i) Editing involves correcting a memo's format, mechanics, grammar, spelling and punctuation.
   (j) Revising focuses on improving the content and sentence structure of a memo.
2. **Study the following situations that require you to write memos. Choose an appropriate organisational pattern (direct/indirect) that you will use while writing each memo.**
   (a) You want to write a memo to your boss to persuade him that you have a solution to a problem facing the company.
   (b) You want to refuse an invitation to attend a seminar in the IT Department of your company because you are very busy.
   (c) You want to invite all your colleagues to a presentation in your department.
   (d) You want to give general guidelines to all your staff about punctuality and discipline in the office.
   (e) You are facing several problems in dealing with some employees of your department and you want to inform the MD of your company of the possible consequences of the situation.
   (f) There has been a fire in one of the offices under you. You want to inform the GM of your company.
   (g) One of the accountants in your company has left the company. You have a solution to the problem and want to share that with the Director, Personnel of your company.
   (h) One of your colleagues has misbehaved with you. You want to complain to the GM (Personnel).
   (i) You have to give historical background of a particular case involving an employee of your company.
   (j) You want to express your acceptance of an invitation to be a key speaker in a seminar organised by the Public Relations Department of your company.

24.2.4 SAMPLE MEMOS

The following are some samples of model memos:

Sample 1

AFRON PHARMACEUTICAL IND.

Ansari Road, Daryaganj, New Delhi-110002

www.afronpharma.ac.in

Interoffice Memorandum

DATE: January 14, 2014

TO: Maya David
District Manager

FROM: Kapil Khandelwal
Regional Manager

SUBJECT: NEW PROCEDURE FOR STOCK VERIFICATION

We are starting a new procedure for stock entry and verification. Instead of keeping three different registers for recording stock of expired medicines, past stock, and new arrivals, we will use only two registers for the three types of entries, one register for expired medicines and one for past stock and new arrivals.

The change will make it easier to record and verify existing stock. This will avoid the present confusion created by triple entries and will save time, space, and energy. District managers will continue to be the stock verification officers for their respective district.

This change will go into effect from March 15, 2014. I am sure the change will make stock entry and verification in our company more organised and logical.

Kapil Khandelwal

Sample 2

S K P Ship Management

Remi Bizourt, VD Road, Andheri (W), Mumbai-400 053

Interoffice Memorndum

DATE: August 7, 2014

TO: Ashish Kumar, Training Manager

FROM: Jerry Massey, Managing Director

SUBJECT: SPECIAL WORKSHOP ON "SHIP MANAGEMENT AND MODERN TECHNOLOGY"

Please refer to your memo dated July 31, 2014, containing the proposal to organise a special workshop on "Ship Management and Modern Technology" for the junior executives of our company. I am pleased to inform you that the Executive Board has approved your proposal.

You may send us the final list of resource persons to be invited in the workshop. You may consider including the names of a few senior executives working in the ship management industry. This may help us in making the workshop more focused and need-based.

I would like to express my appreciation for the effort that you have put in to design the structure of the workshop. Keep up the good work and keep these ideas coming.

Jerry Massey

Sample 3

NATIONAL TOURS AND TRAVELS PVT. LTD.

M-15/6, South Extension, New Delhi-110 049

www.nationaltours.com

Interoffice Memorandum

DATE: June 15, 2014

TO: Preeti Biswas, Training Organiser

FROM: P R Mehta, General Manager

SUBJECT: SPECIAL TRAINING COURSES IN SALES AND MARKETING

As you know, Sarna Corporate Training Pvt. Ltd. Delhi has proposed to conduct special training courses in sales and marketing for our field staff involved in aggressive selling of tour packages. I would like you to select the appropriate course for our sales trainees.

I am sending you the following information as an attachment to enable you to choose the right course for them:

1. List of the courses
2. Duration of each course
3. Structure and content of each course

I would like to discuss this matter with you at the earliest at a mutually convenient time. We need to take a decision by the end of this month.

P R Mehta

Exercise

1. **Assume that you have to write a memo to your office supervisor explaining him (or her) why you are coming late to the office. Mention the following reasons for coming late:**
   - Heavy traffic load
   - A long queue at the company entrance gate
   - The on campus parking problem you are facing
   - In your memo you must take care of all possible steps in designing and styling the memo you learned in this chapter.
2. **Assume that you are Kapil Singhania, the Managing Director of Innovation Software, Limited. You have to write a memo to all your sales staff informing them that the company has decided to give an incentive at the rate of 5 per cent to all the sales staff from July 2014.**
3. **As Mazhar Khan, the Public Relations Officer of Eva Formulations, Pvt Ltd, you have been asked to draft a memo to the office staff about the Company's Annual Business Conference. Include the following information:**
   - Venue of the conference
   - Date and time of the conference
   - Theme of the conference
   - List of special invitees
4. **Assume that you are Pashupati Shah, the Regional Sales Manager of Easy Home Appliances, Mumbai. You have to write a memo to Reena Chatterjee, Assistant Manager (Sales) explaining a new procedure for reporting monthly sales performance. The special features of the new procedure include:**
   - Use of double entry system to record monthly sales performance instead of the existing single entry system;
   - A separate format for sales performance below quota; and
   - A computerised database.

   The new procedure will be go into effect from January 1, 2015.

Key to Progress Check

Progress Check 1

1. (a). True (b) True (c) False (d) False (e) False
   (f) True (g) True (h) False (i) True (j) True

Progress Check 2

1.

NATIONAL TOURS AND TRAVELS PVT. LTD.

M-15/6, South Extension, New Delhi-110 049

www.nationaltours.com

Interoffice Memorandum

DATE: June 15, 2014

TO: Preeti Biswas, Training Organiser

FROM: P R Mehta, General Manager

SUBJECT: SPECIAL TRAINING COURSES IN SALES AND MARKETING

P R Mehta

Progress Check 3

1. (a) False (b) True (c) True (d) False
   (e) False (f) True (g) False (h) True
   (i) True (j) True
2. (a) Indirect pattern (b) Indirect pattern (c) Direct pattern (d) Direct pattern
   (e) Indirect pattern (f) Direct pattern (g) Indirect pattern (h) Indirect pattern
   (i) Indirect pattern (j) Direct pattern

25 CHAPTER

Email Writing

The phenomenal growth in the use of the Internet has resulted in services that millions of people now take for granted, such as e-mail, web browsing, and electronic exchange of business transactions.

—**Gerd Keiser**

LEARNING OBJECTIVES

- Understanding the nature and importance of electronic mail
- Identifying six major advantages of e-mail
- Knowing the five characteristics of successful e-mail messages
- Understanding the different parts of an e-mail message
- Knowing how to write effective e-mail messages
- Understanding standard e-mail practices

25.1 INTRODUCTION

Electronic mail (e-mail) is the medium of communication that sends and receives messages through specially designed computer networks. With the revolution in information technology along with the rapid growth of the Internet, e-mail has become the most popular communication medium. More and more people are spending time on the Net sending e-mail messages. There is no doubt that due to its high speed, low cost, and efficiency, e-mail is today one of the most important channels of communication.

> E-mails are used for quick transmission of information and ideas.

Like business letters and memos, e-mail messages help to reinforce professional and business relations. Everyday business dealings and ordinary activities of business would not be possible without e-mail. E-mail can be used both as a means to reach out to people outside an organisation, and to send information within an organisation. It is used within organisations through specially designed internal computer networks.

> E-mail can be used both as a means to reach out to people outside an organisation, and to send information within an organisation.

We need effective e-mail writing skills because e-mail can be an important communications channel between us and our peers, subordinates, superiors, other colleagues, customers, and several other people we interact with regularly. We may have to write a number of e-mail messages everyday. As e-mails are faster than letters and memos, they are used for quick transmission of information and ideas. They serve several purposes, which may include:

- Conveying routine information, such as new products or services being introduced, new policy changes, introduction of new procedures, new market strategies being followed, and so on
- Requesting information or additional resources
- Inviting the reader to business meetings, conferences, seminars, workshops, or symposiums
- Containing proposals or requests for proposals
- Seeking explanations or clarifications
- Describing problems
- Persuading the reader to take an action
- Giving feedback, suggestions, or recommendations.

25.1.1 Advantages of E-mail

Speed

Speed is the main advantage of using e-mail. Unlike regular mail, which may take days or even weeks to reach its destination, e-mail reaches its destination instantaneously. A message can be sent quickly to anyone anywhere in the world. Distance is immaterial. Just type the name/names and e-mail address/addresses of the recipient and click the mouse on the send button, and your message goes.

Low Cost

Low cost is yet another advantage of using e-mail. As sending e-mail does not involve printing and copying, it is less expensive than any other channel of communication (that is, postal mail, telephone, fax etc.). Ten e-mail messages may be sent in ten minutes and the only cost would be that of using the internet. Moreover, the size of the message or the distance to the recipient does not affect the cost.

Quick Distribution

E-mail makes distribution quick and easy. Messages can be sent to more than one person at the same time. There is no wasting of time and no repetition.

Flexibility

E-mail allows complete flexibility during composing and drafting. While using e-mail, the sender may edit, revise, modify, and redesign his/her message without printing and copying it. He/She can easily reshape e-mail messages before sending them. Moreover, he/she has the flexibility to receive or compose e-mails as per his/her convenience.

Easy Attachments

It is easy to attach files, photographs, clippings, drawings, video clips, sound recordings, and so on to an e-mail. For example, resumes, scanned copies of testimonials, transcripts, and other documents can be attached to job application e-mail.

Easy Upward Communication

E-mail is less formal and structured than letters and memos. It is normally in the form of a private dialogue, where the sender wants to say something and expects a response to the message. Thus, e-mail promotes easier upward communication. While using e-mail the sender need not worry about a formal and fixed style of communication. He/She may follow the norms of any set pattern of writing and is free to choose any style or pattern that suits the content.

25.2 WRITING EFFECTIVE E-MAILS

25.2.1 Characteristics of Effective E-Mail

Professionals need to use e-mail frequently. In fact, the use of e-mail for business and professional communication purposes continues to expand due to its tremendous advantages. It has become the most common professional communication medium. It is replacing printed memos in several organisations by playing a more important role in the dissemination of ideas and information. Good e-mail messages share certain characteristics, which include conciseness, accuracy, clarity, conversational tone, and single theme.

> E-mails are replacing printed memos in several organisations by playing a more important role in the dissemination of ideas and information.

Concise

Conciseness is the most important characteristic of a successful e-mail message. An e-mail should not contain unnecessary information. Unnecessary explanations, repetitions, wordy expressions, and exaggeration should be avoided. Ideas should be organised in such a way that the e-mail makes its point with the fewest words possible. The reader may not be interested, or have the time, in a very long and detailed message.

Correct

Accuracy is crucial to successful e-mail writing. Correct format and structure should be used. Correct e-mail addresses should be written. Messages may bounce if incorrect e-mail address is written. The content of the e-mail should also be checked for factual accuracy. E-mail messages should be edited for spelling, punctuation, and grammar mistakes.

Clear

E-mails should be simple and clear. An unclear and vague e-mail may be immediately deleted. Simple, familiar, direct and specific words, appropriate linkers, and transitional signals should be used to form short sentences and paragraphs.

An unclear and vague e-mail may be immediately deleted.

Conversational Tone

The tone of e-mail messages are usually formal but conversational. It is better to use a tone which gives a personal touch to e-mails. However, one should avoid being too informal or emotional. The challenge is to maintain professionalism without being too formal. Although first person pronouns (that is, I, we) and conversational contractions (you'll, he'll, she'll, can't, don't, doesn't, etc.) may be used, standard writing techniques should be used and professional writing conventions followed.

Single Theme

A successful e-mail message deals with only one topic. In order to be purposive, you need to focus on a single theme. Develop a single theme logically, subordinating related ideas.

Progress Check 1

1. **Read the following statements about e-mail messages and mark True or False against each statement in the light of the above discussion:**
   (a) E-mail is the medium of communication that sends and receives messages through specially designed computer networks.
   (b) E-mail cannot be used as a means to reach out to people outside an organisation.
   (c) Speed is the main advantage of using e-mail.
   (d) The advantages of using e-mail do not include easy upward communication.
   (e) As sending an e-mai message involves using computer, it is more expensive than any other channel of communication.
   (f) You can send your e-mail message to as many people as you want.
   (g) E-mail allows complete flexibility during composing and drafting.
   (h) Attaching photographs, video clips, and sound recordings to your e-mail could be very costly.
   (i) While using e-mail, you may choose any style or pattern that suits your content.
   (j) Your ideas should be organized in such a way that the e-mail makes its point in the fewest words possible.
   (k) The tone of e-mail messages is very informal and emotional.
   (l) A successful e-mail message deals with only one topic.

25.2.2 E-Mail Structure

Formatting e-mail messages demands awareness of current e-mail conventions and standard practices. In order to write an appropriate e-mail, it should be formatted correctly. Standard writing conventions should be followed.

E-mail messages contain six segments: heading (date, from, to, subject, CC, BCC), salutation, opening, body, closing, and signature.

When we receive an Internet e-mail message, it usually contains many lines before the beginning of the actual text. These lines consist of the "header" of the message. Most of it is a record of the path the message took from the sender's computer to the reader's computer. Headers also often contain a time and date stamp and an indication of whether files are attached to the message.

The three most important pieces of information in the header are the e-mail addresses of the sender and the recipient, and a subject line that tells what the message is about. All e-mail messages contain these three pieces of information.

When a person sends an e-mail message, the programme usually inserts him/her name, return e-mail address, and date automatically. Therefore, the sender need not type his/her name, e-mail address, and date again. He/She just needs to fill in the "To" line with the recipient's email address, the "Subject" line with a clear and concise description of the subject of his/her message, the CC line with the e-mail address of anyone who is to receive a copy of the e-mail message, and the BCC line with the e-mail address of anyone who is to receive a blind copy of your e-mail message.

E-mail includes the following:

- Heading
- Salutation
- Body
- Closing
- Signature

Heading

The heading segment of an e-mail includes the following six elements:

- Date
- From
- To
- Subject
- CC
- BCC

Date

The Date line indicates the date the e-mail was written. It includes the day, month, year, and the exact time. While sending an email message, the date line usually appears automatically.

Examples:

Date: Sat, 6 March 2014 12:58:20 + 0100(BST)
Date: Sun, 16 May 2014 07:37:58 –0600
Date: Mon, 19 July 2014 15:01:19 +0400
Date: Wed, 4 Aug 2014 13:16:36 +0100(BST)

From

The From line contains the sender's name and e-mail address. The name does not include any personal title such as Ms, Mrs, Mr, or Dr. While sending an e-mail message, the return address usually appears automatically.

Examples:

From : "Tony Bright" <bright@squ.edu.om>

From : “Christine Coombe” <christine_coombe@hct.ac.ae>
From : “ashraf rizvi” <ashrafrizvi@yahoo.co.uk>
From : “Ian Robertson”<ian@squ.edu.om>

To

The To line includes the recipient’s e-mail address.

Examples:

To : <vaughan@rediffmail.com>
To : <maya@yahoo.com>
To : <beth_wiens@hct.ac.ae>
To : <snmukherjee@perl.ism.ac.in>

Subject

The Subject line summarises the topic of the e-mail in a few words. It includes clear and complete information about the theme of the e-mail in phrase form.

Examples:

Subject : TACON 2014 Proposal
Subject : Return from Extraordinary Leave
Subject : TCS Annual Conference 2014
Subject : Confirmation of participation in SAARC 2005 seminar on Information Technology

CC

The CC line (carbon copy) may include the e-mail address of anyone who is to receive a copy of the e-mail message. It is an optional line.

Examples:

Cc : anmol@cal.vsnl.net.in
Cc : leensthomas@tcs.ac.in
Cc : kmtiwary@yahoo.co.uk
Cc : rowena@infys.vsnl.net.in

BCC

The BCC line (blind carbon copy) may include the e-mail address of anyone who is to receive a blind copy of the e-mail message. The e-mail address(es) mentioned in the BCC line would not visible to other recipients in the To or CC fields. It is an optional line.

Examples:

Bcc: binumathews@yahoo.com
Bcc: rajesh_tandon@rediffmail.com
Bcc: seemat@perl.ism.in
Bcc: ramanathans@squ.edu.om
Figure 25.1 shows e-mail heading.

Mail	Addresses	Calendar	Compose		prmathur@perl.ism.in [Sign Out]	
Check Mail					Search Mail – Mail Options	
Check Other Mail	Previous	Next	Back to Messages		Printable View - Full	
[Edit]	Delete	Reply	Reply All	Forward	Attachment	Move to folder
Folders [Add]	**Date**: Sun, 15 August 2014 16:24:20 + 0100					
Inbox	**From**: "Pramod Mathur" <pmathur@perl.ism.in>					
Draft	**To**: "Naveen Kashyap "< kashyapn@yahoo.co.uk>					
Sent	**Subject**: World Bank Project					
Bulk (Empty)	**Cc**: gsingh@rediffmail.com					
Trash (Empty)	**Bcc**: binumathews@yahoo.com					
My Folders [Hide]						

Fig. 25.1 E-Mail Heading

Salutation

A salutation should be used, as in Figure 25.2, if e-mail is being used as a means to reach out to people outside the sender's organisation. The same name as in the To line can be used with a personal title such as Ms, Mrs, Mr, or Dr. However, salutation may be omitted if the e-mail is being used to send information inside the sender's organisation.

Examples:

Dear Dr Bright,
Dear Professor Vaughan,
Dear Maya
Dear Beth Wiens,

Mail	Addresses	Calendar	Compose		bright@squ.edu.om [Sign Out]	
Check Mail					Search Mail – Mail Options	
Check Other Mail	Previous	Next	Back to Messages		Printable View - Full	
[Edit]	Delete	Reply	Reply All	Forward	Attachment	Move to folder
Folders [Add]	**Date:** Sat, 6 March 2014 12:58:20 + 0100(BST)					
Inbox	**From:** "Tony Bright" <bright@squ.edu.om>					
Draft	**To:** "David Kirk Vaughan"<vaughan@redffmail.com>					
Sent	**Subject:** Business Communication Workshop					
Bulk (Empty)	**Cc:** ian@squ.edu.om					
Trash (Empty)	**BCC:**					
	Dear Mr Vaughan,					

Fig. 25.2 E-mail Salutation

Body

The body of an e-mail message describes, explains, and discusses the central idea of the e-mail. The content of the e-mail should be organised carefully. The first paragraph may begin with a friendly opening followed by a statement of the main point. The next paragraph should begin by justifying the importance of the main point. In the next few paragraphs, justification should be continued along with background information and supporting detail. The closing paragraph should restate the purpose of the e-mail and, in some cases, request some type of action.

Closing

An external e-mail message may be concluded with an appropriate closing such as Best regards, Kind regards, Regards, Sincerely, Yours faithfully, Thank you and regards, All the best, and so on.

Signature

The signature line in an e-mail message generally contains only the writer's name. However, it can also contain the title and organisation of the sender.

Sample E-mail

Figure 25.3 shows the structure of an e-mail message.

Mail	Addresses	Calendar	Compose	christine_coombe @hct.ac.ae [Sign Out]	
Check Mail				**Search Mail – Mail Options**	
Check Other Mail	Previous	Next	Back to Messages	Printable View - Full	
[Edit]	Delete	Reply	Reply All	Forward	Attachment	Move to folder

Folders [Add]
Inbox
Draft
Sent
Bulk (Empty)
Trash (Empty)

From: "Christine_Coombe" <christine_coombe @hct.ac.ae>
To: "ashraf rizvi"<ashrafrizvi@yahoo.co.uk>
Subject: TACON 2014 Proposal
Date: Sat, 6 March 2014 12:58:20 + 0100(BST)
Cc: beth_wiens@hct.ac.ae
Bcc: binumathews@yahoo.com
Bcc:

Dear Dr Rizvi,

We are pleased to inform you that your presentation for the 9th Annual TESOL Arabia Conference to be held in Dubai from March 30–31, 2014, has been accepted. Further details about the schedule for your presentation will follow. Please note that all presenters must pay for membership of TESOL Arabia—either 50AED or 100 AED, depending on your place of employment—and pre-register for the conference.

The last day for the early registration is the 18 March, 2014, and the last date for Pre-registration is the 21 March, 2014. See the TESOL Arabia website for accommodation information and for a downloadable copy of the Conference Registration Form. You can register for the conference and pay membership fees together on this form.

Would look forward to your presentation.

Regards,
Christine Coombe & Beth Wiens
Proposals Co-chairs

Fig. 25.3 Structure of an E-mail Message

Progress Check 2

1. **Study the following e-mail, in which the format is not correct. Reorganise the e-mail, making the necessary changes in its structure and format.**

Mail	Addresses	Calendar	Compose		anindya@rediffmail.com [Sign Out]	
Check Mail					**Search Mail – Mail Options**	
Check Other Mail	Previous	Next	Back to Messages		Printable View - Full	
[Edit]	Delete	Reply	Reply All	Forward	Attachment	Move to folder

Folders [Add]	**Subject:** Return from Leave
Inbox	**Date:** Sat, 14 August 2014 10:12:15 + 0100(BST)
Draft	**Cc:** ronaldpl@ito.ac.ae_
Sent	**From:** "john shannon" <jshannon@ito.ac.ae>
Bulk (Empty)	**Bcc:** <deshpander@ito.ac.ae>
Trash (Empty)	**To:** "anindya sarkar"<anindya@rediffmail.com>
My Folders [Hide]	My name is John Shannon and I am the new Sales Director of the International Trading Organisation Ltd. I am currently planning various activities related to the new Sales Division of the company and it is important that we know your date of return to duty. Would you please contact Ronald and let us know. Thank you and regards, John Shannon Sales Director

25.2.3 Standard E-Mail Practices

As e-mail messages are systematic attempts to collaborate with colleagues and other professionals standard e-mail practices need to be followed. The following suggestions will help in organising and presenting e-mail messages systematically.

> E-mail etiquette or netiquette are essential in writing effective e-mail messages.

Follow Established e-mail Conventions Every organisation maintains certain norms regarding electronic communication. Some organisations may consider certain messages inappropriate for the company e-mail system. In most of the organisations, e-mail is not used to send confidential messages such as confidential employee reports, company secrets, matters related to organisational business, sensitive personal business dealings, and so on. It is important for us to be familiar with the established e-mail conventions of the organization we work in. As a rule, e-mail is not used to send confidential, complex, embarrassing or sensitive information. As e-mail creates a permanent record that can be used against the sender, it should not be used to convey anything that should not be made public.

> As e-mail creates a permanent record that can be used against the sender, it should not be used to convey anything that should not be made public.

Check Mailbox Regularly As speed is the main advantage of using e-mail, everyone wants a quick response to his/her e-mail. We should check our mailbox regularly so that we can read every e-mail message sent to us and respond swiftly. In case, we cannot respond because we do not have enough information, an acknowledgement should be e-mailed.

Be Correct Many people tend to be casual while sending e-mail messages. Special care should be taken about accuracy, which includes, both, accuracy of information as well as accuracy of presentation. It is very important that the sender assures himself/herself of the accuracy of information he/she is sending before clicking the send button. The following should be double-checked:

- The electronic address/addresses of the receiver
- The subject line
- Basic content of the e-mail message
- The attachments.

Also, it is important to review, edit, and revise e-mail messages in order to improve their quality of presentation. E-mail messages should be reviewed to analyse whether they can achieve their purpose. They should be edited to correct their format, mechanics, grammar, spelling, and punctuation. The spelling and grammar check may be used.

Be Brief E-mail may be used effectively to convey non-sensitive simple messages. E-mail may not be very suitable for conveying complex or sensitive information. So, e-mail messages should be short. No one likes to read very lengthy e-mail messages. Unnecessary information, wordy expressions, repetitions, and exaggeration should be avoided. The e-mail message should make its point in the fewest words possible and sentences and paragraphs should be short.

Be Formal E-mail is a formal channel of communication and formal language should be used. Standard writing techniques should be used and professional writing conventions should be followed. Standard English should be used and informality should be avoided even if the sender knows the receiver very closely. Emotional expressions, informal words, personal remarks, humorous statements, jokes, and so on should be avoided. The main purpose should always be borne in mind, and distractions should be avoided.

> Standard writing techniques should be used and professional writing conventions should be followed.

Maintain Readability In order to make a message easy to read, the sender must be able to visualise the computer screen while composing the e-mail message. Design elements such as introductory summary, headings, side-headings, listings, and so on may be used in order to improve the readability of longer e-mail messages. These days many people read their e-mails on mobile phones or tablets. Therefore, readability should be taken care of.

Care About Tone Using a tactless or negative tone can lead to confusion and misunderstanding. A formal but conversational tone, which gives a personal touch to your e-mail is preferable. The sender must adopt his/her expression to the demands of the situation and the needs of his/her readers. First person pronouns (I, we) and conversational contractions (you'll, he'll, she'll, can't, don't, doesn't.) may be used.

25.2.4 E-Mail Writing Strategies

Like letters and memos, e-mail messages are systematic attempts to address key issues and solve problems by quick transfer of information and ideas. As e-mail can be an important communications channel between the sender and his/her colleagues, peers, subordinates, seniors and customers, e-mail messages need to be organised and presented systematically. Although the sender may have to write an email message at a short notice and may not get time to go for detailed planning, a few e-mail writing strategies need to be adopted to help in writing effective e-mail messages.

Sending an E-Mail

In order to write an effective e-mail message, the sender should **identify the problem** that led to the writing of the e-mail message and **analyse his/her audience** to understand their needs. He/She should **determine the scope of the message**, and **prepare an outline of** the main points that he/she wishes to include in the e-mail. Once the sender has determined what he should cover in his/her e-mail, he/she may organise his/her message by **selecting an appropriate organisational pattern**, direct pattern or indirect pattern. The sender may then **write the first draft.** After **reviewing and revising** the first draft, the **final draft** can be written.

Responding to an E-Mail

If a response to an e-mail message has to be written, the message should be read carefully to understand what the writer wants. After determining the scope of the message and organising the message, the first draft may be written. The draft is reviewed, then revised and edited to compose the final draft.

Sample E-mail

Read the following model e-mail message in Fig. 25.4 to understand the way it has been organized.

Mail	Addresses	Calendar	Compose	shannon@uaeu.ac.ae [Sign Cut]
Check Mail				**Search Mail – Mail Options**

Check Other Mail	Previous	Next	Back to Messages		Printable View - Full	
[Edit]	Delete	Reply	Reply All	Forward	Attachment	Move to folder

Folders [Add]	**Date:** Sat, 14 August 2014 10:12:15 + 0100(BST)
Inbox	**From:** "john shannon" <shannon@uaeu.ac.ae>
Draft	**To:** "anindya sarkar"<anindya@rediffmail.com>
Sent	**Subject:** Return from Leave
Bulk (Empty)	**Cc:** <ronaldpl@uaeu.ac.ae>_
Trash (Empty)	**Bcc:** <deshpander@uaeu.ac.ae>
My Folders [Hide]	

Dear Dr Sarkar,

Thank you for your prompt reply. I appreciate the difficulties you are facing and I hope you make a quick recovery.

I look forward to seeing you by 28 August, or earlier if you can manage it. It would be in your interest if you could arrive earlier so as to allow yourself adequate time to prepare the strategy to launch our new product.

Kind regards,

John Shannon

Fig. 25.4 A Sample E-mail Reply Message

Exercise

1. **Assume that you are Niren Bhattacharya, a student doing B.Tech in Mechanical Engineering from IIT, Delhi. Write an e-mail message to Kabir Sahini, the Personnel Manager of Alpha Industries (e-mail address: sahini_kabir@alpha.com) requesting him to allow you to do summer training at the Gurgaon plant of the company. Tell him that you need to do a two weeks training at some company as part of your academic assignments.**
2. **You are Sunil Mehta, Purchase Officer, Central Mining Research Institute, Nagpur. Write an e-mail to the Sales Manager of HCL Limited, Kolkata office. You want fifty HCL Desktop computers at the quoted price of ₹21,327/- each. Request the Sales Manager to send details regarding payment system, freight and handling charges, and the delivery time.**
3. **Suppose you want to take an education loan from Citi Bank. Write an e-mail for the Credit Mangaer of Citi Bank, Mumbai requesting him to send you details regarding educational loans by Citi Bank.**
4. **Assume that you have to write an e-mail to the Librarian-In-Charge of the central library of your university requesting him to send you information regarding new arrivals in the library though e-mail.**

Key to Progress Check

Progress Check 1

1. (a) True (b) False (c) True (d) False (e) False (f) True
(g) True (h) False (i) True (j) True (k) False (l) True

Progress Check 2

1.

<table>
<tr><td>Mail</td><td>Addresses</td><td>Calendar</td><td>Compose</td><td colspan="2">shannon@ito.ac.ae [Sign Out]</td></tr>
<tr><td>Check Mail</td><td colspan="3"></td><td colspan="2">Search Mail – Mail Options</td></tr>
<tr><td colspan="6"></td></tr>
<tr><td>Check Other Mail</td><td>Previous</td><td>Next</td><td>Back to Messages</td><td colspan="2">Printable View - Full</td></tr>
<tr><td>[Edit]</td><td>Delete</td><td>Reply</td><td>Reply All Forward</td><td>Attachment</td><td>Move to folder</td></tr>
<tr><td>Folders [Add]
Inbox
Draft
Sent
Bulk (Empty)
Trash (Empty)
My Folders
[Hide]</td><td colspan="5">DATE: Sat, 14 August 2014 10:12:15 + 0100(BST)
FROM: “john shannon” <shannon@ito.ac.ae>
TO: “anindya sarkar”<anindya@rediffmail.com>
SUBJECT: Return from Leave
CC: <ronaldpl@ito.ac.ae>_
BCC: <deshpander@ito.ac.ae>

Dear Mr Sarkar,
My name is John Shannon and I am the new Sales Director of the International Trading Organization Ltd. I am currently planning various activities related to the new Sales Division of the company and it is important that we know your date of return to duty.
Would you please contact Ronald and let us know.
Thank you and regards,
John Shannon</td></tr>
</table>

26 CHAPTER

Report Writing

A report is a formal document written for a specific audience to meet a specific need.

LEARNING OBJECTIVES

- Understanding the nature and importance of reports
- Knowing the different types of reports
- Being able to identify four report formats
- Knowing the components of formal reports
- Being able to chalk out various strategies of writing a report

26.1 INTRODUCTION

Whether a person is a public servant in a government organisation or a business manager in a multinational company, almost everyone may be asked to write reports at some point of time or the other. Professionals such as administrators, scientists, business executives, and engineers have to write reports for different purposes. A scientist may have to write a technical report that provides scientific data, whereas the sales manager of a company may need to prepare weekly sales reports to answer questions about how effectively sales targets are being achieved. Reports are important because in most organizations executive decision-making is based almost entirely on them.

Reports are important because in most organizations executive decision-making is based almost entirely on them.

Reports may vary from a one-page informal trip report summarising the events of a business trip to a 250-page formal annual report of an organisation. They may be presented orally, electronically, or in a written form. They may also vary in form, content, approach, and purpose. It is, thus, difficult to provide a specific but comprehensive definition of the term 'report'. The literal meaning of the word 'report' is 'a formal or official statement, as of results of an investigation or matter referred' or just 'a statement of facts'.

A report is a formal document written for a specific audience to meet a specific need. It may contain facts of a situation, project, or process; an analysis and interpretation of data, events, and records; inferences or conclusions drawn from objective data; or suggestions and recommendations. Although reports may include a variety of topics and objectives, they all help in the process of decision-making by answering questions and determining ways to improve certain situations. As a common type of communication used during work, reports reinforce, prompt, motivate, and persuade the readers to act. Reports normally move in an upward direction and are used to communicate to the senior levels in an organisations.

A report is a factual and systematic account of a specific business or professional activity.

Reports normally move in an upward direction and are used to communicate to the senior levels in an organisations.

26.1.1 Importance of Reports

The importance of reports for any professional lies in the fact that a number of business decisions and research conclusions are made on the basis of information presented or recommendations made in reports. By helping in dissemination of ideas, views, and suggestions, reports develop information and understanding essential for effective decision-making.

Thus, reports serve several purposes, which may include:

- Presenting data
- Describing problems and suggesting solutions
- Discussing and analysing data
- Recording events and happenings
- Analysing a situation or a condition
- Giving feedback, suggestions, or recommendations.

Reports help in the analysis of a condition, situation, or a problem for an effective solution.

Students will be called upon to write project reports, seminar reports, progress reports, research reports, dissertations or theses. Moreover, effective report writing skills are necessary in order to be successful at the workplace. As a person advances in his/her chosen career, he/she may be called on to prepare different kinds of reports more often and more effectively. Periodic operating reports, situational reports, informational routine reports, investigative reports, feasibility reports, compliance reports, and so on are some of different kinds of reports that may have to be prepared.

26.1.2 Types of Reports

As summarised in Fig. 26.1, reports can be classified as informational and analytical, according to their functions, as routine or special, as per periodicity, as oral and written, according to their communicative form, and as formal and non-formal, based on their nature, scope, and length. Each of these are now discussed briefly.

Informational and Analytical Reports

An informational report presents facts of a case, problem, condition, or situation without any analysis, interpretations, or recommendations. The function of the writer of an informational report is to collect, compile, and organise facts for the readers. He/she is just a compiler who has to present the data as objectively as possible. In order to write an informational report, relevant information should be gathered and presented in a systematic and organised way. Examples of informational reports include conference reports, seminar reports, trip reports, and so on.

Unlike an informational report, an analytical report presents data with interpretation and analysis. The report writer analyses the facts of a case, problem, condition, or situation objectively and puts forward his/her conclusions, inferences, and recommendations. Apart from presenting the facts objectively, the writer must reflect a broader understanding of the subject in order to comment on various aspects related to the report. In order to write an analytical report, the writer should be able to evaluate information and make appropriate inferences. Examples of analytical reports include project reports, feasibility reports, market research reports, and so forth.

Routine and Special Reports

All organisations including companies, institutions, government departments, and research establishments, depend on routine reports for various management decisions. As routine reports are usually prepared on a periodic basis, that is, daily, weekly, fortnightly, monthly, quarterly, or annually, they may also be called periodic reports. The contents of routine reports may vary from simple production information to complex marketing or research data. Routine reports may be informational or analytical depending on the purpose. Examples of routine reports include daily production reports, monthly sales reports, annual reports, and so on.

> As routine reports are usually prepared on a periodic basis they may also be called periodic reports.

Unlike a routine report, a special report is prepared and presented to convey special information related to a single condition, situation, problem, or occasion. Special reports do not contain routine or repetitive information as they are the result of specific circumstances. Some of the most important decisions in an organisation may be taken on the basis of the information contained in special reports. For example, a company might launch a new product based on a report analysing the market demand and presence of competing products in the market. Special reports could be either informational or analytical. Examples of special reports include inquiry reports, research reports, thesis, dissertation, and so forth (Table 26.1).

TABLE 26.1 Types of Reports

Criteria	*Types*	*Description*	*Examples*
Function	Informational	Objective presentation of data without analysis or interpretation	conference reports, seminar reports, trip reports
	Analytical	Presentation of data with analysis and interpretation	project reports, feasibility reports, market research reports
Periodicity	Routine	Presentation of routine information	daily production reports, monthly sales reports, annual reports
	Special	Presentation of specific information related to a single condition, situation, problem or occasion	inquiry reports, research reports, thesis, dissertation
Communicative Form	Oral	Face-to-face presentation of information	accident reports, sales reports, joining reports, conference reports
	Written	Presentation of information in written form	project reports, progress reports, research reports
Nature, scope and length	Formal	Long reports with elaborate description and discussion	annual reports, thesis, project reports, technical reports
	Non-formal	Short reports	laboratory reports, daily production reports, trip reports

Oral and Written Reports

Oral reports are informal and face-to-face presentations of information. Examples may include oral reporting of accidents, sales, production, joining, and so on. Oral reports are useful for presenting brief information related to routine activities, projects, developments, and so on. As oral reports provide quick feedback, they may expedite a work and lead to fast action and decisions. Most organisations nowadays prefer oral reports followed by written versions. This ensures the advantages of oral reporting and avoids the major disadvantages by adding to the permanent records of the organisation.

Most organisations nowadays prefer oral reports followed by written versions.

Written reports are more conventional than oral reports. Most business and technical reports use the written mode of presentation because the organisations using these reports need to maintain proper record for future use and reference. Most reports have a permanent value. For example, a research report is of immense value to future researchers. Similarly, a project or progress report has a permanent value because the organisations using them may need to refer to them during future projects or further evaluation of a particular project. This chapter is mainly concerned with written reports.

Most reports have a permanent value.

Formal and Non-formal Reports

Reports can be formal or informal depending on their nature, scope and length. A formal report is usually the result of a thorough investigation of a problem, condition, or situation. Formal reports are comparatively longer and need elaborate description and discussion. They usually follow a fixed format with predetermined elements, according to the information presented. The length of a formal report may vary from a few pages to hundreds of pages. Formal reports could be informational, analytical, routine, or special. Examples of formal reports include annual reports of companies and organisations, technical reports, project reports, thesis, and so on.

A non-formal report, on the other hand, could be a brief account of a specific business or professional activity. It is usually written to provide introductory information about a routine affair. Non-formal reports are usually short and do not need elaborate descriptions and discussions. As the content is generally insufficient for a formal report, an informal report may involve the use of printed forms, letter formats, or memo formats. Although non-formal reports are usually routine, they may be either informational or analytical and may use the oral or written form. Examples of non-formal reports include laboratory reports, daily production reports, trip reports, and so forth.

An informal report may involve the use of printed forms, letter formats, or memo formats.

Progress Check 1

1. **Which of the following statements are not True in the light of the above discussion about the nature, significance, and types of reports?**
   (a) Executive decisions in the professional world may be based on reports.
   (b) Non-formal reports may be written in letter or memorandum form.
   (c) Professionals do not have to write analytical reports.
   (d) A report is a formal document written for a specific audience to meet a specific need.
   (e) Reports never reinforce, prompt, motivate, or persuade readers to act.
   (f) An analytical report presents facts of a case, problems, conditions, or situations without any analysis, interpretations, or recommendations.
   (g) The most important purpose of a report is to help in the analysis of a condition, situation, or a problem for an effective solution.
   (h) Reports never record events and happenings.
   (i) Routine reports are prepared and presented to convey special information related to a single condition, situation, problem, or occasion.
   (j) Formal reports are generally shorter than non-formal reports.
2. **Study the following table and match different descriptions of reports (left column) with appropriate types of reports (right column):**

Different descriptions of reports	*Types of reports*
1. Lengthy reports	(a) Informational
2. Presentation of routine information	(b) Analytical
3. Data on periodic and situational activities without analysis	(c) Routine
4. Short reports	(d) Special
5. Presentation of specific information	(e) Formal
6. Analysis of data to persuade readers	(f) Non-formal

26.2 WRITING EFFECTIVE REPORTS

26.2.1 Report Formats

As listed in Table 26.2, there are four common formats of reports, that is, printed forms, letter format, memo format, and manuscript format. The choice of format can be made according to the nature, length, scope, and function of the report, and type of audience.

TABLE 26.2 Formats of Reports

Format	*Description*
Printed forms	Forms prepared to record for repetitive and routine data
Letter format	Short informal reports to be communicated to someone outside an organisation
Memo format	Short informal reports to be communicated to someone within an organisation
Manuscript format	Formal reports printed on plain paper

Printed Forms

Printed forms are generally used to collect routine information. For example, a company may keep printed forms for recording daily production or monthly sales. Similarly, an organisation may use printed forms for trip reports, conference reports, laboratory reports, inspection reports, confidential performance reports, and so on. Using a printed form is quite simple because the person filling it is just required to fill in the blanks, or tick against the listed items. Detailed descriptions or discussions need not be provided.

There are three main advantages of using printed forms for reporting. Firstly, they are systematic and make for easy reading. The readers can easily locate and identify important information. Secondly, they are more objective and factual with little scope for the writer to be subjective about the content. There is no subjective interpretation of the material used in the report. Facts are recorded quite objectively. Finally, they save time. It is less time consuming to prepare a report in printed form than preparing reports in other formats. Figure 26.1 gives an example of a report in printed form.

> Printed forms are more objective and factual with little scope for the writer to be subjective about the content.

TOUR REPORT

Report on Participation in Professional Conference

Office order No. 14789/2015 dated 04-01-2015

Name of the officer:	Kumar Abhishek
Designation:	Senior Marketing Manager
Address:	Regional Office, Syndicate Consultancy Services Pvt. Ltd. Nayadeep, Andheri (W), Mumbai-53
Name of the conference:	Emerging Concepts in Sales and Marketing
Name of the Organiser:	Indian Management Association
Place of Conference:	Hotel Tajmahal, Mumbai
Duration of Conference:	January 14 – January 18, 2015
Organisation of Conference:	
(a) Sponsors of the Conference:	1. Tata Consultancy Services 2. Air Sahara 3. Reliance Industries 4. Indian Airlines
(b) Number of Participating companies:	25
(c) Number of sessions:	12
(d) Number of presentations:	32

Date: 27th January, 2015

Signature: Kumar Abhishek

Fig. 26.1 Printed Form

Letter Format

The letter format may be used for short reports that have to be communicated to someone outside an organisation. A letter format contains all the elements of a letter along with some additional sections such as illustrations, references, and so on. Headings may be used in a letter report. The letter format may be used for informational, analytical, routine, special, or non-formal reports. For example, there is an accident on the shop floor in a company and report has to be sent to the insurance company. Other examples of the letter format include evaluation reports, feasibility reports, survey reports, legal reports, and so on. Figure 26.2 shows an example.

> The letter format may be used for informational, analytical, routine, special, or non-formal reports.

ALPHA CONSULTANCY PVT. LTD.
C-21/12, Ring Road, Delhi-110 052
www.alphagroup.com

January 31, 2015

Mr G Ravi Kiran
Chief Safety Officer
NDP Limited, NDPL Building
37-D, Jawaharlal Nehru Road, Kolkata-700 071

SUBJECT: MINE INSPECTION REPORT

Dear Mr Ravi Kiran:

The Alpha Consultancy team inspected the AP section of the IV Seam in NDP Colliery to collect various parameters to determine the Rock Mass Rating (RMR) of the roof. A detailed description regarding different locations visited is given below:

Location A: Shaft Level East I (Rise)

Roof rocks were exposed at this place upto a height of 3 meter by blasting to study the rock types and layer thickness. Three rider seams of thickness varying from 3.5 to 4 centimeter are observed at different horizons. Samples were collected for petrographical study.

1. **Litho types**
   Major litho types observed in sequence were sandy shale, shaly sandstone, sandstone, and grey sandstone. The rider seam 1 (3.5 centimeter thick) occurs in between sandy shale and shaly sandstone. Rider seam 2 (4 centimeter thick) is found between shaly sandstone and sandstone. Rider seam 3 (4 centimeter thick) is observed between sandy shale and grey sandstone. The presence of rider seams in between relatively competent beds is a point of concern from the point of view of the stability.
2. **Joints**
   Three sets of joints were observed. Vertical joints were observed in the roof rocks with a joint intensity of 2.5 numbers per metre length and another joint set spacing was found to be about 4 numbers per metre length. The third joint was found to be oblique to the earlier joint sets. It was also observed that the coal seam just below the roof was well cleated bituminous coal.
3. **Other Structural features**
   A dyke having thickness of 4.5 meter was observed running from North to South throughout the property. Slickensides were seen close to the dyke. Minor slips were also observed.
4. **Water seepage**
   No water seepage was noticed and the roof was completely dry.

(*Contd.*)

Location B: Shaft Level East II (Rise)

Roof fall upto the horizon of rider seam 3 was observed. This fall might have been caused as a result of water seepage (which was at the rate of about 20 ml/min at the time of investigation). Supports were provided at the middle of the gallery with a width of the gallery being 4.6 meter. The location under investigation was proposed to be the haulage point. Roof drilling using electric drills for bolting was attempted in the beginning and it was found that drilling the sandstone roof was difficult due to excess wear and tear of the bit. Thus, roof bolting could not be done.

Location C: Shaft Level East III (Rise)

A fault with a downward throw of 2.5 was seen. Slickensides were seen nearer to the fault upto a length of 5 meter.

Location D: 1 E Dip (North to South)

Upon general inspection of the dip gallery, of width varying from 4 to 4.6 m, it was found that the gallery was stable. Only at some places (gallery and junctions) pit props were provided at the centre of the gallery. No water seepage was seen.

Location E: 2 E Dip /2 L

This is the haulage level with steel pit prop supports placed at 2.2 metre centre to centre.

Location F: 6 D/2 E Level

Face blasting was carried out at this location.

Location G: 2 L

Side fall was observed in the level gallery.

Location H: 2 EL/ID

The galleries are six months old and the roof was found to be dry and intact.

Location I: IR/10 EL near Main Dip

Gallery width is only 4 meter and water seepage from the roof was around 20 ml/min.

Location J: 10LW/ID near Main Dip

Slips were found.

Location K: 7 LW/IR

Junction was observed for its stability. It was found that the roof was intact with a single wooden prop at the centre.

Location L: Drift from IV to V seam

A downthrow fault was observed. The roof rocks were studied for RMR determination. The roof was found to be dry.

The inspection team included Dr Suresh Patra, Dr Seema Biswas, Mr Animesh Kumar and Mr Mohan Srivastava, all senior consultants at Alpha Consultancy.

We at Alpha Consultancy believe that the findings of the team will help you go ahead with your plan to modernise the support system with permanent roadways.

Sincerely,

Sd/-
A P Khemka
General Manager

Fig. 26.2 Letter Format

Memo Format

The memo format can be used for short reports that have to be communicated within an organization. A memo format should contain all the elements of a standard memo. In addition, it may contain a few extra sections. Like a report in the letter form, a memo report should contain headings for easy reading and reference. The memo format may be used for all types of reports, that is, informational, analytical, routine, special, or non-formal. An example has been given in Fig. 26.3.

The memo format may be used for all types of reports, that is, informational, analytical, routine, special, or non-formal.

Innova Solutions Pvt Ltd
Interoffice Memorandum

Date: February 3, 2015

To: Ms. Kavita Kashayap
Director (Sales)

From: Afsar Ali Haider
Chief Training Manager

Subject: INTER- ISPL MEET ON TELEMARKETING STRATEGIES – A

REPORT

Sales managers from all 24 Regional offices of ISPL in India got together between 15 – 20th January 2015, to share their experiences of the use and effectiveness of telemarketing strategies (TMS) in India and to discuss the future plan of action of ISPL in India. There were sessions on Sales Training courses run in the ISPL Regional offices and the activities of the training centres at various parts of India. Sessions were also conducted on TMS materials produced in different ISPL training centres in India and each representative participant received sets of materials produced by the Corporate training centre in Mumbai.

Eminent sales trainers like Mr Anup Khandelwal, Dr N K Das, Ms Savitha Kumar, Coordinator ISPL TMS Scheme, and Mr Naveen Goswami, Coordinator, ISPL Training Centre Scheme, enlightened the participants through their speech and subsequent workshops. The workshops were highly interactive, and the participants actively participated in the deliberations. The question-answer sessions were particularly very interesting. The level of interest and commitment of the participants was remarkable. The meet was very enlightening and successful.

Recommendations

- Many such interactive meetings are necessary to enliven our capacity as sales promoters and to find some tentatvie solutions to some of the common problems that ISPL sales managers in India face.
- The Corporate Training Centre in Mumbai should be asked to produce similar TMS materials for sales trainees of ISPL.
- A few seminars and workshops on telemarketing strategies should be organised by the regional offices.

Fig. 26.3 Memo Format

Manuscript Format

The manuscript format can be used for long and formal reports. These reports are divided into sections and sub-sections, each with a clear heading. These headings and sub-headings are organised in a logical sequence. While preparing a report in manuscript form, the writer needs to be careful about its structure and elements. A structured report will help in thinking clearly and deciding where to put each fact or idea. It also makes reading easy and helps the readers find the information they need. The manuscript format is discussed in detail in the next section.

The manuscript format can be used for long and formal reports.

Progress Check 2

1. Which of the four formats of reports would be the most appropriate for each of the following?

(a) Annual report of a research organisation
(b) A report on the progress of a research project
(c) Daily production report of a lift manufacturing company
(d) A research report
(e) A product launch report to be written by the marketing manager of a company for the marketing director of the company.
(f) Monthly sales report of a pharmaceutical company
(g) A report on the feasibility of launching a new product
(h) A short report examining the problem of poor sales of a new product

26.2.2 Structure of Formal Reports

When writing a formal report, the choice of format as well the parts of the report must be carefully planned. Although the circumstances in which a report is written may determine its structure, the content of the report has to be organised in a logical way to help the readers understand the message clearly.

Formal reports are divided into many components for clarity.

Parts of a Report

A formal report may include the following parts or elements:

1. Title page
2. Preface
3. Letter of Transmittal
4. Acknowledgements
5. Table of Contents
6. List of Illustrations
7. Abstract/Executive summary
8. Introduction
9. Methodology
10. Discussion/Finding/Analysis
11. Conclusion

12. Recommendation
13. Appendices
14. References and Bibliography

Each of these parts of a formal report will now be discussed in detail.

Title Page

A formal report usually begins with a title page. It contains the title of the report, the name of the person or organisation to whom the report is being submitted, the name of the report writer/s, and the date. A Sample Title Page is given in Fig. 26.4.

Title Page

A REPORT ON
Improving Blast Efficiency Through
Performance Analysis
SUBMITTED TO
Department of Science and Technology
Government of India
SUBMITTED BY
Rakesh Kumar
Research Scholar, IIT, New Delhi
DATE
August 16, 2014

Fig. 26.4 Sample Title Page

Preface

The preface is an optional element in a formal report. It introduces the report by mentioning its salient features and scope.

Letter of Transmittal

The transmittal letter is a brief covering letter from the report writer explaining the causes for writing the report. It may contain the objectives, scope, and other highlights of the report. It may also contain acknowledgements if the report does not include an acknowledgement section. Figure 26.5 shows the format of a Transmittal letter.

> The transmittal letter is a brief covering letter from the report writer explaining the causes for writing the report.

Date
Dear ....,

____

____

____

____

Signature

Fig. 26.5 Format of Transmittal Letter

Acknowledgement

The acknowledgement section contains the names of persons who contributed to the production of the report and made the report possible. It is just a 'thank you note'.

Table of Contents

The 'table of contents' provides the reader an overall view of the report and shows its organisation.

This section lists the main headings and the subheadings in the report with page numbers. Figure 26.6 contains a Sample Table of Contents.

TABLE OF CONTENTS

Preface	1
Acknowledgement	2
List of illustrations	3
Abstract	4
1. Introduction	6
2. Methodology	9
3. Discussion	10
4. Conclusion	15
5. Recommendations 19	
Appendices	20
References	28

Fig. 26.6 Sample Table of Contents

List of Illustrations

The 'list of illustrations' gives systematic information about tables, graphs, figures, and charts used in the report. List of illustrations is usually included if the number of these illustrations are more than ten. Figure 26.7 contains a Sample List of Illustrations.

List of Illustrations is usually included if the number of these illustrations are more than ten.

LIST OF ILLUSTRATIONS

Tables		
Table 1	________	1
Table 2	________	8
Table 3	________	12
Table 4	________	14
Figures		
Figure 1	________	3
Figure 2	________	9
Figure 3	________	22

Fig. 26.7 Sample List of Illustrations

Abstract or Executive Summary

An abstract or an executive summary summarises the essential information in the report, focussing on key facts, findings, observations, results, conclusions, and recommendations.

Introduction

This section introduces the readers to the report and prepares them for the discussion that follows by providing background information, defining its aims and objectives, and discussing the scope and limitations of the report. It helps the readers in understanding and analysing the report as it includes facts that the reader must know in order to understand the discussion and the analysis that follow.

Methodology

While writing a report, information may have to be gathered from library and archival sources or through Internet surfing, interviews, surveys, and formal/informal discussions. The section on methodology summarises the methods of data collection, the procedures for investigating the situation/problem, and the criteria of survey.

Discussion/Description/Analysis

This is the main part of the report as it presents the data that has been collected in an organised form. It focuses on facts and findings of the report and may include an objective description and discussion of the problem, an analysis of the situation, and findings of the investigation. It is usually divided into sections and sub-sections with well-structured and clear headings and sub-headings.

Conclusions

This section conveys the significance and meaning of the report to readers by presenting a summary of the discussions and findings, results and conclusions, implications of the conclusions presented, and inferences.

Recommendations

This section contains recommendations that are based on results and conclusions. As they propose a course of action to improve a situation or a condition, they may present several ways to solve a problem or improve a situation. It may also indicate the need and nature for further work in the concerned area.

Appendices

An appendix contains supporting material or data, which is kept separate from the main body of the report to avoid interrupting the line of development of the report.

References and Bibliography

This section may contain references to books, journals, reports, dissertations, or/and published government documents, and other sources used in the report. It may also consist of a list of materials for further reference.

Progress Check 3

1. Study the following table and match different components of a formal report (right column) with their functions (left column):

Functions	*Components of a formal report*
1. Contains suggestions that are based on results and conclusions	(a) Preface
2. Conveys the significance and meaning of the report to readers by presenting a summary of discussions and findings	(b) Letter of Transmittal
3. Presents the data collected	(c) Acknowledgements
4. Summarises methods of data collection and the procedures for investigating the situation/problem, and the criteria of survey	(d) Executive summary
5. Provides background information, defines aims and objectives, and discusses the scope and limitations of the report	(e) Introduction
6. Summarises the essential information in the report	(f) Methodology
7. Contains the names of persons who contributed to the production of the report and made the report possible	(g) Discussion
8. Explains the causes for writing the report	(h) Conclusion
9. Introduces the report by mentioning its salient features and scope	(i) Recommendations

26.2.3 Writing Strategies

Whether one has to write a short informal report or a long formal report, one needs to adopt effective writing strategies. As reports are systematic attempts to discuss problems, situations, or conditions and stimulate thinking or action in individuals and groups, a systematic plan of writing should be followed.

The following steps will help in organising and presenting the report systematically.

Analyse the Problem and Purpose

The process of writing an effective report begins with an objective analysis of the problem that is to be discussed and the objectives of writing the report. In other words, the following two questions need to be answered before beginning to write a report:

1. What do you want to present or discuss in the report?
2. Why do you want to present it?

> The process of writing an effective report begins with an objective analysis of the problem that is to be discussed and the objectives of writing the report.

Answers to these questions will help in identifying the problem that led to the writing of the report and determining the purpose of the report. The problem may be written down in the form of a statement. Expressing the problem in words will provide clarity of purpose and help in writing the report systematically.

> Identifying the specific purpose of a report involves identifying an observable measurable action that the readers would do after reading the report.

Defining the purpose of the report will give it direction and make it focused. Identifying the specific purpose of a report involves identifying an observable measurable action that the readers would take after reading the report. The writer's purpose should be to match the audience's needs, knowledge, expectations, and interests. It should focus on audience behaviour and restate the theme of the report.

Determine the Scope of the Report

In order to keep the report precise and to the point, the amount of information gathered should be limited to the most essential and important facts. It is important to define a reasonable scope of the report. By determining the scope of the report, the writer will be able to decide what should be covered in it, and gather appropriate background information and supporting data. The scope of the report should be narrowed down and made specific so that a reasonable length is maintained.

Determine the Needs of the Audience

When a report is being planned, the writer should know who will eventually read it. A report will be effective only if the writer is able to connect his/her purpose with the interests and needs of his/her readers. When planning a report, the writer should think from his/her readers' perspective. He/she should avoid making false assumptions about his/her readers and should strive to be practical and rational. The following questions are relevant in this context.

> When planning a report, the writer should think from his/her readers' perspective.

- Who is the audience? (age, education, subject knowledge, professional affiliation, status, preferences, biases, attitudes, interests, language level, and so on.)
- How is the report relevant to the audience?
- What is in it for the audience?
- What does the audience expect from the report?
- How much background information will the audience need?

Answers to these questions will provide essential information about the readers that will help the writer to make important decisions about the content, the nature of information that he/she needs, and the level of language that he/she should use in his/her report.

Gather All the Information

> It is important to ensure that the information is accurate, bias free, current, and relevant.

Once the problem and purpose has been analysed, the scope is defined, and the audience has been analysed, the writer is ready to gather information. As he/she knows what he/she is looking for, he/she may not find it very difficult to gather information. He/she may gather information through primary sources (discussions, interviews, observation, surveys, questionnaires, experiments, and so on) or secondary sources (Internet, reports, books, journals, dissertations, magazines, pamphlets, newspapers, and so on). However, it is important to ensure that the information is accurate, bias free, current, and relevant.

Analyse and Organise the Information

Once the information has been gathered, the report writer needs to analyse and organise it. Analysis of information involves evaluating the information objectively, making comparative analyses of different sets of information for obtaining new ideas, and interpreting facts and figures for their relative importance. Organising the information involves using an appropriate logical pattern to arrange the information in the report (Refer to Chapter 4). Before actually organising the information, an outline may be prepared by choosing the central idea, main ideas, the major supporting ideas, and developing the details.

> Before actually organising the information, an outline may be prepared by choosing the central idea, main ideas, the major supporting ideas, and developing the details.

Writing the First Draft

Once the outline has been prepared and the organisational pattern of the report has been decided, the first working draft can be written. While writing the first draft, the following points must be remembered:

- Focus on the scope and purpose of the report.
- Simple and direct language should be used.

Reviewing and Revising

Once the rough draft of the report has been written, it should be reviewed, edited, and revised in order to improve the quality of its content and presentation. Reviewing is the process of analysing whether the report achieved its purpose, whereas editing involves correcting its format, style, grammar, spelling, and punctuation. Revision focuses on improving the content and language of the report.

Writing the Final Draft

Once the rough draft of the report reviewed and revised, the final draft can be composed. When writing the final draft, the following points should be taken care of:

- The report should be simple, clear, concise, direct, and readable.
- Appropriate words, sentences and meaningful paragraphs should be used.
- Appropriate linking devices should be used.
- Graphic highlighting techniques to improve readability and comprehension should be applied.
- Important points should be emphasised.

Exercise

1. **Write brief notes on the following:**
   (a) Significance of reports
   (b) Informational and analytical reports
   (c) Routine and special reports
   (d) Oral and written reports
   (e) Formal and non-formal reports
2. **Identify the format that you will use in the following kinds of reports:**
   (a) Accident report of a company to be submitted to the police
   (b) Annual report of a multinational company
   (c) Weekly production report
   (d) Monthly visit report
   (e) Trip report of a company executive
   (f) A company report examining a problem and its solutions
   (g) A report on benefits of computerisation in railways
   (h) Performance report
   (i) Recruitment report
   (j) Progress report of a construction project
   (k) A research report
3. **Discuss the various elements of a formal report.**
4. **Discuss each of the following steps of report writing process in one paragraph.**

(a) Analysis of the problem and purpose
(b) Determination of the scope of a report
(c) Audience analysis in report writing
(d) Data collection in report writing
(e) Organisation of information
(f) Writing the first draft
(g) Review and revision

Key to Progress Check

Progress Check 1

1. (c), (e), (f), (h), (i), (j)
2. 1e, 2c, 3a, 4f, 5d, 6b

Progress Check 2

1. (a) Manuscript format
   (b) Manuscript format
   (c) Printed form
   (d) Manuscript format
   (e) Memo format
   (f) Printed form
   (g) Memo format
   (h) Memo format

Progress Check 3

1i, 2h, 3g, 4f, 5e, 6d, 7c, 8b, 9a

CHAPTER 27

Proposal Writing

Proposals are written offers to initiate a proposed course of action.

LEARNING OBJECTIVES

- Understanding the nature and importance of proposals
- Knowing the different types of proposals
- Learning about the components of formal proposals
- Understanding the proposal writing process

27.1 INTRODUCTION

> A proposal is a systematic, factual, formal, and persuasive description of a course of action or set of recommendations or suggestions.

Suppose that the new sales manager of a company finds that his company is facing stiff competition from rivals and sales have been decreasing for the last several months. He has a brilliant idea to increase the sales of his company and tells it to his sales director. The sales director is enthused and asks the sales manager to provide a 'proposal'. What he wants is that the sales manager should write about his 'brilliant idea' and provide a 'rationale' for it.

Most people find it very difficult to write a proposal that persuades the readers to accept the proposed course of action. The reason is simple. The given proposal may contain a course of action or set of suggestions but the 'rationale' is either absent or is too weak to be considered. No one is going to accept what a proposal states unless they are convinced about its viability. Thus, it is essential to be persuasive in order to write an effective proposal.

> Proposals initiate new projects, provide fresh ideas, solve problems, or reinforce and prompt innovative strategies.

A proposal is a method of persuading people to agree to the writers view or accept his suggestions. It is a systematic, factual, formal, and persuasive description of a course of action or set of recommendations or suggestions. It is written for a specific audience to meet a specific need. As the main objective of a proposal is to persuade the reader to accept the proposed course of action, it explains and justifies what it proposes. Engineers, scientists, researchers, business executives, managers, and administrators have to write proposals in order to initiate new projects, provide fresh ideas, solve problems, or reinforce and prompt innovative strategies.

Submitting a proposal is usually the first step in going ahead with a new project. Whether an agency needs to be persuaded to work on a project, a business deal has to be initiated with a company, or a potential customer needs to be persuaded to purchase goods/services, a proposal may need to be submitted first. The proposal may be accepted or rejected depending on how effectively it responds to the needs of the situation/problem or the institution/company for whom the proposal is prepared. It is important that the proposal convinces the reader/s that the proposed course of action will lead to future benefits by showing an understanding of readers' needs and offering a viable way to fulfil those needs.

27.2 TYPES OF PROPOSALS

As summarised in Table 27.1, proposals can be classified as **non-formal** and **formal,** according to structure, as **internal** and **external** according to the nature of its audience, and as **solicited** and **unsolicited** according to the source of origin. Each of these have been discussed briefly.

27.2.1 Non-Formal and Formal Proposals

> A non-formal proposal may involve the use of printed forms, letter formats, or memo formats.

Proposals can be formal or non-formal depending on their content and format. A non-formal proposal is a brief description of suggestions or recommendations that are introductory in nature. It is usually written to initiate small projects that do not require elaborate description and discussion. Non-formal proposals are usually short. As the content is generally insufficient for a formal proposal, a non-formal proposal may involve the use of printed forms, letter formats, or memo formats.

Formal proposals, on the other hand, are comparatively longer. They are usually written to initiate big projects and require elaborate description and discussion. Like a formal report, a formal proposal involves use of the manuscript format. It may consist of several sections and sub-sections and can vary from a few pages to hundreds of pages.

Like a formal report, a formal proposal involves use of the manuscript format.

TABLE 27.1 Types of Proposals

Criteria	*Types*	*Description*
Content and format	Non-formal Formal	Short proposals involving small projects Long proposals with elaborate description and discussion
Nature of audience	Internal External	Addressed to readers within an organisation Communicated to people outside an organisation
Source of origin	Solicited Unsolicited	Written in response to a request for proposal Written without any request for proposal

27.2.2 Internal and External Proposals

Proposals can be internal or external, according to the nature of the audience. An internal proposal is addressed to readers within an organisation. It may offer to study a problem, situation, condition, or issue in the company or organisation, and may present different options for solving it. For example, proposing a plan to increase the sales of a company will require preparing an internal proposal. Internal proposals are less formal and elaborate than external proposals.

External proposals are communicated to people outside an organisation. An external proposal may offer a plan to solve a problem or situation of another organisation and give appropriate suggestions and recommendations. External proposals are more formal, detailed, and elaborate than internal proposals.

External proposals are more formal, detailed, and elaborate than internal proposals.

27.2.3 Solicited and Unsolicited Proposals

Proposals may be classified into two types: solicited or unsolicited. A solicited proposal is written in response to a specific request from a client. Many companies, government agencies, institutions, and consultancy organisations solicit proposals for their projects. As they want the best people to take their projects, they may make the request for proposal open to increase competition. They specify their requirements and mention their conditions.

In contrast, unsolicited proposals are written without any request for a proposal. As they intend to propose solutions or recommendations, they are based on an objective assessment of a situation or condition by an individual or a firm. For example, a person noticing a problem in his organisation and wanting to offer his ideas on how to handle it, may submit an unsolicited proposal. Self initiated research and business projects usually involve unsolicited proposals.

Progress Check 1

1. Which of the following statements are true in the light of the above discussion about the nature, significance and types of proposals?

(a) Proposals are oral offers to solve problems.
(b) All proposals are internal.
(c) Proposals never tell how a situation can be handled.
(d) A proposal is a method of persuading other people to agree to your views or accept your suggestions.
(e) Most projects may begin with proposals.
(f) Non-formal proposals may be written in letter or memorandum form.
(g) Professionals do not have to write unsolicited proposals.
(h) A proposal is a formal document written for a specific audience to meet a specific need.
(i) Proposals reinforce, prompt, motivate, or persuade the readers to act.
(j) The most important purpose of a proposal is to describe a situation as it is.

27.3 WRITING EFFECTIVE PROPOSALS

27.3.1 Structure of Formal Proposals

The structure of a formal proposal is similar to that of a formal report. The structure of a formal proposal is discussed here.

> The structure of a formal proposal is similar to that of a formal report.

Parts of a Formal Proposal

A formal proposal may include some or all the following parts:

Title Page

The title page of a proposal contains the title of the proposal, the name of the person or organisation to whom the proposal is being submitted, the name of the proposal writer, and the date (Fig. 27.1).

A proposal on

Submitted to

Submitted by

Date

Fig. 27.1 Structure of Title Page

Table of Contents

This section provides the reader an overall view of the proposal by listing the main headings and the sub-headings in the proposal, with their page numbers (Fig. 27.2).

Fig. 27.2 Structure of Table of Contents

List of Figures

This section includes a list of tables, graphs, figures, and charts used in the proposal, with their page number/s (Fig. 27.3).

Fig. 27.3 Structure of List of Figures

Abstract or Summary

An abstract or a summary is a condensed version of the proposal as it summarises and highlights its major points. However, an abstract is more specialised and technical than an executive summary.

> An abstract is more specialised and technical than an executive summary.

Methodology

The section on methodology summarises the proposed methods of data collection and the procedure for investigating the situation/problem.

Introduction

This section introduces readers to the proposal. It gives the background, states the purpose, and discusses the scope. It may also try to persuade readers by highlighting the major advantages and justifying the proposed course of action.

Statement of the Problem

This section contains an objective description of the problem or situation that the proposal intends to address. As it links the proposed course of action to the needs of the reader and the requirements of the situation, it gives credibility to the proposal and makes it convincing and acceptable.

Proposed Plan and Schedule

This section presents a schedule of activities, highlighting the main course of action.

Advantages/Disadvantages

This section reinforces that the proposal has more advantages than disadvantages by making realistic comparisons. It links benefits to the needs of the situation.

Recommendations/Proposed Solutions

This is the main section of a proposal as it discusses the plan to solve the problem. It is the most persuasive section of a proposal. It is usually the longest section of a proposal, and is logically structured into small manageable sub-sections with suitable headings.

Conclusion

This section presents the final summary of the proposal and focuses on the main points, and the key benefits. It influences readers with a final appeal.

Appendices

Secondary materials are put as appendices in a proposal. This maintains continuity of logical progression and avoids distractions in the main text of the proposal.

Progress Check 2

1. Study the following table and match different components of a formal proposal (right column) with their functions (left column):

Functions	Components of a Formal Proposal
1. Describes the proposed methods of data collection and the procedures for investigating the situation/problem	(a) Abstract or summary
2. Contains secondary material	(b) Methodology
3. Contains an objective description of the problem or situation that the proposal intends to address	(c) Introduction
4. Links benefits to the needs of the situation	(d) Statement of problem
5. Discusses the plan to solve the problem	(e) Proposed plan and schedule
6. Presents a schedule of activities highlighting the main course of action	(f) Advantages/Disadvantages
7. Presents the final summary of the proposal and focuses on the main points	(g) Recommendation
8. Summarises and highlights the major points of a proposal	(h) Conclusions
9. Introduces the proposal by presenting its major aspects	(i) Appendices

27.3.2 Writing Strategies

Apart from using the correct format and structure for the proposal, the proposal should be readable, attractive, and convincing. In order to take any action, the reader/s should be able to understand the proposal. If the proposal is confusing, complex, or too abstract, the reader will not be able to respond to it positively. So, simple and appropriate language should be used to make the proposal readable. Make the proposal attractive and convincing so that reader/s can take a positive decision after reading it. In order to achieve these objectives, a systematic plan of writing should be followed and strategies of good writing adopted.

> Proposal writing is persuasive writing that should involve prewriting, writing, and post-writing.

Pre-Writing

Prewriting of a proposal involves purpose identification, audience analysis, project analysis, scope determination, an analysis of the action desired, and data collection. The writing process should begin with the following questions:

1. Why is this proposal being written?/What are its objectives?
   (*Purpose identification*)
2. Who is the audience?
   (*Audience analysis*)
3. Does the proposal involve any project? What is the project?
   (*Project analysis*)
4. How much information should be included in the proposal?
   (*Scope determination*)
5. What should the reader do?
   (*Analysis of the action desired*)

Once these five questions are answered, the writer can collect data related to the proposal. The writer should do background research, collect relevant information, discuss relevant points with concerned people, make a list of the points that he/she wants to cover, and organise his/her thoughts to help him/her write.

Writing

Writing a proposal involves organising the data that has been collected, outlining what will be presented in the proposal, and writing the first draft. The information may be organised as per the structure of the proposal. A good outline will give the writer a clear picture of his/her proposal and will help him/her to prepare the first draft.

> A good outline will give the writer a clear picture of his/her proposal and will help him/her to prepare the first draft.

Post-Writing

Once the first draft has been written, it is ready to be revised, edited, and evaluated in order to improve its content, layout, and structure. The proposal needs to be edited for grammatical and lexical accuracy. The first draft should be evaluated and critically examined to ensure that the proposal can achieve its purpose. Finally, the final draft is prepared.

27.3.3 Sample Proposal

The following sample shows the structure, components, layout, and style of a proposal. Please note that only some sections of the full proposal have been included here.

TITLE PAGE

A PROPOSAL ON
Development of Erbium Doped Fibre Amplifiers for
Wavelength Division Multiplexed Optical Communication System

SUBMITTED TO
Ministry of Human Resource Development
Bureau of Technical Education
Government of India

SUBMITTED BY
Dr. Vishnu Priye
Department of Electronics and Instrumentation
Indian School of Mines, Dhanbad – 826 004, Jharkhand

OCTOBER 3, 2013

ABSTRACT

The proposed work is experimental in nature with software to be developed based on equations to analyse Erbium doped fibre amplifiers (EDFAs) that are available in literature and also developed by the Principal Investigator as a part of a previous R&D Project on ASE Broadband Optical Source sponsored by the Ministry of Information and Communication Technology, New Delhi.

The main objectives of the proposed project are:

- to fabricate EDFAs having gain ≥ 20 dB, noise figure ≤ 5 dB, and gain flattened for WDM applications in the conventional C-Band using fibres and other components commercially available in the international market,
- to fabricate EDFAs having above specifications, using indigenously developed components at CGCRI, Kolkata, CEERI Pilani, IIT Delhi, and Optiwave Photonics, Hyderabad to make it cost effective for the Indian market, and
- to develop software to estimate the performance and characteristic features of EDFA.

METHODOLOGY

The methodology to be adopted will be as follows:

- Different pumping schemes, erbium doped fibres (EDFs) of different doping levels, and different doping configurations such as clad doped EDFs, different lengths, and other physical parameters will be experimentally investigated to achieve the target of accomplishing optical gain ≥ 20 dB and noise figure ≤ 5 dB at one signal wavelength (1550 nm). For the experiments, commercial as well as indigenous components will be used.

- Using a tunable laser source, the gain spectrum of the above EDFA in the C-Band (1525 – 1565 nm) will be optimised so as to give equal gain and noise figure in the whole wavelength range so that it can be applied in Wavelength Division Multiplexed systems.
  The stipulated period of completion of the project is two years.
- Using wavelength multiplexed signals the response of the module will be investigated for real system application.

INTRODUCTION

Importance of the area of study

EDFAs have assumed importance because they provide format independent gain and have replaced the more expensive and limited electronic regenerators. They are responsible for recent advances in optical communication systems for long haul links. For fibre optic communication systems, they can be used as power amplifiers to boost transmitter power, as in-line amplifiers to increase the system non-repeater reach, or as pre-amplifiers to enhance receiver sensitivity.

Manpower requirement

Manpower is required to carry out experiments, compile results, and write technical details. As the Principal Investigator has teaching load, research load and administrative responsibilities one Project Associate with minimum qualification of BTech/MSc on a consolidated monthly salary of Rs 10,000/- is essential.

Nature of ongoing activities pertaining to project under submission at the Institution.

The Principal Investigator has recently completed an R&D Project titled "Design of Tunable Broadband ASE Fiber Source and Multiwavelength Fibre Laser for WDM System" sponsored by the Ministry of Information and Communication Technology (MICT), New Delhi, which resulted in a Broadband ASE tunable source in C-Band and a Software based on Genetic Algorithm that has been copyrighted by MICT. He is also involved in designing optical modulators, isolators, polarisers, optical networks as R&D, PhD programmes and as B Tech projects. He has recently obtained a minor research project from ISM Dhanbad on Design of—Wavelength—Routed Optical Networks Using Genetic Algorithm. One PhD student is working with him on the application of EDFA to optical networks.

Existing facilities concerned with the project under reference

(a) *Level of infrastructure available with reference to technology under consideration*
At present, the Fibre Optics Laboratory of the Electronic & Instrumentation Department, ISM Dhanbad, has essential equipment such as optical spectrum analyser, splicing machine, 980 nm laser diode modules, wavelength selective couplers, isolators, and few metres of EDF that can be used immediately to start the project in the gestation period of purchase of new equipment/components.

(b) *Library facilities*
Departmental and Central Library facilities are available. However, for successful running of the project, specific technical books have to be procured, which relate to the broad area of optical amplifier and communication.

(c) *Workshop facilities are available*

Linkage with sister institutions, research laboratories, industry, and other agencies

There will be association with CGCRI, Kolkata, CEERI, Pilani, and IIT Delhi in terms of technical discussions, characterisation of modules and visits to one another's laboratories. However no financial obligations will be there. No MOU has been signed.

Self assessment reflecting specific competence for undertaking the project

The Principal Investigator has been involved in research and developmental activities in the area of Fibre and integrated optics' for the past 18 years. During this period, he has developed various analytical and numerical techniques to model optical fibres and integrated optical waveguides, as well as fibre optic components, including isolators, polarisers, polarisation splitters and so on. He is principal investigator of the recently completed R&D project on ASE Broadband Optical Source using EDF sponsored by Ministry of Information and Communication Technology (MICT), New Delhi, which resulted in a Broadband ASE tunable source in C-Band, and a software based on genetic algorithm, which has been copyrighted by MICT.

STATEMENT OF THE PROBLEM

Optical fibre amplifiers with broadband amplification have become important with the continuously increasing number of wavelength channels in optical network systems. Erbium doped fibres (EDFs) are an integral part of present state-of the art optical amplifiers. EDFs consist of silica fibres doped with optically active rare earth erbium (Er^{3+}) ions (typical doping level ~200 mole ppm). The energy levels of the erbium ions in the silica glass host shows excited energy levels corresponding to wavelengths of interest 1530 nm, 980 nm and 800 nm. When a laser beam corresponding to the wavelength of 980 nm is launched in the EDF, the Er^{3+} ions at ground level get excited to upper levels. For Er^{3+} ions in glass host all transitions are non-radiative except between the levels corresponding to wavelength 1530 nm. Hence, most Er^{3+} ions relax down to this level from where they undergo, either, spontaneous or stimulated emission to the ground level. Due to stark split energy levels, the emission occurs in the wavelength range of 1400–1600 nm with relative flat wavelength response in the range 1525–1565 nm.

When EDF (Er^{3+} doping 180 mole ppm) of a given length (~ 12-15 m) is pumped by a 980 nm laser of about 80 mW power, the whole length of fibre is totally population inverted. If a signal at a wavelength in the range 1525 – 1565 nm is launched, it induces stimulated emission and as a result the signal gets amplified. Apart from stimulated emission, there are spontaneous emissions in this wavelength range due to finite lifetime of the atoms in excited states. The photons emitted spontaneously also get amplified and add to the noise of the amplifier.

Presently, international research is devoted to investigating different means to increase the gain and reduce the noise figure of EDFAs by investigating different pumping schemes; different doping levels; different dopants such as ytterbium and phosphate along with erbium; as well as different dopant configuration such as cladding doping, depressed core, and others. The gain flattening is also being investigated so that all signals have equal gain in wavelength multiplexed systems. Schemes are being proposed to reduce cross talks and the effect of non-linearity in fibres.

Research is being done at IIT Delhi as part of the PhD programme and also as research projects. Till 24th March 1999, the principal investigator as a Senior Scientist at IIT Delhi was involved in a Technology Development Mission (TDM) project funded by the MHRD and Planning Commission, towards the technology development of a prototype model of an erbium doped fibre amplifier (EDFA). C-Dot is also involved in development and characterisation of EDFAs. CGCRI, Kolkata, is developing EDFs; CEERI,

Pilani, is developing 980 nm Laser diodes; and IIT Delhi is developing wavelength selective couplers for application in EDFA.

PROPOSED BUDGET

A. NON-RECURRING

Sl. No.	**Equipment/Components**	**Estimated cost In Lakhs (INR)**
1.	980 nm Laser Diode Module (Imported)	3.0
2.	1480 nm Laser Diode Module (Indigenous)	1.0
3.	Tunable laser (Range 1500 –1600 nm) (To be imported)	6.0
4.	DFB Laser (1550 nm) module (Indigenous)	2.0
5.	Multiplexer/Demultiplexer (Imported)	3.0
6.	Erbium Doped Fibres (Both indigenous and imported)	3.0
7.	Wavelength Selective Couplers (Imported)	1.6
8.	Tap Couplers (Imported)	1.0
9.	*Fiber Bragg Grating*	2.0
A.	**Total (Non-Recurring): (Rupees Twenty Two lakhs Sixty Thousand Only)**	**22.60**

B. RECURRING

S. No.	**Head**	**Estimated Cost In Lakhs (INR)**
1.	Consumables	0.30
2.	Travel/Training	0.40
3.	Contingencies (Books + journals + communication services etc.)	0.50
B.	**Total (Recurring): (Rupees One Lakh Twenty Thousand Only)**	1.20

Total cost of the proposed project (A+B):₹ 23.80 (Rupees Twenty three lakhs eighty thousand only)

PROPOSED PLAN

Plan of Execution of Project Under Consideration

Organisational set up

The Institute has an Assistant Registrar (Projects) whose responsibility it is to ascertain the financial transparency related to the project.

Principal Coordinator

Dr Vishnu Priye, Assistant Professor, Department of Electronics and Instrumentation, ISM Dhanbad will be the chief coordinator of the project.

Suggested Plan of action for development of infrastructure

The existing rules of the Institute for purchase will be followed. The acquisition of permanent equipment, systems, and sub-systems will be taken up at the earliest for enhancing the pace of the project. Orders will be placed for required books and journals related to the area of Optical Amplifiers and Optical Communications.

Plan for internal monitoring and evaluation of progress of implementation

For verifying the progress of the proposed project the Institute will take up internal monitoring. Every six months evaluation of the progress of the project can be made by a intra-institute committee. The progress report will be sent to the funding agency as well at regular intervals. The Institute has an officer for auditing the project. It can be further audited by the external audit.

Stipulated period of completion

The stipulated period of completion of the project is two years.

This is a modified version of the original proposal submitted to the Ministry of Human Resource Development of the Government of India by Dr. Vishnu Priye, Assistant Professor, Department of Electronics and Instrumentation, Indian School of Mines, Dhanbad. The proposal has since been approved by the GOI. We are thankful to Dr. Vishnu Priye for permiting us to reproduce the proposal in a modified form.

Exercise

1. **Write short notes on the following:**
   (a) Nature and significance of proposals
   (b) Formal and non-formal proposals
   (c) Solicited and unsolicited proposals
   (d) External and internal proposals
2. **Discuss the different components of a formal proposal.**
3. **Read the sample proposal given in this chapter and rewrite the proposal in the form of a letter, excluding unnecessary details.**

Key to Progress Check

Progress Check 1

1. (d), (e), (f), (h), (i)

Progress Check 2

1. 1 (b), 2 (i), 3 (d), 4 (f), 5 (g), 6 (e), 7 (h), 8 (a), 9 (c)

28 CHAPTER

Technical Article Writing

Technical articles describe, discuss, or analyse a systematic investigation towards increasing the sum of knowledge in a specific field.

LEARNING OBJECTIVES

- Understanding the nature and importance of technical articles
- Learning to identify different types of technical articles
- Grasping the elements of a technical article
- Understanding the various strategies of writing a technical article

28.1 INTRODUCTION

Technical and research articles add to the existing knowledge and understanding of a particular topic or subject.

Technical and research articles are essential to all fields of science, technology, humanities, and management as they add to the existing knowledge and understanding of a particular topic or subject. Writing a technical article that can be published in a professional journal, or presented in a seminar or conference is a challenging undertaking.

A technical article is an important form of technical communication, and it is essential to know how to write a technical article in order to be able to contribute to one's area of interest and specialisation. Technical paper writing skills help in achieving academic and occupational goals by establishing the authors presence in the professional world. Moreover, they give a high degree of professional satisfaction and help in career advancement.

Technical articles present an objective analysis of facts, findings, inferences, recommendations, and conclusions.

A technical article is a written composition describing, discussing, or analysing a systematic investigation towards increasing the sum of knowledge in a specific field. It transfers new research and findings to other scientists and researchers in the field by giving a systematic account of the results of some survey, research, fieldwork, and other activities. As it is an objective presentation of technical information, it distinctly and independently explores one area of research, and presents an objective analysis and interpretation of facts, findings, inferences, suggestions, recommendations, and conclusions.

28.1.1 Technical Articles versus General Articles

Unlike a general article that may follow any form and pattern, a technical article is highly formalised in structure.

Any technical article in a professional journal has the same major sections as all the others.

Technical articles differ from general articles in style, presentation, and objectives. Unlike a general article that may follow any form and pattern, a technical article is highly formalised in structure. For example, any technical article in a professional journal has the same major sections as all the others. On the other hand, two articles from the same film magazine, will be different in structure. Technical articles involve the use of technical vocabulary, specialised terminology, graphic aids, and a particular writing style. Moreover, while writing a technical article, the writing conventions of the particular discipline need to be followed.

28.2 TYPES OF TECHNICAL ARTICLES

As summarised in Table 28.1, technical articles can be classified as journal articles or conference papers depending upon their mode of presentation, and as review articles or research articles according to their approach, content, and functions. Each of these will be briefly discussed here.

TABLE 28.1 Types of Technical Articles

Criteria	*Types*	*Description*
Mode of presentation	Journal articles	Communication of technical information in a structured form as per the established pattern for articles acceptable for publication in a particular journal
	Conference papers	The written form of a technical presentation that the author has presented in a seminar, conference, or workshop
Approach, content and functions	Review articles	Evaluation and analysis of published work on a particular topic
	Research articles	An objective description and discussion based on a research project or on a small scale study

28.2.1 Journal Articles and Conference Papers

A journal article is the communication of technical information in a structured form as per the established pattern for articles acceptable for publication in a particular journal. The form of a journal article is as important as its content because most journals follow a style guide that the technical writer has to use to structure the article. These style guides provide detailed writing instructions that may include guidelines about the preparation of text, organisation, length, referencing system, and use of symbols, abbreviations, illustrations, unit symbols, and so on.

> A conference paper may be published in the "proceedings" of the conference in which it has been presented.

A conference paper is the text of a paper that the author has presented in a seminar, conference, or workshop. As it is the written form of a technical presentation, it follows the pattern in which it has been presented before the audience. It may be published in the "proceedings" of the conference in which it has been presented. However, the academic value of a conference paper is usually less than that of a journal article. The main reason is that the reviewing process of journal articles is usually more formal and systematic than that of seminar papers. Moreover, the editor of a professional journal usually receives a large number of articles, and he or she may adopt strict norms and select only a few of them. In contrast, the organiser of a professional seminar may not have the option of rejecting many conference papers.

> The academic value of a conference paper is usually less than that of a journal article.

28.2.2 Review and Research Articles

A review article is an evaluation and analysis of published work on a particular topic. The main purpose of a review article is to evaluate a published work in order to determine its academic value and research potential. While reviewing a particular piece of published research work, the review writer tries to answer the question, "How does the work under discussion increase the sum of knowledge in a specific field?". The review writer may also comment on the necessity for future research in the concerned area and propose certain directions.

> The review writer may also comment on the necessity for future research in the concerned area and propose certain directions.

A research article, on the other hand, is based on original research carried out by the author. It may be the outcome of a particular research project carried out by the author or the result of a small scale study. The research might have been carried out in the laboratory or in the field. It might be theory based, or a part of action research to develop certain methods, equipment, procedures, systems, and so forth. The main purpose of a research article is to add to the existing knowledge, understanding, and scope of a particular subject. A research article could be either published in a journal or presented in a conference in order to achieve its objectives.

The main purpose of a research article is to add to the existing knowledge, understanding, and scope of a particular subject.

Progress Check 1

1. **Which of the following statements are not True in the light of the above discussion about technical articles?**
   (a) Writing a technical article is a specialised research activity.
   (b) Technical articles add to the existing knowledge and understanding of a particular topic or subject.
   (c) A technical article is a written composition describing, discussing, or analysing a systematic investigation towards increasing the sum of knowledge in a specific field.
   (d) Writing a technical paper does not involve an objective analysis and interpretation of facts and findings.
   (e) A technical article is similar to a general article in style, presentation, and objectives.
   (f) A journal article is the communication of technical information in a structured form as per the established pattern of articles acceptable for publication in a particular journal.
   (g) A professional journal usually follows a style guide providing detailed guidelines about preparation of text, organisation, length, referencing system; and the use of symbols, abbreviations, illustrations, unit symbols, and so on.
   (h) A conference paper is the text of a paper that the author has presented in a seminar, conference, or workshop.
   (i) The main purpose of a research article is to evaluate a published work in order to determine its academic value and research potential.
   (j) A research article may be the outcome of a particular research project carried out by the author or the result of a small scale study.

28.3 WRITING EFFECTIVE TECHNICAL ARTICLES

28.3.1 Structure of Technical Articles

Technical articles are formal technical documents, and are highly formalised in structure. They usually follow fixed-formula pattern to ensure objectivity. The components of a technical article include title, author by-line, abstract, introduction, methodology, results, discussion, conclusion, appendices, and references.

Title

All technical articles begin with a title. The title of a technical article is usually a long phrase that contains keywords and indicates the content of the article. It gives the readers a clear idea of the topic that is discussed in the article. A vague, abstract, or very general title will fail to indicate the content and will not be communicative. It is, therefore, important that the title of a technical article is informative, specific, and comprehensive.

> The title of a technical article is usually a long phrase that contains keywords and indicates the content of the article.

While writing the title of a technical article, sufficient information should be included for the reader to be able to understand the content of the article. This may make the title lengthy, but it is better to use a lengthy title that is clear than to use a short but unclear title. It is important to have a title that is specific and contains keywords that will guide the reader to the article.

Author By-Line

This is the second element of a technical article. It includes the name of the author followed by institutional affiliation/s. The following are some examples:

1 LIZA SMITH
Nicholas Parker UK Ltd
London EC3N 4HJ, UK

2 R. RAVI KUMAR
Department of Organisational Behaviour, Indian Institute of Management
Bangalore, India

3 V. KUMAR and DINESH CHANDRA
Department of Electronics and Instrumentation, Indian School of Mines,
Dhanbad-826004, India

Abstract

The abstract is the most important element of a technical article. There are two kinds of abstracts, that is, descriptive and informative. The descriptive abstract talks about the article and briefly states what the article contains while the informative abstract summarises the essential information in the article, focusing on key facts, findings, observations, results, conclusions, and recommendations. As informative abstracts are more comprehensive and self-explanatory than descriptive abstracts, most professional journals prefer the former to the latter.

> The descriptive abstract talks about the article and briefly states what the article contains while the informative abstract summarises the essential information in the article.

Introduction The main part of a technical article usually begins with an introduction that introduces the reader to the topic or research work under discussion. This section helps the reader to understand the article as it includes facts that the reader must know in order to comprehend the discussion and analysis that follow. A good article introduction may include some or all the following elements:

- **Background**: an objective description of the background of the problem, or events and conditions that led to the problem under discussion
- **Research status**: the status of research related to the problem, and the need of the present research
- **Purpose**: aims and objectives of the research or investigation

- **Significance**: the significance of the work under discussion
- **Methods**: methods or procedures used to carry out the research work, and the rationale for using specific methods of investigation
- **Scope**: the scope and limitations of the problem investigated

Methodology

While writing a technical article, certain methods and materials need to be used to carry out the investigation. The professional value of an investigation largely depends on using appropriate methods and materials. In order to establish the validity of the findings, the materials and methods used need to be described along with the rationale for using them. This may involve an objective description of materials that were used to conduct the investigation, the conditions under which the work was done, the methods of data collection, the procedures for investigating the situation/problem, and the criteria of survey.

Results/Findings

This is the main part of the article as it presents the results or findings of the investigation. This section is concerned with 'what was done', 'what happened' or 'what was looked into'. It focuses on facts and objectively presents the outcome, results, and findings of the research. It is usually divided into sections and sub-sections with well-structured and clear headings and sub-headings. This section should be written as carefully as possible because the value of the article depends on the relevance of its results.

> Results/findings are concerned with 'what was done', 'what happened' or 'what was looked into'.

Discussion

This section presents an analytical discussion of the results and findings of the investigation. It is an extension of the earlier section. As it conveys the significance and meaning of the findings to the reader, it analyses the causes, implications, and significance of these findings. Moreover, it establishes a link between the findings and the existing research in the concerned area.

Conclusion

This section concludes the article by summarising the important highlights of the article. It may contain recommendations that are based on results and discussion. It may also indicate the need and nature for further work in the concerned area.

Appendices

A technical article may contain appendices. An appendix contains supporting material or data that is kept separate from the main body of the article to avoid interrupting the line of development of the article.

References

This section may contain references to books, journals, reports, dissertations, or/and published government documents, and so on used in the article. It may use the referencing method approved in the particular discipline to which the article belongs. Refer to Chapter 18 for a detailed discussion on *Referencing*.

Progress Check 2

1. **Study the following table and match different components of a technical article (left column) with their functions (right column):**

Components of a technical article	Functions
1. Title	(a) identifies the author
2. Author by-line	(b) briefly states what the article contains or summarises the essential information in the article
3. Abstract	(c) introduces the reader to the topic or research work under discussion
4. Introduction	(d) indicates the content of the article
5. Methodology	(e) describes the materials and methods used in the article
6. Results	(f) contain references to books, journals, reports, dissertations, or/and published government documents, and so on used in the article
7. Discussion	(g) presents the findings of the investigation
8. Conclusion	(h) concludes the article by summarising the important highlights of the article
9. Appendices	(i) contains supporting material
10. References	(j) presents an analytical discussion of the results and findings of the investigation

28.3.2 Writing Strategies

A technical article is the formal, structured and objective presentation of technical information and you need to adopt effective writing strategies in order to deliver the material effectively. Whether you have to write a short review article or a lengthy research paper, you need to plan and organize it well. In fact, you need to create a work plan to write your article. The following steps will help you to plan, organize and write your article systematically.

Define the Problem

Planning for an article should start with defining the problem. This is the first step of any systematic inquiry or investigation. In order to write an effective article, the author needs to analyse the problem that he/she wants to discuss objectively. The first question that he/she needs to answer before he/she begins to write his/her article is: "What is the problem that I want to present or discuss in my article?"

> Defining the problem will also help in deciding the approach, content, and methodology. The problem statement could be the guiding principle for writing the article.

Once he/she has answered this question and identified the problem that he/she wants to discuss and explore, he/she will be able to determine the direction of his/her investigation. Defining the problem will also help in deciding the approach, content, and methodology. The problem may be written down in the form of a statement. This problem statement could be the guiding principle for writing the article.

Analyse the Purpose

The purpose of writing an article needs to be defined in order to write a result oriented and need based paper. Why do I want to write this article? This is the most important question that the writer has to answer in order to make his/her article focused. Defining and analysing the purpose will help in making the article relevant and effective. As the aim of the research needs to be mentioned in the abstract of the article, the objective of the research should be written in a sentence.

> Defining and analysing the purpose will help in making the article relevant and effective.

Make Literature Survey

Literature survey is an essential segment of any credible research and is central to the writing of technical articles. Survey of existing literature is essential to be informed about the latest research in the area of investigation, which helps to give a theoretical foundation to the article. It also help to correlate the article to the mainstream of scientific literature in the field.

> Survey of existing literature is essential to be informed about the latest research in the area of investigation.

The following suggestions will help in survey of effective literature:

- Bibliography card should be made for each journal article, book, magazine article, or research report that is closely related to the topic of the article. The entries in the card include the name of the author, title, publication details (place of publication, publisher, date of publication, and so on), identification number, and so forth.
- A literature search of all the related information can be conducted by browsing through relevant journals, books, or magazines. A keyword search through library databases or the World Wide Web and electronic databases is also essential.
- Index cards should be made to record information from both oral and written sources.
- An electronic file should be made to record information from different web sources.
- Personal knowledge, understanding, experience, and exposure can be used as a source of information.
- Research notes should be prepared.

Analyse and Organise the Information

Once the problem and purpose have been defined, literature surveyed, and information gathered, the writer needs to analyse and organise the material. As he/she may have to determine the amount of information that he/she wants to include in his/her article, he/she may evaluate the information objectively, and make comparative analysis of different sets of information for obtaining new ideas, interpreting data for their relative importance. The writer may organise the information by using an appropriate pattern to arrange the information in his/her article. He/she may also develop an outline by choosing the central idea, main ideas, the major supporting ideas, and developing the details.

Write the First Draft

Once an outline has been prepared and the organisational pattern of the article has been decided, the first draft may be written. While writing the first draft, the author need to ensure that his/her article is divided into manageable sections with appropriate headings and sub-headings. Be focused on the objectives of the article and use simple and direct language.

Review and Revise

Once the rough draft of the article has been written, it should be reviewed edited and revised in order to improve the quality of its content and presentation. Reviewing involves the process of analysing whether the article achieved its purpose, whereas editing involves correcting its style, grammar, spelling, and punctuation. Revising focuses on improving the content and language of the article.

> Once the rough draft of the article has been written, it should be revised, edited and revised in order to improve the quality of its contents end presentation

Write the Final Draft

Once the rough draft of the article has been reviewed and revised, the final draft can be written. While writing the final draft, the following points should be taken care of:

- Principles of technical style should be taken care of
- Appropriate key words and technical terms should be used.
- The article should be objective, impersonal, clear, concise, direct, and readable.
- Precise and specific words, short sentences and meaningful paragraphs should be used.
- Appropriate linking devices should be used.
- Graphic highlighting techniques should be applied to improve readability and comprehension.
- Important points should be emphasised.

Exercise

1. **Write brief notes on the following:**
   (a) Conference papers
   (b) Research articles
   (c) Title of a technical article
   (d) Introduction in technical articles
   (e) Methodology in technical articles
   (f) Literature survey and data collection
2. **Expand the following statements into one paragraph each:**
   (g) Technical articles are essential to all fields of science and technology.
   (h) Technical articles differ from general articles in style, presentation and objectives.
   (i) Making literature survey is an integral part of writing technical articles.
   (j) All technical articles should be objective and factual.
   (k) The abstract is the most important element of a technical article.
   (l) The form of a journal article is as important as its content
   (m) A review article is an evaluation and analysis of published work on a particular topic.

3. The following flow diagram summarises the process of writing a technical article, but it is not complete. Fill in the blanks to complete the diagram:

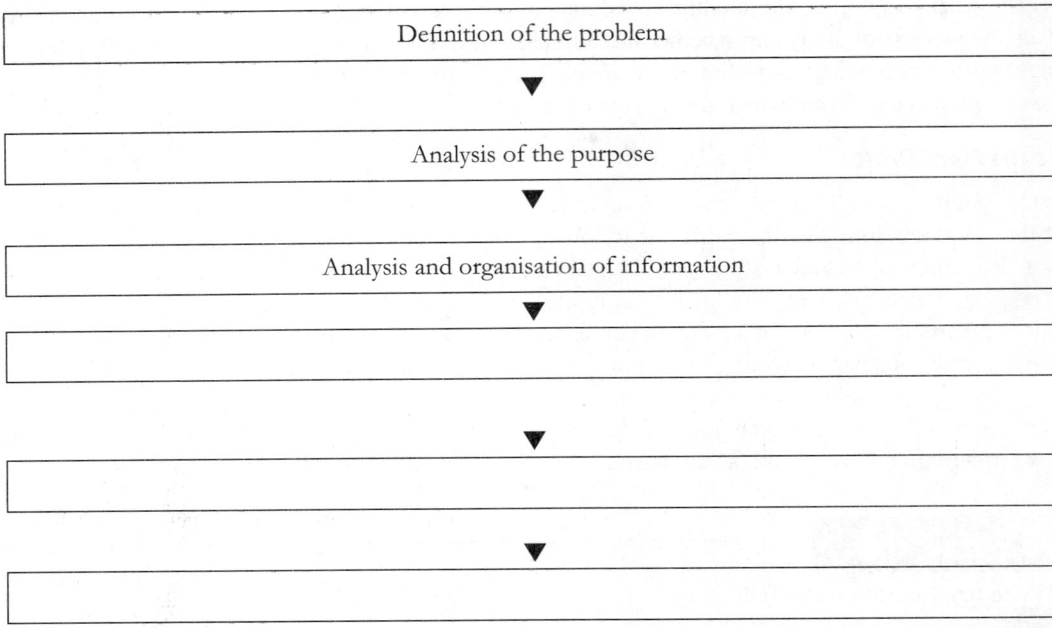

Key to Progress Check

Progress Check 1

1. (d), (e), and (i)

Progress Check 2

1. 1d, 2a, 3b, 4c, 5e, 6g, 7j, 8h, 9i, 10f

SECTION

9

Appendices

CHAPTERS

A APPENDIX

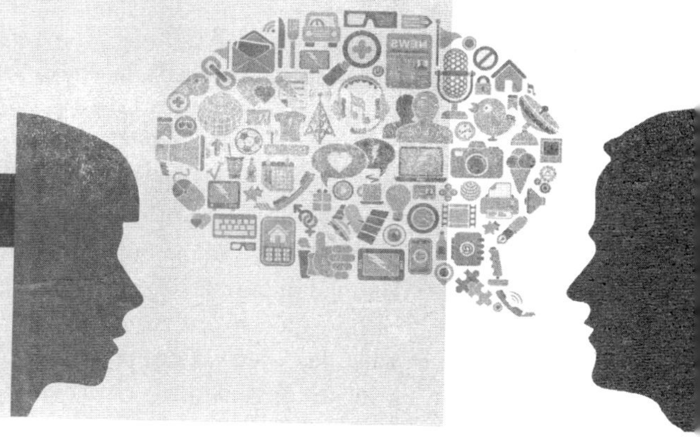

Functional Grammar Review (FGR)

A basic understanding of functional grammar and style is essential for effective technical communication. This appendix is a short manual on functional grammar. It illustrates important grammatical concepts, and explains problem areas and standard grammatical practices. It discusses parts of speech, articles, prepositions, modals, tenses, active and passive forms, concord, conditional sentences, and question tags.

Thorough reading of Appendix A will help in improving readers' understanding of functional grammar, and the exercises given in the practice papers will be helpful in testing the level of understanding.

A.1 PARTS OF SPEECH

The term 'parts of speech' refers to the classification of words into eight groups, that is, nouns, pronouns, adjectives, verbs, adverbs, prepositions, conjunctions, and interjections (Exhibit 1). It is easy to know the definition of each of these groups but it is better to understand them in the proper context because these groups of words function together to communicate meaning. The following short paragraph about fuels helps in understanding how these word groups are used:

"Fuels can be classified according to the phases, solid, liquid, or gas, in which they are available. A gaseous fuel is most convenient to burn while a liquid fuel requires initial heating to vaporise it before combustion begins. A solid fuel requires much more initial heating to ignite. In addition, it requires special equipment to handle it and to dispose off the ash formed."

This paragraph has 64 words. If the words in this paragraph are classified, we will find all parts of speech except interjection, which is normally more commonly used while speaking. We also find a few words known as articles, which are traditionally not included in the parts of speech, but definitely form an important word class.

Interjections are commonly used while speaking.

Table A.1 contains most of the words used in this paragraph to understand the way they can be grammatically classified into parts of speech:

TABLE A.1 Parts of Speech

Examples	*Function*	*Word Class*
Fuels, phases, solid, liquid, gas, heating,	Words that name	NOUNS
combustion, equipment, ash, they, it	Used for other nouns	PRONOUNS
available, convenient, initial, special	Qualify, modify, or add to the meaning of a noun	ADJECTIVES
Can, classified, are, is, burn, requires, vaporise, begins, ignite, handle, dispose	Express action/ condition, or Tell/assert something	VERBS
most, much	Qualify, modify, or add to the meaning of all the words except a noun	ADVERBS
To, in, before, of	Show their relationship to other word/s	PREPOSITIONS
Or, which, while, in addition, and	Connects words, phrases, or sentences	CONJUNCTIONS
		INTERJECTIONS

From this exhibit it is evident that each word class has a particular function, that is, nouns and pronouns name something; verbs assert; adjectives and adverbs modify other words; prepositions show relationships; and conjunctions connect words, phrases, and sentences. This understanding may help us use them more effectively.

Nouns and pronouns name something; verbs assert; adjectives and adverbs modify other words; prepositions show relationships; and conjunctions connect words, phrases, and sentences.

Progress Check 1

1. **Read the following paragraph and identify <u>nouns</u>, <u>main verbs</u>, and <u>adjectives</u> used in the paragraph. Do not repeat the same word.**

   Natural laws, which may be qualitative statements or mathematical formulas, describe observed phenomena. They contrast with legislative laws, which require or prohibit, and which may be 'broken'. There is no room in science for the statement "the exception, which proves the rule." A familiar example of a natural law is the law of gravity. Less familiar examples of laws are those that describe the behaviour of gases. For example, all gases can be compressed, and Boyle's law states that their volume is inversely proportional to the pressure exerted on them. Boyle's law, like the law of gravity, gives no reason for natural behaviour but simply states what the behaviour is.

A.1.1 Prepositions

A **preposition** is a word that shows the relationship between two objects, things, persons, or conditions. Let us take the following sentences:

> A preposition is a word that shows the relationship between two objects, things, persons, or conditions.

The book is <u>on</u> the table.
The book is <u>under</u> the table.
The book is <u>beside</u> the table.
The book is <u>away from</u> the table.

The underlined preposition, in the 1st sentence, states the relationship between the book and the table. A change in the preposition results in change of relationship. The following table summarises the positions in which prepositions are normally used:

Position	*Examples*
Before a question	• <u>To</u> whom are you talking?
	• <u>In</u> which class do you read?
Before a noun or pronoun	• He is afraid <u>of</u> death.
	• There are many important characteristics <u>of</u> compounds having ionic bonds.
	• One way <u>in which</u> the non-ferrous metals differ <u>from</u> iron is in the manner <u>of</u> their occurrence.
Before a gerund	• I am tired <u>of</u> doing the same thing over and over again.
	• He was successful <u>in</u> completing the project within the given time.
After a verb	• He is looking <u>for</u> his notebook.

Uses of Preposition

The following suggestions will help you use prepositions correctly:

- Do not use the preposition '<u>to</u>' after tell, show, or promise.
- If you use a person after the words describe, explain, complain, say, shout, speak, suggest, talk, you should use the preposition 'to' after these words. However, the preposition 'to' need not be used after the words ask, advise, invite, encourage, recommend, request, warn urge, remind, even if you use the person addressed after these words.

- Be careful while using prepositions to describe time, that is, for, since, from, during, at, on, by, in, to, till, until, after, afterwards.
- Distinguish between the following prepositions:
  Besides = in addition to and Beside = at the side of
  Between = two people or things, and Among = more than two people or things
  In = normal position and Into = movement

Table A.2 contains some of the most commonly used prepositions with verbs.

TABLE A.2 Prepositions and the Meanings

Verb + Preposition	*Meaning*	*Verb + preposition*	*Meaning*
Account for	Explain	Carry out	Perform
Allow for	Take into account	Carry on	Continue
Ask for	Request, demand	Close down	Shut
Back up	Support	Close in	Come near
Back out	Withdraw	Close up	Come close
Back for	Move back	Cut down	Reduce in size
Bear up	Support	Cut off	Disconnect
Bear out	Confirm	Cut up	Cut into pieces
Break in	Enter by force	Find out	Discover
Break off	Terminate	Fix up	Arrange
Break out	Spread	Get away	Escape
Break up	Terminate, disintegrate	Get back	Recover
Call in	Ask someone to come	Get over	Recover from
Call off	Cancel	Give in	Stop resisting
Call for	Require	Give up	Abandon
Go ahead	Continue	Give back	Restore
Go away	Leave	Go back	Return
Go on	Continue	Hand over	Transfer
Hand out	Distribute	Hold on	Wait
Keep down	Control	Keep on	Continue
Look after	Take care of	Look into	Investigate
Look back	Consider the background/past	Look for	Search
Make out	Discover the meaning	Make up	Compose
Talk over	Discuss	Think over	Consider

Words Followed by Prepositions

The following list contains some important words followed by prepositions (there could be some exceptions).

Words Used	*Preposition Usually After the Words*
Delight, faith, believe, involved, interested, pride, absorbed, deficient	In
Access, allusion, approach, duty, invitation, alien, contrary, loyal, invite, indifference, Object, grateful, inclined, opposed, attention, equal, compare to (similarities between different things), next, related, similar	To
Accused, afraid, ashamed, aware, conscious, confident, convicted, fond, approve, disapprove, capable, incapable	Of
Ability, affection, ambition, anxiety, apology, aptitude, desire, eligible, except	For
Astonished, surprised, annoyed — a thing	At
Coupled, delighted, agree, bore, disagree, annoyed — a person compare with (differences between similar things)	With
Based, bent, dependent	On

Progress Check 2

1. Read the following sentences carefully and correct errors in the use of prepositions:

(a) Encoding is the process of changing the information at a logical and coded message.

(b) Your weakness to view others about your frame of reference may also lead tc confusion and misunderstanding.

(c) The properties of covalent compounds are quite different with those of ionic compounds.

(d) When alcohol dissolves, in water heat is released in the surroundings.

(e) Certain substances some of the electrons are bound rather loosely with their atoms.

(f) Inside the fuel cells, the chemical energy of the fuel is directly converted with low voltage direct current electrical energy.

(g) Light waves are electromagnetic waves that do not require any material medium to their propagation.

(h) The element iron has an industrial importance, which exceeds that in any other metallic element.

(i) Although there are more than 100 known elements they rarely occur at the pure state.

(j) Plastics have specific properties, which may make them preferable with traditional materials.

2. Read the following paragraph, and fill in the blanks with appropriate prepositions:

Plastics have specific properties, which may make them preferable —1— traditional materials —2— certain uses. —3— comparison —4— metals, for example, plastics have both advantages and disadvantages. Metals tend to be corroded —5— inorganic acids, such as sulphuric acid and hydrochloric acid. Plastics tend to be resistant —6— these acids, but can be dissolved or deformed —7— solvents, such as carbon tetrachloride, which have the same carbon base as the plastics. Colour must be applied —8— the surface —9— metals, whereas it can be mixed —10— with plastics. Metals are more rigid than most plastics, while plastics are very light, —11— a specific gravity normally —12— 0.9 and 1.8. Most plastics do not readily conduct heat or electricity. Plastics soften slowly and can easily be shaped while they are soft.

A.2 ARTICLES

Articles are short words that may be found in almost every sentence. They include 'a' and 'an' (indefinite articles) and 'the' (definite article). We should know how to use them correctly because the wrong use of an article may cause a serious grammatical mistake.

Read the following paragraph and note the use of articles:

> The wrong use of an article may cause a serious grammatical mistake.

A liquid sample assumes **the** shape of its container. **The** kinetic theory explains this property by saying that there are no fixed positions for **the** molecules. **The** molecules in the liquid are free to slide over each other in order to occupy positions of **the** lowest possible potential energy. On earth, gravity pulls the liquid specimen to **the** bottom of its container: in **an** orbiting satellite, intermolecular forces pull **the** specimen into **a** spherical glob.

> The article 'a' is used before a word beginning with a consonant sound while the article 'an' is used before a word beginning with a vowel sound.

Here the indefinite articles 'a' and 'an' are used before singular countable nouns, that is, a liquid, an orbiting satellite, a spherical globe. The article 'a' is used before a word beginning with a consonant sound (that is, a liquid, a spherical globe) while the article 'an' is used before a word beginning with a vowel sound (that is an orbiting satellite).

Also, the definite article 'the' is used before:

- Defined specific nouns (for example, the kinetic theory)
- Superlatives (for example, the lowest possible potential energy)
- A noun that has been mentioned before (for example, the liquid)
- Nouns consisting of noun + noun structure (for example, the shape of the bottom of its container)
- A plural noun to refer to things or people in a particular group (for example, the molecules)
- A 'noun + noun' phrase that refers to a definite noun (for example, the liquid specimen).

The above illustration makes it clear that the use of articles is very significant to communicate meaning and they should be used carefully to avoid errors.

Progress Check 3

1. **Read the following sentences carefully and correct errors in use of articles, if any:**
   (a) When the drop of ink is carefully released in water, there is at first rather sharp boundary between ink cloud and water.
   (b) Tectonic islands are created by movements in Earth's crust.
   (c) Although all the metals react with oxygen, their reactivity is different.
   (d) Silver is best conductor of the heat.
   (e) The vehicular pollution causes serious health problems.
   (f) Poorest conductor among the metals is lead.
   (g) Electrical conductivity is the common property of metals.
   (h) A substance in solid state may be changed into a liquid substance, and one in a liquid state may be changed into a gaseous substance.
   (i) Igneous rocks are formed by cooling of molten material.
   (j) In order to produce and hear sound, we require the source of vibratory energy.

2. **Read the following paragraph and fill in the blanks with appropriate articles:**
——1—— sun emits lights of different wavelengths. If sunlight is passed through —2 — prism, each of these wavelengths is refracted by —3 — different amount. Violet has —4— shortest wavelength, and red has — 5 — longest. — 6 — wavelength of green is midway between that of violet and red. Light whose wavelength is shorter than that of violet is called ultraviolet light. Light whose wavelength is longer than that of red light is called infrared light. About one-third of — 7 —light from — 8 — sun is infrared.
3. **Read the following paragraph carefully and correct errors in use of articles, if any:**
Computer networks are the system of interconnected computers, which to communicate information to one another. Local Area Network (LAN) gained the prominence during 1980's. A LAN can be defined as the group of desktop computers located relatively close to one another through a cabling system to enable them to share the access to computing resources. LANs consist of the workstations connected to central computer called File Server, which is a special purpose computer used to control and manage a network resources that are shared by a network users.

A.3 MODALS

A **modal** is an auxiliary verb used to express the mood of another verb, or the mode of action denoted by the main verb. Modals include the auxiliary verbs shall, will, should, would, can, could, may, might, must, ought, need, dare. Some simple rules need to be remember in order to use modals correctly.

A modal is an auxiliary verb used to express the mood of another verb, or the mode of action denoted by the main verb.

Table A.3 describes some of the uses and functions of these along with examples.

TABLE A.3 Use of Modals

Modal	*Uses*	*Examples*
Shall	Simple future action	I shall send you an e-mail.
Will	Promise, intention, threat,	I will show you what I can do.
	command, determination	I will complete the work tonight.
Would	Past form of 'will'	He said that he would not attend the party.
	Express request	Would you please wait for a minute?
	Express wish	I wish you would get the award.
	Hypothetical condition	You would have got the job, if you had tried for it.
Should	Past form of 'shall'	He said that you should come on time.
	Express suggestion	You should respect your teachers.
Must	Express obligation	You must complete the job by 22nd January.
Ought	Express obligation	You ought to join the duty tomorrow.
Need	Express absence of obligation	You need not come tonight.
Dare	Used as a principle verb to mean challenge	She dares to face the situation.

(Contd.)

	To express venture	Dare he face the crowd? He dare not face the crowd.
May	To express permission	You may leave the class when you have completed the assignment.
Might	'might' as past form in indirect speech	The teacher said that you might leave the class.
	Request for permission	May I come in?
	Express possibility	He may/might attend the meeting.
	Speculation about past action	The letter may/might have reached.
Can	Express permission	
Could	'can' for present and future	You can leave the class now.
	'could' for past	The teacher said that you could leave the class.
	Request for permission	Can/could I meet you tomorrow?
	Express possibility	
	'can' for present and future	The project can be profitable.
	'could' for past	She could be very rude.
	Express ability	
	'can' for present and future	I can drive a car.
	'could' for past	I could complete the assignment. (The assignment was completed) I could have completed the assignment. (The assignment was not completed)
Used	Past habit	He used to come to our office regularly.

A.4 TENSES

Tense refers to the time of an action, that is, present, past, future. It also shows the degree of completeness of the action, that is, continuous, complete, and so on. Tenses include the present tense, the past and perfect tense, and the future tense. Each tense has four forms. However, all the forms are not used. Table A.4 gives the important tense forms.

Tense refers to the time of an action, that is, present, past, future. It also shows the degree of completeness of the action, that is, continuous, complete, and so on.

TABLE A.4 Tense Forms

Present	*Example*	*Past*	*Example*	*Future*	*Example*
Simple present	He works hard.	Simple past	He worked hard.	Simple future	He will work hard.
Present continuous	He is working hard.	Past continuous	He was working hard.	Future continuous	He will be working hard.
Present perfect	He has worked hard.	Past perfect	He had worked hard.	Future perfect	He will have worked hard.
Present perfect continuous	He has been working hard for many years.	Past perfect continuous	He had been working hard.	Future perfect continuous	He will have been working hard.

Eight tense forms that are commonly used are simple present, present continuous, simple past, past continuous, present perfect, the present perfect continuous, past perfect, and future tense.

1. Simple Present Tense

The simple present tense uses the infinitive form of a verb (third person singular number). It is used for the following purposes:

Use	**Example**
Express habitual action	He gets up early in the morning.
Express likes, preferences and dislikes	I like to watch action movies. I prefer tea to coffee.
Express condition in 'if' clauses	If you work hard, you will get A+ grade.
Planned future action	We leave New Delhi on 3rd February and reach Bombay the next day.

2. Present Continuous Tense

The present continuous is formed with the auxiliary verb be + the present participle (verb + ing). It is used for the following purposes:

Use	**Example**
Express an action happening now	He is listening to the radio.
Express present continuous action	I am working very hard to get a good grade.
Planned future action	I am leaving for New Delhi tonight.

3. Simple Past Tense

The simple past tense is formed by adding either d or ed to the infinitive. It is used for the following purposes:

Use	**Example**
Express an action completed in the past at a definite time	He submitted the report last week.

Express an action that occupied a period of time	She lived in New Delhi for three years.
Express a past habit	She always kept a diary.

4. Past Continuous Tense

The past continuous tense is formed with auxiliary verb be (past form) + the present participle (verb + ing). It is used for the following purposes:

Use	**Example**
Express a continuous action in present	She is watching T.V. They are waiting for you.

5. Present Perfect Tense

The present perfect is formed with **has/have + the past participle**. Its uses are given below:

Use	**Example**
Express an action recently completed	He has just submitted the report.
Express past action without a definite time	I have read the report.
Express an action that started in the past and continuous in present	She has lived in Kanpur all her life. She has lived in New Delhi for three years. (She still lives in New Delhi.)

6. Present Perfect Continuous Tense

The present perfect continuous is formed with **has been/have been + the present participle**

Use	**Example**
Express an action that started in the past and continuous in present	I have been working for the company for the last fifteen years.

7. Past Perfect

The past perfect is formed with **had + the past participle**

Use	**Example**
Express complete action in past	He had submitted the report before he received the memo.

8. Future Tense

The future tense is formed with **will/shall + infinitive**

Use	**Example**
Express simple action in the future	I shall meet you tomorrow. He will join the company next year.

A.5 ACTIVE AND PASSIVE VOICE

As both active and passive forms have to be used in writing and speech, it is important to understand the difference between the two forms. Examine Table A.5 containing the active tense forms of the verb 'supply' and their passive equivalents.

TABLE A.5 Active and Passive Forms of the Verb "Supply"

Active Voice	*Passive Form*	*Tense*
Supplies	Is supplied	Simple present
Is supplying	Is being supplied	Present continuous
Supplied	Was supplied	Simple past
Was supplying	Was being supplied	Past continuous
Has supplied	Has been supplied	Present perfect
Had supplied	Had been supplied	Past perfect
Will supply	Will be supplied	Future
Would supply	Would be supplied	Conditional
Would have supplied	Would have been supplied	Perfect conditional
To supply	To be supplied	Present infinitive
To have supplied	To have been supplied	Perfect infinitive
Supplying	Being supplied	Present participle
Having supplied	Having been supplied	Perfect participle

Technical writing involves the use of impersonal language, which demands the use of impersonal passive. The impersonal passive is the most important linguistic device that makes technical communication impersonal, objective, and formal. An impersonal passive construction contains the past participle form of the main verb preceded by the appropriate tense form of the verb 'to be'.

Thus, the structure of the impersonal passive sentence is:

> The impersonal passive is the most important linguistic device that makes technical communication impersonal, objective, and formal.

Object + to be + Verb in past-participle form

Table A.6 contains a list of appropriate 'to be' verb forms according to tense forms.

TABLE A.6 List of applicable 'to be' verb forms

'to be' Verb Forms	*Tense / Verb Form*
Is/ am, /are	Simple present
Is being/are being/am being	Present continuous
Was/were	Simple past
Was being/were being	Past continuos
Has been/have been	Present perfect

(Contd.)

Had been	Past perfect
Will be/shall be	Future
Would be	Conditional
Would have	Perfect conditional
To be	Present infinitive
To have been	Perfect infinitive
Being	Present participle
Having been	Past participle

A passive infinitive may be used to change the auxiliary + infinitive combination into a passive form:

Active: We must not allow water to come into contact with sodium.
Passive: Water should not be allowed to come into contact with sodium.

Active: We ought to place the metal on a dry surface.
Passive: The metal ought to be placed on a dry surface.

Active: We can see several particles of iron and sulphur.
Passive: Several particles of iron and sulphur can be seen.

Active: They should have submitted the project report.
Passive: The project report should have been submitted.

Personal pronouns used as subjects are generally removed in passive constructions. In fact, the doer of the action or the subject is generally not mentioned in the passive form. However, the subject of a sentence should be retained in passive form if it is a material used and not an agent.

Active: Smoke filled the conference room.
Passive: The conference room was filled with smoke.

Table A.7 contains examples of active sentences and their passive equivalents.

TABLE A.7 Examples of Active and Passive Sentences

Active	*Passive*
Friction reduces the efficiency of machines.	The efficiency of machines is reduced by friction.
We use hot dipping as a common method to apply metallic coatings.	Hot dipping is a common method used to apply metallic coatings.
A computer performs fast and accurate calculations.	Fast and accurate calculations are performed by a computer.
We examined the mixture under a microscope.	The mixture was examined under a microscope.
You must complete the assignment by the end of this week.	The assignment should be completed by the end of this week.
We may classify alloy steels as well as plain carbon steels according to their ability to harden.	Alloy steels as well as plain carbon steels may be classified according to their ability to harden.
We use the name quicklime for calcium oxide.	The name quicklime is used for calcium oxide.
We can change a solid into liquid by heating.	A solid can be changed into a liquid by heating.

Progress Check 4

1. Read the following paragraphs and write down the correct forms of the underlined verbs:

(a) In a telescope, the objective and the eyepiece are similarly mount. The focal length of the objective of the telescope is comparatively larger than that of a microscope. The objective form a real, diminished-in-size, and inverted image of a distant object. The position of the eyepiece is so adjust that this image form between the optical centre of the eyepiece and its focus. The eyepiece then form the final image, which is virtual, enlarged, and erect.

(b) These substances are sometimes combine with other chemicals, such as chlorine. By means of pressure and heat, and often with the aid of catalysts, the monomer molecules of the gas or liquid react and, as they combine, form the polymer molecules of the raw plastics, which is generally in the form of a powder or granules. By careful control of the polymerisation, the monomer molecules arrange and join in a number of ways. Thus, the properties of each of the plastic materials modify to suit a wide range of products and applications.

(c) Plastics have specific properties, which make them preferable to traditional materials. In comparison with metals, for example, plastics have both advantages and disadvantages. Metals tend corrode by inorganic acids, such as sulphuric acid and hydrochloric acid. Plastics tend to be resistant to these acids, but dissolve or deform by solvents, such as carbon tetrachloride, which have the same carbon base as plastics. Colour apply to the surface of metals, whereas it mix in with plastics. Metals are more rigid than most plastics, while plastics are very light, with a specific gravity normally between 0.9 and 1.8. Most plastics do not readily conduct heat or electricity. Plastics soften slowly and easily shape while they are soft.

(d) The eyepiece that use in a microscope is a system of convex lenses. It fix in such a way that the image form by the objective lens lies between the eyepiece and its focus. This image acts as the object for the eyepiece, which forms a further magnify, but virtual, image of the object. It is this image that we observe when we look into a slide through a microscope. The final image see remains invert with respect to the object.

2. Read the following paragraphs and complete them by using the correct form of verbs from the options given before each paragraph:

(a) **Force, wash out, give, shake, place, carry**

The simplest method of ore dressing depends on the fact that in general metallic compounds have a higher specific gravity than gangue, and hence settle faster in a stream of water. Gold panning is the simplest illustration of the procedure. On a larger scale, it —1— on in jigs where the ore —2— on a screen and a pulsating stream of water —3— through the screen, causing the lighter gangue —4—. Another form of gravity concentrator is the 'table', consisting of a surface with longitudinal ridges, which —5— a jerking end-to-end motion while a stream of water flows across it laterally. By this means, the heavy ore —6— over the end while the gangue washes off the front.

(b) **Transmit, produce, result, call, transfer**

All sources of sound —1— vibratory energy at frequencies within the audible range of the ear. Some of the most common sound sources are vibrating strings (stringed musical instruments), vibrating air columns (wind musical instruments), vibrating membranes (speakers and drums), and vibrating rods. This vibratory energy —2— to the surrounding medium, normally air, where it —3— from particle to particle to the ear.

Many sound sources have several different natural frequencies or resonant frequencies of vibration. Each different vibratory state —4— a mode of vibration. At these resonant frequencies, a small energy input —5— in a large amplitude.

(c) **Make, displace, release, lose, vibrate, produce, vibrate, depend, stretch, die out**

When a string —1— under tension between two fixed points, we —2— it —3— by —4— it to one side and then —5— it. At most frequencies of vibration the energy —6— rapidly and the vibration —7—. However, when the string —8— at certain natural (resonant) frequencies, standing waves —9— by the interference between the wave and its own reflection from the fixed ends. These resonant frequencies —10— on the length and mass of the string, and the tension in the string.

A.6 CONCORD

The 'subject' of a sentence and its 'verb' must agree with each other for the grammatical accuracy of a sentence. Concord refers to this subject-verb agreement in a sentence. As concord plays an important role in communicating correct meaning to the reader or listener, it is important for the writer/speaker to ensure that the sentences he/she uses do not contain an error related to subject-verb agreement.

> Concord refers to this subject-verb agreement in a sentence.

The following suggestions will help in avoiding errors related to subject-verb agreement:

1. Verbs should agree with subjects. The correct subject should be identified because intervening words and phrases may make it difficult to recognise the subject. The following are some examples:
   - The teacher along with the students was (not 'were') killed in the accident. (The subject is 'the teacher' and not 'the students'.)
   - A teacher's understanding of the problems of his/her students is (not 'are') the key to effective teaching. (The subject is 'a teacher's understanding' and not 'problems' or 'his/her students'.)
2. A singular verb should be used in the following conditions:

• The subject is singular	Example	Ravi is going to attend the session. She is present in the party. He has completed the work.
• The subject begins with an indefinite pronoun, that is, each, every, everyone, neither, either, many a, anyone, anybody, anything, everybody, everything, someone, something, and so on.	Example	Every student is supposed to show his/her identity card during the examination. Neither of the candidates is selected.
• The subject is a noun that is collective in sense but singular in form.	Example	The committee is not able to take a decision.
• The subject consists of two singular nouns which are joined by 'and' but convey a singular sense.	Example	The managing director and chairperson of the company is out of station. The secretary and treasurer has submitted the report.

3. A plural verb should be used in the following conditions:

• The subject is plural	Example	They are not coming to the meeting. Children are playing in the garden. Many students have not submitted the project reports.

- Two subjects are joined by 'and' — Example: Ravi and Sunita are just colleagues.
  He and I are going to join the club.
- The subject is singular in form but plural in number — The people of India love their culture and tradition.

4. Ensure that the verb agrees with the closest subject in the following conditions:
   - Two subjects are joined by 'or' or 'nor'. — Example: Either Ravi or Sunita is to be blamed.
     Neither John nor his brother is responsible for this situation.
5. Make the verb agree with the first subject if two subjects are joined by 'with', together with', 'along with', 'in addition to', 'as well as', 'and not'.

   Examples: The captain along with the soldiers were given the bravery awards.
   The chairman along with the directors of the company are responsible for the growing losses of the company.

Progress Check 5

1. Read the following sentences carefully and edit them:

(a) Communication which is one of the essential conditions of social interaction are a way of reaching others with facts, ideas, thoughts, and values.

(b) The main objectives of horizontal communication is developing teamwork, and promoting group coordination within an organisation.

(c) Effective technical communication is a dynamic interchange that involve a systematic understanding of scientific and technical subjects.

(d) The changes that have taken place in the field of science and technology reflects several developments in the way technical communication skills are viewed.

(e) The prolonged inhalation of carbon monoxide presents in the toxic fumes, released by motor vehicles reduce oxygen carrying capacity of the blood.

(f) The optical density of any transparent medium are a measure of its refractive index.

(g) Air pollution have been a major threat not to the quality of environment but also to human health.

(h) The colour perception of different animals are different due to different structure of rods and cones.

(i) A chemical combination of two or more elements result in a substance called a compound which behaves quite differently from its component elements.

(j) Thermosetting plastics, which becomes rigid on further heating and cannot be softened again, consists of polymer chains which react with one another at points of contact so that they become strongly linked together in three-dimensions.

A.7 CONDITIONAL SENTENCES

A conditional sentence involves the use of conditional expressions. The circumstances in the conditional are connected by certain linkers. These linkers include If, only if, unless, when.

A conditional sentence involves the use of conditional expressions. The circumstances in the conditional are connected by certain linkers.

Examples: If an object is farther than 25 cm, the eye is unable to distinguish fine details; if the object is closer than 25 cm, blurred images are formed on the retina.

An object at rest or uniform motion will remain at rest or in uniform motion unless an unbalanced force acts on it.

When a constant force acts on a body, the acceleration of the body does not change.

Study the following sentence patterns, which involve conditional clauses:

1. Action in simple future + if + Circumstance
   Example: The flow of a liquid will be streamlined (steady) if the velocity at every point in the liquid remains constant in magnitude as well as direction.
2. If + Circumstance + Action in simple future
   Example: If electricity passes through a tube containing a gas at low pressure, it will result in the production of cathode rays.
3. Action in present form + If + Circumstance
   Example: Fumes of nitrogen dioxide are driven out if copper (II) nitrate is heated in a dry tube.
4. Action in present form + If + Circumstance in negative form
   Example: A body is said to be rigid if it is not deformed under the action of external forces.
5. Action in present form + When + Circumstance
   Example: A positive ion results when one or more electrons are removed from an atom.
6. When + Circumstance + Action in present form
   Example: When a body of mass m moves in a circular path of radius r with a uniform speed v, it is subjected to a force F acting towards the centre.
7. Action in simple future (negative) + unless + Circumstance
   Example: A polychromatic light will not split into radiations of different wavelengths unless it is passed through a prism.
8. Action in simple future + only if + Circumstance
   Example: The electron configuration will become more stable only if the removal or addition of an electron results in the symmetrical distribution of electrons in an orbital.

Progress Check 6

1. Complete the following hypothetical statements by using the appropriate forms of verbs given in brackets:

(a) When a simple coil of wire (rotate) in a magnetic field or when a magnetic field through a coil (change), the coil acts as though it had an emf source in it.

(b) If you stretch a material too far, the material (permanently elongate) or perhaps (break).

(c) When an object (elastically stretch), the elongation is proportional to the tensile force.

(d) A rod (break) when the tensile stress in it exceeds its tensile strength.

(e) If a gas (prevent) from condensing to a liquid or solid at very small absolute temperatures, then the molecules would have no motion at absolute zero.

(f) When exposed to humid air, zinc (form) zinc compounds and (protect) the iron from rustings.

(g) When a gamma ray is thrown out, neither the mass nor the charge of the nucleus (change).

(h) When a set of waves (move) from one material to another, the frequency remains the same.

2. Correct the following sentences:

(a) You will achieve professional success if you will be able to communicate effectively.

(b) Iron will rust if it will be exposed to humid atmosphere.

(c) When an object will be allowed to fall freely to the earth from some height, it will accelerate as it falls.

(d) The term 'mass' describes the tendency of an object to remain at rest if it is stationary or to continue in motion if it will be moving already.

(e) When a solid will be heated, the magnitude of these thermal vibrations will increases until they "shake apart" the solid structure and the solid melts, becoming a liquid.

(f) When a ray of light will pass through a prism, it will get refracted

(g) When we can live in the environment and can use the environmental resources, knowingly or unknowingly we will put pressure on the environment.

(h) Whenever you might delete a file, it will temporarily be moved to the Recycle Bin on your desktop.

(i) When molecules will colide, the faster one (with more kinetic energy) might transfer some of this energy to the slower one and causes a transfer of heat energy and a resulting temperature change.

(j) Should a moving vehicle strikes against a wall, a large amount of force acts on the vehicle.

A.8 QUESTION TAGS

Question tags may be used as an effective technique to focus on the meaning of a sentence. However, it is essential to use appropriate tag endings. Read the following question tags and identify the errors:

> Question tags may be used as it is an effective technique to focus on the meaning of a sentence.

1. She is going to buy the flat. Aren't you?
2. You are not going to the party. Aren't you?
3. It's a wonderful place. Is it?
4. They have gone to the college. Hadn't they?

The tag ending in the first sentence does not use the same 'person' as the sentence verb. The correct sentence would be: 'She is going to buy the flat. Isn't she?' In the second sentence, both the sentence verb and the tag ending are negative. If the sentence verb is negative, the tag ending should be positive. The correct sentence would be: You are not going to the party. Are you? In the second sentence, both the sentence verb and the tag ending are in positive. If the sentence verb is positive, the tag ending should be negative. The correct sentence would be: It's a wonderful place. Isn't it? In the last sentence, the tense of the sentence verb is present while that of the tag ending is past. The tag ending has to use the same tense as the sentence verb. The correct sentence would be: They have gone to the college. Haven't they?

There are a few exceptions to these rules, as illustrated by the following examples:

- You ought to work hard. Shouldn't you? ('should' in place of 'ought' in tag ending)
- I am ready. Aren't I? ('are' in place of 'am' in tag ending)
- Let us get started, shall we? (Both in positive)

Key to Progress Check

Progress Check 1

Nouns: laws, statements, formulas, phenomena, room, science, statement, exception, rule, example, law, gravity, examples, behaviour, gases, gases, Boyle's, volume, pressure, reason

Main verbs: describe, contrast, require, prohibit, broken, proves, compressed, states, exerted, gives

Adjectives: Natural, qualitative, mathematical, observed, legislative, familiar, less, proportional

Progress Check 2

1. (a) Encoding is the process of changing the information into a logical and coded message.
   (b) Your weakness in viewing others within your frame of reference may also lead to confusion and misunderstanding.
   (c) The properties of covalent compounds are quite different from those of ionic compounds.
   (d) When alcohol dissolves in water, heat is released into the surroundings.
   (e) In certain substances, some electrons are bound rather loosely with their atoms.
   (f) In fuel cells, the chemical energy of the fuel is directly converted into low voltage direct current electrical energy.
   (g) Light waves are electromagnetic waves that do not require any material medium for their propagation.
   (h) The element iron has an industrial importance that exceeds that of any other metallic element.
   (i) Although there are more than 100 known elements, they rarely occur in the pure state.
   (j) Plastics have specific properties, which may make them preferable to traditional materials.
2. to, for, in, with, by, to, by, to, of, in, with, between

Progress Check 3

1. (a) When a drop of ink is carefully released in water, there is at first a rather sharp boundary between the ink cloud and the water.
   (b) Tectonic islands are created by movements in the Earth's crust.
   (c) Although all metals react with oxygen, their reactivity is different.
   (d) Silver is the best conductor of heat.
   (e) Vehicular pollution causes serious health problems.
   (f) The poorest conductor among the metals is lead.
   (g) Electrical conductivity is a common property of metals.
   (h) A substance in the solid state may be changed into a liquid substance, and one in the liquid state may be changed into a gaseous substance.
   (i) Igneous rocks are formed by the cooling of molten material.
   (j) In order to produce and hear a sound, we require a source of vibratory energy.
2. the, a, a, the, the, the, the, the
3. Computer networks are systems of interconnected computers that communicate information to one another. Local Area Network (LAN) gained prominence during 1980's. A LAN can be defined as a group of desktop computers located relatively close to one another through a cabling system to enable them to share access to computing resources. LANs consist of workstations connected to a central computer called the File Server,

which is a special purpose computer used to control and manage the network resources that are shared by the network users.

Progress Check 4

1. (a) Mounted, forms, adjusted, is formed, forms
   (b) Combined, react, combine , may be arranged, joined, can be modified
   (c) Make, to be corroded, can be dissolved, deformed, must be applied, can be mixed, can easily be shaped
   (d) is used, is fixed, formed, magnified, seen, inverted
2. (a) is carried, is placed, forced, is to be washed out, is given, is shaken
   (b) produce, is transferred, is transmitted, is called, results
   (c) is stretched, can make, vibrate, displacing, releasing, is lost, dies out, vibrates, are produced, depend

Progress Check 5

1. (a) Communication, which is one of the essential conditions of social interaction, is a way of reaching others with facts, ideas, thoughts, and values.
   (b) The main objectives of horizontal communication are developing teamwork and promoting group coordination within an organisation.
   (c) Effective technical communication is a dynamic interchange that involves a systematic understanding of scientific and technical subjects.
   (d) The changes that have taken place in the field of science and technology reflect several developments in the way technical communication skills are viewed.
   (e) The prolonged inhalation of carbon monoxide, present in the toxic fumes released by motor vehicles, reduces the oxygen carrying capacity of blood.
   (f) The optical density of any transparent medium is a measure of its refractive index.
   (g) Air pollution has been a major threat not only to the quality of environment but also to human health.
   (h) The colour perception of different animals is varied due to the difference in the structure of the rods and cones in their retina.
   (i) A chemical combination of two or more elements results in a substance called a compound, which behaves quite differently from its component elements.
   (j) Thermosetting plastics, which become rigid on further heating and cannot be softened again, consist of polymer chains that react with one another at points of contact so that they become strongly linked together in three-dimensions.

Progress Check 6

1. (a) When a simple coil of wire is rotated in a magnetic field or when a magnetic field through a coil is changed, the coil acts as though it had an emf source in it.
   (b) If you stretch a material too far, the material will permanently elongate or perhaps break.
   (c) When an object is elastically stretched, the elongation is proportional to the tensile force.
   (d) A rod will break when the tensile stress in it exceeds its tensile strength.
   (e) If a gas could be prevented from condensing to a liquid or solid at very small absolute temperatures, then the molecules would have no motion at absolute zero.
   (f) When exposed to humid air, zinc will form zinc compounds and protect the iron from rusting.

(g) When a gamma ray is thrown out, neither the mass nor the charge of the nucleus <u>changes</u>.
(h) When a set of waves <u>moves</u> from one material to another, the frequency remains the same.

2. (a) You will achieve professional success if you are able to communicate effectively.
(b) Iron rusts if exposed to humid atmosphere.
(c) When an object is allowed to fall freely to the earth from some height, it accelerates as it falls.
(d) The term 'mass' describes the tendency of an object to remain at rest if it is stationary or to continue in motion if it is already moving.
(e) When a solid is heated, the magnitude of these thermal vibrations increases until they shake apart the solid structure and the solid melts, becoming a liquid.
(f) When a ray of light is passed through a prism, it gets refracted.
(g) When we live in the environment and use the environmental resources, knowingly or unknowingly, we put pressure on the environment.
(h) Whenever you delete a file, it's temporarily moved to the Recycle Bin on your desktop.
(i) When molecules collide, the faster one (with more kinetic energy) transfers some of this energy to the slower one and causes a transfer of heat energy and a resulting temperature change.
(j) When a moving vehicle strikes against a wall, a large amount of force acts on the vehicle.

B APPENDIX

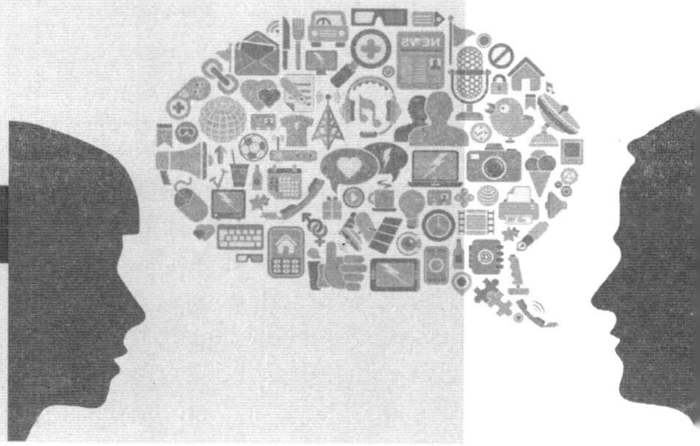

Common Errors

This section contains exercises on common errors. Solve the exercises the answers to which are given at the end of the section.

Exercise 1

1. **Read the following sentences carefully and edit them for grammatical accuracy:**
   (a) There is many solutions to this problem.
   (b) All of us - Ravi, Anil, Arshad, Kavita, and me— are coming to the party.
   (c) If I had time, I will complete the report tomorrow.
   (d) You would not be so upset if you were not choosing your friends carelessly.
   (e) I wish you will not be late for the class.
   (f) You should keep on visit the library for collecting sufficient data for your report.
   (g) If you worked hard, you would have got a good grade.
   (h) We could complete the assignment if it was not so late.
   (i) Dr Anil Sinha eating along with his children, were present in the function.
   (j) Having just taking his dinner, he was not ready to have even a soft drink.

Exercise 2

1. **Read the following sentences carefully and edit them for word structure, grammatical accuracy, and spelling:**
   (a) Any misinterpretation of a message leading to communication breakdown and creates confusion and misunderstanding.
   (b) Organisational competence is the ability to organise information with a logical and structured way.
   (c) Technical communication only makes professional interaction not possible but also directs the flow of technical information and knowledge.
   (d) Different kinds of glass and plastics have different refractive indice.
   (e) Weather varietions are caused by flow of hot air masses in relative to cold air masses.
   (f) Refraction causes a seperation of white light into its componant colours.
   (g) In jet propulsion engines gas turbines are used; only provides the work required for the compressor of the engine.
   (h) Metals are known electropositive elements because they can form positive ions with the loss of electrons.
   (i) The fibre optic cables consist of many glass fibres transport hundred of telephone conversations over long distances.
   (j) The reaction between an acid and a base take place in microseconds.

Exercise 3

1. **In each of the following sentences, a blank has been left to be filled by one of the three alternatives given under it. Select the most appropriate grammatical structure for each blank.**
   (a) If a clean magnesium wire ______________, it catches fire.
      (i) will be heated on a Bunsen burner
      (ii) will heat on a Bunsen burner
      (iii) is heated on a Bunsen burner

(b) Catalysts are substances that alter the rate of chemical reactions ______________.
   (i) without undergoing themselves any overall chemical change
   (ii) without undergoing any overall chemical change themselves
   (iii) without themselves undergoing any overall chemical change
(c) Chemical reactions are accompanied ______________.
   (i) with energy changes
   (ii) by energy changes
   (iii) for energy changes
(d) Equilibrium is always attained ______________.
   (i) through a closed system
   (ii) into a closed system
   (iii) in a closed system
(e) Washing soda has been used ______________.
   (i) for very early times
   (ii) since very early times
   (iii) from very early times
(f) Sodium carbonate is used ______________.
   (i) in removing permanent hardness in water
   (ii) for removing permanent hardness of water
   (iii) for removing permanent hardness in water
(g) Pure calcium oxide, or lime, is an amorphous white solid ______________.
   (i) keeping a high melting point
   (ii) having a high melting point
   (iii) maintaining a high melting point
(h) Photochromatic glass is a special variety of glass that temporarily darkens ______________.
   (i) when it was being exposed to bright light
   (ii) when exposed to bright light
   (iii) when it has exposed to bright light
(i) The properties of steel depend ______________.
   (i) upon the amount of carbon content
   (ii) on the amount of carbon content
   (iii) at the amount of carbon content
(j) Most electrochemical cells ______________ after they are run down.
   (a) would not have been recharged
   (b) could not recharge
   (c) cannot be recharged

Exercise 4

1. **Edit the following sentences to correct faults in word order, grammar, punctuation, and spelling:**
   (a) Photosynthesis and photography involve both light sensitive reactions.
   (b) Light is a form of electromagnetic radiation, that causes the sensation of sight.

(c) Many optical phenomenon observed around us can be understood if we can consider light as waves.
(d) Our retina has a large number of light-sensitive cells; which is having shapes of rods and cones.
(e) An ionic compound is a collection of an equal number of positive and negative ions arranged with a three-dimensional lattice.
(f) Most of the gold and silver produced today are recovered for by-products of lead, zinc, and copper refining.
(g) The simplest method of ore dressing depends on the fact that the metallic compounds having a higher specific gravity than the gangue settles faster in a stream of water.
(h) The dangerous pollutants such as ozone, aldehydes and ketones are the result of a complex chain reaction causing by carbon monoxide, nitrogen oxides and hydrocarbons emitted by motor vehicles.
(i) Unlike springs and pendulums, which only have one resonant frequency, vibrating strings and air columns has an infinite number of different resonant frequencies.
(j) The objective and the eyepiece of a microscope are mounted in the ends of a tube, and the mounting is done in such a way that their axes are common.

Exercise 5

1. Edit the following sentences to correct faults in grammar, punctuation, and spelling:

(a) Wooden beams are used in smaller structures due to they have sufficient strength and are lighter and less expensive than steel girders.
(b) A force is an action that tending to make a stationary object move, or changes the speed or direction of motion of a moving object.
(c) The physical universe is composed entirely of matter and energy which, together is the basis of all objective phenomena.
(d) An object has same mass at any location, for example, its mass is the same on the earth, on the moon, and in free space.
(e) Each atom has a very small core which is extremely dense called the nucleus.
(f) When a solid is heated, the magnitude of the thermal vibrations will increase until they will 'shake apart' the solid structure and the solid melts.
(g) Electricity and magnetism are directly related because both types of phenomena are due to the interactions among electric charges.
(h) After using very high magnifications electron microscopes can reveal some of the details of molecular structure.
(i) When the North Pole of one magnet will be brought close to the South Pole of another the two magnets will attract each other.
(j) The UPS automatically corrects high and low utility voltages as the loads receive voltage within the normal range.

Exercise 6

1. **Read the following sentences carefully and edit them to correct faults in grammar, punctuation, and spelling:**
   (a) In the biological sciences special techniques for preparing specimens mean that, it is possible to look after the internal surfaces of cells that have been fractured open.
   (b) Whether the UPS is overloaded, it will send a constant beep tone.
   (c) Mining is the general term used for separation of an ore from the ground and milling refers processing of the ore into one or more marketable products.
   (d) Magma is original source of most of minerals.
   (e) In very small objects such as viruses and isolated molecules it is possible to prepare them for examination by simply mixing them with a stain that provides a contrasting background.
   (f) If the main voltage will be low, the smart boost corrects it back to its normal range without draining the internal battery.
   (g) It will not be possible for us to remember everything since the process of forgetting is very fast.
   (h) Petroleum occurs widely in the sedimentary rocks of the Earth's crust and may have occurred as a gas, liquid, semi-solid, or solid.
   (i) We can develop some form of technique to help us at the process of remembering what we read.
   (j) A vapour is a gas whose temperature and pressure is such that it is very near the liquid phase.

Exercise 7

1. **In each of the following sentences, the blank can be filled by one of the three alternatives given under it. Select the most appropriate grammatical structure for each blank.**
   (a) Dalton assumed that all matter was made of very tiny particles, which ______________.
      (i) cannot be broken down further.
      (ii) will not be broken down further.
      (iii) could not be broken down further.
   (b) During recent years scientists and policy makers ______________________________ ______ that have the potential to threaten human health or environmental quality.
      (i) paid substantial attention to airborne substances
      (ii) have paid substantial attention to airborne substances
      (iii) did pay substantial attention to airborne substances
   (c) Recent research in air pollution has clearly showed that concentrations of many air pollutants ____ ____.
      (i) can be higher indoors than out.
      (ii) would have been higher indoors than out.
      (iii) could have been higher indoors than out.
   (d) The weight of an object at the earth's surface is not the same as its weight on the moon because the masses and the diameters of the earth and moon __________________________.
      (i) have to be quite different.
      (ii) are quite different.
      (iii) has been quite different.

(e) When a material ____________ to repeated varying loads over a long period, it gradually loses its strength.
   (a) will be subjected
   (b) can be subjected
   (c) is subjected

(f) As the number of users increases, the time it ____________ the computer to do each user's task increases also.
   (i) takes
   (ii) can take
   (iii) should take

(g) The ongoing rise in oil prices appears to be putting an end to the buyer's market that ____________ in the early 1980's.
   (i) was emerged
   (ii) had emerged
   (iii) emerged

(h) The process of metamorphism, ____________ the formation of metamorphic rocks, may generate enough heat and pressure to alter existing mineral deposits of impure or low-grade ores into comparatively more pure and valuable minerals.
   (i) which results in
   (ii) that might result in
   (iii) that will result in

(i) Advances in information technology has provided us with a wide range of effective communication tools, which has made communication easier, faster, and more reliable than ____________.
   (i) it was.
   (ii) it used to be.
   (iii) it had to be.

(j) Distributed processing seems to be the best way ____________ a factory.
   (i) to go about computerising
   (ii) going about to computerise
   (iii) to go about to computerise

Exercise 8

1. Edit the following sentences to correct all language faults, including grammar, punctuation, and spelling:

(a) To understand the structure of the binary number system the first step is to review familiar decimal number system.

(b) For converting a decimal number to binary two common methods are there.

(c) Comparing for the other fundamental forces, gravity is the weakest force of nature.

(d) Electromagnetic force is the force within charged particles.

(e) It is often happening that two or more waves passing simultaneously through the same region.

(f) A common situation, where viscosity does play an important role, is the motion of a sphere in a fluid.
(g) The word potential suggest a possibility or a capacity for action.
(h) Molar masses can be thought as conversion factors among masses in grammar and number of moles.
(i) Energy neither can be created nor can be destroyed; although can be changed from one form to another.
(j) Engineers could have personal computers or engineering workstations on their desks, and could be using available programmes to design and test circuits.

Exercise 9

1. **Edit the following sentences to correct faults in grammar, punctuation, and spelling:**
   (a) Interactive computing is a type of computing environment that originated with commercial timesharing systems and have been refined by the widespread use of personal computers.
   (b) Projectile motion occurs when an object will be freely falling but has an initial velocity that is not vertical.
   (c) Acceleration is a measure of how faster an object's velocity is changing.
   (d) One of the most important and interesting characteristics of Pascal are its abilities to support many different types of data.
   (e) We can calculate the gravitational potential energy of an object by the amount of work it can do in raising another object as it is falling.
   (f) Since energy is the ability to do work we can measure the energy of an object by converting the energy to work.
   (g) Integrated circuits are miniturised circuits contains diodes, transistors, and the other components used in electronics.
   (h) A transistor can be used as an amplifier since the current flowing from the base of a transistor is much smaller than the emitter and collector.
   (i) The output voltage can make much larger than the input voltage in an amplifier.
   (j) X-rays are high energy photons, which can knock an atom outside of a molecule.

Exercise 10

1. **In each of the following sentences, the blank can be filled by one of the three alternatives given under it. Select the most appropriate grammatical structure, to fill in the blank.**
   (a) Plastics can be classified into two groups according to their behaviour ________________.
      (i) when being heated
      (ii) when heated
      (iii) after being heated
   (b) Waves are usually both reflected and refracted as they ________________.
      (i) will go from one material to another

(ii) might go from one material to another
(iii) go from one material to another

3. The chemical properties of an electron are controlled by its outer electrons. ________________.
   (i) aren't they?
   (ii) are they?
   (iii) are they not?
4. Many other materials, ________________________, do not conduct electricity.
   (i) like as non-metallic crystals
   (ii) such as non-metallic crystals
   (iii) as non-metallic crystals
5. ________________________, more valence electrons are above their ground state and are more easily ionised.
   (i) when metals are heated
   (ii) since metals are heated
   (iii) as metals are heated
6. When light tries to go from a more optically dense material to one that is less optically dense, ________________________ if the incident angle is more than the critical angle.
   (i) it will not be refracted
   (ii) it is not being refracted
   (iii) it could not have been refracted
7. Fuels can be classified as solid, liquid, and gaseous, depending on the state ________________________ they exist.
   (i) under which
   (ii) upon which
   (iii) in which
8. Both analog and digital computers include a sub-class of rather simple machines ________________________ only specific simple operations.
   (i) that mechanises
   (ii) that mechanise
   (iii) that is mechanising
9. Chemical reactions may be classified into three types, according to the nature and type of the reactions that ________________________.
   (i) Could produce new substances
   (ii) Produce new substances
   (iii) Might be producing new substances
10. A multi-user mainframe computer has a large memory________________________
    (i) has it?
    (ii) hasn't it?
    (iii) will it.

Exercise 11

1. **Edit the following sentences to correct faults in grammar, punctuation, and spelling:**
   (a) One of the most important consideration in the design of oculars is correction for lateral chromatic aberration.
   (b) The higher the electronegativity, effectively more the atom attracts and holds electrons.
   (c) A non-polar covalent bond exists in between atoms have a very small or zero differences in electronegativity.
   (d) Liquid molecules are able to move and they flow past each other, but their motion is much slower than gases.
   (e) The actual mechanical advantage of a machine is the ratio of output force with the input force.
   (f) The molecules of a solid are closer together than a fluid.
   (g) Unlike solids gases and vapours are higher-energy states of matter they flow to take the shape and to occupy the total volume of any container.
   (h) There are plastic solids flow under the proper circumstances, and even metals may flow under high pressures.
   (i) Using very high magnifications, a transmission electron microscope can provide detailed information about structures such as viruses–most of which are so small to be seen at all with a normal optical microscope.
   (j) When the vector sum of the external forces acting on a system is zero, then the total linear momentum of the system could have remained constant.

Exercise 12

1. **Edit the following sentences to correct faults in grammar, punctuation, and spelling:**
   (a) When you have not used the remote control since a long time, take out the batteries and store them in a cool, dry place.
   (b) When you upgraded from Windows 3.1, Setup automatically transfers your current system settings and installed program.
   (c) An object is said to be in motion if its position changes in respect to the surrounding in course of time.
   (d) If the velocity of a particle changes by unequal amounts in equal intervals of time it is said to move with variable acelleration.
   (e) Friction is the retarding force which is called into play when actually a body moves or tends to move on the surface of another body.
   (f) When a lump of sugar might be crushed, it could be seen that it is made up of small particles of sugar.
   (g) When molecules are formed as a result of interatomic forces between the atoms then there must be some intermolecular forces which must bind the molecules together.
   (h) When a force is applied to a body, it is deformed to a little or great extent depends upon the nature of molecular attraction.
   (i) When a body is fully or partially imersed in a fluid, it could displace the fluid.
   (j) When a liquid heated the thermal agitation of its molecules increases.

Exercise 13

1. **Read the following paragraphs and improve them by correcting grammatical errors:**
   (a) As Manager (Sales and Marketing) at Hyquip Projects Pvt Ltd Hyderabad, I had been being involved at sales and marketing of flat steel products, mainly CR/GP/GC products. I was responsible in creating and build up a strong dealer/distribution network within the North Eastern Region and Eastern states of India, as well as improving institutional sales on all-India basis.
   (b) My greatest strengths is my ability to working under pressure. Whatever may be the circumstances, I am always completing my projects on time. Last month the Director (Sales) of my company had asked me to prepare the Annual Sales Report of our division of the company. We had been to submit the report to the headquarters in a period of three days. I prepared the report in a record time of two days.
   (c) Hello friends. May I could have your kind attention with a few seconds, please? I am sure you are going to agree that we are here to exchanging our views on the reservation policy of the government and we have to complete the discussion within 35 minutes. Because we have already used up more than five minutes, we might begin the discussion now. Shall we be starting?
   (d) In science, our knowledge is usually acquired with systematic observation and measurement. Theories are being developed for attempts to describe these observations and to predicting new results. It can be important that we will have a set of precisely defined standards for measured values, so that we transmitting our knowledge to others.
   (e) A plastics article may be needing to differ in design and appearance with a similar article made from another material such as metal or wood. This is due not only the properties of plastics but also to the techniques employed in fabricate plastic products. These techniques includes injection moulding, blow moulding, compression moulding, extrusion and vacuum forming.
   (f) The sun emits light in different wavelengths. If sunlight will be passed through a prism each of these wavelengths will be refracted by a different amount. Violet has shortest wavelength, and red has longest. The wavelength of green is that of midway from that of violet and red. Light which wavelength is shorter than violet is called ultra-violet light. Light which wavelength is longer than red light is called infrared light. About one-third of light from the sun are infrared.
   (g) We know that nuclear reactions that goes on in the interior of the sun liberates a large amount of energy. Nuclei of deuterium whose is the heavier isotope of hydrogen collides in the sun's interior to produce helium. The energy liberating in these reaction fire the sun, which, in turn, emit lights of different wavelengths. Of these wavelength, it is the infrared wavelengths, which heat up the earth. The reaction which hydrogen in the sun is converted into helium is called a fusion reaction.
   (h) The rotative speed of an impulse turbine is maintain constant through use of a governor. When the load on a turbine may drop the wheel will tend to speed up; this will affect the governor, which, in turn, actuates a mechanism to reduces the power of the jet that impinges on the buckets. In most designs this is accomplished with moving the needle to reduce the flow in the delivery pipe. This may result after serious water-hammer pressures. There are several ways in which this problem might have been avoided.

Key to Exercises

Exercise 1

1. (a) There are many solutions to this problem.
   (b) All of us - Ravi, Anil, Arshad, Kavita, and I— are coming to the party.
   (c) If I have time, I will complete the report tomorrow.
   (d) You would not be so upset if you did not choose your friends carelessly.
   (e) I wish you would not be late for the class.
   (f) You should keep on visiting the library for collecting sufficient data for your report.
   (g) If you had worked hard, you would have got a good grade.
   (h) We could complete the assignment if it were not so late.
   (i) Dr Anil Sinha, along with his children, was present in the function.
   (j) Having just eaten his dinner, he was not ready to have even a soft drink.

Exercise 2

1. (a) Any misinterpretation of a message leads to communication breakdown and creates confusion and misunderstanding.
   (b) Organisational competence is the ability to organise information in a logical and structured way.
   (c) Technical communication not only makes professional interaction possible but also directs the flow of technical information and knowledge.
   (d) Different kinds of glass and plastics have different refractive indices.
   (e) Weather variations are caused by the flow of hot air masses relative to cold air masses.
   (f) Refraction causes a separation of white light into its component colours.
   (g) In jet propulsion engines, gas turbines are used only to provide the work required for the compressor of the engine.
   (h) Metals are known as electropositive elements because they can form positive ions by the loss of electrons.
   (i) The fibre optic cables consisting of many glass fibres transport hundreds of telephone conversations over long distances.
   (j) The reaction between an acid and a base takes place in microseconds.

Exercise 3

1. (a) (iii) (b) (ii) (c) (i) (d) (iii) (e) (ii)
   (f) (iii) (g) (ii) (h) (ii) (i) (i) (j) (iii)

Exercise 4

1. (a) Photosynthesis and photography, both, involve light sensitive reactions.
   (b) Light is a form of electromagnetic radiation that causes the sensation of sight.
   (c) Many optical phenomenon observed around us can be understood if we consider light as waves.

(d) Our retina has a large number of light-sensitive cells, which are shaped like rods and cones.
(e) An ionic compound is a collection of an equal number of positive and negative ions arranged in a three-dimensional lattice.
(f) Most of the gold and silver produced today is recovered as a byproduct of lead, zinc, and copper refining.
(g) The simplest method of ore dressing depends on the fact that metallic compounds having a higher specific gravity than the gangue settle faster in a stream of water.
(h) Dangerous pollutants such as ozone, aldehydes, and ketones are the result of a complex chain reaction caused by carbon monoxide, nitrogen oxides, and hydrocarbons emitted by motor vehicles.
(i) Unlike springs and pendulums, which only have one resonant frequency, vibrating strings and air columns have an infinite number of resonant frequencies.
(j) The objective and the eyepiece of a microscope are mounted at the opposite ends of a tube, in such a way that their axes are common.

Exercise 5

1. (a) Wooden beams are used in smaller structures because they have sufficient strength and are lighter and less expensive than steel girders.
(b) A force is an action that tends to make a stationary object move, or changes the speed or direction of motion of a moving object.
(c) The physical universe is composed entirely of matter and energy, which together are the basis of all objective phenomena.
(d) An object has the same mass at any location; for example, its mass is the same on the earth, on the moon, and in free space.
(e) Each atom has a very small core called the nucleus, which is extremely dense.
(f) When a solid is heated, the magnitude of the thermal vibrations increases until they 'shake apart' the solid structure and the solid melts.
(g) Electricity and magnetism are directly related because both types of phenomena are due to interactions between electric charges.
(h) Using very high magnifications, electron microscopes can reveal some of the details of molecular structure.
(i) When the north pole of one magnet is brought close to the south pole of another the two magnets attract each other.
(j) The UPS automatically corrects high and low utility voltages so that the loads receive voltage within the normal range.

Exercise 6

1. (a) In the biological sciences, special techniques for preparing specimens make it possible to look at the internal surfaces of cells that have been fractured open.
(b) If the UPS is overloaded, it will send a constant beep tone.
(c) Mining is the general term used for the separation of an ore from the ground and milling refers to the processing of the ore into one or more marketable products.
(d) Magma is the original source of most minerals.

(e) In the case of very small objects such as viruses and isolated molecules, it is possible to prepare them for examination by simply mixing them with a stain that provides a contrasting background.
(f) If the main voltage is low, the smart boost will correct it back to its normal range without draining the internal battery.
(g) It will not be possible for us to remember everything because the process of forgetting is very fast.
(h) Petroleum occurs widely in the sedimentary rocks of Earth's crust and may occur as a gas, liquid, semi-solid, or solid.
(i) We can develop some form of technique to help us in the process of remembering what we read.
(j) A vapour is a gas whose temperature and pressure are such that it is very near the liquid phase.

Exercise 7

1. (a) (iii) (b) (ii) (c) (ii) (d) (ii) (e) (iii)
(f) (i) (g) (iii) (h) (i) (i) (ii) (j) (i)

Exercise 8

1. (a) To understand the structure of the binary number system, the first step is to review the familiar decimal number system.
(b) To convert a decimal number to binary, there are two common methods.
(c) Compared to other fundamental forces, gravity is the weakest force of nature.
(d) Electromagnetic force is the force between charged particles.
(e) It often happens that two or more waves pass simultaneously through the same region.
(f) A common situation where viscosity plays an important role is the motion of a sphere in a fluid.
(g) The word potential suggests possibility or capacity for action.
(h) Molar masses can be thought of as conversion factors between masses in grams and the number of moles.
(i) Energy can neither be created nor destroyed, although it can be changed from one form to another.
(j) Engineers can have personal computers or engineering workstations on their desks, and can use available programme to design and test circuits.

Exercise 9

1. (a) Interactive computing is a type of computing environment that originated with commercial timesharing systems and has been refined by the widespread use of personal computers.
(b) Projectile motion occurs when an object is freely falling but has an initial velocity that is not vertical.
(c) Acceleration is a measure of how fast an object's velocity is changing.
(d) One of the most important and interesting characteristics of Pascal is its ability to support many different types of data.
(e) We can calculate the gravitational potential energy of an object by the amount of work it can do in raising another object as it falls.
(f) Since energy is the ability to do work, we can measure the energy of an object by converting the energy to work.

(g) Integrated circuits are miniturised circuits containing diodes, transistors, and the other components used in electronics.
(h) A transistor can be used as an amplifier because the current flowing from the base of a transistor is much smaller than the emitter and collector currents.
(i) The output voltage can be made much larger than the input voltage in an amplifier.
(j) X-rays are high energy photons, which can knock an atom out of a molecule.

Exercise 10

1. (a) (i)	(b) (iii)	(c) (i)	(d) (ii)	(e) (iii)
(f) (i)	(g) (c)	(h) (ii)	(i) (ii)	(j) (ii)

Exercise 11

1. (a) One of the most important considerations in the design of oculars is correction for lateral chromatic aberration.
(b) The higher the electro-negativity, the more effectively the atom attracts and holds electrons.
(c) A non-polar covalent bond exists between atoms having very small or zero differences in electro-negativity.
(d) Liquid molecules are able to move and they flow past each other, but their motion is much slower than that of gases.
(e) The actual mechanical advantage of a machine is the ratio of output force to the input force.
(f) The molecules of a solid are closer together than those of a fluid.
(g) Unlike solids, gases and vapours are high-energy states of matter; they flow to take the shape and to occupy the total volume of any container.
(h) Some plastic solids flow under certain conditions, and even metals may flow under high pressure.
(i) Using very high magnifications, a transmission electronic microscope can provide detailed information about structures such as viruses–most of which are too small to be seen at all with a normal optical microscope.
(j) When the vector sum of the external forces acting on a system is zero, then the total linear momentum of the system remains constant.

Exercise 12

1. (a) When you do not use the remote control for a long time, take out the batteries and store them in a cool, dry place.
(b) When you upgrade from Windows 3.1, Setup automatically transfers your current system settings and installed programme.
(c) An object is said to be in motion if its position changes with respect to the surroundings in course of time.
(d) If the velocity of a particle changes by unequal amounts in equal intervals of time, it is said to move with variable acceleration.
(e) Friction is the retarding force that is called into play when a body actually moves or tends to move over the surface of another body.
(f) When a lump of sugar is crushed, it can be seen that it is made up of small particles of sugar.

(g) When molecules are formed as a result of interatomic forces between the atoms, then there must be some intermolecular forces that bind the molecules together.
(h) When a force is applied on a body, it is deformed to a little or great extent depending upon the nature of molecular attraction.
(i) When a body is fully or partially immersed in a fluid, it displaces the fluid.
(j) When a liquid is heated, the thermal agitation of its molecules increases.

Exercise 13

1. (a) As Manager (Sales and Marketing) at Hyquip Projects Private Limited, Hyderabad, I was involved in sales and marketing of flat steel products, mainly CR/GP/GC products. I was responsible for creating and building up a strong dealer/distribution network within the North Eastern Region and Eastern states of India, as well as Institutional sales on all-India basis.
(b) My greatest strength is my ability to work under pressure. Whatever may be the circumstances, I always complete my projects on time. Last month the Director (Sales) of my company asked me to prepare the Annual Sales Report of our division. We had to submit the report to the headquarters within three days. I prepared the report in a record time of two days.
(c) Hello friends. May I have your kind attention for a few seconds, please? I am sure you will agree that we are here to exchange our views on the reservation policy of the government and we have to complete the discussion within 35 minutes. As we have already used up more than five minutes, we should begin the discussion now. Shall we start?
(d) In science, our knowledge is usually acquired by systematic observation and measurement. Theories are then developed in an attempt to describe these observations and to predict new results. It is important that we have a set of precisely defined standards for measured values so that we can transmit our knowledge to others.
(e) A plastic article may need to differ in design and appearance from a similar article made from another material, such as metal or wood. This is due not only to the properties of plastic but also to the techniques employed in fabricating plastic products. These techniques include injection moulding, blow moulding, compression moulding, extrusion, and vacuum forming.
(f) The sun emits lights of different wavelengths. If sunlight is passed through a prism each of these wavelengths is refracted by a different amount. Violet has the shortest wavelength and red has the longest. The wavelength of green is midway between that of violet and red. Light whose wavelength is shorter than that of violet is called ultraviolet light. Light whose wavelength is longer than that of red light is called infrared light. About one-third of the light from the sun is infrared.
(g) We know that nuclear reactions that go on in side the sun liberate a large amount of energy. Nuclei of deuterium, which is the heavier isotope of hydrogen, collide in the sun's interior to produce helium. The energy liberated in these reaction fires the sun, which, in turn, emits lights of different wavelengths. Of these wavelengths, it is the infrared wavelengths, which heat up the earth. The reaction in which hydrogen in the sun is converted into helium is called a fusion reaction.
(h) The rotative speed of an impulse turbine is maintained constant through the use of a governor. When the load on a turbine drops the wheel tends to speed up; this affects the governor, which, in turn, actuates a mechanism to reduce the power of the jet that impinges on the buckets. In most designs this is accomplished by moving the needle to reduce the flow in the delivery pipe. This may result in serious water-hammer pressures. There are several ways in which this problem may be avoided.

APPENDIX C

Vocabulary Development

This appendix is a manual on vocabulary extension and development and contains comprehensive discussion and explanation of:

- Vocabulary extension methods
- Technical vocabulary
- Formation of new words
- Use of prefixes and suffixes
- Synonyms and antonyms
- One word substitutions
- Words often confused
- Homophones
- Sentence completion
- Anology

This appendix also contains **nineteen vocabulary exercises** to check and improve vocabulary and usage. Answers to the exercises are given in the Key at the end of the appendix.

C.1 VOCABULARY EXTENSION

Vocabulary knowledge is the single most important area of language competence and is of concern to all four language skills. We will not be able to listen or speak confidently or read and write effectively if we do not have reasonable vocabulary competence, which may include our stock of perceptive vocabulary as well as productive vocabulary. All successful communicators do have a reasonable stock of words. We should, therefore, develop our vocabulary.

> Vocabulary knowledge is the single most important area of language competence.

What does vocabulary development mean? What does learning a new word involve? Does it involve knowing just the meaning of the word? Learning or knowing a new word involves knowing its different shades of meaning (both denotation and connotation), use in context, grammatical characteristics, pronunciation, and so on. The following are some general suggestions for vocabulary development:

C.1.1 Learn Words in Context

New words should be learned in context with the help of appropriate phrases. Words in isolation cannot be learned by picking words and their meanings from a dictionary. The only way to learn new words and improve vocabulary skills is by examining the use of words in their context and learning their uses.

C.1.2 Develop Vocabulary Cards

Vocabulary cards are handy aids that help to improve and develop vocabulary. In the course of reading, sometimes we come across, unfamiliar words or phrases, these should be noted down on a card. Any other information, such as meaning, pronunciation in phonetic transcription, a sentence making the use of the word/phrase and so on, should be written down on the back of the card. These vocabulary cards are helpful in recalling the meaning and practising their pronunciation.

C.1.3 Read Extensively

Reading and listening can help in effectively expanding one's vocabulary. While reading something or listening to a structured presentation, we come across a large number of new words and expressions.

C.1.4 Distinguish Between Formal and Informal Words

There are two kinds of words: formal and informal. There are many differences between everyday language and the language used for technical and professional communication. Our choice of words largely depends on our relationship with the person we are talking or writing to.

C.2 TECHNICAL VOCABULARY

The use of formal words, scientific vocabulary, specialised terminology, and formal phrases and expressions is common in technical communication. In fact, technical vocabulary is a specific feature of technical communication. Every field of science and technology has its own list of terms and phrases. The following passage illustrates the use of formal words and technical vocabulary (underlined):

"Magma is the original source of most of the minerals. The constituent minerals, mostly rock-forming silicates and oxides, are deposited at various stages as the magma cools down during its passage. Minerals having nearly similar fusion points segregate and concentrate together, resulting in magmatic segregation. Important deposits of metallic oxides such as magnetite and ilmenite, and sulphides such as pyrrhotite and chalcopyrite are formed in this way. Magmatic segregation may take place at different depths during the travel of the magma and at different temperatures. Most ferro-magnesium silicates and other oxides are formed at depth by magmatic segregation."

It is evident that the technical words and phrases used in the above passage are essential to convey the above information about magma.

Now read the following passage and note the underlined words and phrases:

"The position that an element has in the periodic table tells its electronic arrangement. The electronic arrangement tells us how many shells of electron it has. The group, the atom is in, tells us the number of electrons in its outermost shell. This number tells about many qualities of the atom such as valence, metallic character, the size of the atom, and so on."

It is obvious that the underlined words are too informal and need to be replaced by formal and technical words and phrases to make the language of the passage appropriate and formal. The following is a revised version of the same passage:

"The position that an element occupies in the periodic table defines its electronic configuration. The electronic configuration informs us how many shells of electron it occupies. The group, the atom is in, tells us the number of electrons in its valence shell. This number defines many properties of the atom such as valence, metallic character, the size of the atom, and so on."

The term 'jargon' refers to words or expressions used by a particular group or profession.

The revised passage is clearly more formal and scientific. Therefore, it is important for a writer to be aware of the 'jargon' used in his/her professional field. The term 'jargon' refers to words or expressions used by a particular group or profession.

C.3 RULES OF WORD FORMATION

A combination or a slight modification of words can form new words.

The English language has many words. A combination or a slight modification of these words can also form new words. There are many ways this can happen. Like all other aspects of the language, this one too has some rules.

C.3.1 Compound or Combination Words

Compound or combination words are those words that get formed by the coming together of two or more primary words. For example:

- Tea + Spoon = Teaspoon
- Grand + Father = Grandfather
- Sun + Light = Sunlight
- Lock + Up = Lock-up
- Safe + Guard = Safeguard
- Air + Port = Airport

C.3.2 Clipping and Combining

Sometimes when two words are combined, they are clipped before being merged together. This way, they form new words. For example:

- Breakfast + Lunch = Brunch
- Smoke + Fog = Smog
- Motor + Hotel = Motel
- Europe + Asia = Eurasia

In English, new words can be formed by using suffixes and prefixes.

C.3.3 Suffix

A suffix is attached at the end of a root word to form a new word (care+less = careless). A suffix can change the word-class and meaning of a word. Suffixes may be used to form nouns from verbs and adjectives, and adjectives from nouns and verbs. The following lists contain different suffixes and their uses to form new words.

Nouns from Verbs

Suffix	*Verbs*	*Nouns*
-ment	Appoint, arrange, agree, amend, allot, amuse, amaze, conceal, commit, judge, move, appease, argue, announce	Appointment, arrangement, agreement, amendment, allotment, amusement, amazement, concealment, commitment, judgement, movement, appeasement, argument, announcement
-ion, / -tion	Act, attract, add, adopt, abdicate, affect, Associate, create, combine, connect, select, reject, cultivate, elect, expect, invent, dictate, reveal, collect, narrate, converse	Action, attraction, addition, adoption, abdication, Affection, association, creation, combination, connection, selection, rejection, cultivation, election, expectation, invention, dictation, revelation, collection, narration, conversation
-ance	Abound, assist, attend, assure, insure, defy, rely	Abundance, assistance, attendance, assurance, insurance, defiance, reliance
-al	Arrive, approve, betray, deny, dismiss	Arrival, approval, betrayal, denial, dismissal
-sion	admit, compel, decide, extend, divide, expel	Admission, compulsion, decision, extension, division, expulsion
-ing	Learn, earn, burn, bless, build, beat	Learning, earning, burning, blessing, building, beating
-ure	Fail, furnish	Failure, furniture

Nouns from Adjectives

Suffix	*Adjectives*	*Nouns*
-ity	Able, active, civil, frail, equal, human, inferior, mortal, local, real, rigid, stupid, timid	Ability, activity, civility, frailty, equality, humanity, inferiority, mortality, locality, reality, rigidity, stupidity, timidity
-ness	Busy, bold, calm, good, happy, idle, keen, kind, lame, mean, new, one, quick, red, rude, weak, wet, fond,	Business, boldness, calmness, goodness, happiness, idleness, keenness, kindness, lameness, meanness, newness, oneness, quickness, redness, rudeness, weakness, wetness, fondness
-ance	Abundance, brilliant, distant, ignorant	Abundant, brilliance, distance, ignorance

Adjectives from Nouns

Suffix	*Nouns*	*Adjectives*
-y	Air, bush, cloud, dust, grass, leaf, rain, rose, thorn, wind, worth, oil	Airy, bushy, cloudy, dusty, grassy, leafy, rainy, rosy, thorny, windy, worthy, oily
-ly	Father, hour, man, year	Fatherly, hourly, manly, yearly
-al	Accident, ceremony, classic, essence, face, influence, logic, line, prejudice, practice	Accidental, ceremonial classical, essential, facial, influential, logical, lineal, prejudicial, practical
-ish	Book, black, boy, red, slave	Bookish, blackish, boyish, reddish, slavish
-ful	Harm, beauty, pity, skill, sorrow, thought, use, youthful, cheer, colour	Harmful, beautiful, pitiful, skilful, sorrowful, thoughtful, useful, youthful, cheerful, colourful
-less	Use, pain, life, name, colour, thought	Useless, painless, lifeless, nameless, colourless, thoughtless

Adjectives from Verbs

Suffix	*Verbs*	*Adjectives*
-able	Admire, agree, attain, avoid, believe, compare, consider, love, move, prefer, rely, read	Admirable, agreeable, attainable, avoidable, believable, comparable, considerable, lovable, movable, preferable, reliable, readable
-ful	Thank, boast, help, revenge, use	Thankful, boastful, helpful, revengeful, useful

C.3.4 Prefix

A prefix is attached at the beginning of a root word to form a new word (un+usual=unusual). Prefixes may be used to form new words. They may give adjectives a negative meaning. The following list contains different prefixes and words they are used in.

Prefix	*Meaning*	*Word*	*New Words*
a/ in/ il/ im/ ir/ un	Not	Typical, visible, expensive, Active, legal, literate, possible, movable, rational, regular, cultured, natural, comfortable,	Atypical, invisible, inexpensive, inactive, Illegal, illiterate, impossible, immovable, irrational, irregular, uncultured, uncomfortable
anti	Against	National, climax, civic, body, war, biotic, vitamin, toxin	Anti-national, anticlimax, anti-civic, antibody, anti-war, antibiotic anti-vitamin, antitoxin
auto	Self	Mobile, cut, graph, type, suggestion	Automobile, auto-cut, autograph, auto-type, auto-suggestion
bi	Two, wice	Annual, weekly, lingual, corporate, cycle, lateral, lingual	Bi-annual, bi-weekly, bilingual, bicorporate, bicycle, bilateral, bilingual
ex	Former, out	President, chairman, wife, directory, husband	Ex-president, ex-chairman, ex-wife, ex-directory, ex-husband
hetero	Different	Sexual, genetic, cyclic	Heterosexual, heterogenetic, heterocyclic
homo	Similar	Sexual, cyclic, genetic, logical, phone	Homosexual, homocyclic, homogenetic, homological, homophone
inter	Between	Act, communication, action, connect, change, chain, cross, current, fuse, line, lock, mix	Interact, intercommunication, interaction, interconnect, interchange, interchain, intercross, intercurrent, interfuse, interline, interlock, intermix
intra	Within	Abdominal, capsular, mundane, urban	Intra-abdominal, intra-capsular, intra-mundane, intra-urban
mis	Wrong	Adventure, believe, call, behave, arrange, charge, copy, connect, deal, direct, fit, use, inform, place, lead	Misadventure, misbelieve miscall, misbehave, misarrange, mischarge, miscopy, misconnect, misdeal, misdirect, misfit, misuse, misinform, misplace, mislead
micro	Small	Analysis, analytical, chemistry, chemical, detection, detector, film, organism, wave, structure	Microanalysis, micro-analytical, microchemistry, micro-chemical, micro-detection, micro-detector microfilm, micro-organism, microwave, micro-structure
mono	One	Chord, compound, graph	Mono-chord, mono-compound, monograph
multi	Many	Angular, colour, dimensional	Multi-angular, multicolour, multidimensional
post	After	Script, graduate, entry	Postscript, postgraduate, post-entry

(*Contd.*)

Prefix	Meaning	Word	New Words
re	Repeat, again	Absorb, adjust, admission, allotment, appoint, arrange, arrangement, assign, charge, born, confirm	Reabsorb, readjust, readmission, re-allotment, reappoint, rearrange, rearrangement, reassign, recharge, reborn, reconfirm
semi	Half	Circle, annual	Semicircle, semi-annual
sub	Under	Committee, human, normal, title, heading	Subcommittee, subhuman, subnormal, sub-title, sub-heading

C.3.5 Conversion

Sometimes a new word can get formed by changing its type. For example:

You are always busy texting!

Here, the noun, 'text', is converted to a verb meaning 'sending texts'.

Sometimes, a proper noun gets converted into another form, forming a new word. For example:

You are getting too much into details. Don't be an Aamir Khan!

Here, the proper noun 'Aamir Khan' has been altered to mean 'a perfectionist'.

C.4 SYNONYMS AND ANTONYMS

A synonym is a word that means the same as another (for example, shut and close) whereas an antonym is a word opposite in meaning to another (for example, close and open). A good stock of synonyms and antonyms are essential to be able to use so appropriate and effective language.

C.4.1 Synonyms

In order to use words effectively in speech and writing, the ability to distinguish one word from another with slight change in meanings is essential. Words may have similar meanings but a slight variation in the meaning of a word might make it appropriate in one context but inappropriate in another. Given below is a list of synonyms.

A synonym is a word that means the same as another.

Word	Synonyms	Word	Synonyms
Abandon	Leave, forsake	Abbreviate	Abridge, shorten
Auxiliary	Subsidiary, accessory	Adept	Skilled, expert
Adequate	Enough, sufficient	Admire	Praise, esteem
Assist	Help, support	Amaze	Surprise, astonish
Audacious	Brave, courageous	Bold	Daring, valiant
Candid	Frank, straightforward	Commence	Start, begin
Crazy	Insane, mad	Deadly	Dangerous, fatal
Debase	Degrade, defame	Defer	Postpone, adjourn

(*Contd.*)

Word	Synonyms	Word	Synonyms
Deliberate	Intentional, considered	Delicate	Soft, slender
Devoid	Vacant, empty	Diminish	Decrease, reduce
Distinguish	Differentiate, discern	Deviate	Divert, deflect dubious
	Vague, unclear	Efficient	Effective, able
	Remove, discard	Eliminate	Remove
		Emolument	Salary, remuneration
Endorse	Approve, back	Evidence	Proof, testimony
Fabricate	Forge, construct	Flexible	Changeable, variable
Flimsy	Trivial, ordinary	Fluctuate	Change, waver
Forbid	Prohibit, disallow	Generous	Liberal, kind
Hamper	Block, disturb	Humorous	Amusing, laughable
Ignorant	Ill-informed, unaware	Illegal	Unlawful, illicit
	Unreasonable, childish	Immature	Improper, unfit, inappropriate
Indicate	Show, hint	Infer	Conclude, deduce
Initiate	Start, begin	Invent	Create, originate
Innate	Inherent, inborn	Inhuman	Brutal, barbarous
Intricate	Complex, difficult	Jovial	Merry, hearty
Laudable	Commendable, praiseworthy	Majestic	Dignified, imposing
Necessary	Essential, requisite	Opulent	Rich, wealthy

C.4.2 Antonyms

In order to express a contrast or highlight differences between two objects, things, situations, or persons, antonyms may be used. Antonyms can be formed by using certain prefixes also (for example, usual–unusual, regular–irregular, comfort–discomfort). Given below is a list of antonyms:

An antonym is a word opposite in meaning to another.

Word	Antonyms	Word	Antonyms
Accept	Reject	Absent	Present
Abundant	Inadequate	Skilful	Inexpert
Annihilate	Restore	Arrogant	Humble
Ability	Inability	Abridge	Enlarge
Absurd	Sensible	Abundance	Shortage
Acquit	Charge	Backward	Forward
Brutal	Humane	Careful	Careless
Cheerful	Sluggish	Competent	Incompetent
Encourage	Discourage	Endanger	Defend
Establish	Demolish	Feeble	Strong

(*Contd.*)

Word	Antonyms	Word	Antonyms
Flexible	Rigid	Generous	Miserly
Partial	Impartial	Cautious	Impulsive
Organise	Disorganise	Pacify	Provoke
Pleasant	Unpleasant	Prolong	Decrease
Remarkable	Ordinary	Reverence	Scorn
Scanty	Profuse	Thoughtful	Careless

C.5 ONE WORD SUBSTITUTION

One word may be used in place of several words or phrases. This will help in being concise. The following list contains some one word substitutions.

Words/Phrases	One Word Substitution
That which cannot be expressed in words	Inexpressible
That which cannot be avoided	Unavoidable
That which cannot be believed	Incredible
That which cannot be burnt	Incombustible
That which cannot be divided	Indivisible
That which cannot be recovered	Irrevocable
That which cannot be seen	Invisible
That which cannot be read	Illegible
That which cannot be heard	Inaudible
That which cannot be conquered	Invincible
That which cannot be dispensed with	Indispensable
That which cannot be altered	Irrevocable
That which cannot be perceived by sense	Imperceptible
That which cannot be excused	Inexcusable
That which cannot be allowed	Inadmissible
That which cannot be reached	Inaccessible
A person who knows many languages	Linguist
One who is unable to pay one's debts	Insolvent
A person who leaves his country to settle in some other country	Emigrant
A person who comes as a settler into a foreign country	Immigrant
A person who is not able to be selected or elected under the existing rules	Ineligible
One who is able to make an eloquent speech	Orator
One who always looks at the bright side of life	Optimist
One who always looks at the dark side of life	Pessimist

C.6 WORDS OFTEN CONFUSED

There are several words that may be confusing because they are similar in meaning or pronunciation but have different meanings. Words like accept/except, accede/exceed may confuse the user. The following sentences contain words that are frequently mistakenly interchanged.

1. Accept: agree Except: to exclude
   Except the manager, everyone in the hotel accepted the mistake.
2. Accede: agree Exceed: surpass
   If you do not accede to the government request, you will exceed your limit.
3. Adapt: adjust Adopt: take an idea, habit, etc.
   In order to adapt yourself to a new culture, you need to adopt the ways of that culture.
4. Advice: opinion Advise: to counsel
   Whether you accept or reject my advice, I will advise you.
5. Affect: change, influence Effect: result
   The devastating tsunami has affected the lives of thousands of people and its effect can be seen in several countries of the world.
6. Allusion: reference Illusion: false belief
   He always makes an allusion to his father's ideas because he has the illusion that his father is the wisest person in the world.
7. All ready: all prepared Already: by this time
   You should be all ready to proceed because you are already late.
8. Ascent: the act of climbing up Assent: consent
   Your ascent to this challenging position shows that you have assented to the changes needed to become a high profile executive.
9. Formally: officially Formerly: previously
   If you want to join this organisation formally, you need the recommendation of an existing member of this society or of a person who was formerly a member of this society.
10. Lose: misplace Ioose: not fastened
    If your networking is loose, you will definitely lose customers.

Study the following list of easily confused words and use them in sentences.

Addition	An increase	**Appraise**	Estimate the value or quality of something
Edition	A version of a published book	**Apprise**	Inform
Confidant	Person trusted with knowledge of one's private affairs	**Continual**	Always happening
Confident	Feeling or showing confidence	**Continuous**	Uninterrupted
Dependence	Being dependent	**Disburse**	Pay out
Dependent	Depending		
Dependant	Person supported	**Disperse**	Scatter
Disinterested	Impartial	**Eminent**	Distinguished

Uninterested Not interested
Farther A greater distance
further Additional
Foreword Introductory note
Forward Front of something
Sensual Of physical
Sensuous Affecting the senses

Imminent About to happen
Flounder Move in a confused way/
Founder One who establishes something
Residence A place where a person resides
Resident A permanent inhabitant
Stationary Not moving
Stationery Writing materials

C.7 HOMOPHONES

Homophones are words that are similar in sound and are pronounced in the same way, but are written differently (different spelling) and are different in meaning. The following are some examples:

> Homophones are words that are similar in sound and are pronounced in the same way, but are written differently and are different in meaning.

1. There is no increase in the second class railway **fare**.
   It is not **fair** to discriminate against anyone on the basis of caste.
2. The **riot** has spread to other areas.
   You should consider all the available factors in order to take the **right** decision.
   This is a religious **rite**.

The words 'fair' and 'fare' are pronounced in the same way but they have different meanings. Similarly, the words 'riot', 'right', and 'rite' have different meanings but similar pronunciations.

The following sentences illustrate the use of homophones (underlined):

1. This is an appropriate site for the factory. (ground chosen or used for a town or building)
   His eye sight is weak. (act of seeing or being seen)
   You may cite statements from the report to prove your point. (mention as an example)
2. I have stomach pain. (any unpleasant bodily sensation produced by illness, accident, and so on)
   The pane is broken. (single sheet of glass in a window or door)
3. I cannot wait for the bus now. (defer action for a specified time)
   You have put on weight. (force experienced by a body as a result of the earth's gravitation)
4. You should not waste your time. (use to no purpose)
   The tailor needs the measurement of your waist. (a part of the human body below the ribs and above the hips)
5. I have sent the peon to the post office. (cause to go)
   I have not used a scent. (perfume, pleasant smell)
6. I have not seen him for many days.
   This is a memorable scene. (place in which events, real or fictional, occur)

Now, carefully study the following list of homophones:

Addition – an increase
The addition of teachers in the university will reduce the student-teacher ratio.

Edition – a version of a published work
The new edition of this dictionary is now available in the market.

Allowed – permitted
The company was allowed by the government to bring the new product to the market.

Aloud – speaking audibly	Please speak aloud so that everyone can listen to your talk.
Alter – change	I want to alter the entire plan in order to complete it within the time frame.
Altar – a raised platform	Christians use an altar in worship.
Bare – plain	I am presenting nothing but the bare truth.
Bear – endure	He cannot bear this pain.
Berth – a bed on a train	I got the lower berth in the last train to Mumbai.
Birth – the process of being born	What is your date of birth?
Brake – device to lock the wheels	The brake of the car is not working.
Break – smash	If the glass falls, it will break.
Canvas – cloth used for painting	The painter has brought the canvas to life.
Canvass – solicit votes	All the candidates do not canvass successfully.
Cell – small room	He was confined to the cell for many weeks.
Sell – exchange for money	He wants to sell his old car and buy a new one.
Chord – a group of notes sounded together	He can easily play that chord.
Cord – a string	The dog is tied to the pole with a cord.
Desert – dry area of land covered with sand	The Sahara is the biggest desert in Asia.
Dessert – the last part of a meal	The best part of the dinner was the special dessert.
Know – to discern something	I do not know the manager of this hotel.
No – denial	No, I don't like English movies.
Lessen – to reduce	This medicine may lessen your blood pressure for the time being.
Lesson – a piece of instruction	The first lesson of this course begins with a diagnostic test.
Principal – main	He is the principal actor of this drama.
Principle – law	Every principle of science is based on objective observation and analysis.
Stair – a flight of steps	if you have high blood pressure, you should use the elevator rather than the stairs.
Stare – look fixedly	You should not stare at strangers.

The following are some more examples of homophones in English sentences.

Aid/Aide	Air/Heir	Allusion/Elusion	Ate/Eight
Band/Banned	Bought/Boat	Bloc/Block	Board/Bored
Bold/Bowled	Born/Borne	Bough/Bow	Bread/Bred
Brows/Browse	Cash/Cache	Cast/Caste	Cede/Seed
Cue/Queue	Court/Caught	Dear/Deer	Flour/Flower
Foam/Form	Heard/Herd	Hear/Here	Him/Hymn
Hire/Higher	Knob/Nob	Leach/Leech	Might/Mite
Manner/Manor	Lays/Laze	Pale/Pail	Peace/Piece
Raise/Rays	Read/Reed	Sea/See	Sale/Sail
Sane/Seine	Sort/Sought	Sign/Sine	Sees/Seize

C.8 SENTENCE COMPLETION

This section is best explained with the help of some examples:

1. Petroleum is an extremely ______________ mixture of hydrocarbon compounds.
   (i) positive (ii) difficult (iii) sophisticated (iv) complex
2. A telescope is an ______________ instrument used for magnifying distant objects.
   (i) initial (ii) optical (iii) mechanical (iv) absorbing
3. A computer is an electronic ______________ that stores and processes data.
   (i) machine (ii) tool (iii) instrument (iv) device
4. To ______________ filtration tests, coal fines are mixed with predetermined volume of water and flocculent solution.
   (i) take (ii) do (iii) perform (iv) have
5. Most electrochemical cells cannot be recharged after they ______________.
   (i) break open (ii) run down (iii) break away (iv) run out

Answers

1. (iv) 2. (b) 3. (iv) 4. (iii) 5. (b)

As is evident, one cannot complete such exercises without developing a good vocabulary. Such exercises serve as a good practice for the same.

C.8.1 Analogy

Analogy uses similarities in words for vocabulary development.

Analogy refers to a technique that uses similarities in words for vocabulary development. For example:

Sun : Moon :: Day : Night

Just like the Sun can be seen during the day, the Moon can be seen during the night.

Bowl : Cup :: Soup : ?

Answer: Tea / Coffee

One technique to solve analogy questions is to make a sentence using the relationship that is given, and then fit the relationship with the missing word. For example, the above analogy question can be solved as:

A bowl is used to serve soup.

Similarly, a cup is used to serve tea/coffee.

C.9 VOCABULARY EXERCISES

Exercise 1

1. In each of the following sentences, a blank has been left which can be filled by one of the four alternatives given under it. Select the most appropriate word or phrase that can correctly fill the blank.

(a) The resistance of a material ____________ an important role in electric circuits.
   (i) marks (ii) consists of (iii) plays (iv) shows

(b) The parts or components of an electric circuit ___________ a path for the movement of charges.
(i) provide (ii) show (iii) give (iv) occupy

(c) The components of the an electric circuit are ___________ from material with low resistance.
(i) taken (ii) made (iii) retained (iv) showed

(d) All the food is ___________ the process of photosynthesis.
(i) consisting of (ii) taken (iii) originated (iv) derived through

(e) The oxidation of organic compounds during respiration ___________ carbon dioxide in the atmosphere.
(i) liberates (ii) retains (iii) spreads (iv) controls

(f) The combustion of coal, oil, and other fuels ___________ enormous production of CO_2.
(i) cause (ii) causing (iii) causes (iv) might cause

(g) CO_2 ___________ infrared radiation.
(i) gives away (ii) keeps (iii) displays (iv) absorbs

(h) Chemical reactions ___________ the breaking of bonds.
(i) interface (ii) involve (iii) introduce (iv) show

(i) When chemical reactions occur, a great variety of rearrangements of atoms can ___________.
(i) take up (ii) take off (iii) take place (iv) take on

(j) A decomposition reaction occurs when a molecule is ___________ into smaller parts.
(i) broken open (ii) broken down (iii) broken out (iv) broken away

Exercise 2

1. In each of the following questions, out of the given four alternatives, choose the word that does not express the meaning of the given word.

(a) Accessory
(i) additional (ii) subsidiary (iii) device (iv) auxiliary

(b) Adhesive
(i) glue (ii) gum (iii) sticky (iv) connected

(c) Crafty
(i) reserved (ii) cunning (iii) adroit (iv) artful

(d) Decorum
(i) decency (ii) reverence (iii) gravity (iv) propriety

(e) Designate
(i) name (ii) nominate (iii) posting (iv) appoint

(f) Elegant
(i) Elevated (ii) refined (iii) graceful (iv) tasteful

(g) Enterprise
(i) endeavour (ii) venture (iii) success (iv) undertaking

(h) Intentional
(i) desirable (ii) deliberate (iii) intended (iv) designed

(i) Pragmatic
(i) practical (ii) empirical (iii) reasonable (iv) cultured

(j) Immaterial
(i) useless (ii) spiritual (iii) irrelevant (iv) unimportant

Exercise 3

1. Study the following prefixes and their meanings carefully. Now read the sentences given in the box, and rewrite the underlined words, adding to each the correct prefix to reverse the word's meaning.

Prefix	Meaning
anti	against
un	not
in	not
mis	badly/wrongly
dis	not
im	not
ir	not

(a) Electricity has an important place in modern society.
(b) Your actions show that you are not practical.
(c) Please be comfortable.
(d) This mobile phone is very expensive.
(e) Man is a social animal.
(f) She is very efficient.
(g) Your argument is not convincing.
(h) This is very relevant information.
(i) You should be sensitive to cultural differences.
(j) The process of communication is successful only when the receiver understands the message.

Exercise 4

1. In each of the following questions, out of the given four alternatives, choose the word that is opposite in meaning to the given word.

(a) Accustomed
(i) used (ii) unusual (iii) ready (iv) usual

(b) Arrogant
(i) sincere (ii) grave (iii) humble (iv) vain

(c) Beneficial
(i) injurious (ii) useful (iii) static (iv) dangerous

(d) Cautious
(i) careful (ii) foolish (iii) decent (iv) reckless

(e) Complicate
(i) illustrate (ii) involve (iii) simplify (iv) indulge

(f) Elegant
(i) ugly (ii) refined (iii) graceful (iv) rational

(g) consolidate
(i) weaken (ii) manage (iii) strengthen (iv) undertake

(h) Intentional
  (i) undesirable (ii) deliberate (iii) unintended (iv) designed
(i) Pragmatic
  (i) impractical (ii) rational (iii) wise (iv) cunning
(j) Diligent
  (i) active (ii) lazy (iii) dynamic (iv) honest

Exercise 5

1. In each of the following sentences, a blank has been left to be filled by one of the four alternatives given under it. Select the most appropriate word or phrase that correctly fills the blank.

(a) All substances, solids, liquids, and gases, at temperatures above absolute zero, ——— energy in the form of electromagnetic waves.
  (i) reveal (ii) show (iii) emit (iv) take
(b) Heat transfer by radiation is ______________ from heat transfer by other means.
  (i) apart (ii) differ (iii) distinguished (iv) explained
(c) All matter ______________ space.
  (i) occupies (ii) takes (iii) finds (iv) captures
(d) Fuel oil and natural gas are used to ______________ homes and commercial buildings.
  (i) warm (ii) ignite (iii) heat (iv) burn
(e) The Space Age began on October 4, 1957, when Russia ______________ Sputnik 1 into orbit.
  (i) started (ii) launched (iii) experimented (iv) send

Exercise 6

1. In each of the following questions, out of the given four alternatives, choose the word that does not express the meaning of the given word.

(a) Adequate
  (i) plentiful (ii) enough (iii) absolute (iv) sufficient
(b) Amicable
  (i) friendly (ii) lovable (iii) suitable (iv) introvert
(c) Commensurate
  (i) begin (ii) suitable (iii) applicable (iv) equivalent
(d) Consequent
  (i) resultant (ii) outcome (iii) following (iv) changing
(e) Credible
  (i) believable (ii) true (iii) impossible (iv) probable
(f) Decipher
  (i) translate (ii) cheat (iii) interpret (iv) solve
(g) Deficient
  (i) degrading (ii) lacking (iii) inadequate (iv) wanting
(h) Devoid
  (i) vacant (ii) lacking (iii) empty (iv) diffident

(i) Downright
(i) frank (ii) questionable (iii) blunt (iv) simple

(j) Effective
(i) efficient (ii) dubious (iii) able (iv) capable

Exercise 7

1. In each of the following sentences, a blank has been left to be filled by one of the four alternatives given below it. Select the most appropriate word or phrase to correctly fill the blank.

(a) The operation of many devices, such as ammeters, voltmeters, electric motors, particle accelerators, and television sets, depend on magnetic forces that are ______________ on charges that move through a magnetic field.
(i) given (ii) exerted (iii) pressed (iv) released

(b) Electron microscopes are microscopes that can ______________ up to one million times.
(i) increase (ii) rectify (iii) magnify (iv) reduce

(c) Although some groundwork had been done earlier, AI began in earnest with the ______________ of the modern computer during the 1940s and 1950s.
(i) increase (ii) proliferation (iii) growth (iv) emergence

(d) Pieces of iron, cobalt, and nickel can also become magnetised when they are ______________ many times in the same direction along their length with one end of a magnet.
(i) stroked (ii) released (iii) touched (iv) emmbraced

(e) The magma that is chemically very reactive due to its pressure, temperature, and composition of various minerals ______________ adjacent rocks through which it travels, giving rise to new minerals.
(i) increases (ii) reacts (iii) dissolves (iv) pushes

(f) The scanning electron microscope is extremely useful in ______________ details and contours of different surfaces.
(i) reading (ii) skimming (iii) predicting (iv) studying

(g) If the UPS is in the backup mode and encounters an overload, it will ______________ the output voltage.
(i) turn off (b) turn up (iii) turn down (iv) turn over

(h) If there is no mains voltage present, external devices (for example, servers) connected to the computer interface can ______________ the UPS to shut down.
(i) request (ii) speak (iii) ask (iv) command

(i) This UPS contains potentially ______________ voltages.
(i) hazardous (ii) objectionable (iii) unreasonable (iv) revealing

(j) The battery in this UPS contains lead and poses a hazard to the environment and human health if not ______________ properly
(i) given away (ii) disposed off (iii) given over (iv) retained

Exercise 8

1. In each of the following sentences, a blank has been left to be filled by one of the four alternatives given under it. Select the most appropriate word or phrase to correctly fill the blank.

(a) ______________, crude oil is a mixture of different compounds that boil at different temperatures.
(i) naturally (ii) actually (iii) physically (iv) interestingly

(b) The discovery of electron spin completes the set of ______________ needed to describe an electron in an atom.
(i) qualities (ii) characteristics (iii) standards (iv) patterns

(c) The behaviour of plastics when heated provides the basis for the ______________ between the two main classes of plastics available today.
(i) distinction (ii) similarities (iii) relation (iv) relationships

(d) Heat ______________ in Joules on complete burning of one gram of a fuel is expressed as its calorific value.
(i) created (ii) is (iii) forms (iv) liberated

(e) Carbon ______________ 0.19 per cent of the earth's crust.
(i) created (ii) is (iii) forms (iv) constitutes

(f) The five important characteristics ______________ with each wave are wavelength, frequency, velocity, wave number, and amplitude.
(i) created (ii) included (iii) associated (iv) present

(g) Coal is a natural resource, which constitutes ______________ 85% of the total fossil fuel reserves in the world.
(i) barely (ii) hardly (iii) mostly (iv) approximately

(h) When a gas loses sufficient energy (in the form of heat or by doing work), it ______________ to a liquid.
(i) creates (ii) condenses (iii) forms (iv) liberates

(i) Some of the diesel engines are also stationary engines used in agriculture to power irrigation pumps, and in diesel generating sets, usually, for ______________ electric power generation.
(i) standby (ii) standing (iii) real (iv) temporary

(j) When the shape of a solid is ______________ by external forces, the tangential stresses between adjacent particles tend to restore the body to its original configuration.
(i) deshaped (ii) formed (iii) destroyed (iv) altered

Exercise 9

1. In each of the following sentences, a blank has been left to be filled by one of the four alternatives given under it. Select the most appropriate word, to correctly fill the blank.

(a) Scientists ______________ many experiments and the evidence from these experiments made it clear that an atom is divisible and has a complex structure.
(i) completed (ii) conducted (iii) did (iv) have

(b) Environmental scientists and engineers specialising in air pollution have been ____________ to discover that the highest personal exposures to combustion emissions occur not in urban smog but in homes with unvented combustion appliances.
(i) pleased (ii) startled (iii) excited (iv) unhappy

(c) The mass of an object is ____________ of the quantity of matter that it possesses.
(i) a signal (ii) a symptom (iii) a did (iv) an indication

(d) To avoid structural failures, engineers must know the limitations of the materials they use, and they must be able to calculate the ____________ of any deformations.
(i) extents (ii) limits (iii) magnitudes (iv) wideness

(e) Fatigue is a common cause of ____________ in machinery.
(i) failure (ii) weakness (iii) looseness (iv) strength

(f) About half of the world's oil is ____________ by a fleet of 500 million vehicles whose growth has consistently outpaced that of human population.
(i) absorbed (ii) destroyed (iii) eaten (iv) consumed

(g) In the long run, an increase in the number of vehicles causes oil consumption to rise faster than oil production, resulting in the ____________ of oil supplies.
(i) shrinking (ii) depleting (iii) squeezing (iv) freezing

(h) The production department can have networked computers to keep ____________ of product flow and to control the machines, which actually mount components on circuit boards,
(i) updating (ii) report (iii) refreshed (iv) track

(i) Aluminium is ____________ from bauxite, which contains aluminium oxide.
(i) conducted (ii) extracted (iii) taken (iv) mined

(j) Corporate officers can have personal computers tied into the network so that they can ____________ with any of the other systems on the network.
(i) interact (ii) conduct (iii) connect (iv) relate

Exercise 10

1. In each of the following questions, out of the given four alternatives, choose the word that is opposite in meaning to the given word.

(a) Abridge
(i) shorten (ii) expand (iii) condense (iv) curtail

(b) Absurd
(i) silly (ii) foolish (iii) ridiculous (iv) rational

(c) Accede
(i) refuse (ii) consent (iii) comply (iv) assent

(d) Accelerate
(i) quicken (ii) hasten (iii) reduce (iv) expedite

(e) Accumulate
(i) squander (ii) amass (iii) collect (iv) store

(f) Actuate
(i) impel (ii) stop (iii) instigate (iv) act

(g) Accommodate
(i) reconcile (ii) refuse (iii) fit (iv) suit
(h) Adversity
(i) prosperity (ii) misfortune (iii) distress (iv) hardship
(i) Advertise
(i) conceal (ii) apprise (iii) announce (iv) notify
(j) Affluence
(i) wealth (ii) opulence (iii) riches (iv) poverty

Exercise 11

1. Study the following sentences. The underlined words and phrases are not appropriate. Replace them by using appropriate synonyms of the words:

(a) Ionic compounds can be separated into their constituent ions with little effort.
(b) Through telephone lines, an engineer with a personal computer can approach data in the memory of other computers all over the world.
(c) Microcomputers vary from small controllers that work directly with 4-bit words and can address a few thousand bytes of memory to larger units that work directly with 32-bit words and can address billions of bytes of memory.
(d) The warehouse supervisor can similarly use a personal computer with an inventory programme to keep personal records, and those in the large computer's memory, updated.
(e) Non-renewable resources are those present in limited quantities and, hence, if these are spent injudiciously, we may not find them again.
(f) Some of the more powerful microcomputers have all or most of the qualities of earlier minicomputers.
(g) Molecular interactions cause intermolecular attractive and repulsive forces.
(h) In fuel cells, the intermediate steps of conversion of chemical energy to heat followed by conversion of heat to mechanical work are completely removed.
(i) In these electrochemical devices, the chemical energy of the fuel is directly changed into low voltage direct current electrical energy.
(j) Because the energy change can be carried out isothermally, fuel cell efficiency is not subject to the limitations of Carnot efficiency.

Exercise 12

1. Study the following sentences. The underlined words and phrases are inappropriate. Replace them by using more appropriate and formal words and phrases:

(a) A compound microscope is a device that is used to produce very large enlarged appearances.
(b) Mainframe computers are made to work at very high speeds with large data words, typically 64- bits or greater, and they have massive amounts of memory.
(c) The main function of input devices of a computer is to change information to data and send it to the CPU for further processing.
(d) Boron is a very very hard, low density solid with a melting point greater than 2450 K, and low electrical conductivity.

(e) The physical devices used to connect computer buses to external systems are called ports.
(f) When hydrogen gas gets free from a cylinder into the air, no change is can be seen.
(g) Chromium is one of the less plentiful metals of the earth's crust.
(h) The bulb has a very thin wire called a filament made of tungsten alloy which shut in a vacuum.

Exercise 13

1. In each of the following sentences is a blank that can be filled by one of the four alternatives given under it. Select the most appropriate word or phrase to correctly fill in the blank.

(a) To reduce the risk of fire or shock hazard, do not ____________ this equipment to rain or moisture.
(i) keep (ii) put at risk (iii) subject (iv) expose

(b) Hold down the ENTER and the OFF buttons ____________ until the "▶◀ hold" indication appears in the VCR display.
(i) regularly (ii) simultaneously (iii) continuously (iv) intermittently

(c) When the VCR is ____________ after unpacking and connecting the aerial cable and the mains load, Plug in Auto Tuning starts automatically.
(i) turned out (ii) turned away (iii) turned down (iv) turned on

(d) In order to ____________ electromagnetic interference from the power supply, install the accessory clamp filter on the AC mains lead.
(i) prevent (ii) stop (iii) hinder (iv) avoid

(e) ____________ any optional adjustments to the output size using inches, centimetres, pixels, or a percentage.
(i) do (ii) make (iii) create (iv) bring about

(f) ____________ the Windows 98 CD into your CD-ROM drive.
(i) place (ii) put (iii) insert (iv) keep

(g) Measure the distance between the screen and the mirror in order to ____________ the f (focal length) value of the mirror.
(i) know (ii) determine (iii) settle (iv) decide

(h) A thin aluminium rod (2-mm diameter and 5 cm long) is hung between the poles of a horseshoe magnet using springs, and then the springs are insulated with rubber or plastic sheath ____________ they are not charged.
(i) so that (ii) as (iii) because (iv) since

(i) To ____________ the test, coal fines were mixed with predetermined volume of water and flocculent solution.
(i) carry (ii) perform (iii) do (iv) complete

(j) A leaf is plucked from a plant that was kept in the sun for long and then ____________ boiling water for a few minutes to destroy the enzymes and to make the leaf softer and absorbent.
(i) put in (ii) dipped in (iii) immersed (iv) inserted in

Exercise 14

1. Study the following list of words. All the words in the list are synonyms except one word that is opposite in meaning to the rest of words. Identify this word.

(a) accumulate, amass, collect, distribute, store
(b) recognise, allow, disown, acknowledge, admit
(c) undone, achieve, fulfill, accomplish, execute
(d) loss, advantage, gain, profit, benefit
(e) support, favour, defend, advocate, oppose
(f) lighten, intensify, aggravate, heighten, make worse
(g) straghtforward, candid, partial, frank, fair
(h) praise, censure, condemn, reprimand, reprove
(i) compatible, suitable, consistent, accordant, dissonant
(j) conflicting, consistent, discordant, contrary, disagreeing

Exercise 15

1. In each of the following sentences, out of the given four alternatives, choose the one that <u>does not express</u> the meaning of the given word:

(a) Composure
(i) equanimity (ii) calmness (iii) coolness (iv) excitability
(b) Equip
(i) furnish (ii) provide (iii) divest (iv) array
(c) Commensurate
(i) equal (ii) equivalent (iii) tantamount (iv) opposed
(d) Manifest
(i) clear (ii) obscure (iii) evident (iv) manifest
(e) Precise
(i) exact (ii) inaccurate (iii) correct (iv) strict
(f) Expedient
(i) unadvisable (ii) useful (iii) fitting (iv) suitable
(g) Extract
(i) pull out (ii) draw out (iii) distil (iv) insert
(h) Lavish
(i) restrained (ii) extravagant (iii) excessive (iv) prodigal
(i) Fabricate
(i) construct (ii) forge (iii) invent (iv) realise
(j) Deceptive
(i) delusive (ii) misleading (iii) actual (iv) false

Exercise 16

1. In each of the following questions, out of the given four alternatives, choose the one that <u>does not express</u> the meaning of the given word:

(a) Earnest
  (i) eager (ii) ardent (iii) hesitating (iv) serious
(b) Elucidate
  (i) explain (ii) interpret (iii) illuminate (iv) obscure
(c) Emblem
  (i) error (ii) figure (iii) type (iv) mark
(d) Trespass
  (i) respect privacy (ii) encroach (iii) intrude (iv) trench
(e) Boundless
  (i) endless (ii) infinite (iii) limited (iv) continual
(f) Ratify
  (i) disapprove (ii) endorse (iii) sanction (iv) back
(g) Enhance
  (i) diminish (ii) increase (iii) improve (iv) heighten
(h) Zealous
  (i) ardent (ii) cool (iii) enthusiastic (iv) fervent
(i) Temptation
  (i) enticement (ii) allurement (iii) repulsion (iv) attraction
(j) Momentary
  (i) ephemeral (ii) everlasting (iii) short-lived (iv) transient

Exercise 17

1. In each of the following list of words, choose the word opposite in meaning to the remaining words in the list.

(a) fervour, warmth, coolness, ardour, glow
(b) portion, piece, bit, whole, fragment
(c) fraught, laden, charged, empty, filled
(d) frenzy, madness, rage, fury, sanity
(e) implicate, invlove, exclude, entangle, compromise
(f) imply, denote, exclude, mean, involve
(g) careless, negligent, observant, inattentive, inadvertent
(h) indignant, angry, wrathful, peaceful, exasperated
(i) fluctuate, vacillate, waver, undulate, be constant
(j) laborious, industrious, active, busy, slothful

Exercise 18

1. In each of the following list of words, choose the word opposite in meaning to the remaining words in the list.

(a) Clear, vague, indistinct, dim, ambiguous
(b) Start, initiate, finish, indoctrinate, inaugurate
(c) Insidious, crafty, treacherous, deceitful, honest
(d) Well-flavoured, insipid, tasteless, vapid, flavourless
(e) Look into, examine, investigate, ignore, oversee
(f) Intemperate, uncontrolled, unrestrained, excessive, temperate
(g) Accelerate, stop, hinder, interrupt, break
(h) Distant, intimate, familiar, close, inward
(i) Irrefutable, doubtful, incontestable, indisputable, irrefragable
(j) Segregation, isolation, separation, company, solitude

Exercise 19

1. Find the missing word from the given alternatives.

(a) dog : kangaroo :: pup : ?
  (i) kitten (b) joey (c) cub (d) calf
(b) deer : doe :: chicken : ?
  (i) hen (b) rooster (c) cock (d) duck
(c) thermometer : watch :: temperature : ?
  (i) clock (b) minutes (c) alarm (d) time
(d) child : adult :: school : ?
  (i) picnic (b) driving (c) office (d) party
(e) happy: cheerful :: sad : ?
  (i) gloomy (b) crying (c) pessimistic (d) lonely

Key to Vocabulary Exercises

Exercise 1

1. (a) (iii) (b) (a) (c) (b) (d) (iv) (e) (a)
   (f) (iii) (g) (iv) (h) (b) (i) (iii) (j) (b)

Exercise 2

1. (a) (iii) (b) (iv) (c) (a) (d) (b) (e) (iii)
   (f) (a) (g) (iii) (h) (a) (i) (iv) (j) (b)

Exercise 3

1. (a) unimprtant (b) impractical (c) uncomfortable (d) inexpensive (e) anti-social

(f) inefficient (g) unconvincing (h) irrelevant (i) insensitive
(j) misunderstands

Exercise 4

1. (a) (b) (b) (iii) (c) (a) (d) (iv) (e) (iii)
(f) (a) (g) (a) (h) (iii) (i) (a) (j) (b)

Exercise 5

1. (a) (iii) (b) (iii) (c) (a) (d) (iii) (e) (b)

Exercise 6

1. (a) (iii) (b) (iv) (c) (a) (d) (iv) (e) (iii)
(f) (b) (g) (a) (h) (iv) (i) (b) (j) (b)

Exercise 7

1. (a) (b) (b) (iii) (c) (iv) (d) (a) (e) (iii)
(f) (iv) (g) (a) (h) (iv) (i) (a) (j) (b)

Exercise 8

1. (a) (iii) (b) (b) (c) (a) (d) (iv) (e) (iv)
(f) (iii) (g) (iv) (h) (b) (i) (a) (j) (iv)

Exercise 9

1. (a) (ii) (b) (b) (c) (iv) (d) (iii) (e) (a)
(f) (iv) (g) (iii) (h) (iv) (i) (ii) (j) (a)

Exercise 10

1. (a) (b) (b) (iv) (c) (a) (d) (iii) (e) (a)
(f) (b) (g) (b) (h) (a) (i) (a) (j) (iv)

Exercise 11

1.
(a) Ionic compounds can be dissociated into their constituent ions with little effort.
(b) Through telephone lines, an engineer with a personal computer can access data in the memory of other computers all over the world.
(c) Microcomputers range from small controllers that work directly with 4-bit words and can address a few thousand bytes of memory to larger units that work directly with 32-bit words and can address billions of bytes of memory.

(d) The warehouse supervisor can likewise use a personal computer with an inventory program to keep personal records, and those in the large computer's memory, updated.
(e) Non-renewable resources are those present in limited quantities and, hence, if these are consumed injudiciously, we may not find them again.
(f) Some of the more powerful microcomputers have all or most of the features of earlier minicomputers.
(g) Molecular interactions lead to intermolecular attractive and repulsive forces.
(h) In fuel cells, the intermediate steps of conversion of chemical energy to heat followed by conversion of heat to mechanical work are completely eliminated.
(i) In these electrochemical devices, the chemical energy of the fuel is directly converted into low voltage direct current electrical energy.
(j) Because the energy conversion can be carried out isothermally, fuel cell efficiency is not subject to the limitations of Carnot efficiency.

Exercise 12

1.
(a) A compound microscope is a device that is used to produce very large magnifications.
(b) Mainframe computers are designed to work at very high speeds with large data words, typically 64 bits or greater, and they have massive amounts of memory.
(c) The main function of input devices of a computer is to convert information to data and send it to the CPU for further processing.
(d) Boron is an extremely hard, low density solid with a melting point greater than 2450 K, and low electrical conductivity.
(e) The physical devices used to interface computer buses to external systems are called ports.
(f) When hydrogen gas escapes from a cylinder into the air, no change is visible.
(g) Chromium is one of the less abundant metals of the earth's crust.
(h) The bulb contains a very thin wire called a filament made of tungsten alloy, which is enclosed in a vacuum.

Exercise 13

1. (a) (iv) (b) (ii) (c) (iv) (d) (i) (e) (b)
(f) (iii) (g) (ii) (h) (i) (i) (b) (j) (b)

Exercise 14

1. (a) distribute (b) disown (c) undone (d) loss (e) oppose
6 lighten (g) partial (h) praise (i) dissonant (j) consistent

Exercise 15

1. (a) (iv) (b) (iii) (c) (iv) (d) (b) (e) (b)
(f) (a) (g) (iv) (h) (a) (i) (iv) (j) (iii)

Exercise 16

1. (a) (iii) (b) (iv) (c) (a) (d) (a) (e) (iii)
   (f) (a) (g) (a) (h) (b) (i) (iii) (j) (b)

Exercise 17

1. (a) coolness, (b) whole, (c) empty, (d) sanity (e) exclude,
   (f) exclude, (g) observant, (h) peaceful, (i) be constant (j) slothful

Exercise 18

1. (a) clear, (b) finish (c) honest (d) well-flavoured, (e) ignore,
   (f) temperate (g) accelerate, (h) distant, (i) doubtful, (j) company,

Exercise 19

1. (a) (ii) (b) (i) (c) (d) (d) (c) (e) (a)

Index